THE COLLINS GUIDE TO
FRANCE

THE COLLINS GUIDE TO
FRANCE
EDITED BY JOHN ARDAGH

WILLOW BOOKS
Collins, 8 Grafton Street, London W1
1985

Contributors

John Ardagh
France Today, Gastronomy, Alsace-Lorraine,
Languedoc-Roussillon, Provence

Arthur Eperon
Alps/Savoy, Poitou-Charentes, Dordogne and Lot,
Loire/Centre, Lower Loire, Corsica

Douglas Johnson
History

Alex de Jonge
Literature

Marc Jordan
Art

John Musgrove
Architecture

Robin Hunter Neillands
Jura/Franche-Comté

Nesta Roberts
Normandy, Ile-de-France, Champagne/Ardennes
Aquitaine, Pyrenees

Andrew Sanger
Burgundy, Massif Central, Lyon Area, Picardy and
Nord

Keith Spence
Brittany

Elisabeth de Stroumillo
Paris

Steven Spurrier
Wine

Willow Books
Wm Collins Sons & Co Ltd,
London · Glasgow · Sydney · Auckland
Toronto · Johannesburg

First published in Great Britain 1985
Copyright © Robert Adkinson Limited, London

British Library Cataloguing in Publication Data

The Collins guide to France.
  1. France—Description and travel—1975–
  —Guide-books
  I. Ardagh, John
  914.4'04838   DC29.3
  ISBN 0-00-218164-9

Designed and produced by
Robert Adkinson Limited, London
Editorial Director   Clare Howell
Editor   John Gilbert
Art Director   Christine Simmonds
Designer   Roy Williams
Designer Assistants   Anita Plank
                          David Powell
Illustrations   Thelma Lambert
Cartography   MJL Cartographics

Phototypeset by Tradespools Limited, Frome

Illustrations originated by East Anglian Engraving
Limited, Norwich

Printed and bound by Brepols, Turnhout, Belgium

Measurement Conversions	
1 kilometre	= 0.621 miles
1 metre	= 3ft 3¼in
1 hectare	= 2.471 acres

CONTENTS

INTRODUCING FRANCE

GAZETTEER

FRANCE TODAY

France today is in many ways a highly modern country. Whereas twenty years ago its antiquated telephone system was a sad joke, France now leads Europe in the practical pioneering of videophones, home viewdata systems and other marvels of electronics and telecommunications. It is the land of Airbus and Ariane, of the La Défense skyscrapers outside Paris, and of Europe's largest hypermarkets. Yet, for all their pride in modernity, realized with fine technical flair, the French remain, too, a very conservative people, clinging for security to old habits and rituals. Thus, the new franc (100 old francs) dates from 1959, yet many people today, even those born after the change, still calculate in old currency.

The French have not lost their peasant roots. The change from a basically rural to an industrial society is very recent. Since the war, French agriculture has been extensively modernized and three-quarters of the former, huge farm population has moved to the towns or switched to other occupations. France has seen the type of urban revolution that Britain experienced in the 19th century, and many cities have trebled their size.

Yet many people find it difficult and painful adapting to conditions in the lonely new suburbs. Today, in the 1980s, modernism is becoming unfashionable and 'quality of life' is all the rage. In cities, the vogue is less for new skyscrapers than for creating traffic-free zones with trees and coloured paving. The French are seeking to renew contact with their rural origins and traditional values. Some take jobs in small towns or in the country; a few city students and intellectuals have even given up the rat-race and turned to hill-farming in poor areas. Others are devoting themselves to ancient handicrafts, to the revival of folklore and festivals, and to the restoration of old buildings.

One of the most dramatic changes in post-war France is the way in which Paris, since the 1950s, has been losing ground to the provinces. In this most centralized of lands, Paris used to suck the life-blood from the regions: it was the sole seat of political power, prestige and culture, possessed all the banks and controlled much of the nation's industry. The railways all converged on Paris, with few cross-country main lines. Since the war, however, France's great economic revival has centred mainly on the provinces, with the building of new factories and universities, and the creation of a more vibrant social and cultural life. Paris, that beloved monster, has grown *too* noisy, hectic and congested, and many people have come to realize that life outside the capital can actually be more fun – a strange reversal after those centuries of Parisian contempt for provincials. Middle-class Parisians happily migrate to new jobs in the regions, especially the sunny south: today it is almost smarter to say that you live and work in Aix-en-Provence than in the Faubourg St-Germain.

This strong trend of regional reaction against modern monolithic bureaucracy – evident in many other countries – is partly cultural, aiming to revive the old local languages and traditions, partly political. In certain regions – notably, Brittany, Languedoc and Corsica –

Left Rural and city *milieux* are moving closer together today. There is a distinct trend for city dwellers to buy up empty farmsteads or to build country villas for weekend and holiday use.

separatist movements have emerged, sometimes resorting to violence; but they appeal only to tiny minorities. The vast majority of people in such areas do not want full independence from Paris, merely a little more say in their own local destinies, less domination by anonymous bureaucrats in the distant capital. French governments since the 1960s have recognized this feeling; but in a nation with so strong a tradition of centralism, political devolution has not been easy to achieve. The de Gaulle, Pompidou and Giscard regimes took a few half-hearted steps, slightly relaxing the tight grip of the Paris-appointed prefects over local budgets and policies, and grouping the 90-odd Napoleonic *départements* into 22 new regions. But this did little to change the basic pattern. It was left to the Socialists, coming to power in 1981, to introduce a much more radical set of reforms that are gradually being enforced. The prefects have lost much of their power; locally elected councils have won a large measure of autonomous control; and the regions are at last getting directly elected assemblies with real powers. So France is finally moving, if not to a German-style federal structure, at least towards the kind of regional system adopted recently in Italy and Spain.

Yet in other ways this remains a rigid and stratified society. Despite some relaxation, class divisions still remain sharper than elsewhere in northern Europe, except possibly for Britain. Income disparities, too, are greater: wage differentials between manager and skilled worker, approximately 4:1 in Britain and Germany, are 6:1 in France. The Socialist introduction of new taxes on wealth after 1981 did little to change this. France is also a land of hierarchies, where the right diplomas, contacts and background count for a great deal. Education, some 83 per cent of it in state hands, is theoretically the same for all, and free: but in practice the places at the top Grandes Écoles, those élitist colleges that provide an entry to the best careers in politics and administration, still go mainly to the bourgeois privileged few. The Socialists modified this to an extent, appointing trade union leaders to some public posts; but the unions, weak in membership and politically at loggerheads, remain far less influential than in many countries, such as Britain. The Grande École system, though arguably providing efficient rule by a talented élite, is essentially unjust and undemocratic, perpetuating a gulf between rulers and ruled, between senior and junior grades, leading to resentment and apathy at the lower levels.

Below There has been an energetic rebuilding programme in France since the end of World War II. In the past two decades the skyline of Paris has been modified by the appearance of high-rise buildings, such as this Front de Seine development.

Above The French still remain strongly attached to traditional ways of preparing food in spite of the introduction of modern production methods.

The education system has been modified repeatedly since the war, notably after the shocks of the 1968 student revolt. The universities, hitherto tightly run by the state, now have a little more autonomy. In schools, the traditionally rigorous academic obstacle-race has been eased, in line with modern educational thinking – and possibly at the expense of standards. All this is consistent with post-war social and domestic changes. Although the family, as in other Latin countries, remains a tighter unit than in Britain, life at home has certainly become more relaxed and parents less authoritarian. Teenagers have enjoyed a new permissiveness and sexual morality is less formal. According to surveys, some 44 per cent of young couples now live together openly before marriage, against 17 per cent in 1969; in pre-war days it was rare indeed. Women have won a fuller emancipation; after a long struggle, birth-control and abortion have been legalized. The Catholic Church, though becoming more liberal (often despite Rome), is losing influence: in Paris, only 10 per cent of people now attend Mass each week. Yet those who remain practising Christians tend to be more sincere in their faith, less convention-bound, than in former days.

All these changes in some ways derive from France's post-war economic revolution. The 1950s and 1960s saw a 'French miracle', with an astonishing industrial modernization programme, stimulated by Jean Monnet's famous Plan. The EEC, which has benefited France hugely, then provided another spell, enabling her industry to surmount the challenge of open German competition. The recovery lasted until the first oil crisis shocks after 1973. Since then the economy has run into trouble, for complex reasons. France has few native energy resources, many sectors of industry remain outdated and poorly organized, and high inflation is organically rooted. Unemployment has been rising, passing the 2 million mark in 1982. The Socialists tried to remedy matters, first by Keynesian reflation, which failed, then by introducing more classic austerity measures, which simply made them unpopular with their own supporters.

The Socialist victory of 1981 followed 23 years of uninterrupted Right-of-centre rule, under de Gaulle, Pompidou and Giscard, by which time change was badly needed. The alternation of power, normal and healthy in a democracy, and characteristic of such countries as Britain, Germany and the US, has proved peculiarly difficult in France, partly because of the 'threat' posed by a large Communist Party, partly because of the French tendency to polarize, to split into warring camps of Left and Right, thus leading to a lack of national consensus. Although some of the Socialist reforms have been gratuitous and doctrinaire (e.g. the nationalizations), others have been liberal and positive (e.g. decentralization). There has also been a sharp decline in Communist support. By and large it has been a healthy development, suggesting that France may perhaps be moving towards consensus and a greater measure of political realism.

HISTORY

The history of the land we know as France is considered by many to have begun in AD843, the year when Charlemagne's empire was divided, at the treaty of Verdun, and a separate country established. This became known as France, the land of the Franks. But prior to that, at the time of the Roman empire, the region was known as Gaul. And the true origins go back far beyond the Roman period, to prehistoric times, as is evident from the abundant signs of early habitation.

Indeed, the first reliable evidence of the presence of modern man in Europe comes from south-west France. The earliest finds include a mandible from Montmaurin, a cave in the lower Pyrenees, and the fragments of two skulls at Fontéchevade, east of Angoulême. Skeletons have been discovered in Dordogne at Le Moustier, La Chapelle-aux-Saints and at La Ferrassie, whilst other finds have occurred in the valley of the river Somme and at Chelles, near Paris.

The most clearly recognizable example of an advanced human type was Cro-Magnon man. It was in 1868 that workmen in Périgord unearthed a number of skeletons in a rock shelter called Cro-Magnon, near Les Eyzies-de-Tayac. It was estimated that these individuals lived between 20,000 and 30,000 years ago, Similar finds were made at Aurignac in the lower Pyrenees. In the valley of the river Vézère in Dordogne archaeologists have found a wealth of material, notably tools and weapons, associated with the cultures of these early settlers. And it is in this region – at La Madeleine, La Mouthe, Font de Gaume, Les Combarelles, Lascaux and other sites, of which Les Eyzies is the centre – that astonishing cave paintings and drawings have also been revealed. Other painted caves have come to light at Angoulême and Cahors, and in the Pyrenees. All provide a wonderful insight into the life of these primitive societies.

The period of cave-dwellers extended over several thousands of years, as is shown by the developing styles of the decorations in caves such as Pech-Merle, near Cahors. But these cultures were superseded, around 8000BC, by that of the Neolithic era. The people of the New Stone Age learned to live by agriculture, to dwell in houses and villages, to make pottery and weave cloth. They used the wheel, built boats and eventually forged and cast metals. There is evidence of this civilization in the tumuli, or mound graves. But their most remarkable remains are the series of huge stone monuments that are scattered throughout western Europe.

The so-called megalithic culture (from the Greek *megas*, great, and *lithos*, stone) began to spread across France from about 2500BC onwards. Because most famous monuments have appeared in Brittany, they are usually called by Breton names. A single upright stone is called a *menhir*, flat stones placed on top of upright stones form a *dolmen*, and a *cromlech* consists of a series of upright stones in a circle. At Carnac, some 8km from Auray, the alignments of megaliths consists of more than 4000 stones, stretching for a distance of several kilometres. Similar monuments exist in southern France, as in the Ariège

Left Bonaparte as First Consul, the office to which he acceded in 1799, painted by Antoine-Jean Gros (1771–1825).

11

département. They testify to a mysterious culture, and certainly one that was highly organized and technically advanced.

Peoples from the eastern Mediterranean began to appear on the coasts of France around 1000BC. The Phoenicians established trading posts in such places as Monaco and Port Vendres. In about 600BC the Greeks founded Massilia (Marseilles) and their trade routes extended far inland, as is shown by the great bronze vase found at Vix, near Châtillon-sur-Seine, in Burgundy.

Predating the Greek settlements were the Celtic invasions. The Celts, coming from the mountainous regions of central Europe, succeeded in conquering the whole of Gaul. But with their varied origins and histories, they were organized into many dozens, perhaps hundreds of tribal groups; and topographical features – dense forests, swamps and rivers – ruled out any semblance of unity. The names of certain tribes are recognizable in modern French names, the Carnutes in Chartres, the Andegavi in Angers, the Pictavi in Poitiers and the Veneti in Vannes. Amongst the Celts, only the order of the Druids, with their religious, judicial and educational functions, provided some form of cultural uniformity to peoples who were politically fragmented.

The Romans began their conquest of Gaul around 120BC, responding to an appeal from the people of Massilia who were being threatened by local Gallic tribes, and they soon dominated the entire Mediterranean coast. They called it Provincia, the province, from which comes the present French name of Provence. It was this part of France which became most deeply imprinted with Latin culture.

The Pont du Gard built by the Romans across the ravine of Bonègre as part of a 25-mile long aqueduct bringing water from Uzès to Nîmes.

Between 58 and 50BC Julius Caesar conquered Gaul, his task facilitated by superior military strength and the feuds that divided the Gauls. His only serious challenge came from the chief of the Avernes, Vercingetorix; but the latter was eventually encircled and forced to surrender at Alésia (Alise-Ste-Reine, near Semur in Burgundy). For the first time Gaul had a unified system of government, soldiers and tax

collectors were despatched to every corner of the country, and Lugdunum (Lyon), at the meeting point of the rivers Rhône and Saône, founded in 43BC, became the nucleus of a road system and the administrative capital.

There are countless testaments to the highly sophisticated Roman civilization, notably in Provence, with examples such as the Pont du Gard, part of an aqueduct system, the vast arena and Maison Carrée at Nîmes, and the theatre and triumphal arch at Orange. In addition there are innumerable temples, monuments, tombs, amphitheatres, statues and baths, and the remains of ordinary houses adorned with mosaics, columns and other decorations. But Gaul was too big to be completely Romanized. Parts of the country, like the interior of the Massif Central, were less affected. Yet the Romans lost no opportunity to found towns and establish communications. Even in Brittany they developed both a coastal and river trade, and places like Nantes (which had some 13,000 inhabitants by the 3rd century), Rennes and Vannes, became prosperous. It is possible to find important remains in what are today small villages, such as Corseul, near Dinan, which was then a junction of several roads and the centre of much activity.

The impact of Rome was further modified by the collaboration of the Celts with their conquerors. The tribes remained important, as is evident from the fact that their names have endured whereas the Latin names have fallen into oblivion. Thus Reims, Amiens and Limoges are references to the Remi, the Ambioni and the Lemovices. The Celtic religion also persisted, its goddesses, for example, never being absorbed into Roman mythology; and just as the Romans sometimes carved representations of their gods on menhirs, so there are sculptures and decorations that show an assimilation of Roman and Celtic art. Thus it is sensible to talk of a Gallo-Roman civilization.

The origins of Christianity in Gaul are obscure, but it seems to have appeared in several of the main towns towards the end of the 1st century and to have become important in the 2nd century. By the beginning of the 4th century the church in Gaul was officially tolerated and the new religion spread from the towns to the rural areas. The church in Gaul venerated the most popular of all the French saints, St Martin of Tours.

The rise of Christianity coincided with the decline of the Roman Empire. The Germanic tribes proved fatal to an ailing Rome, and a variety of invaders roamed across France, some of them remaining permanently. The Visigoths settled in Aquitaine, between Bordeaux and Toulouse, and spread further eastwards. In the 5th century the Alamanni settled in Alsace, the Burgundians took possession of the land between the Rhône and the Saône, and Celts fleeing from Britain occupied the Roman province of Armorica which became known as Brittany. But after a short-lived invasion by the Huns, the Franks, arriving from the north, established their authority. They made agreements with the Gallo-Roman bishops who were the principal authorities in the towns, and in 496, when their leader Clovis was baptized, they became the champions of the Gallo-Roman Christians. Clovis founded the Merovingian dynasty, but with his death in 511 the kingdom fell apart and was divided into regions. The concept of unity, however, lingered on, and the capitals chosen by Clovis's sons were Reims, Orléans, Paris and Soissons, all located in the geographical area of the Paris basin. A confused period of conflict during the 6th and 7th centuries ended at Poitiers in 732 when one of the chiefs of the Austrasian Franks, Charles Martel, defeated a Moslem force that was advancing into France from Spain. His son, Pepin, became king of the Franks and was anointed by the pope. He united much of the kingdom, and his son Charles, who became king in 768, brought together all the Christian peoples of the west under his rule. This was Charlemagne, who on Christmas Day 800, was crowned Holy Roman Emperor by the pope in Rome.

A contemporary bronze of Charlemagne, king of the Franks and later crowned Holy Roman Emperor in 800; he was credited with the revival of intellectual life in Christian Europe.

It is likely that this was an empire in name only. One feature of Charlemagne's rule was to encourage the system of vassalage, the procedure whereby a warrior would bind himself to a lord by personal agreement. In return he might receive some land. Charlemagne wanted the lords similarly to bind themselves to him. This arrangement of bonds between one man and another (feudalism) was a move away from the Roman system of direct state authority. The certain fact is, however, that at Charlemagne's death (814) his empire was divided up and eventually, by the treaty of Verdun (843), France was separated from Germany and from Lotharingia which lay between them (the name exists today as Lorraine). Charlemagne's son, Louis the Pious, had already signed an agreement with Nominoë, the Breton ruler of Vannes, who became duke of Brittany and went on to expand his possessions. This form of agreement, whereby regional or local leaders achieved an official independence, was frequently repeated.

In the 9th and 10th centuries, France also had to contend with invading Vikings (Norsemen) from Scandinavia who established themselves in Terra Northmanorum, later known as Normandy. Within a century of their first appearance in the Seine valley in 820, their leader had been baptized in the name of Robert and had signed a treaty with the Carolingian king which gave him the title of duke of Normandy. He re-established the monasteries founded by the Franks in the 5th and 6th centuries, which earlier marauding Vikings had destroyed. Eventually, when the Carolingian royal line had died out, it was a descendant of Robert, Hugh Capet, in 987, who was elected king by an assembly of notables. This was the beginning of the royal house of France.

The Capetian kings gradually increased their power. At first they were masters of a collection of lands, châteaux and towns, called the royal domain. Other principalities in the kingdom were bigger. In 1066 the duke of Normandy, William the Conqueror, became king of England, and thus a much greater personage than the king of France. From the 11th century onwards, some of the most famous religious buildings in Europe were built in Normandy, such as the cathedrals of Coutances and Bayeux, and the abbeys of Bec and Jumièges, so adding to the prestige of the Norman rulers. Other principalities, such as

Detail from the celebrated Bayeux tapestry showing William, duke of Normandy, embarking for his invasion of England, 1066.

Brittany, Gascony and the county of Toulouse, had been founded on the basis of cultural or ethnic ties. Then there were centres of power which were the creation of enterprising individuals, such as the count of Flanders. But the Capetian domain was a region that included Paris and Orléans. It was at the heart of a prosperous area and was well placed both commercially and strategically. Through the efforts of several able and patient rulers, the Capetians gradually achieved supremacy.

The first famous monarch of this dynasty was Philip II (reigned 1180–1223), known as Philip Augustus, because he expanded his territories. He fought the English kings, the Plantagenets, who by inheritance, marriage and conquest, had established their rule over a large part of France stretching from Picardy in the north to the Pyrenees in the south. The other was Louis IX (1226–70), who won battles against the English and against his own rebellious aristocracy. His role as a Crusader gave him a great reputation for piety and he was to be canonized as St Louis.

When St Louis died the Capetian monarchy held undisputed power in the kingdom. New institutions had been set up, including the *parlements*, which were intended to deal with legal matters. From the 13th century onwards Paris had become a favourite and logical residence for the king, who lived on the Île de la Cité, in the Louvre fortress, or at Vincennes. Louis had expressed his religious zeal by two buildings in Paris, the hospital of the Quinze-Vingts, founded to house 300 blind persons, and the Sainte Chapelle, a repository for the relics of the Passion of Christ. The Gothic architecture of Notre-Dame in Paris and of later cathedrals such as Chartres, Amiens and Reims, reflects the country's prosperity and confidence.

Capetian power could at times be brutal, as with Philip the Fair (1285–1314), who tried to manipulate the papacy to his advantage. He secured the election of his candidate as pope in 1309, but the new pontiff, fearing the hostility of the Roman population, took up residence in Avignon. His successors, who were also French, remained

Louis IX embarks on the Seventh Crusade, 1248. Scene from a fourteenth-century manuscript.

15

Charles VII (1403–61) was inspired in his campaign against the English by Joan of Arc and was crowned king at Reims in 1429. Painting by Jean Fouquet (1420–81).

there for almost a century, and this city, with its papal palace, became unique in France.

The Capetian line died out in 1328 and Philip of Valois founded a new dynasty. From 1337 to 1453 the so-called Hundred Years' War was fought between England and France as the kings of England laid claim to inherit the French throne. The French were defeated at Crécy (1346), at Poitiers (1356) and at Agincourt (1415), but later, inspired by Joan of Arc, they rallied. Charles VII, who had taken refuge in Bourges, was persuaded by Joan to take the offensive and to capture Orléans and Reims, in which town he was crowned and anointed king in 1429. Even after Joan had been captured by the forces of the powerful duke of Burgundy and handed over to the English who burned her at Rouen in 1431, the royal fortunes continued to recover. After the death of Charles VII, Louis XI (1461–83) won control of Burgundy, Provence, Artois and Picardy. His successor, Charles VIII (1483–98) married Anne of Brittany, and after his death she married his successor and cousin Louis XII (1498–1515); thus the duchy of Brittany became a permanent part of the kingdom of France.

Both Charles VIII and Louis XII had invaded Italy, laying claim to Naples and Milan, but François I (1515–47) and Henri II (1547–89) transformed the Italian wars into a struggle for European supremacy against Charles V, the Holy Roman Emperor and ruler of central Europe, Spain and much of Italy. But the accidental death of Henri II and the absence of suitable heirs ushered in a period of some thirty years of civil warfare in which France's neighbours also intervened. The conflict was all the more bitter and complex because of the religious issue. The two most prominent rival families were the Guises, who were the leaders of the French Catholics, and the Bourbons, some of whom were members of the Protestant faith which had entered France, mainly under the influence of Calvin, from the 1540s onwards. The violence and brutality symptomatic of these religious disputes culminated in the massacre in Paris, on St Bartholomew's day in 1572, of thousands of Protestants.

When Henri III (1574–86) was assassinated, Henri of Navarre, a Bourbon and a Protestant, became the only rightful heir. He renounced his Protestantism and became king as Henri IV (1586–1610). He granted religious toleration to the Protestants with the Edict of Nantes (1598).

During this protracted period of warfare, France benefited from having many different centres of cultural and artistic activity. After Charles VII had settled in Bourges, the region of the Loire became noted for its fine châteaux. Jacques Coeur, the richest man in France, built himself a magnificent house at Bourges. Under François I Italian artists were encouraged to work in France, and to the great châteaux of the Loire such as Amboise, Blois and Chambord, he added that of Fontainebleau. Burgundy, too, boasted a culture that was independent of the royal court and which asserted itself with the ambitious buildings of Dijon and the original conception of the 'hospices' at Beaune. In the capital itself Henri IV had the Place Royale (now the Place des Vosges) built as a formal setting for residence and for public gatherings, and the Pont Neuf across the Seine was also completed.

When Henri IV was assassinated in his turn, there was a further period of rebellion, since his son Louis XIII (1610–43) was only nine years old and the queen mother, Marie de Médicis, an unpopular figure. In 1614 an Estates General, representing the three orders of the nation, the clergy, the nobility and the commons, presented an impressive list of grievances to the virtually powerless king. Only ten years later did Cardinal Richelieu become the chief minister and set out to curb the activities of unruly nobles. They were particularly active in

A contemporary print of the events of St Bartholomew's night, August 24 1572, when thousands of Huguenots were massacred in Paris and the provinces.

Three portraits by
Philippe de Champaigne
(1602–74) of Cardinal
Richelieu who, obsessed
with the idea of State
supremacy, devoted his
life to the services of
Louis XIII and the
aggrandisement of
France.

those parts of France where they were allowed to maintain local
assemblies or estates, which fixed taxation levels. These were Languedoc, Brittany, Burgundy, Provence, Normandy and the Dauphiné.
Richelieu used special agents, known as Intendants, to enforce the will
of the central government.

In 1643 Louis died, shortly after Richelieu, and history repeated
itself as Louis XIV (1643–1715) was aged only four and his mother
Anne of Austria was assisted by Cardinal Mazarin. A series of revolts,
known as the Frondes, took place, which involved members of the
royal family, nobles, the *parlements* which were anxious to maintain
their privileges, the Paris mob and the peasantry. About 90 per cent of
the sixteen million people who made up France at the beginning of the
17th century were peasants. Because of their precarious livelihood,
they would often explode into insurrection; and because they were so
influential, their risings were often joined by other social classes.

When Mazarin died in 1661, the young king took over the
government himself and was to rule as well as reign for the next fifty-
four years. He became the epitome of kingliness, living a life of
constant parade, dominated by etiquette – the Sun King who was so far
above his subjects that he required to be worshipped. The temple
where the worship was most clearly organized was the palace of
Versailles which was the supreme artistic accomplishment of the age,
bringing together architecture, sculpture, painting, furniture and
landscape gardening.

Through long wars and adroit diplomacy, Louis worked energetically to increase France's territory and wealth. Even such an important
minister as Colbert, who sought to bring order into France's financial
and commercial life, had little influence over policy. Yet Louis was not
always successful. He failed to unite the kingdoms of France and
Spain, and his revocation of the Edict of Nantes compelled many
Protestants to flee from France. By the time of his death there was
widespread discontent in his kingdom. There are those who would
argue that the real achievements of his reign are to be found in the plays

State portrait of Louis XIV by Hyacinthe Rigaud, one of the most successful portrait painters of Louis's reign.

Built on a vast and opulent scale, the palace of Versailles housed the centralized court of Louis XIV, reflecting the triumph of his monarchy by Divine Right. Painting by Pierre-Denis Martin (1663–1742).

Louis XV was five when he ascended the throne in 1710, and France was ruled by the Regent Philippe d'Orléans. This painting by Nicolas Lancret shows the majority of the king and the Bed of Justice ceremony in parliament, 1723.

of Corneille, Molière and Racine, the philosophy of Descartes, the glories of Versailles and the buildings of Paris, such as the Invalides.

The 18th century demonstrated the contradictions underlying the despotic rule of the French kings. Louis XV (1715–74) and Louis XVI (1774–93) attempted to make the government more efficient, but failed. The vast cost of the many wars which France fought in Europe, North America and India, together with the general inflationary movement of the century, made it necessary for the government to increase its revenue. Thinkers such as Voltaire responded to this drastic situation by criticizing all the nation's institutions, whilst Rousseau put forward new ideas about man's rights and obligations in society.

By 1789 the government was close to bankruptcy. For the first time since 1614 the Estates General was summoned and the Third Estate (the commons) saw this as a chance to air its grievances and assume what it considered to be its rightful place in French society. Already certain of the provinces had shown hostility to the central government and the nobility had been particularly recalcitrant. During the spring and summer of 1789 there were disturbances in many parts of the country. On 14 July the mob captured the Bastille in Paris, symbol of state authority, and the countryside became seized by agitation. The result was an attempt to establish a constitution whereby the king would share his power with the elected representatives of the wealthier citizens. In a system of rational government there was to be equality before the law and the administrative confusions of the preceding centuries were swept away as France was divided into 83 *départements*. The financial crisis was to be solved by nationalizing and selling church property, and social problems resolved by abolishing much of the feudal system.

The Catholic church and many of the nobility nevertheless opposed the Revolution, and some European powers threatened to intervene in support of the royal family (the queen, Marie-Antoinette, was a Hapsburg). This led to war against enemies abroad and enemies within; and as a consequence the Revolution became more violent. New leaders such as Danton and Robespierre assumed supreme

Marie-Antoinette, aged 17, painted in 1773 when she was still Dauphine.

A popular engraving by Carnavalet of the Fall of the Bastille, June 14, 1789.

Napoleon, Alexander I, Frederick William III and Queen Louise of Prussia at Tilsit in 1807. The Tilsit treaties signalled Napoleon's total domination of Europe.

power; the king and queen were executed and France became a republic. In the period known as the Terror the guillotine was used against the enemies of the Revolution and civil war broke out as a counter-Revolution was organized in the west. The patriotic fervour of the defenders of the Revolution is commemorated by the song which was sung by those who marched to Paris from Marseilles, the Marseillaise; places in Brittany, such as Nantes, Auray and Quiberon preserve the memory of the counter-Revolution.

By 1794 the war crisis diminished and moderation returned. From 1795 to 1799 central power was divided among several Directors (hence this period was known as the Directory). But it proved impossible to establish stable government at home or to apply a consistent foreign policy. A young and victorious general of Corsican birth, Napoleon Bonaparte, was able to turn the desire for security to his personal benefit and in 1799 he seized power.

Initially assuming the title of first consul, then consul for life, and finally, in 1804, accepting the crown as Emperor Napoleon I, in Notre-Dame, with the pope standing by and giving his blessing, France's new ruler aimed to make his regime the rallying point for all French citizens. But his government was a personal affair, wholly dependent on his energy, his rapid mind, his mastery of detail. Inevitably he came to rely heavily on the bureaucracy, and sought to extend and improve the centralized system of government that he inherited from the past. He issued a code of laws, made the imperial university the authority for the whole educational system, and laid special emphasis on the *lycées*, secondary schools for boys, which would provide France with future officials. He had always admired the Romans, and his neo-classical tastes were reflected in architecture, notably in such buildings as the Arc de Triomphe, the church of the Madeleine, and the column of Vendôme which bore his statue.

Nevertheless it was as a soldier that Napoleon achieved his greatest fame. The legend of the little man in the grey coat leading his armies across the continent has its basis in fact. Defeat was fatal to him. In 1814 he was exiled to the island of Elba. The next year, always the adventurer, he escaped and returned to France as emperor. But his defeat at Waterloo was final and there was no attempt to get his young son to succeed him.

After 1815, Louis XVI's brother was returned to the throne as Louis XVIII, and established a parliamentary regime in which a small number of wealthy men had the vote. His brother, Charles X, who succeeded him in 1824, grew impatient with this system and tried to restore royal authority. In July 1830 a rising of the people in Paris forced him off the throne (the tall column that stands in the middle of the Place de la Bastille commemorates those who died in this revolution). The Orléans branch of the Bourbons took over the throne in the person of Louis Philippe, but he never succeeded in gaining the support of the whole nation. He was accused of governing in the name of the upper bourgeoisie. In 1848 a revolution with socialist undertones forced him off the throne and he was the last king ever to rule over France.

The second Republic was not long-lived. Napoleon's nephew, Louis Bonaparte, was elected president but in 1851 he declared himself emperor, with the title of Napoleon III. The bourgeois king had been replaced by a bourgeois emperor who believed in making the country prosperous. He sought to modernize the economy by building railways, promoting public works, developing banks, and encouraging the opening of large departmental stores. Paris, becoming all the more important as the centre of the railway system, was transformed by Baron Haussmann. Its streets were made into wide, straight boulevards (which would be useful in putting down riots) and it was beautified by the creation of parks and the building of a new opera house.

Possibly because he was a Bonaparte, Napoleon III determined to conduct an active foreign policy, against Russia in the Crimea and against Austria in Italy (which enabled him to annex Nice to France). But in 1870, provoked by Bismarck, he declared war against Russia, was defeated and captured. A Republic was proclaimed on 4 September 1870.

The first task of the new government was to make peace with the Germans who had besieged Paris. This was followed by a working class rising in Paris known as the Commune (1871), which was ruthlessly crushed by French troops. But thereafter the Third Republic consolidated itself. It was always weak, because it tried to combine a centralized administration with a parliamentary system and because French people were very divided, both socially and ideologically. It was also weak economically because the pace of French industrialization was slower than that of other countries and because the French population did not increase as rapidly as others. Yet it overcame its greatest crisis, the 1914–18 war. The Germans invaded France and occupied about one-tenth of her territory. The worst battles of the war, such as Verdun, were fought in France. By the time the Allies had won in 1918, France had lost 1,325,000 dead, some 10 per cent of its able-bodied male population.

Thus it was a seriously weakened country that emerged from the war. The lost generation could not be replaced. Pre-war prosperity could not be regained. No political consensus could be attained. France could no longer stand on her own as a great power. After going reluctantly to war with Hitler's Germany in 1939, France was unable to withstand the German offensive of May 1940. The French army was completely broken. France signed an armistice and accepted that much of her territory should be occupied by Germany. In one short but devastating campaign, a long historical process had been temporarily reversed.

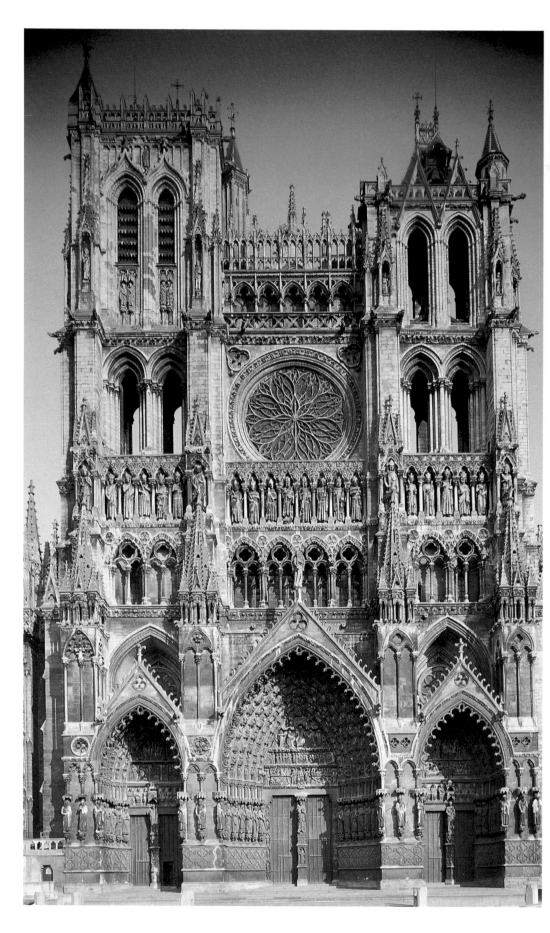

ARCHITECTURE

The traveller in France moves through an immense time perspective. Most of western Europe's prehistoric settlements were in what we now call the Dordogne where the many cave paintings, especially around Les-Eyzies-de-Tayac in the Vézère valley exemplify a high level of representational skill thousands of years before the appearance of anything of equivalent quality elsewhere. The Lascaux cave near Montignac is perhaps the best known prehistoric site in Europe, if not the world.

The cave paintings are over 20,000 years old, but it was not until the Neolithic period that standing megaliths in ritualistic patterns were planted on both sides of the Channel. Near Carnac on the Brittany coast there are thousands of these stones, erected about 1500BC; some weigh several tons and they are arranged in accurately oriented lines.

It is the Roman buildings of Transalpine Gaul, however, which represent the first significant surviving architecture of France. By 120BC the Romans controlled the northern Mediterranean seaboard from Spain to Thessaly, and the Provincia Romana (Provence) was firmly established. Although there are, of course, Roman remains right across France, it is in those favoured early locations around the Rhône delta in modern Provence and the Languedoc that the best preserved and most impressive monuments are to be found.

Arles, at the junction of the Aurelian Way from Rome to Spain and the Agrippan Way to the north, and with a canal linking it to the sea, became the capital of the province. The great elliptical arena has lost its upper (third) storey but still dominates much of the old town. The nearby theatre, still in use, has been much restored and modified over the original lower levels. The podium of an imposing forum and a necropolis cemetery on the outskirts of the town indicate the status of Roman Arles.

Opposite The soaring west front of Amiens cathedral, one of the glories of the second period of French Gothic and a lasting tribute to the anonymous craftsmen who built the great medieval churches of northern France.

Below Though it now lacks its upper storey, the massive amphitheatre at Arles remains a powerful reminder of the Roman presence in Provence.

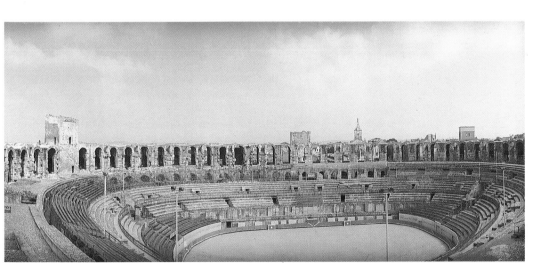

Nîmes was a principal
centre of Roman
civilization in Provence;
the city's famous Maison
Carrée is one of the finest
and best preserved of all
Roman provincial
temples.

The most spectacular Roman provincial buildings of the Augustan age, however, are in and around Nîmes (Nemausus) on the river Gard. The Maison Carrée is probably the best preserved of all Roman temples, and the amphitheatre, too, is almost complete. In the Jardin de la Fontaine stands the Tour Magne, and below it the so-called Temple of Diana, in fact a part of the baths with a barrel-vaulted roof and vaulted aisles, prototypes of the nave-aisle arrangement of Christian basilican churches for over a thousand years. Twenty kilometres north-east is the most majestic of all Roman architectural-engineering achievements, the Pont du Gard, part of a 30km aqueduct, its water channel at this point nearly 50m above the level of the river bed.

At Orange (Arausio), founded by Augustus on the site of an earlier town, there is a Roman theatre capable of seating 10,000, and one of the largest of all triumphal arches. St-Rémy-de-Provence, Roman Glanum, has a unique cenotaph mausoleum 20m high with carved stone panels of extraordinary beauty and vigour. Fréjus, which also boasts Augustan remains, provides a rare link between Roman imperial and Christian architecture in the form of a late Roman-Christian baptistry, now a part of the cathedral; there is another, perhaps rather more restored example at Aix-en-Provence, earliest of all Roman settlements in France. These early Christian buildings are among the first to demonstrate the unadorned forms appropriate to the Christian ethic.

The last Roman governor was defeated by Clovis at Soissons in AD486, and another thousand years was to pass before the first great period of French architecture reached maturity; and it was the Christian foundations and communities who brought it into being. The full glory of high Gothic did not emerge until the designers of the great churches ceased looking back to the forms of Roman engineering and abandoned the round for the pointed arch. There was little secular building until the mid-9th century when warring factions began building castles and fortifications, the symbols of emergent feudalism. Little remains in France of early Christian and Byzantine architecture, although we know from the writings of Gregory of Tours, Bishop Namatius and others that fine basilican churches were built, for example at Tours and Clermont. Many early buildings used timber in their construction and thus fell easy prey to the marauders of the 9th and 10th centuries.

The Romanesque style in France started late and only accelerated significantly in the second half of the 11th century after William of

Normandy conquered England, and there followed a period of comparative peace in northern France. There seems to have been a desire to replace and augment buildings destroyed in the preceding 200 years or so in more permanent materials, as well as to celebrate the growing assurance of the Christian communities. The church builders responded magnificently to the challenge to roof ever larger spaces in stone. The earlier Romanesque buildings reflected many of the diverse influences of the Mediterranean region. The Moors were in south-west France by AD720 and their direct influence can be seen in the domed churches such as the cathedral at Cahors (Midi-Pyrenees) so reminiscent of the Byzantine church of St-Irene at Constantinople. The cathedrals of Périgueux, Angoulême and, further north, Fontevrault Abbey, all have domed naves, and although they were all much restored in the 19th century remain among the finest examples of Romanesque aisleless churches in Europe.

Direct Roman influence, on the other hand, can be seen in the Romanesque churches of Arles – St-Gilles-du-Gard and St-Trophime – not only in their barrel-vaulted naves but also in their west fronts which recall the earlier triumphal arches. The influence is more residual in the great Romanesque churches of the Auvergne and Burgundy. Clermont-Ferrand is often cited as the most typical of the basilican churches from which the high Gothic evolved. It has a simple stone barrel-vaulted roof and a high triforium. Other churches of the region such as those at Issoire and Le Puy share with Clermont the inlaid decoration made from the coloured lavas of the Puy-de-Dôme district.

Little remains of Burgundy's best known medieval monastery at Cluny, but some of its features, which included very early pointed arches, can be seen in other nearby churches – the cathedral at Autun, St-Madeleine, Vézelay, and St-Philibert at Tournus, earliest of the Burgundian barrel-vaulted churches. Autun is indeed a miniature version of Cluny, its nave covered with a pointed barrel vault on transverse arches, and at Vézelay the entrance narthex has one of the earliest pointed cross-vaults in France. The church stands above the town and its radiating east-end chapels combine to give one of the most dramatic examples of church architecture in the world.

Although cross-vaults in aisleless churches are to be found in west-central France, for example at Angers, Saumur and Poitiers, it is the 11th and 12th-century churches of the north-west which most immediately portend the appearance of the Gothic style itself in the Île-de-

Above The church of St-Philibert at Tournus, notable among Burgundian churches for its early pointed arches and barrel-vaulting.

Left A masterpiece of Burgundian ecclesiastical art: the carved tympanum in St-Lazaire, the cathedral of Autun, depicting the Last Judgment.

The vaulting of Laon cathedral, one of the great churches of the first, or Primaire, period of French Gothic.

France. The two great Norman churches of Caen are the best known examples and along with St-Denis, near Paris, are the most significant in terms of architectural development. The Abbaye-aux-Dames was founded by Matilda, wife of William the Conqueror, about 1062. Its twin towers rise in beautifully proportioned arcaded stages, their masses balanced by a square tower at the crossing. The Abbaye-aux-Hommes, begun a few years later by William himself is a vaulted basilican church with an ambulatory and radiating chapels of later (12th century) date, an arrangement to be developed as a feature of so many of the great Gothic churches. Its west-end spires and pinnacles characterize the ethereal quality of William's church. It is also worth looking for the fascinating smaller churches in Normandy, many with vaulted naves and towers, which give architectural character to towns such as Bernières-sur-Mer, Ouistreham and Boscherville.

If the Normandy churches presage the coming high Gothic, it is the Abbé Suger's reconstruction and extension of St-Denis which moves the centre of architectural interest to the Île-de-France. He is credited with the introduction of the 'ogival' system of the choir roof, earliest of the rib-vault constructions developed to carry the weight of stone roofs via flying buttresses, weighted with pinnacles and onto increasingly slender column-clusters, forming a stone frame, so that, as in modern buildings, the panels between become screens only, and in the major Gothic buildings are filled almost entirely with stained glass, until the whole fabric assumes an insubstantial, soaring appearance.

The earliest of the French Gothic cathedrals, Laon, Lisieux and Notre-Dame-de-Paris, although exciting, still retain an air of great solidity – the heavy Corinthianesque columns and a feeling of the Romanesque in their decoration. This is the Primaire period, sometimes called 'à lancettes', distinguished by narrow-pointed and geometric traceried windows. There are other examples at Noyon, at Sens, where the lofty cathedral was built by that same master mason William who built Canterbury, and at Senlis. As the sophistication of the stone technology improved, the great naves reached unprecedented levels of daring and virtuosity.

Interior of Laon cathedral which, though distinctly of the first Gothic period, still retains some elements of Romanesque 'heaviness'.

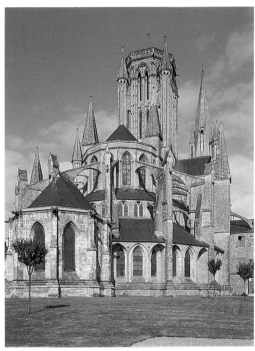

By the early years of the 13th century, the skills of the French master masons coincided with the burgeoning aspirations of the civil communities to produce the masterpieces of Gothic architecture. This is the Secondaire, 'rayonnant' period during which were built Reims, Amiens, Bourges and most of Chartres. Bourges is often regarded as the supreme example of pure French Gothic, its single spacious volume uninterrupted by transepts, its semi-circular chevet a fitting climax to the aspiring perspective of the nave. Superlatives do not exist to do justice in a few words to the glories of Reims and Amiens, or to convey the wonder which goes with the first sight of the spires or the stained glass of Chartres. And if the 60m ridge of Amiens with its timber flèche does not set you back on your heels, travel a little south and stand amazed inside all that remains of Beauvais cathedral, its vault some 48m from the floor, and try to envisage its open-work spire which collapsed for want of a nave to buttress it almost as soon as it was built. Here, too, the transept demonstrates the third stage of French Gothic architecture, Tertiaire or 'Flamboyant', which marked the beginning of its decline over the next two centuries. Yet the period includes such wonderful buildings as Rouen's two major churches, St-Ouen and St-Maclou, the latter with perhaps the richest of all Flamboyant interiors. And whilst still in Normandy, keep an eye open for the churches with intriguing mixtures of periods and styles from Romanesque to Flamboyant Gothic in their make-up – they are everywhere – Évreux, Troyes, Dol, St-Pierre at Caen, Coutances, Bayeux and many others.

Not all French Gothic architecture is ecclesiastical: the earlier centuries produced many fortified towns. Carcassonne was already important in the Romanesque period, the 13th-century walls of Aigues Mortes in the Languedoc and romantic Mont-St-Michel both conjure up stories of the troubadours, to say nothing of the 14th-century papal city of Avignon with its machicolated walls and towers. By the 15th century, fortified castles began to give way to country houses. The Château d'Amboise, built almost entirely in the 15th century, was the first royal residence in France, and Josselin in Brittany has a fine Flamboyant courtyard facade built later in the century. Sixteenth-century civic buildings include Hôtels de Ville at Arras, Bourges, Dreux and Compiègne, and the Palais de Justice at Rouen, much damaged in 1944. A number of fine town houses have survived. The

Above left One of the glories of Chartres cathedral is the stained glass which embellishes what many regard as one of the most beautiful buildings in the western world. This illustration shows a panel from the Charlemagne window.

Above right Many notable Norman churches, like this one at Coutances, display an interesting *mélange* of architectural styles, from the Romanesque to successive phases of Gothic.

The châteaux of the Loire valley represent one of the finest flowerings of French Renaissance architecture with few examples more impressive than Chenonceaux, here seen from its gardens instead of the more usual river view.

Bourgtheroulde house at Rouen and the Chambellan house at Dijon with its characteristic carved figures on the street facade are among the better known examples. Smaller half-timbered houses of the period can be seen at St-Lô, Caen and Beauvais.

It was to the Château d'Amboise that Charles VIII returned from Italy towards the end of the 15th century with a number of Italian artists and craftsmen in his train. He ushered in the early period of French Renaissance architecture associated with the châteaux of the Loire (most of them built in the first quarter of the 16th century) and with the reign of François I. The masters of the new repertory of decorative forms were Philibert de l'Orme, Pierre Lescot, Jean Bullant and Cerceau the Elder; their Loire valley châteaux range from the additions to Blois, through a list of names which are synonymous with

Painted panels by Primaticcio decorate the King's staircase of Fontainebleau, massively redeveloped in the early 16th century by François I.

the elegance of the period – Chambord, Chenonceaux, Azay-le-Rideau and Villandry.

François I also began the work of redeveloping Fontainebleau: he commissioned Gilles le Breton and established the colony of artists whose work was to become influential across the whole of western Europe. Primaticcio, an Italian artist from Mantua, joined the group in 1532 and was largely responsible for designing the stucco and painted panels which are so much a characteristic of French Renaissance interiors. Fontainebleau's exterior facades, on the other hand, are unimpressive, although its courtyards, terraces and gardens portend the coming formalism of the classical period. Other interesting buildings of the time include the early 16th-century Hôtel de Ville at Orléans, the Hôtel de Ville at Beaugency and the Hôtel Assézat at Toulouse. There are also a number of ecclesiastical examples, such as St-Pierre at Caen, St-Étienne-du-Mont and St-Eustache in Paris, and the tomb of the Cardinales d'Amboise at Rouen.

The architects of the period visited Rome and the age of rational classicism associated in literature with Corneille, and in painting with Poussin, began. It had been heralded in the early years of the 17th century by Salomon de Brosse in the Luxembourg Palace, in his facade to the late Gothic church of St-Gervais in Paris and in the Palais de Justice at Rennes.

In 1546 François I gave Pierre Lescot the first commission for remodelling the Louvre palace, which with the Tuileries was to form that vast complex of royal palaces along the north bank of the Seine, destined not to achieve its present form until almost the end of the 19th century. But even as the work of François Mansart epitomized the high classical tradition in the Orléans wing at Blois and in the symmetry of the Château de Maisons (in the 1630s), the Baroque was already in the air, and can be sensed in his church of Ste-Marie in the Rue St-Antoine, Paris. This was to be the style of Louis XIV and Colbert, boosted when they commissioned further development at the Louvre and at Versailles. Jules Hardouin Mansart (nephew of François) and Louis le Vau were to be the purveyors of the new 'official' style, and the former remained Louis's principal architect for over forty years. At Versailles, the park facade, the great galleries and the gardens by Le Nôtre are more Baroque in spirit than any other manifestation in

French architects of the 17th and 18th centuries proved themselves exceptionally adept at solving the problems of large-scale urban planning. The Louvre, developed over a long period, forms a striking termination to the Jardin des Tuileries.

French art of the time. There is a consistency in the mastery of the style in the Grand Trianon, the Orangery and the chapel, and it is noticeable also in J.L. Mansart's other buildings, for example, his dome to Les Invalides. All possess the Baroque understanding of space and movement and are unsurpassed even by Bernini himself in Rome.

The work of Mansart's contemporaries had already established a tradition of handling large-scale urban design problems. Mansart's own Place de la Vendôme and Claude Chastillon's Place des Vosges, amongst others, pointed the way. There are, for example, civic schemes at Nancy by de Corny linking earlier buildings by Boffrand, rebuilding at Rennes following the 1720 fire, and the Place Royale at Bordeaux, these last two by Jacques Gabriel, father of Jacques-Ange who was to design the Place de la Concorde in Paris.

The 18th century saw the beginning of the Rococo and the so-called Louis XV style. As well as winning the competition for the Place de la Concorde, J.A. Gabriel designed the Petit Trianon at Versailles. He was a master of rococo detail, used extensively in his interiors, and it tempered the somewhat severe external classical forms with a handling of scale reminiscent of the Baroque: the giant classical orders of the twin palaces of the Concorde are excellent examples of his work. This brilliant balance between form and decoration, so typical of French architecture in the last two or three decades of the 18th century, can be appreciated in such buildings as Soufflot's Panthéon, completed in 1792, in Antoine's building for the Mint and the Palais de Justice in Paris, both finished in the late 1770s, and in Victor Louis's theatre at Bordeaux (1773–80), for more than a century regarded both aesthetically and technically as a model for theatres all over Europe. And although few of their buildings remain, of major importance to the future development of architecture are the visionaries, Boulée and Ledoux. The latter was one of the king's architects, and his Paris Barrières, such as that at La Vilette (1785), presage the futuristic projects in which he proposed that architecture should be purified by the use of simple unadorned geometrical forms – the beginnings of the Modern Movement in the 18th century.

With the Republic and Napoleon came an interest in Roman models of the republican era, and the 19th century was ushered in with Percier's Arc du Carrousel, closely followed by Chalgrin's Arc de Triomphe of 1808, some three years after Napoleon was crowned emperor. The use of Roman precedents is perhaps best exemplified by the Madeleine, completed over the next few years. Designed by

Built from 1687 onwards by Hardouin-Mansart and Robert de Cotte, the Grand Trianon at Versailles is a reduced version of the main palace, to which the sovereign could escape from court etiquette.

The interior of the library of Ste-Geneviève, a notable mid 19th-century cast-iron frame building, notable also for a facade in Italian Renaissance style.

Vignon, it literally imitates an octastyle Roman temple, but its impressive interior owes little to republican Rome – it is lit imaginatively from a most elegant series of saucer domes.

The period from the eclipse of Napoleon to the mid-19th century was one of eclectic revivals in France, as elsewhere in Europe, but was also notable for the development of new building materials, especially cast iron, concrete (originally following Roman models), and eventually steel. In Paris, perhaps the most distinguished building of the mid-century is the library of Ste-Geneviève by Henri Labrouste, in which a building with a completely cast iron frame is combined with a facade of nearly perfect early Italian Renaissance style. There are also many examples of fine cast iron construction in the galleries and market halls of the 1840s and 1850s. But the heavy quasi-Baroque of the Second Empire hung on for many years in parallel with buildings of almost every style from the past, the high Renaissance being perhaps the most memorable, for example in the great railway stations, and Charles Garnier's Paris Opera House. This style was also encouraged by contemporary publications such as Letarouilly's *Édifices de Rome Moderne* of 1864, and to its acceptance France owes much of her impressive urban development of the later part of the century. This is best characterized by the large areas of Paris transformed by Haussmann between 1853 and 1868, at the expense, unfortunately, of so many fine buildings of the ancien régime. The revivalist schools continued alongside the exciting developments in structure under the influence of engineers such as Eiffel – the Paris Opera predates Bon Marché by only two years – and produced such varied buildings as the Gothic St-Epvre, Nancy, and the Sacré Coeur whose white Byzantine domes on the heights of Montmartre reflect Paul Abadie's detailed knowledge of St-Front, Périgueux.

It was, however, an associate of Labrouste, Eugène Emanuel Viollet-le-Duc, whose writings brought together the rational design developments represented by iron-framed buildings and the remaining, often debased neo-classicism of the Second Empire. He argued that construction and structural techniques should be the basis of good design and should lead to the establishment of a true 19th-century style. But the practical amalgamation of the new functionalist attitude with the neo-classical tradition of French architecture was only achieved at the turn of the century in the work of Auguste Perret, who was also one of the founding fathers of the Modern Movement in architecture.

Meanwhile, the linear forms of cast iron encouraged a peculiarly French manifestation of the short-lived Art Nouveau. The sinuous metal plant forms which entwine the structure and break up the glass lines of the Samaritaine, and Guimard's Métro entrances, their structures almost hidden amongst the convoluted lines of doors and display panels, are eloquent of the fin-de-siècle search for new idioms.

As elsewhere in Europe, the new century began with architects seeking a symbolism more in keeping with engineering developments, but in France the evolution of new idioms was related closely to the development of reinforced concrete. From early Perret to the system-built grand ensembles of the 1960s it is concrete which characterizes French avant-garde architecture. Just as the older townscapes take on their character from the vernacular idioms of the periods in which they grew, from the soft colour-washed walls and warm faded reds of Roman pantiles in Provence to the harsher but often equally romantic mixtures of yellow stone Gothic and grey Romanesque in Normandy, most of the modern architecture of post-war France takes its character from the reinforced concrete of the heroic engineering period of the second half of the 19th century. The names of François Coignet, whose first patents date from 1855, François Hénebique, whose important work on concrete was published in 1879, and Freyssinet (pre-stressed concrete) are still associated with concrete building systems today.

It is the work of Auguste Perret, however, which best expresses the changes which introduce the Modern Movement. His apartment building at 25b, Rue Franklin in Paris (1903) and his garage in the Rue Ponthieu, demolished in 1968, in their early 20th-century context must have been quite staggering to a public used to the urban aesthetic of 19th-century Paris. Whilst the Champs Élysée Theatre (with Henry Van de Velde) is untypical in having marble facing, the foyer begins to indicate the neo-classical flavour of Perret's later work; but it is hardly apparent in the two churches built immediately after World War I, Notre-Dame, Le Raincy, and Ste-Thérèse, Montmagny, both near Paris. The churches have west-end towers quite unlike anything that preceded them and both have thin concrete wall panels with filigree glazing direct to the concrete. The gridded windows and the increasingly neo-classical character of the later work such as the Musée de l'Assistance publique, are among the strongest influences to be discerned in the flood of anonymous urban buildings between the wars.

Le Corbusier worked in Perret's office for a time in 1908, but his earliest work is associated with the cubists, Léger, Ozenfant and Picasso. His first buildings, workers' houses for Henri Fruges at Lège near Arachon and at Pessac, a few kilometres from Bordeaux, express in cubist terms the ideas about planning and structure which informed much of his later work and his influential writings. The hundred or so houses at Pessac have been much modified by successive owners, but like the better known private villas, Les Terraces at Garches and the Villa Savoye at Poissy, correspond to the popular concept of modern architecture. The Pavillon Suisse at the City University of Paris, with its juxtaposition of cubist and fluid shapes, has generated a thousand

The International Style is also represented in Paris, notably in the UNESCO building of 1958 by Marcel Breuer and Pier Luigi Nervi.

pale imitations, some of them in the late 1930s, others in the last forty years during which the international style has spread to almost every country in the world.

After World War II, Le Corbusier introduced the bolder, more deeply modelled facades exemplified by the Unité d'Habitation at Marseilles. The Dominican monastery at Éveux-sur-l'Arbrêsle, near Lyon, is a smaller building in the same genre but in a sense is a late example, because the Jaoul house at Neuilly already heralds the return to humanist values now affecting architecture everywhere, and enshrined in the jewel-like church of Notre-Dame-de-Ronchamp. Meanwhile contradictory design attitudes thrive side by side and make the architectural scene more exhilarating. What could provide greater contrast than Spoerry's Port Grimaud with its modern vernacular Provençal images compared with La Grande Motte, half a day's drive way into the Languedoc, where the space-age concrete pyramids, echoing Niemeyer's Brasilia, come as something of a shock in that dreaming landscape. No more of a shock perhaps, than for the visitor to Paris who has not previously seen the down-town scale intrusion of La Défense when viewed along the grand vista of the Élysées; but Paris would not have been complete without its own international modernismus across the Périphérique, its mighty Fiat building and the Dallas dazzle of the Manhattan Tower. For France as a whole, the changing scene is perhaps best illustrated by comparing the UNESCO Secretariat building of 1958, which brings together other famous names of the Modern Movement (Marcel Breuer and Pier Luigi Nervi), with the Centre Pompidou. The former demonstrates well the power and influence of the fathers of the modern face of Europe which may be seen by driving through almost any French town, especially those which have doubled their size in twenty or so years as a result of recent industrialization. The Pompidou Centre, on the other hand, with its romantic cast iron imagery, whilst perhaps a relevant symbol of the high-tech 1970s, is already being overtaken by a new interest in the historic past.

One of the most controversial buildings constructed in Paris in recent years is the massive high-tech Post-Modernist centre for the arts, the Centre Pompidou.

ART

Deep in the south of France, in the rather musty museum at Villeneuve-lès-Avignon, just across the Rhône from Avignon itself, hangs a magnificent 15th-century altarpiece depicting *The Coronation of the Virgin*. It was painted by Enguerrand Quarton (c.1410–66), one of the first French painters whose name has come down to us. In Paris, in the Salon Carré of the Louvre, hangs the famous *Pietà* which, like *The Coronation of the Virgin*, was originally painted for the Gothic Charterhouse at Villeneuve. It too is sometimes attributed to Quarton, though there is no firm evidence to prove this. But whoever was the artist of the Villeneuve *Pietà*, with its mourning figures of the Virgin, St John and Mary Magdalene leaning bleakly over the dead Christ, there is no doubt that it is among the most moving religious images ever painted, anywhere. It is also the first masterpiece in the story of painting in France which can be described as characteristically French. In its quiet and unblinking confrontation with the facts of suffering and death, the picture seems the very embodiment of that *sens du vrai*, that feeling for reality, which Manet once told Marcel Proust was the essence of French art.

If it seems surprising that this early masterpiece should have been painted not in Paris but in Provence, it is worth remembering that Paris has not always been the hub of artistic life in France. During the later Middle Ages after Agincourt, the French kings were at their weakest. Their depleted realm extended little beyond the Île-de-France and was under constant threat from the English and from powerful independent nobles like the Duke of Burgundy. For much of the time there can have been little peace of mind or leisure either at court or in the impoverished city for the pursuit of the arts. This is why so many of the surviving early works of 'French' painting come from the fringes of modern France; from the south, Provence and Roussillon, and the north-east, Burgundy and Lorraine, areas of relative peace and prosperity.

At Perpignan, tucked in under the Pyrenees, in the little Musée Rigaud, is the 15th-century *Retable of the Trinity*, a devotional work painted for the *consuls de mer* of the town and including a rather idealized view of the still surviving *loge de mer* or stock exchange. For a century or more before this picture was painted, this corner of south-west France, Roussillon, belonged to the Spanish kingdom of Catalonia. The splendid Perpignan *Trinity* is entirely Spanish in feel, but remembering the Villeneuve *Pietà*, we can see how something of the dark realism of Catalan painting must have penetrated to neighbouring Provence.

Provence was early on a channel for another stream that flowed into French painting. In the 14th century, the presence of the popes at Avignon, in self-imposed exile from the quarrels of the noble families of Rome, made the region an independent centre of a sophisticated culture with closer links to Italy than France. Petrarch lived many years of his life at Avignon; while Simone Martini (c.1284–1344), the greatest Sienese painter in the generation after Duccio, worked with a

Left The labours of the French countryside as well as the elegance of courtly life in the 1400s were portrayed by the Limbourg brothers in the month of *August* from the *Très Riches Heures du Duc de Berri* (Musée Condé, Chantilly).

team of assistants on the frescoes which can still be seen in the Palace of the Popes. It was from this city that their elegant and refined style, called International Gothic, found its way to Burgundy and eventually Paris. And, as we have seen, the culture was still vigorous enough after the popes left to produce the simplified, monumental painting of Quarton and his associates.

Kenneth Clark has called the *Très Riches Heures du Duc de Berri*, the illuminated book of hours which is the greatest masterpiece of the International Gothic style, one of the miracles of the history of art. Its pages were painted in about 1416 by the Limbourg brothers for the most important artistic patron of the time, the Duke of Berry, uncle of the unhappy King Charles VI. This fragile work, which is in the Musée Condé at Chantilly, just outside Paris, is indeed a miracle, not just in the fact of its survival, but in the extreme beauty of its highly wrought miniatures of hawking and hunting, feasting and amorous dalliance, the whole romanticized ritual and parade of life at the duke's sophisticated late-medieval court.

The Duke of Berry and his powerful brother, the Duke of Burgundy, who also employed the Limbourgs, were able to monopolize the talents of the best artists of their time because of the weakness of the French crown. But with the return of strong government in the second half of the 15th century under Charles VII, Paris and the royal châteaux in the surrounding region were increasingly to become the main sources of patronage and main dynamos of artistic development.

Outstanding among the painters who worked for Charles VII was Jean Fouquet (c.1420–81), who stands just this side of the divide between the medieval and modern worlds. His most interesting work, *The Melun Diptych* of about 1450, which depicts an almost shockingly secular and sexy Virgin (sometimes said to be the king's mistress Agnès Sorel) is, alas, no longer in France. But Fouquet's incisive portraits of Charles and his thuggish chancellor Guillaume Jouvenel des Ursins hang in the Louvre. They show that the artist had not only absorbed the new and realistic monumental conventions of Italian and Flemish portrait painting, but that he was capable of using them to describe this generation of ruthless *realpolitikers* with unflattering objectivity.

Art in 16th-century France was dominated by the inexhaustible energy and ambition of one man, François I, who has been described as the first modern Frenchman. François was avid for all the new learning, manners, science and art of Renaissance Italy. He invited Benvenuto Cellini to France. He bought sculpture from Michelangelo. He even persuaded the aged Leonardo to come to Amboise, bringing with him, incidentally, the *Mona Lisa*. The king's collection of Italian painting, which forms the nucleus of the Louvre museum, was a formative influence on French artists in the royal service. It is somehow difficult to believe that this *uomo universale* was the contemporary of Henry VIII.

A number of very able native painters were employed by François, including the portraitists Jean and François Clouet. The son, François (d.1572), probably painted the well-known portrait of the king in middle age which is in the Louvre; while the father, Jean (d.1540), made the remarkable series of red and black chalk drawings of court notables which can be seen at Chantilly. These have something in common with the contemporary portrait drawings by Holbein at Windsor Castle.

The grandeur of the new Renaissance style imported by François can, however, best be appreciated today in the Galerie François Premier of the château at Fontainebleau, where he began on the first of those enormous building campaigns to which French monarchs right up to the time of Napoleon III became addicted. The gallery is decorated with allegorical paintings in elaborate stucco frames, and recent cleaning has removed a good deal of the 19th-century 'restorations' which disfigured them. This extremely successful and modish

scheme is the work of two Italian artists, Rosso Fiorentino (1494–1540) and Francesco Primaticcio (1504–70). Rosso, who had worked under Andrea del Sarto, was an artist of considerable standing in Florence and Rome before he fled to France in the aftermath of the sack of Rome in 1527. Primaticcio, the younger man, had been an assistant to Giulio Romano in the decoration of the Palazzo del Tè at Mantua. They were thus well versed in all that was most advanced in Italian art.

The style in which the two Italians worked at Fontainebleau in the middle years of the 16th century belongs to that late, sophisticated, nervy phase of Renaissance art so aptly called Mannerism. The immediate effect of Rosso and Primaticcio's art on French painters was to produce a spate of pictures which imitated the elegant elongations of their nude figures and the strange harmonies of their boiled-sweet colours without any real understanding of the broad principles of Classical structure which underpinned their stylishness. But in the longer term the Italian influence decisively shaped the direction to be followed by French painting in its 17th-century golden age.

We tend to think of the 17th century in France as the age of Louis XIV. Yet though Louis was responsible for one of the major artistic enterprises of the century, the building and decoration of Versailles; although it was at his instigation that the Royal Academy of Painting and Sculpture was founded; and though many able and talented artists worked for him during his long reign, all the most brilliant artistic achievements of that brilliant century had been made before he came to the throne or before he reached his majority. When the period of

Above An astonishingly sophisticated integration of painted and sculptural decoration in the Italian manner, the sixteenth-century Galerie François Premier in the Château at Fontainebleau has recently been restored to something like its original splendour.

personal rule did begin in the 1660s, Louis was determined to run the arts as a branch of the civil service for the aggrandisement of the state. And the truth is, perhaps, that the arts are resistant to this kind of bureaucratization.

Certainly the outstanding painters of the 17th century were what we would describe today as 'independents'. The most intriguing of them all is undoubtedly Georges de La Tour (1593–1652), a painter who was almost completely forgotten until eighty years ago, but who is now one of the most popular French artists. La Tour worked in the provincial milieu of the prosperous town of Lunéville, near Nancy in Lorraine, and his output was tiny, not more than about forty paintings being known. His grand but simple figure style is based on Caravaggio's work, so it has been assumed that he must have travelled early in his life to Italy, or, more likely, to the Low Countries where Caravaggio had many imitators. But whereas the dramatic lighting effects for which the Italian painter is so famous were designed to shock, La Tour's biblical candlelight scenes, like *Job and his Wife* at Épinal and *The Nativity* at Rennes, have a still, contemplative quality, which suggests that the artist was a man of deep religious convictions.

The dignified simplicity of La Tour's pictures of the 1640s and 1650s has been connected with a Franciscan religious revival taking place in Lorraine in the first half of the 17th century. And this, in a curious way, connects him with a very metropolitan painter, Philippe de Champaigne (1602–74). Champaigne had been trained in Brussels but came to France as a young man. He is best known as a portrait painter, although he also painted large religious canvases and designed a number of ambitious decorative schemes for Parisian churches. Champaigne worked chiefly for the court and is often compared with his fellow Fleming, Van Dyck. But even in his most formal portraits of his

Georges de La Tour's religious canvases often combine a noble simplicity of composition with virtuoso lighting effects derived from Caravaggio. The result as here in the *Dream of St Joseph* is visually and emotionally compelling (Musée des Beaux-Arts, Nantes).

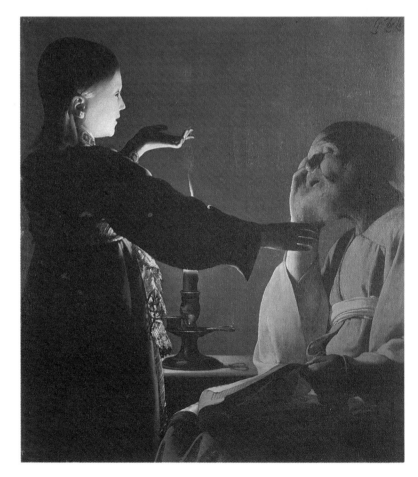

patrons Louis XIII and Cardinal Richelieu, there is none of the Baroque swagger and flourish of Van Dyck's nearly contemporary paintings of Charles I and his courtiers. In Champaigne we find an innate tendency to austerity which became especially marked in the later 1640s when he began an association with the convent of Port Royal, a centre of the puritanical Catholic doctrines of Jansenism. Some of Champaigne's finest portraits are of the chief figures of the Jansenist movement, like that of the Abbé de Saint-Cyran in the museum at Grenoble. But his great *tour de force* is the Louvre's extraordinary *Two Nuns of Port Royal* of 1662, part portrait and part religious offering. Painted to celebrate his daughter's miraculous recovery from paralysis (she is the younger of the two nuns, the other, praying for her, is the prioress Agnès Arnauld), the extreme simplicity of this picture's composition and the eloquent austerity of its almost monochromatic colouring, broken only by the red crosses on the nun's habits, seems to sum up that strand of rationality so characteristic of the French mind in the 17th century. We have only to think of the flamboyant theatricality of a contemporary Roman work, Bernini's swooning statue of St Theresa in Ecstasy to appreciate the Classical restraint with which Champaigne treats religious themes.

The genre scenes of peasant life in the Dutch manner painted by the Le Nain brothers, Antoine (c.1588–1648), Louis (c.1593–1648) and Mathieu (c.1607–77), are as agreeable to 20th-century taste as La Tour's seemingly artless canvases. But a look at Louis Le Nain's *The Traveller's Rest* in the Louvre will show that our satisfaction comes not simply from the unpretentious subject matter but also, as with La Tour as well as Philippe de Champaigne, from the discreet but strong underpinning of rational composition which derives ultimately from the intellectual principles of Italian Renaissance painting.

A deep reverence for those principles and for the sculpture of Greek and Roman Antiquity is the foundation of the painting of one of France's greatest artists, Nicolas Poussin (1594–1665). Poussin, like the more romantically minded Claude Lorraine (1600–82), chose to spend much of his life away from the increasingly despotic milieu of the French court, in the congenial artistic and intellectual atmosphere of Rome. Poussin in part and Claude wholly, expressed their artistic ideas in the medium of landscape, a genre not previously very highly regarded in French painting.

Claude's landscapes are elegiac idealizations of the countryside around Rome, painted in the cool light of sunrise or the tender tones of fading day. His figures, reduced to the status of picturesque punctuation, are Arcadian shepherds or Virgilian heroes. Such is the skill with which Claude draws the eye past tree and lawn and ruined temple into his infinite luminous distances, that we are almost tempted to step into paintings like the Grenoble museum's beautiful *Landscape with Shepherds* of 1644. These highly artificial compositions, which in less sensitive hands could, and did, become very tired formulae, were to dominate French landscape painting well into the 19th century; and through the activity of British collectors in the 18th century deeply influenced the men who laid out the great English landscape gardens.

Nicolas Poussin, as Anthony Blunt pointed out, is the key to the whole later evolution of French art; French painters up to our own time have either taken his Classicism as their ideal or reacted against it with a violence that testifies to the continuing strength of his influence. Poussin's very intellectual art is, frankly, difficult, but it is also correspondingly rewarding. His Classical landscapes and his scenes from Greek and Roman mythology, or taken from the Stoic historians, can seem at first stiff, cold and remote. Poussin's colouring is often hard and his figures have the frozen air of marble sculpture. Yet looking at the Rouen museum's *Venus Arming Aeneas* of 1639 or the Louvre's *Diogenes Throwing Away his Bowl* of 1648, two of his greatest pictures, there is something deeply satisfying about these compositions which are so lucidly organized that to change a single element would, we feel, cause a crashing discord. And that, perhaps, is the clue to understanding Poussin's painting; it is a search for harmony. Like his contemporary Descartes, Poussin believed that under the apparent chaos of experience there was a pattern, a governing structure to the universe which also extended into the moral realm. His canvases are both an attempt to impose order on the flux of visual perception and an affirmation of faith that harmony does indeed exist. That Poussin's life-long search for order was a very human enterprise can be judged from the tense and anxious face which looks out from the artist's self-portrait in the Louvre.

Such high-minded universal considerations as engaged Poussin would not have interested Louis XIV. He was after grandeur of effect on an unprecedented scale. At Versailles a team of skilled craftsmen, sculptors and painters laboured for years under the command of the director of the Académie Royale, Charles Le Brun (1619–90), to carve and paint and gild a decorative ensemble in which every detail glorified the Sun King. The result is rather like a well-trained and highly professional orchestra playing the popular classics under a disciplinarian conductor: it is all superbly done but lamentably lacking in individual character.

A more approachable face of painting under Louis XIV's regime can be found in the portraits of Hyacinthe Rigaud (1659–1743) and Nicolas de Largillière (1656–1746). Both artists could be exceedingly grand in the Baroque manner when occasion demanded – witness Rigaud's state portrait of the ageing king painted in 1701 (Louvre) or the wonderfully opulent *Cardinal de Bouillon* in the museum at Perpignan, the artist's birthplace. But they could also achieve effects of remarkable immediacy and grace. Rigaud's Rembrandtesque double-portrait of his mother, in the Louvre, done in 1695 in preparation for a marble bust by the sculptor Coysevox, and Largillière's much later and very beautiful portrait of a young woman, known as *La Belle Strasbourgeoise*, in the Musée des Beaux-Arts in Strasbourg, are

Nicolas Poussin was perhaps the greatest and is certainly the most influential painter ever produced by France. The Classical subject and lucid organization of pictures like *Diogenes throwing away his Bowl* (Louvre, Paris) reflect his life-long search for order in the flux of experience.

Loveliest and most graceful of all French pictures of the eighteenth century Watteau's *Pilgrimage on the Island of Cythera* (Louvre, Paris) has seemed to many to sum up the light-hearted spirit of the Rococo style.

excellent examples.

These two long-lived artists went on painting well into the 18th century and their styles came to reflect the new feeling of *détente* which followed the death of Louis XIV. There was a general flight from the formality and pomposity of Versailles, and Paris became the centre of an elegant, stylish and altogether more civilized way of life. The ease of manner and urbanity of French life under Louis XV, *le bien-aimé*, as he was tagged, can be felt vividly in the polished portraits of Rigaud and Largillière's successors in fashionable esteem, Maurice-Quentin de Latour (1704–88) and Jean-Baptiste Perronneau (1715–83). Their sitters positively shine with that look of wry amusement which seems to have been the habitual mask of the age of Voltaire. Latour worked exclusively in pastel and many of his most stunning efforts in this virtuoso medium can be seen in the museum at St-Quentin near the Belgian border. Perronneau also worked in pastel, though in a less showy manner, but his masterpiece, a portrait of the magistrate Daniel Jousse, is in fact an oil painting in the fine collection of 18th-century portraits at Orléans.

But this is to leap ahead; for the painter whose art has seemed to many to sum up the new light-hearted spirit of 18th-century France is Antoine Watteau (1684–1721). After the acres of sombre allegorical canvas at Versailles, Watteau's pictures were of a size to hang on the walls of a drawing room or a boudoir. Their colours were tender pinks and blues, pearly greys and opalescent whites. After the desiccated Classicism of the Académie's theories, a travesty of the principles of Raphael and Poussin, Watteau's compositions were based on the easy flow of the serpentine Rococo curve, and his brushwork evoked the lush, painterly touch of Rubens, betraying perhaps Watteau's Flemish origins in the border town of Valenciennes.

Watteau's apparently diffuse fantasies of the *dolce fa niente* of courtly love on endless summer afternoons were felt to be so novel that the Académie had to invent a new category of painting, the *fête galante*, to accommodate them. For from the Academic point of view, Watteau's pictures had, literally, no subject. And this is precisely the place where the difficulty with Watteau begins. More critical ink has been spilt on the probably insoluble riddle of the meaning of Watteau's painting than on any other problem in the study of French art. We can be certain that the many paintings which can be seen in French collections by Watteau's followers and imitators – Jean-Baptiste Pater (1695–1736) and Nicolas Lancret (1690–1743) chief among them – have no other aim than to please the eye. But in Watteau's case the critics have consistently detected a melancholy, autobiographical, but elusive, subtext to this tubercular painter's depictions of amorous dalliance; a whole body of literature has been built on this romantic foundation. Yet confronted with the Louvre's *Pilgrimage on the Isle of Cythera* of 1717 (one of Watteau's three or four most accomplished works, and ravishingly beautiful since its recent cleaning) the unprejudiced observer might be forgiven for feeling that just as many signs point to this being a robust and grown-up look at the profit and loss account of love and marriage as to its being a wistful poem of amorous regret. It may be, however, that not the least engaging quality of Watteau's art is that such contradictions can never be fully resolved.

Love, in its erotic rather than sentimental guise, was the subject of much of the painting of the first two-thirds of the 18th century in France. François Boucher (1703–70) was by far the most prolific and inventive purveyor of Rococo nudities by the middle years of the century. His creamy-fleshed, rosy-cheeked nymphs and goddesses with the unmistakable baby face of Mme Boucher are ubiquitous; though it could be that the more chaste but more exuberant canvases of Jean-Honoré Fragonard (1732–1806) – his *Blind Man's Buff* in the Louvre is a case in point – are more authentically erotic.

In contrast to what Diderot called the 'agreeable vice' of Boucher's mythological canvases are the still-lives and bourgeois genre scenes of Jean-Baptiste-Siméon Chardin (1699–1779). Pictures like the Louvre's famous *The Tobacco Box* of 1737, or even the exquisite little still-life to be found quite unexpectedly in the museum at Carcassonne, are among the greatest glories of French painting. With them we are back with that quiet contemplation of things as they are, Manet's *sens du vrai*, which unites Chardin in the French tradition with such seemingly disparate artists as Georges de La Tour and the anonymous painter of the Villeneuve *Pietà*.

If love may be said to have been the presiding genius of French art in the earlier 18th century, then duty was the more exacting god who dominated the decades leading up to the Revolution of 1789. The prevailing style, Neo-classicism, began after the excavations at the buried Roman cities of Pompeii and Herculaneum as a fashionable alternative to the Rococo. It ended as a campaign for artistic and moral rearmament. Pictures like Joseph-Marie Vien's (1716–1809) *The Merchant of Loves* of 1763 (it can be seen in the château at Fontainebleau) are every bit as titillating, for all their chic Classical accessories, as a canvas by Boucher. But by the time Jacques-Louis David (1748–1825) painted his *Belisarius Begging Alms* (now at Lille) in the early 1780s, French painting was once more dealing with subjects of the highest seriousness, stern illustrations of Roman civic virtue, painted in an elevated style derived from the revered Poussin.

David, who became a kind of self-appointed commissar of the arts, dominated French painting in the Revolutionary and Napoleonic epochs. His best-known work is probably the Louvre's formidable *The Oath of the Horatii*. Some critics, influenced by David's subsequent active involvement in the politics of the Revolution, have been tempted to read this potent and stirring picture as a Republican call to arms, though it was in fact painted five years before the fall of the Bastille.

David's art, however, is not all as declamatory as this. He was a notably brilliant and acute portrait painter in an age which set very high standards in this sphere. His beguiling portrait of Mme Recamier in the Louvre is only the most famous of a large number of portrayals of his contemporaries. They range in mood from the informal *Dr Leroy in his Study* in the Musée Fabre at Montpellier to the dramatic, wind-swept *Napoleon Crossing the Alps* at Versailles.

It was perhaps inevitable that David's dictatorship of the arts should eventually produce an extreme reaction among the younger generation of painters. And when Napoleon was defeated at Waterloo in 1815, the tattered remnants of the heroic and patriotic ideals which had inspired the painting of the Davidian school were finally discredited. The great

adventure was at an end; and in the decades after 1815 the artistic mind in France was turned in on its own resources. Those resources often proved to be both bizarre and violent.

For this reason the conventional image of French painting in the first half of the 19th century as a battleground fought over by the implacable enemies, the Classicist and pupil of David, Jean-Auguste-Dominique Ingres (1780–1867) and the Romantic, Eugène Delacroix (1798–1863) is misleading. Delacroix, though he had been a friend and passionate admirer of the short-lived Théodore Géricault (1791–1824), the young Turk of the Romantic movement, was himself always reluctant to be labelled a Romantic. And in a sense he was a very traditional artist. Standing in the Louvre in front of two of his biggest canvases, one, *The Death of Sardanapalus*, a work of his youth inspired by a poem of Byron, the other, *The Entry of the Crusaders into Constantinople*, painted in his maturity, we can see that these are pictures painted by an artist who is heir to the great tradition of European painting; the tradition, that is to say, of Raphael and Michelangelo, of Titian and Veronese and Rubens, which Delacroix has absorbed and understood without doctrinaire prejudice. Yet Delacroix's pictures, despite their grandeur, are disturbingly introspective and personal; poems of eroticism and violence, as Baudelaire put it. And for all the richness of the brush-work and deep sonority of colour of his boldly composed canvases, Delacroix's art, like the piano music of his close friend Chopin, is deeply pessimistic.

Delacroix was the greatest colourist France has ever produced. Ingres was one of its three finest draughtsmen, sharing the honours with Poussin and Degas. The drawings on display in the museum devoted to him in his home town of Montauban in the Périgord are quite astonishing in their purity. And his paintings seem almost to have been conceived as line drawings to which the colour has been added as an afterthought. Ingres' insistence on the primacy of line over colour, of the essential world of forms over the merely contingent world of sensation, would appear to ally him to his artistic heroes, Raphael, Poussin and David. It seems unlikely that the big mythological and religious pictures on which he staked his reputation, like *Jupiter and Thetis* in the gallery at Aix-en-Provence or *The Martyrdom of St Symphorian* in the cathedral at Autun, will ever again be anything but elephantine curiosities. But his portraits and nudes, often highly wrought reworkings of Raphaelesque models, are justly admired. The strangeness of the painting of this self-proclaimed Classicist is that no one looking at the Louvre's nude *La Grande Odalisque* or portraits like *Mme de Senonnes* at Nantes can fail to be struck by their bizarre distortions of anatomy or impossible contractions of space. Ingres' compositions seem to be struggling as to whether they are depictions of three-dimensional forms in space or two-dimensional patterns across the surface of his canvas. And the violence of this unclassical tension

Above left High seriousness and a return to the Classical style of Poussin are typical of French painting in the decades leading up to the Revolution of 1789. Jacques-Louis David's formidable *Oath of the Horatii* (Louvre, Paris) is a stirring call to put civic duty before domestic affection.

Above right Delacroix's paintings despite their grandeur are disturbingly introspective and personal. None more so than the Louvre's violent and erotic *Death of Sardanapalus*, one of the masterpieces of the flamboyant Romanticism of the 1820s.

between two and three dimensions is positively flaunted. Ingres saw himself as the embattled successor of Raphael. But the contemporary who described him as a painter from China astray in the ruins of Athens perfectly caught the idiosyncratic, paradoxical nature of his art.

Ingres and Delacroix were both still painting in the 1860s. But by this time a newer, more democratic movement in art was challenging the traditional assumptions of the Classicists and the Romantics. The new movement, Realism, was led by Gustave Courbet (1819–77), a man of prodigious, brusque energy in all aspects of his life (he was eventually to be exiled from France for his part in the demolition of the Vendôme column during the Communard uprising of 1871). Courbet, like many of the radical generation of 1848, wanted an end to pictures with subjects drawn from the conventional repertoire of mythology and history, the bible and the poets. He was unrepentant in his desire to find and paint what was heroic in *modern* life. In the Louvre, in the same gallery as some of Delacroix's finest masterpieces, with their subjects drawn from Byron, from medieval history and the exotic world of the oriental harem (all considered novel sources in the 1820s and 1830s), is Courbet's *The Burial at Ornans*. This was his attempt to show that a monumental museum-sized picture could be made from the material of everyday mid-19th century life; in this case a peasant funeral in his native Franche-Comté.

Painted in 1849, the year following the revolution which toppled the stolid, bourgeois monarchy of Louis-Philippe and established the short-lived Second Republic, *The Burial at Ornans* was understandably a controversial work which enraged many of the old guard. Courbet continued to provoke fierce controversy with his radical approach to art and his radical politics for the rest of his life. Yet Courbet's artistic radicalism, seen from the standpoint of his successors, the Impressionists, was limited. His pictures are composed on traditional lines. And though his subject matter is refreshingly down to earth, it is concerned in the main with rural life and does not touch on the factories, railways, cafés and theatres, the facts of modern urban life, which were so to fascinate Manet, Degas, Renoir and Monet. Nevertheless, the enduring impression left by Courbet's enormous output is of unquenchable vitality, and also of an engaging child-like vanity of personality quite different in kind from the introspection of the Romantics. In one of his finest paintings, and certainly one of his best-loved, *Bonjour, Monsieur Courbet*, at Montpellier, the artist, without a trace of embarrassment, raises himself to the status of hero in his own picture.

The landscape painter Camille Corot (1796–1875) was as modest and self-effacing as Courbet was robust and self-centred. Corot is the quiet genius who transformed French landscape painting from unimagina-

Brusque, energetic and an outstanding manipulator of paint Gustave Courbet was determined to make monumental art from the everyday facts of mid-nineteenth-century life. His *Burial at Ornans* (Louvre, Paris) was universally denounced for its ugliness when it was first exhibited in 1849.

tive imitation of the formulae of Claude into one of the most innovative art forms of the 19th century. While there is some truth in the often heard criticism that Corot's later work can be vapid and sentimental, in such pioneering pictures as the Louvre's view of Ville d'Avray of about 1838, the artist shows such uncanny precision in his painterly instincts that it can almost be said that he perceives his subject not essentially as form or colour but as pure tone.

But far from being simply 'tone poems', Corot's best landscapes have that pungent sense of place which soon became such a characteristic of French 19th-century landscape painting. With the spread of the railway and the invention of ready-prepared paints in metal tubes, artists could leave the studio and paint *en plein air*. At Barbizon in the Forest of Fontainebleau a group of landscape painters formed itself around Théodore Rousseau (1812–67) and Jean-François Millet (1814–75). The Normandy coast became a favourite summer haunt of painters from Paris, Corot among them; and so a little later did the wilder landscape of Brittany, where by 1880 the town of Pont-Aven had become the most famous and crowded artists' colony in Europe.

The rural, however, had little appeal to Édouard Manet (1832–83), the urban and urbane painter who eventually found himself forced into the slightly uncongenial role of father-figure to the Impressionists. Like Courbet, Manet was a Realist determined to create art every bit as grand as that of the Old Masters from the rebarbative facts of everyday life. But unlike Courbet, Manet was a Parisian who relished the sophisticated pleasures of the Second Empire. He wanted to find, in a memorable phrase of Baudelaire's, the beauty that lurked in the black frock coats and polished boots of his time. With his deep love of the art of the past (in particular the bold, painterly effects of Velazquez) Manet joined the old and the new, in such famous and controversial pictures of the 1860s as *Le Déjeuner sur L'Herbe* and *Olympia*, in a new and dynamic relationship which is both reverential and ironic. Manet, like the Impressionists who so much admired him, can be seen at his best in Paris at the Musée du Jeu de Paume.

Of all the well-known painters, Renoir (1841–1919), Sisley (1839–99), Pissarro (1831–1903), Degas (1834–1917) and Cézanne (1839–1906), who showed their work at the Impressionist exhibitions of the 1870s and 1880s, the most purely enjoyable as well as the most consistently innovative is Claude Monet (1840–1926). Indeed it was an oil sketch by Monet called *Impression, Sunrise*, now in the Musée Marmottan in Paris, which got this loosely knit group of painters its, at first derogatory, name. Manet had worked largely in the traditional way in his studio. So did two other artists who shared his interest in modern subject matter, Edgar Degas (a rather unusual American scene *The New Orleans Cotton Exchange* can, incidentally, be seen in the museum at Pau) and the much younger Henri de Toulouse-Lautrec (1864–1901), whose work can be seen to great advantage in the delightful museum at Albi near Toulouse. But for Monet, whose pictorial obsession was light and to whom the ostensible subject-matter of his paintings became increasingly irrelevant, there was only one place to paint, and that was outdoors. Manet had already begun to purge the French palette of its old, dark colours but the extraordinary vaporous brilliance of Monet's townscapes and landscapes was unprecedented.

The flickering touch with which Monet rendered the contour-dissolving play of light and colour over the surface of objects, as in the Lille museum's *The Houses of Parliament, London: Stormy Sky*, took visual naturalism about as far as it could go. For Paul Cézanne, who began his career as an Impressionist, the problem of painting soon ceased to be how to render the *coup d'oeil*, the momentary perception of the shifting kaleidoscope of visual impressions, but how to achieve a structural integrity within the work of art. Cézanne, in fact, took up that struggle with composition which arises from the paradox that the

Cézanne's *L'Estaque, View of the Bay of Marseille* is among the famous collection of Impressionist and Post-Impressionist pictures to be moved from the crowded Jeu de Paume to the new Musée d'Orsay when it opens on the Left Bank in Paris in 1986.

painter must represent three-dimensional objects on a flat surface. It is not surprising that the two painters he admired above all were Poussin and Ingres.

Searching for the highest degree of stability and pictorial unity in his paintings of still-life, nude bathers and the famous views of the Montagne Sainte-Victoire near Aix, Cézanne tried by rigorous analysis to reduce what he saw to the simplest geometrical shapes and relationships. His intention, in his own words, was 'to do Poussin again, from Nature'. The result, which comes at moments close to complete abstraction, still looks radical today.

Paul Gauguin (1848–1903) represents another much more romantic and emotional strand in Post-Impressionist painting, but one which was to be almost as important for the art of our own century. During his years at Pont-Aven in Brittany, and later in Tahiti, Gauguin, like Cézanne, worked to free himself from the conventions of naturalistic painting. The bold, expressive contours and simple, strong colours of pictures like the Lyon museum's exotic *Nave nave mahana* ('Delicious Days') were derived from sources as various as the decorative art of the Far East and the primitive sculpture of the South Seas. The result was painting with a deeply voluptuous and subjective atmosphere, yet quite without the preciosity of older and more conventional Symbolist painters like Gustave Moreau (1826–98) who form the link between Gauguin and the interiorized world of Delacroix.

With the succession of the Post-Impressionists, the story ceases to be a history of French painting, and becomes instead the story of international painting in France. Long before Cézanne's death in 1906, the prestige of French art had made Paris the Mecca of young painters from all over Europe and America. From the arrival of the youthful Picasso from Barcelona in 1900 until the fall of France in 1940, Paris was the art capital of the world; and through those forty years the School of Paris was synonymous with Modern Art.

Looking back down the perspective of the painting of the 20th century from the vantage point of the national collection of Modern Art at the Pompidou Centre in Paris or the outstanding new Musée d'Art Moderne at Troyes, what is most apparent is not the iconoclasm at which some contemporary critics shrilled, but the sense of continuity with the past. When painting at the end of the 19th century found that it had freed itself from the obligation to be a direct transcription of visual experience, artists turned with relish to explore new and exciting solutions to some very old preoccupations. To say that Pablo Picasso (1881–1973) and Georges Braque (1882–1963) in their Cubist paintings took up where Cézanne left off, is only to underline that with their fractured and carefully rearranged images they were exploring some of the same fundamental problems of the painter's art which had exercised Poussin and Ingres. The endlessly inventive technical innovations of Surrealists like Max Ernst (1891–1976), and Salvador Dali's (born 1904) strange perversions of traditional illusionistic technique were used to express in post-Freudian terms the hidden impulses of the mind; a subjective theme in French art which, as we have seen, can be traced back through Gauguin and the Symbolists to Delacroix. And few artists have had such a reverence for the art of the past as Henri Matisse (1869–1954), probably the greatest painter of the 20th century, and yet have remained so strikingly themselves. It is a tribute to the wealth of French painting through its long history and to its central place in the European tradition that the outstanding painters of the 20th century have drawn from it their sustenance and inspiration.

As in *Large Red Interior* of 1948 (Musée National d'Art Moderne, Centre Georges Pompidou, Paris) Henri Matisse insisted on the flat surface of his canvases with bold black lines and brilliant colour. Yet his paintings always depict the seen world with a typically French relish.

LITERATURE

French literature starts early in the Middle Ages, and it is a curious irony that its first masterpiece should have been written in England, at the dawn of the 12th century, and discovered in its most complete form in Oxford's Bodleian library as late as 1837. *La Chanson de Roland*, which has become the national epic of France, is founded upon undoubted historical event – the Spanish expedition of Charlemagne in 778. After crossing the Pyrenees and capturing Pamplona, he was beaten back from the walls of Saragossa. On the return, his rearguard, led by his nephew Roland, was surprised by Basques in the valley of Roncesvalles, and lost to the last man. If you cross the Pyrenees at Puerto de Ibañeta, you will pass through Roncesvalles on the Pamplona road. It is, quite visibly, a cruel place for an ambush.

The 4000-line poem narrates a classic tale of tragic foolhardiness, courage and treachery. Charles's expedition is here a crusade against the Saracens who number over 400,000 men when they ambush Roland and his comrade in arms, the trusty Oliver. Roland is betrayed by his father-in-law, the treacherous and envious Ganelon, who encourages the leader of the Saracens to attack Charlemagne's rearguard, having arranged for Roland to lead it. When he comes under attack, Roland, despite the urgings of Oliver, obstinately refuses to sound his horn to summon the main body of Charlemagne's army, because this would bring dishonour upon himself and his companions. By the time they have been attacked by three waves of Saracens and fought to the last man, the dying Roland has just enough strength to put a horn to his lips and call back Charlemagne's army to avenge him and bring about the triumph of French Christians over the infidel.

The characters and narrative techniques of medieval literature are so different from our own that it is sometimes hard to respond to what we read. *Tristan et Iseut*, dating from late in the 12th century, is a remarkable exception. Béroul, author of one of the earliest versions, was a professional entertainer or *jongleur*, who combined the skills of professional story-teller, singer and on occasion acrobat, juggler and animal tamer. In his fragment of the Tristan legend, Iseut, who is married to King Mark of Cornwall, has been united with the knight Tristan in a passionate and all-consuming love by a love potion which they have drunk together by mistake – it should have been taken by Iseut and Mark to consolidate their marriage. The story effectively becomes a painfully penetrating analysis of two lovers who cannot help betraying and deceiving a man whom they both like and respect.

Béroul's fragment contains references to King Arthur, whose exploits and those of the knights of the Round Table were recounted in a series of verse works, written in the 12th and 13th centuries. The forest of Broceliande, mentioned in these *Romans de la Table Ronde*, once covered the whole of Brittany. All that remains today is the Forêt de Paimpont, situated between Rennes and Ploërmel. Legend has it that the wizard Merlin is imprisoned here, in the rocky ravine known as Le-Val-Sans-Retour.

Left Thirteenth-century stained glass window in Chartres cathedral showing Roland fighting the giant Ferragus (detail).

Later medieval literature saw the development of the tradition of courtly love, notably in the Arthurian poems of Chrétien de Troyes (1135–90). This is one of the most sophisticated explorations of desire not for fulfilment, but simply for its own sake. *L'amour courtois* is a disciplined and reasoned passion, directed towards an object worthy of it, a beautiful and virtuous woman. The love is described as ennobling and uplifting, an ordeal to be welcomed, and governed by a strict code of conduct. Perhaps the most substantial work devoted to the theme is the 22,000-line allegorical poem *La Roman de la Rose*, the first part written about 1235 by Guillaume de Lorris, the second about 1275 by Jean de Meung, which was immensely popular at the time, but which has lost some of its force over the centuries.

There is much else to enjoy in medieval French literature, such as Froissart's chronicle of the chief events of the Hundred Years' War, which he composed between 1325 and 1400. But if there is one writer of this period who towers above the rest, and who belongs in the company of the very great, it is François Villon (1432–1463?), arguably the finest poet that France has ever known. Villon was brought up by a foster father and priest, Guillaume de Villon, whose name he assumed. He was a student at the Sorbonne but seems to have spent many hours in the company of criminals and down-and-outs. He later spent some time in prison, from which he was released and then arrested again twice. The second time he was sentenced to be hanged, but although the sentence was quashed on appeal it brought forth a poem, *Ballade des Pendus*, which depicts the poet and his companions swinging slowly back and forth on a creaking gibbet. His main work consists of two mock wills, the *Lais* and *Le Testament*. In them he looks back on his life which, practically speaking, was a disastrous failure, and makes various bequests to friends, drinking companions and enemies.

Thanks to the upheavals of the Hundred Years' War, the new learning of the Renaissance began to manifest itself in France only in the early 16th century. The new humanism is first reflected in literature, in the extraordinary, imaginative works of François Rabelais (1494–1553) who was born near Chinon in Touraine, on the farm of La Devinière, the setting for much of his work, and which can still be seen today. *Pantagruel* (1532 or 1533) and *Gargantua* (1534) are parodies of medieval tales about adventurous giants. Frequently preposterous – the giant Gargan is born through his mother's left ear, a birth precipitated by her over-indulgence in an abundant dish of tripe –

Épitaphe dudit Villon
Freres humains qui apres no[9] viues
Napez les cueurs contre no[9] enduercis
Car se pitie de no[9] pouures auez
Dieu en aura plustoft de vous mercis
Vous nous voies cy ataches cinq six
Quāt dela chac q trop auōs noutrie
Elleft piera deuource et pourtie
et no[9] les os deuenōs cēdres a poulsie
De noftre mal persōnne ne sen rie
Mais pues dieu que tous nous veueil
It abjoulsie   g iii.

Right Ballade des Pendus by François Villon.

Far right Portrait of François Villon (1432–after 1463).

The title page of the first edition of Rabelais' *Pantagruel*, thought to have been written in 1532 or 1533.

much of the work glories in a celebration of man and his natural functions, to the extent that refined literary scholars of an earlier age found the work entirely unacceptable. But beneath his humour and his celebration of the splendid food and drink of the area, with its *andouillettes* and its *matelotes*, still to be found in Chinon itself, there is a wonderfully optimistic belief in man, his natural decency, his capacity for honour, goodness and self-improvement, combined with a rejection of all the rules and restrictions that prevent him from living his life to the full.

The French Renaissance saw the beginnings of secular theatre and also a renewal of poetic form by the poets of the *Pléiade*, notably Pierre de Ronsard (1524–85) a Vendômois, and Joachim du Bellay (1522–60) a gentleman from Anjou, who attempted to free the language from its medieval antecedents and realign it upon the patterns of classical Greece and Rome. They are accomplished poets who send their echoes down the ages, establishing ways of working with words that have remained a vital part of French poetic practice to this day.

Yet the outstanding writer of the latter half of the age, and one who provides a sombre answer to the optimism of Rabelais, is the essayist, philosopher and one-time mayor of Bordeaux, before he retired to his family château in Périgord, Michel de Montaigne (1533–92). Montaigne lived through a period when there was little reason for optimism, as France was torn by savage wars of religion. It was also an age in which certainties and long-held beliefs seemed to evaporate. In his essays Montaigne comes to the conclusion that we cannot know anything for sure, that our truths are only approximate, and that all we have is our knowledge of constantly changing selves. Montaigne expresses an attitude rather than a philosophy through a rambling combination of self-portraiture and conversation with his readers that makes for a wise, honest and civilized work of quite exceptional human dignity. Although the Château de Montaigne, near Castillon-la-Bataille in the Bordeaux region, was damaged by fire in the late 19th century, the rooms in which the writer worked were spared and can be visited today.

The 17th century in France saw the development of political absolutism and of rules governing different literary genres, especially tragedy. One of the major dramatic writers of the period, Pierre Corneille (1606–84), did not, however, live very easily with the conventions relating to the unities of time, place and action. Born and raised in legal circles in Rouen, Corneille had an extravagant exuberance that is closer in feel to Jacobean drama than to the elegant stillness of French classical tragedy. His works, still part of the French theatrical repertoire, are centred on passionate conflicts that build to the climax of a meeting of irresistible force and immovable mass. Characters are torn between their passions and their sense of obligation toward some code or set of beliefs by which they are possessed. In *Le Cid* (1637), for example, Rodrigue and Chimène love each other, but Rodrigue is obliged by his father to challenge the father of Chimène to a duel, and kills him. Chimène feels bound to call on the king of Spain for Rodrigue's head although she still loves him. When related in cold blood, the conflict may appear contrived and artificial, but the stylizations are no more preposterous than those of grand opera, which the form greatly resembles.

Pierre Corneille (1606–84).

Where Corneille was a robust creator of extravagant conflict, Jean Racine (1639–99), arguably France's greatest dramatist, is a poet, with a magical feel for words, and a sense of tragic myth that puts him on a par with the ancients. He writes as if the unities were made for him, using them to intensify emotions which he catches at the moment. In plays such as *Andromaque*, *Iphigénie en Aulide* and *Phèdre*, he has left us some of the most beautiful verse in French literature.

The 17th century was also the golden age of French comedy; most notable were the works of Jean-Baptiste Poquelin, known as Molière (1622–73). While his plays contain elements of knock-about farce, many – such as *L'Avare*, *Le Tartuffe* and *Don Juan* – are also profound explorations of human weaknesses and obsessions. Molière was an accomplished actor and ran his own theatre company, the ancestor of France's National Theatre. Indeed, the Comédie-Française is also known as La Maison de Molière.

Jean Racine (1639–99).

Part of the Palais-Royal was given to Molière's troupe by Louis XIV, who also welcomed performances of comedies and tragedies at court, first at the Louvre, then at Versailles. The latter, with its gardens designed by Le Nôtre, is often said to epitomize the splendour and formality of French Classicism.

French literature in the 18th century, the age of enlightenment, is very much a literature of ideas. The French reading public was the most educated and sophisticated in Europe, and it took a genuine delight in intellectual discussion with a political colouring. The philosopher Denis Diderot (1713–84), is best known for his role as the editor of France's first Encyclopedia (1751–80), itself a monument to the values of the new age.

Most of the major works of the period are indeed concerned with ideas and the quest for social justice. One of the greatest thinkers and authors of the age of enlightenment was the Baron de Montesquieu (1689–1755). He spent most of his life in the exquisite 13th century

54

family château of La Brède in the Gironde. His *De l'esprit des lois* (1748), a study of law as a social institution, is one of the seminal texts of sociology, and had immense influence upon the founding fathers of the United States of America.

Rousseau's *Discours sur les origines de l'inégalité* (1754) and his *Du Contrat Social* (1762) are vital to the development of political philosophy, and are the precursors of major socialist thinkers of the 19th century, such as Marx.

Ideas play a part, but a part only, in the works of the greatest playwright of the age, a man whose biography reads like an adventure story. Pierre-Augustin Caron (1732–99) was a clockmaker whose talents attracted the attentions of a rich widow who married him, giving him the name Beaumarchais, after a property she owned. He then embarked upon an extraordinary switchback career, first losing his wife and her fortune, then becoming music master to the king's daughters before making another fortune of his own. His life went on to include spells in prison, a dramatic lawsuit, spying for the crown and personally financing the French contribution to the American War of Independence. He also wrote plays; *Le Barbier de Séville* (1775) is a development of Molière-style knock-about farce. *Le Mariage de Figaro* (1784) is as much a masterpiece as Mozart's operatic version of the play. Enormously long, it never drags, the pace is breakneck and the dialogue snappy enough to win the admiration of Oscar Wilde.

The best-known figure of the French enlightenment, the 'immortal Voltaire' (1694–1778), as Beaumarchais calls him, has given us the finest work of its kind written in any language – the short novel *Candide* (1758). The eponymous hero is a naïve figure, who starts out in life with the belief that all is for the best in this best of all possible worlds. He is obliged to endure a whole panorama of disaster, from war and earthquake to the operations of the Inquisition, in a despairing search for his long-lost love, Cunégonde. By the time he finds her, she is horribly ugly and a shrew to boot, a discovery that brings him to the conclusion that it is useless to hope, or even to wonder what the world is like or how it should be; all we can do is 'cultivate our garden'.

The works of Voltaire, Rousseau, Diderot and the other philosophers who questioned accepted values both reflected the growing unrest of the 18th century which culminated in the French Revolution and contributed to it. The First French Republic became 'Le Premier Empire' in May 1804 and in December of that year, Napoleon I was

Above left Jean Baptiste Poquelin, known as Molière (1622–73).

Above right Voltaire (1694–1778).

crowned in Notre-Dame. Although Bonaparte has come to be seen as the typical, brooding Romantic hero, he favoured Neó-classicism in the arts. It might, in fact, be argued that the Napoleonic era was partly responsible for Romanticism coming late to France, its heyday falling between 1820 and 1840.

The *Méditations poétiques* by Alphonse de Lamartine (1790–1869), who went on to become the first President of the Second Republic in 1848, are considered as marking the rebirth of lyric poetry in France. He wrote one of the best-known elegiac poems in French literature – *Le Lac* – its title referring to the beautiful Lake Bourget by Aix-les-Bains in Savoy.

Alfred de Musset (1810–57) also exploited the lyrical vein, especially in the four poems known as *Les Nuits*, but many of his works contain bitter irony and pessimism.

Victor Hugo (1802–85).

The major figure of the Romantic period is Victor Hugo (1802–85) who, in fact, dominates the century. His plays (*Hernani* and *Ruy Blas*), his novels (*Notre-Dame de Paris* and *Les Misérables*), and his collections of poetry (*Les Contemplations* and *La Légende des Siècles*) have made him France's most famous man of letters. Hugo was also an extraordinary pictorial artist, as is evident from the drawings and paintings on show in the Musée Victor Hugo, in the Place des Vosges, Paris.

Another poet of the Romantic age worthy of mention is Gérard de Nerval (1805–55), an eccentric, reputed to have once taken a pet lobster for a walk in the Bois de Boulogne. He also wrote magical prose and produced beautiful evocations of the Valois region, its customs, its folk poetry and its dreamy, watery countryside, that make for some of the finest nature writing in the language.

For many, however, the most influential poet of the 19th century is Charles Baudelaire (1821–67), author of *Les Fleurs du Mal* (1857) and one of the most perceptive art-critics of his age. He has been described as the first poet of the modern city.

Charles Baudelaire (1821–67).

Over half a century before English language poetry starts, with T.S.Eliot, to address themes of everyday urban reality, lamplit cities through which the wind blows rubbish on a cold November night, Baudelaire was using his genius to turn the muddy cityscapes of Second Empire Paris into the subject matter of great art, exploring the stranger aspects of human experience and sexuality.

This was also the golden age of the novel, one in which three names stand out, Stendhal, Balzac and Flaubert. Stendhal (1783–1842), a Grenoblois, was a professional civil servant who rose to great heights under Napoleon I and subsequently became French Consul in Civita-Vecchia. A delightful man, as sensitive as he was ugly, he had little success with women though he displayed an amazing capacity to fall in love with them. He combined sensitivity with great intelligence, a cold sardonic wit with a love of passionate energy; it was this strangely contradictory blend of characteristics that shaped his great novels. *Le Rouge et le Noir* (1830), set in the Besançon area and contemporary Paris, tells the story of a peasant's son, Julien Sorel, who is determined to take his revenge upon a society that has denied him his rightful place, but discovers finally that his capacity to love and to act spontaneously is more powerful and more valuable than cold ambition. Stendhal's second great novel, *La Chartreuse de Parme* (1839), is set mainly in the small Italian principality of Parma but also gives us the first modern account of war, when the young hero Fabrice del Dongo tries to fight at the battle of Waterloo, only to discover that battles do not resemble military paintings.

Stendhal (1783–1842).

Where Stendhal left a handful of novels, Balzac left a world. A Tourangeau like his adored Rabelais, Honoré de Balzac (1799–1850) was possessed by extraordinary creative energy. The series of novels known as *La Comédie Humaine* (1842–48) is the story of an entire generation. As Balzac said, 'The history of a generation is a drama with four or five thousand prominent characters; that drama is my book.'

Honoré de Balzac (1799–1850).

He provides a panorama of French society from the Consulate to the July Monarchy, in which over two thousand characters from every walk of life appear and reappear in various volumes, shifting from background to foreground at differing stages in their lives, revealing a society in which money is the driving force and self-interest the supreme motive. Many of Balzac's best-known novels were written in the Château de Saché, near Azay-le-Rideau on the Loire, where his workroom can be visited.

If Baudelaire was the father of modern poetry, Gustave Flaubert (1821–80) stands in the same relation to the modern novel. He begins the tradition of 'difficult' prose, which explores the ambiguities of narration, whereby you can never be quite sure that what you are reading is 'the truth'. Flaubert's dedication to literature was as total as that of a hermit who withdraws from the world to save his soul. Indeed, he lived a hermit-like existence in his family home of Croisset, on the Seine near Rouen. His faith was a belief in the absolute value of style; as a result he reworked his novels with the agonized attention of an obsessive, spending hours, days sometimes, over a single paragraph. Yet despite his obsession with technique, his novels were wonderfully moving. *Madame Bovary* (1857) tells the pathetic and comic story of a stupid yet warm and vibrant woman who tries to realize her bookish dreams of escape and fulfilment in the dead world of provincial Normandy, married to a country doctor whose limited horizons are only matched by his unlimited capacity for love. She tries to escape through adultery with hopelessly inadequate partners, and ends by taking her own life when her debts, not her affairs, catch up with her. Yet for all the flatness of its subject matter, and its dreadful evocations of French provincial life, the book is dreamy and poetic notwithstanding the repugnance that Flaubert makes us feel for his characters. *L'Éducation sentimentale* (1869) is another study of failed dreams, the failure of a young man of means to find fulfilment in Paris. It is a historical novel, set in the 1840s, and culminating in Louis-Napoleon's *coup d'état* of 1851.

The novels of the meridional Émile Zola (1840–1902) are more robust and less demanding than those of his predecessors: the *Rougon Macquart* series (1871–93) traces the fortunes of two branches of a family during the Second Empire. Zola's native Aix-en-Provence served as a model for the fictional Plassans, from which the family stems. Other carefully documented settings for the novels in the series are the different *quartiers* of Paris and the industrial north. Zola covers the whole range of society from its corrupt leaders to its exploited workers, writing in a manner that combines great attention to detail, sensationalism, and extraordinary imaginative power.

Although Marcel Proust (1871–1922) wrote *À la recherche du temps perdu* in this century (1913–27), it is a work that marks the end of an era, catching the disintegration of the old world of stable French bourgeois and aristocratic society as it crumbles apart in World War I. Beginning with the greatest of all French literature's evocations of childhood, based on Proust's enchanted recollections of his beloved Illiers near Chartres, now renamed Illiers-Combray, after its fictional counterpart, and visited each year by countless Proustiens. The fifteen volumes of *À la recherche du temps perdu* combine a skein of social observation and satire that is gloriously rich and funny with a very different theme. The work is written as the autobiography of a character named Marcel whose life we follow through to middle age. On the one hand we find him accepting experiences as they arrive, on the other he is also the middle-aged narrator looking back on them, with a full understanding of their significance. It is only in the last volume that the full meaning of the work becomes clear; namely that all these experiences have served to prepare Marcel to be the writer who one day will create something very close to the work we are reading. The title of the book derives from Marcel's understanding that he is

Gustave Flaubert (1821–80).

Émile Zola (1840–1902).

Marcel Proust (1871–1922).

possessed of an 'involuntary memory' which can be suddenly unlocked by a sensation, a taste, or a stumbling footstep, to bring the past flooding back in all its richness, demonstrating that nothing is lost for ever, and enabling him to triumph over the apparent passage of time.

Proust's contemporary, André Gide (1869–1951), is a fascinating and elusive personality within whose works the interplay of sincerity and self-deception play an extraordinary game of hide and seek, and whose opinions on literature are always worthwhile. Yet as a novelist the notes he strikes ring hollow all too often.

Mme Colette (1873–1954), on the other hand, is a writer of the very highest order, with a magnificent talent for the analysis of human relationships and for a delicate and unsentimental rendering of a woman's point of view. Although novels like the *Claudine* series, (1900–03), *Chéri* (1920), *La Fin de Chéri* (1926) and *Julie de Carneilhan* (1941) seem deceptively slight and trivial, they have a humane wisdom, and a remarkable sense of poise and timing. Her

Colette (1873–1954), on the left, photographed in the 1920s.

understanding of human emotion and the wit of her dialogue are only equalled by her beautiful evocations of her childhood and adolescence among the 'bois chéris' of St-Sauveur-en-Puisaye in northern Burgundy.

This century has seen the flourishing of excellent local novelists, who make no claim to belong to world literature. The Catholic novels of François Mauriac (1885–1970), so often set in the flat, sandy, stifling region of Les Landes; Jean Giono's evocations of pastoral life in his native Manosque in the Durance Valley; or the curiously stark and desperate evocations of Paris between the wars by Louis Ferdinand Céline and Drieu La Rochelle, both of whom were to collaborate with the Nazis, all have much to offer, but they remain of local interest only. As much is true, in another sense, of Alain-Fournier (1886–1914) whose *Grand-Meaulnes* (1913) gives us a dreamy and magical evocation of the Sologne that rivals Nerval's descriptions of the Valois.

Where the 19th century gave us giants, the 20th, in retrospect, will be seen to have left us with a series of schools and -isms. The first, surrealism, was in many respects the most ambitious attempt ever to use the imagination to free man from the dull confines of ordinary waking and working existence. Poets such as André Breton, Louis

Aragon and Paul Éluard tried to liberate man, break down barriers between dreaming and waking, sense and nonsense, liberating the human spirit from the disciplines of reason. They encouraged the process of automatic writing, free association, which brought together disconcerting combinations of image and juxtaposition, releasing writer and reader from the world of sense.

The last great French -ism of any significance was existentialism, a second Left Bank, indeed a St-Germain-des-Prés, movement which flourished in the late 1940s, its principal literary exponents being Sartre, Camus and Simone de Beauvoir. Philosophically speaking, Jean-Paul Sartre (1905–80) maintained that we are all 'condemned to be free', that it was up to each man to define himself; born into a void, he must make of it what he can. Essentially a philosophy of action, Sartre believed that man, in order to live authentically, must engage himself in action, in which process he creates his own values. A prolific thinker, playwright and novelist, and above all a representative of the Parisian haut-bourgeois intellectual, his *Chemins de La Liberté* (1945–49) and *La Nausée* (1938) require no knowledge of his philosophy to be read with pleasure.

Perhaps the hardest of all these writers to evaluate is the Algerian-born Nobel Prize winner Albert Camus (1913–60), a latter day humanist rather than an existentialist proper. His novel *L'Étranger* (1942) still has an extraordinary impact on sensitive adolescent minds. It depicts a man who is condemned to death, less for a murder he has committed than because he refuses to conform to the behaviour patterns of a society from which he feels himself to be alienated. A second work, *La Peste* (1947), tells the story of a community in Oran, North Africa, struggling to fight an epidemic of the plague. It seems to conclude that even though men are ultimately powerless to deal with such afflictions, all human dignity and decency depend upon their working together against them as best they can. The plague has often been taken to be a symbol for the German occupation – Camus was very active in the French Resistance. His last work, *La Chute* (1956), takes a darker view of the human race, being an analysis of the innate hypocrisy and vanity of the ostensible do-gooder, based upon Dostoevsky's definition of man as 'a creature who walks on two legs and is ungrateful'.

The most recent literary movement in France seems to resume all that great culture's idiosyncrasies and weaknesses. *Le nouveau roman* is highly cerebral, abstract even, as is so much French literature, and displays that careful regard for a set of 'rules' that has been a part of French writing since the 17th century. Moreover, like so much literature since the Pléiade, it is the creation of a group or school. But unlike the writing of earlier ages, it is ultimately sterile. In the late 1950s and early 1960s a group of novelists, including Alain Robbe-Grillet (b.1922) and Nathalie Sarraute (b.1902) arrived at the view that there was something false about traditional forms of the novel, which took for granted assumptions about character and plot and claimed to hold up a stable and accurately reflecting mirror to the world, and which presumed that narration required a beginning, middle and an end. They set out to write novels that did not aim at offering an easily decoded picture of the world. The most successful exponent of the new forms has probably been Robbe-Grillet, notably in film scripts such as *L'année dernière à Marienbad* (1961) because his technique of scrambling narrative sequences and time frames lends itself better to cinema than to the printed word.

We have come a long way from the moment that Roland put the horn to his lips in France's first masterpiece. That French writers should have continued to produce outstanding works of literature, despite the vicissitudes of history, including wars and revolutions from the twelfth to the twentieth century, is surely one of the great achievements of European culture.

Albert Camus (1913–60).

GASTRONOMY

France is *the* land of gastronomy, and good eating is one of the greatest pleasures of a holiday there. This is true whether the meal be a sumptuous 400-franc-a-head adventure in a luxury restaurant, a tasty peasant stew in a simple country inn, a light lunch of freshly caught shellfish with Muscadet in a Breton fishing-village, or a woodland picnic of cheese, pâté and fruit bought in a local market. Endowed by nature with a fertile soil and a mild climate, the French have developed a richly varied agriculture and have used their creativity and love of good living to evolve a cuisine of unequalled diversity and subtlety. Gastronomy is part of the French heritage: it is regarded as one of the noblest of the arts in a land where great chefs are revered as leading national figures, on a level with famous painters or opera singers. The French have gastronomy in their bones, so that a housewife knows almost instinctively the correct ingredients for a *daube* or *pot au feu*.

Despite the fact that since the war this grand tradition has to some extent been threatened by the fad for convenience foods and the popularity of mass eateries, France is still the land where you eat better than anywhere else – especially in the provinces.

The regional diversity of French cooking is quite amazing. It is true that some dishes are common to most parts of France: but each region also has its own elaborate array of specialities, rooted in peasant history and usually based upon local produce, dependent on soil and climate.

Left Michel Guérard, the pioneer of the new French cuisine and proprietor of Les Prés d'Eugénie at Eugénie-les-Bains, north of Pau.

Below Fruit stall in the Latin Quarter of Paris

The abundance and variety of Mediterranean fish has inspired the creation of many great recipes in Provence, notably *bouillabaisse*, the truest version of which comes from Marseille.

Some of these specialities are described in the introductions to the regional chapters, but a brief summary is worth giving here. Broadly speaking, the cuisine of southern France is more spicy and sharply flavoured than that of the north; in the south, olive oil often replaces butter in cooking, and garlic and herbs are much more widely used. In all wine-growing areas, wine tends to enter into the preparation of many main dishes, whereas in Normandy it may be cider and in Flanders beer. Beef, pork and chicken are the commonest meats of the north; in the south, you are as likely to find lamb, rabbit and goose.

The pungent cuisine of Provence is famous for garlicky fish stews such as *bouillabaisse* and *bourride*, local mountain lamb with wild herbs, and a wide range of spicy salads, often served as a lunchtime hors d'oeuvres buffet. The Nice area, formerly part of Italy, has its own special dishes such as ravioli, anchovy tart and *salade niçoise*. To the west, the cuisine of Languedoc has much in common with that of Provence, while the Toulouse/Carcassonne area is the heartland of Languedoc's special glory, *cassoulet*, a rich and complex goose-and-bean stew with subtle local variations.

Throughout the south-west, from Périgord to the Pyrenees, *pâté de foie gras*, *confit d'oie et de canard* (preserved goose and duck) and *magret de canard* (duck steak) are regular dishes, while the proud and individualistic Basques have their own specialities such as *civet de palombes* (woodcock stew) and *piperade* (a kind of tomato omelette). Upland Auvergne offers a simple but plentiful peasant cuisine (e.g. tripe, stuffed cabbage and thick soups). In the Loire valley, around Tours, the cooking is more refined and sophisticated, based largely on the excellent and varied fruit and vegetables of this 'garden of France'. In Brittany, the accent is on local fish, notably shellfish, eaten either uncooked (oysters and shrimps), marinated in wine (mussels), or in a variety of strong sauces (lobster and monkfish). The rich Norman cuisine makes lavish use of cream and butter, and sometimes also of cider or calvados, for preparing veal, chicken and the local fish, such as sole, in many inventive ways. Picardy and the Nord may not be as distinguished gastronomically, yet they too have interesting local dishes, such as beef braised in beer (common also in Belgium) and *ficelle picarde*, a kind of ham and mushroom pancake.

The Alsatians, enthusiastic eaters, make much culinary use of their white wines, notably in *coq au riesling* and in the ubiquitous *choucroute* (pork with sour cabbage). Neighbouring Lorraine is best known for its *quiches*, but has much else as well. In Burgundy, the fruity red wines feature strongly in the cooking – notably in *coq au vin*, perhaps the best known of all French classic dishes – and in *boeuf bourguignonne*. Snails in garlic and parsleyed ham are other highlights of Burgundy's redoubtable gastronomy. In mountainous Savoy, the local lake and river fish are cooked in many interesting ways. And so finally to the Lyon area, often regarded as the heartland of French cuisine: here even the humble pig's trotter, or a hot garlic sausage, becomes a major delicacy for gourmets, while pork, veal, pike and crayfish form the basis of many subtle dishes. As for Paris itself, the French capital has few specialities of its own; but many of its best restaurants are owned and run by émigrés from the French regions, who serve their local dishes and often obtain their produce from farms back home.

French cooking runs the gamut from the *haute cuisine* of the smart classic restaurants, by way of *nouvelle cuisine* and *cuisine bourgeoise*, to the *cuisine paysanne* of little country inns. Most regional cooking falls into the *cuisine bourgeoise* category (good ingredients, well prepared as by a bourgeoise housewife in her kitchen) or else *cuisine paysanne* (simpler materials, perhaps leftovers or scrag meat, ingeniously reworked so as to bring out their flavours, as poor peasants have, by necessity, long learned to do). These peasant dishes are often spicy and heavy, with much use of garlic and herbs. Nevertheless, it would be wrong to infer from this that all French cooking is rich and thus hard to digest. Very often its secret is meticulous simplicity. In many a rural *auberge* you can enjoy a delicious meal without trying anything more exotic than, say, home-made vegetable soup or a tomato salad, trout lightly sautéd, roast lamb or grilled farm chicken with tarragon, *haricots verts* in butter, Camembert and a home-made cherry or apple tart.

Fresh black cherries are used in the Auvergne for this traditional fruit *clafouti* (cherries baked in batter).

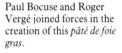

Among the great chefs first practising nouvelle cuisine were Jean and Pierre Troisgros.

The great classic restaurants of Paris, such as *Lasserre* and the *Tour d'Argent*, offer *haute cuisine* – the expensive, sophisticated style of cooking devised for smart society in the 19th century, using plenty of rich sauces with cream, butter, flour and perhaps brandy. But this is gradually going out of fashion. Today's gourmets are more diet-conscious, and have thus provided a ready custom for the major culinary revolution of the past twenty or so years: *la nouvelle cuisine française*. This inventive style marks a return to a lighter, purer manner. It discards most heavy sauces that mask the real taste of the meat, and spurns flour and carbohydrates as well. It relies on very fresh ingredients, rapidly cooked in their own juices, almost in the Chinese manner, so as to bring out their true flavours. Vegetables are served crispy, half-cooked. It encourages the chef to deviate from classic recipes and try out adventurous new blends: for example, a purée of mixed spinach and pear, preserving the fresh taste of both.

The school of *nouvelle cuisine* was pioneered by the late Fernand Point, the great owner-chef of the *Pyramide* restaurant at Vienne, south of Lyon. Today its leading exponents include most of the greatest chefs of France, such as Paul Bocuse, Roger Vergé, Pierre Troisgros and Alain Capel. The trend has become so popular with the public that well over half of the smarter restaurants in France now follow it, although very many of them – for instance, Bocuse's own famous establishment in the Lyon suburbs – provide a mixture of 'new' and more classic dishes. This 'new' cooking is nearly always expensive, for it demands the highest-quality ingredients as well as much time and skill. Nor is it

Paul Bocuse and Roger Vergé joined forces in the creation of this *pâté de foie gras*.

Cassoulet, the most famous of all Languedoc specialities, is based on white kidney beans.

universally appreciated; portions tend to be small and rather too daintily served – for example, five or six different vegetables arranged in patterns on the plate, almost like flowers. For such reasons, many gourmets, disliking such over-refinement, prefer the more robust tastes of traditional, if less nutritive, dishes such as *cassoulet*. Moreover, while *nouvelle cuisine* in the hands of a master chef like Bocuse can certainly produce sublime results, it has also led to many absurdities, since the free licence to invent has been abused by many inferior or inexperienced chefs. The leading French gastronomic critic and writer, Henri Gault, himself a key apostle of the new cooking, has admitted this: 'Young cooks striving for instant fame are doing horrible things in the name of *la nouvelle cuisine*, like serving sweetbreads raw, or putting steak with strawberries. The cult of innovation for its own sake is silly.' Even so, the overall legacy of the new cooking has certainly been positive. It has given a needed shot in the arm to a gastronomic tradition that was growing stale, and has helped to revive a wider public interest in food.

How can the foreign visitor tell whether a given restaurant is serving new or classic cuisine? Only by having a knowledge of French cooking vocabulary and then looking at the menu, always posted up outside. If you want classic dishes, make sure that these are on the menu before you step inside. And you will rarely find *nouvelle cuisine* in country *auberges*, traditional brasseries, or anywhere with set menus for less than about 80 francs.

Lunch tends to be the main meal of the day in France. In the provinces this is still very often a leisurely two-hour family affair: but elsewhere, especially in the cities, the trend is increasingly towards the quick-lunch system in snack-bars and canteens. The French do, however, remain conservative about their times of eating meals: lunch in Paris is always strictly at 1.00 (rather earlier in the provinces), while among all social classes and in all regions the evening meal is rarely before 7.30 or 8.00 p.m. There is no equivalent of the English high tea; nor do the French eat snacks between meals, except for the occasional afternoon pâtisserie. Thus restaurants are open for meals only at set

La Pyramide, Vienne, owned by the late Fernand Point, pioneer of the school of *nouvelle cuisine*.

hours, and even in big cities such as Paris, it is hard to get a hot meal at, say, 4.00 or 5.00 p.m.

The French generally eat a full three- or four-course main meal, starting with soup or *hors d'oeuvre*, then a fish or meat dish (indeed *both*, for a special meal or on an extensive menu), and always cheese *before* dessert. This is a question of taste, on the assumption that cheese goes better than sweet as a balancing contrast after meat, and that you can continue drinking the same red wine with both, perhaps switching to a white with the dessert. In the evening the French generally start with soup, and at lunch with an *hors d'oeuvre* or salad dish – often *crudités*, mixed raw vegetables with dressing. Meat is generally served on its own, or with just one vegetable specially chosen to harmonize with it (e.g. flageolet beans with roast lamb, or lentils with *petit salé pork*) and does not come smothered by several ill-assorted vegetables in the Anglo-Saxon manner. Note also that French taste is to eat meat rare *(saignant)* or medium rare *(à point)*; a serious restaurateur may even refuse to serve a 'barbarian' who insults his cooking by asking for it well done *(bien cuit)*.

When choosing a restaurant, it is best to realize that the smart places are not necessarily where one eats best, for the French tend to set less store by comfort and gloss than by the kitchen itself. So do not judge by an imposing facade or the number of waiters in tails. Look first at the menu outside, then venture in: if the place seems to be full of *French* people, that is a good sign. Nowadays, many smart-looking places on holiday routes tend to be tourist-traps, so unless the reliable French guidebooks suggest otherwise – try to avoid them.

Restaurant menus in Paris are generally *à la carte*; in the provinces they are *prix fixé* too, and this usually offers much better value, for a three- or four-course set meal will cost no more than one *à la carte* main dish. The best menus are very often the shorter ones, with relatively little choice: except in large, international places, beware of long standardized menus which too frequently imply reheating, precooking and over-use of tins or the deep-freeze. The French prefer fresh ingredients, freshly cooked, and often you will do best by taking the patron's *plat du jour*. By and large, French restaurants offer excellent value and are not expensive: in a family-run *bistro* in the provinces, you can still get a very good meal with wine for a mere 60–80 francs – and the paper tablecloths on which the waitress perhaps scrawls the bill are all part of the fun. The bill almost always comes with service included: but you generally leave two or three francs extra, especially if service has been good. Waiters and waitresses may seem brusque at first, notably in Paris – that is their style – but are generally helpful and friendly if you show an interest in the food. Unlike so many staff in Britain, they *know* what the dishes are and how they are cooked.

Restaurants vary enormously in kind and price. For a special gastronomic treat, ignoring the cost, it might be worth trying out one of the places awarded two or three rosettes in the red Michelin guide. This book gives its top, three-rosette rating to some eighteen restaurants, twelve of them in the provinces. But you can also eat very well far more cheaply, for example by consulting Michelin's list of value-for-money, moderate cost restaurants, denoted by a red 'R'. A *brasserie* is a town café-beerhall-restaurant, often large, bright and bustling, serving solid conventional food; a rural *auberge* will usually be cosier and more charming, but the food may not be better. In the provinces, some of the best cooking is frequently found in sedate commercial hotels; and if you don't mind rough simplicity, the lorry-drivers' pull-ins on main roads (*relais routiers*, denoted by red-and-blue signs) often offer good value. Avoid, if you can, the modern mass-catering motorway restaurants which, as in other countries, are none too good.

French eating habits are today in a state of transition. Depending on your viewpoint, the French may either seem still to be loyal to their gastronomic traditions or fast deserting them. Certainly they are eating lighter, healthier meals than in the past; and young housewives, less prepared than were their mothers or grandmothers to spend long hours on some *plat mijoté*, will as readily toss a steak under the grill. It is true that the past ten years or so have seen a revival of interest in serious cooking, as witness the massive sales of cookbooks and the fact that, despite economic crisis, *good* restaurants are today fuller than ever. But this revival is no longer a matter of daily routine, being reserved for the once- or twice-weekly special meal in a really good restaurant, the ritual Sunday lunch or the dinner party for a few friends. On such occasions, the French are exacting as ever: but for routine meals during the rest of the week, they seem prepared to let standards slip.

The shorter lunch-break, along with other modern trends, has inevitably produced a spate of new snack-bars, fast-food eateries and down-market hamburger joints, all quite alien to the French tradition. Although most of these are horrible, some of the big self-service restaurants do serve tolerably good French food rather than imitation American junk-food: you can queue up for *andouillettes, tripes à la mode de Caen* and even *quenelles*. Anglo-American influences have led to the invasion of Paris and other cities by English 'pubs' (quite phoney and with dreadful food) and also by 'drugstores' which are often quite good in their way, even if nothing like the genuine American article. They are simply large multiple restaurants, in a ritzy modern setting, plus boutiques, open late, and often serving authentic French food, good salads and ice-creams.

So-called 'drugstores' and 'pubs' are not the only new foreign influences. The French once maintained that only their own national cuisine was any good, despising all foreign cooking, but this attitude has been changing. From their foreign holidays they have now discovered a taste for moussaka, paella, lasagne, kebabs, etc, trying out these dishes in their own homes, and eating them in the foreign restaurants which are fast opening up in Paris and other cities. Most numerous are the Vietnamese and south Chinese, followed by Italian, Spanish, Greek, North African, etc. There are also many modest-priced pizza houses, often run by Corsicans, and hordes of restaurants serving North African dishes such as couscous, most of them run by French repatriates from Algeria.

One of the great delights of a French holiday is surely buying a picnic in a local shop or market and then eating it in a lovely setting –

fresh crunchy French bread, *pâté* or *charcuterie*, fresh cheese such as Brie, juicy tomatoes, a ripe pink sweet Cavaillon melon, or strawberries, and, naturally, wine. So where to buy all this? The local open-air markets are, of course, still an attractive feature of most French towns, especially in the south, either daily or on one or two days a week; and they provide food that is fresher, more interesting, and markedly cheaper than in the shops. Small grocers and greengrocers tend to be unsatisfactory: but not so the more specialized local stores selling *pâtisseries*, *charcuterie*, fish, and the like. The range of fresh fish in French shops is marvellous, far wider than in Britain – but to enjoy these to the full, you need to be on a self-catering holiday in a villa or flat. Above all, do not spurn the French hypermarkets, which are the biggest and some of the best in Europe, with a wonderful range of fresh foods – the delicatessen, *charcuterie* and cheese counters are as long as a bowling alley – and a wide variety of frozen foods as well. Although they still prefer fresh food, the French are gradually coming round to deep-freezing. However, they are not interested in freezing basic foods such as peas or fish-fingers, going in more for expensive pre-cooked and frozen dishes such as *coq-au-vin*, *cassoulet* or even frogs' legs *provençale*. These may not be quite as good as the same dishes freshly cooked in a restaurant, but are still very tasty, and worth trying if you have the kitchen facilities. So the French are harnessing modern deep-freeze techniques to their traditional gastronomy.

Some specialized French food shops:

Charcuterie (cooked meat shop): here the choice will be staggering, with the accent on pork by-products. Besides *pâtés* and *terrines*, try *rillettes* (a soft *pâté* of spiced pork), white and black pudding *(boudin blanc, boudin noir)*, *andouillettes* to eat with mustard, salami-style *saucisson sec*, or strong red peppery *chorizo* sausage from the Basque country.

Fromagerie (cheese shop): France is the land of 300 cheeses (de Gaulle once said that is what makes it so impossible to govern) and any good dairy or grocery will have a wide selection. Apart from the better known regional cheeses, it may be worth looking out for: *Livarot*, a pungent cheese from Normandy; *Époisses*, from Burgundy, even more smelly; salty goats'-milk *Venaco* from Corsica; and of course *fromage blanc* and *fromage frais*, a kind of semi-curdled cream, taken with sugar and delicious in summer.

Below A stall in Périgueux shows the wide variety of *charcuterie* available in the Dordogne region.

Boulangerie et pâtisserie (bakery and cake shop): many purists feel that French bread is not as good as it used to be; but there is still something splendidly chewy about it, so long as it is really fresh. Of the long loaves, the thinnest and crustiest is the *ficelle*; then comes the standard *baguette*, good for sandwiches; then the fatter *pain de livre*. Many other kinds of bread are also available such as rye bread *(pain de seigle)* or huge, broad country loaves *(pain de campagne)*. As an alternative to *croissants* for breakfasts, try *brioches*. *Pâtisseries* are made in every shape, size and colour and are usually beautifully served even in the tiniest local shop, with an elaborately tied ribbon around the carton – another small example of French pre-eminence in style.

Above The character of goat cheese changes almost daily. In France, it is sold according to age and taste. The best goat cheeses come from the Poitou.

Left Bread is indispensable to the balanced French diet. Local bakers produce a large selection of different loaves. Here we see a typical range: *baguettes, ficelles, croissants* and *pains de campagne*.

WINE

France is the second largest producer of wine in Europe, from the renowned vintages to the more modest *vins de table*, the choice is enormous. Wine is available so freely in France that it is actually easier than buying bread, but a few hints will help you to get the best value for your money.

When travelling through France, the local wine is always the best buy. Surprisingly enough, the French drink a lot of *vin ordinaire*, usually cheap and with no regional character whatsoever. This should be avoided. If you are on a tight budget, buy the Vin de Pays from the *département* that you are travelling through. Most regions, particularly those towards the south, produce wines under the VDQS *appellation*, midway between the Vins de Pays and the fully fledged AOC wines. These cost a little more than the former, but offer few disappointments. In the AOC category more care is needed, as the difference between a dull and a good example is often very little in francs but a good deal in flavour.

There are three main places to buy wine in France; in a grocery or supermarket, at a specialist wine shop, and from the vineyard or cooperative. The first is the most convenient but probably offers the most risk and not always the best value; the second should give you sound advice as well as showing a wide range; the third is the most fun, but you have to purchase more than a couple of bottles. Almost every wine-growing commune in France has a *cave coopérative* and if you are staying some days in one place, it is worth tracking it down. The prestigious Châteaux in Bordeaux and the important Domaines in Burgundy apart, most wine-growers welcome visitors into their cellars for a small tasting and it is merely courtesy to buy a bottle or two when you leave.

Buying wine to take home with you demands even more care. One rule is, never buy the cheapest, since the basic costs of bottles, corks, labels, transport and so on are virtually fixed and you will get more wine for your money by spending a little more. Another rule is to buy wines you will enjoy at home, avoiding those that are *only* good with the local shellfish. The third is to buy something you are proud of, since if you get tired of it yourselves, it will make a good present, unlike a bottle of *vin ordinaire*.

The trend of the 1980s, as far as wine is concerned, is the emergence of the wine bar. In Paris, for example, there have always been cafés specializing in regional wines, generally as an accompaniment to *charcuterie* and a few *plats du jour*. These wines, Sancerre, Pouilly, Beaujolais, Chinon and so forth were generally bought in barrel, bottled on the premises, and sold at low prices. Many of these cafés-à-vin are still thriving. Since the late 1970s a number of bistros-à-vin, specializing in better wines and serving appropriately good food as accompaniment, have opened in the capital. They have an agreeable atmosphere, are run by knowledgeable people who place wine first, cater for women as well as men, and are well worth patronizing.

There are few parts of France that are not wine-growing regions, and there are countless books providing general and specialized information for both the amateur and the connoisseur. Only a very brief geographical survey is possible here.

Champagne/Ardennes

The ancient province of Champagne produces wines of the same name from the most northerly vineyards in France. Four-fifths of the land under vines is in the *département* of the Marne, where the two Champagne towns of Reims and Épernay vie with each other for importance. Reims is much the larger, yet despite the presence of such *grandes marques* as Veuve Clicquot, Taittinger and Krug, the champagne trade is centred on Épernay where Moët et Chandon, Pol Roger and Perrier-Jouët, amongst many others, make up l'Avenue de Champagne.

Champagne, the only AOC wine in France that does not have to put *appellation contrôlée* on the label, is a white or pink wine that must be made sparkling by the process of secondary fermentation in the bottle, known as the *méthode Champenoise*. Grapes used are the Pinot Noir and Chardonnay, the noble grapes of Burgundy, and the Pinot Meunier. If the Chardonnay alone is used, the wine may be termed a *blanc de blancs*. Still wines, red, white and a very little rosé, are also made in Champagne and carry the *appellation* Coteaux Champenois.

The finest wines come from the Montagne de Reims and the Côte des Blancs. Certain villages, such as Ay, Bouzy, Cramant and Le Mesnil, benefit from Grand Cru status and champagne made from one of these villages alone is known as a *monocru*. However, the fame of the world's best known sparkling wine lies in the art of blending, and several dozen wines from different vineyards and different vintages will make up the non-vintage *cuvée* of a prestigious champagne house.

The 'Trianon' summer house known as the Orangerie at Moët & Chandon where guests are entertained.

Alsace and Lorraine

The Vosges mountains are the key to the climatic differences in this north-eastern corner of France. To the east, sheltered by the mountain range from the winds and rain of the north, are the vineyards of Alsace, centred around Colmar. To the west are the almost forgotten vineyards of Lorraine. Here, the Côtes de Toul, red, white, rosé and especially *gris*, are pleasantly fruity and refreshing wines, while the

Vins de Moselle, also a VDQS, making light reds and slightly tart whites, are never seen outside the region. Across the Vosges, however, the picture is quite different: the wines of Alsace are world renowned and offer a notable range of styles thanks to the propitious climate, the different types of soil and the large number of grape varieties planted. Almost all Alsace wine is white, although there is a little red or rosé made from the Pinot Noir, and it is all grown, made and bottled in the *départements* of the Haut and Bas Rhin. The beautiful *route de vin* stretches 100 kilometres from Strasbourg to Mulhouse and each village possesses its own microclimate and special type of soil to suit the various grapes. Sylvaner, light and thirst-quenching, is better in the north around Barr and Mittelbergheim; the Pinot Blanc (locally known as Clevner), and Pinot Gris (confusingly known as Tokay), fuller and more aromatic wines, are especially good south of Colmar near Pfaffenheim; the Muscat, dry and delightfully scented, best as an apéritif, is excellent at Eguisheim; the Gewürztraminer, exuberant and heady, even spicy, is at its best from Turckheim and Wintzenheim, while the noble Riesling, with its stylish fruit and lemony acidity, is perfect from around Ribeauvillé and Riquewihr.

Above Riquewihr, the celebrated Alsatian wine village, produces some of the best Riesling.

Lower Loire
The city of Nantes is the capital of le Pays Nantais, the birthplace of Muscadet. Muscadet is the most popular wine in France, crisp, dry and refreshing, divided between three *appellations*, Muscadet, Muscadet des Coteaux de la Loire and Muscadet de Sèvre et Maine. Even slightly 'greener' than Muscadet is the Gros Plant du Pays Nantais which should be drunk the year after the vintage. Also in the Loire-Atlantique *département* are the little known red, white and rosé wines of Ancenis, light, local wines that do not travel.

The modern-day *département* of Maine-et-Loire corresponds roughly to the ancient royal province of Anjou. Historically, the white wines have always been in greatest demand, and the sweet, honeyed wines of Bonnezeaux, Quarts de Chaume and Coteaux du Layon are now justifiably regaining popularity. The *appellation* Anjou may account for dry, semi-sweet or sweet whites, reds and rosés, and while the ever popular Rosé d'Anjou is still being produced, it is better to drink the raspberry-scented red wines, served at cellar temperature. The wines

Above Grape harvest in the Loire valley.

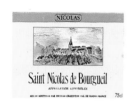

of Saumur often have more in common with those of Touraine: the whites are generally dry or demi-sec and much of it is sold as Saumur Mousseux, a very good alternative to champagne. The finest white wine of the Saumurois is the delightfully flowery Savennières. The best red wine is Saumur Champigny, deep-coloured and fruity, with a distinctive earthy taste.

Loire Centre

One of the pleasures of travelling in France is discovering or re-discovering wines that are not available outside their region of origin. The Orléanais wines are a case in point. These light red, delicious, almost colourless rosés known as *vins gris*, and lively whites are now only to be found on the spot and in Paris.

The wines of Sancerre, however, are so popular around the world that the vignerons have already sold their crop by the time of the next vintage. The white is particularly good with a brochet from the river or the local *crotin de Chavignol*. There is a little Sancerre red and rosé made with the Pinot Noir. Similar in style to Sancerre are the white wines of Quincy, Reuilly and Menetou-Salon.

The widest range of wines comes from the Indre-et-Loire *départe-ment*, otherwise known as Touraine or the Garden of France. The Chenin Blanc is at its best here, as can be seen from the wines of Vouvray, ranging from very dry to honey-sweet. Touraine is itself an *appellation*, whose wines often state the name of the grape on the label – Sauvignon, Gamay – and to which certain communes can add their names – Amboise, Azay-le-Rideau, Mesland – the latter wines being particularly good.

Major red wines on this route include the deep, earthy Bourgueil, Saint Nicolas de Bourgueil and Chinon. Their raspberry or violet scented bouquet and clear fruit make them some of the most delicious of French wines.

Throughout the region, the light, refreshing Vins de Pays may be sold under the name Jardin de la France, or under the name of their *départements*.

Burgundy

This region encompasses the whole of the wines of Burgundy, excluding Beaujolais, and even some wines properly classified in the Loire, so it is not possible to deal with them all in any detail.

Driving south from Paris, the first vines one sees are those of the Yonne. The vineyards of Chablis and the Auxerrois are the most northerly in Burgundy. The soil is a limestony-chalk, which gives Chablis more in common with Champagne than with the more clayey soil of central Burgundy. The white wines are crisp and dry, even slightly austere, with good fruit but none of the 'fleshiness' of the Chardonnays from further south. The famous Chablis region is separated into four *appellations*, in ascending order of quality: Petit-Chablis, Chablis, Chablis Premier Cru and Chablis Grand Cru.

Throughout the Burgundy region, i.e. the *départements* of the Yonne, Côte d'Or and Saône-et-Loire, there are regional or generic *appellations*. For white wine there is the crisp dry Bourgogne Aligoté and the sparkling Crémant de Bourgogne, while for reds Bourgogne-Grand-Ordinaire is the most minor *appellation*, followed by Bourgogne Passetoutgrains and Bourgogne. These generic wines are inexpensive and, if bought from a reputable *négociant* (dealer) or a reliable grower, good value for money. The finer wines from Burgundy, however, carry the name of the village from which they come – Pommard, Chambolle-Musigny, Volnay, Meursault – and the finest of all will be from a specific Premier Cru or Grand Cru vineyard.

Burgundy proper is divided into the Côte de Nuits and the Côte de Beaune. From Dijon to Chalon, the names of these wines are synonymous with Burgundy at its best: Fixin, Gevrey-Chambertin,

Chambertin, Morey-St-Denis, Chambolle-Musigny, Clos de Vougeot, Vosne-Romanée, Nuits-St-Georges, Aloxe-Corton, Beaune, Pommard, Volnay, Meursault, Puligny and Chassagne-Montrachet, Santenay, Mercurey and Givry. White wines are made exclusively with the Chardonnay, reds with the Pinot Noir. The vineyards are small in comparison to Bordeaux, and the holdings parcellated. The key to Burgundy is to know the producer, who bottles his wine and puts his name on the label. *Négociants* will buy wine in barrel and bring it up in their cellars, bottling it under their own name, but often retaining the name of the actual vineyard or *climat*, and here the name of the *négociant* is often more of a guarantee than the name of the wine. The centre of the wine industry is in Beaune. The reputation of the wines of the Côte de Nuits and the Côte de Beaune has been acquired over many centuries, and lesser known wines offering perhaps better value for money are to be found in the hills around St Aubin and in the Côte Chalonnaise.

Above Oak casks maturing in the cellar of a *négociant* in Beaune.

At the southern end of the Saône-et-Loire *département* are the wines of the Mâconnais. While Mâcon Blanc and the vastly overpriced Pouilly-Fuissé are much appreciated, Mâcon Rouge has been superseded by the wines of Beaujolais, making it all the more interesting to sample on the spot. The white wines of the Mâconnais, Pouilly-Fuissé excepted, are quite delicious and not too expensive. The Nièvre *département* produces one of the most perfect examples of the Sauvignon grape, Pouilly-Fumé, around the town of Pouilly-sur-Loire.

Jura/Franche-Comté

Only the *département* of the Jura now produces wine in the ancient province of the Franche-Comté. Jura wines are not well known outside France, but their lack of notoriety is well compensated by their originality. They can be red, white, rosé, *gris* and sparkling, with a varied, distinctive style. The better known *appellations* are Arbois and Côtes de Jura, while the little town of L'Étoile has an *appellation* to itself for a delicious white wine rarely seen outside the area. The great rarities of this region, however, are the *vin de paille*, an astoundingly rich, amber-coloured dessert wine only sold in half bottles or *pots*, and the extraordinary *vin jaune*, a wine of intense, sherry-like concentration. It is worth looking for the Vins de Pays du Franche-Comté, light reds and rosés, and refreshingly crisp whites.

Cognac

Poitou-Charentes

The excellent Cave Coopérative at Neuville de Poitou produces the Vins de Haut Poitou – red, dry white (still and sparkling) and rosé. The two most successful whites are the Chardonnay and the Sauvignon. The red is light in colour and should be drunk young and cold.

The *départements* of the Charente and Charente-Maritime are the home of the Cognac industry. Centred on the market town of Cognac and the sleepy village of Jarnac, the world's best known *eau-de-vie* is produced by twice distilling a thin acid wine made from the overproduction of Ugni Blanc grapes. It is forbidden to sell single-vintage Cognacs in France, so age is determined by a system of stars, or phrases such as 'Vieille Réserve', 'Hors d'Age'. It is best to stay with the well-known Grandes Marques such as Hennessy, Martel or Delamain, or better still, try the single Domaine Cognacs bottled by the growers themselves.

Massif Central

The Massif Central is geographically recognizable but viticulturally difficult to define. The wines from the north-west *départements* of the Allier and the Puy-de-Dôme are classified as Loire wines and those from the Aveyron are linked with the south-west. In style, the delightful wines of Saint Pourçain have more in common with Burgundy than with the Loire. The whites are crisp and flowery, the reds and rosés fruity. Just to the south, from the region of Clermont-Ferrand and Riom, the Côtes d'Auvergne wines are particularly agreeable. The reds have much in common with the Saint Pourçains and more than a hint of Beaujolais, and the rosés are justifiably popular. The better wines from this region can add the name of the commune, such as Boudes, Chanturgue, Corent and Madargues. The Vins de Pays du Puy-de-Dôme are light and quaffable.

To the south of the Massif Central, the character of the red wines becomes more rustic, and the whites more aromatic. The best known wine is Marcillac, a VDQS, from around the town of Rodez, mostly red, deep-coloured and full of a rough fruit that goes well with the local cuisine. Two very little known VDQSs from the Aveyron, the Vins d'Entraygues et du Fel and the Vins d'Estaing, red, rosé and a very little white, are a must at the local restaurants. Even more obscure is the Vin de Pays des Gorges et Côtes de Millau.

The Lyon area

Among the many well-known wines from this part of France, by far the most popular is Beaujolais. A little white Beaujolais is still made in the Saône-et-Loire *département* to the north; but in the Rhône *département*, all Beaujolais is red, a fruity, usually refreshing wine (when it does not have too much alcohol), made from the Gamay grape. Beaujolais-Villages comes from the region of Villefranche and between here and Mâcon are the nine villages whose wines are superior Beaujolais, with *appellations* of their own: Brouilly, Côte-de-Brouilly, Morgon, Chiroubles, Fleurie, Chénas, Moulin-à-Vent, Juliénas and Saint-Amour. From the outskirts of Lyon come the pleasantly fruity Coteaux du Lyonnais and the slightly lighter Côtes de Forez.

South of Lyon is the Côtes du Rhône region. From terraced vineyards on either bank of the river, between Vienne and Valence, come the finest wines of the Rhône valley, indeed some of the finest in France: the intensely aromatic Condrieu, with its bouquet of apricots and almonds, and the miniscule Château Grillet, one of France's rarest wines. The wines of Côte-Rôtie are distinguished by a velvety richness and great length of flavour, and are rivalled in the northern Rhône only by the powerful, deep red Hermitage. Hermitage, from around Tain l'Hermitage and Tournon, can also be white, at once flowery and firm. The wines of Crozes-Hermitage are good, but not in this league, either for quality or price. Saint Joseph is known for its spicy reds and

fragrant whites, while Cornas, in the Ardèche *département*, produces a solid, uncompromising, long-lived red wine. The delightful white wines of Saint-Péray are mostly sparkling, to be drunk locally. None of these wines are cheap, but they are all of high quality. Lighter and easier on the pocket are some excellent Vins de Pays des Coteaux de l'Ardèche, red, white and rosé.

Above The Beaujolais is the most southern vineyard area of Burgundy and is also the largest.

The Loire *département* produces some fruity reds and rosés around Roanne, under the VDQS Côtes Roannaise *appellation*; and from the north of the *département* the Vins du Pays d'Urfé, reds, rosés and whites, are all for drinking young.

The Ain *département* is the home of the Vins de Bugey – perfect picnic wines – light and fruity, the whites especially good around Montagnieu and Cerdon.

Alps and Savoy

The *département* of the Savoie and the Haute-Savoie produce some crisp, smoky dry white wines, but also a range of fuller whites, very good reds and rosés, and some excellent sparkling wines. The light white wines of Crépy, with just a hint of natural sparkle, are lively and elegant. The little town of Seyssel produces a violet-scented white wine that is delicious with fish and local cheeses. The basic *appellation*, however, only upgraded in 1973 from VDQS, is Vin de Savoie, which may be red, white, rosé or sparkling. Certain villages have the right to use their name on the label. The best whites are Abymes, Apremont, Ayse (with its own sparkling wine), Chignin, Chignin-Bergeron and Ripaille; the best reds and rosés are Chautagne and Montmélian.

In the midst of these vineyards, the town of Chambéry has given its name to a clean, aromatic vermouth, sometimes served with a dash of *liqueur de framboise*.

To the south-west of the region, there are some pleasantly fruity reds, and some lively whites from Chatillon-en-Diois, but the wine to drink here is Clairette de Die, aromatic and not quite dry, delicious on its own or with desserts, served very cold. Two Vins de Pays from this region are Palmes Dauphinoises and Coteaux du Grésivaudan.

Dordogne and the Lot

The two best known wines from this part of France are Bergerac and Cahors. Cahors is a slightly rustic, full-bodied wine which can be drunk young, even the year after the vintage, while the finest *cuvées* are kept for three years in cask and may use the *appellation* 'Vieux Cahors'. Also from the Lot *département* comes some good Vins de Pays

Above The vineyards of Cahors are some of the oldest in France, being already well established by the Romans.

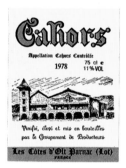

Château Margaux.

des Coteaux de Quercy, perfect for picnics.

The wines of Bergerac are softer than those of Cahors, and the *appellation* covers both reds and rosés, with the excellent dry whites carrying the *appellation* Bergerac Sec to distinguish them from the sweet Côtes de Bergerac Moelleux. Bergerac is full of fruit and charm and may be drunk young. The red Côtes de Bergerac is a little firmer, while the more rare Pécharmant, the best red wine from the Dordogne, is at its best at 3–6 years. Another interesting *appellation* is Côtes de Duras, producing Bordeaux-style reds and dry and sweet whites.

The luscious, honey-sweet wines of Monbazillac once rivalled the great Sauternes, and are again worth discovering. An almost forgotten wine is Montravel – white, dry, demi-sec or sweet – making a charming apéritif. Even rarer are the semi-sweet white wines of Rosette, mostly drunk locally. Finally, the Vins de Pays de la Dordogne and the Coteaux de Glanes are light, fruity and refreshing.

Aquitaine

To write about all the wines from Aquitaine would take a book, and a lifetime of visits would be necessary to sample all the 3500 or so wines from the Châteaux of Bordeaux, to say nothing of the wide variety of country wines from the surrounding *départements*. This, then, is the briefest of surveys.

The Bordeaux wine-producing region, enclosed in the *département* of the Gironde, with some 100,000 hectares under vines and producing 500 million bottles a year, all *appellation contrôlée*, is the largest fine wine region in the world. The range covers the simple red, white and rosé Bordeaux, usually drunk a year or two after the vintage, through the more important generic *appellations* such as Saint Émilion, Médoc and Graves, to the prestigious Châteaux like Margaux, Lafite-Rothschild, Pétrus, etc. Geographically, the Bordeaux vineyards are divided into three regions: those to the left of the river Garonne, running from south of Langon to the tip of the Gironde estuary; those on the right bank of the Dordogne and to the right of the estuary; and those between the Dordogne and the Garonne rivers, an area known as 'Entre-deux-Mers'. From the first region come the luscious sweet wines of Sauternes and Barsac, the fine dry white and red wines of the Graves and, passing around Bordeaux, the classic, long-lived wines of the Médoc and the Haut-Médoc, including Listrac, Moulis, Margaux, Saint-Julien, Pauillac and Saint-Estèphe.

The wines from the right bank, based on the Merlot grapes as opposed to the Cabernets for the Médoc and the Graves, are rounder and softer. The top *appellations*, Saint-Émilion and Pomerol, have often been referred to as 'the Burgundies of Bordeaux', hinting at their extra weight and warmth. The great Châteaux from this region rival in expense and quality those from the left bank, while there are excellent values to be found amongst the lesser known Montagne-Saint-Émilions, Fronsacs, rather more concentrated Canon-Fronsacs, and the reliable Côtes de Bourg, Côtes de Blaye and Côtes de Castillon.

While over 90% of the wines produced in these two areas is red, this is not true of the region known as Entre-deux-Mers. Opposite Langon, luscious sweet wines are made at Loupiac and Sainte-Croix du Mont, but the majority of the white wines are now dry. The reds, sold mostly under the *appellations* Bordeaux and Bordeaux Supérieur, provide classy everyday drinking at a modest price.

The surrounding *départements* have sensibly kept to producing wines of individual quality from local grape varieties. In the Landes *département*, around the towns of Geaune and Aire-sur-Adour, the VDQS red, white and rosé wines of Tursan are worth looking out for. Below the Landes, the Pyrénées-Atlantiques *département* harbours some of the best regional wines of France. Sweet Jurançon is more lemony but as rich as some of the best Sauternes; dry Jurançon is crisp and fruity with a hint of honey.

The Lot-et-Garonne *département* offers some very good alternatives to Médoc from the excellent Cave Coopérative at Buzet, the fruity Côtes de Marmandais are a good match for a simple Bordeaux and less expensive, and the Vins de Pays Agenais have considerable character.

Above Pruning vines in Bordeaux.

Below Bringing in the harvest at Château Latour

Pyrenees

The wines of this region are firmly 'south-west' in character. Perhaps the best known is Madiran, a dark-coloured, meaty red wine from the north-west of Tarbes and north-east of Pau. From the same region comes the very rare Pacherenc de Vic Bihl, a dry or slightly sweet white wine not unlike Jurançon. A relatively new *appellation* is the Côtes du Frontonnais, red and rosé wines from a small but expanding vineyard area north of Toulouse. Similar to it is the VDQS wine of Lavilledieu. The VDQS Côtes de Saint Mont produce reds not unlike a simple Madiran, and whites that are flowery and appealing. The Cave Coopérative at Plaimont is the largest producer, whose Vin de Pays des Côtes de Gascogne is particularly good value. Other worthwhile regional wines are the Coteaux et Terrasses de Montauban, Condomois, Côtes de Montestruc and Saint-Sardon. All these may be also sold under the name of Vins de Pays du Comté Tolosan.

More famous than the often excellent country wines is Armagnac, the pride of the region. The finest comes from the area around Condom known as the Bas-Armagnac. There are some big companies here, such as Samalens and Janneau, but the real *eaux-de-vie* to look for are the vintage Armagnacs of Lafitte, Laberdolive and Darroze.

Above Vines near Mamazet. The Hérault is one of the most densely planted regions in France, producing a high proportion of the country's table wines.

Languedoc-Roussillon

This region covers one of the densest vineyard areas in France, but before taking a look at the wines of 'le Midi', we should try those from some of the oldest vineyards in France, Gaillac in the Tarn *département*. Grown around the towns of Albi and Castres, the wines of Gaillac are quite diverse: fruity aromatic reds and rosés, clean dry whites, sweet whites and wines that are fully sparkling, slightly sparkling or simply *perlé*.

A very different style of wine is made in the Pyrénées-Orientales, the hottest and driest *département* in France. Starting with the wonderful fortified wines from Banyuls or the heady Muscats de Roussillon and Rivesaltes as an apéritif, one would follow with a white Côtes de Roussillon, continue with a sturdy red from the same *appellation*, and finish on an old Collioure (the finest table wine in the region) with the cheese. For the less ambitious palates, the Vins de Pays des Pyrénées-Orientales are reliable, the best from the Val d'Agly. The wines from the Aude *département*, mostly red, are a little less sun-baked, and the best-known names here are Corbières, Fitou and Minervois for the reds and the lovely, sparkling Blanquette de Limoux for the whites. A lesser known wine is the Côtes de la Malepère, from the region of Carcassonne, and among a plethora of local wines, mostly under the global name, Vins de Pays de l'Aude, are Coteaux Cathares, Coteaux de Peyriac, Val de Cesse and Val d'Orbieu.

Whereas in the Aude, the Corbières reigns above the other *appellations*, in the Hérault it is the Coteaux de Languedoc (red and rosé). Both are VDQS, and will surely be upgraded to AOC in the near future. The two AOCs in the Hérault are the wines of Faugères and Saint-Chinian, but they are not noticeably better than those from the eleven communes that go to make up the Coteaux du Languedoc selection. A particularly good white wine is La Clape, which outclasses the rather lighter Picpoul de Pinet. Vins de Pays are to be found everywhere, either split between 28 separate communes or grouped under the label Vin de Pays de l'Hérault.

Provence

Provence, which here is taken to include the southern Côtes du Rhône, is, with the exception of the hilly country of the Hautes Alpes, virtually a sea of vines, making many different types and styles of wine, each

particular to a region or commune. From the Ardèche come the lively Coteaux de Vivarais, while the Drôme at this point produces mainly Vin de Pays, with the exception of the heady Côtes du Rhône at Valréas. As one crosses into the Vaucluse, vines stretch as far as the eye can see. The better wines, from specific villages such as Cairanne, Laudun, Rasteau, Sablet, Vacqueyras, Vinsorbes and Visan, can either use these names on the label, or sell under the *appellation* Côtes du Rhône Villages. All are warm and robust. A super version of these is Gigondas, a massive, deep-coloured meaty wine. Its only rival for supremacy in the Vaucluse is the magisterial Châteauneuf du Pape, justly famous the world over. A meal with Châteauneuf du Pape as the main wine should be preceded by the nectar-like Muscat de Beaumes de Venise, with its heady aroma of ripe peaches.

Châteauneuf du Pape apart, the best known wine from the southern Rhône is the rosé from Tavel, the perfect accompaniment to a summer meal. Next door to Tavel is Lirac, whose rosé is lighter but just as fruity as Tavel and whose red wine resembles a light Châteauneuf. In the Gard *département* the wines of Costières du Gard are basically red, although the whites and rosés are lovely if they are drunk young, and there is a particularly good white wine called Clairette de Bellegarde. The number of Vin de Pays from the Gard and the Vaucluse, too numerous to mention, are improving with each vintage.

The *département* of the Bouches-du-Rhône provides a wide choice of wines including one of the best whites that Provence has to offer: Cassis. The wines from Coteaux d'Aix-en-Provence are full of fruit and, with the exception of the extraordinary Château Vignelaure, very good value for money. The more full-bodied wines of Coteaux des Baux-en-Provence have recently acquired full AOC status, yet still remain inexpensive, Along with the perfect-for-everyday wines from the Côtes du Ventoux and the Côtes du Luberon, in the Vaucluse, and the Côteaux de Pierrevert, in the Hautes-Alpes, these offer virtually guaranteed pleasure.

The Var *département* is notable for Provence's finest red wine, Bandol. Until the Côtes de Provence received *appellation* status in 1977, Bandol was one of only four AOCs in Provence. The better Côtes de Provence reds can approach Bandol in quality, particularly the single Domaine wines, and the Provence whites are steadily improving. The classic wine here, however, is the Rosé de Provence. Of the many Vins de Pays in Provence, the Vins de Pays du Var are good, but the Coteaux Varois are better and have recently been awarded VDQS status. Côtes de Provence comes in many fancy-shaped bottles, often with over-enthusiastic labels. It is best to stick to wines bottled in the classic Bordeaux or Burgundy shape.

Corsica

Vines were first planted here by the Greeks, so that the Corsican vineyards are the oldest in France. Production has been steadily decreasing, partly owing to the falling local consumption, partly to difficulties of transport to the mainland, but also due to the dull, heavy, tired wines that many growers and *coopératives* tended to produce. Vinification is now improving, and there is an awareness that the summer visitor does not wish to be knocked out by a wood-aged 15 degree rosé, but would prefer something light and refreshing. Corsican wine can be red (the best), rosé, dry and semi-sweet white, and there is even some very good Vin Doux Naturel.

Over 60% of the production is of the delightfully named Vin de Pays de l'Île de Beauté, although the *appellation* Vin de Corse covers the whole country, Recently, the following regions have gained their own *appellations*: Calvi, Coteaux d'Ajaccio, Coteaux de Cap Corse, Figari, Patrimonio, Porto-Vecchio and Sartène. With few exceptions, Corsican wine is now of good quality, and while it is at its best drunk 'sur place', it travels as well as any wine from the south of France.

GAZETTEER

The gazetteer which now follows is intended principally to provide the traveller and tourist with extensive background information on the most worthwhile places to visit in France.

The guide does not contain information about hotels nor does it give times of opening and closing of tourist sights. It is, rather, 'before' and 'after' reading presented in a form which has been considered most useful for the visitor. Thus, the precise geographical boundaries of the twenty-two French administrative regions have not been strictly followed in the division of the gazetteer; they have, instead, been modified to form 'tourist' regions, making each part more immediately useful and interesting to the traveller. The two Normandy regions, for instance, have been presented as one. Similarly, Picardy and Nord-Pas-de-Calais have been combined, and Lorraine has been treated with Alsace. In contrast, Dordogne has been taken out of Aquitaine and here appears as a region on its own, since so many tourists tend to take holidays within its bounds. The boundaries of the Pyrenees and Massif Central have also been changed to make more coherent areas for the traveller.

Within the entries themselves, many other places and sites located in the neighbourhood of the main subject have been included. In other cases, a town or village may be found described in an entry relating to a whole area or connected group of places; for instance on the entries on the 'wine routes'.

The maps show the location of all the main entries listed within a given region together with principal rivers and main roads.

1	PAS-DE-CALAIS	25	SEINE-ET-OUSE
2	NORD	26	SEINE
3	SOMME	27	EURE-ET-LOIR
4	AISNE	28	EURE
5	ARDENNES	29	ORNE
6	SEINE-MARITIME	30	CALVADOS
7	OISE	31	MANCHE
8	MARNE	32	MAYENNE
9	MEUSE	33	ILLE-ET-VILAINE
10	MEURTHE-ET-MOSELLE	34	CÔTES-DU-NORD
11	MOSELLE	35	FINISTÉRE
12	BAS-RHIN	36	MORBIHAN
13	VOSGES	37	LOIRE-INFÉRIEURE
14	HAUT-RHIN	38	VENDÉE
15	TERR DE BELFORT	39	MAINE-ET-LOIRE
16	HAUTE-SAÔNE	40	DEUX-SÈVRES
17	DOUBS	41	SARTHE
18	HAUTE-MARNE	42	INDRE-ET-LOIRE
19	CÔTE-d'OR	43	VIENNE
20	AUBE	44	LOIR-ET-CHER
21	YONNE	45	INDRE
22	NIÈVRE	46	CHER
23	SEINE-ET-MARNE	47	ALLIER
24	LOIRET	48	SAÔNE-ET-LOIRE

49	JURA	71	CHARENTE INFÉRIEURE
50	AIN	72	GIRONDE
51	HAUTE-SAVOIE	73	LANDES
52	SAVOIE	74	BASSES-PYRÉNÉES
53	ISÉRE	75	GERS
54	HAUTES-ALPES	76	TARN-ET-GARONNE
55	DRÔME	77	HAUTES-PYRÉNÉES
56	RHÔNE	78	HAUTE-GARONNE
57	ARDÈCHE	79	TARN
58	LOIRE	80	ARIÈGE
59	HAUTE-LOIRE	81	AUDE
60	PUY-DE-DÔME	82	PYRÉNÉES-ORIENTALES
61	LOZÈRE	83	HÉRAULT
62	AVEYRON	84	GARD
63	CANTAL	85	BOUCHES-DU-RHÔNE
64	CREUSE	86	VAUCLUSE
65	CORRÈZE	87	BASSES-ALPES
66	LOT	88	VAR
67	HAUTE-VIENNE	89	ALPES-MARITIMES
68	CHARENTE	90	HAUTE-CORSE
69	DORDOGNE	91	CORSE DU SUD
70	LOT-ET-GARONNE		

ENGLISH CHANNEL

ATLANTIC

OCEAN

MEDITERRANEAN SEA

Kilometres
0   50   100   150

BRITTANY

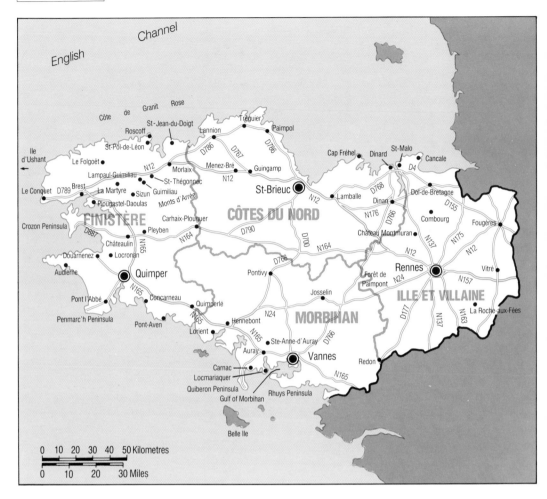

A granite bastion on the western edge of Europe, Brittany has the feeling of a world apart. Its 1200km rocky coastline is cut into innumerable deep estuaries, bays and sandy inlets which for centuries has determined its maritime economy and now makes it a favourite holiday playground. Inland there are continual contrasts and surprises, with alternations of harsh upland plateaux where the bones of underlying granite break through the sparse covering of soil and gentle river valleys where forgotten villages and small stone chapels shelter from the wind. Above all, Brittany has retained its sense of timelessness, both in its ancient man-made remains, the finest of which are the standing stones of Carnac, and in the legends of vanished cities, holy men, magicians and monsters that still haunt its shores and forests.

Brittany is slightly bigger than Wales, with just over three million inhabitants. Geographically, it is part of France, but in geological terms it is far older than the rest of the country, created when a cataclysm about 500 million years ago heaved up an immense mountain range known as the Armorican Massif. The ancient peaks of Brittany would have rivalled the much younger Alps and Himalayas, but aeons of erosion by wind and rain have

worn them down to stumps, so that none today even rise as high as 400m.

Granite has shaped the landscape of Brittany, dictating the form and texture of its buildings, from astonishing churches and calvaries to massive sea-walls, austere farmhouses and humble cottages.

The Bretons themselves display the same granitic durability. A race of fishermen and farmers, accustomed to wresting a hard living from hostile seas and a thin soil, they are as independent in outlook as the Welsh, with whom they share a common Celtic ancestry. The Celtic sense of mystery is expressed in a host of legends and a doomed fatalism summarized by stories in which their figure of Death, the Ankou, plays a major role. The brighter side of life is celebrated in their own forms of music and dance, their local costumes and their unique brand of religious festival, the *pardon*. Centuries of war, peaceful collaboration and intermarriage with outsiders from France have nevertheless made them intensely practical; and although to the foreigner they may seem suspicious and reserved, once the barriers are down they show a warmth and hospitality found in few other regions.

Although Brittany has been inhabited since remote prehistoric times, perhaps as far back as 500,000BC, the earliest man-made artefacts date from Neolithic times, the standing stones (menhirs) and burial mounds (dolmens) being among the most spectacular remains in Europe. The Celts of the 6th century BC called the coastal parts Armorica ('land by the sea') and the inland areas Argost ('land of forest'), and under Roman occupation it was Gallia Armorica. The Celts who invaded the land from Britain in the 5th and 6th centuries AD called it Petite Bretagne or simply Bretagne, bringing with them their own form of Church organization led by an army of saints who founded chapels, monasteries and hermitages.

For almost seven centuries Brittany was an independent duchy, attacked by land from France and harried from the sea by England. In 1532 François I united the region with France, and it retained its own parliament. The 17th and 18th centuries were years of intense maritime activity, Breton fleets sailing to South America, the Indian Ocean and the Far East. The Stamped Paper revolt of 1675, protesting against a royal tax for foreign wars, was brutally repressed. During the Revolution the Bretons sided with the royalists and the insurgent Chouans fought on till 1795.

After the Revolution Brittany ceased to exist as a political entity and was divided into *départements*. With the Gaullist reform of 1964, the new 'region' of Brittany comprised four *départements*: Finistère, Côtes-du-Nord, Ille-et-Vilaine and Morbihan. The Loire-Atlantique *département* (cap. Nantes), traditionally regarded by many people as part of Brittany, was hived off to the Pays de la Loire region – to the fury of many Bretons.

The Bretons suffered grievously in two World Wars but since 1945 they have achieved an astonishing economic revival. The fishing industry, although it no longer holds pride of place, remains important. Industrial development has been remarkable and during the 1970s the government poured money into the region, modernizing communications and encouraging research in modern areas such as tidal generated electricity, space electronics, nuclear energy and the quest for offshore oil, the last thus far without result.

Agriculture, traditionally based on livestock, dairy farming, poultry and vegetables, has also been modernized extensively in the post-war period and flourishes as never before (with exports ever increasing) despite the departure of three-quarters of the farm population to Paris and other towns. Spearheading the agricultural revival was a young Morlaix farmer named Alexis Gourvennec who led a protest in 1961 against middlemen and unfair farm prices, culminating in the setting up of a farmers' sales cooperative, now the most powerful in France, which subsequently launched Brittany Ferries, with services from Roscoff to Plymouth and Cork and from St Malo to Portsmouth.

The government supported Gourvennec's campaign partly because it was motivated by economic rather than nationalistic considerations. Yet the Bretons still feel strongly independent and conscious of their nationhood. Few of them would advocate secession (which is, of course, unlawful), apart from the extreme fringe represented by the Front de Libération de la Bretagne (FLB), which advocates and practises violence. Most Bretons do not support the terrorists but still want more say in their own affairs.

Lacking an influential political party to promote their nationalistic aspirations, the Bretons have concentrated on economic growth, welcomed the prosperity brought by tourism, and devoted them-

selves to reviving their language and culture. Breton, an ancient tongue modified by centuries of contact with France, is still spoken in Basse Bretagne, the western half of the country, whereas the eastern part, Haute Bretagne, is French-speaking. There are estimated to be some 800,000 Bretons who speak their native language, though only about 10,000 can read it; the *bretonnants* are mainly old people, for whom it is a first and often only language, and students, since it is officially taught in schools.

Traditional music and dance are also part of the cultural revival, although the old Breton costumes – broad hats and baggy trousers for men, elaborate lace head-dresses *(coiffes)* for women – are reserved for special occasions, notably the village *pardon*, when the statue or relics of the local saint are paraded through the streets and countryside with much festivity.

Compared with the rest of France, Brittany is not renowned for its gastronomy. Most restaurants serve the standard French *cuisine*, with cider accompanying the meal, for Brittany produces no wine of its own. Even so, there are many excellent local delicacies based on marvellously fresh vegetables, fish and seafood (notably prawns, clams, lobsters and oysters). There is an appetizing fish-stew known as *cotriade*, a dish of beef and vegetables called *potée bretonne*, lamb *gigot* with *haricots blancs* (from the coastal salt-pasture sheep), and a varied *charcuterie* of local pork products. Most popular of all are the ubiquitous wheat or buckwheat *crêpes*, served either plain or with ham, cheese, jam or honey.

Breton 'coiffe'

ARRÉE, MONTS D'
FINISTÈRE

The highest hills in Brittany, though nowhere reaching more than 384m, the Arrée Mountains are the worn-down stumps of a once-gigantic range, comparable in height to the Alps. At their centre is a marshy area known as the Yeun Ellez, surrounding a lake that since 1966 has been used to cool the Brennilis atomic power station. Overlooking the lake is a superb natural viewpoint, the Montagne St-Michel, crowned by a chapel dedicated to St Michael.

The main village of the Monts d'Arrée is **Brasparts**, which has a fine 16C parish close. A little way N of the village, a farm complex has been turned into a craft centre, where more than 200 artists and craftsmen show and sell their products.

AUDIERNE
FINISTÈRE Pop 3600

Prettily situated at the mouth of the Goyen estuary, at Brittany's western corner, Audierne was once a major tunny-fishing centre, but is now mainly a port for lobsters and crayfish. It is also a popular seaside resort, with several fine waterfront hotels and restaurants. *Pardon* last Sun. in Aug. Beyond Audierne, some 15km W, is Brittany's own 'Land's End', the **Pointe du Raz**, where Finistère

meets the Atlantic in a maelstrom of churning water and shattered rock. From here, on a good day, the **Île de Sein**, 8km out to sea, is clearly visible. This low-lying, treeless island was used by the Druids as a burial site and was still pagan in the 17C. In June, 1940, after France surrendered to the Germans, every man of fighting age left Sein to join de Gaulle's Free French army in England.

Some 7km NW of Audierne, on the other side of the peninsula, the majestic cliffs of **Cap Sizun**, towering 70m above the sea, form one of Brittany's major seabird sanctuaries. During the spring breeding season cormorants, puffins, gulls, choughs and many other species perch, squabble, scream and brood on the narrow ledges high above the waves.

AURAY
MORBIHAN Pop 10,400

A delightful little town, on the river of the same name, Auray has played a more prominent part in Breton history than its sleepy appearance would suggest. In 1364 the battle of Auray decided the succession to the much disputed dukedom of Brittany for Jean de Montfort. 400 years later, in 1776, Benjamin Franklin landed at St Goustan (the medieval part of the town) on his way to Paris, to arrange a treaty between France and the United States. A plaque on one of the quayside houses commemorates his landing.

Auray's town centre, with its spectacular 17C

Belle-Île

church of St-Gildas, is up the hill on the opposite side of the river to St-Goustan, crossed by a medieval stone bridge. A zigzag footpath winds up to the town, from where there are superb views of the ancient quayside and the moored boats.

BELLE-ÎLE
MORBIHAN   Pop 4300

Belle-Île is the largest of Brittany's offshore islands, measuring about 17km long by 9km wide. It is an ideal away-from-it-all place for a holiday, with some 80km of varied coastline, where rocky headlands contrast with sandy beaches and creeks. From the mid-19C on, it became a favourite resort of writers such as Dumas, Flaubert, Proust and Colette and the artists Matisse, Derain and Monet, while the actress Sarah Bernhardt owned an old fortress there for a number of years. From the 16C citadel reinforced by Vauban there are fine views of Le Palais, the main town, and the coast.

Belle-Île is reached by boat from Quiberon in about 45 minutes.

BIGOUDEN, PAYS
FINISTÈRE

If any region can be described as containing the essence of Brittany, it is this small segment of SW Finistère, stretching roughly from the river Odet to Audierne. In the 'Bigouden Country' the Bretons keep more to their ancient traditions than elsewhere – for example, many of the older women still wear their immensely tall *coiffes* or head-dresses.

The chief town of the region is **Pont-l'Abbé** (pop. 7700), named after a bridge built by a medieval abbot. The town's fine 14C château contains a museum devoted to Bigouden life and culture. One of the nearby villages, **Pouldreuzic**, was the birthplace in 1914 of the Breton writer Pierre-Jakez Hélias, whose best-selling *Le Cheval d'Orgueil (The Horse of Pride)* gives a detailed picture of the harshness of Bigouden life in the early part of this century.

BREST
FINISTÈRE   Pop 172,000

For more than 2000 years, since Roman times, Brest's magnificent harbour site has sheltered warships and merchantmen. In the 17C, under Louis XIV, it was the chief port of the French navy. The old harbour grew up along the banks of the Penfeld river, now crossed by the largest vertical-lift bridge in Europe, but little survives from former times, since Brest was almost totally destroyed at the end of World War II.

The most prominent of the survivals is the 15C tower called the Tour Tanguy, which guards the harbour entrance and now contains an excellent historical museum. The naval dockyard (barred to foreigners) stretches upstream along both sides of the river. Modern Brest now spreads east and west

Brest

along the Rade de Brest, and is mainly built in the featureless modern style of the post-war years.

Brest's university is closely involved with the revival of Breton language and culture, while its oceanographic centre is one of the world's leading institutes for marine research.

CANCALE
ILLE-ET-VILAINE Pop 5000

This attractive small port is renowned for its oysters, grown in the rich silt of the Bay of Mont St Michel. Louis XIV was so fond of them that he had them sent twice a week by special convoy to Versailles. Today's holidaymakers can eat them in one of Cancale's excellent waterfront restaurants, or buy them freshly opened at the stalls along the quayside.

The oyster growers collect them from the mud of the bay in flat-bottomed boats (*chalands*), then place them in stone-walled tanks of mud-free water to get rid of the impurities. In common with other European oyster fisheries, the Cancale beds were attacked by disease in the 1920s, and young oysters are now mainly bought from Auray and cultivated in the bay.

A little way north of Cancale, the headland of the **Pointe de Grouin** gives magnificent views along the coast. The small island of **Landes** off the headland is a nature reserve and seabird sanctuary.

CARHAIX-PLOUGUER
FINISTÈRE Pop 9000

Carhaix-Plouguer is a workaday market town, at the centre of a road network that made it important even in pre-Roman times, when it was the capital of a Gaulish tribe called the Osismii. The Romans built an aqueduct there, and in the 6C it was the capital of Count Comorrus, known as the 'Breton Bluebeard' for his habit of cutting the heads off a succession of wives.

In 1743, one of Brittany's home-grown heroes, Théophile-Malo Corret, known as La Tour d'Auvergne, was born at Carhaix. A pioneer in the revival of the Breton language, he was a soldier as well as a scholar, and won undying military fame when Napoleon named him 'the first grenadier of France'. He was killed in action in 1800. Some of his relics are kept in the Carhaix *mairie*, and there is a statue of him in the main square.

CARNAC
MORBIHAN Pop 3700

The astonishing prehistoric stone monuments of Carnac are thought to date from about 2000BC – that is, from the same period as Stonehenge and Avebury – and to be connected in some way with observations of the heavenly bodies, and hence with the right times to sow crops and to harvest.

There are three main rows (*alignements*), consisting almost entirely of menhirs (single standing stones), as opposed to the dolmens (two uprights with a horizontal laid across) found elsewhere in the Morbihan. The principal alignment of Ménec is over 1km long and 100m wide and consists of 1099 menhirs, the tallest of which is 4m high. Further along the same road are the Kermario lines which are only slightly shorter than Ménec, and beyond those are the lines of Kerlescan, a semi-circle of 39 menhirs followed by a row of a further 540 stones. Surveying the ranks of stones, and just E of the town, is the Tumulus St-Michel, a huge, prehistoric burial mound over 120m long, now crowned by a small chapel.

Carnac itself is an attractive little town (though choked with traffic in summer), linked to the seaside resort of Carnac Plage. The Musée Miln-le Rouzic, named after two archaeologists, contains Stone Age artefacts discovered in the region. The 17C church is dedicated to St Cornély, the patron saint of horned animals. A statue of the saint between two oxen can be seen on the outside wall of the church. *Pardon* 2nd Sun. in Sept. Gregorian chanting can be heard at the abbeys of **St-Michel-de-Kergonan** (Benedictine nuns) and **Ste-Anne-de-Kergonan** (Benedictine monks), 3km and 3.5km respectively NE of the town.

Carnac

CHÂTEAULIN
FINISTÈRE   Pop 6500

Once known as 'La Cité-sur-Aulne', Châteaulin is a peaceful riverside town, built on the banks of the meandering river Aulne. It used to be the main town for salmon fishing in Brittany, with so many fish caught that farm workers stipulated that they should be fed salmon only three times a week. After a dramatic decline in numbers, the salmon has started to revive during the 1980s. Notre-Dame church, on a bluff above the town, contains several outstanding statues of St Anne and other saints.

COMBOURG
ILLE-ET-VILAINE   Pop 4700

The pointed turrets of Combourg's château, rising above a dense canopy of trees, make a romantic picture when seen across the lake on the outskirts of the little town. Built originally in the 11C by one of the Bishops of Dol, the château was the childhood home of François-René de Chateaubriand (1768–1848). One of the high priests of Romanticism in literature, Chateaubriand has left a vivid picture in his autobiography *Mémoires d'Outre-Tombe* (*Memoirs from Beyond the Tomb*) of life at Combourg in the years leading up to the French Revolution. His isolated room in one of the turrets would have given most children nightmares for life, but Chateaubriand said that it sharpened his imaginative powers.

The little town, clustered round the château, has two or three streets of fine old houses. The park, full of large, old trees, is attractively informal.

Château de Combourg

CONCARNEAU
FINISTÈRE   Pop 18,200

Concarneau's unusual name derives from the Breton *Konk-Kernev*, meaning the 'Creek of Cornouaille' – a legendary name, like Cornwall, that is also applied to much of southern Finistère. The old, walled town or Ville Close, built on an island and linked to the mainland by two small bridges, dominates the natural harbour. The island was first fortified in the 13C, and the massive walls were strengthened under Louis XIV in the 17C. They still form a complete circuit, making an ideal place for a stroll on a fine summer's afternoon.

Concarneau's involvement with the sea is displayed in the fascinating Musée de la Pêche, which has complete examples of traditional fishing vessels among its exhibits. On the third Sun. of Aug. the week-long Fête des Filets Bleus begins. Held in and around the Ville Close, the festival includes folklore displays of all sorts. The town is now a flourishing seaside resort, as well as a major historic site.

CONQUET, LE
FINISTÈRE   Pop 1900

The westernmost town in Brittany, Le Conquet is a pretty little estuary port, with a small fishing fleet that goes to sea after lobsters and crayfish. From here, boats are available to the islands of Ushant (q.v.) and Molène. Nearby are several good sandy beaches, which have made Le Conquet increasingly popular as a quiet seaside resort. Nothing survives of the medieval town, as it was burnt by the British fleet in 1558.

Just to the south is the imposing headland called the **Pointe de St-Mathieu**. At its summit is a lighthouse, a war memorial and the ruins of a 13C abbey which, during the Middle Ages, kept the skull of St Matthew as its most treasured relic.

CROZON PENINSULA
FINISTÈRE

The Presqu'île de Crozon is the central of the three peninsulas that jut into the Atlantic at the western end of Brittany. In its turn, it is divided into three headlands, like the points of a flattened trident. Northernmost of these is the **Pointe des Espagnols**, guarding the narrows that open out into the Rade de Brest and taking its name from a Spanish expeditionary force that made a brief landing there in 1594. The central headland is the dramatic **Pointe de Penhir**, 70m high, while to the south, jutting into Douarnenez Bay, is the **Cap de la Chèvre**.

The peninsula's chief town is the old port of **Camaret-sur-Mer**, with a fine harbour protected by a natural bank of shingle, the Sillon de Camaret. At the end of the shingle is a fortified tower, the Tour Vauban, now a small museum, and nearby is a pretty little chapel, the Chapelle de Rocamadour, which has been a sailor's shrine for hundreds of years. Its belfry was decapitated by an English cannonball in 1694. Camaret is the subject of a famous, obscene drinking song, *Les Filles de Camaret*.

About 11km SE of Camaret, the small resort of **Morgat** has several fine beaches and some spectacular wave-eroded caves.

At the eastern end of the peninsula, the **Menez-Hom**, a 330m dome-shaped hill, stands like a sentinel, affording wide-ranging views, on fine days, both inland and out to sea across the Rade de Brest and Douarnenez Bay. Beside the road that runs below it, the little chapel of Ste Marie du Menez-Hom contains fine carved woodwork. A folklore festival is held on the summit on 15 Aug.

Dinan

DINAN
CÔTES-DU-NORD Pop 17,000

With its streets of medieval houses, its delightful situation on the river Rance and its excellent hotels and restaurants, it is not surprising that Dinan is the most frequented tourist town in the whole of Brittany. Holidaymakers started to come here from Britain as long ago as the 1830s, and its popularity has never faltered since. Lovingly restored and cared for, Dinan exudes a timelessness that epitomizes the best of ancient Brittany.

The town was built for its strategic position guarding the first feasible crossing of the Rance. During the perpetual wars between France and England in the Middle Ages, it was much fought over. Its hero is the great French general Bertrand du Guesclin, who, in 1359, in the main square of the town, beat the English knight Sir Thomas of Canterbury in single combat. His statue rides proudly among the market stalls and parked cars in the Pl. du Guesclin at the upper end of the town.

Dinan is normally approached across a high-level road viaduct leading into the upper level of the town. The ancient harbour is well worth exploring, and is reached on foot either down the medieval Rue du Petit Fort, or down the path from the tree-shaded Jardin Anglais. The town's massive walls and ramparts are virtually complete, and still have fifteen of their towers and gates. The finest of the ancient streets is the Rue de l'Horloge, named after a tall clock tower 60m high, from the top of which there are wide-ranging views over the town and the Rance valley.

A short walk away is Dinan's main church, the Basilique St-Saveur, which combines the Romanesque and Gothic styles and has a fine 12C W doorway. In the N transept is the 'heart shrine' of du Guesclin; after his death in 1380 the heart was removed from his body and laid to rest in his home town. The château, at the south-west corner of the

walls, is not so much a castle as a powerful, fortified tower. Known as the Tour de la Duchesse Anne, it houses a museum of local history and costume.

Dinan makes good use of its river, with frequent pleasure cruises down the beautiful valley of the Rance to Dinard and St-Malo.

DINARD
ILLE-ET-VILAINE Pop 9600

During the early years of this century, Dinard was the Brittany holiday resort *par excellence*. Several of the larger hotels date from those far-off, spacious days, and Dinard's sweeping beach, backed by the casino and rows of dignified buildings, harks back to a more leisurely epoch.

Until the mid-19C, Dinard was a fishing village, but in about 1850 it was 'discovered' by the British and its prosperity began. In 1906 a French writer called it 'the most aristocratic and elegant beach resort in northern Europe'. In recent years modernity has reached it in the form of a small airport and a tidally operated hydroelectric barrage *(usine marémotrice)* across the mouth of the Rance. The road to St-Malo runs above it.

DOL-DE-BRETAGNE
ILLE-ET-VILAINE Pop 5100

An ancient frontier town, where Brittany confronts Normandy, Dol is an attractive little place with rows of half-timbered houses and an unusual and striking cathedral. It owes its origins to a monastery founded by St-Samson, who came from Britain in the 6C and is one of the 'seven founding saints' of Brittany. In 848 Nominoë, the first duke of an independent Brittany, was crowned there. During the Middle Ages it was besieged on several occasions. The last bishop of Dol was shot in 1795, for anti-Revolutionary activities.

St-Samson's cathedral, just off the main street,

is an imposing building, built mainly in the 13C. The W front has a curiously lopsided appearance due to the different heights of its twin towers. On the S side are two remarkable porches, one large and one small. The lofty interior has some superb arcading and holds eighty 15C oak choir stalls, carved with leaf motifs and human heads.

Just north of the town is **Mont Dol**, a flat-topped granite outcrop rising above the plain. Once a Celtic holy place, both St Michael and the Devil are said to have left their footprints in its rocks. At its summit is an old semaphore tower, now turned into a chapel.

The coastal plain north of Dol, known as the **Marais de Dol**, was once covered by an immense forest, the Forêt de Scissy, inundated by the sea some time during the Dark Ages. This marshland began to be reclaimed in the Middle Ages and the work still continues.

DOUARNENEZ
FINISTÈRE   Pop 19,300

Somewhere out in Douarnenez Bay, so the legend goes, lies the sunken city of Ys, flooded by the sea, it is said, when the Devil opened the sluice gates that once protected it. On calm summer nights the muffled bells of its churches can still be heard, chiming from the sea-bed – sounds magically brought to life by Debussy in his piano prelude *La Cathédrale Engloutie*.

However, modern Douarnenez is far from such fancies, as it is a practical town, the fifth most important fishing port in France, with a fleet of trawlers and smaller vessels and its own canning plants. Though today's port now faces the open

sea, old Douarnenez grew along the banks of the Port-Rhu estuary, now mainly used by pleasure craft. Across the estuary are the beaches of Tréboul, the holiday offshoot of Douarnenez.

FOLGOËT, LE
FINISTÈRE   Pop 2,253

During the 14C a simpleton called Salaün or Solomon lived in a wood 2km outside Lesneven, north-east of Brest, surviving on bread dipped in spring water, and constantly invoking the name of the Virgin Mary. After his death, a lily took root in his mouth, with the words 'Ave Maria' miraculously appearing on its petals. A chapel was built on the site, and called Le Folgoët (Breton for 'the Fool in the Wood') after Salaün. The present chapel, in lavish Flamboyant Gothic style, dates mainly from the 15C. Still one of the main pilgrimage centres in Brittany, Le Folgoët has an important annual *pardon* on the first Sun. after 8 Sept.

FOUGÈRES
ILLE-ET-VILAINE   Pop 27,700

Few castles in France, or indeed in the whole of Europe, are more redolent than Fougères of the great days of knightly prowess and feudal splendour. The most powerful of the chain of castles that protected Brittany from Normandy and the rest of France, Fougères owes its phenomenal strength' to Baron Raoul II of Fougères, who rebuilt it in 1173, after it had been destroyed by Henry II of England. Its thirteen noble towers were added in the 14–15C.

When first rebuilt, the castle was surrounded by

Douarnenez

Château de Fougères

water, and was thus even more impregnable than it appears today. The oldest part of the town, including the beautiful St-Sulpice church, is down on this lower level. The modern town is built on the high ground above the castle. For centuries Fougères has been a centre of footwear manufacture, and the castle contains a small museum devoted to this industry. *Son-et-lumière* displays are held in the castle during the summer.

Some 3km NE of the town is the magnificent state-owned woodland of **Fougères Forest**, which has a number of prehistoric standing stones in clearings among the trees.

FRÉHEL, CAP
CÔTES-DU-NORD

The grandest headland of the noble north coast of Brittany, Cap Fréhel towers some 70m above the waves boiling and crashing at its foot. On clear days it is visible from St-Malo, more than 20km away, while from the Fréhel lighthouse the view extends as far as the Cherbourg peninsula 50km E. The rocks on the eastern side of the headland are a sanctuary for gulls, guillemots, cormorants and other seabirds.

A little way to the SE is **Fort la Latte**, a formidable castle standing on a wave-battered promontory. Built by the Counts of Matignon in the Middle Ages, it was 'modernized' in the 17C to fit it for the age of artillery.

GRANIT ROSE, CÔTE DE
CÔTES-DU-NORD

The 'Coast of Pink Granite', so named for its extraordinary rock formations, takes in the bulbous peninsula at the north-west corner of the Côtes-du-Nord, between the resorts of **Perros-Guirec** and **Trébeurden**. The strangest of the rocks are found round Trégastel and Ploumanac'h, where millennia of erosion by wind and sea have worn gigantic boulders into shapes that have given rise to such names as 'Napoleon's Hat', 'Death's Head', 'Elephant without a Trunk' and many other fancies.

Perros-Guirec is the main resort on this stretch of coast. It has several fine beaches, a fishing

harbour and a casino, and is the starting point for boat trips to the offshore **Sept Îles** seabird sanctuary. Guirec, from which the town gets half its name, was a Welsh monk (St Curig in Welsh) who sailed to Brittany from Wales in the 6C, legend says, in a stone drinking trough. A small oratory dedicated to him stands on the beach of St-Guirec, at **Ploumanac'h**.

GUIMILIAU
FINISTÈRE   See PARISH CLOSES

GUINGAMP
CÔTES-DU-NORD   Pop 10,800

At the centre of a road network radiating to all parts of the Côtes-du-Nord, Guingamp is an ancient town whose name – in Breton, *Gwen Camp* or White Camp – probably derives from its fortifications in the Dark Ages. The town centre consists largely of granite Renaissance houses, clustering round a superb and highly original church, the basilica of Notre Dame de Bon Secours. Built in a mixture of the Gothic and Renaissance styles, it was partly rebuilt in the 1530s, after the south tower collapsed. The north porch contains a rare Black Madonna, carved from black stone, while the floor is inlaid with a maze design.

Near the church, in the Pl. du Centre, is a fanciful Renaissance fountain, festooned with nymphs and monsters and crowned by a statue of the Virgin. The lower stages of Guingamp's castle walls survive, but it was mainly demolished by Cardinal Richelieu in the 17C.

Guingamp stands on the dividing line between French and Breton-speaking Brittany. In 1909 the Gorsedd of the Breton Bards was founded here, and each year, on the last Sun. in Aug., the town holds a Festival of Breton Dance. *Pardon* on evening of first Sun. in July.

HENNEBONT
MORBIHAN   Pop. 12,500

Not much survives of old Hennebont, since the town was greatly damaged during the Liberation at the end of World War II. Its name comes from the Breton *Hen Bont*, meaning 'old bridge'; originally it was the first point upstream at which the river Blavet could be conveniently crossed by a bridge.

The main street runs uphill from the ramparts of the medieval castle to the imposing basilica of Notre Dame de Paradis, built in the 16C in Flamboyant Gothic style. The tower is enormously tall (65m to the top of the spire), as is the western entrance porch below it.

On the edge of the town is the **Haras National** (National Stud), which can be visited; it stands in the grounds of a 13C Cistercian abbey, the Abbaye de la Joie.

JOSSELIN
MORBIHAN   Pop 3000

Josselin's château is the most famous castle in Brittany, and on a fine summer's afternoon hordes of tourists gather in the little town that lies above and around it. Its three towers, and the curtain wall linking them, rise sheer from the living rock, and originally dropped straight to the river Oust; the present road at the castle's foot is a later addition.

Château de Josselin

Various earlier castles stood on the site, before the present superb fortifications were built towards the end of the 14C by Olivier de Clisson, nick-named the 'Butcher of the English'. Clisson's wife was Marguerite de Rohan, and the château still belongs to the Rohan family. Their motto, *À Plus* ('More and More'), is carved into the ornate stonework of the Gothic *corps-de-logis* in the inner courtyard, which dates from about 1500, and is in delicate and luxurious contrast to the somewhat grim exterior of the castle. The fortifications were demolished early in the 17C under Richelieu, but restored in the 19C. *Pardon* second Sun. in Sept.

Halfway between Josselin and Ploërmel, 3km E, a monument called the **Colonne des Trente** stands on an island between two lanes of the dual carriage-way. This commemorates the famous battle in 1351 between 30 English and 30 Breton knights, known as the *Combat des Trente*. At that time the Bretons under Jean de Beaumanoir held Josselin, while the English had seized Ploërmel. The two squadrons met under an oak tree and hacked away at each other hand to hand all day, until the English survivors were routed and led back, defeated, to Josselin.

LAMBALLE
CÔTES-DU-NORD   Pop 5500

This quiet old town still has a few of its medieval houses, notably the 16C Maison du Bourreau (Hangman's House), now the Syndicat d'Initia-tive. At either end of the ancient town centre are two fine medieval churches, the Flamboyant Gothic Église St Jean, with an octagonal tower added in the 17C, and the older Notre Dame de Grande Puissance, consecrated about 1220 and once the chapel of Lamballe's castle, demolished in the 15C.

Nowadays Lamballe is best known for its Haras National (National Stud). Founded as long ago as 1825, it is a centre for breeding the powerful Breton draught horses (the Trait Breton).

LAMPAUL-GUIMILIAU
FINISTÈRE   See PARISH CLOSES

LANNION
CÔTES-DU-NORD   Pop 18,000

At Lannion old Brittany meets the latest in modern technology, since in recent years the town has become the centre of a flourishing electronics industry. Built on the banks of the wide river Léguer, the town centre has a feeling of spacious-ness. A small part of medieval Lannion survives in the streets that run up the hill from the river to the 16C church of St-Jean-du-Baly. Not far from the centre, a flight of 140 granite steps leads up to Brélévénez church, founded by the Templars in the 12C and greatly enlarged in the 16C.

About 7km N of Lannion, the huge white radome of the **Pleumeur-Bodou** satellite-tracking station looms above a stretch of wild heathland. This telecommunications centre, opened in 1962, can be visited daily during the summer.

About 10km SE of Lannion are the mighty ruins of **Tonquédec Castle**, rising from the trees above the Léguer valley, and the **chapel of Kerfons**, with a fine Renaissance rood-screen and 16C stained glass.

LOCMARIAQUER
MORBIHAN   Pop 1300

This pretty little fishing village, at the western end of the Gulf of Morbihan, stands on a peninsula that is crammed with fine prehistoric remains. Quar-ried, hewn and hauled into position by the Neo-lithic civilization that produced the alignments of Carnac (q.v.), a few kilometres away, they include burial mounds and chambers, and standing stones of every type and size.

Just N of the village is the Grand Menhir Brisé (the Great Broken Menhir), now in four pieces, which together weigh about 350 tons and are estimated to have stood some 20m high. The Table des Marchands is an impressive chamber tomb, carved in places with symbolic designs; while the Mané-Lud dolmen takes the form of an under-ground chamber, likewise symbolically carved. South of the village is the burial mound known as the Tumulus de Mané-er-Groac'h (Witches' Hill).

LOCRONAN
FINISTÈRE   Pop 700

A picture-postcard little town of superb granite houses, mainly 16–17C, Locronan well deserves its popularity among tourists who crowd its narrow streets to admire its architecture and buy lace, pottery and other examples of traditional Breton crafts. The town gets its name from St Ronan, a 5C monk from Ireland who had a nearby woodland hermitage. The church, dedicated to the saint, is a magnificent 15C building with a stone-vaulted ceiling; it contains St Ronan's empty tomb and has some fine carvings.

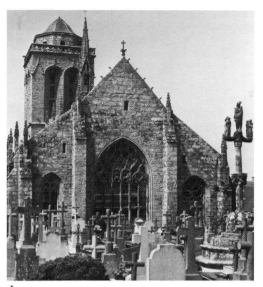

Locronan

The chapel on the Montagne de Locronan above the town is the destination of the local *pardons*, known here as *troménies*. There is a processional *Petite Troménie* every second Sun. in July and a *Grande Troménie*, encircling the hill and halting at twelve stations, on the third Sun. in July every six years (the next in 1989).

LORIENT
MORBIHAN Pop 72,000

Origially known as l'Orient (The East), Lorient was founded by Louis XIV in 1666, as the ship-building centre for the Compagnie des Indes Orientales (France's East India Company). Its splendid harbour site, on the estuary where the rivers Scorff and Blavet meet, has ensured its leading position as a port for the past three centuries. At the end of World War II it was fiercely defended by the Germans, and the centre virtually destroyed. Like Brest, it was rebuilt in a character-less modern style, though a few buildings from the time of the Compagnie des Indes survive at the heart of the town. Lovers of bagpipe music flock to Lorient in Aug., when the Festival Interceltique des Cornemuses is held there.

During summer there is a regular boat service from Lorient to the island of **Groix**, about 7km offshore. With a coastline of tall cliffs sheltering sandy beaches, Groix is a popular place for day excursions.

Across the estuary, the formidable encircling walls of **Port-Louis** (pop. 3700) seem far too imposing for such a small, remote town. Named after Louis XIII, Port-Louis was built in the early 17C under Cardinal Richelieu as the first head-quarters of the French East India Company, but its fortifications lost their significance when the company later moved across to Lorient.

The Citadel, guarded by angular granite bastions, now houses the Musée de l'Atlantique, devoted to France's maritime glories.

MARTYRE, LA
FINISTÈRE See PARISH CLOSES

MENEZ-BRÉ
CÔTES-DU-NORD

Though Menez means 'mountain' in Breton, this isolated hill, in the countryside 8km W of Guingamp, hardly qualifies for such a title, since it is only 302m high. At its summit is a small chapel to St Hervé, a popular Breton saint, protector of horses, who was invoked against terrors of all sorts, especially those induced by prowling wolves.

MONTMURAN, CHÂTEAU
ILLE-ET-VILAINE

A short way off the main road from Rennes to St-Malo, near Hédé, Montmuran was begun in the 12C by the lords of the nearby town of Tinténiac. The chief medieval survival is the 14C gate-tower, which still has its drawbridge in working order. The great soldier Bertrand du Guesclin was knighted in this castle chapel in 1354.

Some of the finest stained glass in the whole of Brittany is to be found in the church of **Les Iffs**, 1km from Montmuran. Inspired by Flemish glass, the nine 16C windows show the Nativity, the Last Judgment and other biblical scenes.

Château Caradeuc, some 10km W of Montmuran, has been nicknamed the 'Versailles of Brittany', both for the classical 18C symmetry of its facade and for the elegance of its park, laid out partly in the formal French style and partly in the more naturalistic English fashion.

MORBIHAN, GULF OF

Morbihan means 'Little Sea' in Breton, and is an apt title for this landlocked expanse of water, dotted with islands that seem to float on its lagoon-like surface. With only a single channel leading to the open sea, and protected along its southern edge by the Rhuys Peninsula (q.v.), the Morbihan is a favourite playground of small-boat sailors, who revel in its 200km of muddy shoreline, and its dozens of island anchorages. The largest island is the tranquil **Île-aux-Moines** (pop. 600), once a monastic fief, now a delightful seaside resort.

Brittany's main prehistoric sites (see *Carnac* and *Locmariaquer*) lie around or near the gulf, and the small island of **Gavrinis** has one of the finest burial mounds in Europe, consisting of a stone pass-ageway leading to a burial chamber, probably a royal tomb. In 56BC Julius Caesar decisively beat the Gaulish fleet in a battle off the mouth of the gulf, paving the way to his conquest of Brittany.

In spite of the Morbihan's scenic beauty and mild climate, there is only one major town, **Vannes** (q.v.), along its shores.

MORLAIX
FINISTÈRE Pop 21,000

The chief town of northern Finistère, Morlaix lies in a valley, at the head of an estuary – a position that made it a major trading harbour during and after the Middle Ages. It still has a wealth of fine, half-timbered and granite merchants' houses, but its most striking feature is a superb railway viaduct, built in 1864, which bestrides the valley on lofty arches.

Morlaix's easy access to the Channel made it a natural target for attack and pillage from England. One such raid is commemorated in the town's punning motto 'S'ils te mordent, mords-les' ('If they bite you, bite them back'). In 1522 an English raiding party found the town undefended, looted the houses and drank themselves senseless; and when the inhabitants returned from a local festival, they massacred the raiders – hence the motto.

The oldest church, St-Melaine, built in Flamboyant Gothic style, lies in the shadow of the viaduct. Most of the medieval buildings are upstream from the viaduct, including the Jacobin Museum, originally the church of a 13C Dominican (Jacobin) convent. Its collections cover religious art, shipbuilding, and all aspects of bygone life in north Finistère.

Downstream from the viaduct is maritime Morlaix, where the quaysides, once crowded with merchant shipping, are now given over to small boats. A tobacco factory, founded here in 1736, is still in operation.

With its radiating network of main roads, Morlaix makes an excellent centre for visiting the great parish closes (q.v.), the Monts d'Arrée (q.v.) and the remoter parts of central Brittany.

Morlaix

PAIMPOL
CÔTES-DU-NORD   Pop 8500

This little fishing port, with a well-sheltered harbour, reached its heyday towards the end of the 19C when a fleet of sailing trawlers made an annual journey to the Icelandic cod-banks. The harsh lives of Paimpol's fishermen were vividly described in Pierre Loti's novel *Pêcheur d'Islande (The Iceland Fisherman)*, published in 1886. Today Paimpol is both a popular tourist resort, and the home of a training school for merchant navy officers.

Some 6km N is the **Île de Bréhat**, reached by ferry in 10 minutes from the Pointe de l'Arcouest. Traffic-free and with a climate mild enough to grow oleanders and other Mediterranean plants, Bréhat is one of the prettiest places on Brittany's north coast.

PAIMPONT, FORÊT DE
ILLE-ET-VILAINE

The 6500ha of Paimpont Forest are the last ves-

tiges of the ancient forest of Armorica, which once covered much of central Brittany. During the Middle Ages it became famous under the name of Brocéliande – the mythical forest where King Arthur presided over the Round Table, and where his knights roamed the groves and thickets, fighting monsters and ogres, and rescuing damsels in distress.

Arthurian echoes still linger round Paimpont, in names such as the Pont du Secret, where Guinevere declared her love for Lancelot, the Perron de Merlin (Merlin's Threshold), a large stone by the remote Fontaine de Barenton, and the manorhouse of Brocéliande. From the lake that stretches in front of the Château de Comper, Sir Lancelot took his name 'Lancelot of the Lake', while in the church at Tréhorenteuc is a painting of the Holy Grail appearing to King Arthur's knights.

The village of Paimpont is built round an imposing abbey, founded in the 7C. The present buildings are mainly 17C.

PARISH CLOSES
FINISTÈRE

The parish close *(enclos paroissial)* is an architectural phenomenon unique to Brittany. During the Middle Ages many parish churches became embellished with various additions, including stone Crucifixion carvings *(calvaires)* outside the church, ossuaries for storing the bones of the dead and triumphal arches as entries to the enclosure surrounding the church. In the 15–16C this complex became stylized, mainly in Finistère, reaching its high point in magnificent 17C examples such as the close at Pleyben.

Three of the finest parish closes, within a few kilometres of one another, have been conveniently grouped together to form the signposted 'Circuit des Trois Enclos', about 16km S of Morlaix. From W to E they are: **Lampaul-Guimiliau**, whose church contains numerous statues of saints; **Guimiliau**, where the 16C calvary is covered with more than 200 stone figures telling the story of the Crucifixion in three-dimensional tableaux; and **St Thégonnec**, the largest, dominated by an enormous church tower in Renaissance style.

There are other splendid closes at **Pleyben**, **Sizun** and **La Martyre**, and less spectacular examples throughout Finistère, either with all the elements combined, or just with a calvary or triumphal arch. Among the best of the calvaries is the one at **Plougastel-Daoulas**, with almost as many figures as at Guimiliau.

The great series of *enclos* came to an end before 1700, with the decline of Brittany's trade, when there was insufficient money to finance such grandiose constructions.

PENMARC'H PENINSULA
FINISTÈRE

A forgotten corner of Brittany, this peninsula is named after the town of Penmarc'h, once an important harbour but now quietly sinking into decay. Beyond the Pointe de Penmarc'h are treacherous rocks, covered at low tide. The tall lighthouse above the rocks is called the Phare d'Eckmühl, after the Prince of Eckmühl, whose daughter left the money to build it.

Just north of the Pointe is the exquisite chapel of **Notre-Dame-de-la-Joie**, built on the sea wall and almost within reach of the waves. A few km up the coast, beside the chapel of **Notre-Dame-de Tronoën**, is the oldest, loneliest and most evocative of all the Breton calvaries, dating from about 1465.

PLEYBEN
FINISTÈRE See PARISH CLOSES

PLOUGASTEL-DAOULAS
FINISTÈRE See PARISH CLOSES

PONT-AVEN
FINISTÈRE Pop 3500

The woods round Pont-Aven and the banks of the little river Aven are still as pretty as they were when Gauguin came there to paint a century ago, but nowadays the narrow streets where he and his friends strolled, and the village square where they sat outside to drink, are often solid with traffic. The Gauguin tradition is maintained during the summer months at the town hall, where exhibitions of work by the Pont-Aven school are held each year.

Just above the town, in the secluded Trémalo chapel, is the yellow-painted wooden figure of Christ on the Cross that inspired one of Gauguin's finest paintings, the *Christ Jaune*.

PONTIVY
MORBIHAN Pop 14,500

Despite its situation at the mid-point of Brittany, Pontivy has never attained much importance. In 1805 Napoleon enlarged it to a grid pattern, and it was briefly renamed Napoléonville. A few old houses survive, clustered round the Flamboyant Gothic church. The chief medieval survival is the castle, whose massive walls and pointed towers were built at the end of the 15C by the powerful Duc de Rohan. It is now an exhibition centre.

Pontivy stands on the Nantes-Brest Canal, and is a popular centre for river holidays and trips.

North of Pontivy is the picturesque **Lac de Guerlédan** which, although it appears wholly natural, was, in fact, created artificially from the river Blavet by means of a dam 45m high at its eastern end, near the pretty little town of **Mur-de-Bretagne**. The tour around the lake (67km) takes about three hours.

At the western tip of the lake, a minor road winds northward through the wild and sombre **Gorges de Daoulas**, where the swift-flowing river Daoulas has cut a channel through the rock of the surrounding hills.

QUIBERON PENINSULA
MORBIHAN

The Presqu'île de Quiberon juts like a pointing finger from the Morbihan coast. Once an island, it is now linked to the mainland by a narrow isthmus.

Quiberon Peninsula

Its two sides provide a remarkable contrast: on the west, the rocks of the Côte Sauvage face the fury of the Atlantic storms, while on the east a sandy beach shelves gently into the sheltered waters of Quiberon Bay.

During summer the whole peninsula becomes a holiday playground, centring on the resort of Quiberon at its southern tip. Windsurfers and dinghies scud across the bay, while devotees of strange rock formations can explore the grottoes and sculpted arcades of the Côte Sauvage.

Quiberon is famous in Breton history as the setting for a last-ditch stand by Royalists against the Revolutionary forces. In 1795 an Anglo-French expeditionary force landed in Quiberon Bay and linked up with the Chouans (Breton Royalists). After some initial success, they were defeated by General Hoche. More than 900 Chouans were taken to a field 2km north of Auray and shot without trial; the field, known as the **Champ des Martyrs**, is still consecrated to their memory.

QUIMPER
FINISTÈRE Pop 61,000

The administrative centre of Finistère and the capital of the ancient region of Cornouaille, Quimper combines the attractions of a tourist centre with the bustle of a provincial capital. The Breton name *Kemper* means 'river junction', referring to the point where the river Odet joins a stream, now piped underground, called the Steir. Its origins go back to Brittany's legendary past, when the good King Gradlon, fleeing from the flooded city of Ys (see *Douarnenez*), founded a new city on the banks of the Odet.

Not far from the river is Quimper's magnificent 13C cathedral, dedicated to St Corentin, a miracle-working hermit who became the first bishop of the city. Though the Gothic cathedral appears to be all of a piece, the pair of noble spires that dominate the town centre were added as recently as 1855. At the foot of the cathedral the medieval Bishop's Palace has been turned into the Musée Breton, which covers the prehistory, history and art of western Brittany.

The square in front of the cathedral is the starting-point for several of Quimper's medieval streets, of which the most impressive is the Rue Kéréon, forming the spine of the old city. The Middle Ages live on in several of the street names here, among them the Pl. au Beurre (Butter Square) and the Venelle du Poivre (Pepper Lane). Across the square from the cathedral, the Beaux-Arts gallery combines Old Master paintings with works by Breton artists.

On the other side of the river the tree-covered Mont Frugy forms a green rampart above the wide Pl. de la Résistance. This is the setting each July for the week-long Fêtes de Cornouaille, Brittany's main festival of folk music and dance, which ends with a grand *fest-noz* (night festival) in the streets. Below Mont Frugy, alleys of plane trees lead alongside the river to Locmaria, the oldest part of Quimper, which has been inhabited since Roman times and probably much earlier. Locmaria has a superb Romanesque church, largely 11C, with a peaceful little cloister beside it. Nearby is the famous Quimper pottery, where the characteristic sturdy, colourful Quimper wares have been made since the 17C (guided factory tours throughout the year).

The popular seaside resort of **Bénodet**, at the mouth of the Odet, is 15km by road from Quimper. The best way of getting there is to abandon the car and go by boat down the romantically wooded river valley.

Quimper

QUIMPERLÉ
FINISTÈRE   Pop 11,000

This delightful little town is linked with the far larger Quimper in an old saying: 'If Quimper is the smile of Cornouaille, Quimperlé is surely its kiss.' Its name (likewise from the Breton *Kemper*) refers to the junction of the rivers Ellé and Isole, which meet in the centre of Quimperlé. From here, jointly renamed the Läita, they flow southward to the sea down a prettily wooded valley.

Quimperlé is famous among lovers of unusual buildings for its abbey church of Ste-Croix, built in the 11C in Romanesque style and largely reconstructed in the 1860s. Its plan, in the form of a rotunda with rounded apses, is modelled on the church of the Holy Sepulchre in Jerusalem. The Ville Basse, down at river level, retains several alleys of fine half-timbered medieval houses.

The Ville Haute, across the river, is mainly later in construction, though it does have its own medieval church.

REDON
ILLE-ET-VILAINE   Pop 11,000

For centuries Redon has been an important cross-roads town, standing at a point where major highways meet, and at the junction of the Nantes-Brest canal and the Vilaine river. However, not much indication of its ancient origins survives today, apart from the splendid Romanesque church of St-Sauveur at the heart of the town. It stands on the site of an earlier Benedictine abbey church, founded in 832 and destroyed by the Normans.

The most notable feature of the present church is the magnificent 12C Romanesque central tower, squat and rugged, and built in a startling contrast of dark granite and red sandstone. It is thought to be the only Romanesque tower with rounded corner-angles not only in Brittany, but in the whole of France. At the SW corner of the church is a 15C Gothic bell tower, isolated from the main building since a fire destroyed much of the nave in 1782.

RENNES
ILLE-ET-VILAINE   Pop 206,000

The Victorian travel writer Augustus Hare remarked of Rennes: 'There is never any life or movement in Rennes, and there is nothing whatever worth seeing.' Fortunately things have improved over the past century. Rennes, which is both the capital of the Ille-et-Vilaine *département* and of the whole of Brittany, has grown far livelier in recent years, with expanding industries, the inevitable high-rise blocks of flats and offices, a large university, fine shops and a go-ahead museum and art gallery.

Architecturally, the centre of the city is still on the dull side, though much enlivened by flower-planting. Most of its buildings are in the ponderous 19C manner, and little survives from before the 18C because a disastrous fire in 1720 burnt a huge hole in the medieval town centre, destroying most of the ancient buildings. Old Rennes, with its medieval street layout, lies north of the Quais along the river and around the cathedral. The rest of the city conforms mainly to a grid pattern.

For centuries Rennes disputed the position of Brittany's first city with Nantes, away to the south on the banks of the Loire. But since Nantes became the capital of the Pays de la Loire in the 1960s, Rennes has reigned supreme. It is, in fact,

Palais de Justice, Rennes

an ancient city; known as Roazon in Breton, the name derives from the tribe of the Redones, conquered by Julius Caesar. The Romans recognized its strategic importance and built a fortified town at the confluence of the Ille and Vilaine rivers, with its centre roughly where the cathedral now stands.

After the Romans left, it remained important. The Franks fortified it, the Normans plundered it and, in the Middle Ages, the dukes of Brittany made it one of their chief cities. The Pl. des Lices ('Square of the Lists'), where tournaments were held, dates from this period, as do a few old streets (Rue de la Monnaie, Rue St-Guillaume) and the Flamboyant Gothic St-Germain church, just E of the old town centre. The cathedral itself, built far later, is a dull building, with a baroque exterior and a heavy 19C interior.

From the 15C until the French Revolution, Rennes was the seat of the États, Brittany's parliament, which had a considerable amount of autonomy. Those great days are recalled by the soberly impressive 17C Palais de Justice, formerly the parliament building. Not far away is another splendid 17C building, the Abbaye de St-Georges, only a short walk from the Jardin du Thabor, a superb example of the French formal style of public garden.

S of the river, on the Quai Émile Zola, is the Palais des Musées which contains both the Musée des Beaux-Arts and the Musée de Bretagne. The former contains an important collection of art works from the 16C to the present day, including paintings by Veronese, van Heemskerk, Rubens, de la Tour, Chardin, Greuze, Corot, Sisley and Gauguin. The latter museum is a 'must' for anyone interested in Breton art, history and culture.

The modern Maison de la Culture is an imaginatively designed complex containing a theatre, a cinema, an exhibition gallery and a discothèque.

RHUYS PENINSULA
MORBIHAN

The Presqu'île de Rhuys, which protects the S side of the Morbihan Gulf (q.v.), remains off the tourist beaten track. Its only town of any size is **Sarzeau** (pop. 4000) which still has a handful of fine 17C houses. Near the Atlantic coast is the magnificent **Château de Suscinio**, built between the 13C and 16C, one of the castles of the dukes of Brittany. Further round the coast the village of **St-Gildas-de-Rhuys** is now remembered for its associations with Peter Abélard, the 12C philosopher and teacher, who was appointed abbot of St-Gildas and spent a tormented term of office there.

The road and the peninsula both end at the little harbour and resort of **Port-Navalo**, a good starting-point for boat trips round the gulf. A nearby hill, called the Butte de César, is said to be the vantage-point from which Julius Caesar in 56BC watched his galleys defeat the Gaulish fleet.

ROCHE-AUX-FÉES, LA
ILLE-ET-VILAINE

The 'Fairies' Rock' is far more imposing than its folksy name might suggest: it is, in fact, one of France's finest megalithic monuments, dating from around 2000BC. It consists of a covered way of huge standing stone blocks, with roofing stones laid across them. There are 48 blocks, of which the heaviest weighs about 45 tons; the interior is divided into two separate chambers, presumably for important burials. The locals believed that the rock was built by fairies, and young engaged couples would visit it at new moon, being promised happiness only if they completed the circuit, each counting the same number of stones.

ROSCOFF
FINISTÈRE   Pop 3500

This rugged 'nest of corsairs', as a local poet called it, is now full of tourists fresh off the cross-Channel ferry from Plymouth. Its dour granite houses are built round a splendid church with an elaborate and fanciful tower. Part of the medieval town wall survives beside the seafront, unchanged since Mary Stuart (later Mary, Queen of Scots) landed there in 1548 as a five-year-old, on her way to Paris to be engaged to the Dauphin.

Roscoff's greatest curiosity is Le Grand Figuier, a giant fig-tree planted c.1620 in the garden of the Capuchin convent, with its sprawling branches supported on a forest of granite columns. However, most of the plantings round Roscoff are less spectacular in scale: the region's prosperity depends on the farming of artichokes and cauliflowers.

The Marine Biological Centre, an out-station of Paris University, has an aquarium which can be visited.

Just offshore is the lonely, windswept island of **Batz** (pronounced 'Ba'). The church on Batz still preserves the stole of St Pol (St Paul-Aurélian), who among his many miracles tamed a dragon that was terrifying the people of Batz.

Mary Stuart's turret, Roscoff

ST-BRIEUC
CÔTES-DU-NORD   Pop 57,000

No one would claim that St-Brieuc is a picturesque town, and few tourists nowadays visit it. Yet as the capital of the Côtes-du-Nord it is full of life and bustle. Its centre is built on a superb plateau site between two rivers, and it has its fair share of ancient buildings.

St Brieuc or Brioc, one of the 'Seven Founding

St-Malo

Saints' of Brittany, was a Welsh missionary who set up a monastic community not far from the sea c.AD580. The town that grew up round the monastery was constantly threatened with destruction throughout the Middle Ages. Its history is summed up in the architecture of St Stephen's cathedral, completed c.1230, which looks more like a fortress, with machicolations and arrow-slits. In later centuries St Stephen's was much altered and rebuilt, the nave as recently as the 18C.

Much of the old town centre has been pedestrianized, and there are superb public gardens nearby (the Grandes Promenades). In May St-Brieuc holds Le Mai Breton, an important folklore festival.

ST-JÈAN-DU-DOIGT
FINISTÈRE   Pop 700

In about 1440 an imposing church was built here in Flamboyant Gothic style as a shrine for the miracle-working finger of St John the Baptist. The relic arrived in Brittany miraculously, under the skin of a young man from the nearby village of Plougasnou. In former times touching the finger was reputed to restore sight and hearing and to cure all kinds of diseases. An important *pardon* is still held here each June, during which the finger is carried in procession round the village. Thomas Adolphus Trollope, brother of the famous novelist, attended the *pardon* in the 1830s and described the 'hideous deformity and frightful mutilation' of peasants hoping for a cure.

Just outside the church is an attractive Renaissance fountain, decorated with statues of Christ and John the Baptist.

ST-MALO
ILLE-ET-VILAINE   Pop 46,000

St-Malo is one of the wonders of northern France, both for its architecture and for its magnificent site on a rocky promontory, guarded by a reef of small islands. Gustave Flaubert called it 'a crown of stone above the waves', but it is more like a ship of stone, especially when viewed from the sea, with its encircling walls forming the ship's hull, and its tall houses like a grey granite superstructure.

Despite its venerable appearance, St-Malo is mostly of recent construction, since it was virtually annihilated by bombardment in August 1944, in the final stages of World War II. But it was rebuilt so massively, and with so much care for its original appearance, that the old corsairs would still feel thoroughly at home in its narrow streets. The people of St-Malo (known as Malouins) have a saying that sums up their local patriotism: 'A St-Malo man first, a Breton perhaps, a Frenchman if there's anything left over.'

St-Malo was founded in the 6C by a Welsh monk, Maclou or Malo, who landed here to convert the pagan inhabitants. The first settlement was on the little island of Aleth, now part of nearby St-Servan; but attacks by the Franks and later by the Norsemen drove the inhabitants across the harbour to the site of the present town, then an island separate from the mainland. Strongly fortified and almost impregnable, St-Malo was for centuries the breeding-ground of formidable sailors, who preyed on shipping in the Channel and further afield. Returning home laden with plunder, they built themselves houses both within the city walls (intra muros) and in the suburbs and country outside (extra muros). Seamen from St-Malo, incidentally, were the first to discover the distant Falkland islands, which the French still call Les Malouines and the Argentinians Las Malvinas.

A walk round the ramparts provides superb views out to sea and over the town, and passes statues of the town's most famous inhabitants: corsairs Duguay-Trouin and Surcouf, and the explorer Jacques Cartier, discoverer of the St Lawrence river. At the heart of the old town is the former cathedral, an attractive mixture of building styles from the 12C onwards, with an exceptionally graceful chancel.

St-Malo's powerful castle was built by the dukes of Brittany outside the walls of the town, as much to keep a check on the ambitions of the Malouins as to defend them from outside attack. Two of its massive towers are now museums, the Grand Donjon devoted to the town's maritime history, while the oddly named Quic-en-Groigne contains waxworks tableaux of the exploits of the corsairs. Its name derives from a remark by the Duchess Anne, who built it around 1500. When the Malouins complained at its size and strength, she replied: 'Qui qu'en groigne, ainsi sera.' ('Complain as much as you like, that's how it will be.')

S and E of the walled town is the harbour area, where yachts crowd the marina below the walls, cargo ships unload in the inner basins, and the cross-Channel ferry disgorges its daily horde of cars and passengers.

Across the causeway that links St-Malo to the mainland are the popular seaside resorts of **Paramé** and **Rothéneuf**. On the other side of the bay, **St-Servan** is a small town in its own right, though joined to St-Malo by a continuous commercial and housing development. At St-Servan, the 14C Tour Solidor has been turned into a museum devoted to the round-the-world sailing ships.

ST-POL-DE-LÉON
FINISTÈRE   Pop 8100

This thriving agricultural town is the main centre of the rich stretch of farmland known as the Ceinture Doré. It is the headquarters of the Sociétés d'Intérêt Collectif Agricole (SICA) set up by Alexis Gourvennec (see *Introduction*) after the 'artichoke war' of 1961, with a virtual monopoly in an area producing 70 per cent of the nation's artichokes and cauliflowers. The town's twofold name derives from St Paul-Aurélian (see *Roscoff*) and Léon, the ancient N Finistère bishopric abolished at the time of the Revolution.

The vegetable fields, stretching for miles around, are dominated by the enormous tower and spire, almost 80m high, of St-Pol's Kreisker chapel, built in the 15C. Near by is the town's cathedral, a fine Gothic building of the 13–14C, with twin towers 50m high. The long, narrow nave is built of Caen limestone and the rest of the building of local granite. Behind the choir are small boxes, each containing the *chef* (skull) of a cathedral canon.

Although Roscoff is St-Pol's harbour, the town has its own small waterfront at nearby **Pempoul**.

About 20km SW of St-Pol, set in remote countryside, is the noble Renaissance **Château de Kerjean**, approached through a huge park and avenue of superb beech trees. The granite walls, pierced for cannon, rise from a dry moat. Inside, much of the *corps-de-logis* and other buildings were destroyed by fire in 1710, but there has been restoration over the years and some rooms are now open to the public.

ST-THÉGONNEC
FINISTÈRE   See PARISH CLOSES

STE-ANNE-D'AURAY
MORBIHAN

About 6km N of the town of Auray (q.v.), Ste-

Anne is the focus of Brittany's main religious gathering. For two days each year, on 25 and 26 July, thousands of pilgrims converge on its vast 19C basilica and enormous assembly area. Nearby is an immense war memorial to the 250,000 Bretons killed in World War I.

Ste-Anne has been a pilgrimage centre since the 17C. In 1623 a local peasant, Yves Nicolazic, had a vision of St Anne, mother of the Virgin Mary and the patron saint of Brittany, ordering him to build a chapel on the site of one destroyed during the Dark Ages. Nicolazic did so, and two years later was led by a sign to discover an ancient statue, which he set up in the sanctuary. The clergy took an interest, followed by Louis XIII, and the future of Ste-Anne-d'Auray was assured. The statue was burnt during the Revolution, and so its age and provenance will never be known, though there is a theory that it may have represented Ana or Dana, the pre-Christian Celtic mother-goddess.

SIZUN
FINISTÈRE   See PARISH CLOSES

TRÉGUIER
CÔTES-DU-NORD   Pop 3700

One of the most attractive old towns in northern Brittany, Tréguier stands high above the river Jaudy, crowned by the lofty spire of its medieval cathedral. It was the seat of the bishopric of Trégor from the 9C until the Revolution, and still breathes the atmosphere of more leisurely times. Below the cathedral, streets of old houses, some of them half-timbered, drop down to the waterfront.

The cathedral's striking spire is pierced with holes to lessen resistance to the wind. Dedicated to St Tugdual, who rid the countryside of a formidable dragon before founding a monastery at Tréguier, the cathedral dates from the, 14–15C, though part of it is in the older 10–11C Romanesque style. It contains the tomb of St Yves (Yves Hélory) who was born near Tréguier in 1253 and spent most of his life as Tréguier's *Official* (ecclesiastical judge). Renowned for the honesty of his judgments at a time when most of his colleagues

Tréguier

were corrupt, he was canonized soon after his death and became the patron saint of lawyers. He is usually depicted between a rich man and a poor man, as in a statue in the cathedral. Each year, on 19 May, lawyers from all over France march in solemn procession through Tréguier in his honour.

A very different personality, Ernest Renan, the agnostic and free-thinker, was born at Tréguier in 1823. His statue stands in the square by the cathedral, and his birthplace is now a museum devoted to his life and writings.

USHANT
FINISTÈRE   Pop 1450

Ushant (Île d'Ouessant) is known to the Bretons as *Enez-Heussa*, the 'Island of Terror', and with good reason, since down the centuries its rock-bound coast, fringed with savage reefs, has been the graveyard of countless ships. Some 20km out to sea beyond Brittany's northern peninsula, Ushant lies at the point where the Atlantic and the Channel meet, and is battered by swirling currents and continuous winds.

Because of its remote position, Ushant remained pagan longer than the rest of Brittany, and the Druid cult survived until the 5–6C AD. In historic times it was the custom of the women rather than the men to propose marriage, since the latter were away at sea; and for the same reason the farms were cultivated by the women, who wore a black costume unique to the island.

Today it is known for its weather station, its powerful lighthouse (Phare du Créac'h), its flocks of migratory birds, and its small breed of sheep which feed on the salt-laden grass and make excellent mutton. Along with the smaller island of **Molène**, Ushant forms the westernmost part of the Armorique Regional Nature Park.

VANNES
MORBIHAN   Pop 45,000

As the southernmost of the four Breton *départements*, the Morbihan is the most relaxed in atmosphere, and Vannes is its suitably relaxed capital. Although far from the sea, on the inner fringe of the Gulf of Morbihan, it is still a harbour town, with a busy quayside thronged with small boats during the summer. A good third of the medieval town wall survives, as do two of the powerful fortified gatehouses. Vannes seems to care more about its past than many equally ancient Breton towns; much of the centre is free of traffic, and there is a comprehensive restoration scheme for its historic buildings.

Its name derives from the Veneti, one of the Gaulish tribes defeated by Julius Caesar in 56BC. During the 9C, Nominoë, first duke of Brittany, declared his country's independence from France at Vannes; and between 1456 and 1532, during the final years of Breton independence, it was the seat of the États (Breton parliament). Many superb town houses survive from the late Middle Ages, among them the Château Gaillard, where the États assembled, the Hôtel de Roscanvec, now an excellent museum of Morbihan prehistory, and La Cohue (The Hubbub), a covered market restored in the 1970s. Below the town walls is a unique medieval survival – the slate-roofed *lavoirs* where the washerwomen of Vannes once scrubbed their laundry.

The town's patron saint is the Spanish missionary St Vincent Ferrier, who died here in 1419. The Spanish town where he was born is recalled in the Pl. Valencia, in the heart of medieval Vannes. The southern gateway (Porte St-Vincent) is named after him, and tapestries in the cathedral portray his miracles. The cathedral, dedicated to St Peter, is a mixture of architectural styles from Romanesque to Renaissance; St-Vincent's tomb and relics are in a chapel on the N side.

The modern administrative buildings are W of the old town, across the broad Rue Thiers. Below the ramparts, on the E side of the old town, the broad moat has been grassed over and planted with elaborately formal flower-beds. Beyond this is a tree-shaded public garden (Jardins de la Garenne), a good place to relax after walking round the streets.

VITRÉ
ILLE-ET-VILAINE   Pop 13,000

Like Fougères (q.v.) some 30km N, Vitré was a fortified frontier town guarding Brittany against the rest of France. Its magnificent castle, triangular in plan, was begun in the 11C; the present impregnable-looking curtain wall and turrets date mainly from the 15C. There is a small historical museum in one of the towers. Apart from the castle, Vitré is worth seeing for its streets of ancient houses, and its gabled and pinnacled church, in 15C Flamboyant Gothic style.

The famous 17C letter-writer Mme de Sévigné, who for almost half a century chronicled life at the court of Louis XIV, had a town house in Vitré, and has left a vivid picture of the meetings of the États (Breton parliament) held from time to time in the town. While in Brittany, she often stayed at her country château of **Les Rochers**, 6km S of Vitré. Built in the 14C, it was remodelled in the 17C, partly by Mme de Sévigné herself, who added the small chapel. The gardens, with well-kept alleys and avenues of trees, were her creation. Some rooms in the château can be visited, including Mme de Sévigné's workroom, now a museum.

Vitré

101

NORMANDY

It has been said that the result of the battle of Hastings was not so much that a Norman duke became king of England but that the kings of England became dukes of Normandy. Which is another way of saying that Normans and English have shared a good deal of history.

After the Conquest, the two peoples were united politically; yet to a large extent they were already united racially. The Normans who landed at Hastings were the descendants of the Vikings who, a few generations earlier, had first raided and then settled in northern France while their compatriots were doing the same in eastern England. France naturalized them sooner than did England. Less than a hundred years after the Vikings first came up the Seine, reaching Paris, Rollo the Dane was baptized in the name of Robert and signed with Charles the Simple the treaty of St-Clair-sur-Epte, which made him duke of Normandy. The Scandinavian settlers who moved into the new dukedom turned into Frenchmen with remarkable speed. Robert's grandson, the third duke, had to be sent to Bayeux to learn the Norse language, which had died out elsewhere; and the Norman knights who crossed to England with the Conqueror would have found there more surviving Norse customs

than they had left behind.

Gains came with the Conquest. The Normans were natural lawyers – they still are – and they gave England excellent government; they were builders and they imported the milky Caen stone to build Canterbury Cathedral as well as introducing the Romanesque style of architecture for the churches we still call "Norman". In exchange, a good deal of English money crossed the Channel to help build churches in Normandy. The dukedom kept its administrative autonomy after it lost its independence upon being united with the French crown in 1204. After the Revolution, when France was divided into new administrative units, it lost even the autonomy, but there was no question of losing its identity. The history of the five *départements* of the Seine-Maritime, Eure, Orne, Calvados and Manche was too solidly founded, the character of their people, steady and dependable, too firmly established in the minds of the French for there to be room for doubt about the individuality of Normandy.

The character of the landscape is remarkable above all for its variety: it is hard to think of any area of comparable size which can offer so much contrast, from the rolling plateau of the Pays de

Caux to the craggy valleys of the Suisse Normande, from the great beech forests of the interior to the flats of the lande de Lessay in the Manche *département*. The chalk cliffs of the Côte d'Albâtre mirror the white cliffs of Dover; at the north-west tip of the Cotentin peninsula the rocks that plunge into the turbulent sea are Breton granite. There are miles of sand, a childhood paradise, on the coast of Calvados, clean shingle beaches ideal for swimmers around Étretat and Le Tréport, sand again, and high fashion with it, off the Côte Fleurie. Inland stretches some of the most fertile agricultural land in Europe, with miles of cereal and root crops and lushly green pastures where the pied dairy cattle have their heads down from dawn till dusk. There is horse-breeding in the Cotentin, the Perche, the Pays de Caux and the Pays d'Auge, the horses ranging from thoroughbreds to that superb draught horse, the dappled Percheron. Everywhere there are orchards, garlanding the whole province with blossom during April and May, rose and palest pink for the apple trees, bridal white for the pears that are cultivated around Domfront. Through the autumn they are gemmed with fruit, golden and greenish ivory and brilliant scarlet.

So many centuries of prosperity, along with a plentiful supply of building stone, have made Normandy one of those rarely fortunate areas where, almost without exception, nature has been embellished rather than marred by the hand of man (in passing, one may speculate whether the intensive industrial development between Rouen and the mouth of the Seine will have as happy an outcome). Charming small towns are built of local materials, châteaux and, above all, churches and cathedrals are masterpieces. Even after the damage of World War II, which destroyed many of the characteristic timbered houses, the history of Normandy can be traced today in its buildings, from the great abbeys first founded in the Seine valley in the 6th century, when the monks began their mission of civilization as well as evangelization,

through the medieval fortresses that still mark the old border between France and Normandy, to the Gothic and Renaissance glories of churches and châteaux.

Art and literature have flourished here along with architecture. Poussin and Géricault were Normans, Millet was born near Cherbourg and Boudin at Honfleur; and the whole Impressionist School found its nursery if not its birthplace under the shifting skies of the Channel coast. Malherbe was born at Caen, Corneille and Flaubert at Rouen, Maupassant at Fécamp.

Strictly, perhaps, cooking is a craft rather than an art, but the best Norman cooks surely deserve the status of artist-craftsmen. The whole province is renowned for good eating, its reputation resting less on elaborate dishes, though the *canard au sang* of Rouen and the *tripes à la mode de Caen* are justly famous, than on superb raw materials and on the lavish use of butter and cream. The seafood is unrivalled, the cheeses are many and memorable, and there is the delicious prospect of a Calvados, the apple brandy of Normandy, to round off the meal.

ALENÇON
ORNE Pop 35,500

The state lace factory founded by Colbert gives this market town on the Sarthe its prestige, though its living comes substantially from manufacturing kitchen appliances. The 14–15C château of the dukes of Alençon, with machicolated gate towers and a curiously turreted central tower, is now a prison. The 18C Hôtel de Ville houses an interesting art collection, which includes pictures by Ribera and Géricault, and a fraction only (for lack of space) of the town's lace collection.

The church of Notre-Dame has a 14C W porch with triple gables and a carved balustrade which represents the Flamboyant at its superb peak. Unhappily, after a fire in 1744, the E end was rebuilt in a banal classical style.

Alençon is an excellent centre for exploring the miniature **Alpes Mancelle**, a stretch of rugged country to the SW. The **Forêt d'Écouves**, to the N, 14,000ha of oak, beech, fir and pine, is populated by red and roe deer.

Ste Thérèse de l'Enfant Jesus was born in the town.

ANDELYS, LES
EURE Pop 8200

The white walls of the Château Gaillard flashing on their height above the lovely curve of the Seine, flowing between wooded banks, make Les Andelys, on the D313, one of the most memorable sights of Normandy. Richard Lionheart built the fort in 1196, to strengthen the defences of Normandy against France, and, specifically, to bar the route to Rouen. It is said to have been completed within a year. Richard declared that his *château gaillard* (bold or strong castle) with its moat 15m deep and the 5m-thick walls of its keep, was impregnable, and even today, when only one of the original five defensive towers remains, the claim does not seem extravagant. When, after his death,

Château Gaillard, Les Andelys

it did fall to the French king, Philippe Auguste, after a five-months' siege, it was because a few of the attackers entered the enceinte by way of the latrines and let down the drawbridge. In 1603 Henri IV ordered the castle to be demolished.

Le Petit Andelys has some good timbered houses and an impressive Gothic church, St-Sauveur. The organ was built by Ingout of Rouen in 1674. The church of Notre-Dame in Le Grand Andelys, remarkable for being Flamboyant on the S side and Renaissance on the N side, has renowned 15C glass.

François Blanchard (1753–1809), the pioneer balloonist who invented the parachute, was born at Les Andelys and the artist Nicolas Poussin (1594–1665) at the neighbouring hamlet of Villers.

ARGENTAN
ORNE   Pop 18,000

The battle of Normandy ended in the broad valley of the Dives, 10–15km NE of Argentan, when, on 19 Aug. 1944, the British forces advancing from the NW made their junction with the Franco-American units coming from the S and the remains of the German army were trapped in the pincers. Happily, both the town's churches, St-Germain, with a lantern tower and a spectacular Flamboyant N porch, and the Gothic-Renaissance St-Martin, which has an octagonal tower, escaped irreparable damage during the fighting.

Point d'Argentan lace is made by the nuns of the Benedictine abbey of Notre-Dame.

AVRANCHES
MARCHE   Pop 10,400

Set on sloping ground overlooking the Selune estuary, Avranches offers from the terrace of its attractive Jardin des Plantes a memorable view of Mont-St-Michel (q.v.). The founder of the abbey was the 8C bishop of Avranches, St Aubert, who, says pious legend, was instructed by the archangel Michael himself to build a church on the summit of the Mont. When Aubert questioned the authenticity of two visitations, the archangel materialized a third time and gave him a smart rap on the head.

The bishop's skull, with a visible dent in it, is in the treasury of the church of St-Gervais. There are ancient MSS from the monastic library, including the *Sic et Non* of Abélard and a 9C copy of Cicero's *De Oratore*, in the museum and library housed in the old bishop's palace. Today Avranches has neither bishop nor cathedral. All that remains of the building which collapsed at the end of the 18C is a broken pillar and, beside it, a tablet marking the spot where, in 1192, Henry II knelt to do penance for the murder of Thomas-à-Becket and to receive papal absolution. A more spectacular monument records the breakthrough of General Patton's Third US Army in 1944. The soil on which it stands, like the trees set in it, were brought from the different states of the Union.

BAGNOLES-DE-L'ORNE
ORNE   Pop 800

With the adjoining commune of Tessé-la-Madeleine, Bagnoles, on the D20, is the biggest spa in W France, and a vintage specimen of the genre. Its situation, on the borders of the Forêt d'Andaine, is highly attractive and its amenities include a casino and a boating lake. According to tradition, the first patient to be rejuvenated by the sulphurous and radioactive water of the warm spring was the horse of Hugh, lord of Tessé, who came upon the spring by lucky chance. These days it is used in the treatment of circulatory ailments.

BARFLEUR
MANCHE   Pop 630

This small seaside resort and former fishing harbour on the NE end of the Cotentin peninsula was an ancient cross-Channel port much favoured by Anglo-Norman royalty. According to tradition, the *Mora*, the vessel which carried William, duke of Normandy, to Hastings, was built at Barfleur: a plaque near the lifeboat slipway commemorates the 900th anniversary of his sailing in her. From Barfleur, too, in 1180, the White Ship sailed, to sink with Prince William, son and heir of Henry I of England, and half the court.

BARNEVILLE-CARTERET
MANCHE   Pop 2300

These twin towns set on either side of the Gerfleur estuary are one resort with three sandy beaches, of which the Plage de la Vieille Église extends for eleven unspoiled kilometres. Barneville has an 11C church which still has its orginal carved capitals despite much rebuilding. At **Portbail**, 8km NE, the remains of a 6C baptistry have been uncovered near the harbourside church of Notre-Dame, which is itself 11–12C.

BAYEUX
CALVADOS   Pop 15,300

This beautifully preserved, historic town, known by the Romans as Augustodorum, is principally famous for the wool-embroidered scroll, called the 'Bayeux Tapestry', which tells the story of the events before and during the Norman conquest of

England in 1066. The town is interesting, too, for its lovely old houses and its splendid Norman Gothic cathedral.

The tapestry, kept in a late-17C seminary near the cathedral, measures 70m long and 50cm wide; it consists of 58 colourful scenes – the central strip recounting the main narrative of the events culminating in the invasion, and the bands along top and bottom depicting everyday events, pictures of fantastic animals, etc. It was probably commissioned by Bishop Odo of Bayeux, William the Conqueror's half-brother, around 1080, made by Saxon craftsmen and first mentioned as an item in the cathedral's inventory in 1476. Visitors can hire earphones with French and English commentaries.

Facing the tapestry exhibition is the S porch of the cathedral, an impressive, sombre grey stone edifice, mainly 13C and later. The twin W towers, piers and arches of the nave, and the crypt are late 11C. The interior, 102m in length and 22m in height, is a blend of Romanesque and Gothic, and the nave, with its sturdy piers, contains carvings, many in a humorous vein, in the spandrels of the arches. The 13C chancel, with its slender columns, is surmounted by a clerestory of tall windows. The raised choir has carved 16C stalls and a 17C bishop's throne. The tiled floor of the chapterhouse is arranged as a maze and the crypt contains some 13C frescoes.

There are many 15–18C houses, some of them beautifully preserved, in the cobbled streets of the old town.

In World War II Bayeux was the first French town to be liberated by the Allies, in June 1944.

Some 14km SW of Bayeux is the 17C **Château de Balleroy**, built by François Mansart, with grounds laid out by Le Nôtre. The walls and ceiling of the state reception room are decorated by Mignard. The castle contains a ballooning museum.

BEC-HELLOUIN, LE
EURE

In past years state as well as church in England owed much to this Benedictine abbey, 4km N of Brionne, founded in the 11C by the knight Herluin, or Hellouin. In 1042 the Italian scholar-priest, Lanfranc, joined the community. Soon the abbey became a school for diplomats and royal officials as well as theologians, and Lanfranc himself had become the trusted counsellor of the young duke of Normandy, on whose behalf he interceded with the pope for the removal of the sentence of excommunication (see *Caen*). William appointed him first abbot of his new foundation at Caen, the Abbaye aux Hommes. Some years later Lanfranc was to be appointed archbishop of Canterbury, and was regent in England when the king was abroad. His successor at Bec was another Italian, Anselm, and he, too, became archbishop of Canterbury. During the 11–12C Herluin's abbey was to give England a third archbishop of Canterbury, three bishops of Rochester and seven abbots.

All that remains of the ancient buildings, apart from the bases of the pillars and part of the blind arcade of the transept of the abbey church, is the detached bell tower of St-Nicolas, which dates from the 15C. The monastic buildings, impressive-

ly restored, are those of the 17C Maurist reform: they include the cloister and the wonderful 18C Night Stairway. The altar of the present church, of green Carrara marble, was a gift from St Anselm's native region of Aosta. On the N wall a slab from Canterbury recalls Bec's English connection. There is a motor museum, with models from 1921 onwards, at the abbey gates.

BERNAY
EURE   Pop 11,000

This town in the valley of the Charentonne, which grew up round the abbey founded in the 11C by Judith de Bretagne, grandmother of the Conqueror, was the birthplace of the 12C troubadour, Alexandre de Bernay, who evolved the iambic line of twelve syllables, known as the alexandrine. The abbey is being restored after deconsecration during the Revolution and two centuries of neglect. The 14C church of Ste-Croix contains statues and tombstones from the abbey of Bec.

The château of **Beaumesnil**, 13km SE of Bernay, set in a classical French park, which has been called "a dream of stone" (though it is part-brick) was built in 1633 on the site of a medieval fortress.

BRICQUEBEC
MANCHE   Pop 3800

After Agincourt Henry V gave the château of this ancient market town some 20km S of Cherbourg to William de la Pole, Earl of Suffolk, who, in 1429, had to return it to the French as part of his ransom. The fortified enceinte, with flanking towers, and the ten-sided 14C donjon have survived intact. Notre-Dame-de-Grace, 2.5km N of the town, is one of the few Trappist monasteries in Normandy.

CABOURG-DIVES-SUR-MER
CALVADOS   Pop 3300

Something of the elegance of the Belle Époque persists at **Cabourg**, a seaside resort at the mouth of the River Dives, with a glorious sandy beach. This was the model for the Balbec of that part of Marcel Proust's great novel entitled *À l'ombre des jeunes filles en fleurs*; and if its modern holiday clientele is more democratic than that which frequented it in the early years of the century, the wide lawns of the Casino and the Grand Hotel are still velvet green and the villas that line the avenues fanning out from it have lost none of their architectural fantasy. The one addition is the building of a marina in the river mouth.

Dives, on the E bank of the river, was the port from which William the Conqueror sailed for Hastings in 1066. It is no longer a port; the mouth of the river has silted up so that the town is a couple of kilometres from the sea. The names of William's companions in arms may be read at the W end of the church of Notre-Dame. Notre-Dame, which was Proust's "church of Balbec", dates from the 14–15C, with a portion of an 11C abbey church incorporated in it. The market hall, with its russet-tiled roof and ancient rafters, is almost as old as the church. The Hostellerie de Guillaume le Conquerant, once a posting inn, is 16C.

CAEN
CALVADOS Pop 118,000

"The Athens of the North" – the familiar description does justice to Caen's long-established eminence as a seat of learning but covers neither its martial past nor its thriving present as a port on the Orne Canal, still less the triumph of its post-war restoration. During the Allied offensive of June 1944, Caen was more than three parts destroyed. The outstanding success of its rebuilding was due both to the quality of the planning and to the use of the creamy Caen stone, which has so long been valued as a building material that it was brought from Normandy to construct both the Tower of London and Canterbury Cathedral.

Caen is the Conqueror's city, where one of his first recorded acts, in 1061, was to declare "the truce of God", the edict that, in the ecclesiastical province of Rouen, there must be no war between Wed. evening and Mon. morning. The penalty was excommunication, which William had already incurred by his marriage, within the bounds of consanguinity, with his cousin, Matilda of Flanders. Through the good offices of abbot Lanfranc of Bec, the pope was persuaded to raise the excommunication provided that William and Matilda, for penance, each founded an abbey. The result was two of the finest Romanesque churches in France. Lanfranc, an Italian, is thought to have had a hand in the designing of William's foundation, l'Abbaye aux Hommes, dedicated to St Étienne, and certainly the austerity of the W front, with its four massive buttresses, has counterparts in N Italy. By contrast, the two octagonal towers, added in the 13C, are luxuriantly decorated. The E end, also added in the 13C, is a Gothic marvel, with superimposed turrets and flying buttresses. Inside, the Romanesque and the Gothic meet in perfect harmony. Before the high altar a marble slab marks the place of the Conqueror's tomb. It was violated by both the Protestants and the Revolutionaries and the bones scattered. From 6 June to 9 July, 1944, hundreds of townspeople took refuge in the abbey church and the conventual buildings.

Matilda's foundation, l'Abbaye aux Dames, dedicated to the Sacred Trinity, is wholly Romanesque except for a 13C chapel in the transept. The two W towers lost their spires during the Hundred Years' War. The carvings of the capitals in the apse include one of an elephant – was this done from hearsay or had the Normans discovered the Far East in the 11C? Matilda lies at the entrance of the choir under the slab of black marble which was set there in 1083. Of Caen's many other churches, the Gothic and Renaissance St-Pierre is a rich man's church, elaborately decorated, and St-Nicolas, in its almost rustic churchyard, is purest Romanesque.

The château on a spur of rock, which William built and later generations enlarged, has been rescued from ruin and dominates the town magnificently. The Beaux Arts Museum, at its entrance, is a comprehensive collection particular'_y_ strong in 16–17C works. The Musée de Normandie, housed in a 17–18C building which was formerly the governor's house, has an outstanding collection relating to regional art and craft.

Caen University, whose modern buildings occupy a 30ha campus, was founded in 1432 by Henry VI or strictly, by his regent in France, the duke of Bedford. A few old houses escaped the destruction of 1944, notably the Renaissance Hôtel d'Escoville, now the Syndicat d'Initiative.

The poet François de Malherbe (1555–1628) was born at Caen. From Sept. 1830 to March, 1832, Beau Brummel, once ruler of fashionable society in England, was British consul here. He died, penniless and demented, in the convent hospital of Le Bon Sauveur in 1840.

CAUDEBEC-EN-CAUX
SEINE-MARITIME Pop 2500

This trim little resort on the Seine, about halfway between Rouen and Le Havre, has been almost wholly rebuilt since World War II, when all but three of its typically Norman timbered houses, and the 13C House of the Templars, were razed. The church of Notre-Dame, which escaped irreparable damage, is a Flamboyant tour de force, built between 1426 and 1539. It has a superb triple porch, with carving at once delicate and luxuriant, and a tower and spire rising to 101m. Of its series of 16C windows, that of Our Lady with SS Michael, George and Catherine, was the gift of Fulke Eyton, the last of the English captains to command the garrison here. It is one of the very few examples of English glass in France. The seven-ton keystone pendentive in the Lady Chapel, carved from a single block of stone, is perhaps remarkable rather than precious. Antoine Josselyne, of Rouen, built the great organ in 1542: it still has most of its original stops.

Across the river is the **Forest of Brotonne**, which is now a Regional National Park. The suspension bridge upstream, opened in 1977, is as graceful as that of Tancarville.

CERISY-LA-FORÊT
MANCHE

The abbey of Cerisy, one of the great buildings of Normandy, is 14km NE of St-Lô. There was a religious foundation here in the 6C: it was refounded in 1032 by the Conqueror's father, Robert the Magnificent. The present nave, shorn of five of its original eight bays, is late 12C; the superb choir, with stalls dating from 1400, was added about 1100.

CHERBOURG
MANCHE Pop 30,000

Lacking both a natural harbour and shelter from the NW gales, Cherbourg, on the tip of the Cotentin peninsula, was converted into a major port by heroic labours. They included the building, two miles offshore, of a breakwater two-and-a-quarter miles long, which Napoleon I, who inherited the task from Louis XVI, described as "recreating at Cherbourg the wonders of Egypt". The wonders were, in fact, not completed until 1853. During the Allied invasion of Normandy in 1944, the harbour was mined and badly damaged by the

Cherbourg

retreating Germans: it was restored as a supply port for the Allied armies, where Pluto, the undersea oil pipeline from Britain, came ashore. Today, when commercial shipping has dwindled, it is important chiefly as a naval dockyard which builds France's nuclear-powered submarines.

The mid-19C Fort du Roule has a Museum of the War and the Liberation which includes a map room showing the progress of the Allied armies after the landings. In the Musée des Beaux Arts there is a room devoted to Jean François Millet (1814–75), the painter of peasant life, who was born in the neighbouring village of Gruchy and had his first art training at Cherbourg.

Two châteaux within easy reach of Cherbourg are the Renaissance **Tourlaville**, 5km SE, which has an attractive wooded park, and **Nacqueville**, about the same distance to the W, a late 16C house, with pepperpot towers and a rosy tiled roof. The historian and political scientist, Alexis de Toqueville (1805–59), lived here.

CONCHES-EN-OUCHE
EURE   Pop 3900

Set on its spur of rock rising out of the forest, Conches, with its many old houses, is a lookout over the valley of the Rouloir. The elegantly intricate 15–16C church of Ste-Foy, built on the site of an earlier one, has a series of windows which are recognized as being some of the finest existing examples of 16C glass painting. Among them is the golden window of St-Adrian and St-Romain, by Arnoult de Nimègue, and the seven choir windows by Romain Buron, the "Master of Gisors," who worked at Beauvais. The most celebrated, the Mystical Wine Press, in the S aisle, is from a Paris workshop. There are fine 15C English alabasters in the aisles.

COUTANCES
MANCHE   Pop 13,500

The tranquillity of Coutances, two-thirds of the

way down the Cotentin peninsula, which has been almost wholly rebuilt since World War II, is a perfect setting for the cathedral of Notre-Dame, which is the most perfect, and perfectly simple, Gothic church in Normandy. Constantia, as it then was, became a see in 471. In the 9C the Viking raiders drove out the bishop and clergy and destroyed the cathedral. Its successor owed much to the enterprise of a soldier-priest, Geoffroi de Montbray, who went to Hastings with the Conqueror. To raise funds for the new cathedral he travelled to Calabria to appeal to the generosity of three knights from the Cotentin, the brothers Guillaume Bras de Fer, Robert Guiscard and Roger de Hauteville, who had conquered the whole of S Italy. It proved so bountiful that cathedral and bishop's palace were completed by 1056.

When that Romanesque cathedral was largely destroyed by fire in 1218, the present Gothic cathedral was built over and around it, so that the surviving W towers were scaffolding for the airy Gothic spires, and the pair of massy pillars in the transept were adorned with slender columns. The impression of the interior is of purity of line with an emphasis on soaring verticals, the whole flooded with light from the clerestory windows and from the domed lantern tower over the crossing. The cathedral has fifteen 13C windows; one of the oldest, in a chapel of the N transept, has scenes from the life of Thomas-à-Becket.

Coutances has an unusually attractive public garden laid out in formal 17C style. From it there is a view of the medieval aqueduct. During the summer there are *son-et-lumière* spectacles.

DEAUVILLE
CALVADOS   Pop 4800

One of twin resorts at the mouth of the river Touques, Deauville, on the W bank, has the cachet, Trouville (q.v.) the charm. Deauville was created by a consortium of businessmen, headed by the Duc de Morny, illegitimate half-brother of Napoleon III, to be a fashionable and expensive resort, and has more than fulfilled their hopes. Its attractions include two racecourses, the casino, the Pompeian baths, a vast new marina and lavish floral displays; also, for the curious, the chance of observing the rich and/or famous who frequent it during the high season. This starts in July and ends with the Grand Prix on the fourth Sun. in Aug. The yearling sales, which take place in Aug. and Nov., are world-famous.

DIEPPE
SEINE-MARITIME   Pop 23,700

Favoured resort of the English since the early 19C, Dieppe, at the mouth of the Arques, is also a busy commercial and fishing port. In the 16C, when its sailors were privateers and explorers, it was a centre for shipbuilding; the fleet built for Jean Ango, banker and governor of the town, captured 300 Portuguese ships.

The château of flint and sandstone which looks down from the W cliff on the long curve of the beach, with the green esplanade above it, has one tower which was part of the castle built by Duke

Richard I; the rest is variously 14–16C. It has been both a prison and a barracks since the time when it was the residence of the governors of Dieppe, and is now a museum with a remarkable collection of carved ivories. The art developed locally during the 16–17C, when tusks from India and Africa were landed here. There were then 350 artist-craftsmen working in ivory in Dieppe: only one or two remain.

At the foot of the cliff, in the green Square du Canada, a memorial, one of many in the town, records the Dieppe raid of 19 Aug. 1942, in which a mainly Canadian force of more than 6000 men suffered murderous losses. Its aim was to destroy enemy defences and equipment, capture invasion barges and seize documents from the German divisional HQ. In the event the strength of the German defences proved to have been grossly underestimated, the landing beaches were swept by withering fire and the tanks could not manoeuvre successfully on the pebbles and shingle of the beach.

Thanks to a bombardment by the British navy in 1694, Dieppe is an 18C town: the tall houses are seen to advantage along the arcaded quays, with their excellent fish restaurants, and in the main shopping thoroughfare, the pedestrian Grande Rue. The Pl. du Puits-Salé, overlooked by one of the best of the 18C buildings, the Café des Tribuneaux, is the lively centre of the town. The church of St-Jacques, of almost cathedral size and splendour, was started in the 13C and completed in the

16C. Jean Ango's tomb is in one of the chapels of the S side. The other chapels were offered by the town's shipowners: the luxuriant ornament of the apsidal chapel is another testimony to their wealth. 16–17C St-Rémy has an organ which is one of the finest in France: Saint-Saëns (1855–1921) was once its organist.

Sickert lived and worked in Dieppe from 1899–1905, and many of the Impressionists painted here. Oscar Wilde, during his exile, spent some time in the town. Dieppe's culinary reputation rests on its superb seafood and particularly the delectable *sole dieppoise*, which has now become a classic.

Jean Ango's country house, the Manoir d'Ango, a steep-roofed Renaissance building in patterned brick and flint, is at **Varengeville-sur-Mer**, 7–8km W of Dieppe. The tiny clifftop church of St-Valéry has a Jesse window by George Braque (1882–1963), who is buried in its churchyard, as is the composer Albert Roussel (1869–1937).

Arques-la-Bataille, 6km S of Dieppe, has a château built by an uncle of the Conqueror between 1035 and 1083. Today there is only a ruin behind the deep fosse, but the scale of the entrance towers, which were added in the early 16C, makes plain why this fortress was considered impregnable. The battle took place in 1589, when Henri de Navarre, though heavily outnumbered, defeated the Duc de Mayenne and an army of the Catholic League. The town has attractive old houses and a Flamboyant Gothic church.

Dieppe

DOMFRONT
ORNE Pop 4600

Only two walls of the keep still stand of the fortress of this medieval border town built along a rocky ridge above the river Varenne, with grand views over the bocage. It was among the strongest in Normandy and was used by many of the Anglo-Norman kings. Originally twenty-four towers defended the walls of the town: some of those that remain are now dwelling houses.

There is an interesting modern church, St-Julien, with an octagonal tower, in the town and, in the valley below, a near-flawless Romanesque one, the 11C Notre-Dame-sur-l'Eau. It misses perfection only because of the vandalism which led the authorities to truncate four bays of the nave in order to build the road from Domfront to Mortain.

Domfront is in the heart of the pear-growing country: the local *poiré* (perry) is renowned.

ÉTRETAT
SEINE-MARITIME Pop 1250

This popular resort on the Alabaster Coast, picturesquely situated between two enormous cliffs, the Amont and the Aval, at either end of a shingle beach, still retains the 19C elegance which attracted many writers and painters. The church of Notre-Dame is partly 11–12C, though spoiled by a 19C tympanum. On the Amont is a small chapel commemorating the first attempt, with fatal results, to fly the Atlantic in 1927.

ÉVREUX
EURE Pop 48,700

Évreux has suffered fire and destruction from the 5C, when it was sacked by the Vandals, to World War II, when it was devastated successively by the Germans and the Allies. Almost unbelievably, there are still portions of the 12C cathedral, itself the town's third, inside the present one, where continual rebuilding and restoration has resulted in an amalgam of styles from early Gothic to Renaissance. Work still in progress has given the facade its towers once more, though not yet their spires. Luckily, the 14–15C glass, which is the glory of the building, was removed to safety during the war. The Municipal Museum in the Bishop's Palace of 1481 has many Gallo-Roman remains found in the district. The pinnacled belfry which rises above the river Iton is from 1490. The bell is older, founded at Mantes in 1406.

There is 16C glass in the church of St-Taurin, which was originally that of a Benedictine abbey founded in the 7C, though the present building is 14–15C. The treasure here is the Chasse de St Taurin, a silver gilt reliquary presented to the abbey by St Louis. Taurin's reputed tomb is in the 11C crypt.

FALAISE
CALVADOS Pop 8800

The magnificently theatrical equestrian statue of William the Conqueror is one of the few features of this town above the valley of the Ante, which was

Falaise

his birthplace, to have escaped damage during the climax of the battle of Normandy in Aug. 1944. Tradition says that his father, the future duke Robert the Magnificent, looked down from the castle which dominates the town from its spur of rock, saw "la belle Arlette", daughter of a local tanner, doing the household washing at a spring below the ramparts which is still a public wash-place, and exercised the *droit du seigneur*. After the birth of William the Bastard, a marriage was arranged for her with a Norman noble by whom she bore William's half-brother, Bishop Odo. Today's castle, with its twelve-towered enceinte, is largely 11C but the donjon includes part of the 10C building where the Conqueror was born. In a chapel built into the thickness of the wall a modern bronze plaque records the names of the 315 companions who followed him to Hastings. The dungeon where Prince Arthur, King John's nephew, was imprisoned and murdered is still to be seen.

The town's two most interesting churches, Romanesque-Gothic St-Germain, with a fine 12C lantern tower, and the 13–16C La Trinité, with a curious triangular Gothic porch, have been successfully restored. The suburb of Guibray, with a 12C church, was formerly the site of one of the most famous fairs in France.

FÉCAMP
SEINE-MARITIME Pop 21,700

Before the establishment of Mont-St-Michel, Fécamp, on the Alabaster Coast, was the most important pilgrimage centre in Normandy: ten years ago it was still France's foremost port for deep-sea cod-fishing. Pleasure craft have now replaced most of the trawlers, but pilgrims still come on the Tues. and Thurs. after Trinity. The object of veneration is a phial containing a few drops of the Holy Blood, which, says legend, was hidden in the trunk of a fig-tree by a nephew of Joseph of Arimathea and consigned to the waves, to be cast up off Fécamp. From the 7C it was kept in a convent which, early in the 11C, was succeeded by a Benedictine abbey, with a splendid Romanesque church, destroyed by fire in 1168. Two of its chapels are incorporated in the majestic early Gothic church of La Trinité, built between 1175 and 1220, of cathedral proportions, whose only flaw is the classical W front added in the mid-18C. Externally, it is distinguished by a lantern tower rising to 60m above the crossing, and by the contrast between the relative austerity of the nave and the exuberantly Flamboyant Lady Chapel. The interior, high and light and harmonious, has a remarkable 15C group of the Dormition of the Virgin and exquisitely carved stone screens in the ambulatory chapels. The shrine of the Holy Blood forms part of the early 16C marble high altar by the Genoese sculptor, Girolamo Viscardo, to which was added, in the 18C, an airy baldachino of gilded wood.

The secret of distilling the liqueur Benedictine was discovered in 1510 by a monk of the abbey, Bernardo Vincelli. It is now manufactured commercially; the process, with upwards of 800 examples of counterfeit Benedictine, may be seen in the outrageous 19C-antique buildings of the museum attached to the Benedictine distillery.

The novelist and short story writer, Guy de Maupassant (1850–93) was born at Fécamp, though, by a hasty journey almost immediately after the birth, his mother managed to have him registered at the more desirable address of the **Château de Miromesnil**, some 8km S of Dieppe.

Château de Miromesnil

FONTAINE-HENRY
CALVADOS

This château, 16km NW of Caen, has a strong claim to be rated the finest example of Renaissance domestic arhcitecture in Normandy. It was built for the Harcourt family in the 15–16C, on 11–12C foundations, and is distinguished by its enormous mitred roof, deeper than the walls it crowns, and the elegantly decorated facade of the main building. The attractions of the interior include a François I spiral staircase and a collection of pictures with works by Rigaud, Philippe de Champaigne, Poussin, Watteau, Mignard and Hubert Robert. The chapel dates from the 13C.

FORGES-LES-EAUX
SEINE-MARITIME   Pop 3800

This sedately pleasant spa set between the rivers Andelle and Epte, in the Pays de Bray, produced iron from Gallo-Roman times until the 15C. Since the later 16C it has prospered on its chalybeate waters. Its early patrons included Cardinal Richelieu, Louis XIII and Anne of Austria: the three springs are named after them. The royal couple had come in the hopes that the waters would make their union fruitful after eighteen childless years, but the future Louis XIV was not born for another six years. There are attractive timbered houses in the town and graceful 17–18C facades near the thermal park.

GISORS
EURE   Pop 8900

There was a château at Gisors, on the Epte, in the 10C, but in 1096 William Rufus employed the great military engineer, Robert de Bellême, to build a more powerful fortress on the border between France and Normandy. Henry Beauclerc built the walls round the huge enceinte, now a public garden, and Henry II strengthened them and added two storeys to the donjon. From its summit there are panoramic views over the valley of the Epte. In the donjon of the Prisoner's Tower two captives held respectively in the 15C and 16C carved in the soft stone of the walls a series of pictures ranging from a tournament to a Crucifixion, and a poignant 'Mater Dei, memento mei'. From the terrace of the castle there is a downward view of the church of St-Gervais-et-St-Protain, in which the styles of five centuries, the latest the 16C, have achieved harmony and coherence. There is wonderful carving, without and within.

GRANVILLE
MANCHE   Pop 15,000

There is a Breton flavour about Granville, seaside resort and commercial port on the Atlantic coast of the Cotentin, and there is a Breton-style Pardon of the Corporations de la Mer here on the last Sun. in July each year. It was the English who, in 1439, fortified the old town on its Gibraltar-like Roc, hoping to use it as a base from which to attack Mont-St-Michel. They further strengthened the defences by cutting a ditch, still known as the Tranche aux Anglais, across the isthmus that joins the Roc to the lower town. They were soon expelled; during the 17–18C Granville was the home port of the corsairs who harassed the British navy as well as of the fishermen who had been catching cod off the Newfoundland Grand Banks since the 16C. The old town, granite-built and still enclosed by its walls, has some good 17–18C houses: the 16–17C church has a window depicting the procession of the Grand Pardon. There is excellent material illustrating the history of the town in the Musée du Vieux Granville. The Jardin Public Christian-Dior was once the property of the couturier's family, who lived here.

12km SE of the town, the 12C Premonstratensian abbey of **Lucerne** is being restored.

HARAS-DU-PIN, LE
ORNE

Colbert founded, and Jules Hardouin-Mansart designed, the buildings of the National Stud set in magnificent forest 12km E of Argentan. The stables, where upwards of a hundred stallions are at stud, may be visited, and the horses are exercised in the forest rides. On the first Sun. of Sept. and the second of Oct. there are race meetings which include harness classes.

HAVRE, LE
SEINE-MARITIME Pop 198,000

Of the town which François I built at the mouth of the Seine when the ports of Harfleur and Honfleur were silting up, all that now remains is the old quarter of St-François, which preserves the excellent pattern of neighbourhood planning adopted by the Italian engineer, Girolamo Bellarmato. The

Le Havre

rest was flattened during the battle for liberation of the town in Sept. 1944: the port, which is now the second in France, was out of action for two years. Auguste Perret, the architect who was commissioned to construct the new Havre, had been a pioneer in the use of reinforced concrete: he employed it on the heroic scale for his town, which, while it kept to Bellarmato's chessboard pattern, was conceived as a gigantic, if not gargantuan complex. Its guiding principle was the balance of space and the alternation of horizontals and verticals; there are many who find the vast blocks and towers simply dehumanizing. The two most striking buildings are the Hôtel de Ville, whose 72m tower rises above one of the most enormous squares in Europe, and the church of St-Joseph, which Perret saw as the pivot of the town. Its tower is 109m tall, and the interior of the church is irradiated with colour from the mosaic of narrow slabs of glass in the tower and walls. A building in a far different and brilliantly successful modern idiom is that of the Museum of Modern Art, in which glass, steel and aluminium are manipulated to provide ideal space and lighting for pictures. The collection includes some 300 paintings and drawings by Eugène-Louis Boudin (see *Honfleur*) and a large number of the works of Raoul Dufy (1897–1953), who was born at Le Havre and

found many of his subjects on the Normandy coast.

The seaside resort of **Ste-Addresse**, just E of Le Havre, was the seat of the Belgian government during World War I. At **Granville** there is an 11–13C abbey church. **Harfleur**, now a suburb of Le Havre, was a major port from the 9–16C. It has a church with a striking Flamboyant spire rising to 83m.

There are international regattas at Le Havre during July.

HONFLEUR
CALVADOS Pop 8400

Still a fishing port, though nowadays on a reduced scale, when working craft share the port with yachts, Honfleur, with its ancient, slate-hung houses and its tiny inner harbour built in the 17C might be a specific antidote to the ferroconcrete brutalism of Le Havre on the opposite bank of the Seine estuary. It was a walled town in the 13C; during the 16–17C its seamen roamed the world. Early in the 17C Samuel de Champlain (1567–1635), navigator and explorer, was commissioned by Henri IV to colonize Canada, which had been a French possession since 1535. He sailed from Honfleur to found Quebec in 1608, and men from the port were among those who later helped to populate the new colony.

The inner harbour, or Vieux Bassin, is surrounded by narrow, tall houses, some reaching seven storeys, and many slate-faced as well as slate-roofed. The 16C Lieutenance at the harbour mouth, which was once the home of the governor of Honfleur, is all that remains of the old fortifications and one of the town gates has been incorporated in it. The church of Ste-Catherine, one of the very few surviving timber churches in Normandy, is a triumph of the shipwrights' craft.

Old harbour, Honfleur

JUMIÈGES, ABBAYE DE
SEINE-MARITIME

The surviving W towers, rising to 43m, are a dramatic entrance to the noble ruin of the Benedictine abbey of Jumièges, 15km W of Rouen. St Philibert established a religious community here in 654 and the monks were soon engaged in their civilizing mission of clearing the forest and farming the land. In the 9C the abbey was demolished by the Viking raiders; in the 10C their descendants, transformed into Normans, encouraged its refounding. In 1067 the rebuilt abbey church of Notre-Dame was dedicated in the presence of the Conqueror, who endowed it with various properties in his new possession of England. The abbot of the period, Robert Champart, later became archbishop of Canterbury. During the following 700 years, despite a period of decline, the abbey kept the reputation for charity which had earned it the title of Jumièges l'Aumônier (the almoner). It was closed during the Revolution and the buildings were later systematically cannibalized for their stone. Thanks to an enlightened mid-19C proprietor, the walls of the roofless nave remain standing behind the facade, as does the great arch supporting one wall of the lantern tower. Otherwise there are only foundations and fragments of walls and arches from which we may judge the size and magnificence of the whole.

Abbaye de Jumièges

LESSAY
MANCHE   Pop 3000

This little town at the mouth of the River Ay has one of the most perfect Romanesque abbey churches in France, founded in 1050 by Turstin Haldup, seigneur of La-Haye-du-Puits. It escaped destruction during the Revolution only to be wrecked during World War II. The restoration was an exact reconstruction: every fragment of the original material which could be salvaged was used, and was supplemented by material as nearly identical as possible. Craftsmen even worked with tools like those used in medieval times. The result has recreated a masterpiece and enhanced it with details like the windows in tones of grey, ochre and pale yellow, the pebble mosaic in the floor of the baptistry, and the high altar which is a monolithic slab.

During the second weekend of Sept. each year the flat lande de Lessay, S of the abbey, is the scene of the Holy Cross Fair, one of the most important in Normandy, which was founded by the Benedictines in the 13C.

LILLEBONNE
SEINE-MARITIME   Pop 9700

The château of Lillebonne, 8km NE of the bridge of Tancarville (q.v.), is the spot where William of Normandy assembled his barons before the invasion of Britain. His château was rebuilt during the 12–13C, but the donjon is that of the first castle. The town was the Roman Juliobona: its remains include a theatre which could seat 10,000 spectators. There is an archaeological museum.

LISIEUX
CALVADOS   Pop 25,900

Capital of the Lexiovi tribe under the Roman Empire and for long a prosperous market town, Lisieux, in the fertile valley of the Touques, was a cathedral city long before it became a pilgrimage centre. The pilgrimages date from the short life of Thérèse Martin (1873–97), the Carmelite saint and mystic, who entered the local Carmelite convent when she was fifteen. She wrote the story of her spiritual pilgrimage, *L'Histoire d'une Âme*, shortly before her death from tuberculosis. In 1925 she was canonized as Ste Thérèse de l'Enfant Jésus, but before that the soldiers of World War I spontaneously adopted her as their patron. Since then she has become the secondary patron of France. Visitors see her childhood home, Les Buissonets, and her relics in the Carmel. The enormous basilica consecrated in 1954 to accommodate the pilgrims who flock to Lisieux has no more aesthetic merit than the average pilgrimage church built during the past century. On summer evenings it stages a history of the saint.

The church of St-Pierre, which lost its cathedral status at the end of the 18C, was completed in the mid-13C in exemplary Norman Gothic style. The Flamboyant Lady Chapel was rebuilt during the 15C at the order of Pierre Cauchon, who became bishop of Lisieux shortly after he had condemned Joan of Arc to death. In the adjoining Bishop's Palace the episcopal robing room, justly called the Chambre Dorée, has a coffered ceiling and walls lined with Cordoba leather, both lavishly gilded.

LOUVIERS
EURE   Pop 19,400

Once a centre for clothmaking, an industry established in the 12C, Louviers, some 30km S of Rouen, now lives by modern light industry. Its prosperity as a textile town enabled it to build and later to enlarge the church of Notre-Dame. Nave and choir, both plain and sober, date from the 13C; the NW tower, which was never finished, was begun early in the 15C. The end of that century produced the glorious Flamboyant decoration of the S side, whose masterpiece is the porch. The interior is rich in works of art, among them a 14C Pietà and two Nottingham alabaster panels. The fresco of St Christopher on the baptistry wall is 16C. There is a well arranged survey of the local textile industry, also outstanding ceramics, in the Municipal Museum.

LYONS-LA-FORÊT
EURE   Pop 740

Some 10,000ha of the most magnificent beech forest in France surround the little resort town of Lyons, about 30km SE of Rouen, to which timbered houses as well as an enviable setting give an almost excessive charm. Timbered, too, is the bell tower of the church, 12C though extensively altered in the 15C, which has interesting statues, and the splendid 18C market hall. It was at Lyons that Henry Beauclerc died of the surfeit of lampreys which he had eaten at the Cistercian abbey of **Mortemer**, 4km S. The 12C gatehouse of the abbey and a dovecote of the same period are still intact. Visitors see the park, with its farm, and the lake where, no doubt, the lampreys originated.

During World War II the forest was a centre of the Resistance; its clearings were frequently used for clandestine landings or for parachuting agents into France.

MONT-ST-MICHEL
MANCHE   Pop 80

For the French, the secondary title of the abbey of Mont-St-Michel is "La Merveille"; and whether it is considered as an act of faith or a feat of civil engineering, the building of a great church on the summit of a peak of granite rising 80m out of the sea is a marvel indeed. During the twelve and half centuries since the first oratory was founded here, midway between Normandy and Brittany, it has been monastery, fortress and prison. Today it is both a monument that every year receives more visitors than any other in France except Versailles, and an abbey church where, once more, Benedictine monks say mass daily.

The oratory which Bishop Aubert established on the island in 708 (see *Avranches*) was succeeded by a Carolingian church, Notre-Dame-Sous-Terre, which later served as one of the crypts which were built against the steep flanks of the rock to provide foundations for the Romanesque church raised on its narrow summit. This was completed before the end of the 12C, despite an early collapse of its N side, only to be largely destroyed by fire in 1203. The Gothic abbey, its walls rising like a cliff, seeming to grow out of the rock rather than to be superimposed on it, was built within twenty-five years, and for the next three centuries was to be both fortress and religious community, as testified by the ramparts defending the small town at the base of the rock. The Mount was never taken; it withstood, among other attacks, three assaults by the English.

After the Revolution – the community, like others in France, had already dwindled almost to extinction – the abbey became a prison. There were weaving sheds in the monastic buildings and, in the church, which was divided into two storeys,

the prisoners made straw hats. Restoration began after the abbey was declared a national monument in 1874.

Originally the nave of the abbey church was twice its present length of 70m: the unfortunate classical facade was built when it was shortened after 1780. The terrace which has replaced the destroyed W end affords unforgettable views of the Breton coast as far as Mont Dol, and the exquisite E end is compensation for almost anything. The celebrated Escalier de Dentelle, with its open balustrade, leads up one of the buttresses to the base of the spire from whose summit the figure of St Michael brandishes his sword. Inside, the lack of ornament in the Flamboyant choir and the relative lightness of the Romanesque nave gives the church an unexpected unity. On the same level are two other wonders, the perfectly proportioned early 13C refectory, lit by rows of tall lancet windows, and the cloister, built between 1225 and 1228, poised between sky and sea, with rich carving above its arches and slender columns set staggered in a double arcade. There are two great Gothic halls in the middle storey, the Salle des Hôtes, the chief guest chamber of the abbey, where St Louis was received, and the Salle de Chevaliers, which was the monks' scriptorium.

The Mount is approached by a causeway and, owing to the silting up of the bay, rises from sand flats as often as from the waves; but the spectacle at the equinoxes, when the rise and fall is about 14m, is impressive.

During July and Aug. there is a series of concerts: Les Heures Musicales du Mont-St-Michel. At Michaelmas each year there is a festival in which, in true medieval tradition, faith and folklore mingle.

Mont St-Michel

MORTAIN
MANCHE Pop 3000

When Mortain, roughly halfway between Dom-front and Mont-St-Michel, was three parts des-troyed during the German counterattack of Aug. 1944, the superb collegiate church of Saint-Évroult escaped. Like most of the town, it is built of granite, in the pure, early style of Norman-Gothic; both exterior and interior are faultless. The church's treasure is the chrismale, a small coffret of gilded copper, used either as a reliquary or a portable pyx, which is 7C work, possibly Anglo-Irish.

The town, set above the narrow gorge of the Cance, with its two picturesque waterfalls, the **Petite** and the **Grande Cascade**, is a good centre for those with a taste for river and forest scenery. The **Abbaye Blanche**, a Cistercian foundation, has a beautiful 13C church and parts of a 12C cloister.

Further W, at **St-Laurent-sur-Mer**, the US military cemetery, with close on 10,000 graves, bears witness to the heavy losses suffered by American units of the 5th Corps of the 1st Division of the First Army, who landed at Omaha Beach. Offshore currents swept the landing craft beyond their calculated disembarkment point and pebble ridges proved impassable by tanks. The sheer rock face of the Pointe du Hoc seemed equally impreg-nable, but men of the 2nd Rangers Battalion scaled them and silenced the German batteries. Mulberry A, built here, was destroyed by a storm on 19 June. The battlefield has been left unchanged, its craters and shattered defences a more telling memorial even than the Monument du Débarque-ment at Les Moulins. Utah Beach, NE of Caren-tan, was the scene of the less tragic American landing, when units of the 7th Corps of the 4th American Division were able to liaise with units of the 82nd and 101st Airborne Divisions dropped at **Ste-Mère-Église**. Within three weeks they had liberated the Cotentin peninsula. Ste-Mère Église has a museum of the landings.

NEZ DE JOBOURG
MANCHE

Normandy ends in this rugged headland 128m above the savage seas off the NW tip of the Cotentin peninsula. Near the lonely village of Jobourg, with its 12C church, with saddle-back tower, is one of France's atomic centres, producing chiefly plutonium. There is continuing anxiety, both in Normandy and in the Channel Islands, over the amount of water, its radioactivity reduced but not eliminated, which the centre discharges into the **Raz Blanchard**, 5km from the coast.

NORMANDY LANDING BEACHES
CALVADOS

From **Riva-Bella** at the mouth of the Orne to **Colleville-sur-Mer**, some 15km E of the Pointe du Hoc, the coast of Normandy is almost a single beach, with the miles of sands and the small, simple resorts which make for ideal family holi-days. Since 1944 names like that of **Courseulles**, which is renowned for its oysters, **Langrune-sur-Mer**, whose air is healthily iodized by the carpets of seaweed uncovered at low tide, and **Bernières-sur-Mer**, with its 13C church spire, 67m high, have taken on a new resonance. This coastal strip was the scene of the Allied landings which even-tually brought about the end of World War II.

The launching of over 4000 craft on 6 June 1944 was the culmination of more than a year's pre-paration, which had included the construction of two artificial ports known as Mulberry Harbours. Of the five landing areas the two westernmost, **Utah**, in the Cotentin peninsula, and **Omaha**, E of the Pointe du Hoc, were assigned to the Ameri-cans; **Gold**, **Juno** and **Sword** beaches, farther E, to British, French and Canadian units. During the night of 5–6 June, units of the 6th Airborne Division captured the bridge over the Orne and the Caen Canal, since known as **Pegasus Bridge**, and held the line which they consolidated until 17 Aug., at a cost which is recorded in the British military cemetery near **Barneville**, with 2175 graves. Sword Beach was sheltered by the sinking of twelve blockships. Franco-British commandos came ashore at Colleville-Plage, henceforward to be known as **Colleville-Montgomery**, in honour of General Montgomery, **Lion-sur-Mer** and **St-Aubin**. Juno Beach was the target of the Canadians

Omaha beach

of the 3rd Division, who landed at Bernières and were the first troops to enter Caen on 9 July. At Courseulles, whose little port was used before Mulberry Harbour B became operational, twelve days after the first landings, a granite monument commemorates the return to French soil, on 14 June, of General de Gaulle. The most vivid impres-sion of the landings is conveyed at **Arromanches**, keypoint of Gold Beach, which was taken by British troops of the 50th Division. Construction of the two Mulberry Harbours, for which 146 cais-sons, 33 pontoons and 16km of floating bridges were towed across the Channel, began on D-Day plus one. An admirable museum, with films, describes the operation. The remains of Mulberry B can still be seen offshore.

Remains of Mulberry Harbour, Arromanches

OUISTREHAM
CALVADOS   Pop 6300

Once the port of Caen, which is now approached by the Orne canal, Ouistreham has developed into an international yachting centre, with a 15ha harbour. The 12C church of St-Samson, massive as a fortress, with a splendid W front, was built for the nuns of La Trinité, Caen, and has some resemblance to the abbey church.

PONT-AUDEMER
EURE   Pop 10,200

Timbered houses leaning over the many branches of the river give character to this small town 13km above the mouth of the Risle, long famous for its tanneries. The great church of St-Ouen, with an 11–12C choir and a 15C nave, is a monument to ambitions foiled by inadequate means. It was designed by Rolland Le Roux, architect of the porch of Rouen cathedral: the exquisitely luxuriant decoration reaches its peak in the triforium. At that point funds ran out; the clerestory is modest in the extreme, the roof could not be vaulted and the facade was never completed. There are some Renaissance windows and also some by the modern master, Rex Ingrand.

ROUEN
SEINE-MARITIME   Pop 105,000

Capital of the Celtic Veliocassi, named Rotomagus under the Romans, capital of the duchy of Normandy under Rollo, Rouen has risen from the embers of wartime devastation as a prosperous and enterprising regional capital. It is also a major port, with 18km of docks on the Seine to continue its ancient trading vocation. Also it has so triumphantly repaired the damage to its architectural treasures that it still has the right to the title of "the museum city."

The cathedral of Notre-Dame is a handbook of 12–16C Gothic architecture and also a rich visual experience. The first Christian church here was built by the bishop, St Mellon, at the beginning of the 4C. The present building was begun in the 12C, rebuilt in the 13C after a disastrous fire, embellished and in part rebuilt again during the 14–15C, and finally salvaged after World War II by heroic efforts of rescue and reconstruction. The Tour St-Romain, on the N side, is early 12C, its upper storey 15C. It is restrained by contrast with the Butter Tower on the S, so called because its cost was partly met with money paid by the not over-austere faithful for permission to eat butter during Lent. The facade between them is a delicate marvel of gables, galleries, turrets and pinnacles. Both N and S sides have doorways remarkable for their 13–14C carving. The cast-iron spire topping the 15C lantern tower was added in the 19C: it is

Rouen

Notre-Dame, Rouen

the tallest but hardly the most distinguished in France. By contrast with the riot of ornament on the exterior, the interior of the cathedral is sober. There are wonderful 13–14C windows in the Lady Chapel and ambulatory, two of which are by Clément, glass painter of Chartres. The Lady Chapel has two splendid 16C tombs, on the S side that of Louis XIII's minister, Cardinal Archbishop Georges I d'Amboise and his nephew, Georges II, on the N that of the Seneschal Louis de Brézé, husband of Diane de Poitiers, who was later to console herself with Henri II. The tombs of the first dukes of Normandy, including Richard Lionheart, are in the ambulatory. Apart from that of Rollo, all the effigies are 13C.

St-Ouen, the oldest of the great abbeys of pre-Viking Normandy – it was a Merovingian foundation – might be a second cathedral; it is, indeed, slightly larger than Notre-Dame. The present church, built over two centuries from 1315, has an interior memorable for the purity of its proportions. The exterior provides a contrast in the exotic carving of the Portail des Marmousets, leading into the S transept, and the fragile-seeming flying buttresses of the apse.

Rouen's third Gothic masterpiece is the Flamboyant church of St-Maclou, built between 1437 and 1520, precious and elaborate as a reliquary with its delicate gables and pinnacles and arcades. Its cloister, near by, whose low buildings set round a court are now used by the École des Beaux Arts, was a medieval charnel.

Newest of Rouen's many churches – it was completed in 1979 – is that built in the Old Market Place which was the scene of Joan of Arc's martyrdom on 30 May 1431. After her capture by the Burgundians at Compiègne, she was brought to Rouen and imprisoned in the 13C castle of which only the donjon remains. The church is built like an inverted ship's hull; its 16C windows come from the church of St Vincent, which was destroyed in 1944. The medieval ground level of the market has been restored and the historic remains uncovered include the site of the stake at which Joan was burned. The large cross which now marks it is a national memorial.

More than 700 of Rouen's patrimony of timbered houses, dating from the 15C to the late 18C, have been restored. Some have the overhanging upper storeys forbidden after 1520, a few have carved timbers. There is a concentration of them in the Rue de Gros-Horloge, now a lively pedestrian precinct. The clock itself, gilded and painted, was originally placed in the adjoining belfry tower built in 1489. In 1527 it was moved to a Renaissance clock house which bridges the street. In the clock tower are the two 13C bells which rang for the peasant rising called La Harelle in 1382. One of them still rings curfew at nine each evening. The city's most remarkable secular building is the Palais de Justice, built for the parliament of Normandy between 1508 and 1526. The elaborate fretted carving of its facade is seen at its best when floodlit. The Hôtel de Bourgthéroulde, a sumptuous Gothic-Renaissance house, now used as a bank, has carvings showing the meeting of Henry VIII and François I at the Field of the Cloth of Gold.

Museums are many and important. The Musée des Beaux Arts is a major collection of painting, particularly strong in 17C and 20C work, and has remarkable ceramics. The Musée de Secq-des-Tournelles, set in the old church of St-Laurent, is devoted to every kind of metal craft; exhibits range from the 3C to the 19C and the presentation is exceptional. The Musée des Antiquités ranges from the mosaic of *Apollo in Pursuit of Daphne* from Lillebonne through Nottingham alabasters to 17C furniture and silver. The Musée Corneille is in the house where the dramatist, Pierre Corneille (1606–84) was born and lived for 56 years. The Musée Flaubert et d'Histoire de la Médecine is in the building of the Hôtel-Dieu, where the novelist, Gustave Flaubert (1821–80), whose father was a surgeon at the hospital, was born. Some 5km out of the town, at **Croisset**, there are other Flaubert relics in the summer pavilion which is now all that remains of the riverside house where the author wrote *Madame Bovary* and *Salaambô*. The 17C house where Corneille spent his summers stands intact at **Le Petit Couronne**, 14km SW of the town centre. Rouen was also the birthplace of the painter Théodore Géricault (1791–1824).

RY
SEINE-MARITIME   Pop 550

This village, 20km NE of Rouen, is generally held to have been the model for the "Yonville-l'Abbaye" where Flaubert set his *Madame Bovary*. A so-called Museum of Automata, with 300 figures representing characters in the novel, supported, more seriously, with documents relating to the people and plans mentioned, has been set up in a converted 18C building. The 12C church of St-Sulpice has a Renaissance porch of carved wood which is considered to be the finest in Normandy.

ST-LÔ
MANCHE Pop 25,000

The mutilated towers which are all that remain of
the twin spires of the cathedral of St-Lô, on its rock
above the Vire, at the strategic centre of the
Cotentin peninsula, stand as a memorial to the
devastation which the town suffered during the
battle of Normandy in July 1944. When it
ended with the American breakthrough, 80 per
cent of St-Lô was in ruins. The new town within
the ramparts, which have been successfully restored and laid out with gardens, has rather more
ferroconcrete than some might wish, but it is
planned for space and order. Notre-Dame, a 14–
15C church, escaped total destruction and has been
rebuilt, apart from the W front and the N spire.
The rare Gothic exterior pulpit survived 1944
without damage. The windows include one in the S
aisle which is said to have been the gift of Louis XI
and a modern one by Max Ingrand in the chapel of
St Thomas of Canterbury.

The National Stud, apart from the period mid-
Feb. to mid-July, has up to 200 stallions on view.
During the season there are galas and driving
displays on Sats.

ST-SAUVEUR-LE-VICOMTE
MANCHE Pop 2300

The novelist and critic Barbey d'Aurevilly (see
Valognes) was born and died at St-Sauveur, some
25km SE of Cherbourg. There is a museum
devoted to him in the postern of the château whose
14C keep survived the bombing of 1944. The
church, whose oldest parts are 13C, has a number
of interesting statues, notably a 15C St Jacques de
Compostelle and an Ecce Homo of 1532.

ST-VAAST-LA-HOUGUE
MANCHE Pop 2400

Vauban created the great defences of the agreeable
small resort and fishing port of St-Vaast (pronounced St Va') on the E coast of the Cotentin
peninsula, but only after the destruction, in 1692,
of the French fleet which was to have taken part in
a projected landing on the English coast to restore
the exiled James II to the throne. The oyster beds
of the bay are famous.

ST-VALÉRY-EN-CAUX
SEINE-MARITIME Pop 5800

The monument of Balmoral granite on the Falaise
d'Amont, to the E of the harbour of this small port
and seaside resort on the Alabaster Coast, commemorates those who fell during the desperate rearguard action of the 51st (Highland) Division during the Allied retreat to Dunkirk in 1940. On the
W cliff, the Falaise d'Aval is a memorial to their
comrades of the French 2nd Cavalry Division. The
Renaissance Maison Henri-IV, where the king is
said to have lodged, survived the bombing which
destroyed much of the rest of the town. The
successes of the rebuilding include the striking
small church of Notre-Dame-du-Bon-Port.

ST-WANDRILLE
SEINE-MARITIME Pop 1200

The earliest of the great abbeys to be founded in
the Seine valley, St Wandrille, 3km E of Caudebec, is once more a functioning religious community. When it was established in 649 by Count
Wandrille, a member of King Dagobert's court, it
was known as the abbey of Fontenelle. Only on its
rebuilding in 960, after it had been destroyed by
the Vikings, did it take Wandrille's name. The
monks were dispersed at the Revolution but the
buildings were not destroyed, though at one period
they were used as a spinning mill. Only the 13C
abbey church fell into ruin. The 14C cloisters have
now been restored to their original use, as has the
remarkable 12C refectory, with its lovely blind
arcading. To replace the abbey church, the monks
took down a 13C tithe barn at Canteloup, some
50km distant, and reassembled it here. Within the
abbey grounds is the tiny chapel of St-Saturnin,
whose foundations are probably Merovingian,
though the chapel itself is 10C.

Before the return of the monks in 1931, Maurice
Maeterlinck (1862–1949), who wrote *The Bluebird*,
lived here.

Abbaye de St-Wandrille

SÉES
ORNE Pop 5200

The calm of this little town some 20km NE of
Alençon, a species of ecclesiastical lagoon, studded
with convents and seminaries, is as attractive as its
small but exquisite Norman-Gothic cathedral of
Notre-Dame. There is 13–14C glass in the windows of the choir and the ambulatory chapels, and
a surpassing treasure in the late 13C figure of
Notre-Dame-de-Sées. The delicately graceful choir
has at its SE end a pillar whose capital is composed
of some thirty human heads, most of them comic.

About 7km W of Sées, the three pavilions of the
Château d'O, respectively late Gothic, early
Renaissance and 18C, are reflected in a wide moat.
The last of the family of O to occupy it was
François, finance minister successively to Henri III
and Henri IV, despite which he died bankrupt.

TANCARVILLE, PONT DE
SEINE-MARITIME Pop 1200

Both industry and tourism have gained from the opening of this bridge over the Seine estuary in 1959, but the visitor is likely to be impressed above all by its beauty. It is one of the biggest suspension bridges in Europe, with an overall length of 1400m, the taut arc of its single span, 48m above high water, measuring 608m. The Eagle Tower above the bridge is all that remains of a 10C castle owned by the Tancarville family.

Pont de Tancarville

TRÉPORT, LE
SEINE-MARITIME Pop 6600

Two thousand years ago the outport of the Roman city of Augusta, modern Le Tréport, at least during the season, is almost Paris-on-sea, so large are the crowds flocking from the capital, 170km away, to its pebble ridges and broad sands. The white cliffs behind mark the beginning of the Alabaster Coast, which extends as far as Le Havre. The port is still active, partly with commercial cargoes, partly with coastal fishing. In the upper town the 16C church of St-Jacques, diamond-patterned in flint and sandstone, has elegant pendant bosses in the nave.

Le Tréport

TROUVILLE
CALVADOS Pop 6000

Trouville, across the estuary from Deauville (q.v.), was the favoured resort of Napoleon III; and it was from here, in 1870, that the Empress Eugénie escaped from France in the yacht of an English friend, Sir John Burgoyne. Flaubert stayed at Trouville both as a schoolboy with his parents and as an adult, and met here Mme Schlesinger, the love of his life. The Musée Montebello has a good collection of pictures and engravings by artists associated with the area. Somewhat less fashionable than Deauville, its fine sands and good bathing make it a popular family seaside resort, and it is still a fishing port. A concession to the modern age is the Olympic-size swimming pool.

Trouville

VALOGNES
MANCHE Pop 7000

The town, in the heart of the dairying area of the Cotentin, has seen much rebuilding since World War II, but a number of its fine *hôtels particuliers* have survived to recall its 18C past as a centre of provincial fashion, boasting one hundred noble families. The best of them are the Hôtel Beaumont, built just after the mid-18C, and the Hôtel de Grandval-Coligny, which was for some years the home of Barbey d'Aurevilly (1808–89), the novelist of the Cotentin, who used it as the setting for one of his books. The regional cider museum in the town illustrates the process of its manufacture since the days when the fruit was crushed in primitive fashion between giant half-moons of stone.

VERNEUIL-SUR-AVRE
EURE   Pop 6900

Henry Beauclerc built Verneuil to form, with Tillières and Nonancourt, a defence line between France and Normandy. Its broad market place is dominated by the splendid Flamboyant tower of the church of La Madeleine, its three storeys peopled by statues and crowned by a double diadem of a lantern. It was built between 1470 and 1570 and can rank beside the Butter Tower of Rouen cathedral. The church has good 15–16C glass and statues which include the memorable Vierge à la Pomme, of the 15C or very early 16C. The church of Notre-Dame, 12C but much defaced by later building, is a veritable museum of sculpture, both wood and stone, of which the most outstanding piece is the 12C or 13C Virgin of the Calvary. The massive Tour Grise, of 1120, was the donjon of Beauclerc's castle. There are many timbered houses in the town.

VERNON
EURE   Pop 23,500

Rollo the Dane founded Vernon, in the Seine valley, and the piles of the old bridge still visible above the surface of the river (here studded with wooded islets) date from the 12C. The donjon with pepperpot towers was part of the bridge's defences. Of the castle which Henry Beauclerc built in 1123, all that remains is the much-restored Tour des Archives. The church of Notre-Dame, whose building extended from the 11–17C, has a lovely rose window in its graceful Flamboyant facade. A number of good timbered houses survived World War II.

The château of **Bizy**, 2km SW, has been reconstructed since it was built in the 18C for the grandson of Fouquet, Louis XIV's finance minister, but it is set in a delightful park, which merges into the forest, and has good 18C furniture.

At **Giverny**, a few kilometres upstream, where Claude Monet lived and painted from 1881 until his death in 1926, the water garden which was his model for the great series of the *Nymphéas* in the Orangerie, Paris, has been recreated.

VILLEDIEU-LES-POÊLES
MANCHE   Pop 5000

Copper kitchen utensils have been made at Villedieu, at the crossing of the N175 and the D924, since the 17C: bell-founding, which is also practised here, has a longer history. In our own day the foundry has sent bells to cathedrals and churches as distant as Korea and the USA. The Musée de la Poeslerie traces the history of the craft. There are many old houses, some with inner courts, in the town, which is largely built of granite, like the church of Notre Dame. This is mostly Flamboyant, but still has portions of the original church of the Knights of Malta, one of whose earliest Commanderies was founded here in the 13C. Every four years, on the second or third Sun. after Whitsun, there is a ceremonial commemoration of the founding. The next is due in 1987.

VILLEQUIER
SEINE-MARITIME   Pop 770

About 5km down the Seine from Caudebec-en-Caux, Villequier was the scene of the boating accident in 1843 in which Victor Hugo's nineteen-year-old daughter and her young husband, Charles Vacquerie, were drowned. They were victims of the tidal bore on the Seine, the *mascaret*, which has almost disappeared since the damming of the river. The Vacquerie family house is now a Hugo museum; the two young people are buried in the churchyard.

VIMOUTIERS
ORNE   Pop 5100

Since 1928 a statue of Marie Harel, the farmer's wife who, at the end of the 18C, first made Camembert cheese, has stood near the church of this small town some 16km S of Lisieux, which markets it. The bombing of 1944 decapitated the statue, since when another Marie Harel, soubrette rather than housewife, has stood beside her, the gift of workers in a factory which makes Camembert in Ohio. The farmhouse, Beaumoncel, where she worked her miracle, is near the village of **Camembert**, 5km SW of Vimoutiers.

VIRE
CALVADOS   Pop 14,000

This ancient town, former capital of the Bocage, is situated on a hill overlooking woods and river valleys. It was almost destroyed by Allied bombing in World War II but many of its historic buildings have been restored, including the Gothic church of Notre-Dame. The 15C clocktower and its 13C gateway survived.

A 14C clothworker named Olivier Basselin was renowned for his bawdy tavern songs which were later collected under the title of Les Vaux de Vire, by which name the valley of the river Vire is known. The corruption of this name later gave rise to the word 'vaudeville'.

YVETOT
SEINE-MARITIME   Pop 10,900

In the Pays de Caux, 12km NE of Caudebec, whose centre has been almost wholly rebuilt after the devastation of 1940, Yvetot is known for its round church of concrete and glass, built in 1951–56 to the design of Yves Marchand. All that relieves the exterior of the domed drum is a huge figure of St Peter the Fisherman in high relief over the porch and a 30m bell tower beside it. The interior is an iridescent dazzle of colour from the twenty-one windows by the contemporary master, Max Ingrand. It resolves itself into a central Crucifixion, surrounded by Our Lady and the Apostles, the colour deepening through reds and purples to the intense crimson and gold and yellow of the Crucifixion. Behind the Lady Altar greens and pale shades of violet are used with the deepest blue in a window depicting scenes from the life of Our Lady. But no detail surpasses the jewelled radiance that is the visitor's first impression.

PICARDY AND NORD

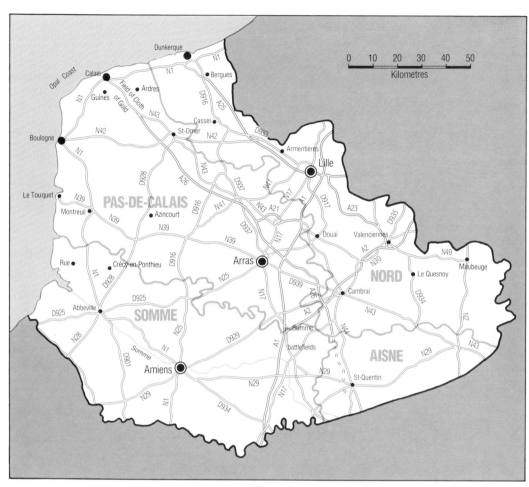

Though just across the Channel, Picardy, Artois, and Flanders are more often traversed than visited by travellers, and remain relatively undiscovered. Flat and melancholy in places, with some grim industrial landscapes and many reminders of a battle-scarred history, this is nonetheless one of the most peaceful and rural regions of France.

Country lanes weave through gently rolling farmland, quiet villages, and green wooded valleys. The coast, handsome with white cliffs and broad sandy beaches, is scarcely developed. In the little inland towns the lavishly ornate Flemish art and architecture, seen especially in grand town halls with their tall belfries, is matched by extravaganza of Gothic.

This airy, open countryside has seen more than its share of war and conflict. The worst onslaughts came in this century, when the area north of Amiens was devastated during World War I: beautiful old towns were half-destroyed, whole villages taken off the map, and hundreds of thousands of soldiers and citizens died to prevent the German occupation of northern France. Fewer died, though still more damage was done, hardly more than twenty years later in World War II, for the same reason – and once again it was the same area which suffered most.

Now tranquil, the villages calm and rustic, the rebuilt towns pleasantly bustling, it might seem impossible that such events had ever happened. Only the well-cared-for military cemeteries and memorials everywhere serve as a constant reminder.

More Flemish than French in their history, this northern people developed distinctive customs and traditions. Many towns have their annual *Fêtes des Géants*, dating from the 16C, in which huge wickerwork models of giants, attired in medieval costume, are brought out of their year-long seclusion (usually inside the town hall) to be wheeled through the streets at the head of lively processions. Each giant is invidividually named, and is often thought to commemorate some local hero.

Cuisine is characteristically hearty and substantial, rich and meaty. Specialities include sausages and black puddings, tripe, pâtés, smoked fish and pungent cheeses. Typical dishes, seen on many a restaurant menu, might be *potje*, a mixed pâté of veal, rabbit, and chicken, followed by *hochepot*, a heavy stew of veal, lamb, pork, and vegetables. French vegetables – called *hortillons* – are important here. From Amiens comes the popular *ficelle picard*, a sort of crêpe with ham inside and a mushroomy cheese sauce on top.

ABBEVILLE
SOMME Pop 26,000

On the banks of the Somme, Abbeville is today a bustling industrial town (textiles, sugar beet, metals) with a pleasant atmosphere. Totally destroyed by German bombing in May 1940, the town was completely rebuilt on its original street plan.

Parts of the 15C Gothic Flamboyant church of St-Vulfran, though in the centre, did survive the bombing, but reconstruction work on the rest of the building has kept most of it swathed in tarpaulins for years. The elaborate and ornate facade and the heavily carved doors are impressive, but the choir, later than the rest and on a smaller scale, gives the church an oddly ill-proportioned look. On the SE edge of town, the elegant 18C Bagatelle, a folly in the form of a little château in beautiful gardens, built between 1752 and 1790, has a pastel-coloured exterior and contains some good wood-panelling. The Musée Boucher-de-Perthes has an interesting local archaeology section and a considerable art collection.

At picturesque **St-Valéry**, 20km NW, the river Somme reaches the sea in a huge estuary. The town still has its old ramparts, from which there are excellent views, and to the E and W along the estuary are the sand dunes called the **Mollières**.

AMIENS
SOMME Pop 136,000

Capital of Picardy, mercilessly battered in both world wars, Amiens survives as a thriving modern textile-manufacturing town on the river Somme. In the midst of it all rises up the elegant and graceful 13C cathedral of Notre-Dame, largest (and widely regarded as the finest) cathedral in France, among the most important examples of Gothic art, and one of the earliest to move towards the Flamboyant style. Though struck by nine shells, it escaped from World War I virtually intact. The two 15C towers, of unequal height and technically unfinished, and the 16C spire, blend perfectly with the rest. Statuary crowds the ornate entrance porch and its tympanum. No less remarkable is the high, bright interior (42m) with superb stained glass windows. The nave is the longest in France (145m). Detailed painted reliefs show scenes in the life of St Firmin, who brought Christianity to Amiens in AD301.

Inside the cathedral are memorials to the men who died in this region during World War I. The battlefields were only a few miles outside town (see *Somme Battlefields*).

Unrestored older parts of Amiens, such as the Quartier St-Leu, look much as they must have done in the Middle Ages, but these streets, though picturesque, tend to be rather squalid.

19C English essayist John Ruskin was deeply impressed with this city, and wrote a guide to its cathedral. Writer Jules Verne lived most of his life here, becoming an influential member of the town council. A small regional museum, with an art collection and an unusual assembly of local historic documents, is next to the cathedral in a 17C mansion, Hôtel de Berny. The much larger and grander Musée de Picardie has a number of rooms devoted variously to archaeology, sculpture, and some large collections of painting, especially local works.

In Pl. Léon Gontier, the Maison de la Culture, an unusual modern complex (1966) in front of a sports centre, houses theatres, cinema, exhibition rooms, and (own entrance) tourist office.

Just beyond the town boundary lies an extensive and fascinating area of waterways and tiny market gardens known as *les hortillonages*. Most of these colourful patches of cultivation, on which the owners used to live in shacks, are accessible only on the network of canals, along which the farmers travel in punts. Boat tours of the *hortillonages* leave daily from Amiens, or you can glimpse them by walking the riverside path on the N bank of the Somme.

ARMENTIÈRES
NORD Pop 26,000

Now an unpretentious industrial town on the Belgian border, Armentières has gone into music-hall history as the home of a *mademoiselle* who took the fancy of British soldiers during World War I, when it was just two miles from the front. There is still a well-cared-for British cemetery and an evocative monument to the French Resistance.

ARRAS
PAS-DE-CALAIS Pop 45,400

Capital of Artois, within the battlefields area of both world wars, and scene of 17C battles between French and Spanish forces, Arras also suffered much during the Revolution.

Extremist Revolutionary leader Maximilien de Robespierre was born here (1758), and in the Pl. du Théâtre the guillotine was erected for mass executions during the Terror which he masterminded. Sober memorials recall the more recent events: the Arras Memorial to the Missing, numbering 36,000 men, and the Mur des Fusillées, where 200 Resistance members were lined up and shot.

The cathedral, once completely destroyed, has been rebuilt. The Palais St-Vaast, former Benedictine abbey and now a Fine Arts museum, with sculpture, porcelains, and a 15C tapestry of the type called 'Arras' which made the town famous in the Middle Ages, has twice risen from its ruins – in the 18C and again in the 20C.

Two magnificent squares, Grande Place and Petit Place or Place des Héros, surrounded by tall stone-and-brick gabled 17C mansions, and popular shops and cafés along arcaded sidewalks, give the town much character. Both squares fill with stalls for the lively Wed. and Sat. morning markets. Hidden beneath the squares is an amazing network of vaulted tunnels and rooms called Les Boves or Les Souterrains (guided tours daily). This labyrinth, 1000 years old in parts, has often served as a refuge for the people of Arras. The entrance to the tunnels is inside the town hall, Pl. des Héros, which was restored to its 16C appearance after World War II.

AZINCOURT
PAS-DE-CALAIS

The tiny village of Azincourt – or Agincourt – 16km NE of Hesdin, was the scene of the historic battle on St Crispin's Day (25 Oct. 1415), when King Henry V's army of 6000 men, including many skilled archers equipped with the new long-bow, ambushed a French force of many times their number. It took hardly three hours to arrive at a decisive English victory, with 10,000 French soldiers lying dead on the field.

BERGUES
NORD Pop 4800

Bergues, 9km S of Dunkirk, is a lovely little town, much restored after World War II damage, with attractive reconstructed buildings in the Flemish style, including the Belfry and the Hôtel de Ville. The museum building (good paintings) is a 17C survival. The town is still enclosed by medieval ramparts and defensive waterways, enlarged by 17C military architect Vauban.

BOULOGNE
PAS-DE-CALAIS Pop 48,400

The historic old seaport of Boulogne-sur-Mer has been largely rebuilt since heavy World War II damage, in a functional modern style. Today it is a sizeable industrial centre, and the biggest fishing port in France: trawlers leave here for deep-sea fishing of herring, mackerel, cod, etc. There is a major cold-storage centre. After Calais (q.v.), Boulogne is also the leading French port for car and passenger traffic with Britain.

Local farmers put up their market stalls in the Pl. Dalton each Wed. and Sat. Above the modern town, the old town (Ville Haute) stands high on a hill within its fine ramparts, which largely escaped the 1940–45 destruction. Here medieval gateways lead into cobbled streets; at one corner is a 13C moated castle, and next to it the black dome of the basilica of Notre-Dame, dominating the town. This big church has a fine painted cupola; in the crypt, corridors and a room with painted walls are the sole remains of an older Romanesque church. There are even some remnants of a Roman temple. Boulogne was a major Roman harbour: here Caesar in 54BC launched his successful invasion of Britain. Napoleon had similar plans, and his army waited here three years before he changed his

Boulogne-sur-Mer

mind. He stayed several times in the 18C Hôtel Desadrouins within the ramparts. Also worth a visit are the museum (Greek vases), the sailors' calvary and the **Colonne de la Grande Armée** on a hill 3km NE. There are good views from the walkway along the top of the ramparts.

The nearby stylish modern resort of **Hardelot**, 15km S, has a good beach fringed by pines and sand dunes. The forest of **Desvres** has marked footpaths and picnic tables.

CALAIS
PAS-DE-CALAIS Pop 77,000

Most popular port of arrival for British visitors to France, and the largest of French ports in terms of passengers, Calais belonged to the English crown

Calais

for over 200 years; when it was won back by France in 1558, Mary Tudor was so distressed that she declared: 'When I am dead and opened you shall find "Calais" lying in my heart.' That historic Calais was destroyed once and for all (ironically, by British bombers) during World War II, and the town today is entirely modern.

One of the rare relics of the past is the plain and uninspiring Tour du Guet, a 13C watchtower, in Pl. d'Armes. A more distinctive landmark, visible from miles around, is the ornate Flemish-style town hall standing by the bridge which links Calais-Nord (the original Calais) and Calais-Sud (the more commercial post-war area). In front of the town hall, Rodin's 'Burghers of Calais' depicts the six prominent citizens, starved and ragged after a long siege by the English (1347), offering to sacrifice their own lives if Edward III would, in exchange, spare the rest of the town's population. He accepted their offer, but was then persuaded by Queen Philippine to spare the six burghers as well.

The city museum, by Richelieu Park, has a good art collection, including more works by Rodin. In Parc St-Pierre, across the bridge, an interesting war museum preserves documents, posters, and other moving reminders of the Nazi occupation.

CAMBRAI
NORD Pop 36,600

This once-beautiful fortified town was badly damaged both in 1918 and 1944. Now rebuilt, industrialized, and lacking much of architectural interest (little remains even of the ramparts), Cambrai still has some fine town squares, and its church of St-Géry contains a Renaissance rood screen and an impressive *Entombment* by Rubens.

HOBBS Rosemary Jean (née Davies) on 2nd July in hospital, aged 78. Widow of Anthony, mother of Michael, Angela and the late Diana, grandmother of Anna, Jack, Elliot and Molly. Service at St Margaret's Church, Ockley on Thursday 19th July at 12.30pm. Family flowers only. Donations to The Children's Society, Edward Rudolf House, Margery Street, London WC1X 0JL.

HORTON See Dunn.

HUNTER Philip Brown 28th June 2007 in his 99th year. Husband of the late Joyce Mary Hunter and father of Pippa, Charles, James and Kate. Funeral service and interment at St. Mary's Parish Church Ysceifiog, nr Holywell on Tuesday 17th July at 11.30am. Family flowers only but donations, if desired, to Parkinson's Disease Society. Enquiries 01352 741265

JAMES David Douglas. FRICS. Died quietly on 3rd July with his wife Audrey and daughter Jennifer and the support of his two granddaughters Katie and Anna. All enquiries to William Emery & Sons Funeral Directors. Tel 01785 251205.

JONES Catherine, peacefully on 6th July 2007. Wife of the late Herbert Alan Jones and greatly loved mother of Charles and Celia. Funeral service at Putney Vale Crematorium on Monday 16th July at 11am. Family flowers only. Donations, if wished, to Trinity Hospice. All enquiries to H J Bent, Funeral Directors Telephone 0208 969 1170.

KER Elizabeth peacefully with her family around her on 6th July aged 88 in Chelsea and Westminster Hospital after a long and brave struggle, widow of Hugh Ker and previously of George Morgan, first Baron Trefgarne, adored mother of David, Trevor, Mary and Gwion, much loved grandmother, great-grandmother and mother-in-law. Funeral at St Saviour Church, Valley End, near Chobham (GU24 8TB) on Tuesday 24th July at 11.30 a.m. Family flowers only, donations, if desired, to Cancer Research UK or Friends of Chelsea and Westminster Hospital. Enquiries to Chelsea Funeral Directors

PINCHES John Harvey, M.C. died peacefully at home 2nd July aged 91. Beloved husband of Rosemary, father of Joanna and Sarah and grandfather of Leonora and Harriet. Private cremation. Service of Thanksgiving at Holy Cross Church, Ramsbury, Monday 23rd July at 3pm.

PRINCE-SMITH William Richard, aged 78, fourth baronet dearly beloved husband of Ann and father of Elizabeth (Lilla) and grandfather of Katie, died peacefully at his home on 28th June, in Rancho Mirage, Palm Springs, California, after a long period of ill health.

ROWLES Peggy passed away peacefully on 2nd July 2007, aged 86. A much loved wife of Arthur and mother of Mark. Funeral service on Friday 13th July at Kent & Sussex Crematorium, Tunbridge Wells at 10.30 am. Family flowers only. Donations, if desired, to Cancer Research UK or The Hospice in the Weald c/o Francis Chappell & Sons, 27 London Road, Sevenoaks TN13 1AR. Tel: 01732 450203

RUDGARD Barbara Anne (née Keay). Tristan, Charles and Emma's Mum, Annabel and Olivia's Ganny. Died on Saturday 7th July 2007 peacefully at her home Trembach. Her life was jam-packed full of laughter and very special. Anyone who knew Barbara is very welcome to come to her funeral on Friday 13th July at 3.30pm at St Mary's Church, Twyford near Winchester. She wanted no flowers, we are collecting donations for a memorial seat. Enquiries and cheques to "Richard Steel & Partners", Alderman House, 12-14 City Road, Winchester, SO23 8SG (01962 862333).

SHORE Margaret Alison known as Alison. Passed away peacefully on 4th July 2007, aged 94 at Oakdene Nursing Home, Three Legged Cross, Dorset. Dearly beloved mother of Janet and Peter, and adored grandmother and great-grandmother. Memorial Service on Wednesday, 18th July at 2.30 pm at the Church of The Holy Ascension, Hyde, Fordingbridge. Family flowers only. Donations in her

Weather Eye Paul Simons

Rain helped Henry V win the battle of Agincourt

The rains this summer have been a thorough misery, but rain has come to the rescue of the English at some decisive moments in history.

Downpours played a vital role in the battle of Agincourt, in October, 1415. Having invaded France, Henry V met a formidable army at Agincourt, a village in the north east. The odds against him seemed hopeless — his troops were exhausted, hungry, suffering from dysentery and hopelessly outnumbered by the enemy. Their plight grew even worse the night before battle, when rain pelted down and, with very little shelter, the English were left soaking wet.

However, the downpour also turned the battlefield into a quagmire. With no cavalry of his own, Henry V was unconcerned with horses trying to move through the thick mud. Instead, he stationed his archers, equipped with longbows, close to woods on either side of the narrow battlefield and launched an attack.

The French retaliated with a cavalry charge but, weighed down with heavy armour, the horses lost their footing in the mud and fell or ran into each other. Under salvos of arrows and with little room to manoeuvre, the cavalry were left in utter disarray and ran into their advancing infantry. The English tore into the French ranks and within a few hours they had won a stunning victory.

CASSEL
NORD   Pop 2400

Hilltop Cassel delightfully preserves its 17C Flemish character, little spoiled either by war or industry. It was here, in the battle of 1793, that the 'Grand Old Duke of York' marched his 10,000 men to the top of the hill but was forced to march them down again.

In Grand' Place, the long and broad main square, some splendid mansions are grouped together. Nearby there are imposing town gates and picturesque back streets, and the church of Notre-Dame, in the distinctive Flemish Gothic style. An 18C windmill, of all things, stands in the public gardens.

CLOTH OF GOLD, FIELD OF

Between the villages of Guînes and Ardres is the celebrated plain where Henry VIII and François I met in 1520 for peace talks. The site was so named because of the lavish efforts that each made to outshine the other in the richness of encampment and entourage. Such rivalry bode ill from the start and the meeting was a failure.

Nearby **Guînes** lies beside an extensive forest, with paths and picnic areas. **Ardres** is a pretty and charming fortified town.

CRÉCY
SOMME   Pop 1500

The village of Crécy, close to the site of the battle of 1346 when Edward III's English army of 20,000 defeated a French army of 60,000, is unremarkable save for the curious brick Lanterne des Morts, erected in 1189 by Eleanor of Aquitaine, wife of Henry II, to commemorate her sons, Richard Lionheart and John Lackland, presumed dead but actually still alive, away on crusade. It was the English attempt to reestablish their weakening control over Ponthieu and Aquitaine that subsequently led to the battle. The village lies at the edge of the tranquil oak and beech forest of Crécy.

Crécy

DOUAI
NORD   Pop 44,500

A historic town on the canalized Scarpe, now heavily industrialized (chemicals, food processing, sheet metals, and in a major colliery region), Douai preserves two of its old city gates, the 14C Porte d'Arras and the 15–17C Porte de Valenciennes, as well as several Flemish buildings. Its lofty Gothic town hall, topped by the Lion of Flanders, has 62 bells which chime the quarter-hours and on which brief recitals are given every Sat. (and Mon. evenings in summer).

The Direction des Houillères du Nord (Northern Coalfields Administration) is located at Douai, its offices being in the Louis XIII-style Hôtel de la Tramerie.

An interesting group of 16–18C buildings of the former Chartreuse includes the Flemish-Renaissance Hôtel d'Abancourt-Montmorency, which houses the museum about which Augustus Hare was so scathing in 1890 ('an unusual amount of rubbish'). Today it has distinguished collections of sculpture, ceramics, religious art of the 15–16C, and numerous good paintings, mainly 16–19C French and Flemish.

Douai's *Fête des Gayants*, on the Sun., Mon. and Tues. following 5 July, is the most spectacular of the Flemish 'Giant Festivals': the 8m-tall Father Gayant, his consort Marie-Canegon, and their three children lead big street processions.

DUNKERQUE
NORD   Pop 73,300

The old fortified seaport of Dunkerque (Dunkirk) was in the 17C a repair of pirates, led by the famous sea captain Jean Bart (his statue stands in the central square that bears his name). Largely destroyed in World War II, the town today is a big industrial centre, with oil refineries, chemical and steel works (many of these are open to visitors). The commercial port is the third largest in France. The city museum has works by Van Dyck, Cranach, Corot, etc.

The long sandy beaches E of the town were the scene of the epic events of May–June 1940, when, in a single week, an armada of little boats from England rescued 350,000 men from the encircling German army.

LILLE
NORD   Pop 157,600

Capital of the Nord-Pas-de-Calais region, Lille is the centre of a huge industrial conurbation of over a million people that also includes Roubaix and Tourcoing. There are several universities and a new Métro system; textiles, metalwork, food-processing and brewing are among the main industries. A workaday town, maybe, but also a very lively one, with an active night life, much culture, and far more of interest to tempt the visitor than might appear at first sight. The ambience is strongly Flemish – you could easily be in a Belgian city such as Ghent – with zigzag house facades, cobbled streets and wood panelling in the cafés.

Around the cental Pl. du Général de Gaulle

The Old Bourse, Lille

stand several important buildings – notably, the Old Bourse, an exquisite example of 17C Flemish baroque, with galleries round a courtyard and a bronze statue of Napoleon made from guns captured at Austerlitz. To the north of the square is the 15th-century Hospice Comtesse, housing a museum of folk art; and the 'new cathedral' of Notre-Dame, begun in 1854 and still incomplete. Graceful Flemish houses line the Rue de la Monnaie, in the old quarter. Further south, the Blvd de la Liberté leads from the Porte de Paris (1682), splendid former gateway to the city, to Vauban's massive 17C citadel, the most impressive of all the great fortresses built in France by that military engineer, and still today a military camp (you can walk round its battlements).

Along the boulevard stands Lille's chief cultural glory, the Musée des Beaux Arts, with one of the best painting collections in France (works by Van Dyck, Rubens, Delacroix, Goya, Dufy and others, as well as floors devoted to sculpture, tapestries and Delft china).

Lille's greatest son was Charles de Gaulle, born here in 1890. More recently, Pierre Mauroy, Socialist prime minister in 1981–84, was for many years mayor.

At nearby **Tourcoing**, the 85m belfry houses 49 bells on which recitals are given on fête days (and sometimes Suns). In the former village of **Hem**, now in the Lille suburbs, the simple and elegant chapel of La Sainte-Face contains superb modern stained-glass murals by Gustave Manessier.

MAUBEUGE
NORD Pop 36,200

Ancient fortified Maubeuge, near the Belgian frontier, was completely destroyed in World War II, but rose again to become an important iron and steel producing town, centre of a highly industrial region. Parts of Vauban's defences survive, sheltering pleasant gardens. There is a twelve-day beer festival here in the second and third weeks of July.

MONTREUIL
PAS-DE-CALAIS Pop 2900

From within massive hilltop ramparts, Montreuil-sur-Mer, as it is still called, looks towards the sea which has receded several miles since Roman days when this was an important harbour town.

Along the encircling walls, overgrown and grassy, there is a lofty walkway – it takes about an hour to go all the way round. Within the town, old houses line cobbled streets and squares, including some interesting religious buildings, particularly the often repaired, originally 11C church of St-Saulve, and, secure behind separate moated walls, the ancient Citadelle refortified by Vauban. This contains some interesting buildings and ruins, and a fine view over the rooftops of the town into the wooded valley of the Canche and out across the surrounding farmland.

The nearby peaceful valley of the Canche continues to **Hesdin**, an attractive small town. The less familiar valley of the Course wanders through country even more tranquil and rustic.

OPAL COAST
PAS-DE-CALAIS

From Calais to the Somme, the Channel coast is named 'Opal' for its clear, pale waters, but the stretch N from Boulogne (about 20km) is by far the most beautiful. The winding coast road follows spectacular chalk cliffs gnawed by the sea, passing pretty coastal villages, harbours and small old-fashioned resorts backed by sand dunes: **Wimereux**, with modest beach and breezy promenade, through **Ambleteuse**, a picturesque port with 17C **Fort Mahon** above, to **Cap Gris-Nez**, a high promontory of rock projecting boldly into the sea. This is the closest point to England, only 11.5km away. From Cap Gris-Nez, through **Wissant** (good sandy beach), the road climbs to **Cap Blanc-Nez**, with superb views, and then descends to Calais via **Blériot-Plage**, the sandy beach from which Louis Blériot made the first cross-Channel flight in 1909, and **Sangatte**, the planned exit of the Channel Tunnel. Earthworks mark the spot where work on the project was begun, then halted, a few years ago.

Cap Blanc-Nez

QUESNOY, LE
NORD Pop 4900

Situated in a wood, and built entirely within ancient brick fortifications (with additions by Vauban), Le Quesnoy is a pleasant little Flemish town. Below the walls are defensive waterworks, ditches and shaded footpaths. The nearby **Mormal Forest**, over 850ha, mainly of oak and beech, takes in the hamlet of **Locquignol**.

RUE
SOMME

Rue, small and quiet, some 8km inland from the Somme estuary, was an important seaport in the Middle Ages. The Chapelle du St-Esprit, with abundant, delicate sculpture and tracery, and extraordinarily ornate vaulting, represents 15C Flamboyant Gothic at its most unrestrained.

The lovely nearby coastal **Marquenterre Ornithological Park** was opened in 1973. Populated by resident wildfowl and frequented by over 300 species of migratory birds, the 2300ha park is divided into three areas – walking, aviaries and lakes, and observation.

ST-OMER
PAS-DE-CALAIS   Pop 15,500

A few corners of St-Omer, close to the Channel ports, preserve its Flemish character. The main shopping streets form a pedestrian zone. Pleasant public gardens cover a remnant of the town's fortifications. There are several buildings of interest, including the 13–15C cathedral of Notre-Dame, with a 50m belfry, good sculpture in the S portal, and a spacious interior with excellent stained glass and wood panelling, galleries in the choir and transepts, 15–16C tombs, 13C paving and sculpture, and an astronomical clock of 1558. The handsome 18C Hôtel Sandelin houses a Fine Arts museum with an important collection of Delftware, as well as an assortment of local archaeology, old guns, furnishings, painted medieval sculpture, and some good Flemish painting.

N of the town is a large area of drained marshland, long ago turned into patches of cultivation and an intriguing network of canals, called the *watergangs*. Just over 1km from St-Omer is the **Fôret de Rihour-Clairmarais**, ancient woodland around a lake.

ST-QUENTIN
AISNE   Pop 65,000

Modern, industrial, war-damaged, yet St-Quentin in eastern Picardy has charm and many interesting things to see. The town hall, in the popular main square, has an extraordinarily Flamboyant facade. The collegiate church of St-Quentin is a superb Gothic edifice, grand and spacious, with excellent stained glass, a fine organ loft, and the tomb of Saint Quentin in the crypt. The Musée Lecuyer has a considerable collection of the work of local 18C portraitist Maurice-Quentin Delatour. The Entomological Museum contains 600,000 insects.

SOMME BATTLEFIELDS

In the long and cruel trench warfare of 1914–18, much of the worst fighting took place on the rolling high ground N of the river Somme, where British and Empire troops attacked en masse in July 1916 and lost thousands of dead for every hundred yards they pushed back the German line. From **Albert**, a signposted 25km drive on country lanes, the **Circuit du Souvenir** visits the principal memorials

Canadian monument, Vimy ridge

and cemeteries of the area. On a hilltop at **Thiepval** stands the largest British memorial, designed by Sir Edwin Lutyens. Some 5km N is the Newfoundland Regiment's memorial park at **Beaumont-Hamel**, watched over by a statue of a caribou, where many of the original trenches have been preserved.

TOUQUET, LE
PAS-DE-CALAIS   Pop 5500

Le Touquet was one of Europe's smartest resorts in the railway era, before 1939, when rich and fashionable people from London and Paris found it fairly easy to reach. No longer so exclusive, it is still a busy, much-frequented resort, with polo-ground, racecourse, two casinos, a big congress hall, and some gorgeously old-fashioned hotels. The huge sandy beach is often windy, hence ideal for sand-yachting (sail-driven go-karts).

Just inland is the fishing-port of **Étaples**, on a river. To the S, on the coast, **Bagatelle Zoo Park** has funfair attractions and animals; farther S lies **Berck**, a resort with seawater health cures.

VALENCIENNES
NORD   Pop 41,000

This heavily industrialized town by the Belgian border remains proud of its former title, 'The Athens of the North', which reflected the town's traditional interest in the arts. Several painters and sculptors were born here, including Antoine Watteau, and Valenciennes today has a good Musée des Beaux-Arts. Unfortunately the old town centre of wooden buildings was destroyed in World War II, leaving few interesting features.

The nearby Regional Park (or Forest) of **St-Amand-Raismes** is a popular leisure area, mainly attractive woodland, with footpaths, botanic gardens, and a small game enclosure. **St-Amand-les-Eaux**, on the other side of the park, has relics of a partly 7C Benedictine abbey with curious ornate Flemish additions: a tall belfry housing 47 bells, and the Échevinage, with its Watteau Room (but note that the paintings are by Louis Watteau, not the more famous Antoine who was his uncle). St-Amand is still visited as a spa. The Établissement Thermal, with baths, hotel, and casino, lies outside the town beside the forest.

ÎLE-DE-FRANCE

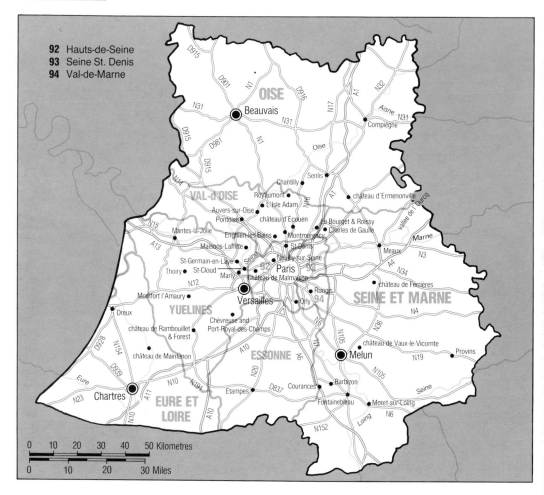

92 Hauts-de-Seine
93 Seine St. Denis
94 Val-de-Marne

OISE

Beauvais

Aisne
Compiègne

Chantilly
Senlis
VAL-d'OISE
Royaumont
château d'Ermenonville
Auvers-sur-Oise
L'Isle Adam
Pontoise
château d'Ecouen
Le Bourget & Roissy
Mantes-la-Jolie
Charles de Gaulle
Enghien-les-Bains
Montmorency
Maisons-Laffitte
St-Denis
Meaux
Marne
St-Germain-en-Laye
Neuilly-sur-Seine
Thoiry
St-Cloud
Paris
Marly
Château de Malmaison
Montfort l'Amaury
Rungis
château de Ferrières
Versailles
Orly
SEINE ET MARNE
Dreux
YUELINES
Chévreuse and
Port-Royal-des-Champs
château de Rambouillet
& Forest
château de Vaux-le-Vicomte
Provins
château de Maintenon
ESSONNE
Melun
Barbizon
Eure
Courances
Chartres
Etampes
Fontainebleau
Moret-sur-Loing
EURE ET
LOIRE
Loing

0 10 20 30 40 50 Kilometres

0   10   20   30 Miles

The region around Paris known today, as it was in medieval times, as the Île-de-France, is a comparatively small area, covering eight *départements*. It was so named because it was largely surrounded by water, being bounded by three great rivers, the Marne, the Seine and the Oise. This is France's royal heartland, a treasure store of architectural marvels – châteaux, palaces, cathedrals and abbeys, parks and gardens – enshrining some two thousand years of the nation's history.

In spite of the modern encroachment of the capital's sprawling suburbs, the commuter belt and the new towns, the ring-roads and motorways and airports, much of the region still retains a timeless fascination and charm. Agriculture is of prime importance, and over half the area consists of farmland, from the immense cornfields of the Beauce around Chartres to the market gardens south of Paris; and almost a quarter is covered by glorious oak and beech forests, formerly royal hunting preserves, nowadays state-owned, lovingly tended for universal enjoyment. In this gentle landscape of river and woodland, shimmering in the incomparably clear light that induced Corot, Millet and the Impressionists to paint so many masterpieces, architecture plays a determinant role.

AUVERS-SUR-OISE
VAL D'OISE   Pop 5800

This village, about 5km SW of L'Isle Adam, was a favourite subject of many Impressionist painters. It was the home of Dr Paul Gachet, physician, psychiatrist and friend of many artists, with whom Vincent Van Gogh stayed for the last five years of his life. Van Gogh finally committed suicide and was buried here.

BARBIZON
SEINE-ET-MARNE   Pop 1200

Barbizon's situation on the edge of the forest, 9km NW of Fontainebleau, ensures its popularity as a quiet yet still fashionable weekend retreat from Paris. In the 19C it was the centre of the *plein-airistes*, the new school of landscape painters who took their subjects from peasant life and worked out of doors. The founders of the Barbizon School were Théodore Rousseau and J.F. Millet, and members included Daubigny, Diaz and Troyon.

BEAUVAIS
OISE   Pop 54,000

This important crossroads town, capital of the Oise *département*, 76km N of Paris, is the site of the Cathedral of St-Pierre, planned to be the biggest Gothic church of its day. The daring architectural conception was never completed. The pillars of the choir, begun in 1247, were set too widely apart and only massive buttressing in 1284 prevented its total collapse. The transept was not built until after the Hundred Years' War and this was crowned with a huge 153m tower and spire which, unsupported by a nave, collapsed after five years. Lack of funds prevented further work on the cathedral which remains truncated, with transept, choir (the highest in the world), apse and seven apse-chapels. Yet the building is astonishingly impressive, with a superbly decorated S porch, 16C stained-glass windows, a 20C rose window by Max Ingrand over the N door, and a precious collection of tapestries. The famous mid-19C astronomical clock was constructed by an engineer aptly named Verité.

The nearby church of St-Étienne has a Romanesque nave and transept, and a Gothic choir containing splendid Renaissance stained glass.

Beauvais was virtually rebuilt after heavy bombing in 1940, when the cathedral miraculously escaped damage.

LE BOURGET & ROISSY/ CHARLES DE GAULLE
SEINE-ST-DENIS

The Musée de l'Air, with a collection of 140 aircraft, is installed at the old airport of Le Bourget, which itself has a storied past. On the night of 21–22 May, 1927, Charles Lindbergh landed his monoplane *Spirit of St Louis* here after the first W to E Atlantic crossing. Three years later, on 1 September, 1930, Costes and Bellontes achieved the first E–W flight.

NE of Le Bourget is the immense and technically sophisticated Roissy/Charles de Gaulle international airport complex, opened in 1974 to share incoming and outgoing air traffic with Orly.

CHANTILLY
OISE   Pop 10,200

A racecourse, a museum and art gallery of remarkable variety and quality, a château reflected in a moat as wide as a lake: Chantilly, 43km N of Paris, offers all these things. The present château is the fifth to have been built here over the past 2000 years, the most splendid of them being the Renaissance palace created in the 16C for Constable Anne de Montmorency, and rebuilt for the Great Condé, inheritor of the property in 1643, by Mansart. The building was razed after the Revolution, only the mid-16C Petit Château and the vast 18C stable block built for the Great Condé's grandson, the Duc de Bourbon (who apparently believed he would be reincarnated as a horse) being spared. Between 1875-81 the château was rebuilt by the Duc d'Aumale, who inherited the property after the death of the last of the Condés. He filled it with his art treasures and, on his death in 1897, left it to the nation. The immense collection in the Musée Condé include jewels, tapestries and stained glass, the 15C illuminated manuscript *Les Très Riches Heures du duc de Berry*, the forty miniatures from the *Book of Hours* of Étienne Chevalier, treasurer of France, reputedly by Jean Fouquet, and an unrivalled collection of royal and other portraits. The Cabinet des Gemmes has the famous Condé rose diamond. The interior of the château is itself a museum of period decor, as in the chinoiserie of the Salon des Singes and the 18C woodwork and rocaille of the Appartements des Princes. The park is one of Le Nôtre's most brilliant achievements, with ornamental water and vast parterres sheltered by avenues of limes, contains a prototype of the 'hamlet' later installed by the same great landscape gardener at Versailles.

The stables, which could accommodate 240 horses, now house a Museum of the Horse. Some 3000-3500 horses are trained in the racing stables. The beautiful racecourse has held meetings since 1836 and the two most important races of the season, the Prix du Jockey Club and the Prix de Diane are run in June every year.

Château de Chantilly

The 2100ha Forest of Chantilly, with a series of lakes at its S fringe, is largely an enclosed state forestry reserve.

CHARTRES
EURE-ET-LOIR   Pop 41,200

The two spires of what has been called the most beautiful church in the world, the Cathedral of Notre-Dame, are visible from afar across the cornfields of La Beauce. The cathedral is the principal tourist attraction of the town of Chartres, capital of Eure-et-Loir, some 85km SW of Paris, and stands on the site of an ancient Druidic place of worship. A pre-Christian cult of the Mother Goddess was subsequently converted into that of Notre-Dame-Sous-Terre, to whom the 11C crypt, the largest in France (over 200m long), was dedicated. This Romanesque church was destroyed by fire in 1194, only the W front and towers surviving. The Clocher Vieux, rescued intact, is 105m high, the tallest Romanesque steeple in the world. The Clocher Neuf has a slightly taller (115m) Gothic spire, added in the early 16C. The triple porch, the Portail Royal, of the W front is a superb monument of Romanesque sculpture, with supporting columns in the form of tall, attenuated statues of biblical kings, queens, prophets and patriarchs. The present rose-window and upper part of the facade are early 13C. The N and S doorways, devoted respectively to the Coming of Christ and the Last Judgment, have the greater decorative freedom of the 13C. All the portals and statues would originally have been painted and gilded.

The initial impression as one enters the vast nave, the broadest of any French cathedral (16.4m), is a vibrant blaze of blue, unique to Chartres. The nave is illuminated by more than 160 richly coloured stained-glass windows, most of them 13C. The three W windows below the rose-window are rare examples of 12C glass, as is the magnificent window portraying the Virgin and Child on the S side. The superb stone choir-screen, begun in 1514 and completed under Louis XIV, has 40 sculpture groups depicting the Life of

The rose-window, Chartres Cathedral

Christ and of the Virgin.

The town still possesses interesting old houses, some with stair turrets, in the narrow streets sloping down to the river. The 12–13C church of St-Pierre has an impressive E end and glass from the later 13C and 14C.

Jean Moulin, the most famous leader of the Gaullist Resistance in France, murdered by the Gestapo, was prefect of the town in 1940.

CHÉVREUSE AND PORT-ROYAL-DES-CHAMPS
YVELINES

The Valley of Chévreuse, SW of Versailles, is associated with the quarrel between Jesuits and Jansenists which tore the religious life of France apart during the 17C. The 13C abbey of Port Royal, the few remains of which can be seen at Port-Royal-des-Champs, about 8km NW of the small town of Chévreuse (pop. 4200), had returned to the rigour of the Cistercian rule under the influence of a reforming abbess, Mère Angelique, and became the centre of the Jansenist movement. In 1648 the nuns were joined by a group of theologians known as the 'solitaires', who set up their Petites Écoles in the farm of Les Granges to practise their methods of education. Pascal, Racine and Philippe de Champaigne were among those associated with them. Influenced by the Jesuits, Louis XIV ordered the eviction of the nuns. In the following year the abbey buildings were destroyed. The history of the Jansenist movement and of the abbey is presented in the nearby Musée National des Granges de Port-Royal.

About 4km W of Chévreuse is the **Château de Dampierre**, built in 1675–83 by Jules Hardouin-Mansart for the Duc de Chévreuse, a former pupil of the Petites Écoles and Colbert's son-in-law.

COMPIÈGNE
OISE   Pop 43,300

The historic town of Compiègne lies 75km NE of Paris, and its royal palace is surpassed in importance and splendour only by Versailles and Fontainebleau. On the town side its rather bleak facade conveys no idea of the luxuriance of its interior or of its superb outlook over one of the most beautiful forests of France. The original château, used as a royal hunting lodge, dates from the 14C. Louis XIV, though complaining that at Compiègne he was 'housed like a peasant', often stayed at the château; Louis XV and Louis XVI, who first met Marie-Antoinette here, transformed it into a palace. The splendour and extravagance date from the following century, when Napoleon adopted the château as an imperial residence and was introduced here to his second wife, Marie-Louise of Austria. The magnificent entertainments held here by Napoleon III and the Empress Eugénie were terminated abruptly by the Franco-Prussian War.

The interior has a corresponding mixture of styles: charming Louis Seize in the royal apartments, where Marie-Antoinette's Salon des Jeux contains the original furniture with silk curtains woven at Lyon, and weightier gold and mahogany of the Empire in Napoleon I's quarters. There are Gobelins tapestries in the Galérie des Chasses. The Musée National de la Voiture has a heterogeneous collection of horse-drawn vehicles from 1740 onwards, primitive bicycles and vintage cars.

Compiègne was badly damaged during World War II, but its notable buildings escaped. The Hôtel de Ville, from the turn of the 15–16C is a Gothic extravaganza whose belfry, topped with a slate spire, contains the original bell of 1303. Three early 16C figures called Picantines strike the hours and the quarters.

The Musée de la Figurine Historique has close on 100,000 lead soldiers illustrating military uniform from Vercingétorix onwards. The Tour de Beauregard was reputedly the prison of Joan of Arc after she had been captured by the Burgundians outside Compiègne in 1340.

The **Forest of Compiègne** (14,450ha), with its broad tree-lined avenues, rocks, brooks and tiny lakes, once a royal hunting reserve, is a delightful place for strolling.

In the **Clairière**, a clearing of the forest 8km from the town, is a replica of the railway carriage serving Marshal Foch as an office in which, on 11 November, 1918, the Armistice which ended World War I was signed. On 14 June, 1940, in the same carriage, Hitler received the French capitulation in World War II. It was later taken to Berlin, where it is believed to have been destroyed by bombs.

The **Château de Pierrefonds**, some 10km S of the clearing, is the work of Viollet-le-Duc, who, between 1857–84, reconstructed Louis d'Orléans's late 14C fortress, with its massy angle towers and double rampart walks. Some 8km further SE is the former abbey church of **Morienval**, a near-perfect 11C Romanesque building which has one of the earliest ogival vaults in France.

COURANCES
ESSONNE

The brick-and-stone château 5km N of Milly-la-Forêt was built in the 16C and rebuilt in the 17C, while the horseshoe staircase, copied from Fontainebleau, was added in the 19C. The gardens were designed by Le Nôtre and the perspective of the long approach drive set between twin canals, bordered by limes, is magnificent. The château was briefly the HQ of General Montgomery after the World War II Liberation.

DÉFENSE, LA

Variously condemned as 'an aesthetic outrage' and hailed as 'the most ambitious and exciting new urban project in Europe', La Défense, with its metal and glass skyscrapers of all shapes and sizes, colourful traffic-free piazza, immense shopping precinct (said to be the largest in Europe), ring-roads and underground railway is a controversial but bold and grandiose project. Built on a 1700-acre site across the Seine beyond Neuilly as a major new commercial and residential area, the main high-rise scheme is almost completed. Most of the projected thirty tower blocks, some over forty

storeys high, are already occupied as offices by giant firms such as Esso, Fiat, IBM, etc.

La Défense

DREUX
EURE-ET-LOIR   Pop 34,000

This busy industrial town on the borders of Île-de-France and Normandy was formerly a frontier post, both during the English Wars, when it was taken by Henry V, and in the Religious Wars, when after a three-year siege it was captured and extensively burned by Henri IV. The local Metézeau family of architects were largely responsible for the 13C church of St-Pierre, much rebuilt over the centuries, with some good 15–16C glass, and for the early 16C Renaissance Beffroi. The Royal Chapel of St-Louis, on the site of an old château W of the town, is the burial place of the Orléans family.

ÉCOUEN, CHÂTEAU D'

The château, 20km N of Paris, was one of two glorious houses built during the 16C for the Constable Anne de Montmorency, the other being Chantilly (q.v.). After it was confiscated during the Revolution, Napoleon converted it into the first school for daughters of members of the Legion of Honour. Since 1962 it has accommodated the Musée de la Renaissance, exhibiting the best of the decorative arts of the 16C and early 17C from Italy, France and the Netherlands. The château's painted chimney pieces are apparently products of the School of Fontainebleau, and there is an outstanding series of 16C Brussels tapestries depicting the story of David and Bathsheba.

ENGHIEN-LES-BAINS
VAL-D'OISE

A spa little more than 6km from industrial St-Denis, Enghien offers pleasures other than the most powerfully sulphurous water in France, held to be sovereign against rheumatism. There is a racecourse and a casino, and boating on the 40ha lake. At the Château St-Gratien, to the W, the Princess Mathilde, Napoleon's niece, who was sympathetically portrayed by Proust in *À la Recherche du Temps Perdu*, held a brilliant salon. She is buried in the parish church.

ERMENONVILLE, CHÂTEAU D'
OISE

A caravan site in the park does not improve the atmosphere of the estate S of Senlis where the Marquis de Girardin, a disciple of Jean-Jacques Rousseau, created a landscape garden, but the main features of it survive. Rousseau himself died here in 1778, while he was a guest, and was buried on the Île des Peupliers on the lake. Six years later the state removed his body to the Panthéon, which he would undoubtedly have deplored.

Some 3km N of Ermenonville is the **Mer de Sable**, a curious stretch of sand dunes where there is a small zoo. Nearby are the ruins of the 12C Cistercian abbey of Châalis. The 18C abbey buildings were converted into a château: its last owner was Mme Jacquemart-André, who with her husband, founded the Paris museum bearing their name (q.v.).

A pine forest near Ermenonville was the scene of the worst air disaster in history on 3 March, 1974, when a Turkish Airlines DC-10 crashed after take-off from Orly, killing 346 people.

ÉTAMPES
ESSONNE Pop 19,500

This old town, 40km from Paris on the old Orléans road, preserves an atmosphere of calm thanks to a traffic bypass. Looming over the town, with many old buildings, is the 12C Tour de Guinette, where King Philippe-Auguste imprisoned his enemies and also, from 1201 to 1212, his Danish queen Ingeborg, who refused him a divorce. The 12C church of Notre-Dame, fortified in the 13C, has a fine S porch.

FERRIÈRES, CHÂTEAU DE
SEINE-ET-MARNE

Baron James de Rothschild, founder of the French branch of the banking family, employed Joseph Paxton, architect of the Crystal Palace in London, to design his new château, some 30km E of Paris and to lay out the wooded park. It was completed in 1859: eleven years later the château was the scene of France's request for an armistice from Bismarck at the end of Franco-Prussian War. With part of the park, it now belongs to the University of Paris.

FONTAINEBLEAU
SEINE-ET-MARNE

This royal house, nearly 70km SE of Paris, is François I's palace as unmistakably as Versailles is that of Louis XIV. But whereas Versailles is vast and imposing in its open setting, Fontainebleau, surrounded by forest and irregular in plan, gives an impression of attractive informality. Kings of France have lived here at least since the 12C; Henri IV gave it a Grand Canal sixty years before that of Versailles was built; Napoleon loved it and looked upon it as the true royal home.

The 12C manor was little more than a hunting

Fontainebleau

lodge built near a spring known as the Fontaine de Bliaud, or Blaut, hence the present name. In later centuries the manor was fortified, Thomas à Becket consecrated a chapel, St Louis founded a monastery for the *mathurins*, or Trinitarians. Save for the old keep, almost all the medieval buildings vanished when, in 1528, François I commissioned from Gilles le Breton a massive programme of construction. It produced two groups of buildings around the Cour Ovale and the present Cour de Cheval Blanc, or des Adieux, then known as the Basse Cour, which were joined by a gallery. For their decoration he imported two Italians, Giovanni Battista Rosso, a Florentine, who had worked under Andrea del Sarto, and Francesco Primaticcio, a Bolognese. They were the founders of the so-called First School of Fontainebleau, a combination of Mannerist painting and stucco decor.

Leading to the W front of the central building, with the famous horseshoe staircase designed by Jean de Cerceau for Louis XIII, is the huge Cour du Cheval Blanc, also known as the Cour des Adieux, since it was here that Napoleon made his farewell to his heartbroken Old Guard before departing for Elba. The pure spring still rises in the Cour de la Fontaine beyond it, though the fountain itself is less than 200 years old. The Cour Ovale, oldest of the courts, was once that of the medieval castle; the 12C keep, all that remains of the original buildings, was incorporated into its W end. It was here that François I had his bedroom. The celebrated Porte Dorée of 1528, once the main entrance to the château, opens on to this court; it is a typical Renaissance porch, with François I's device, the salamander, carved on the tympanum.

The great gallery of François I, linking the two buildings of the Cour de la Fontaine, has the original decor; Rosso's paintings and stucco reliefs were finished after his death by Primaticcio who, amid the scenes of love and war, found a place for a small picture of the château. The adjoining Salle des Gardes also has its Louis XIII ceiling. Louis XV built the Escalier du Roi in 1747, but retained the existing decoration of its upper part, which had once been the bedroom of the Duchesse d'Étampes, François I's mistress; the frescoes showing François I as Alexander the Great were painted from Primaticcio's designs, by his assistant, Nicolo dell' Abbate. Both men also collaborated on the magnificent Salle de Bal, built for François I but decorated for his son Henri II, as indicated by the many monograms of the king and his favourite, Diane de Poitiers. Here the ceiling design, of walnut decorated with silver and gold, is repeated in the parquet floor put in under Louis Philippe. A lighter style distinguishes the Appartements de la Reine, where, particularly in her boudoir, Marie-Antoinette inspired the height of luxurious elegance in interior decoration. There are a number of Napoleonic relics in the Emperor's apartments, including the table on which he signed his abdication.

The Forest of Fontainebleau (about 17,000ha), chiefly of oak and beech, has sandy clearings, rivers and outcrops of rock which have made it a popular training ground for climbers. Winter visitors may see the picturesque *Chasse à courre* (stag hunt) in action.

L'ISLE ADAM
VAL D'OISE Pop 10,000

Two of the greatest families of France, Montmorency and Condé, lived in the 11C château of this small town some 25km W of Paris, which was destroyed during the Revolution. Today L'Isle Adam is a popular weekend resort, with sailing and swimming in the Oise and a forest to E and S.

MAINTENON, CHÂTEAU DE
EURE-ET-LOIR

Maintenon, on the Eure, some 10km SW of Épernon, was the gift of Louis XIV to Françoise d'Aubigny, shortly to become Madame de Maintenon and the king's morganatic second wife. Her descendants, the Noailles family, still live in it. The keep of the 12–13C *château fort* which originally stood on the site still remains; the three brick towers which complete the quadrangle are 14C and the rest of the building is French Renaissance. Le Nôtre laid out the park, just beyond which are the ruins of the colossal aqueduct by which the king hoped to convey the water of the Eure for the first part of the 110km to Versailles.

Château de Maintenon

MAISONS-LAFFITTE
YVELINES Pop 23,800

The mid-17C château of Maisons-Laffitte, about 4km N of St-Germain-en-Laye, is one of the best examples of the work of François Mansart, distinguished particularly for its interior decoration. It was visited by royalty in the 18C, and Voltaire was a guest here when he wrote *Marianne*. The château was bought in 1818 by the banker Laffitte, who added his name to it. It is now owned by the state.

The racecourse, close to the Seine, and training stables, in what remains of the original park, are second only to Chantilly in importance.

MALMAISON, CHÂTEAU DE
HAUTS-DE-SEINE

Malmaison, 15km W of Paris in the suburb of Rueil-Malmaison, the most intimate of the châteaux associated with Napoleon, was the property of his first wife, Josephine Beauharnais. The modest house, built in 1622, was surrounded by gardens which Josephine tended personally – she had 255 varieties in the rose garden, duly painted by Redouté – and here, during the early years of his marriage Napoleon enjoyed what were probably his happiest hours. Divorced and defeated, he spent a few days at Malmaison between Waterloo and his departure for St Helena. Josephine had died during the previous year.

The château, now restored, with much of its initial furniture reassembled, is a Napoleon museum. The dining room, with its frescoes of Pompeian dancers, and the library retain their original decoration. The First Consul's room, which is a reconstruction of Napoleon's bedroom at the Tuileries, has the authentic furniture and hangings. The museum has on view both the imperial throne from Fontainebleau and the bed in which Napoleon died on St Helena; among the personal souvenirs are his desk and armchair and a collection of books from his private library. The rose garden has been replanted and the cedar which Josephine planted after the victory of Marengo still stands.

MANTES-LA-JOLIE
YVELINES Pop 43,600

Few today would call the industrial town of Mantes 'la jolie', but the rebuilding after massive World War II damage was tastefully done. It was here that William the Conqueror suffered the riding accident which led to his death. Later, Henri IV took at Mantes his final decision to renounce Protestantism, with the famous reputed remark, 'Paris is worth a Mass'. The collegiate church of Notre-Dame, which Corot painted, has the scale and splendour of a cathedral; it was built in two stages between 1170 and 1325. The original windows, most of which were destroyed during the last war, have been replaced by striking modern ones. The Romanesque church of Ste-Anne of Gassicourt has outstanding 13C glass.

MARLY
YVELINES

Only the park, with its lawns and lakes, remains to remind us of the château 5km W of St-Germain-en-Laye which Hardouin-Mansart designed for Louis XIV, who used it as a refuge from the formal splendours of Versailles. Guests were lodged in twelve small *pavillons*, leaving the Sun King in sole possession of the royal one. Along with the building of the château went the construction of the 'machine of Marly', which raised the water of the Seine 163m and conveyed it by aqueduct to the fountains of Versailles. The Forest of Marly was a royal hunting preserve, and the old village was popular with artists and writers during the 19C.

MEAUX
SEINE-ET-MARNE   Pop 46,000

The chief attraction of Meaux, 45km E of Paris, is the great Cathedral of St-Étienne, which is a text book illustration of various periods of Gothic architecture from the late 12C, when building started, to the 16C, when the W front was completed. Meaux has been a bishopric since the 4C. The most famous occupant of its chair was Bossuet (1627–1704), the great 17C preacher and religious writer. The 12C former Bishop's Palace is now a Bossuet museum; its gardens are built over part of the old ramparts which contain Gallo-Roman work. Meaux is situated in the rich farming district of Brie and has produced Brie cheese since the early 13C.

MELUN
SEINE-ET-MARNE   Pop 39,800

Industrial Melun, 45km SE of Paris, remains the administrative capital of the Seine-et-Marne *département*, although the New Town of Melun-Sénart, a group of dispersed communities, has grown up to the NE, among the woodlands of the forests of Sénart and Rougeau. The town is a Gallo-Roman foundation; the church of Notre-Dame, built on an island in the Seine, is 11C, but has been considerably altered. The Melun region produces one of the four classic types of Brie cheese.

MONTFORT L'AMAURY
YVELINES   Pop 2800

This ancient small town 13km N of Rambouillet, nowadays a smart residential commuter area, is an excellent centre for exploring the forest. The ruined 11C fort was built by Amaury de Montfort, ancestor of Simon de Montfort. Anne de Bretagne was responsible for rebuilding the church of St-Pierre at the end of the 15C: the S facade has a splendid Renaissance doorway and the stained glass is outstanding. The composer Maurice Ravel lived at Montfort from 1920 until his death in 1937. His house, Le Belvédère, is now a museum.

MONTMORENCY
SEINE-ST-DENIS

5km NW of St-Denis, is now an outer suburb of Paris: in 1756, when Jean-Jacques Rousseau settled there to write *La Nouvelle Héloïse*, it was a pleasant hilltop village, popular with excursionists. Montlouis, the second house which he occupied there, where he wrote *Émile* and *Du contrat social*, is a museum.

The collegiate church of St-Martin, built in the 16C but heavily restored, is the mortuary chapel of the Montmorency family.

MONT VALÉRIEN
HAUTS-DE-SEINE

The fort of Mont Valérien, on the site of an earlier pilgrimage chapel, overlooking St-Cloud, SW of Paris, dates from the reign of Louis-Philippe and had a brief period of military glory during the defence of Paris in 1870–71. During the German Occupation of 1940–44 some 4500 members of the Resistance and hostages were executed here. In 1960 it was inaugurated as a Memorial to Fighting France.

MORET-SUR-LOING
SEINE-ET-MARNE   Pop 3100

Alfred Sisley spent the last twenty years of his life in this riverside village, E of the Forest of Fontainebleau, which still retains part of its old ramparts and two of its 14C gates. The church of Notre Dame has a 12C choir consecrated by Thomas à Becket: the belfry was not completed until the 15C. There is remarkable carving in the organ loft. On summer Sat. evenings there is *son-et-lumière* beside the river which Sisley so often painted.

Moret-sur-Loing

NEUILLY
HAUTS-DE-SEINE

Modern blocks of flats have largely destroyed the character of the suburb of Neuilly, W of the Bois de Boulogne; the elegance of the villas laid out in what was once the park of Louis-Philippe's château is now hard to seek. The pleasing stone bridge over the Seine, by the 18C engineer Jean-Rudolphe Perronet, replaced one built in 1606 after Henri IV and Marie de Médicis had a narrow escape from drowning. Just N of the bridge is the Île de la Grande Jatte which Seurat painted in 1884.

ORLY
VAL-DE-MARNE

Until the 1960s Orly airport, SW of the village of Orly, 16km S of Paris, to which it is linked by a special branch of the Autoroute du Sud, was Europe's major airport. Its contemporary installations, plus hotels, restaurants, chapel and cinema, almost constituted a village in themselves. Despite the scale of Orly's development the volume of traffic eventually outstripped its capacity. The Roissy/Charles de Gaulle airport complex (q.v.), was therefore built N of Paris to cope with the saturation. Since 1974 international air traffic has been shared by the two airports.

OURCQ, VALLÉE DE L'
SEINE-ET-MARNE

The valley of the Ourcq, running NE from Meaux, and the plateaux to the W of it, were the scene of the first battle of the Marne in Sept. 1914, at the beginning of World War I. The Germans had advanced beyond the river and the Canal de l'Ourcq before the French and British forces counter-attacked and finally drove them back over the Marne. It was to the Nanteuil-le-Hardouin sector, in the NW of the area, that General Gallieni ferried 6000 men from the garrison of Paris in the famous 'taxis of the Marne', 600 of which were taken from the streets of the city, each to make two trips.

PONTOISE
VAL D'OISE   Pop 29,500

Pontoise, 33km NW of Paris, has only the shell of its medieval château, but still retains part of the ramparts which, in 1437, when the town was under deep snow, English soldiers, wearing white camouflage, approached unnoticed. They took the town and held it for four years. The 15–16C cathedral of St-Maclou has a spectacular Flamboyant tower crowned by an elaborate dome, with turrets. There is some 12C work in the choir. Camille Pissarro lived and worked at Pontoise from 1872–84.

PROVINS
SEINE-ET-MARNE   Pop 13,100

The distant view of the 12C ramparts of Provins, 84km SE of Paris, with the Tour de César rising to 44m, has more in common with the town's noble medieval past than with its quiet provincial present. In the 13C it was one of the seats of the counts of Champagne and a centre for the fairs (see *Champagne*) which brought prosperity to the province. The English Wars and the Wars of Religion successively caused its eclipse. The Romanesque-Gothic church of St-Quiriace (he was the Bishop of Jerusalem who, traditionally, found the True Cross) was built in the late 12C; the 13C nave, conceived on a vast scale, was never completed. The dome was added in the 17C.

Provins was the nursery of the red rose of Lancaster. Count Thibault IV of Champagne was said to have brought home from the Fourth Crusade the rose of Jericho and cultivated it at Provins.

RAMBOUILLET, CHÂTEAU AND FOREST
YVELINES

The Château of Rambouillet has had royal associations since the mid-16C, when François I died here as the self-invited guest of Jacques d'Angennes, captain of his guard. In 1706 Louis XIV purchased it from the Angennes family for his son the count of Toulouse; in 1783 Louis XVI bought it for himself. Since 1897 it has been the official country residence of the President of the Republic. All that now remains of the 14C castle built for the Angennes is the machicolated tower in which François I died. Otherwise the building, red brick with flanking stone towers, is largely the result of modernization in the mid-16C and the enlargements made by the count of Toulouse at the beginning of the 18C.

ROYAUMONT
OISE

St Louis (King Louis IX) founded the Abbey of Royaumont, 8km SW of Chantilly, and gave it to the Order of Cîteaux. He was married in its church in 1234, and regularly visited the abbey to share in the life of the monks, even taking his turn at serving them at table. The church was demolished during the Revolution and the works of art which, as a royal foundation, it had accumulated, were dispersed. The foundations indicate its immense size; all that now remains above them is the stair turret of the N transept. At one period the abbey buildings were used as a cotton mill. They are now used as a cultural centre, staging concerts, exhibitions, etc, and for congresses and seminars, but a number of the original rooms are open to visitors. Foremost among them is the fine 13C refectory, with seating for sixty monks. The double nave is divided by a line of pillars: the pulpit of the lector remains though it has lost its balustrade. Also open to the public are the 13C cloister, its graveyard now converted into a garden, the splendid kitchen, with three vaulted naves and the 14C statue of the Virgin of Royaumont, and a chapel which was formerly the sacristy.

RUNGIS
VAL-DE-MARNE

The immense new site of Paris's wholesale markets for fresh food is 11km SE of the capital, near Orly airport, replacing the ancient and picturesque market of Les Halles in 1969.

ST-CLOUD, PARC DE
HAUTS-DE-SEINE

On high ground overlooking the Seine, 12km W of Paris, the Parc de St-Cloud (450ha) is rivalled only by the Parc de Sceaux as the most attractive open space within easy reach of the city centre. It was landscaped by Le Nôtre, but its most important feature, the Grande Cascade, with the water descending three great ramps to be thrown up in fountains, was the work of Lepautre and Mansart.

The château, where Henri III was assassinated by a fanatical monk in 1589, where Napoleon in 1799 established the Consulate with his coup of 18 Brumaire, and where he married Marie-Louise in 1810, was destroyed during the Franco-Prussian War: its site is marked by clipped yews. The world-renowned Sèvres porcelain factory and the museum of Ceramics are to the SE of the park. Interpol has its HQ in the town of St-Cloud.

ST-DENIS
SEINE-ST-DENIS

The present majestic basilica, the first great Gothic church of Europe, was the work of the Benedictine abbot of St-Denis, Suger, and Pierre de Montreuil, architect of the Sainte Chapelle. Before the end of the 12C the W front, whose rose window was the first of its kind in any church, two bays of the new nave and the chancel and crypt had been added to the Carolingian nave. By the end of the 13C the work had been completed. The survival of the cathedral after centuries of neglect, wanton damage during the Revolution and a disastrous attempt at restoration which destroyed the 13C spire, is due to Viollet-le-Duc's work during the 19C.

ST-GERMAIN-EN-LAYE
YVELINES

For more than five centuries St-Germain, some 20km W of Paris, was the country residence of the kings of France. Louis VI built the first castle here on the site of a convent dedicated to St Germain which dated from 1020. When it was destroyed during the Hundred Years' War, Charles V restored it; less than two centuries later François I transformed it into the Renaissance château which we see today, the so-called Château Vieux, which had the first rooftop terrace in Europe. All that remains of its predecessors are the donjon of Charles V's château and the exquisite Sainte Chapelle, which was built for St Louis in 1230; this predates by about ten years that of Paris, and is by the same architect, Pierre de Montreuil, but lacks the stained glass. In the later 16C Henri II built the

Forest of St-Germain

Château Neuf (now destroyed), which was a celebrated pleasure palace, and the royal family occupied both indifferently. Louis XIV, who moved the court to Versailles in 1682, was born at St-Germain, Mary Queen of Scots spent ten years of her childhood and girlhood here, and James II died here, having sought refuge with his cousin Louis XIV; his heart is buried in the parish church. The Château Vieux now houses the Musée des Antiquités Nationales, covering periods from the paleolithic to that of Charlemagne. Le Nôtre laid out the park, the finest feature of which is the Grande Terrasse, NE of the château, a promenade bordered with lime trees which has a memorable view over the Seine to distant Paris.

Claude Debussy was born at St-Germain and Alexandre Dumas wrote *The Three Musketeers* and *The Count of Monte Cristo* here. The Forest of St-Germain, once a royal hunting preserve, has attractive green rides and walks.

SCEAUX, PARC DE
HAUTS-DE-SEINE

Nothing now remains of the château which Louis XIV's great finance minister, Colbert, with Claude Perrault as his architect, built at Sceaux, 12km S of Paris, in the 17C. The château was destroyed during the Revolution, and its replacement, of no architectural interest, now houses the excellent Musée de l'Île-de-France, a repository of folk culture, containing pictures by artists who worked in the region, among them Hubert Robert, Bonington, Utrillo and Dunoyer de Segonzac. The great park laid out by Le Nôtre has been restored to its original magnificence. Its most spectacular features are the Grandes Cascades, a series of ten waterfalls dropping into the Bassin de L'Octagone, and the Grand Canal, enclosed between ranks of poplars.

Lovers of roses will want to visit **L'Haÿ-les-Roses**, 2.5km E of Sceaux, with its beautiful gardens and rose museum.

SENLIS
OISE   Pop 15,300

The narrow streets and alleys of Senlis, 44km NE of Paris, still breathe an air of bygone tranquillity. This Gallo-Roman city became a favourite residence of Merovingian and Carolingian monarchs, and in 987 Hugh Capet was elected to the throne of France here. The site has been fortified since the 1C and sixteen towers of the Gallo-Roman precinct remain. The château is now an assortment of ruins but retains its Roman square keep. The exquisite cathedral of Notre-Dame, begun in 1153, has an elegant 78m spire and a Romanesque W door with marvellous carvings from the Life of the Virgin. The interior is remarkable for its beautiful gallery high on either side of nave and choir. The former church of St-Pierre, retaining one Romanesque and one Renaissance tower, and a 15C spire, is now a covered market. The 10C church of St-Frambourg has recently been restored and is now used as a concert hall, its crypt housing an archaeological museum.

THOIRY
YVELINES

The 16C château of Thoiry, 45km W of Paris, has been occupied by the same family, the Comtes de la Panouse, for four centuries. It has elegant 18C furniture and gardens planned by Le Nôtre, but the main attraction for the public is the vast safari park, the largest in Europe.

VAUX-LE-VICOMTE, CHÂTEAU DE
SEINE-ET-MARNE

The 17C château of Vaux-le-Vicomte, 6km NE of Melun, was, though not intentionally, a rehearsal for Versailles. It was built for Nicolas Fouquet, Louis XIV's first finance minister, some 18,000 workmen were employed, with Le Vau as architect, Le Brun as decorator and Le Nôtre as gardener. When the château was completed he invited the young king to a fête, the splendours of which included a dinner service of solid gold, 1200 fountains jetting in the park, and Molière and his troupe performing *Les Fâcheux*. Nineteen days later Louis arrested Fouquet for peculation and he was imprisoned for life. Le Vau, Le Brun and Le Nôtre were then set to work on the new and even more magnificent royal château of Versailles.

Inside the château, privately owned, the finest of the furnished rooms on view is the domed Grand Salon. The formal gardens, on descending levels, display Le Nôtre's marvellous handling of perspective by means of lawns, avenues, trees, pools, fountains and cascades.

VERSAILLES
YVELINES

The majestic complex of buildings, gardens and parkland that makes up Versailles, some 20km SW of Paris, is one of the greatest and most rewarding tourist attractions in France, or indeed the world. Built for the glorification of the Sun King, Louis XIV, Versailles was, from 1682 to 1789, the political capital of the nation, a glittering focal point of social and cultural life which embodies the ethos of the *ancien régime* and illustrates the reason for its collapse.

It was Louis XIII who built a small shooting lodge at Versailles, later having it enlarged to the brick and stone manor which can still be seen in the Cour de Marbre. Louis XIV, commanding the services of Le Vau, Le Brun and Le Nôtre as architect, painter and gardener respectively, transformed it into a palace which could accommodate the entire court, consisting of 3000 to 4000 people. The original small palace was enclosed on three sides by new buildings containing the Grands Appartements where the king and queen led their semi-public life. There was a ceremonial rising and retiring, the *lever* and the *coucher*, with courtiers in attendance; when Marie-Antoinette gave birth to her first child, only screens held off the crowds who filled the room. The Chambre du Roi is again as it was under Louis XIV, who died in the royal bed in 1715.

The Grands Appartements include Le Vau's great Galerie des Glaces (Hall of Mirrors), 75m

Versailles

long, with seventeen high arched windows looking out on to the gardens and, on the opposite wall, seventeen corresponding mirrors framed in marble arcades. Roof paintings by Le Brun record the events of the first seventeen years of Louis's reign. The Salon d'Hercule, formerly used as the chapel of the palace, has two paintings by Veronese. The ceiling paintings by François Lemoyne were designed to harmonize with them; the work took him three years, at the end of which he committed suicide. The gold and white Chapel was begun by Hardouin-Mansart and completed after his death by his brother-in-law, Robert de Cotte. The Opéra, which was completed in 1770, in time for the marriage of the future Louis XVI and Marie-Antoinette, is a masterpiece by Jacques-Ange Gabriel, shaped like a truncated oval (the first oval room in France) and lit by crystal chandeliers, with the decor entirely of gilded wood or wood painted to resemble marble. A restoration in 1957 – in time for Queen Elizabeth II to attend its opening – has made it the most elegant of state theatres.

Le Nôtre's gardens and park, which cover about 100ha, were constructed on the most unpropitious marshy site, which had to be levelled, cleared and drained, with hills shifted, fountains channelled and thousands of trees brought in and planted. The original classical pattern, with its balance and symmetry, has been retained, though nowadays there are far fewer than the 150,000 bedding plants of Louis XIV's day. Hardouin-Mansart's Grand Trianon, built in 1687, is a one-storey palace with a colonnade in which pale stone alternates with pink and white marble. Here Louis XIV organized intimate dances and supper parties. Later Napoleon was to occupy the former private royal apartments; the furniture is largely and, in the Chambre de l'Empereur, entirely of his period, although the restored decor is from the time of Louis XIV. The Petit Trianon, the work of Jacques-Ange Gabriel, was Louis XVI's gift to Marie-Antoinette. Here she retired from the constraints of court etiquette to live simply with her children and close friends. The hamlet, a group of thatched houses, with dairy, barn and mill, created by the queen's favourite architect, Richard Mique, fostered the illusion. It was here that the Queen received news of the Revolution and fled, never to return.

The fountains of Versailles, which consume a million gallons of water an hour, play on the first and third Sundays of the summer months. Four times in the summer there are Fêtes de Nuit, ending with fireworks.

PARIS

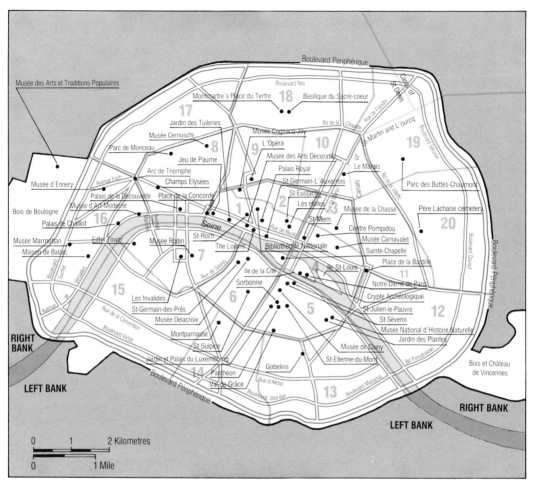

Musée des Arts et Traditions Populaires
Boulevard Périphérique
Boulevard Ney
Montmartre's Place du Tertre 18 Basilique du Sacré-coeur
Canal St Denis
St Denis
Jardin des Tuileries
Musée Cernuschi
17
Bd de la   Chapelle
Rue de Flandre
Boulevard Sérurier
Parc de Monceau
Musée Cognacq-Jay
St Martin and L'ourcq
Musée d'Ennery
Jeu de Paume 8   L'Opéra 10   19
9   Musée des Arts Décoratifs
Arc de Triomphe Palais Royal   Le Marais
Avenue Foch   Champs Elysées   St-Germain-L'Auxerrois   Parc des Buttes-Chaumont
Palais de la Découverte   Place de la Concorde   St-Eustache
Bois de Boulogne   Musée d'Art Moderne   Les Halles
Musée de la Chasse   Père Lachaise cemetery
Palais de Chaillot 16   St-Merri 3
Seine   1   2   Centre Pompidou   20
Musée Marmottan   Rue de Rivoli   Musée Carnavalet   Boulevard Davout
Eiffel Tower   Musée Rodin   St-Roch   Bibliothèque Nationale   Sainte-Chapelle
Maison de Balzac   The Louvre   Place de la Bastille
Boulevard Suchet   7   Ile de la Cité   Ile St-Louis   11
Avenue de Lattre   Rue de Sèvres   Sorbonne   4   Notre-Dame de Paris
15   Les Invalides   6   Crypte Archéologique   12
St-Germain-des-Prés   5   St-Julien-le-Pauvre   Boulevard Périphérique
Rue de la Convention   Musée Delacroix   St-Séverin
Boulevard Victor   Montparnasse   Musée National d'Histoire Naturelle
RIGHT   St-Sulpice   Jardin des Plantes
BANK   Musée de Cluny
Jardin et Palais du Luxembourg   Gobelins   St-Etienne-du-Mont   Bois et Château de Vincennes
LEFT BANK   14   Panthéon   Rue d'Alésia   Bd Poniatowski
Val-de-Grâce   13   RIGHT BANK
Boulevard Périphérique   Boulevard Jourdan   Boulevard Masséna   LEFT BANK

0   1   2 Kilometres
0   1 Mile

Motorists understandably tend to give capital cities a wide berth, but Paris infinitely repays the temporary abandonment of any car, for it possesses the rare quality of being able to fulfil and even exceed a wide variety of preconceived expectations.

Picture-postcard images of the Eiffel Tower and the Arc de Triomphe, of Montmartre's Place du Tertre and the bookstalls along the Seine, of the Madeleine flower-sellers and the Rue de Rivoli, all turn out to be even better than envisaged, because they are so magically enhanced by something no postcard can convey – the sweeping perspectives of Paris.

Cultural Paris lives equally well up to expectations: the Louvre, the Modern Art museum and the myriad lesser museums and galleries, Notre-Dame and the Sainte-Chapelle, the theatre and the opera, all provide feasts of unparalleled richness.

Lovers' Paris is still vibrant and pulsating across a thousand café tables and along the *quais* of the Seine; high-fashion Paris continues to flourish in the salons of the great couturiers and in the chic boutiques; gastronomic Paris is alive and well and ever more innovative despite the proliferation of fast-food outlets.

Yet Paris is more than the sum total of preconceived images: it is also a mosaic of past history and of dozens of very different contemporary communities, which are nevertheless united in love and pride for their city. The smartly turned-out shop and office workers, heels tapping along the pavements, the old men dozing on benches in quiet corners, the polyglot street entertainers, the women carefully shopping for the midday meal and the children scurrying about with their school satchels; the blacks and the Algerians, the students, and the despondent down-and-outs are all part of the intensely alive fabric of Parisian life that has little to do with sights and monuments and the arts but is an equally important aspect of the city.

So, too, are the ordinary streets where these people live, among the village-style shops, bars, bistros and markets, the slightly faded older apartment buildings and mansions and the aggressively new ones, the parks and playgrounds, the half-hidden courtyards and alleyways. And so is the atmosphere of restlessness that is an integral part of the Paris scene: the preoccupation with novelty, the delight in change, the sensation of perpetually being on the brink of some new discovery – all adding up to a tinglingly electric sensation that is unique.

The history of Paris started with a Gallic tribe, the Parisii, who erected rough fortifications around their settlement on what is now the Île de la Cité. The Romans razed it and built their city of Lutetia, gradually extending it across the river to the present Latin Quarter. Subsequent Hun invasions were repelled by the intercession of Sainte Geneviève, later the city's patron saint, but she permitted the besieging Franks and their Christian king Clovis to make Paris their capital in AD508.

Charlemagne shifted his capital to Aix-la-Chapelle in the 8C but the Capetians, heirs of Hugh Capet (elected king of France in 987) moved back to Paris and reigned for 350 years from their palace on the Île de la Cité, where the Conciergerie now stands. To this period belong Notre-Dame Cathedral, the Sainte Chapelle, St-Denis and the foundation of the Sorbonne university. As English power became a threat, the first Louvre fortress and city walls were built. Parisians suffered from the wars with England (who held the capital from 1429 to 1439) and from visitations of the plague; but they benefited from the Italian Renaissance ideas and inspiration that François I introduced at the beginning of the 16C, when the Louvre was enlarged and many fine churches and secular buildings were founded.

In the 17C, under Louis XIII and Louis XIV, Paris entered a golden age to which the Luxembourg Palace, Palais-Royal, Invalides, Pont Royal, Comédie Française and Place Vendôme still testify. Corneille, Racine and Molière brought lustre to the theatre, Pascal to philosophy, Mme de Sévigné to letters; academies of music, painting and sculpture were established.

Public building and the arts continued to flourish in the 18C, with painters such as Watteau, Fragonard and Boucher, musicians like Rameau and Gluck (German-born but a Paris resident), and writers and philosophers such as Voltaire, Rousseau and Montesquieu. Wars in the colonies, financial problems and repressive government nevertheless fuelled popular discontent, culminating in 1789 in the Revolution and subsequent years of terror that lasted until Napoleon assumed power in 1809.

Under Napoleon, order was restored, prosperity returned, new industries were developed and the arts revived. In the half-century after Napoleon's fall in 1815, despite periods of political and popular unrest, modernization continued with the building of canals and railways, markets (including Les Halles), gas lighting and sewers. New boulevards were laid out and bridges erected under the supervision of Baron Haussmann, prefect of the city; schools and museums opened, the Orangerie and Jeu de Paume pavilions were built and parks were created. The latter part of the 19C brought the Prussian wars and the people's Communard Revolt of 1871, when thousands died or were later imprisoned or transported. Yet within twenty years Paris had recovered sufficiently to build the Eiffel Tower (1889) and hold a World Exhibition alongside it, while the first Métro line opened a decade later. The arts burgeoned anew with the Impressionist painters and a wealth of musical talent; it was the heyday of Montmartre.

Two World Wars and enemy occupation left Paris comparatively undamaged but economically depressed; and although the city was the cultural hub of the world in the 1920s and 1930s, general recovery was slow. Drastic redevelopment in the 1960s and 1970s resulted not only in the Blvd Périphérique ring-road but also the insensitive skyscrapers of Montparnasse and La Défense, and the destruction of the graceful Les Halles buildings when the markets were moved. It has to be said, however, that redevelopment of certain areas was inevitable, to accommodate a growing population (now approx. 2,170,000) in the suburbs and combat the ever-increasing traffic congestion in the city centre. Recent rebuilding, fortunately, has been on a more human scale, much attention has been paid to cleaning and restoration, and there has been notable improvement of services and facilities – most recently the huge new Palais Omnisports complex in the Bercy area, used for entertainment as well as sport.

View over St-Sulpice

Arc de Triomphe

Principal Sights and Tourist Areas

Arc de Triomphe Focal point from all twelve of the avenues that radiate from it, this colossal monument (50m high and 45m wide) vies with the Eiffel Tower for the honour of being the prime symbol of postcard Paris. Conceived during the Revolution, it was not begun until 1806 when Napoleon approved the plans submitted by Chalgrin, and it was not finished until 1836, after his death. Four huge sculptural compositions in high relief decorate the pillars, of which Rude's "La Marseillaise" (on the right, seen from the Champs-Élysées) is the best. Above are friezes in lower relief commemorating Napoleon's major campaigns and a mass of decorative motifs that include shields inscribed with the names of Revolutionary and Napoleonic victories. Inside the arch are carved the names of lesser military triumphs and of 558 generals; the names underlined are of those who died in the field. Beneath the arch is buried the Unknown Soldier, commemorating the dead of two World Wars, for whom an eternal flame is kept burning. Inside the upper part of the arch is a museum of its history.

Arènes de Lutèce In a quiet little square in the heart of the Latin Quarter, the grassy remnants of this Gallo-Roman amphitheatre constitute one of the very few relics of Roman Paris. The date of its building is not known but it appears to have been destroyed in AD280 and lay forgotten until the Rue Monge was being laid out in the 19C. Now thoroughly excavated and restored, its stage area, wings and tiered seats clearly visible, it is a peaceful place.

Bastille, Place de la Nothing remains of the medieval fortress with its eight towers that for 400 years was used as a prison – mainly for well-born miscreants, such as the Marquis de Sade, or political enemies of the establishment, such as Voltaire – and was the first purely symbolic target of the Revolutionary mob on 14 July 1789. It was demolished immediately thereafter and only a line of stones, tracing its outline on the surface of the square, recalls it. Central point of the busy, rather dreary square today is the 52m bronze July Column, topped by an allegorical figure of Liberty in memory of Parisians who died during the briefer revolutions of 1830 and 1848. Currently the old railway-station site that flanks the Place is being redeveloped with an ambitious new opera house (Opéra de la Bastille) to commemorate the 200th anniversary of the Revolution.

Place de la Bastille

Billettes Cloister The only remaining medieval cloister in Paris is just a short walk away from the Pompidou Centre and Halles area, alongside an unremarkable 18C church. Giving on to a small courtyard, its lines are graceful and harmonious.

Canals of St-Martin, St-Denis and l'Ourcq Work began on the oldest canal, de l'Ourcq, in the 16C: its first lock was designed by Leonardo da Vinci. Not until Napoleon's time, however, when Parisian water supplies had become critically short, was work resumed, and the Canal St-Martin was finally opened in 1825. Thanks to local pressure, a plan to pave the canals over has been dropped and the entire area, formerly seedy, is now enjoying a regeneration. Canal cruises were recently started, the most popular being the three-hour trips by La Patache along the Canal St-Martin in spring and summer. Part of the route was paved over in the time of Baron Haussmann, architect of modern Paris in the late 19C; north of his tunnel, on the Quai de Jemmapes, is the facade of the Hôtel du Nord, made famous by Marcel Carné's 1938 film of the same name.

Cemeteries The principal cemeteries of Paris were created under Napoleon in his first drive to reorganize the city: its existing and too-central burial grounds were cleared and their incumbents' skeletons deposited in ossuaries created from ancient Gallo-Roman quarry workings – now the Catacombs. These can be visited on Sat. afternoons in summer (every other Sat. in winter), whereas the cemeteries themselves, park-like places whose often splendid memorials evoke a host of historic, literary and artistic figures, are normally open during daylight hours.

In **Montmartre** lie buried the painter and sculptor Degas; writers Stendhal, the younger Dumas, Gautier, Murger (author of the book on which the opera *La Bohème* was based) and Zola; musicians Berlioz, Delibes and Offenbach; actors Louis Jouvet and Sacha Guitry; dancers Taglioni and Nijinsky. Nearby is the smaller **St-Vincent** cemetery where that most evocative of Montmartre painters, Utrillo, is buried.

Montparnasse contains the graves of writers de Maupassant and Sainte-Beuve; of the poet Baudelaire; of musicians Saint-Saëns and César Franck; of artists Bourdelle, Soutine and Zadkine; of World War II Vichy-France premier Pierre Laval, and of the eponymous inventor of the Citroën motor car. Among its monuments is Brancusi's charming sculpture, 'The Kiss'.

In **Passy**, a green oasis behind the Palais de Chaillot, lie painters Manet and Berthe Morisot and composers Debussy and Fauré.

Père Lachaise, biggest and best-known of all, needs an entire morning or afternoon just for its principal monuments, which range from a sentimental memorial to the medieval lovers Abélard and Héloïse to the mass grave of Communard rebels executed in 1871, and the cult-centre tomb of a famous spiritualist. Others include those of Oscar Wilde (by Epstein) and writers Colette, Balzac, Proust, La Fontaine (of *Fables* fame) and Molière; composers Chopin, Rossini, Bizet and Cherubini; artists Corot, Modigliani and Delacroix; tragedienne Sarah Bernhardt and cabaret star Edith Piaf.

Père Lachaise cemetery

Champs-Élysées, Avenue This broad sweep, running for 2km from Pl. de la Concorde NW to the Arc de Triomphe (with the new skyscrapers of La Défense visible behind it) constitutes one of the most famous views in Paris. The lower end, between Concorde and the traffic circus known as the Rond-Point, was laid out by Louis XIV's landscape artist, Le Nôtre, in the late 17C, and is still bordered by park-like areas. In the early 19C only about half a dozen mansions stood on it and its reputation was insalubrious; 100 years later, it had assumed its present aspect, lined with cinemas, airline offices, car showrooms, shopping centre, bars and cafés. It is a natural processional route: Napoleon's funeral cortège in 1840 and countless others since, including the invading German army in 1940 and the triumphantly returning French, led by General de Gaulle, in 1944.

Champs-Élysées

Churches The principal churches of Paris are the following:

Dôme see *Invalides.*

Notre-Dame See main entry.

Madeleine See *Concorde/Madeleine area.*

Sacré-Coeur, Basilique du Crowning the summit of Montmartre hill, the Butte, and as much a symbol of Paris as the Eiffel Tower or Arc de Triomphe, the pale, neo-Byzantine bulk of the Sacré-Coeur was built by a number of Catholics as an act of affirmation after the devastating Franco-Prussian war of 1870, funded by public subscription, and consecrated in 1919. Perhaps it is a measure of the piety with which it was regarded that nobody seems to have raised any protest at its design and its unfortunate effect on the city skyline, as they did with the Eiffel Tower. Nowadays, of course, Paris is unimaginable without it, and the views from its terrace, or from the dome, are stunning. The interior is profusely decorated with mosaics and frescoes – all of which causes most visitors to ignore a nearby church of very real worth, St-Pierre-de-Montmartre (q.v.).

St-Denis, Basilique See *Île-de-France* section.

St-Étienne-du-Mont Built between 1492 and 1628 to replace the former abbey church of Ste Geneviève, the variety of architectural styles reflect the inordinate length of time taken over its construction. The interior, particularly, has some lovely features, chief of them the beautifully-carved stone rood-screen, framed at either end by spiral stairs to the galleries; the pulpit; and the 17C stained glass cloister windows. A chapel to Ste Geneviève contains a fragment of her original sarcophagus and there are memorials to Pascal and Racine, who are buried there.

St-Eustache The huge former parish church of the old Halles, built between 1532 and 1640 in a mixture of Gothic and Renaissance styles, now serenely dominates the brash new Halles quarter. It is full of historical associations: Cardinal Richelieu, Molière and the future Mme de Pompadour were christened there; the funerals of Molière and La Fontaine were held there; and Louis XIV took his first communion there. Its soaring, richly decorated interior is best appreciated during one of the concerts whose chief feature is the magnificent organ upon which Berlioz used to play.

St-Germain-l'Auxerrois Located just behind the Louvre, this much-altered church dates back to the 12C from which the Romanesque bell-tower survives, and spans the following four centuries of architectural styles. The 15C Flamboyant Gothic porch is charming, as is the medieval stained glass in the transept windows, and the carved royal pews and pulpit. Many artists are buried here, including Boucher, Nattier, Le Vau, Soufflot and Gabriel.

St-Germain-des-Près Once the heart and hub of Paris's most ancient and powerful abbey, founded in 542 to shelter holy relics brought by King Childebert to France and named for its first bishop, St Germanus, this marvellous church towers over the tawdry commercialism around it. Behind its 12C Romanesque belfry the mainly Romanesque nave yields gracefully to the Gothic choir and ambulatory, the harmony of unsweeping lines fortunately overwhelming the 19C frescoes. Several columns in the upper chancel arches are the oldest elements in the church, which also contains the tomb of Descartes and those of two Scotsmen who served French monarchs: William Douglas, Earl of Angus (d1611) and Lord James Douglas (d1645).

St-Julien-le-Pauvre This is one of the earliest of Paris churches, dating from the late 12C and standing in a shady garden with views across to Notre-Dame. A sense of pious humility pervades the simple interior where medieval pilgrims once prayed before setting out on the long journey to Santiago de Compostela. An iconostasis (altar screen) shuts off the chancel today, for the church is now used by Greek Catholics; it is also the venue for concerts during the Paris summer festival.

St-Merri Built in the first half of the 16C in the Flamboyant Gothic style which had reached its

Sacré-Coeur

peak at that time, and rather over-embellished in the 18C, this nonetheless fine church succeeds triumphantly in bridging the gap between the Renaissance piety that gave it birth, and the explosive modernity that now surrounds it, in the form of the Pompidou Centre and its precincts; it is the venue for numerous lectures, concerts and recitals, and its organ, on which Saint-Saëns played, is a joy to hear.

St-Nicolas-des-Champs, near the Arts et Métiers museum on Rue St-Martin, dating mostly from the 15C, retains its splendid Flamboyant Gothic W portal and belfry but is elsewhere somewhat smothered by later additions.

St-Pierre-de-Montmartre Too often overlooked by the crowds of visitors to the Sacré-Coeur next door, this exquisite little Romanesque church is probably the oldest unaltered sanctuary in Paris. Four Roman columns help to support the interior of the W front, and other noteworthy features include the ancient column-capitals in the nave, and the beautiful chancel arches.

St-Roch Louis XIV himself, in 1653, laid the foundation stone of this oddly elongated church, built to serve the newly burgeoning parish to either side of the Rue St-Honoré, but as it was not completed until some 60 years later, it incorporates many Baroque features into its basically 17C design. The playwright Corneille is buried here, as is Le Nôtre, designer of the Tuileries gardens.

St-Séverin One of the most altered churches in a city notoriously given to remodelling its sanctuaries, St-Séverin, standing in a partly pedestrianized Latin Quarter square close to the Musée de Cluny, incorporates the styles of four centuries, from the 13–17C, yet reconciles them all into a triumphant harmony. Particularly stunning is the ambulatory, its Flamboyant Gothic vaulting springing like palm-leaves from a crowd of columns, the central one delicately twisted. The adjacent garden, formerly the cemetery, is flanked by the arches of the original charnel house, and in this now-peaceful spot the first gallstone operation was performed in 1474: the patient, a prisoner, received a pardon in return for allowing the operation to take place. Regular concerts are given here on the organ once played by Fauré and Saint-Saëns.

St-Sulpice The mismatched towers of the W facade of St-Sulpice dominate the square and its surrounding web of old streets between St-Germain-des-Prés and the Luxembourg Gardens, and add a much-needed light touch to the somewhat ponderous facade. This is another church that took over a century to achieve its present form, under numerous successive architects: it was started in 1655 and not completed until just before the Revolution – when it was promptly converted into a Temple of Reason. Despite this lack of homogeneity, its sheer size gives it a unity and grandeur, emphasized by fine murals (some by Delacroix) and an immense organ (regular concerts are held). Two huge shells that serve as holy-water stoups were presented by François I; a diagonal line that

runs across the transept floor is precisely lit by the sun through a S transept window at midday during the winter solstice.

Val de Grâce At the S edge of the Latin Quarter (q.v.), this fine example of the French Classical style was built by Anne of Austria, wife of Louis XIII, in gratitude for the belated birth, after 23 barren years, of a son, Louis XIV. Much of the convent of which it was part is still preserved, including a beautiful cloister, but it was turned into a hospital during the Revolution and remains the centre of a large medical complex to this day.

Conciergerie Once the Royal Palace, built by Philippe le Bel in the early 14C on the Île de la Cité, it was later used as a prison and much restored and enlarged in the 19C. The exterior, reflected in the Seine, makes an imposing sight flanked by its two oldest towers, the round Tour Bonbec and the square Tour de l'Horloge, which had the first public clock in Paris. Its somewhat oppressive atmosphere within is heightened by the lugubrious commentaries of the guides, who dwell with relish on the famous prisoners incarcerated here, from Ravaillac, who assassinated the popular Henri IV in Rue de la Ferronnerie in 1610, to Marie-Antoinette and the Revolutionary leaders who eventually followed her inside its walls. Parts of the building date back to the 14C and are magnificent, particularly the superbly vaulted anteroom, the Salle des Gardes, in which visitors assemble for the guided tours, the vast Salle des Gens d'Armes beyond it, and the massive medieval kitchens from which upwards of 3000 people could be fed. Marie-Antoinette's cell is preserved, partly as a chapel, and contains mementoes of the unfortunate queen; next door is the cell which held first Danton and then Robespierre.

Concorde/Madeleine area **Place de la Concorde** is by far the largest square in Paris, huge enough even to dwarf somewhat the murderous traffic that constantly swirls about it. It was designed by the architect Gabriel in 1755 for Louis XV, whose statue stood at the centre; this was pulled down by the Revolutionaries and replaced by the guillotine. In 1831 the tactfully non-committal Egyptian obelisk from Luxor was erected; from its base there is a splendid view, framed by Coustou's beautiful marble horses originally carved for Louis XIV's palace at Marly, of the Champs-Élysées and the Arc de Triomphe. The fountains that flank the obelisk were also installed in 1831, but the eight plinths bearing statues dedicated to important French provincial cities were part of Gabriel's original design, as were the two beautifully proportioned buildings on the N side of the square, now housing the Navy Ministry and the **Hotel Crillon**. The view S from the obelisk extends across the **Pont de la Concorde** bridge to the **Palais-Bourbon**, where the National Assembly sits; to the N, between Gabriel's colonnaded facades, it is up **Rue Royale** to the **Madeleine**. This church, with its neo-classical facade, at the heart of one of the city's most chic areas, was conceived at the same time as Pl. de la Concorde to replace an earlier church, but was not consecrated until 1842. In the intervening

141

Place de la Concorde

years it narrowly failed to become a memorial to Napoleon's armies, a theatre, and a railway station. Its full name is Ste-Marie-Madeleine and its interior is unexpectedly opulent. Outside, one of its walls is flanked by flower sellers, and off the Rue Royale, just a few paces from its facade, leads the chic **Rue du Faubourg St-Honoré**, lined with beautiful shops and the splendid buildings housing the Presidential Palace (the Élysée), and the **British Embassy**. The **Élysée Palace**, built in 1738 for the Comte d'Evreux, was subsequently enlarged and became a dance hall during the Revolution. Napoleon signed his abdication here in 1815 after Waterloo. Since 1873 it has served as the official residence of the French president.

Eiffel Tower (Tour Eiffel) So completely has this 321m-high monument, composed of 9700 tons of material, integrated itself into the Paris scene that it is hard to envisage the furore that bridge-builder Gustave Eiffel's masterpiece caused when it was first erected, to commemorate the 100th anniversary of the Revolution. Many demanded its demolition, and only its strategic importance as a radio/telegraphic tower in World War I saved it. Recently overhauled, facelifted and ready for its own centenary, with new lifts, refurbished restaurants, shops, a museum-cinema and a post-office where souvenir postcards can be franked, it is again fully open to sightseers. Over 100 million visitors have now visited it, most of them ascending to the topmost stage (where the view, incidentally, is less clear than from the second stage). To the NW it overlooks the **Pont d'Iéna** bridge and the **Chaillot Palace**; in the opposite direction the views are across the **Champ de Mars** and the **École Militaire**. The Champ de Mars (Martian Field) was laid out on an area previously occupied by market gardens as a military parade-ground by the same architect, Gabriel, who designed Pl. de la Concorde. It also served as an exhibition area and fairground, and at the beginning of this century was converted to a public park with ponds, lawns, trees and some pleasantly peaceful corners.

Gobelins (tapestry workshops) In a dignified complex of buildings just beyond the Latin Quarter in SE Paris are housed the state-owned tapestry workshops of Gobelins (originally founded here in the 15C by a dyer named Jean Gobelins), and Beauvais (moved here after World War II) plus the former royal carpet workshops of Savonnerie. Guided tours are available on Wed., Thurs. and Fri. afternoons.

Halles, Les Only the name recalls the fact that the markets of Paris stood here for over 800 years. For the last century of their existence they were housed in a series of iron-and-glass halls, designed by the architect Baltard under Napoleon III, with storerooms beneath them and linking covered passageways. In the period of redevelopment, largely necessitated by extreme traffic congestion, that followed World War II, these halls were entirely demolished and the markets moved in 1969 to Rungis, outside Paris, leaving an enormous and desolate gap, both visually and spiritually, in Parisian life. Now, slowly, the area is being regenerated – traditionalists would not say improved. Between the bulky rotunda of the 18-19C **Bourse du Commerce** (commodity market) and the church of **St-Eustache** (q.v.), along **Rue de Turbigo**, **Rue Pierre Lescot** and **Rue des Halles**,

Forum des Halles

old narrow houses have been restored and the gaps between them filled with new ones that attempt to echo their austere lines; a cultural centre has been built and a huge semi-underground shopping centre, the **Forum des Halles**, created on four levels, surrounded by glazed arcades that strive to recall Baltard's buildings. Pavilions and pergolas have shot up in some of the empty spaces, most of them pedestrianized, and future plans envisage a park, indoor swimming pool and other amenities. Faint echoes of the old Halles can be found in some of the smaller surrounding streets: the famous kitchenware shop of **Dehillerin** still exists in Rue Coquillière; there are still a few food merchants, and some of the traditionally atmospheric old restaurants, notably *Pharamond* and *Au Pied de Cochon*. The beautiful Renaissance **Fontaine des Innocents**, which was built in 1549 and stands on the site of the medieval communal cemetery, has been restored, but sadly an inevitable tinge of garishness has invaded the area, with tatty souvenir shops, sex shops and cheap boutiques vying for attention with fast-food outlets and more genuine attractions. Nevertheless, it is a lively district, popular with young people.

Îles de la Cité and St-Louis Lying in mid-Seine, linked to each other and to the river banks by fourteen bridges, these two islands and the atmospheric *quais* facing them on either side constitute one of the city's most fascinating districts. The Île de la Cité is the cradle of Paris, site of the earliest Gallic inhabitants, and was for centuries the city's royal, administrative, judicial and ecclesiastical centre. The medieval core of the Cité, with its numerous churches, chapels and theological schools, remained intact almost until the reign of Napoleon III. In the process of modernization, Baron Haussmann demolished the centre of the Cité and removed 25,000 of its inhabitants to make room for street-widening and immense new public buildings. Yet despite the changes wrought by the centuries, the Cité still survives as the very heart of

the capital. At the extreme downstream end, the tiny **Vert-Galant** square, with its statue of Henri IV (the name being an allusion to his prowess as a lover), is backed by the **Pont Neuf** and the *quais* beyond. Between them is the leafy **Pl. Dauphine** with its attenuated stone-and-brick 17C houses; and behind that the vast complex of the **Palais de Justice** (Law Courts) and the **Conciergerie** (q.v.) enfold the exquisite **Sainte Chapelle** (q.v.). Dwarfed by the bulky outlines of the **Hôtel-Dieu** hospital, the Police Headquarters and the Commercial Courts, the **Pl. Louis-Lépine** blazes unexpectedly with a cheerful flower market. Beneath the **Pl. du Parvis Notre-Dame**, facing the great cathedral (q.v.), lie relics of an earlier Paris in the **Crypte Archéologique** (q.v.), and alongside the cathedral to the N is the meticulously restored medieval **Ancien Cloître** quarter with one of the city's oldest churches, the tiny **St-Aignan** chapel. This area and the little garden squares at the upstream end of the Cité are less frequented by strollers and sightseers than other parts of the island, and one can find even greater seclusion by crossing the **Pont St-Louis** to the smaller and utterly peaceful island of the same name. Formerly two islands, they were joined in the first half of the 17C and the land developed in the classical style; many of the original buildings remain unchanged and none of the later ones threaten the architectural harmony of this delicious spot. Two notable 17C mansions are the **Hôtel de Lauzun**, briefly occupied by Baudelaire and Gautier, with sumptuously decorated ceilings, panelling and tapestries; and the **Hôtel Lambert**, once the home of Voltaire. The latter building stands at the far end of the island's main thoroughfare, the Rue St-Louis-en-l'Île, which leads to the Baroque church of **St-Louis-en-l'Isle**. The richly decorated interior boasts fine gold, marble and enamel-work, paintings and English alabaster. In spite of the absence of major sightseeing features, the island emanates an atmosphere of elegant self-sufficiency unmatched anywhere else in Paris.

Île de la Cité

Invalides, Les Conceived in the grand manner by Louis XIV to house soldiers wounded in his service, the Invalides was realized to perfection by the architect Libéral-Bruand and later crowned by Hardouin-Mansart with the addition of the arrestingly cupolaed **Dôme** church. Originally the building housed over 5000 invalided soldiers; today the number has shrunk to fewer than 100 and the remainder of the space is occupied by Napoleon's tomb and by military museums. Napoleon's body was brought here in solemn procession after its return from St Helena in 1840 and his ashes interred in the crypt of the Dôme in no fewer than six coffins, one inside the other, all encased in a red porphyry sarcophagus surrounded by reliefs and statuary.

Latin Quarter This vibrant, mosly youthful and slightly raffish district grew up in the 12C on the site of the Roman settlement of Lutetia when the monk Abélard broke away from the rigid teaching-pattern established on the Île de la Cité to form the core of a more liberal university. In 1253 Robert de Sorbon founded a college there for poor students which eventually became the Sorbonne, among whose teachers was St Thomas Aquinas. The name of the district derives from the fact that in former times students, and even their servants, had to converse in Latin, and until Baron Haussmann drove the broad boulevards **St-Germain** and **St-Michel** through it, it was a cobweb of narrow, insanitary streets whose main artery was **Rue St-Jacques**, the old Gallo-Roman road and start of the medieval pilgrims' way to Santiago (St Jacques) de Compostela. Today the Latin Quarter is no longer the university headquarters, for around 1969 the University of Paris was decentralized and split into thirteen new units; but it still has a large student population studying at the (largely rebuilt) **Sorbonne**, the **Collège de France**, and the **Lycée Henri IV**. Boutiques, clubs and fast-food outlets of every nationality spatter the area but echoes of the past can be found in its many bookshops and in some of its older streets: **Rue de la Harpe**, **Rue des Grands-Augustins**, **Rue Séguier**, **Rue Gît-le-Coeur**, **Rue St-André-des-Arts** and **Rue du Chat-qui-Pèche**, among others. It is rich in important sights and churches: the **Musée Cluny**, **Arènes de**

Students in Left Bank bookshop

Lutèce and **Panthéon** (qq.v.); the churches of **St-Séverin**, **St-Julien-le-Pauvre**, **St-Étienne-du-Mont** and the **Val-de-Grâce** (qq.v.); plus the **Grand Mosque** of Paris, near the Arènes de Lutèce, and **St-Médard** at the foot of **Rue Mouffe-tard** (see *Markets*). Inside the Sorbonne building is the elegant chapel where Cardinal Richelieu is buried, and inside the Lycée Henri IV (closed to the public) are the remains of the original abbey of **Ste-Geneviève**.

Place des Vosges

Marais, Le One of the most typical, least spoiled, old-Parisian districts, the Marais takes its name from the marsh that covered this area; it was drained in the 12C. Its development as a residential district started in the late 16C when Henri IV laid out the beautiful **Pl. des Vosges** (then Pl. Royale) around which the rich and famous subsequently built magnificent mansions. By a miracle, Baron Haussmann's 19C replanning of Paris stopped short of the Marais, which gradually dwindled into a slum, and by another miracle it was declared a conservation area in the early 1960s by the then Minister of Culture, André Malraux, and was consequently saved from post-war redevelopment. Restoration has been taking place ever since and the narrow streets of this quarter, stretching up from the Seine with the **Pompidou Centre** at its W edge and the **Canal St-Martin** to the E, are lined with beautiful old mansions *(hôtels)*, many of them museums (see *Museums*); others, like the **Hôtels du Sens, de Lamoignon, des Ambassadeurs de Hollande, d'Albret**, and many more, are seldom, if ever, open but can be viewed from outside and from their courtyards. **The Hôtel de Béthune-Sully** at No 62 Rue St-Antoine now houses the information office of the Historic Monuments department, and its interior can be visited on Wed., Sat. and Sun. afternoons. Notable churches in the Marais include the Jesuit **St-Paul-St-Louis**, **St-Gervais-St-Protais**, **Notre-Dame-des-Blancs-Manteaux**, and **St-Merri** (q.v.). At the heart of the area is the wonderfully harmonious Pl. des Vosges with its mellow red brick facades and arcaded pavements; its houses have sheltered a number of famous people, including Mme de Sévigné, Cardinal Richelieu, and Victor Hugo who lived at No 6.

Market on Place Maubert

Markets Central to Parisian "village" life, the open air street markets, selling mostly food, of **Rues Lepic**, **Mouffetard** and **Buci** and of **Place Maubert**, **Blvd Raspail** and **La Muette**, make colourful spectacles. Two well-restored 19C covered **food markets** are to be found in the 10th *arrondissement*: **St-Quentin**, near the Gare de L'Est, and **St-Martin** on Rue Bouchardon behind the Blvd de Strasbourg. Most famous of the **Marchés aux Puces** (flea markets) – selling furniture and all sorts of bric-à-brac – is the huge one beyond the Porte de Clignancourt Métro station; while no longer a place for amazing bargains, it still yields good buys. Other flea markets, mostly at weekends, function at the Porte de Vanves and Porte de Montreuil. A **pet market** is open daily along the *quais* du Louvre and Mégisserie, opposite the Île de la Cité; on the island itself, **birds** are sold in Pl. Louis-Lépine alongside the flowers and there are other **flower markets** in Pl. de la Madeleine, Pl. de la République and Pl. des Ternes. **Books and prints** are sold from boxlike stalls all along the left bank of the Seine from the Pont Royal to the Pont St-Michel and along the *quais* du Louvre and Mégisserie on the right bank; there is a **stamp market** on Ave. Gabriel, parallel with the Champs-Élysées, (Thurs, Sat, Sun) and a weekend **textile market** in Montmartre on the Pl. St-Pierre.

Métro-station entrances The Paris underground or Métro is the easiest and quickest way of getting round the city, with quiet trains, clean stations and excellent information facilities. There is a standard fare for all inner network services, no matter how many changes are made. The Métro, which is being continuously improved and modernized, is integrated with the *Réseau Express Régional* (RER) which provides an extra-fast service across Paris and out through the suburbs, including a line to Versailles, with extensions planned and in progress. When the first Métro opened in 1900, every station entrance was graced with *art-nouveau* canopies by Hector Guimard. Most have now disappeared but a few have been restored or replaced with reproductions. They can be seen at the following stations: Gare de Lyon, Bastille, Châtelet, Louvre, Palais-Royal and Tuileries (on Line 1); Père-Lachaise, Ménilmontant, Barbes-Rochechouart, Anvers, Pigalle, Nation, Blanche, Clichy, Monceau and Ternes (Line 2); République, Temple, Opéra, St-Lazare and Wagram (Line 3); Gare du Nord, Château d'Eau, Étienne-Marcel, Cité, St-Michel, Raspail, Denfert-Rochereau (Line 4); Place d'Italie (Line 5); Picpus, Daumesnil, Pasteur, Boissière and Nation (Line 6); Porte d'Auteuil, Mirabeau, Église d'Auteuil (Line 10). There are good reproductions at Kléber, on Line 6, and Abbesses, on Line 12.

Métro entrance, Place des Abbesses

Steps leading down from Montmartre

Montmartre The name is a condensation of 'Mont des Martyres' recalling the martyrdom of Paris's first bishop, St-Denis, who was beheaded on the slopes of the 130m-high hill. In the 12C a Benedictine abbey was established there in memory of him: the tiny **Chapelle du Martyre** in Rue Yvonne le Tac (not open to the public), where the Order of Jesus was founded in 1534, is a relic of it, as is the church of **St-Pierre** (q.v.). Around it a village grew up where wine, cereals and vegetables were cultivated and flour milled for the city, which eventually engulfed it in the 19C. Following the horrors of the Communards' Revolt of 1871, which started in Montmartre, artists started to move out there, attracted by its picturesqueness and its cheapness; and its heyday as a bohemian quarter, when Toulouse-Lautrec, Utrillo, Renoir, Signac, Seurat, Picasso and Braque painted there, lasted until past the turn of the century. Today parts of it have become thoroughly sleazy, particularly along **Blvd de Clichy**, **Pl. Blanche**, site of the famous *Moulin Rouge* music hall, and **Pl. Pigalle**, with the notorious 'hot streets' leading off it; and parts have become self-conscious touristy parodies of their erstwhile prettiness, notably **Pl. du Tertre** and its surroundings. Yet other Montmartre streets – **Rue Lepic**, with its market, and those around the back of the hill, below **Rue Caulaincourt** – retain their cachet and, in addition to the churches of the **Sacré-Coeur** and **St-Pierre**, and the famous Montmartre cemeteries, there are still plenty of absorbing sights. The **Musée du Vieux Montmartre** is one, installed in an old house that was at one time a bistro and is full of mementoes; another is the **Historial** waxworks museum and yet another the **Musée de l'Art Juif** (Jewish Art). The only vineyard in Paris, the **Montmartre Vineyard**, celebrates its *vendange* in early Oct. each year; the **Lapin Agile** café near it still recalls the former village and the **Moulin de la Galette** and the **Bâteau-Lavoir** studios (rebuilt) evoke memories of Renoir and of the Cubist painters respectively.

Montparnasse Following World War I, when Montmartre had become too expensive and chic, artists and literati started to gravitate S of the Seine to Montparnasse, named after Mount Parnassus, home of the Muses, by the 17C students who frequented it and gave recitals of their poems there. Its hill was flattened when **Boulevard du Montparnasse** was laid out, but cafés and entertainment-centres moved in and its light-hearted reputation was born (recalled, in name only, by Rue de la Gaieté). Its heyday lasted well into the 1930s when it was frequented by artists such as Rodin, Modigliani, Léger, Soutine, Chagall and Rousseau-le-Douanier; writers such as Sainte-Beuve, Apollinaire, Rilke, Romain Rolland, Cocteau, Ernest Hemingway and Henry Miller; and political exiles Lenin and Trotsky. Their stamping grounds were the famous boulevard cafés, *Le Dôme, Le Sélect, La Rotonde, La Coupole,* and the *Closerie des Lilas* – the last three still retaining something of their former atmosphere. After World War II the developers moved in and subjected the quarter to some of the ugliest rebuilding ever seen, exemplified by the spiky new **Tour Montparnasse**, the modern railway station and the growing complex of skyscrapers around them. Among the district's sights are, of course, its famous cemetery (q.v.) and a trio of small museums: **Musée Zadkine**, in Rue d'Assas, where the sculptor lived for 40 years; **Musée Bourdelle**, in Rue de Bourdelle, also in the sculptor's former studio; and the nearby **Postal Museum** in Blvd de Vaugirard. A notable landmark at the crossing of Blvd Raspail and Blvd du Montparnasse, is a splendid statue of Balzac by Rodin.

Museums Space permits only a brief mention of the major museums and their contents. Other smaller museums are alluded to elsewhere under appropriate main entries.

Armée, Musée de l' Housed in the Invalides and rarely closed, this enormous collection of military memorabilia spreads over three floors in two wings, and covers the evolution of arms and armour from the Middle Ages to World War II. Particularly fascinating is the collection of miniature soldiery and weaponry in the main museum, and the scale models of forts and fortified French towns in the adjacent Musée des Plans-Reliefs.

Art Moderne, Musée Nationale d' Occupying the third and fourth floors of the Pompidou Centre (q.v.), this collection is rivalled only by New York's Museum of Modern Art as the biggest in the world and covers the development of painting and sculpture from 1865 to the present day, from Fauvism through Cubism, Abstract Expressionism, Dadaism and Surrealism to contemporary Action and Pop art. Opening off the main galleries dedicated to each art movement are smaller spaces devoted to particular artists or groups of artists. It is worth taking a guided tour on the first visit, to gain an insight into the method of presentation.

Art Moderne de la Ville de Paris, Musée d' Housed in the Palais de Tokyo and completely reorganized following the removal of many works to the Pompidou Centre, this excellent collection focuses on artists linked with Paris or who were members of the Paris School: Dufy, Picasso, Braque, Matisse; the pointilliste painters Signac, Seurat, Vuillard and Bonnard; Modigliani, Soutine, Rouault, Van Dongen and Vlaminck. In addition, there are temporary exhibitions of contemporary art and occasional lively manifestations of other art forms.

Arts Africains et Océaniens, Musée des   Originally called the Colonial (Outre-Mer) Museum when it was established (by the Bois de Vincennes, Métro Port Dorée) in 1931, it houses some superb examples of ethnic art, notably from Islamic and black Africa and the Pacific.

Arts Décoratifs, Musée des   Enclosed within the Marsan wing of the Louvre, entered from Rue de Rivoli, and entirely reorganized between 1980 and 1985, its object is to show the evolution of taste in the applied arts from the Middle Ages onwards. This is done in a succession of rooms representing every major phase of decorative styles, including everything from furniture and fabrics down to the smallest bibelot. Some of the best exhibits are of French styles, but other European countries are also represented, as is Islamic decorative art.

Arts et Métiers, Conservatoire des   Paris's science museum occupies part of the ancient priory of St-Martin-des-Champs in Rue St-Martin and many of the exhibits are within the former church. On prior application, permission can be obtained to see the beautiful 13C former refectory, designed by Pierre de Montreuil and now the library.

Arts et Traditions Populaires, Musée des   Located at the N end of the Bois de Boulogne, off Route du Mahatma Gandhi, this somewhat clinical display of French ethnography and folklore includes regional costumes, crafts and domestic artefacts, agricultural tools, and even aids to witchcraft.

*Balzac, Maison de (*see *Passy–Trocadéro)*   One of the main attractions of this house for the perpetually hard-up author of the *Comédie Humaine* must have been its two entrances: the main one off Rue Reynouard and a back one lower down, on Rue Berton, enabling him to avoid his creditors. Full of atmosphere and memorabilia, it also contains a comprehensive library.

Beaux Arts de la Ville de Paris, Musée des   Housed in the Petit Palais and built for the Paris Exhibition of 1900, this highly eclectic collection ranges from ancient sculptures through medieval and Renaissance furniture and paintings to 18C porcelain. Its best section comprises French works of art of the 19–20C.

Bibliothèque Nationale, Rue de Richelieu, Cardinal Mazarin's former palace (see *Palais Royal)* today houses a collection of medallions and temporary exhibits.

Bourdelle, Musée, Rue Antoine-Bourdelle (see *Montparnasse).*

Bricard, Musée, Rue de la Perle. One of the great mansions of the Marais (q.v.), turned into a museum in the course of restoration, this Hôtel, the Libéral-Bruant, built in 1685 for his own residence by the architect of the Invalides, contains a charming collection illustrating the development of the locksmith's and metalworker's art.

Carnavalet, Musée   Another marvellous Marais mansion, built in the Renaissance style, partly remodelled by the architect Mansart and from 1677–96 occupied by Mme de Sévigné, its imposing courtyard opens off Rue de Sévigné and its collection illustrates the history of Paris and the daily life of its citizens over the centuries. Furniture, paintings, frescoes, maps, old prints and sketches, old tradesmen's signs, a reconstruction of an old café and of a chemist's shopfront, are displayed in a series of well-arranged rooms that include Mme de Sévigné's own apartments.

Cernuschi, Musée   On the edge of the Parc Monceau in Ave Velasquez, the house and its rich collection of Chinese art-objects, dating back to earliest times, belonged to a 19C Italian banker.

Chaillot, Palais de, Pl. du Trocadéro   Built in the 1930s in the shape of an archer's bow, with the charming Trocadéro gardens running down to the river from it, the Palais de Chaillot contains four museums: Cinéma, de l'Homme (mankind), de la Marine (navy), and the Monuments Français – plus a theatre and an aquarium. The site is of some interest: Catherine de Médicis had a country house there which later became a convent, much frequented by ladies of noble birth expiating their sorrows. Napoleon conceived the idea of building a palace for his son there and razed the site, but the plans were abandoned when his son died. The area was briefly occupied by a pavilion used for the 1878 Paris Exhibition and called the Palais du

View from the Palais de Chaillot

Trocadéro. The Cinema museum not only illustrates the technology of film-making but also includes a wealth of sets, props, costumes and other evocative material, plus a theatre in which old films are shown. The Musée de l'Homme is a wide-ranging anthropological and ethnographic survey richly illustrated with all sorts of objects including rock-paintings from the Sahara, Easter Island cult-carvings and a mummified Inca from Peru. The Maritime museum (de la Marine) is a comprehensive chronicle of the history of seafaring generally, with an array of model ships and old figureheads. The Monuments Français museum, far more absorbing than its name might suggest, sprang from an idea of Viollet-le-Duc, the 19C art historian who restored so many of France's great buildings, and who needed scale models from which to work. An array of amazing models traces the development of art and architecture in France.

Chasse, Musée de la A museum of hunting might seem of limited appeal but this one, housed in Mansart's stunning mid-17C Hôtel Guénégaud in Rue des Archives, is something else. One of the first Marais mansions to be rescued from dereliction in the early 1960s, its saviour was François Sommer, himself an enthusiastic hunter, and the exhibits, which include paintings related to the hunting theme as well as stuffed trophies, weapons, and fine objects from former royal hunting-lodges, fit appropriately into their superb setting.

Cluny, Musée de One of the gems of Paris, located where Blvd St-Michel and Blvd St-Germain intersect on the edge of the Latin Quarter, the medieval building was raised by a 14C abbot of Cluny to house visiting dignitaries from that great abbey in Burgundy. It is built above the ruins of a huge 3C Gallo-Roman bath-house, the Thermes de Lutèce, and at various times was occupied by Mary Tudor and by Cardinal Mazarin. Its last private owner was a wealthy 19C collector, and it was turned into a museum in 1844. The bulk of its collection is medieval: ecclesiastical treasures, furniture, original sculptures ripped from Notre-Dame at the time of the Revolution, metalwork, objets d'art, jewellery (including some rare Visigothic pieces) and, above all, tapestries, among them the famous "Lady with the Unicorn" series. The former abbots' chapel is preserved on the first floor. Below and in the gardens are the remains of the thermal baths, including some of the original vaulting.

Cognacq-Jay, Musée An oasis of civilized calm is this former draper's shop on the Blvd des Capucines (see *Opéra quarter*). It belonged to the founder of the Samaritaine department stores, a compulsive collector. The house is decorated in pure 18C style with panelling, furniture and furnishings of the period, and the works of art are mostly of the same epoch.

Crypte Archéologique One of Paris's newest museums, this is buried beneath the square in front of Notre-Dame and consists of the excavations made there. Reliefs, fragments of statues, cellar-walls of medieval houses and relics of Roman ramparts, inscriptions and gravestones, are

all admirably linked and explained with the help of models and plans.

Découverte, Palais de la Occupying part of the Grand Palais on Ave Winston-Churchill, which together with its smaller companion, the Petit Palais, was built in the grandiose style of the period for the Paris Exhibition of 1900, the museum's exhibits relate to scientific discovery in all fields and include a splendid planetarium.

Delacroix, Musée (see *St-Germain quarter*) Evocations of the great Romantic artist in the apartments where he ended his life.

d'Ennery, Musée Outstanding among the exhibits, collected by a 19C dramatist in his sumptuous home on Avenue Foch, close to the Bois de Boulogne, and only open on Sun. afternoons, are the *netsuke* (traditional ivory ornaments from Japan). Most of the other furniture, porcelain and art objects, all Oriental, are more interesting for their sheer and rather endearing profusion. The Armenian museum, in the same house, is open similar hours.

Grand Palais (see *Découverte, Palais de la*).

Grévin, Musée (see also *Opéra and Grands Boulevards*). To call this museum on Blvd Montmartre the Paris equivalent of Madame Tussauds in London only tells part of the story. Founded by an early 19C caricaturist, waxworks of famous personalities do constitute the main part of the exhibits, but there are also magic and illusion shows and other flights of fancy. A branch of the museum has recently opened in the Forum des Halles (see *Les Halles*).

Guimet, Musée The 19C industrialist and traveller, Émile Guimet, presented the core of this Oriental collection, located on Pl. d'Iéna, to the state in 1884. Under the management of the Louvre, it has been considerably augmented by other collections and by works from the parent museum and forms one of the richest assemblies of Far Eastern art in existence. Works displayed there include rare Cambodian sculptures, items from Pakistan and Afghanistan, Tibet and Nepal, Indian bronzes, and Chinese porcelain.

Histoire de France, Musée de l' (also known as the Archives Nationales). A magnificent Marais mansion, the Hôtel de Soubise on Rue des Francs-Bourgeois occupies the site of a medieval manor built in 1375, and incorporates its original gateway into the Rue des Archives facade. For over 100 years it belonged to the Guise family until it passed into the hands of the Princesse de Soubise at the end of the 17C. It was acquired to store the National Archives in 1808, thus escaping the dilapidation that other Marais mansions suffered. There are imaginatively mounted displays of documents illustrating French history: the Edict of Nantes, which brought religious freedom to France, and the later Revocation, which sparked off the religious wars; letters from Joan of Arc, Marie-Antoinette and Voltaire; the wills of Louis

XIV and Napoleon and much more. The National Archives also spill over into the nearby Hôtel de Rohan which the state acquired in 1927 and where temporary exhibitions are often held; its courtyard is stunning, as are the splendidly restored state apartments.

Histoire Naturelle, Muséum National d' A quartet of galleries flanking the S edge of the Jardin des Plantes (q.v.) house this museum's departments of Entomology (insects), Mineralogy (fossils and gems), Palaeobotany (petrified plants) and Palaeontology (animal skeletons and reconstructions of prehistoric "monsters"); there are also temporary exhibitions in a nearby annexe.

Invalides, Hôtel des (see *Armée, Musée de l'*).

Jacquemart-André, Musée Banker Édouard André built this imposing mansion on Blvd Haussmann during the latter half of the 19C; now the property of the Institut de France, it houses the magnificent collection accumulated by him and his wife, portraitist Nélie Jacquemart. On the ground floor are sumptuous examples of 18C French art: furniture, objets d'art paintings, tapestries and other treasures; the staircase and several upper rooms have frescoes by Tiepolo.

Jeu de Paume One of the two Second Empire pavilions at the W end of the Tuileries gardens, this houses the Louvre's collection of Impressionist art – the late-19C movement that took its name from Claude Monet's hauntingly misty painting entitled "Sunrise: Impression" (now in the Marmottan museum, q.v.). By no means all the Louvre's Impressionist collection can be accommodated here – the new museum of the 19C projected for the refurbished Gare d'Orsay in 1986 will, it is hoped, give them more space – but despite overcrowding and occasional apparently illogical hanging (when pictures from various bequests or donations are hung together, rather than alongside individual artists' works) it affords a rich and colourful overview of the movement and its offshoots. Artists represented include Bazille, Boudin, Fantin-Latour, Jongkind, Manet, Monet, Pissarro, Renoir, Sisley and Toulouse-Lautrec, among the "pure" Impressionists; Degas and Van Gogh, on the periphery of the movement; Cézanne, Seurat and Signac among the post-Impressionists; and Gauguin, whose style is quite unclassifiable.

Louvre, Musée du Perhaps the world's richest collection – though in great need of the rebuilding and reorganization currently under way – it occupies the most palatial premises of any of the world's national museums. Looked at from the Tuileries gardens, or from the riverbank Quai du Louvre, the vast building gives an impression of architectural unity that is not far short of miraculous, since it took over six centuries to achieve its present form. Begun as a fortress in 1200, and converted and enlarged by Charles V into a royal residence in the 14C, it was pulled down and rebuilt in the 16C at the instigation of François I who was an amateur of Italian Renaissance art and wanted a suitable setting for his sizeable collection (which included the *Mona Lisa*, called *La Gioconde* in France). The SW corner of the central Cour Carrée dates back to his time, but successive monarchs all added to the building. Henri II's wife, Catherine de Médicis started to build the continuation of the Cour Carrée along the riverside and was also responsible for the extreme ends of the two wings – the Pavillons de Flore and de Marsan, originally part of her own Tuileries Palace. Louis XIII and Louis XIV completed the Cour Carrée, and Napoleon was responsible for the Rue de Rivoli wing and for other additions. Each ruler in turn added to the contents: Louis XIV and Napoleon amassed the greatest numbers of treasures, but Henri IV set a style in royal patronage of the arts by installing artists and craftsmen on the premises. It was made into a museum after the Revolution and its collections have grown ever since. Now more space is to be made for them by reclaiming the wing currently occupied by the Finance Ministry, and by creating a new underground "reception" area beneath the

The Louvre

Cour Napoléon, lit by a fountain-encircled glass pyramid. It is advisable to take one of the guided tours on the first visit, to get an overall view, and to return later for more detailed viewing – avoiding Sundays, if possible, when admission is free and crowds immense. Briefly, the collections subdivide into six main sections. Greek and Roman Antiquities, including the Venus de Milo, Victory of Samothrace and the much earlier Hera of Samos, now share most of the ground-floor galleries with the Oriental Antiquities department (mostly Middle-Eastern) and with part of the immense Egyptian Antiquities section, founded, after Napoleon's Egyptian campaigns, by the great French archaeologist Champollion. The Sculpture department, depicting the evolution of French sculpture through the ages but also including some magnificent examples from other countries, occupies the end part of the S wing, including the Pavillon de Flore. Paintings, an incredibly rich and comprehensive section, occupy most of the upper floors and include many more Leonardos than the *Mona Lisa*, plus works by other Italian Renaissance artists such as Raphael, Titian and Veronese; the Spanish, Flemish, Dutch and German schools are also represented, but French paintings from the 14–19C are the most numerous. Objets d'art and furniture comprise the sixth section and include the Crown Jewels; they are now displayed on the first floor in the richly frescoed and panelled galleries around the Cour Carrée.

Marmottan, Musée Overlooking the shady Ranelagh gardens from its location on Rue Louis-Boilly at the edge of the Bois de Boulogne, this 19C mansion was owned and furnished by wealthy art-lover Jules Marmottan and his son, who bequeathed it to the Institut de France. Its finely displayed salons, mainly furnished in the style of the First (Napoleonic) Empire, exude a faintly and undeservedly neglected air, however, for most visitors come here to view the fantastic Monet collections which were bequeathed to the Marmottan during the post-war years. They include some of the artist's most stunning flower-border and water-lily paintings, plus important works by his friends and contemporaries.

Mode, Musée de la Changing exhibitions of costumes, highlighting the evolution of fashion, occupy the 19C Palais de Galliéra, built in the Italian Renaissance style with a charming garden on Avenue Pierre-I-de-Serbie.

Nissim de Camondo, Musée Like so many smaller Paris museums, including the Cernuschi, which is also on the edge of the Parc de Monceau, this was originally a private collection. The house, on Rue de Monceau, was inspired by the Petit Trianon at Versailles and that 18C period was the principal passion of its builder, the wealthy Count Moise de Camondo. It is a wonderfully homogeneous collection, beautifully maintained by the Musée des Arts Décoratifs.

Picasso, Musée The most recent transformation of a great Marais mansion is that of the 17C Hôtel Salé, on Rue de Thorigny, to house the works of that colossus of modern art, Pablo Picasso. A French resident for most of his life, he was also a prudent collector of his own works, and many of these were handed over to the French government after his death to discharge his tax liabilities. They constitute a fascinating microcosm of his prodigious output and changing styles, as well as of his astonishing versatility. A few works are by other artists, mostly his friends and contemporaries.

Rodin, Musée One of the very few mansions of the St-Germain quarter (q.v.) that can be visited is the Hôtel Biron, on Rue de Varenne, which Rodin occupied from 1907–17. Built in 1730 to designs by Gabriel, it was owned towards the end of the century by Marshal Biron and briefly became, after his execution in 1793, a music hall. Much of its decoration was later removed by order of nuns who subsequently occupied it, but has been partially restored. The state acquired the mansion early in this century and made it available to artists, and the house and garden make a beautiful setting for Rodin's sculptures.

Victor-Hugo, Musée The great French writer and national hero lived at no 6, Pl. des Vosges, from 1833–48 and the house is full of mementoes of his life and work, most interesting and unexpected of which are probably his drawings and paintings, and idiosyncratic pieces of furniture he designed from old fragments.

Notre-Dame-de-Paris The great cathedral on the Île de la Cité was begun in 1163 but not completed for 165 years. Thus it enshrines all aspects of the pure Gothic style and its architectural influence can be seen all over Europe. Saint Louis lay in state there, Henri IV was converted to Catholicism there, French kings – and one English king, Henry VI – were crowned there, as was Napoleon when he became emperor in 1804; and countless royal marriages have taken place there, including that of Mary Stuart of Scotland to the young Dauphin (later, briefly, to become François II). During the Revolution most of its statues were smashed and its treasures looted; half a century later, it was sweepingly restored by the 19C arch-restorer, Viollet-le-Duc, but only narrowly escaped severe fire-damage during the Communards' revolt of 1871. The W front, crowned by its two towers, is composed of three tiers, the lower pierced by three vaulted doorways with magnificent portals. From left to right, they depict the Virgin, the Last

Notre-Dame de Paris

Judgement, and St Anne. Above them is the frieze of statues called the Kings' Gallery, in which almost all the figures are reproductions because the Revolutionaries had supposed them to be kings of France rather than kings of Judaea and Israel. Some original pieces can be seen in the Musée Cluny (q.v.). Above this, the great rose window is flanked by two pierced Gothic bays, and above them a screen of carved narrow arches links the two towers. High points of the N and S facades are the Cloister Portal opening into the N transept with a beautiful original figure of the Virgin above it and the St-Étienne portal on the S transept. The apse radiates elegant 14C flying buttresses; the lantern-spire is a Viollet-le-Duc vaulted replica. Inside, the cathedral's breadth and simplicity are enhanced by tiers of arches rising to the vaulted ceiling and suffused with soft light from the three great rose windows of the transepts and the W front; the N transept rose is nearly all 13C. Among the treasures to look for are a beautiful 14C statue of the Virgin and Child against the southern-most pillar at the chancel entrance; the 14C chancel-screen reliefs; many of the later statues and paintings in the ambulatory chapels, and the 18C carved wood choir-stalls. Finally, a visit to the towers affords not only fine views over the Île de la Cité but also close-ups of many a grotesque gargoyle.

Opéra and Grands Boulevards quarter The mid-19C **Opéra**, designed by Charles Garnier, dominates this part of Paris by the sheer glitter of its ornate facade. Inaugurated in 1875, its interior is equally grandiose, with a huge foyer, a magnificent marble staircase, sumptuous chandeliers, acres of gold leaf and plush, and an auditorium whose ceiling was frescoed by Chagall in 1964. If the Opéra itself is the visual focal point of its area, this is due as much to the planning of Baron Haussmann as to the architect: Haussmann laid down the broad boulevard that bears his name, the quadrangle of streets that enclose the Opéra building, the huge square in front of it and the avenue leading away from it. The **Blvd des Italiens** was already a centre of entertainment, taking its name from an older theatre specializing in Italian light opera, of which Rossini was briefly musical director. Now it boasts numerous cinemas and the **Opéra Comique** is just off it, behind the ornate Crédit Lyonnais bank building. To the W of the Opéra, the broad avenue becomes **Blvd des Capucines**, with the **Cognacq-Jay museum** (q.v.) of paintings and objets d'art and the famous **Café de la Paix**; the boulevard leads eventually to the Madeleine. N of the Opéra on **Blvd Haussmann** are the two massive department stores, **Au Printemps** and **Galeries Lafayette**; just past its junction with Blvd des Italiens, the Rue Drouot leads in a very few paces to the newly rebuilt **Drouot auction rooms**. Beyond this junction, still on Blvd Haussmann, is the **Musée Grévin**.

Palais Royal This lovely and unexpectedly peaceful enclave with its gardens, fountain and arcaded pavements seems miles from the Paris of today swirling round it, yet it has not always been so other-worldly. Built originally by Cardinal Richelieu as his personal residence in 1629, it

Palais Royal

eventually passed to Philippe d'Orléans, regent for the young Louis XV, who held orgiastic parties there that scandalized the city. The E wing was virtually destroyed by fire in 1763 and Philippe's descendant, the future Philippe-Égalité, decided to raise the money for its rebuilding by enclosing the gardens with galleries of shops on the ground floor and apartments to let above them, and these are the buildings to be seen today. Revolutionaries held meetings and staged demonstrations in the gardens towards the end of the century, and after the Revolution the entire premises became notorious for its brothels and gaming-houses. It again suffered damage both in the 1848 revolution and during the Commune; today, with the **Comédie Française** rebuilt into its SW corner, its little curio shops and its restored gardens, it is a welcome oasis. To the N is the beautiful covered **Galerie Vivienne** shopping arcade, and across Rue de Richelieu is the **Bibliothèque Nationale** (National Library) in a mansion whose marvellous reading room, its ceiling supported by cast-iron columns with tops that fan out like umbrella-spokes, can be admired through glass doors; there is also a small museum (q.v.). Also nearby is the charming **Pl. Louvois** with a very delightful fountain, designed by Visconti, and **Pl. des Victoires**, designed in honour of Louis XIV.

Panthéon In gratitude for having recovered from an illness in 1744, Louis XV vowed to build a magnificent shrine for Ste Geneviève and Soufflot was commissioned to design it. Lack of money delayed its construction and other misfortunes plagued it; as a result it was not finished until 1789, after Soufflot's death. The Revolutionary Assembly then decided to convert it into a mausoleum for the heroes of French liberty, and caused many of the windows to be filled in. Mirabeau was the first incumbent, followed by Voltaire, Rousseau and Marat. Twice thereafter it was briefly rededicated as a church but in 1885 it reverted to being a lay monument, which it is today. Shaped like a Greek cross and sombre within, its vaulted crypts are now the resting place of scores of great Frenchmen, including Victor Hugo, Zola, Soufflot himself, and Louis Braille (inventor of the reading system for the blind).

Luxembourg palace and gardens

Parks and Gardens

Bois de Boulogne On the edge of Paris (with the Blvd Périphérique ring-road only partially buried beneath it), this enormous area of 863ha (over 2000 acres) was originally a royal hunting-ground which Louis XIV opened to the public and which Napoleon III presented to the city. Baron Haussmann directed its landscaping and installed the two racecourses of Longchamp and Auteuil and various other entertainment facilities. With many more roads and tracks criss-crossing it now, and even a camping ground, it is no longer so natural-looking, but lakes and waterfalls, shady walks and cycle-paths (bikes as well as boats can be hired), and rural-seeming restaurants, make it a welcome summer escape from the city – though at night parts of it are distinctly unsafe. Three mini-parks are contained within the Bois: the Jardin d'Acclimatation, a children's play area; the Pré Catalan, with magnificent old trees; and the delicious Bagatelle. The last, erected in 1779 by the Comte d'Artois, later Charles X, who also built the folly of a house, subsequently belonged to the wealthy English collector Sir Richard Wallace, whose treasures (the Wallace Collection) are in London. Among its delights are a rose-garden, water-gardens, parterres and shrubberies; an orangery and a pagoda; and a restaurant discreetly installed in the former stables.

Buttes-Chaumont, Parc des This original and beguiling little park is also a creation of Baron Haussmann and built not only over some former quarries but also on top of what had later become a vast and insalubrious rubbish dump. Huge quantities of detritus had to be shifted but, instead of levelling it, the landscapers had the inspired notion of creating a series of sharp little hillocks that culminate in a steep-sided and rocky artificial island set in a moatlike lake and reached by two high-arched bridges. There is a fine view from a neo-Classical folly of a temple at the summit of the island.

Luxembourg, Jardin et Palais du On the S edge of the St-Germain quarter, the widowed Marie de Médicis built herself a palace in grounds she bought from the Duc de Luxembourg in 1612. Oppressed by the Louvre Palace following the assassination of her husband, Henri IV, she sought to recapture in her new home echoes of her native Italy. In 1625 she moved in, presenting the original 16C mansion on the estate to her son Louis XIII's chief minister, Cardinal Richelieu, who then turned against her and engineered her banishment. After the Revolution, it became the seat of the parliamentary assemblies and, after considerable alteration and enlargement in the 19C, housed the French Senate, as it does to this day. It can be visited on Sundays but, apart from the gilded Cabinet Doré which retains original decor from the widowed queen's time, is of little interest. The garden, on the other hand, with its terraces and pools, its lovely Medici fountain, its myriad statues and its unexpected hidden corners, is perfectly charming and Parisian to the core: it was Parisians in their thousands, indeed, who petitioned to prevent it being entirely annihilated during Haussmann's replanning of Paris. Now it is a favourite haunt of Parisians of all ages and types, from countless generations of children who have watched its famous marionette theatre, to the students who sit in discussion upon its benches and hold hands under its trees, the joggers who circumnavigate it and the old people of the surrounding *quartier* who sit gossiping and watching the passing scene. From the S end there is a splendid view up the broad tree-lined avenue to the Observatoire, and at the N end the original ducal mansion, now called the Petit Luxembourg, is the residence of the head of the Senate.

Monceau, Parc de Parisians term this a "jardin anglais", but even to those unversed in the art of English landscape gardening this delicious folly of a place looks unmistakably French. Originally laid out in the 18C on the immense property of the Orléans family, it is still surrounded by nobly conceived mansions that once housed members of their court, notably the Musée Cernuschi (q.v.) in Ave Velasquez, the neighbouring Nissim de Camondo museum (q.v.), and no 5 Ave Van-Dyck, which has kept its magnificent gilded railings. Among the park's artfully ruched contours, trees and shrubs, a host of amusing frivolities from the original ducal garden have been romantically arranged: a pagoda and a pyramid, a small lake with a curious fragment of a colonnade alongside part of it, statues, and an archway from the old Hôtel de Ville.

Plantes, Jardin des Lying at the E edge of the Latin Quarter, near the river, and originally established as a medicinal herb garden by Louis XIII in 1626, it was gradually embellished and enlarged and opened to the public towards the end of that century. Its greatest curator was Buffon, in the 18C, who planted a wealth of rare and ornamental trees and added an amphitheatre, a maze and various other amenities. Children flock there to visit its delightful little zoo; botanists come to study its plants; students ponder over the exhibits in the Muséum d'Histoire Naturelle (q.v.); and people of all ages come just to enjoy its shady walks.

Tuileries, Jardin des Apotheosis of the French-style formal garden, running from the Louvre W to the Pl. de la Concorde and flanked by the Seine and the Rue de Rivoli respectively, the Tuileries faithfully preserves the layout originally designed by Louis XIV's landscape artist, Le Nôtre, whose bust is among a host of other statues. It had been a garden for a hundred years before that, however, having originally been created by Catherine de Médicis to complement her Tuileries Palace. All that now recalls the palace is its former main entrance, the Arc de Triomphe du Carrousel, which was installed to commemorate Napoleon's victories in 1807; the palace itself was burned by the rioting Communards in 1871 and its two remaining wings, the Pavillons de Flore and de Marsan, were later incorporated into the Louvre.

Vincennes, Bois et Château de The lung of SE Paris, Vincennes was, like the Bois de Boulogne, originally a royal hunting-ground in the 11C; 200 years later, St Louis forbade the killing of animals there and, by popular tradition, held court for his subjects under one of its oak trees. Successive monarchs enlarged and remodelled the original manor house (but retained Charles V's chapel, copied from the Sainte Chapelle). Henry V of England died there in 1422, of dysentery; Louis XIV spent his honeymoon there. After Versailles was built, however, Vincennes was abandoned; for a brief period it housed a porcelain factory, which later moved to Sèvres, then a prison, and eventually an arsenal. Napoleon III retained the arsenal but presented the park to the city of Paris in 1860, when it was laid out with lakes and streams and pathways; nowadays it also has a fine zoo, a racecourse, university buildings, a Buddhist centre, various sports facilities and a Floral Garden. The château, which had been extensively remodelled during its period as an arsenal, began

to be restored in the 19C by Viollet-le-Duc and, after several vicissitudes (including being partly blown up by the Nazis) now conveys an excellent idea of its erstwhile grandeur with a fine medieval keep, the 14C chapel, the 17C pavilions and colonnades, and a small museum.

Passy/Trocadéro The former village of Passy, in the smart 16th *arrondissement* on the right bank of the Seine, was incorporated into Paris in 1859 and rapidly became a wealthy residential area of large houses with private gardens. Most have now given way to blocks of flats, but it still has many an attractive leafy street, and some good boutiques along its main artery, **Rue de Passy**. To the S, **Rue Reynouard** contains several interesting houses: at No 66 lived Benjamin Franklin, who erected the capital's first lightning-conductor on its roof, and at No 47, half hidden below the street in a mass of greenery, is the house where Balzac lived from 1840–47 (see *Museums*). Its back door opens on to the atmospheric **Rue Berton**, at a lower level still, and on the opposite side of that street stands the Turkish Embassy in the former park of the Princesse de Lamballe, confidante of Marie-Antoinette. At the foot of the hill is the narrow river-island known as the **Allée des Cygnes**. Back uphill, **Rue Franklin** has at No 8 the **Musée Clemenceau**, preserved much as it was when the great French statesman lived there, from 1895 to 1929. The same street leads on past **Passy cemetery** with a statue of Benjamin Franklin opposite it, to **Pl. du Trocadéro** and the **Chaillot Palace** (see *Museums*). Leading out of the opposite side of Pl. du Trocadéro, **Ave du Président Wilson** leads first to **Pl. d'Iéna** and the **Musée Guimet**, then to the **Musée de la Mode** (qq.v.), and comes down to the river at **Pl. de l'Alma**, where is the entrance to the Paris sewers.

Pompidou Centre (see also *Art Moderne, Musée d'*) Officially the Centre National d'Art et Culture Georges-Pompidou, and also known as Beaubourg from the area it occupies, this extraordinary building, designed by one British and one Italian architect, and opened in 1977, still outrages traditionalists but nonetheless has become the animated centre of an animated district. All the building's utilities – heating, ventilation, water, gas, electricity, and even the escalators – are on the outside and often painted in bright primary colours, giving a general impression of some gigantic child's toy – but allowing maximum space for the exhibitions inside. As well as the Museum of Modern Art, it contains a library, a children's

Centre Pompidou

centre, space for temporary exhibitions relating to industrial design, an Acoustic and Musical Research institute, a re-creation of the sculptor Brancusi's studio, and a self-service restaurant with marvellous views on the top floor. Outside the building, the open spaces are pedestrianized and surrounded with souvenir shops and cafés, and in the central piazza all sorts of performances regularly take place: folk groups, mimes, fire-eaters, magicians, acrobats and jugglers vying for the attention (and the donations) of the passing crowds. Just S of the Centre, towards the church of St-Merri, the newest addition to the area is a large rectangular pool full of pop-art mobile sculptures.

Sainte Chapelle   Now tucked away in a courtyard among the Palais de Justice buildings and deconsecrated, the chapel was originally built (to enshrine holy relics) by St Louis in 1245–48, to designs by Pierre de Montreuil. It was an adjunct to the then Royal Palace and its upper storey was connected directly to the kings's apartments; the lower part (painted in the 19C) was used by lesser worshippers. Nowadays one enters through the lower part and climbs a narrow winding staircase to emerge in the chapel proper, a jewel of Gothic art, its tall stained glass windows (dating from the 13–14C, restored in the 19C) separated by slender, fragile-seeming pillars. The brilliant windows, the oldest in Paris, should be examined clockwise, starting on the left of the entrance: they start with a representation of Genesis and continue through both Old and New Testaments as far as the fifteenth, which depicts St Helena and the True Cross and St Louis with the holy relics. The final window, the rose at the W end, is a 15C rendition of the Apocalypse.

St-Germain quarter   The oldest part of this quarter is around the church of **St-Germain-des-Près**, where in the Middle Ages there stood a huge and populous monastery surrounded by farmlands. Students from the university encroached on some of these lands for recreational purposes and Parisians would take a ferry (*bac*) across the Seine, terminating where **Rue du Bac** now finishes, in

Café Deux-Magots

order to enjoy the fresh air. It was not until Louis XIV started work on the Invalides, and had built the Pont Royal, that the wealthy started to build mansions there, some of which exist to this day, and the Faubourg (suburb) St-Germain developed into a rival of the Marais as the most fashionable residential area. Today the **Blvds St-Germain** and **Raspail** slice through it but the character of the district has remained virtually intact in a number of dignified old streets: **Rue de l'Université**, **Rue St-Dominique**, **Rue de Grenelle**, **Rue de Varenne** and **Rue de Lille**. Dozens of splendid mansions line these streets: the **Hôtel Matignon** in Rue de Varenne is the office and home of France's prime minister while in the same street the **Hôtel de Boisgelin** is the Italian Embassy, and the **Hôtel de Biron**, one of the few that can be visited, is the **Musée Rodin** (q.v.). Near the junction with Blvd Raspail, the charming 18C **Quatres-Saisons fountain** is on Rue de Grenelle; farther along it, the **Hôtel de Courteilles** houses the Ministry of Education. Down near the river is the **Hôtel de la Légion d'Honneur**, with a small museum on one side, and the splendid turn-of-the-century **Gare d'Orsay**, being transformed into a museum of the 19C, on the other. Walking E either along **Quai Voltaire** or **Rue de Lille**, one comes to the **École des Beaux-Arts**, established by Louis XIV, with the **Institut de France** beyond it and, beyond that again, another majestic mansion, the **Hôtel des Monnaies**, which houses the Mint and another small museum. Leading away from the Seine is a cobweb of narrower, atmospheric old streets: **Rue des Saints-Pères**, **Rue de Seine**, **Rue des Beaux-Arts** (where Oscar Wilde died), **Rue Jacob**, **Rue Mazarine** and its continuation, **Rue de l'Ancienne Comédie**. Here stood the original Comédie Française, and opposite still stands the 300-years-old *Café Procope*, patronized by Molière, Corneille, Racine and many another literary figure: the entire area is haunted by memories of famous writers and artists. A few steps W along Blvd St-Germain is the heart and soul of the area, the great church of St-Germain-des-Près (q.v.); behind it, in the tiny, shady **Rue de Furstenberg** is the studio where the 19C Romantic painter Delacroix worked, which is now a museum. The open space in front of St-Germain-des-Près is frequently animated by young street performers, and just along the boulevard are the post-war "literary" cafés, *Flore* and the *Deux-Magots*, made famous by Jean-Paul Sartre and the Existentialists. Across the road, the equally famous *Brasserie Lipp* still keeps its cachet. Behind it, more delightful old streets full of little Italian and Greek restaurants (**Rue des Ciseaux**, **Rue des Canettes**, **Rue Grégoire de Tours**) lead to the church of **St-Sulpice** (q.v.); further S again are the (reconstructed) **Théâtre de l'Odéon**, the **Luxembourg Palace** and gardens (q.v.) and the **Paris Observatory**, built by Louis XIV.

St-Jacques, Tour   Marooned in a square off Rue de Rivoli, this former bell-tower is all that remains of the 16C church that was once the starting point for medieval pilgrims making their way down Rue St-Jacques and heading for the Pyrenees, Spain and the shrine of St James at Santiago de Compostela. It now has a meteorological station inside it.

The Seine

Seine, River The Seine describes a huge curve through central Paris, making the traditional division between the Right Bank, to the N, and the Left Bank: a few decades ago the Right Bank was considered fashionable and the Left Bank intellectual, but the divisions are more blurred today. The river has always played an important part in Parisian life: in pre-Roman times there was an association of merchant boatmen in the city; one of its symbols is a ship, and in the Middle Ages members of the watermen's guild took over its administration and remained involved with it until the reign of Louis XIV, when the king dissolved all municipal institutions and brought Paris under state rule. Headquarters of the watermen's guild, and of city administration, was on the Pl. de Grève (now **Pl. de l'Hôtel de Ville**) where the first food-market stood as well as the first town hall (built 1337). The present **Hôtel de Ville** is a somewhat more ornate copy of its predecessor, which was burned down during the Communard revolt of 1871. The *quais* of the Seine, particularly downstream of the **Hôtel de Ville**, have lost much of their ambience since the advent of heavy traffic, but in the older parts of the city there are still many delightful stretches to wander along, and the stalls of the *bouquinistes* (see *Markets*) offer agreeable browsing. Some of the most historic and interesting Paris bridges are those connecting the two Seine islands with the river's outer banks: oldest is the **Pont-Neuf** (1607), followed by **Pont Marie** (1625). **Pont de la Tournelle**, with its statue of Ste-Geneviève, is a 1925 reconstruction; **Pont St-Michel** was rebuilt in 1857. Its continuation, **Pont au Change**, built two years later, is another replacement for a much older bridge while the **Petit-Pont** (1853) and its continuation, **Pont Notre-Dame** (1913) follow the line of the oldest Seine fording-point. Further downstream, the more important bridges are the pedestrian **Pont des Arts** (1803); **Pont Royal (1685); Pont de la Concorde** (1790); **Pont Alexandre III** (1900), built for the Paris Exhibition of that year; **Pont de l'Alma** (rebuilt 1972) which incorporates an earlier Zouave figure on which high-water marks are registered; and **Pont d'Iéna** (1813).

Rue de Rivoli/Vendôme area Running from **Pl. de la Concorde** alongside the **Tuileries** gardens (see *Parks*) and the **Louvre** (see *Museums*), past the former royal church of **St-Germain l'Auxerrois** (see *Churches*) and – by this time shedding some of its elegance – past the **Hôtel de Ville** (see *Seine*) and into the Marais, this is one of the city's longest thoroughfares. Its first stretch, laid out at the beginning of the 19C with its dignified colonnades, is also one of the capital's most famous streets. Among its discreet shops are a few that still traditionally sell gloves and handkerchiefs, a tea-room descended from the famous Rumpelmayer's, and two bookshops. Also here is the **Hôtel Meurice** which served as German Army headquarters during World War II; near it, **Pl. des Pyramides** has a gilded statue of Joan of Arc. Just behind Rue de Rivoli, up **Rue de Castiglione**, is the most elegant square in Paris: **Pl. Vendôme**, designed by Mansart at the end of the 17C and now boasting the **Ritz Hotel**, the Ministry of Justice, and a handful of the world's most expensive jewellers. A statue of Louis XIV originally stood at the centre, but it was destroyed in the Revolution and replaced, on orders of Napoleon, by the present column (a copy of Trajan's in Rome) on which his Austerlitz campaign is commemorated in bronze. The statue of Napoleon at the top is a replica.

Rue de Rivoli

CHAMPAGNE/ARDENNES

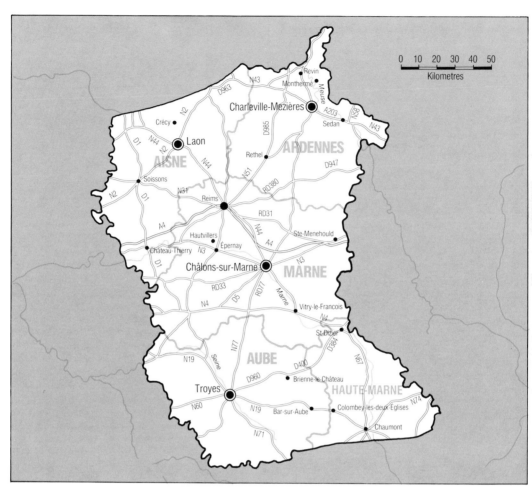

The fertile agricultural province of Champagne, bordering Belgium and extending southwards to Burgundy from the mountains of the Ardennes, derives its name from the Latin 'campania' or 'flat country'. It comprises a chalk plain defined on the west by the so-called 'cliff' of the Île de France, a line of low hills on the slopes of which lie the vineyards with the grapes that produce the province's most famous export. The plain grows abundant cereal and root crops: and the 'damp' south-east is an area of stock-farming. Nobody has described it better than General de Gaulle, who looked out from his study window (see *Colombey-les-Deux-Églises*) at a landscape of 'huge, blurred, wistful horizons of wood and meadow, ploughland and mournful fallow' ('vastes, frustes et tristes horizons, bois, prés; cultures et friches mélancholiques'). The Ardennes, geologically, is the continuation of the mountain range which runs from the Rhineland through Belgium. The forest which Julius Caesar called 'the most extensive of Gaul', and where Charlemagne hunted, has dwindled, though there are still extensive woodlands of oak, beech and poplar that shelter deer and wild boar. Most of the timber, however, is sold to other parts of France or exported abroad and with little

reafforestation, soil erosion poses a threat to the environment.

The region was populated early; there are many Stone Age and Iron Age remains. Julius Caesar found it inhabited by a number of tribes, among them the Celts and the Belgae. Huns, Franks, Carolingians, Normans and Hungarians subsequently fought to dominate the territory, and it was not until the 12th century that the counts of Champagne emerged as major feudal lords. Champagne was a staging post on the trade route between northern Europe and the Mediterranean, and towns such as Troyes, Lagny, Provins and Bar-sur-Aube held annual fairs attended by merchants from Italy, Flanders, England and Germany, where cloth from the north was exchanged for silks, spices, dyes and other luxuries from the south. Transactions were made by promissory note, payable at future fairs, and by the 13th century the fairs of Champagne had virtually become international banking centres; the prosperity they engendered was even more important to the province than its own industries of cloth-making, leatherwork and dying.

Union with France by dynastic marriage failed to bring peace to Champagne. For nearly four centuries English and Burgundians, the Spaniards of Charles V, Protestants and Catholics turned the province into an almost permanent theatre of war. In the 19th century came a second period of prosperity which brought, among other achievements, the great expansion of the champagne trade, typified by the first exports of the wine to Imperial Russia by Nicole-Barbe Clicquot-Ponsardin, familiarly known as the widow (Veuve) Clicquot of Reims.

Following the scars of two world wars, one marvels at the riches that have survived so much turbulent history. If the Ardennes appeals for its solitude and simplicity, and the glowing colours of its autumn woods, Champagne is memorable primarily for architecture. Reims's cathedral is recognized as one of the great buildings of Christendom, but many visitors to France are unaware of the treasures to be found in Troyes, Laon and Châlons-sur-Marne. Neither region has a reputation for great cuisine, but the Ardennes is notable for its game and trout and Champagne boasts some hearty peasant dishes. Visitors will certainly enjoy the experience of drinking champagne produced by modest but honest growers, and, at the other end of the scale, the adventure of discovering the great still champagnes, such as the red Bouzy and Mareuil, which are rarely encountered abroad. Nor should it be forgotten that the secondary wine of the region is a light, blond, bitter and excellent beer.

BAR-SUR-AUBE
AUBE Pop 7200

Bar-sur-Aube, 21km E of Troyes, has exchanged its medieval ramparts for a girdle of boulevards. The late 12C church of St-Pierre, whose tower is crowned by a dome added in the early part of the 18C, has along its S side and part of the facade a timbered market hall which was added in the 14C. The church of St-Maclou, also mainly 12C, was once the chapel of the château of the counts of Bar.

BRIENNE-LE-CHÂTEAU
AUBE Pop 4100

Brienne, largely rebuilt since 1940, lies 2km from the right bank of the Aube. Napoleon Bonaparte took his first communion in the 14–15C local church and was a pupil at the École Militaire from the age of ten to fifteen (1779–84). He left a legacy of 1,200,000 francs to the town, where there is now a Napoleon museum. The tiled and timbered market hall dates from the 13C. The late 18C château crowning the hill, from which the small town takes its name, is now a psycho-therapeutic centre, not open to visitors.

CHÂLONS-SUR-MARNE
MARNE Pop 54,400

Châlons, a busy industrial, commercial and administrative centre in the heart of the Champagne, some 35km SE of Reims, has the charm of a town threaded by waterways – a canal and two small tributaries of the Marne, as well as the river itself – and blessed with gardens and green walks allied to a historic past. Catalaunum, as it was then known, was a bishopric in the 3C and, by the 4C ranked as the third city of Gallia Belgica.

Some timbered houses survive, and there are three old stone bridges over the Marne's tributaries, but the town takes its character essentially from its substantial 17–18C buildings. They include the mid-18C Préfecture, once the hôtel of the Intendancy of Champagne, and the Hôtel de Ville, of 1771. The elegant 17C Hôtel des Gouverneurs de Châlons today accommodates the municipal library, which has a notable collection of 12–15C illuminated manuscripts.

The mainly 13C cathedral of St-Étienne, built on the site of an early fortified church, retains a Romanesque tower from an earlier building; the W front was added in the 17C. The interior, memorable for the lightness and purity of its soaring arches, has a series of stained glass windows dating from the 12–16C.

Even more impressive is the church of Notre-Dame-en-Vaux, whose twin spires are reflected in the canal. This was built between the early 12C and early 13C and the development from Romanesque to early Gothic can be seen in the nave, choir and apse. There are good 16C stained glass windows and a carillon of 56 bells.

Some 20km E of Châlons, the great basilica of **Notre-Dame-de-l'Épine**, extravagantly Flamboyant Gothic without, elegantly restrained within, has been a centre of pilgrimage since the early 15C. The exterior has a remarkable collection of gargoyles representing the vices being banished from the church.

CHARLEVILLE-MÉZIÈRES
ARDENNES Pop 61,600

These two towns, set on either side of a curve of the Meuse, near the Belgian border, now form a single unit though both keep their individual character, respectively commercial and administrative. Charleville was created by the Spanish duke Charles de Gonzaga: the symmetrical streets of his

'New Town', laid out in 1606, open on to the splendour of the Pl. Ducale, with a swaggering equestrian statue of himself in its centre. The harmony of the arcaded brick and stone buildings, with steep-pitched slate roofs is marred only by the Hôtel de Ville on the W side, built in 1843 on the site of the unfinished ducal palace.

N of the square, built over the Meuse in the style of a massive town gateway, is the Vieux-Moulin, the ducal mill, which now houses a small museum devoted to the 19C poet Arthur Rimbaud, who was born and buried at Charleville. The restored basilica of Notre-Dame d'Espérance at Mézières is mainly Flamboyant Gothic, with a Renaissance tower. The citadelle, built in the late 16C, was modified by Vauban in the 17C. During World War I the neighbouring Préfecture served as the GHQ of the occupying German army.

CHÂTEAU-THIERRY
AISNE   Pop 14,900

This small town, set on either bank of the Marne, was the birthplace of the 17C author Jean de La Fontaine, renowned for his *Fables*. The house, a 16C hôtel, is now a La Fontaine museum. The ramparts of the 8C fort built by Charles Martel provide a fine view of the Marne valley.

CHAUMONT
HAUTE-MARNE   Pop 28,400

Its position on the edge of the plateau that divides the Marne from its tributary, the Suize, and the three-storey viaduct that rises 50m above the latter river are the most striking features of Chaumont. The donjon of the 12C castle remains and a number of old houses with corbelled stair turrets survived the bombing of 1940 and 1944. The basilica of St-Jean-Baptiste, dating from the 13C, has a notable 15C Entombment, with more than life-sized figures.

Chaumont

COLOMBEY-LES-DEUX-ÉGLISES
HAUTE-MARNE   Pop 350

Colombey, a tranquil, red-roofed village on the borders of Burgundy and Lorraine, and thus on the classic invasion route, owes its fame to the fact that in 1933 Charles de Gaulle, then CO of the 507th Armoured Regiment stationed at Metz, bought a modest country house here. After World War II, during his two periods as President of the Republic, General de Gaulle used 'La Boisserie' as a private retreat, and it was his permanent home while he was out of power and from 1969 until his death the following year.

After the simple village funeral, from which de Gaulle explicitly excluded any notables, and his burial in the family grave in the village churchyard, Colombey was transformed into a secular Lourdes. The village souvenir shop is crammed with the general's likeness in every imaginable form and medium. 'La Boisserie' has been kept as it was during his lifetime, and visitors can see the salon, the library and the study with his work desk.

The simple and totally private family tomb, which also records the general's wife Yvonne and their handicapped daughter Anne, who died at the age of twenty, is in striking contrast with the national memorial – a great granite Cross of Lorraine – which stands on a hill outside the village.

Épernay

ÉPERNAY
MARNE   Pop 28,800

Little of historic interest survives in Épernay, a strategically situated town on the Marne which has repeatedly suffered from fire and sword, but its architectural character is prosperous 19C and it is pleasantly laid out amid much greenery. Surrounded as it is by undulating vineyard country, notably the Côte des Blancs to the S and the Montagne de Reims to the N, Épernay, like Reims, devotes its activity almost wholly to the production of champagne. Over 100km of great chalk vaults, maintained at constant temperature, run beneath the town and the great champagne firms established here are open to visitors, several of them organizing conducted tours of their caves. Wine has, in fact, been produced on the slopes of the neighbouring hills since before Roman times.

The former Château Perrier, built in the mid-19C, now houses a museum of prehistory and of champagne.

HAUTVILLERS
MARNE

Set among the vineyards of the Montagne de Reims, 6km NE of Épernay, this delightful village has attractive old houses with arched porches and wrought-iron signs. In the Benedictine abbey founded by St Nivard in 660, Dom Pérignon, cellar-master from 1688 to 1715, literally put the fizz into white wine, carrying out research and experiment in blending wines and developing the process of double fermentation which culminated in the discovery of sparkling wines from which champagne, as we now know it, evolved.

LAON
AISNE   Pop 29,000

Laon, 45km NW of Reims, set on a dramatic spur of rock 100m above the plains of Picardy and the Champagne, is a rare example of a medieval city preserved virtually entire within its three miles of ramparts. It was the birthplace of St Rémi, the archbishop of Reims, who baptized Clovis, and was itself a bishopric from the end of the 5C, its bishops being dukes with the right to attend the monarch during the ceremonies of coronation. During the 9–10C, when the last Carolingian kings lived here, Laon was the capital of France.

The old city clusters round the 12–13C cathedral of Notre-Dame, one of the oldest and most splendid Gothic cathedrals of France. Two of its seven towers were lopped during the Revolution: of the remaining five the W pair, airily pierced by tall, narrow bays, have at their corners statues of oxen, recalling the legendary beast which appeared to help a team in trouble during the building of the cathedral. The facade, with its three deep porches, is renowned for its statuary, and the interior is worthy of it, with a nave of four storeys and 13C glass in the windows of the apse and N transept. There is a complex of ecclesiastical buildings around the cathedral, including the partly 13C, partly 17C former Bishop's Palace, which is now the Palais de Justice. Its 12C chapel is on two levels, the lower orders being confined to the ground floor. There are ancient houses in the surrounding streets of the old Cité.

At least as old as the cathedral is the tiny, octagonal Templars' chapel. The neighbouring museum has an outstanding archaeological gallery and paintings including 17C works by the three brothers Le Nain who were born at Laon. The 12–13C church of St-Martin was once a Premonstratensian abbey: its 18C abbatial buildings now house the municipal library, which has a notable collection of manuscripts.

Three of the city's original nine fortified gates survive. A cable railway links the lower town with the city on the rock.

During the second and third weeks of Sept. each year Laon stages the 'Heures médiévales', a festival of theatre, music and exhibitions.

MONTHERMÉ
ARDENNES   Pop 3100

Monthermé, just below the confluence of the Meuse and the Semoy, is an excellent centre for exploring the valleys of both rivers, also the forests of the Ardennes. The valley of the Meuse, where the river follows a twisting course through a narrow gorge, is outstandingly picturesque, with rocky outcrops affording wide views, though the most dramatic panorama is from the so-called Château du Diable above the Semoy valley. Monthermé has many old houses and a church, part 12C, part 15C, dedicated to St Léger.

REIMS
MARNE   Pop 182,000

Cathedral of Notre-Dame, Reims

If one accepts the romantic dictum that 'France was born of an act of faith on a battlefield', here is its cradle. On Christmas Day, AD496, Reims saw the baptism by its archbishop, St Rémi, of the Frankish Clovis, founder of the French monarchy. After the accession of Hugh Capet in 987, almost every French king was to be crowned in the cathedral of Reims, the most famous ceremony being the coronation of Charles VII in the presence of Joan of Arc in 1429.

In Gallo-Roman times, Reims was an important provincial capital, Durocortorum, and already a centre of the wool trade, a far older local industry than the champagne for which it is pre-eminent today. The Porte Mars, a triumphal arch of the 3C or 4C, survives from this period. In 406 the Vandals destroyed the city and martyred its bishop, Nicasius, on the threshold of his newly built cathedral. The baptism of Clovis marked the beginning of a more peaceful era.

During World War I the city was devastated. The rebuilding, if it produced no very distinguished architecture, has given it pleasant boulevards and shopping streets.

The cathedral of Notre-Dame was built during the 13C to replace a Romanesque building which had been destroyed by fire; only the towers were added respectively in 1445 and 1475. During World War I it was to be ravaged once more: happily the restoration has been triumphantly successful. The sumptuous W front has three deeply-set, gabled doorways which are marvels of 13C sculpture. They are topped by a great rose window and that by the third-storey 'gallery of the kings', which has the baptism of Clovis at its centre. Most of the figures (some of which are replicas) have a naturalism which makes it seem invidious to single out, as is customary, the 'Smiling Angel', in the N porch. The interior is austere, but the perfect proportions of the narrow lofty nave call for no ornament other than the statues at the W end. From Easter to All Saints Day the walls of the nave are hung with seventeen 16C tapestries of the Life of the Virgin (they spend the winter in the Musée des Beaux Arts). There are three windows by Chagall in the apsidal chapel.

The former Archbishop's Palace, Palais du Tau, is now the cathedral museum, housing the statues damaged by war or time, which have been removed from the cathedral.

The oldest church in the city is the basilica of St-Rémi, consecrated by Pope Leo IX in 1049. Originally an abbey church, it was built on the site of the chapel where St Rémi was buried and conceived on a scale to accommodate the pilgrims who visited his tomb. In spite of a 19C rebuilding of the central gable and the N tower, the W front retains its stern 11–12C Romanesque aspect. The interior has the sober elegance of the Benedictine tradition, with the Romanesque of the lower storey of the nave contrasting with the pointed arches above. The late 12C choir is one of the earliest examples of the Champagne style of Gothic. St Rémi's tomb is behind the high altar. The great Crucifixion window of the apsidal chapel is 12C.

A museum of Archaeology has been set up in the buildings of the former abbey on the N of the basilica. The Musée St-Denis (Beaux-Arts) is an important collection, particularly strong in French painting. It also has a remarkable series of portraits of German princes by the Cranachs, father and son. Exhibits associated with the history of Reims are displayed in the 13C buildings of the Musée Le Vergeur. The art section contains a fine series of Dürer engravings.

The Salle de Guerre, 12, Rue Franklin-Roosevelt, is the room where General Eisenhower witnessed the signing of the German capitulation in 1945, and is open to the public.

The Foujita Chapel of Notre-Dame-de-la-Paix is named after the Japanese painter, Léonard Foujita.

Reims was the birthplace (1619) of Jean-Baptiste Colbert, who became Louis XIV's finance minister.

Reims rivals Épernay for the title of wine capital of Champagne. Several of the more important champagne houses arrange guided tours through their subterranean cellars tunnelled for many kilometres into the chalk. Newer industries include chemicals, metallurgy and wholesale groceries.

RETHEL
ARDENNES   Pop 8900

With a history that goes back to the 10C, when the castle, now in ruins, was built, Rethel, on the Aisne, some 20km NE of Reims, is today a new town, having been almost wholly rebuilt after the damage of World War II. The Gothic church of St-Nicolas, in fact two churches set side by side, one 12–13C, the other 15–16C, has been well restored. The poet Paul Verlaine taught here from 1877 to 1879.

REVIN
ARDENNES   Pop 10,600

Revin, built on two peninsulas of the curving Meuse, near the Belgian border, was once a Spanish town, and, until 1679, an independent republic. From the neighbouring heights, the Rocher de la Faligeotte, and, notably, Mont Malgré Tout, there are panoramic views. The Monument des Manises, on a height E of the town, commemorates 108 local members of the Resistance who were shot by the Germans in June 1944.

ST-DIZIER
HAUTE-MARNE   Pop 37,400

This industrial town, set between the right bank of the Marne and the Marne-Saône Canal, has a martial past. In 1544 its garrison of 25,000 held off Charles V with an army of 100,000; and in 1814 it saw Napoleon's last victory on French soil. At **Villiers-en-Lieu**, 8km NW, the French Motor Car Museum has about 100 vintage models.

STE-MENEHOULD
MARNE   Pop 5800

Here, in 1715, Dom Pérignon (see *Hautvillers*) was born, and here, 76 years later, King Louis XVI was recognized during his attempted escape from the Tuileries, so that he and the royal family were intercepted and arrested at Varennes. A fortified town from the 13C, Ste-Menehould today is largely 18C, having been almost wholly rebuilt after a disastrous fire in 1719.

SEDAN
ARDENNES   Pop 24,500

The fort of Sedan, dominating a curve of the Meuse near the Belgian border, is claimed locally to be the largest in Europe. Ironically, the two landmarks customarily pointed out to visitors when they mount to the battlements are the Château de Bellevue, where Napoleon III signed the capitulation of 1870, after the Prussians had defeated his heavily outnumbered army, and the point where the Germans broke through in 1940.

The fort was built in the 15–16C on the foundation of an 11C church and round a 13C keep which still stands. The fortress was once the palace of the princes of Sedan, and Marshal Turenne was born in the royal apartments in 1611. The successive stages of the building are set out in the historical museum.

The town, which was occupied during 1914–18, was badly damaged in the fighting of 1940, when most of its 17–18C houses were destroyed; a few original ones survive in the Rue du Mesnil. Since the 16C Sedan's mainstay has been the textile industry, particularly the manufacture of the black cloth known as 'sedan'. Today metallurgy and chemical works flourish alongside it.

SOISSONS
AISNE Pop 32,200

Soissons, in rich agricultural country on the Aisne, has been the see of a bishop since the 3C and a battleground through much of its history, as the nearby village cemeteries testify. Clovis defeated a Roman army here in the 5C; in modern times the town was largely destroyed during World War I. According to (dubious) tradition, the shoemaker saints, Crispin and Crispinian, recalled by Henry V before Agincourt, were martyred here in the 3C.

The cathedral of St-Gervais and St-Protais, begun in the 12C, but because of war not completed until early in the 14C, impresses by the scale and the harmonious simplicity of the nave. There is 13–14C glass in the lancet windows of the choir and in the N transept. Also on the N side is Rubens's *Adoration of the Shepherds*.

Royal and episcopal vandalism destroyed the abbey church of St-Jean-des-Vignes, demolished in 1805 by imperial decree in order that the stone might be used for work on the cathedral. Public outcry saved the glorious W front, with its Flamboyant towers and the huge, empty rose window. The 13C refectory of the abbey was spared and two wings of the 14C cloister remain.

TROYES
AUBE Pop 64,800

Troyes, on the Seine, 130km S of Reims, has a distinguished heritage of art and architecture. It was converted to Christianity in the 3C, and in 451 St Loup, its bishop, turned Attila from its gates, apparently by sheer force of character. As the capital of Champagne from the 10C the city became a centre for the international fairs which were established by the counts, and, through their princely generosity, was magnificently endowed with churches and hospitals. They also encouraged the arts: in the 12C Chrétien de Troyes, who wrote of courtly love, found a patron in Count Thibaut, and there were important schools of sculpture and glass-painting.

The old centre of the town has a complex of narrow streets bordered by timbered, turreted, corbelled houses scarcely to be rivalled in northern France. The cathedral of SS Peter and Paul is one of the finest Gothic churches in the province – the Gothic predominates, though building lasted from the 13C to the 17C and the W front is Renaissance.

The interior has a series of windows which provide a survey of the art of glass painting in Champagne from the 13C to the 16C.

Ste-Madeleine, the oldest church of Troyes, is mid-12C, with a Renaissance W tower. The glass here is 16C, and superb. Of the same period is the stone rood which is a triumph of intricate and exquisite carving.

The 13C basilica of St-Urbain was built by order of Pope Urbain IV, son of a local shoemaker, who is buried on the N side of the choir.

St-Pantaléon, part Gothic, part Renaissance, with a timber vault, has a collection of about 60 statues, of varying quality, taken from churches which were destroyed during the Revolution.

The church of St-Jean, with a 14C clocktower, was the scene, in 1420, of the marriage of King Henry V of England with Catherine of France, daughter of Charles VI.

The Renaissance Hôtel de Valuisant now houses the Musée Historique de Troyes et Champagne (interesting sculpture and glass) and the Musée de la Bonneterie, dealing with the history of the manufacture of hosiery, which has for centuries been the town's most thriving industry.

The Musée des Beaux Arts and the municipal library are in the former abbey of St-Loup. The former includes works by the 17C brothers Nicolas and Pierre Mignard, who were born here. Thanks largely to its acquisitions from monastic libraries after the Revolution, the latter, founded in 1651, is of major importance.

Hôtel de Valuisant, Troyes

VITRY-LE-FRANÇOIS
MARNE Pop 18,800

This town, on a junction of waterways – the Marne and the Saulx and the Marne-Rhine and Marne-Saône canals – takes its name from François I who rebuilt the town 4km NE of the original site after it had been destroyed by the troops of Charles V in 1544. Today's new town, built after the destruction of 1940, follows the original plan of the Italian engineer employed by François I. The 17–18C church of Notre-Dame has an impressive classical facade.

ALSACE-LORRAINE

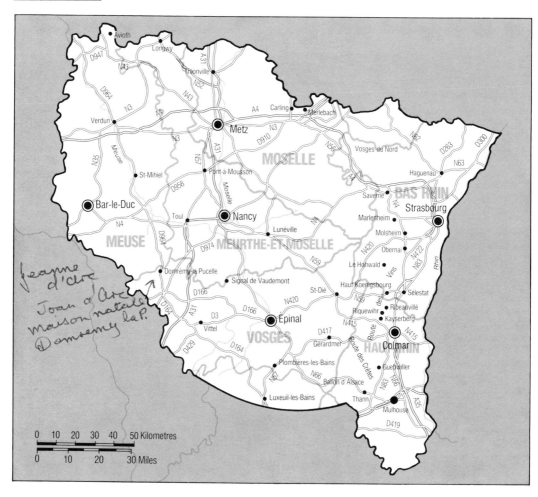

Alsace and Lorraine, very different in character, are linked by the common fate of being the only French provinces to share a frontier with Germany. This has deeply marked their history, for although effectively united with France since the 17th century, they have repeatedly suffered German pressures and invasions: Alsace and north-eastern Lorraine (Metz, but not Nancy) were annexed by Germany from 1871 until 1918. Souvenirs of past wars are on every side – the forts above Metz, the battlefields of Verdun, and that sad folly, the Maginot Line, built so confidently in the 1930s to keep out *les Bosches*, but in 1940 so swiftly outflanked by Guderian's panzers. Today its underground fortresses can be visited as tourist attractions. Nowadays the Germans are friends, and Alsace can wear with an untroubled conscience the basically Germanic style of its dialect, culture and architecture: but both provinces are proudly French. Lorraine remains, as ever, a land that enshrines French patriotism – the land of Joan of Arc, of the sacrifices of Verdun, of Barrès's *Colline Inspirée*, and of the double-barred Cross of Lorraine that French kings bore into battle in the 15th century and de Gaulle later adopted as his symbol of *La France Libre*.

The two provinces are separated by the Vosges, running north to south for 150km. They are more like high hills than mountains, for nowhere do they rise more than 1425m and their rounded summits can easily be climbed on foot: in fact, a good road runs along the central spine. Much of the range is thickly forested, mainly with pine: but there are upland pastures, too, where cows graze, and slopes used by skiers in winter. On the west, the Vosges descend gently to the plateau of Lorraine; to the east, they drop more sharply to the plain, and here the noble Alsatian vineyards lie for miles along the slopes, at the foot of ruined castles and the walls of lovely ancient villages. The plain stretches to the Rhine, that natural frontier with Germany busy with commercial traffic. Here, set back from the west bank, are Alsace's two main industrial cities, Mulhouse and Strasbourg, the latter also a capital of the new Europe.

More than any other part of mainland France, even Brittany, Alsace has the look and feel of a foreign, non-French country. The older houses, half-timbered, many with wooden balconies, look exactly like those across the Rhine in Baden. These lovely buildings are everywhere – in the old part of Strasbourg, in the centre of delightful Colmar, and in scores of smaller places. The Alsatians are a people of Allemanic origin, close cousins to the nearby Badeners and Swiss-Germans, so it is not surprising that their *patois*, too, is very similar, as are their German-sounding place and family names. Their local costumes, the style of jollity in their wine-festivals, even the style of the wine itself, almost entirely white, much of it from Riesling grapes – are all reminiscent of south-west Germany. Yet the Alsatians suffered so much from German occupations – notably in 1940–4 when Hitler brutally tried to annex the province – that they have acquiesced in Paris's post-war policy of Frenchification. Alsatian dialect is not taught in schools, although you will still hear it spoken, especially by older people, in rural areas; the younger generation in towns do not speak it.

Alsace's climate is fairly mild and damp, and the people are exuberant, talkative, fond of colour (their balconies are gay with flowers) and good living, with hearty appetites. They are artistic, too – like the south Germans – traditionally talented wood-carvers and sculptors, as is evident from the ornate decor of the many fine Romanesque churches, and secular buildings such as the curious 'Metzig' in Molsheim. To see Alsace at its most typical, follow the Route du Vin through the wine-villages, which hold high-spirited festivals, some-times with free wine flowing from the fountains. On the roofs and towers of some villages there are still old storks'-nests; but, alas, the storks today are few and far between.

In Lorraine the people are more dour and reserved, influenced in part by the climate, which is harsher. Yet the plateau of southern Lorraine is pleasant undulating country, full of woods and lakes, cornfields, and orchards of plums, pears and cherries. Here are famous spas such as Vittel, and,

in the Vosges foothills, little textile towns that have seen better days. Northern Lorraine, thickly popu-lated, is one of France's main regions of traditional heavy industry – but this, too, is now in difficulty. Towards the Saarland frontier, many coal mines have closed, but at least new modern factories have taken their place. Much the worst-hit area is the large iron-and-steel belt north-west of Metz, vic-tims of Europe's steel recession: here unemploy-ment is high and the towns look woebegone. But the Lorrains are a hard-working, adaptable people, hopeful of better times to come. Theirs is a proud province – in the Middle Ages the kingdom of Lotharingia, then a key duchy. Culturally, its golden age was the 18th century, when Duke Stanislas developed Nancy as one of the most beautiful of French cities, and Duke Leopold built the château at Lunéville on the modal of Versailles. Other fine buildings, such as Toul cathedral, date from earlier periods.

Lorraine, like anywhere in France, has its share of good restaurants, but few special dishes of its own save its ubiquitous and unremarkable *quiche*. In Alsace, the cuisine is far more varied and interesting, making plenty of use of the local wines. The Alsatians have robust appetites and are constantly devouring huge platters of *choucroute* (sour cabbage with pork and sausages). They also enjoy *coq au Riesling*, spicy sausages, and game in rich sauces – yet their palates are not unsubtle, as witness their love of *foie gras*, made from the livers of local geese, cruelly force-fed. Soft yellow Muns-ter and square Carré de l'Est are the best cheeses. The abundant local fruit is used for lavish, gaily coloured tarts and flans, also for excellent white *eaux-de-vie*, notably *kirsch* and *mirabelle*. Whether for art or hedonism, the province offers quite a little taste of paradise.

Strasbourg

AVIOTH
MEUSE

A hamlet near the Belgian frontier, noted for its remarkable 14–15C Gothic church with two richly sculpted portals, two towers, and 14C frescoes above the choir; beside it is an unusual little hexagonal chapel, the Recevresse. **Montmédy**, a small town 5km S, is overlooked by a Renaissance fortress later strengthened by Vauban.

Avioth

BALLON D'ALSACE
TERRITOIRE-DE-BELFORT

This mountain N of Belfort forms the most southerly part of the Vosges range. The upper areas today are pastureland, studded with alpine flowers, but there are also many forests ('*ballon*' in French normally means 'balloon' but here comes from the Alsatian '*bolong*' meaning 'long wood', i.e. '*bois long*'). Good roads wind up to the Ballon from N, S and E. You can drive to within 15 minutes' walk of the top (1250m) where there are marvellous views of the Vosges, Black Forest, Jura – and even, on a clear day, Mont Blanc.

BAR-LE-DUC
MEUSE   Pop 20,000

Noted, oddly enough, for its redcurrant jam, this industrial town has fine 15–18C houses around the prefecture and the Pl. St-Pierre. Here in the Gothic church of St-Étienne is the weird 'Skeleton' statue of René de Châlon, a prince of Orange, the work of Ligier Richier: as the prince lay dying in battle in 1544, his last wish was for this effigy of his decomposing corpse to be erected above his tomb.

The N35 leading NE from Bar was in 1916 the only supply route left open to the besieged garrison at Verdun. The French Army used it to pour in reinforcements, thus averting defeat. The road is still known as the 'Voie Sacrée'.

CARLING-MERLEBACH
MOSELLE

An important industrial area beside the German frontier (Saarland): its traditional coal-mines have inevitably been contracting, but diversification has brought in many new chemical and other factories, notably German. At Carling is the imposing Émile-Huchet power station. To the S, by the road to St-Avold, is one of the largest American cemeteries in Europe (16,000 dead from the 1944–5 battles). **Forbach**, to the E, has attractive 1950s housing designed by Émile Aillaud.

COLLINE INSPIRÉE, LA
MEURTHE-ET-MOSELLE

This horseshoe ridge has long been a focus of French nationalist feeling, religious in its intensity – partly because it lies just inside the part of S Lorraine that was not annexed by Germany in 1871 and thus came to symbolize freedom for the Lorrains. The nationalist writer Maurice Barrès (1862–1923) coined for it the name 'colline inspirée' (inspired hill), and wrote a novel with that title. There is a monument to Barrès at the summit, the Signal de Vaudemont (fine views). The 18C church at **Sion**, 3km N, has been the scene of major nationalistic pilgrimages in 1873, 1920, 1946 and 1973, though the theme of the last was at least reconciliation with Germany.

COLMAR
HAUT-RHIN   Pop 63,000

Colmar, the most 'typically Alsatian' of the province's larger towns, has an old quarter of great charm, beautifully preserved, with many of its small squares and narrow streets now closed to traffic. Here are many gabled houses with carved wooden fronts: most notably, in the Rue Mercière, the quaint Maison Pfister, built in 1537 for a local hatmaker, and the Maison Schongauer where the painter of that name lived (see below); in the Rue des Têtes, the Maison des Têtes (1608), so called because of the many carved heads on its facade; in the Grand' Rue, the Maison des Arcades (1609), with its two little angle-towers; and the handsome former customs house (1480). Just S is the pretty 'Little Venice' where old houses are brightly reflected in the narrow river Lauch: best view is from the Pont St-Pierre, looking N.

Colmar contains two famous and masterly works of religious art. The first, in the Musée d'Unterlinden, is the *Isenheim Altarpiece*, painted c.1510 by a German artist, Mathias Grünewald, of whom almost nothing is known. Made for the Isenheim monastery, which was destroyed in the Revolution, it was moved to Colmar in 1793. Besides three gilded wood sculptures of saints (the work of Nicolas of Haguenau), the ensemble consists of hinged wooden panels showing New Testament and other religious scenes. The *Crucifixion* panel is movingly realistic; others show a fanciful imagination. Grünewald used bright, luminous colours very unusual for that period. His portraits of Christ and the Holy Family are sympathetic: but he used a noticeably more satirical brush for bishops and other prelates, and it is thought that he may have been sharply critical of the church of his day (he was a contemporary of Luther).

The museum that houses this work is a former 13C monastery, with a charming cloister. It also contains local history and folklore exhibits, and many paintings, notably a 24-panel *Passion* by Martin Schongauer which, like the Grünewald, stands in the former chapel. Colmar's other great work is Schongauer's *Virgin and the Rosebush* (1473), with its intricate background of birds and rose leaves: it is housed in the Dominicans' church which also has some fine stained glass. Another church with good glass is St-Martin, 13–14C Gothic, noted too for the sculptures on its portal.

Colmar was the birthplace of the 19C sculptor Bartholdi who made New York's Statue of Liberty (his house is a small museum), and of Baron Haussmann who rebuilt so much of Paris in the 1860s.

The wine fair is held 5–15 Aug., and the *choucroute* fête in early Sept. On Thurs. summer evenings concerts are staged in the Unterlinden cloister.

Colmar

DOMRÉMY-LA-PUCELLE
VOSGES Pop 205

Quite a flourishing Joan-of-Arc industry now centres on this tiny village by the Meuse where the Maid *(La Pucelle)* was born in 1412 (6 Jan., so it is said). You can visit her cottage birthplace (with little museum). The church has been much altered

since her time, but preserves the font where she was baptized. The basilica of **Bois-Chénu**, 1.5km S, was completed in 1926 on one of the spots where she is said to have first heard her 'voices'. A pilgrimage takes place here in May.

Basilica of Bois-Chénu

The little town of **Vaucouleurs** (Meuse), 20km N, is where, in May 1428, Joan first came to ask the support of the local governor, Robert de Baudricourt. After winning him over, in February 1429 she rode out through the Porte de France (partly extant) to meet the Dauphin at Chinon. You can see the relics of de Baudricourt's castle; also the Chapelle Castrale, rebuilt in 1929 above a 13C crypt, containing the statue of Notre-Dame-des-Voûtes before which Joan prayed.

ÉPINAL
VOSGES Pop 40,000

The phrase 'image d'Épinal' in French means cliché or naive stock opinion, and comes from the industry of popular prints and engravings of stereo-

Print in Épinal museum

typed figures that has flourished since the 18C in this pleasant town on the upper Moselle. You can visit the Imagerie Pellerin, a works founded in 1796 that still produces these prints today. And the town's museum has a large and changing exhibition of woodcuts, prints and engravings from many countries, giving the history of this kind of printing; also drawings, paintings and Gallo-Roman relics.

Capital of the Vosges department, Épinal is a centre of cotton-weaving. The old part of the town lies around the attractively arcaded Pl. des Vosges; to the E rises a wooded hill with a small zoo. Across the river, note the big modern stained glass window in the rebuilt church of Notre-Dame.

GÉRARDMER
VOSGES   Pop 9000

A sizeable summer and skiing resort, beautifully situated at one end of the largest lake in the Vosges, with a backdrop of pine-clad hills. The town also has textile industries. It was burned down by the Germans during their retreat in Nov. 1944, but has been rebuilt. Plenty of excursions in the area, e.g. to the **Saut des Cuves** waterfall.

GUEBWILLER
HAUT-RHIN   Pop 11,000

An industrial town noted also for its wine, on the river Lauch where the Vosges foothills meet the plain. There are three fine churches: St-Léger, 12–14C, with two dissimilar towers and a remarkable W portal; Notre-Dame, late-18C, with many sculptures and wood-carvings; and the Dominicans, now deconsecrated, with a rood-screen and frescoes dating from the 15C (classical concerts are held here in summer). The town hall (1514), Flamboyant Gothic, has an unusual five-sided loggia; the Florival museum contains a fine 13C Virgin and a 15C altarpiece.

At **Murbach**, 5km W, in a lovely wooded valley, stand the graceful twin towers of a 12C Romanesque Rhenish church, once part of the powerful abbey of St-Pirmin that stood here. The nave has gone, but the choir, transepts and unusual flat apse survive. The road NW from Guebwiller ascends the beautiful Lauch valley, past another fine Romanesque church, at **Lautenbach**, then climbs up to the artificial lake of Lauch in a glorious wooded setting.

HAGUENAU
BAS-RHIN   Pop 29,000

This town on the Rhine plain has museums of Alsatian crafts and history, and a church, St-Nicolas, dating from 1189, with a finely carved pulpit. Longfellow visited the town and wrote 'The Cobbler of Haguenau'.

HAUT-KOENIGSBOURG
BAS-RHIN

Rivalling Mad King Ludwig's Neuschwanstein in Bavaria, this vast and splendid folly of a fairy-tale fortress stands high (757m) on a wooded promontory of the Vosges, dominating the plain of Alsace and affording grandiose views. It dates from 1480, with a 12C keep: but in 1899 the town of Sélestat donated it to Kaiser Wilhelm II who then rebuilt it, rather too thoroughly, and often stayed there. You can inspect his rooms and antique furniture: over the chimney-piece in the Salle des Fêtes is the revealing inscription he made on his final visit, in April 1918, when the war was going badly: *'Das habe ich nicht gewollt'* (I didn't want this)! It is thus most apt that Jean Renoir used the castle for location shooting of his great anti-war film, *La Grande Illusion* (1938).

Haut-Koenigsbourg

HOHWALD, LE
BAS-RHIN   Pop 400

A summer and skiing resort in a beautiful part of the Vosges SW of Obernai. Meadows with orchards, and vineyards lie in the fertile valleys between high forested hills. There are ruined castles to explore – notably **Spesbourg** and **Haut-Andlau**, W of Barr; and **Guirbaden**, just N of the Obernai-Schirmeck road. A scenic road runs SW from Le Hohwald to the panorama point of **Champ du Feu**. Other notable views are from **Neuntelstein**, 3km N of Le Hohwald, and the **Signal de Grendelbruch**, 2km W of Grendelbruch.

KAYSERBERG
HAUT-RHIN   Pop 2700

An attractive little wine town in the valley of the river Weiss, overlooked by the ruins of a feudal castle. Albert Schweitzer, doctor, missionary, organist, Nobel prizewinner, was born in 1875 at 124 Rue du Gén.-de-Gaulle, the main street: the house is now a small museum of his life. From here the street winds down between lovely old buildings, over a 15C fortified bridge with a tiny chapel on it, past the Renaissance town hall and the 12–15C church with its splendid altarpiece. In the courtyard of 54 Grand' Rue is a Renaissance fountain with the inscription, 'Too much water at table chills the stomach: better drink an old and subtle wine and leave my water to me.'

LONGWY
MEURTHE-ET-MOSELLE   Pop 17,000

A former fortified town in a deep valley by the Belgian border. Till recently a prosperous steel-making centre, it has now fallen on hard times: in 1979, when plans for closing the main steelmills were announced, the workers replied with riots that lasted weeks, but finally lost their battle to save the mills.

About 13km SW, S of the Chiers valley, is the fort of **Fermont**, one of the major bastions of the Maginot Line, captured by the Germans on 27 June, 1940, after heavy fighting. You can visit the underground barracks and defence systems.

LUNÉVILLE
MEURTHE-ET-MOSELLE   Pop 23,000

A town on the river Vezouze, where in the early 18C Duke Leopold of Lorraine built a small-scale imitation of Versailles – a château and a formal park with fountains and walks. Later it became the favourite residence of Stanislas (see *Nancy*) who added more adornments, entertained in style, and died there in 1766. The place then fell into decay, but has recently been well restored. The château has a museum of porcelain and other treasures; a *son-et-lumière* in the park in summer evokes the spirit of Stanislas.

Baccarat, 25km SE, has been famous for its heavily ornate glass since 1764. A museum gives details of the glass-making process.

Château de Lunéville

LUXEUIL-LES-BAINS
HAUTE-SAÔNE   Pop 10,000

The waters of this old spa town, known to the Romans, treat gynaecological and blood disorders. The Irish monk Columbanus founded an important monastery here in 590, of which no trace remains. Fine Renaissance buildings include the Hôtels des Échevins and du Cardinal Jouffroy, and the Maison François I. A big air base lies 3km S.

METZ
MOSELLE   Pop 118,000

Metz

Lorraine's capital, though hardly a tourist centre, is a city of great character and interest, at once tough and graceful. Sited at a natural strategic point on the Moselle, it has long been a defence post against invaders from the east. The Romans fortified it to defend their empire; in 1944 the Germans, now on the retreat, held up the American advance here for two-and-a-half months. The city is still girt by strong forts.

Charlemagne was especially fond of Metz and had his wife buried here. In the 12C it was the capital of a small republic. Today it is a lively, progressive city with a new university, and the government has recently rewarded its dynamism by making it the official capital of the Lorraine 'region', rather than its larger but sleepier rival, Nancy.

Finest of the many fine buildings is the lofty Gothic cathedral of St-Étienne, whose marvellous stained-glass windows, ranging from the 13C to 20C, create miracles of light and colour; best of all is the huge rose window at the W end. On the S side, the high Mutte Tower (closed to visitors) is now the municipal belfry: its bell, the famous 'Dame Mutte', cast in 1605 and weighing 10,943kg, is rung on special occasions.

The Esplanade, a small park, affords pleasant views over the river. Here the church of St-Pierre-aux-Nonnains is reputed to be the oldest in France: it stands on the foundations, still partly visible, of a 4C Roman basilica and belonged to a 7C Benedictine abbey. At the other extreme of age and styles, the shed-like church of Ste-Thérèse in the S suburbs was completed in 1954 and is flanked by a soaring needle-like spire. In the old quarter, the charming Pl. St-Louis has arcaded 14–16C buildings. To the E is the Porte des Allemands, a 13–15C fortress astride the river Seille. The Musée d'Art et d'Histoire, in a former monastery near the cathedral, has French and other paintings (including Delacroix and Corot) and a good Gallo-Roman archaeological collection: note here the 13C painted ceilings of the Hôtel de Voué.

At **Scy-Chazelles**, 4km W, is the former country home (open to visits) of Robert Schuman, the great Lorrain who played so large a part in creating the European Community and died here in 1963.

MOLSHEIM
BAS-RHIN Pop 7000

A charming old town near the N end of the Route
du Vin (q.v.), at the foot of Riesling-producing
vineyards. It has remains of ramparts and an old
fortified gateway. In the Pl. de l'Hôtel de Ville is
the 'Metzig', a curious Renaissance building put
up in 1554 by the butchers' corporation who held
meetings and sold meat there. Truly Alsatian in
style, it has big voluted gables, a perron, a graceful
balcony, and a loggia crowned by a belfry where
two angels strike the hours. The first floor is now a
small museum, the ground floor is devoted to
wine-tasting. Note also the big 17C church formerly run by Jesuits, and the new Bugatti factory
in the outskirts.

MULHOUSE
HAUT-RHIN Pop 114,000

Alsace's second largest city is noted mainly for its
diverse industries: linen spinning, printed fabrics,
chemicals, machinery and automobiles (Peugeot).
There is a big new university and research complex
in the SW suburbs. The town has changed colours
several times: from the 13C it declared itself a 'free
city', then joined the Swiss Confederation in 1648
but in 1798 voted freely to become French; it was
German against its will in 1871–1918, and is now

Mulhouse

French again. Alfred Dreyfus of the 'affair' was
born here in 1859.

There are several interesting museums, some
unusual: a museum of over 400 vintage cars,
including 117 Bugattis and an 1892 Panhard; a
railway museum; a museum of printing on cotton
(the technique was pioneered here, in 1746);
museums of history and Beaux-Arts, the latter with
some good Dutch and Alsatian paintings. The
Protestant church of St-Étienne has 14C stained
glass, the 16C *mairie* has a fine painted facade – and
a well-stocked zoo will appeal to the young.

NANCY
MEURTHE-ET-MOSELLE Pop 99,000; with suburbs,
266,000

Place Stanislas, Nancy

A small central part of Nancy is as elegant as any
town in the French provinces: the rest is a rather
grey, dull northern city, with a crisscross grid of
streets, and new suburbs sprawling up the nearby
hills. It has a fair-sized university and several other
major centres of learning and research, such as the
famous École des Mines. But it is not a very
dynamic place, and its long historic role as Lorraine's capital has recently been transferred to its
rival, Metz – to Nancy's fury.

It was founded in the 11C by Gérard, first duke
of Lorraine, who made it his capital. In the 18C its
beautiful central zone was built not by a Frenchman but a Polish exile, Stanislas Leszczynski.
Father of the wife of Louis XV, he also became
king of Poland, but had to renounce the throne in
1737. In compensation, Louis made him duke of
Lorraine, on condition that the province returned
to France on his death. Stanislas, a man of taste,
set about planning an ensemble that compares on a
smaller scale with Versailles. He was helped by
two master artists, the architect Emmanuel Héré,
and the ironsmith Jean Lamour.

The Pl. Stanislas, as the main square is now
called, is a harmonious array of palaces, fountains
and superb wrought-iron railings with lanterns.
The palace along the S side, now the town hall, has
an imposing stairway leading to the Salle des Fêtes,
which offers a fine view of the square: on summer
evenings it is floodlit, and there are commented
guided tours. The Arc de Triomphe, on the N
side, was put up by Stanislas in honour of his son-
in-law. It leads to the long Pl. de la Carrière, lined
with stately 18C houses, also Héré's work. Beyond
again is the former Palais du Gouvernement with
its ornate colonnade, and beside it the old 13C
Ducal Palace, which has a sumptuous Renaissance
doorway. This building now houses the remarkable Lorraine Historical Museum, giving a varied
and vivid picture of the province and its life.

The church of the Cordeliers, next to the palace,
holds the tombs of many of the dukes of Lorraine,
richly carved in stone: best of them is the tomb of
the Duchess Philippa de Gueldre, by Ligier
Richier (16C). To the N of the church is the half-

ruined Porte de la Craffe, a relic of the 14C city ramparts; to the E, the Pepinière, a formal park with rose-garden, zoo, and statue by Rodin of the painter Claude Lorrain (Claude Gellée), born near Nancy in 1600. Take a look too at the 18C cathedral, the Musée de Beaux-Arts (a good collection, from Italian primitives through to Modigliani), and the unusual museum of the Nancy School (turn-of-the-century decorative arts).

An international festival of experimental drama, the leading one of its kind in Europe, is held in May; and there is a biennial summer jazz festival.

In the centre of the little industrial town of **St-Nicolas-de-Port**, 12km SE, there rises the unlikely spectacle of the two lofty towers of a 16C church, a splendid example of Flamboyant Gothic.

OBERNAI
BAS-RHIN   Pop 9000

Perhaps the most enchanting of all smaller Alsatian towns. It still has its old ramparts, shaded by lime-trees: you can walk round them, admiring the view of vines, orchards and forested hills. Around the big Pl. du Marché are many attractive buildings: a 16C corn-market with a storks' nest on its roof; a Renaissance *mairie* with sculpted balcony; a 13C belfry with corner-turrets; and a strange 16C well whose three wheels each lift two buckets. Pretty wooden houses in the Rue des Juifs. In the church, 19C, is a casket that since 1921 holds the heart of Mgr Freppel, former bishop of Angers: before he died in 1981 he asked that his heart be transferred to his native Obernai, but only after Alsace's return to France.

PLOMBIÈRES-LES-BAINS
VOSGES   Pop 900

Montaigne, Voltaire, the Empress Josephine, Baudelaire and Berlioz are among those who have taken cures at this celebrated little spa in the pretty Augronne valley. Its radioactive waters treat rheumatism and digestive disorders, and were known to the Romans, whose relics can be seen in the Bain Romain.

PONT-À-MOUSSON
MEURTHE-ET-MOSELLE   Pop 15,000

An industrial town at a key crossing-point of the Moselle, where a bridge has stood since the 19C, and where for two weeks in Sept. 1944 the Ger-

Abbaye des Prémontrés, Pont-à-Mousson

mans tenaciously resisted Patton's advance. On the E bank, the imposing ex-monastery of the Prémontrés, 18C, is now a cultural centre and the home of the European Centre of Religious Art. The building has a pleasant cloister and three attractive stairways. In the arcaded 16C Pl. Duroc, note the House of the Seven Deadly Sins, symbolized by pretty caryatids. Major pipeline factory of the St-Gobain group.

RIBEAUVILLÉ
HAUT-RHIN   Pop 4000

There is much of varied interest in this old Alsatian wine town, known for its Riesling and Traminer wines. At its SE entrances are two old towers where storks still nest. From here the Grand' Rue winds up between old houses to the tiny main square and the Butchers' Tower, a 13C belfry. One of the oldest surviving Alsatian folk festivals, the 'Pfifferdaj', takes place here on the first Sun. in Sept., with much music and dance; from the fountain in the square there flows free wine for all.

On the hill c.3km NW of the town stand three ruined castles. First drive up a narrow track to the lonely little monastery of **Dusenbach**, still in use. Leave the car there, then climb a steep path to the 12–14C château of **St-Ulrich**, a well-kept ruin. Fine view from the summit of its keep.

RIQUEWIHR
HAUTE-RHIN   Pop 1000

Riquewihr

The most celebrated of Alsatian wine-villages. Although incredibly picturesque, it is no museum-piece but a lively community, producing some of the best Riesling. Harvest is a good time for a visit – if you don't mind the tourist hordes. Partly walled, its cobbled streets closed to traffic in summer, Riquewihr looks much as it probably did in the 17C. Everywhere there are fine old buildings with gables, balconies, bow windows. Finest is the

An old walled town EGUISHEIM we have stayed in photo picture on wall in Peter's room with a storks nest on the church. of a wide valley with geraniums in window box

Dolder Gate (1291), which houses a museum of local history. The postal museum, in the old château, traces the history of communications in Alsace since Gallo-Roman days.

ROUTE DES CRÊTES

This well-built crest road, clearly signposted, winds from peak to peak along the spine of the S Vosges, offering many splendid views. In 1871–1914 the Franco-German frontier was here, and the road was first built by the French Army in 1914 for supply purposes. The route starts at the **Col du Bonhomme**, W of **Kayserberg**, and turns sharp right at the **Col du Calvaire** where a road to the left leads to the **Lac Noir** and **Lac Blanc**, two lakes in a grandiose setting of granite cliffs, today used for hydroelectricity. The crest road passes the **Lac Vert**, tinted green by lichen, then the skiing-centre of **Col de la Schlucht**, to reach **Le Hohneck**, one of the highest points in the Vosges (1362m: marvellous view from the summit, reachable by car). The road then runs past **Le Markstein**, another ski station, to the **Grand Ballon**, highest peak in the range (1424m): a 15-minute walk takes you to the summit, where the view covers the **Vosges**, **Black Forest**, **Jura** and, on a clear day, the **Alps**. Further S you come to **Vieil-Armand**, the name given by French soldiers to the **Hartmannswillerkopf**, a steep ridge above the plain that saw bitter fighting in 1915 (30,000 dead). There are French and German memorials.

ROUTE DU VIN D'ALSACE

The touristic 'wine road', well signposted, winds for 180km through some 40 wine towns and villages, from **Marlenheim**, W of Strasbourg, down to **Thann**, W of Mulhouse. To the W rise the wooded Vosges, to the E lies the plain, stretching to the Rhine; and all around are the famous vineyards on the slopes, producing mainly wines of quality, based on Riesling, Sylvaner, Traminer and other grapes. Harvest is an ideal time for a visit: but at any season the drive offers a beautiful picture of traditional rural Alsace. Some places have entries of their own in this chapter (Molsheim, Obernai, Ribeauvillé, Riquewihr, Kayserberg, Guebwiller and Thann), but there are many other points of interest. Among them, N to S:

Wangen has arched courtyards, old houses, twisting streets. **Avolsheim** has a church said to be Alsace's oldest, and a 9C Romanesque baptistry. **Rosheim**: among its many old buildings, the 'House of the Pagans' is said to be the oldest dwelling in Alsace (12C). The church, Alsatian Romanesque, has a fine octagonal tower. **Boersch**: three old gateways, lovely houses in the main square. **Ottrott** produces red wine, rare in Alsace, and has *two* medieval châteaux. **Barr** has a wine fair, 14 July, in the handsome 17C *mairiel*; harvest fête, 1st Sun. in Oct., when the fountain flows with free wine. **Andlau**: 12C church with remarkable Romanesque sculptures on its porch; remains of a famous monastery. **Dambach**: old walled town with three tower-topped gates.

Bergheim: remains of ramparts, 14C fortified gateway; German cemetery (1939–45) to W. **Hunawihr**: fortified church, once used by both Catholics and Protestants. **Bennwihr**: modern church with a vivid stained-glass window stretching right across S wall. **Sigolsheim**: 12C church with Romanesque portal; French Army cemetery (1944). **Kientzheim** has a gateway with a sculptured head that sticks its tongue out. **Ammerschwihr**, mostly rebuilt (in Alsatian style) after wartime bombing, preserves an old gateway with storks' nest and sundial. **Turckheim's** varied delights include a large papermill, a singing nightwatchman, a storks' nest above an old gateway, and Renaissance houses around a charming main square, the Place Turenne (named after the general who in 1675 here won a key victory over a much larger German army, thus winning Alsace for France). **Eguisheim**: a charming old town of fountains and alleys, overlooked by three red towers of a ruined castle. The stained glass in the modern church depicts the life of Pope Leon IX, born either here or at Dabo in 1002. **Rouffach**: Witches' Tower with storks' nest, Renaissance ex-*mairie*, and other old buildings.

Turckheim

ST-DIÉ
VOSGES Pop 26,000

A town in a fertile valley W of the Vosges, flanked by pine-wooded sandstone hills. The pink sandstone cathedral, restored after 1944 damage, has Romanesque nave and S portal, 14C choir and aisles; next door is a large and attractive Gothic cloister. Important library.

ST-MIHIEL
MEUSE Pop 5000

This town on the Meuse was captured by the Germans in Sept. 1914 in their bid to outflank Verdun, and was not retaken till 1918. The sculptor Ligier Richier (1500–67) was born here and has left two fine works: a Virgin in the church of St-Michel, and an Entombment in the church of St-Étienne.

We have also stayed at WINTZENHEIM while Brian was in BASLE. 1984

STE-ODILE
BAS-RHIN

This hilltop convent is the most-frequented tourist spot in the Vosges, because of its links with Ste-Odile, Alsace's patron saint. Legend has it that she was born blind at Obernai in 670. Her father, the duke of Étichon, gave orders for her to be killed, but she escaped with her nurse to a convent, where at her baptism she recovered sight. When adult, after more adventures, her father repented and gave her his hill-castle of Hohenburg which she turned into a convent. It was destroyed by fire in 1546 but rebuilt a century later and is now again used as a convent. A chapel survives from the 11C, and an 8C stone tomb venerated as Ste-Odile's. The nuns run a guesthouse, open to tourists as well as pilgrims. There is a major pilgrimage on 12 Dec., the saint's day.

S of the convent a short path leads to a view of the strange 'Pagan Wall', a looping 9km circuit of rough stones: its origin is a mystery, but it may have marked the bounds of a Celtic or Gaulish encampment.

SAVERNE
BAS-RHIN Pop 10,000

This town on the river Zorn has an impressive pink sandstone château, an abode of the prince-bishops of Strasbourg from the 13C until the Revolution: Cardinal Louis Rohan (see *Strasbourg*) rebuilt it after a fire in the 18C and lived there in grand style. It now belongs to the state and holds a small museum of history. Its majestic N facade (not the one visible from the road) has high Corinthian pillars and looks over a park. To the W, off the Route de Paris, is a rose-garden.

The ruined 13C castle of **Haut Barr**, built on three great rocks on a hilltop and affording excellent views, stands 3km SW. From **Saverne** a road runs SW through a wooded valley and up on to the lovely scenic plateau around **Dabo**, where there are sweeping views from the top of the imposing Rock of Dabo. At **Marmoutier**, 6km SE of Saverne, is an unusual old abbey church with an 11C façade in Lombardic style.

SÉLESTAT
BAS-RHIN Pop 15,000

Sélestat has modern industries around it, but is an old centre with remains of ramparts and Renaissance houses. In the 15C it had a university and was a key centre of Humanism: its important Bibliothèque Humaniste, dating from that time and today open to visits, has a 7C Merovingian lexicon and many other rare MSS, including 2000 books that belonged to Beatus Rhenanus, native of Sélestat and friend of Erasmus. Of the two fine churches, Ste-Foy is 12C Romanesque, St-Georges is Gothic with lovely stained glass.

The ruined feudal château of **Kintzheim**, 5km SW, has an aviary with 80 eagles and other birds of prey: visitors can watch them being trained. At **Markolsheim**, 15km SE, by the Rhine, is a museum of the Maginot Line, adorned with a Sherman tank and a Soviet cannon. At **Illhaeusern**

by the river Ill, 13km S of Sélestat, you have one of France's most gastronomically celebrated and beautifully sited restaurants: the brothers Haerberlins' luxury *Auberge de l'Ill*.

STRASBOURG
BAS-RHIN Pop 252,000; with suburbs, 409,000

Alsace's capital, lying just W of the Rhine, is a pleasant and dignified old city full of character. The sprawling suburbs are modern and industrial: but the central area round the cathedral, forming an island within two arms of the river Ill, has many lovely buildings and much of interest.

Strasbourg has had remarkably little history until recent times. It was repeatedly burned, pillaged and occupied by invaders, usually German: but today it has become the very symbol of Franco-German reconciliation and of the new united Europe. The city has become the seat of the Council of Europe and, more important, the main venue of the European Parliament, and so one of the EEC's three capitals, along with Brussels and Luxembourg. The smart new Palais de l'Europe, housing these bodies, is in the NE suburbs and can be visited on appointment. To the E, the *port* of Strasbourg, France's largest river port after Paris, can also be visited. E again is the Rhine and the rebuilt Pont de l'Europe, leading into Germany. Strasbourg also has important universities.

Main point of interest for the visitor is the pink sandstone Gothic cathedral, one of Europe's finest, with its tower and spire soaring to 142m. Its majestic façade, begun in 1284, has three portals richly decorated with carvings of biblical scenes.

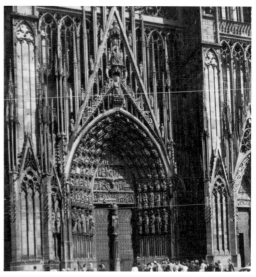

Notre-Dame, Strasbourg

There were to have been two towers, but the one on the S side was never built. Anyone fit and unafraid of heights should climb the 328 steps of the external spiral stairway to the platform at the base of the tower, for a wonderful view over Strasbourg and the far mountains (Goethe, a student in the city in 1770, used to climb it regularly in order to fight against his feelings of vertigo).

The cathedral's spacious interior is artistically rich: stained-glass windows from the 12–20C; 14

superb 17C tapestries depicting the life of the Virgin; a Flamboyant Gothic pulpit; and the superbly carved 'Pillar of Angels' in the S transept. Above all, visitors are drawn to the famous Astronomical Clock (1838) whose complex mechanical figures perform at noon each day: Death strikes the hour, Christ blesses the Apostles, and the cock crows to mark Peter's denial.

A walk round the city from the cathedral could start at the square in front, where you find the Pharmacie du Cerf (1268), said to be the oldest pharmacy in France, and the charming Maison Kammerzell with its carved timbers (restored) and 15C doorway: it is now an excellent restaurant. Here the Rue Mercière leads to the Pl. Gutenberg, where a statue of the inventor of the printing-press commemorates the fourteen years, 1434–48, that he spent here as a political refugee from his native Mainz. Just SE of the cathedral is the vast 18C Château des Rohan, now a museum but formerly home of the cardinal-bishops of the Rohan family, notably the handsome and sophisticated Louis de Rohan (1734–1803), friend of Cagliostro, whose profligate ways shocked Marie-Thérèse. From here you can walk via the pretty little Pl. du Marché-aux-Cochons-de-Lait (sucking-pigs' market) to the Pont du Corbeau over the Ill, so named because in medieval days murderers were here drowned in iron cages, their bodies left for crows to eat.

The King's Chamber, Château des Rohan

From here you can walk right along the river to the enchanting Petite France, most picturesque quarter of old Strasbourg, where the gables and balconies of 16C houses are reflected in the quiet waters of canals. To the W, by the Ill, are four towers, formerly linked by covered bridges, that were part of the 14C city ramparts; to the N, the charming Rue du Bain-aux-Plantes with its Renaissance houses, formerly the tanners' quarter; to the E, the Protestant church of St-Thomas, containing the tomb of Marshal Saxe, a highly dramatic sculpture by Pigalle (1777). N from here lies the broad Pl. Kléber, busy heart of the modern city. NE again, at 4 Pl. Broglie, a plaque on the Banque de France building marks the spot where in 1792 a young army officer, Rouget de Lisle, composed the patriotic hymn now called *La Marseillaise* (see *Marseille*).

Principal museums of Strasbourg:
Château des Rohan: after admiring the rich 18C decor of the Rohans' living-rooms, you can visit a large, varied and important museum that is in three parts: (a) Beaux-Arts: paintings from the Middle Ages to 18C: Italian primitives and Renais-

sance; a notable Mater Dolorosa by El Greco; Dutch works by Marmion, Van Dyck, etc. (b) Archaeology: local finds. (c) Decorative arts: major collection of ceramics, mainly Alsatian.

Musée de l'oeuvre de Notre-Dame: virtually the cathedral's own, devoted mainly to Alsatian art of the Middle Ages and Renaissance: stained glass and other relics from the earlier Romanesque cathedral (note a 'Head of Christ' dated to 1070, one of the oldest extant pieces of figurative glass); paintings and sculptures by Witz, Schongauer, etc.; documents relating to the cathedral's history.

Musée Historique: military souvenirs, plus drawings, maps, etc. of old Strasbourg.

Musée d'Art Moderne (in the former customs house): Renoir, Degas and other Impressionists; Modernists (Klee, etc.); modern stained glass and sculptures (Arp, Moore, etc.).

Musée Alsacien, in three old houses, one with a charming galleried courtyard: Alsatian folklore and folk art.

Festivals include an international music festival in June; European Fair first half Sept.; and a Christmas Fair on Pl. Broglie.

In summer there are regular sightseeing boat-tours on the Ill.

THANN
HAUT-RHIN   Pop 7000

An old town on the river Thur, noted for its large collegiate church of St-Thiébaut, arguably the finest Gothic building in Alsace. The N and W portals have rich and realistic statues and carvings; the 15C stained glass is also remarkable, but the church is famous above all for its splendid 15C choir-stalls with their lively and humorous carvings. On a hill to the N is the ruined feudal castle of **Engelbourg**, one of whose round towers was blown up by Turenne in 1674: it now lies on its side, the aperture looking from afar like a giant eye – so it is known as 'the Witch's Eye'.

THIONVILLE
MOSELLE   Pop 41,000

This old fortress town on the Moselle, S of Luxembourg, was a favourite residence of Charlemagne and is today capital of Lorraine's troubled iron and steel industry.

To the SW, in the valleys of the Fensch and Orne, notably around Hayange and Rombas, the giant steelmills were built in happier days beside rich iron-ore deposits. Today the deposits are mostly exhausted, and in face of world recession many mills have been closing down. Some new factories have arrived, but not enough to avert massive unemployment. Here industrial decay hits you in the face. Rail tracks to closed factories are lost in weeds. Grimy canals, once busy with barges, stagnate in disuse. Derelict mineshafts crown the hills, above valleys where the surviving furnaces belch their black, pink and orange fumes over the ugly terraced houses. In ghost towns, many shops are shuttered. The steel towns, oddly, have names like Hayange, Uckange, Gandrange – but these are angels with dirty faces.

Some 20km E of Thionville, at **Le Hackenberg**,

N of the road to Saarlouis, is another sad memorial to the past, of a different kind: the remains of the largest of the fortifications of the Maginot Line, able to hold 1200 men and supplies for three months. In 1940 it held out till 4 July, and surrendered only when France as a whole capitulated. The underground fortress, now with a small museum, is open to visits Sat., Sun.

TOUL
MEURTHE-ET-MOSELLE   Pop 17,000

An old ramparted town above the Moselle, once both a key military post and a major bishopric. Its magnificent former cathedral, 13–16C, was badly damaged in 1940 and 1944, as was the old bishop's palace next door, now the *mairie*. Work on restoring the cathedral is still incomplete. It has a superb Flamboyant facade, two high octagonal towers, and lovely cloisters. The nearby church of St-Gengoult, 13–15C, also has fine cloisters, in Flamboyant style, as well as 13C stained glass.

VERDUN
MEUSE   Pop 24,000

Strategically placed in the narrow Meuse valley, Verdun has been a fortified town since Gaulish and Roman days, and by 1914 was the strongest fortress in France. It was heavily damaged in the 1916–18 battles (see below); but its 12C Romanesque cathedral has been well restored and has a fine cloister. The former bishop's palace, next door, houses a museum of local history. The nearby citadel contains big underground rooms where soldiers took turns to sleep and rest during the long battles.

The main sites of the battle of Verdun are c.5–10km N and NE of the town. Verdun was already encircled on three sides when, in February 1916, the German Army launched its great frontal assault from the N, in a bid to capture this key bastion. The Germans made some progress, taking the fort of Douaumont, and later those of Vaux and Thiaumont: but French resistance, under the command of General Pétain, was much stiffer than they had expected. By July the German advance had been halted and Verdun was saved. In 1917 the French counter-attacked and regained much of the lost ground. In all, these 1916–17 battles were the most terrible trench-warfare episodes of the First World War, worse even than the Somme and Ypres battles. Almost 400,000 French soldiers died, and about the same number of Germans. Eight villages were destroyed and have not been rebuilt.

It is well worth touring the battlefields, which are on high ground above the river, now replanted with forests. Several of the old fortresses have been preserved, and they and other memorials are open to the public – notably, the forts of **Vaux** and **Douaumont**; the ossuary of Douaumont that holds the bones of 100,000 men; the memorial and museum of the battle, S of Douaumont. All is clearly signposted. The dank forts with their gun-emplacements and underground galleries are a grim sight. To the W of the river, the hills of **Le Mort-Homme** and **Côte 304** were also the scenes of furious fighting. On the hill of **Montfaucon**, to

the NW, a former German fort and lookout post, the US Government has erected a giant memorial to mark the American victories in the area in 1918: you can climb to the top of its Statue of Liberty.

VITTEL
VOSGES   Pop 6000

This well-known spa town lies amid lovely country, and its large thermal baths are set in a handsome park. As at the neighbouring spa, Contrexéville, the waters are used to treat migraine, arthritis and liver and kidney complaints. The bottling factory, producing one of France's most popular mineral waters, can be visited. Of the many hotels, the largest is now a Club Méditerranée 'village'.

VOSGES DU NORD

A number of interesting places (notably, ruined castles) lie close to the German frontier in a hilly, forested area that forms the N part of the Vosges du Nord regional park. From W to E: The town of **Bitche** (pop. 7000) has a fortress, rebuilt in 1679 by Vauban, that successfully resisted the Prussians in 1870–1; 4km W is the fort of **Simserhof**, one of the major underground bastions of the Maginot Line.

From Bitche, the road SE to Niederbronn passes below the ruined castles of **Falkenstein** (fine view from its belvedere) and **Wasenbourg**. A road running NE goes close to the frontier, traversing the picturesque villages of **Obersteinbach** and **Niedersteinbach**, to reach the ruined 13C castle of **Fleckenstein**, built on a rock and partly carved out of the rock. The road goes on to **Wissembourg** (pop. 6000) a frontier town of true Alsatian character, with a colourful carnival on Whit Mon.: the large Gothic church of St-Pierre-et-St-Paul has an octagonal tower, a 12C rose window, and a mural painting of St-Christopher 11m high. The town was the scene of a decisive Prussian victory in 1870. To the S are the very pretty Alsatian villages of **Oberseebach**, **Hunspach** and **Hoffen**.

Wissembourg

LOWER LOIRE

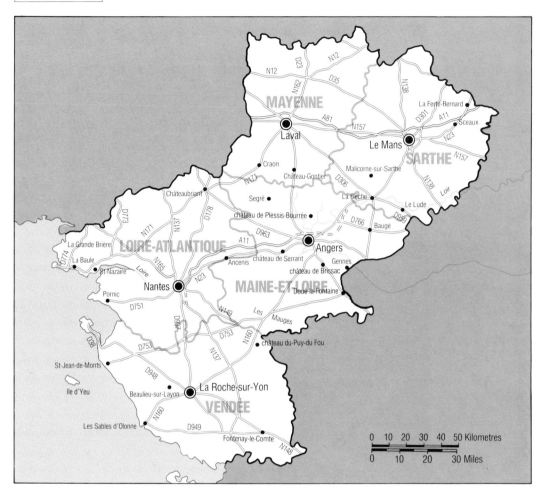

The western Loire from Saumur to the sea, the Vendée south of Nantes, even Maine and the Sarthe valley, are worlds away from the Loire Valley as tourists know it. Not only did these regions miss the tourist revolution, which came with the family car, but all except a few cities missed the industrial revolution as well.

The wars in this part of France were fierce and dragged on for centuries. In the 10–11C the powerful counts of Anjou fought the counts of Touraine for power and Paris could do nothing. Then the marriage of Eleanor of Aquitaine and Henry Plantagenet in Angers in 1152 sealed the fate of Anjou. Two years later Henry was king of England and not only this area but Aquitaine as well became English for the next three centuries.

The end of the Hundred Years' War, with the English finally driven from France in 1453, brought peace, but a century later Calvin was preaching reform and the Wars of Religion found the whole area divided. The skilled artisans mostly supported the Protestant cause. When in 1685 the Edict of Nantes, giving them religious and personal freedom, was revoked and persecutions began, they fled abroad – mostly to the Netherlands and England.

The peasants of the Vendée were staunch Catholics and Royalists. After the Revolution and the execution of Louis XVI they were so angry at the new Republic's persecution of priests that they rose in protest. Armed mostly with pitchforks and scythes, the Chouans, as they were called, reached Le Mans before being defeated and put down with savage reprisals by the Republican General Turreau, who was later guillotined for it – too late.

The Vendéans, still strongly Catholic, have remained through the centuries a people apart. But that is gradually changing, at least on the coast, as holiday-makers arrive in increasing numbers, lured not only by the clean sand beaches backed by pines but by the superb seafood, the Muscadet wine of the Nantaise, the butter, cream and cheese from the Loire estuary, and the beef from the Charolais cattle fattening in the Mauges bocages.

In Maine, especially around Le Mans, they produce *rillettes*, the splendid potted pork, and still grow the lovely Reinette apple, the one regional variety to have stood its ground against the encroaching American Golden.

Unlike the Loire, which has 'existed to look beautiful' since the arrival of railways, the Sarthe from Le Mans to Angers was a fairly important waterway until World War II and is still navigable by hire cruisers. In places it has parallel canals. It passes through woodlands and meadows, with some arable patches producing mostly potatoes and cabbages, and there are some pleasant villages on the way.

Far more spectacular is the Mayenne Valley from Laval to Angers, which winds and twists through deep-sided valleys and is particularly attractive around Écluse and Ménil. It keeps away most main roads and towns, passing tiny hamlets, watermills, some still working, and secretive reaches shaded by trees. Work is progressing to repair locks north of Laval for pleasure boats.

ANCENIS
LOIRE-ATLANTIQUE   Pop 7300

This pleasant little town in a half-circle N of the Loire was for long plagued by traffic but the motorway from Nantes to Angers has brought blessed relief. Some traffic still uses its fine suspension bridge. Its old houses rise in tiers above the river and it has remains of a castle, including a Renaissance wing with overhanging turret. Once it was a vital river crossing, and busy port, making sailcloth. Now it is an important pig market and wine producer, mostly Muscadet white but some Gamay red and rosé, and a little Cabernet. Coteaux d'Ancenis Gamay is light, sometimes acid.

ANGERS
MAINE-ET-LOIRE   Pop 141,100

The old capital of the dukes of Anjou prospers through a changing world. Always a centre for wine, fruit, vegetables, herbs and flowers, it now produces textiles, electronics, TV sets, car ports and umbrellas. It stands on the banks of the river Maine which is just 8km long and is really the meeting place of the Sarthe, Mayenne and the little Loir before they reach the Loire 8km away. But the main city is on the big hill, not beside the water, though a new river port is becoming important.

Angers was tied to England when Foulques Nerra, count of Anjou, married his son Geoffroy, first of the Plantagenets, to Mathilde, granddaughter of William the Conqueror. Although she lost her fight for the throne of England to Stephen, their son became Henry II of England and, through marriage to Eleanor, of Aquitaine.

Philippe-Auguste took Angers for France in 1205. His grandson Louis IX (St Louis) built the present château around 1220 in the style of the Crusaders' forts in Palestine, with a kilometre-long outer wall flanked by seventeen round towers.

Angers is a city of tapestries and the greatest is in the castle – 'The Apocalypse', woven in Paris in 1375–80 from cartoons by Hennequin of Bruges, who took a few small liberties with St Paul's text. Though not complete (it was originally 168m long, but was vandalized during the Revolution), 100m remains, displayed in a special room, and visitors can either admire the whole or move from one sequence to the next, using commentaries provided in several languages. It has extraordinary depth of colour and precision, portraying surrealistic fantasy. More magnificent tapestries are in the

Angers

Logis Royal (including the 15C richly colourful Flemish 'The Passion') and Logis du Gouverneur ('Lives of the Saints').

A modern masterpiece is in the Musée St-Jean in the old hospital – ten tapestries called 'Le Chant du Monde' are 78m long and took nine years to weave. The work, its black background exploding in intense colours, remarkable for purity of line and scintillating design, is by Jean Lurçat, greatest of modern tapestry artists, who was planning another seven hangings when he died in 1966. He wrote a commentary, on sale in English translation. You will need it.

The 12–13C cathedral of St-Maurice is of a transitional Gothic-Renaissance style. The Calvary to the left is by Jean-Pierre David, the early 19C sculptor known as David d'Angers. Most of his works are in the Musée des Beaux Arts in the 15C Logis Barrault, with some good 18C French paintings (Watteau, Fragonard, Boucher and others).

The cathedral's stained glass windows cover this art from the 12C to the present day, but many, alas, are too high to be seen properly. One shows the life of Thomas à Becket.

Angers is rich in old buildings. Curnonsky (real name Maurice-Edmond Sailland), the French 'Prince of Gastronomes', was born in Angers in 1272; his Tournedos Curnonsky is sautéed with bone marrow and tomatoes.

BAUGÉ
MAINE-ET-LOIRE   Pop 3900

The market town for lush green country between La Flèche and Angers, it has attractive old houses and a 15C château now used as town hall and museum. It was the favourite residence of Yolande d'Aragon, protectress of Joan of Arc, and her son Good King René, duke of Anjou, count of Provence and king of Sicily, who was no warrior but one of the most cultivated men of his time. He more or less handed Anjou to his nephew Louis XI and went to live in Aix-en-Provence. The château has an interesting turret staircase and overlooks a big square with gardens. The Hôpital St-Joseph beyond has a dispensary with a collection of decorated pottery medicine jars. The old hospital chapel now contains a piece of the Cross brought from the Holy Land by a crusading local overlord. It has two arms, was originally called the Cross of Anjou, then adopted as the double-cross of Lorraine, emblem of the Free French Forces under General de Gaulle in World War II.

Le Vieil-Baugé, the neighbouring village which has a church with a leaning spire, was the site of a battle in 1421 when the English lost to the French and the Scots under the Earl of Buchan, later High Constable of France.

BAULE, LA
LOIRE-ATLANTIQUE   Pop 14,700

A resort since the 1880s, La Baule has remained fashionable and elegant even in this age of jet travel, thanks in large measure to the beauty of its bay and 8km of clean sands, protected by 400ha of maritime pines planted in the 19C to settle the dunes. Other attractions are the interesting fishing ports nearby, and the high standard of international sporting events backed by the authorities, including tennis championships, golf tournaments, show jumping and racing. It keeps something of its snob-appeal – lively, but never brash or vulgar. The casino thrives, and the pleasure boat harbour between sea and salt marshes came long before the marina boom.

La Baule-les-Pins, also planted with pines, was added in 1930 and has a fine flower park. **La Pouliguen**, to the W, is an old fishing port with narrow streets which became a resort back in 1854. The beach is sheltered by woods. Fishing boats still land white fish, crab and lobsters on the noisy quay.

Batz-sur-Mer comes next, between sea and salt marshes, a very Breton town of granite houses with a tall 17C church belfry as landmark. Three sandy beaches break the rocky coast.

Le Croisic, its neighbour, is a photogenic, busy little white fishing port and resort, with 17C houses lining the quay, boats landing shellfish, coastal traffic and pleasure yachts. The town was once entirely surrounded by water.

Pornichet, E of La Baule, was a salt-marsh workers' village which became a resort in 1860, the haunt of Paris journalists. It is at the end of the bay's long sand beach, and has a well known racecourse.

Inland from Batz in the salt marshes is **Guérande**, a fortified medieval town built by the de Montfort family, with its ramparts from the Middle Ages still intact, flanked by eight towers and

pierced by four fortified gateways. The old moats are now a circular promenade.

The **Marais Salents**, marshes between Guérande and Batz, was a sea-covered bay when Julius Caesar's galleys under Brutus defeated the becalmed sailing boats of the Veneti by hooking them and landing men aboard. Caesar then wiped out the whole Veneti tribe.

BEAULIEU-SUR-LAYON
MAINE-ET-LOIRE   Pop 950

The attractive Layon valley runs N into the Loire just downstream from Angers and its slopes produce fine dessert wines, with vineyards sometimes separated by fruit trees, mostly plum, peach and walnut. The grape harvest can take from early Oct. to mid-Nov. Fermentation can last up to six weeks and the wine reach 15 per cent alcohol or more. Beaulieu is the centre of the vineyards.

BRISSAC, CHÂTEAU DE
MAINE-ET-LOIRE

Château de Brissac

The 12th duke of Brissac lives in this château 8km S of Angers. His military family have owned it since 1502. The present château was started in 1606 in the ruins of the 15C castle, by the second duke. Because the formidable primitive towers of the old castle could not be pulled down, he built between them, giving it the present patchwork effect. He died with it unfinished and it was damaged in the Revolution. Restorations began in the 19C.

The interior is magnificent. The huge guard room is superbly proportioned, with richly carved wooden beams, the bedrooms have tapestry-hung walls and early poster beds, and the ceilings are painted and gilded. The family portrait gallery includes Mme Clicquot, the champagne widow. Vineyards surround the park and you can taste the local wine in the château cellar.

CHÂTEAUBRIANT
LOIRE-ATLANTIQUE   Pop 14,400

An old fortified town among woods and pools in the attractive Chère valley. Its castle is in two parts – remodelled medieval, with a large square keep, and a good-looking 16C Renaissance house built by Jean de Laval, with esplanade and gardens down to the river.

La Baule

At the town gates is a memorial to 27 local hostages murdered by the Nazis in 1941.

Châteaubriant

CHÂTEAU-GONTIER
MAYENNE   Pop 8400

This pleasant old town on the Mayenne river S of Laval has a damaged 11C château, a much-restored Romanesque church and, each Thurs., the biggest cattle market in France, especially for calves, with 4000–5000 head sold weekly. Beautiful trees adorn the gardens and river quays.

CRAON
MAYENNE   Pop 5000

A delightful little-known town astride the Oudon river, SW of Laval in the Mayenne bocage country-side where cattle are raised. It has an elegant and symmetrical 18C château built in the white tufa of Saumur, which grows whiter with the centuries, in a lovely setting of a French formal garden surrounded by an English park with gentle grassy slopes. The park and gardens are open.

La Frenouse, 14km NE, is a restored farm-house reached by an avenue bordered by giant, totem-like statues, all by Robert Tatin.

DOUÉ-LA-FONTAINE
MAINE-ET-LOIRE   Pop 6800

An extraordinary town 17km from Saumur, known for roses and its network of underground quarries and galleries cut out of limestone rock, started by the Romans. In the Douces quarter is an arena, originally a quarry, transformed in the 15C by cutting rows of seats in the rock, now used for musical and theatrical performances and a mid-July rose show. A zoo on the Cholet road, open in the summer, has a collection of snakes and birds of prey, including vultures.

FERTÉ-BERNARD, LA
SARTHE   Pop 10,000

This delightful old Sarthe market town has been rescued from terrible traffic problems by the motorway, which takes most of the Paris–Le Mans traffic. Ferté means a small fortress. It belonged to the Guise family and the Catholic League. When the League were defending it against the troops of Henri IV in 1590, the women were sent out of the town when food ran low. Seeing them eagerly invited into the enemy camp, the League commander sent out 200 men disguised as women (the 'Lambs of Ferté'). Outside they attacked the enemy who fled in dismay.

Park by the medieval gatehouse (Porte-St-Julien) and walk under it through narrow shopping streets and Renaissance houses to the market square, where a big food and wine market is held every Mon.

The superb church of Notre-Dame-des-Marais is a classic example of the meeting of Flamboyant Gothic and Renaissance, built between 1450 and 1596.

FLÈCHE, LA
SARTHE   Pop 16,400

Pleasantly situated on the banks of the Loir, this market town for fruit is famous for its military college (Prytanée Militaire), founded originally in 1607 as a Jesuit college by Henri IV, whose parents had lived here. Descartes was a pupil. It became a military school in 1762 when Jesuits were expelled from France and in 1808 was made a high school for sons of officers and civil servants.

Tertre-Rouge zoo, 4.5km SE, has 700 live animals and 700 stuffed museum specimens. **St-Germain-du-Val**, 1km N, was the birthplace in 1836 of ballet and opera composer Léo Delibes. The Scottish philosopher Hume wrote his *Treatise on Human Nature* at the manor of Yvandeau.

FONTENAY-LE-COMTE
VENDÉE   Pop 16,700

This quiet town on the banks of the Vendée river was an intellectual centre of the Renaissance, an English stronghold bravely defended in 1372 by the beautiful wife of the English governor against Du Guesclin.

Fontenay, now industrialized, has always been a literary centre. Rabelais, a monk at the monastery, was expelled for owning books supporting reform. The 16C poet Nicolas Rapin was born and lived here; and in 1648 Molière acted at the theatre. In the 18C the Marquis de Sade, stationed at the garrison, wrote his novel *Justine* before fleeing after fighting a duel with a magistrate. Georges Simenon wrote some of his Maigret novels here during the German occupation of World War II.

GENNES
MAINE-ET-LOIRE   Pop 1900

A pleasant Loire riverside town on the slopes of a hillock, known chiefly for four dolmens (prehistoric burial chambers) in the hills behind and its little suspension bridge across the Loire to Les Rosiers. This replaces one of three across the river (the others at Saumur and Montsoreau) blown up by 1200 men and 800 cadets of the Saumur Cavalry School who for a while held up a German force, destroying a number of tanks, after Paris had capitulated in 1940.

Nearby **Les Rosiers** is a delightful little town possessing a 13C church with Renaissance spire, some old houses, and Albert Augerau, an institution of the Loire. Albert is patron-chef of the hotel-restaurant *Jeanne de Laval*, reviver of old regional recipes, defender of Loire cooking and wines, and holder of a Michelin star.

GRANDE BRIÈRE, LA
LOIRE-ATLANTIQUE

More than one-third of this regional nature park of 6600ha, between La Chapelle-des-Marais and the port of St-Nazaire, consists of marshland, with 'islands' between. It was originally a forest flooded by the sea, which receded to leave peat bog as vegetation decomposed over centuries; 5000-year-old fossilized tree trunks have been found. Over the five centuries water was pumped, drainage was improved and it became the common property of local people who caught fish and eels, shot wildfowl, cut peat, gathered rushes for thatching and wickerwork, propelling their flat-bottomed boats, 'blin', for transporting cows and sheep to pasture. Locks and roads have now been built, and marsh turned into pasture.

LAVAL
MAYENNE   Pop 53,800

An agreeable town astride the Mayenne at the N end of the winding, deeply-banked Mayenne valley down to Angers. The old town on the W bank surrounds the castle, which is in two parts. Vieux Château, from the 11C, contains a mixed-bag museum, with tools of medieval craftsmen and naïve paintings, including a work by Henri Rousseau (Le Douanier) born here in 1844. Château Neuf, with Renaissance facade, was restored and enlarged in the 19C to serve as law courts. Grande-Rue, down to the river, is lined with half-timbered houses with overhangs and stone Renaissance houses with decoration. It reaches the river at Pont Vieux, a hump-backed bridge, once fortified. One of the old *bateaux lavoirs* (laundry boats) the 'St Julien', used until 1970, is a museum.

The unattractive Romanesque cathedral has been much altered but has some good artistic works, including fine 17C Aubusson tapestries. St-Vénérand church over the bridge has fine Renaissance windows, but the most attractive church is the Gothic-Renaissance Notre-Dame d'Avénières,

Laval

with huge wooden statues of Christ and St Christopher, and modern windows by Max Ingrand.

Former Laval citizens include the Renaissance surgeon Ambroise Paré, who started ligature of arteries during amputations, Henri Rousseau and his friend the eccentric writer Alfred Jarry, innovator of the Theatre of the Absurd, and Alain Gerbault, tennis doubles partner to Jean Borotra and sole round-the-world sailor, lost in the Pacific in 1941.

Trappe du Port-du-Salut, 7km S, is the monastery where Port-Salut cheese was made until 1959. This is now produced in a factory at nearby **Entrammes**, although the monks still make their own cheese.

LUDE, LE
SARTHE   Pop 4500

In the park of the château, beside the river Loir, a spectacular *son-et-lumière* takes place on some summer evenings, involving almost everyone in the little town.

The attractive castle looks Renaissance, but that is a facade. It has wings from three periods – Louis

Château le Lude

XII, François I, Louis XVI – with huge round corner towers. It is a feudal fortress turned into a stately home, still lived in, beautifully kept and richly furnished. It has an interesting collection of costumes and Henri IV's bedroom retains its original furnishings.

MALICORNE-SUR-SARTHE
SARTHE   Pop 1800

In the Sarthe valley between Le Mans and Sablé, it is in a pleasant riverside position and has a 12C church and 17C château with small turrets, surrounded by a moat, in a fine park. Local potters specialize in reproduction faience period pieces.

MANS, LE
SARTHE   Pop 150,000

There is a lot more to this big industrial and business city than motor racing, but the 24-hour race, started in 1923, is still one of the great international events of any year. The 13.5km circuit is S of the town. Within it are Les Hunaudières horse-racing course from which Wilbur Wright attempted one of his early flights and the 4km Circuit Bugatti, used for car testing and motor cycle racing. A large motor museum has some magnificent old cars.

The Romans fortified the town in the 3–4C and well preserved Roman walls can be seen at several points. Le Mans was taken by William the Conqueror, whose granddaughter married Geoffroy Plantagenet. Their son, Henry II of England, was born in the town and retired there in old age but was expelled by his rebellious son Richard Lionheart. The medieval town is within these ramparts and has many beautiful and interesting old mansions.

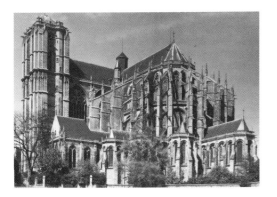

St-Julien, Le Mans

The cathedral of St-Julien, dedicated to the saint who brought Christianity here in the 4C, is imposing and architecturally interesting. Parts are beautiful but the high Gothic transepts of the 14–15C are in slight discord to the low, 11–12C Romanesque nave.

The capitals in the nave are covered with fantastic animals, monsters and hideous masks while the high Gothic chancel is surrounded by twelve chapels with stained glass in vivid blues and reds, and 16C tapestries hang above the choir stalls.

The tomb of Queen Berengaria, widow of Richard Lionheart, with a small dog at her feet, is in the transept. She was given the Maine district by Louis-Philippe of France after he took it from King John of England.

In the cathedral precincts is the house where Paul Scarron, the 17C poet and satirical writer, lived. A witty and pleasure-loving young man, he was made impotent by paralysis before he was 30 and his wife, Françoise d'Aubigné, became Louis XIV's mistress – Madame de Maintenon.

In 1793 the royalist Chouans were defeated here by the Revolutionaries; and in 1871 the Prussians defeated the French here and made the relief of besieged Paris impossible.

MAUGES, LES
MAINE-ET-LOIRE

A secretive area of rocks, ravines, woodlands and pasture between the Loire, the manufacturing town of Cholet and the Layon river, rearing cattle sold at a huge Sat. market. **Cholet** is known for shoes, handkerchiefs, radio and electronic components, toys and tinned meat. Centre of heavy fighting in the Vendéan counter-revolution, it has a war museum from the time.

Chemillé is another livestock market town and produces medicinal herbs, with an exhibition gar-

den by the Mairie. Here the Vendéans beat the Republicans. **Beaupréau**, in the heart of Les Mauges on the river Evre, has narrow winding streets and a restored 15C château which has two round towers with cupolas.

Though only 210m high, **Le Puy de la Garde**, a ridge between the villages of Gardes and St-Georges, affords fine long views over the Mauges, even to the Loire and Layon valleys.

NANTES
LOIRE-ATLANTIQUE   Pop 248,000

Rebuilding after World War II damage, though tastefully done, removed some of this industrial and commercial town's historic character, yet much of its ancient charm still survives. Gone are the little trains which used to move goods from the quays and send frustrated drivers mad, three tributaries of the Loire have gone underground, and the two islands have been swallowed by the city. This has improved traffic flow, but there are still horrific parking problems.

The port, at the mouth of the Loire, is navigable by large vessels and the shipyards, with those at St-Nazaire, make naval and commercial vessels, especially dredgers. There are sugar refineries, canneries, and factories producing refrigeration plants, oil-boring equipment, telephones, electronics, chemical products and ships' boilers. The first ship's engine using nuclear energy was produced here. The city also distributes Muscadet and Gros Plant wines.

A Gallic and then Roman town, Nantes vied with Rennes through the Middle Ages for the title of capital of Brittany. The dukes of Brittany and the French kings squabbled over it until the daughter of Duke François II, Anne of Brittany, married Charles VIII and subsequently Louis XII. Although just inside Brittany, Nantes was detached from it after the Revolution and made capital of the non-Breton Loire-Atlantique *département*. Today it is the capital also of the Pays de La Loire region, entirely separate from Brittany, whose capital is Rennes. The two towns are bitter rivals.

François II began the Château des Ducs in 1466 and Anne continued it. A severe fortress, its most pleasant part is the Renaissance Tour de la Couronne d'Or, with fine Italian-inspired loggias. Henri IV signed the Edict of Nantes here in 1598, giving religious and personal freedom to Protestants. When Louis XIV revoked the charter in 1685, the terrible massacre and persecution of Protestants started and many fled from France. In World War II Nantes was a persistent centre of the French Resistance.

The castle now houses the Musée d'Art Populaire, with absorbing collections from Breton culture and life, from head-dresses to furniture and interesting cooking equipment; and the Musée Salorges, a maritime museum, with models of the 17–18C slaver and sugar boats which made the town's fortune. Slaves were taken from Guinea and sold in the Antilles, and cane sugar was bought to be refined at Nantes.

The Musée des Beaux Arts has a superb collection of Renaissance and later schools of painting, including Rubens, Tintoretto and some Impressionists.

The Gothic cathedral of St-Pierre-et-St-Paul, begun in 1434, finished 1893, has an austere, dull facade but the inside is impressive, with vaults over 35m high. The tomb of François II, by Michel Colombe (1502), with the duke and his duchess reclining on a black marble slab, is one of the greatest Renaissance masterpieces of France.

A museum devoted to the novelist Jules Verne, born here in 1828, is at 3 Rue de l'Hermitage.

The covered way with shops, steps and statues, Passage Pommeraye, is a lovable piece of ostentation. Nantes has a lively carnival just before Easter.

Tomb of François II

PLESSIS-BOURRÉ, CHÂTEAU DU
MAINE-ET-LOIRE

Jean Bourré became treasurer of France under Louis XI, so had money to build himself several châteaux, this one being started in 1461. Though a fortress, with conical topped round towers, it has a pleasant outline and was designed inside for comfort and refinement. The white stone was dragged from near Angers (20km) at enormous expense. It is approached across a bridge of many arches over a wide moat.

Nearby, 13km NW of Angers, is **Château du Plessis-Macé**, built in the 11C as a fortress, turned into a residence in 1510 but still looking like a fort from outside. From inside the courtyard, it looks like a country house, with a charming balcony in one corner for spectators at entertainments or jousts. The ground floor is hung with 17–18C tapestries, some from Angers cathedral. The chapel was built in 1472.

PORNIC
LOIRE-ATLANTIQUE   Pop 2300

This delightful fishing port forms an amphitheatre around an inlet S of St-Nazaire. The natural harbour is crowded with fishing boats and there is a new yacht marina under a corniche.

The small beach lies below a 13C castle which belonged to Gilles de Rais. Hero of the siege of Orléans with Joan of Arc, marshal of France at 25, he became rich by marriage, ran through his fortune and was accused of terrorizing much of Brittany, kidnapping women and boys for his orgies and killing them. He was hanged at Nantes, but modern lawyers studying the evidence at his trial, believe he was almost certainly 'framed'.

Noirmoutier is a narrow isle 19km long, mostly of sand dunes and salt marshes, with market gardens and a small sardine-fishing port. It can be reached either by road or by boat from Pornic.

PUY-DU-FOU, CHÂTEAU DU
VENDÉE

This château, half in ruins after being sacked by government forces in the Chouan uprising, stages a spectacular night pageant throughout the summer, with hundreds of costumed performers, recounting the violent and bloody story of the Vendée wars. It is well worth a detour.

ROCHE-SUR-YON, LA
VENDÉE   Pop 48,000

After the 1793 counter-revolt of the Chouans (the Vendéan peasants) against the Revolution had been savagely suppressed, Napoleon decided in 1808 to build a garrison town to keep order. He chose La Roche because he thought it must have rock for building; but the builders had to use clay, and the town, named Napoléon-Vendée, was nicknamed 'Town of Dirt'. It was planned on the lines of Washington, D.C., with a great square fed by roads placed geometrically at right-angles.

When Napoleon fell, they changed the name smartly to Bourbon-Vendée, then back to La Roche. A museum traces the history of the Vendéan wars.

An important stud, with thoroughbred stallions and French trotters, is open all the year. Local industries include washing machines and plastics.

SABLES D'OLONNE, LES
VENDÉE   Pop 16,700

Increasingly popular beach resort with Parisians in particular, with 1km of fine sands and an informal attitude to dress in shops and little restaurants. An embankment promenade behind the beach (Le Remblai) was built to protect the town but is now lined with fashionable boutiques, cafés, hotels and pricy flats. Once famous for its cod-fishing boats, Olonne is still a fishing port with boats landing tunny, sardines and sole. One of its more infamous sons was the brutal buccaneer of the Spanish Main, Jean-François Nau, nicknamed L'Olonnois, who was born here in 1630 and was hacked to pieces by Carib Indians.

ST-JEAN-DE-MONTS
VENDÉE   Pop 5600

Expanding beach resort N of Les Sables d'Olonne with a firm sand beach, backed by dunes and pines, which joins others to make a long stretch of sands along this Vendéan coast.

Challans, 16km NE, has an interesting Tues. duck market; the ducks are often incorrectly called 'Nantais'.

ST-NAZAIRE
LOIRE-ATLANTIQUE   Pop 70,000

Built for ships which became too big to reach
Nantes, St-Nazaire is a port and industrial town.
Although there is at present quite a slump in its
shipbuilding activities, it produces ships for the
French Navy, especially submarines, diesel en-
gines and turbines for ships and railways. The
residential part of the town is separated from the
industrial zone.

The submarine base was built by the Nazis
during World War II occupation, mostly with
slave labour, and had a covered lock to allow U-
boats to come and go in secret. The base withstood
an enormous tonnage of Allied bombs and is now
used by industry.

In March 1942 the Royal Navy and British
Commandos raided the docks of St-Nazaire, fighting in the streets for two days and causing enormous damage. The old destroyer *Campbeltown*
filled with explosives was rammed into the huge
gates of the Louis-Joubert dock, where transatlan-
tic liners such as the *Normandie* docked in peace-
time, and blown up, putting the port out of action
for some time. Local people helped the raiders and
the Germans took terrible reprisals against the
town.

Bridge near St-Nazaire

SEGRÉ
MAINE-ET-LOIRE   Pop 7200

Centre of an area of wooded land with mixed
farming SW of Laval, Segré has a modern town
grafted on to the old. By the river are ancient quays
and attractive bridges, overlooked by tiers of old
houses of schist stone. The big neo-classical church
at the top was built in 1820.

Château de la Lorie just S was built by an 18C
provost-general of Anjou who married an American heiress. The grand Italian ballroom, with
marble and mirrors, was the scene of great fêtes
when the house was later owned by the duke and
duchess of Fitz-James; their title came from Mar-
shall Berwick, bastard son of James II of England,
who became a French general and got a dukedom
from Louis XIV. The lovely gardens and park,
with little lakes, were laid out later by Édouard
André, the great landscape gardener.

SERRANT, CHÂTEAU DE
MAINE-ET-LOIRE

This grand Renaissance mansion beside a lake
which feeds its moat, in a beautifully kept park, is
still occupied, but is partially open to the public. It
is at St-Georges-sur-Loire, off the tourist track,
18km from Angers. Brown schist stone and white
tufa contrast cleverly in one building and two
massive round towers capped by cupolas give it a
remarkable symmetry considering it was built over
three centuries, 16–18C.

A fine panelled Renaissance stairway leads to
first-floor apartments with coffered ceilings, tapestries in the dining room, big bedrooms with 18C
furniture, magnificently furnished formal drawing
room, decorated in green with a carved ceiling,
and a handsome library with 20,000 volumes. It
also has a picture of Bonnie Prince Charlie leaving
for Scotland and the abortive '45 uprising.
Anthony Walsh – Antoine de Walsh – who supplied the frigate to carry the Young Pretender is
saying farewell. For this service, Louis XV made
Walsh count of Serrant.

His great grandfather, James Walsh, an Irish
boat owner, had brought James II into exile from
England in 1688, settled in Nantes and made
money from shipping. His grandson James bought
Serrant and left it to 'Antoine'. Théobald de
Walsh, count of Serrant, had the gardens laid out
in 1820. The Duc de la Trémoille inherited it by
marriage and the family still live there.

YEU, ÎLE D'
VENDÉE   Pop 5000

This fisherman's isle, 10km long by 4km wide,
20km off the Vendéan coast, 60km S of St Nazaire.
It has a gentle climate until the wind really blows;
then seas breaking over the rocks on the southern
Côte Sauvage are fearsome.

Car ferries run from the mainland at **Fromen-
tine**, near Beauvoir, and take $1\frac{1}{4}$ hours (book well
ahead). They land at **Port-Joinville**, which has a
tunny-fishing fleet. The little S harbour, **Port-de-
la-Meule**, in a sheltered cover, has lobster boats.
Pierre-Levée fort was the prison from 1945 of
Marshal Pétain, hero of World War I who made
peace with Hitler on Montoire-sur-Loire on 24
Oct. 1940, and was President of France during the
Nazi occupation. He died here in 1951, aged 95,
and was buried in the island cemetery.

Port-Joinville, Île d'Yeu

LOIRE/CENTRE

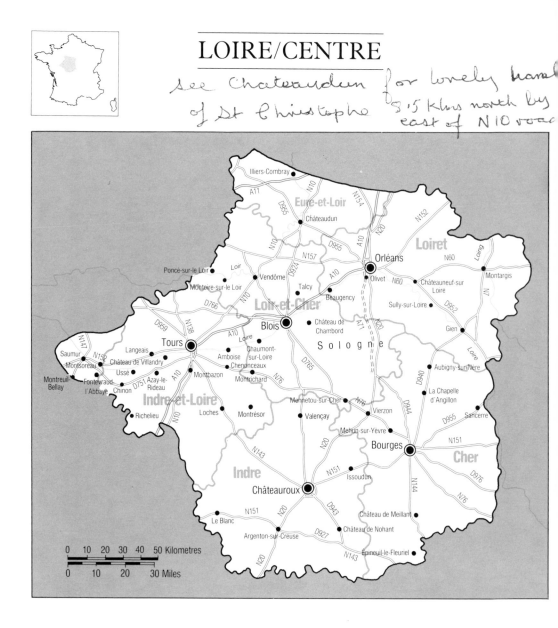

The Loire and its surrounding countryside are beautiful and the climate kindly, with short warmish winters, spring arriving as early as March, hot summers, and autumn days made delicious as early morning mist gives way to sun.

This good-tempered climate is one of the main reasons why the centre of France has seen through the centuries as much of France's important historic action as any area, even Paris. Its climate and garden-like lands drew northern invaders – Huns, Visigoths and Normans. Monarchs from Charles VII to Henri III preferred it to Paris not only for its weather and well-stocked game forests but its security from the plotters and restless citizens of Paris. Though François I built Fontainebleau, he also built or took over several great châteaux in the Loire as "hunting lodges" and moved huge convoys of courtiers, retainers, their luggage and even furniture into them. Even after building his beloved Versailles, Louis XIV visited Chambord, and Madame de Pompadour acquired and converted Méhars.

If the châteaux of the Loire, as we know them today, were made for love, leisure and hunting, they were not always so. Many of the earlier ones, similarly to those of the Dordogne, were built

originally for war, and converted or replaced later to be fit for comfortable living. The future of France was decided in fighting around here – hardly surprising, for the Loire divides France as we know it in half, and made a natural defence barrier.

The powerful counts of Blois and Anjou could almost ignore Paris, and they fought each other for power. It was a count of Anjou, Godfrey Plantagenet, so called because he wore a twig of *genêt* (golden broom) in his hat, who wed a granddaughter of an English king, and their son became Henry II of England in 1154. Astutely he had married Eleanor of Aquitaine after the king of France had renounced her, and so Aquitaine came under the English crown.

The fight between the Plantagenets and the French crown was inevitable and much of the fighting was around the Loire. Although after Richard Lionheart's death in 1199 the astute Philippe Auguste of France soon subdued John of England, who preferred pleasure to war, England kept Aquitaine and English kings retained their ambition to rule France. The Loire was terribly vulnerable. Touraine was part of France but Anjou was a duchy merely owing France allegiance.

182

From 1357, the Hundred Years' War was fought almost as much around the Loire river area as around the Dordogne, and it was Joan of Arc's triumph at Orléans in 1429 which paved the way to eventual French victory, the English suffering total defeat in 1453 at Castillon. Anjou joined France in 1481. It was in Anjou that some of the fiercest fighting of the French Revolution took place between Republicans and Royalists.

Travel on the Loire was for many centuries easier than by road. People called the river the road that moves. The fleet was only replaced as railways developed.

The river looks lazy but is not easy to navigate, for it swirls round islands and sandbanks and can be very bad-tempered. It can rise suddenly and rage as heavy rain in the Massif Central or quick-melting snows bring water pouring down its tributaries. Roads follow huge dykes which can look laughable when the river dawdles along beside beaches where children play and girls sunbathe in the briefest bikinis. But floods have been known to sweep away those dyke walls.

The Loire valley is not truly one region. The infertile Sologne is a world apart from the richly fertile Petite Beauce between Orléans and Beauce, a land for farmers rather than tourists. Touraine boasts lush pastures, flower gardens, vineyards, magnificent castles and manors, and a few choice industries. Anjou, rich in history, has its horticultural valley along the Authion, strawberries near Saumur, soft fruit and artichokes near Angers, and hillsides of soft stone south of the river where vines are grown and wine is stored in caves.

Orléans itself has been very much attached to Paris since it was the property of each king's second son. Now it supplies Paris with flowers, lettuce, cucumbers and tomatoes.

In the 1950s many small farmers, market gardeners and farm workers left the land for the Paris factories. New factories in places like Tours have stemmed the rural exodus, but the population is ageing somewhat as Parisians avail themselves of its pleasant scenery and milder climate on retirement or buy themselves second homes here. The A10 motorway has brought it all nearer to Paris but blessedly keeps most of the hurrying through-traffic away from the pleasanter small roads and villages.

The old lands of Berry, Indre and Cher are still little known and, apart from the historic city of Bourges and a few market towns, are given over to farmers. Unlike the cosmopolitan people of the Loire valley, who are used to tourists, these are retiring people, in no hurry, and you do not get to know them in a hurry, either. But the land has some charm and much variety – forests, wheat prairies, rich pastures and grassy hillsides watered by thousands of small streams. Beyond Loches and Vierzon, where most tourists abandon them, the valleys of the Indre and Cher rivers are equally unfamiliar.

It is a calm, secretive, sometimes mysterious land which has appealed more to imaginative storytellers from George Sand to Alain-Fournier rather than writers of guide books. But it played a vital role in French history when Joan of Arc's beloved Dauphin hid there and was scathingly called "King of Bourges" until she persuaded him to be crowned at Reims. And it was a Bourges banker, Jacques Coeur, who paid for the upkeep of the entire campaign against the English.

Berry cooking is hearty, straightforward, but hardly plain, being rich in game, chicken, pâtés and pies. *Poulet en Barbouille*, with chicken blood added to the sauce, is rich; filling soups are on every farmhouse cooker and potatoes are made into a heavy cake called *truffiat*, and pumpkins into pies. As nearer the Loire, there are good river fish, including lampreys. The now-universal *beurre blanc* of shallots and wine vinegar mixed with butter came originally from the Loire, where it is served with river pike, carp and shad.

The Loire is known as the Garden of France and is rich in fruit – William pears, Reinette apples from Le Mans, Saumur strawberries, quinces from Orléans, peaches, apricots, grapes and melons. The Sologne forest produces game for Orléans and here the *tarte tatin*, the upside-down apple pie, was invented. It is a land of goat's cheese, too, including Chabichou, Chavignol of Sancerre, Livroux in pyramid shape, and St-Maure.

Each town has its own *rillette* – pork cooked in its own fat with herbs, pounded and kept in jars.

The Loire produces good flowery light summer wine but many others besides. The dry spicy Sauvignon white wines of Sancerre and the Fumé of Pouilly are now fashionable, Reuilly and Quincy from the same area less known. Muscadet, from the grape of that name, has spread eastward from around Nantes and is one of the most popular wines in Europe. Saumur makes some of the best Champagne-method white wine (and the first made outside Champagne), and Vouvray has a world reputation for sparkling, pétillant and still white wines. Red wines of the centre of France are becoming popular again – Chinon, beloved by Rabelais, and dark red Bourgueil, both made from the fruity Cabernet Franc grape.

From its great châteaux days of royal courts, the Loire has inherited festivals, and they are legion. Oldest is the Festival of Joan of Arc in Orléans on 7–8 May, celebrated for five centuries. Saumur has its traditional Tattoo of the Black Squadron, once for cavalry, now for tanks as well, in late July. Touraine's classical music festivals are in June and July, Anjou has a great summer festival of music, dancing and art, Cheverny has a concert of horn music and hunting horns on Saturdays in July and August, and Doué-la-Fontaine's medieval arena is the site, in mid-July, of one of the world's biggest rose shows, with 100,000 blooms of 500 species.

Son-et-lumière started at Chambord castle and nowadays in summer ten Loire châteaux put on shows, with the biggest at Le Lude.

The biggest fête in central France, however, is still held at Le Mans in mid-June – the 24-hour motor race.

AMBOISE
INDRE-ET-LOIRE   Pop 11,400

Amboise is the most attractive and evocative of the Loire's bigger towns. Most is on the left bank of the river and you see it best from the right bank or the bridge. Though much demolished after the

183

Amboise

Revolution, the château perched above the river is still impressive and interesting. Once it covered seven times the ground. Charles VII stole it from the counts of Amboise. Charles VIII, who had married Duchess Anne, ruler of Brittany, started to rebuild it. Two years later he set off to conquer Italy.

Defeated, he came back with Italian furniture, textiles and works of art, and Italian artists and craftsmen of the Renaissance who changed French artistic styles. The superb little chapel of St-Hubert, last of the French Gothic buildings, begun in 1491, has a magnificent doorway showing the saint's conversion while out hunting. The artist is not known.

In 1498 Charles cracked his head on a low lintel and died. Louis XII continued the château. François I turned it into a centre of court junketings, with magnificent festival balls, masquerades, tournaments, even fights between wild animals. He brought Leonardo da Vinci here, and the great artist finished his life at the nearby manor house, Château Clos-Lucé. François bought two of his masterpieces after his death – the *Mona Lisa* and *Virgin of the Rocks*.

The widowed queen Catherine de Médicis brought here her boy-king son François II and his girl-wife Mary, later Queen of Scots, when Protestants were rising up in angry protest following St Bartholomew's Day massacres.

In 1560 a foolish Protestant from Périgord arranged for others to meet him at Amboise to start a revolt. Betrayed to the all-powerful duke of Guise ("Scarface"), they were hunted down, tortured, broken on the wheel and hanged from castle balconies. Royals and court would come out after dinner to watch them. The duchess of Guise warned Catherine: "What vengeance is here being stored up for the future!" And the royal family paid – the boy king François II died within months, his brother Charles IX died in terror and remorse after a bloodstained reign, the duke of Guise and Henri III were both murdered, and Mary was beheaded. The midsummer *son-et-lumière* depicts François I's merrymaking, not the Guise's bloodbath.

The 15C **Château Clos-Lucé** is full of little treasures, including da Vinci's bed, copies of his drawings, and in the basement models made recently from his own drawings of his inventions – a swing bridge, a clockwork driven motor-car for two, an air-conditioning plant, a flying machine, a turbine, a projector, a jack, a paddle-boat and a parachute. A man three centuries ahead of his time.

The island in the river, now a high-grade camping site, was the spot where in the 6C King Clovis of the Franks, backed by the church, met Alaric II of the Visigoths to feast and swear eternal peace and friendship. Like most summits, it preceded war, with Clovis killing Alaric and swallowing his kingdom. **Chanteloup Pagoda** (3km) is all that remains of the duke of Choiseul's château. He built it to mark the loyalty of friends from court who came when he was banished here by Louis XV after he fell foul of Mme du Barry, the royal mistress. It is 44m high, with fine views from the top.

ARGENTON-SUR-CREUSE
INDRE Pop 6100

Photogenic town of mainly old buildings round a curve of the river Creuse and a good centre for seeing the Creuse valley, including Le Pin bend in a background of hills and rocks, the beautiful Gargilesse valley, **Lake Chambon** watersports centre and the ruins of **Crozant** castle.

Argenton-sur-Creuse

AUBIGNY-SUR-NÈRE
CHER Pop 5700

A town of old houses with steep pitched roofs in higgledy-piggledy streets and big squares, it now makes lingerie and electric motors. For long it was a Scottish town; Charles VII gave it in 1423 to John Stuart of Darnley for helping him fight the hated English, and Scots craftsmen set up glass-making and wool weaving. The Stuarts, prominent in French diplomacy and war, stayed until 1672, when the last male heir died. The Stuart château is now the town hall, and their arms are on the vault of the church. The most interesting old house, **Maison du Bailli**, was theirs, too, as was the isolated lakeside **Château de la Verrerie** (11km SE).

Louis XIV gave all the property to Louise de Kéroualle, the baby-faced Bretonne who became mistress of the English Charles II, and mother of Charles Lennox (duke of Richmond). A later duke of Richmond sold it in 1834.

AZAY-LE-RIDEAU
INDRE-ET-LOIRE Pop 2900

The 16C château has been described as "a lovely houseboat made of stone". Though not quite so lovely as Chenonceaux (q.v.), it is a Renaissance gem of grace and strength with a Gothic outline. White walls and blue-grey slate reflect magically in the ornamental lake and Indre river, from whose bed the castle rises on one side.

The original castle was destroyed in a fit of temper by Joan of Arc's supposedly "gentil Dauphin" when aged 15. Believing he had been insulted by a Burgundian sentry, he executed the garrison of 350 soldiers and burned down the town. Azay was called Azay-le-Brûlé (Azay the Burnt).

The new castle was built from 1518 by Gilles Berthelot, treasurer-general of France and related to Catherine Briçonnet who built Chenonceaux and Jacques de Semblençay, the king's treasurer. Semblençay was accused by François I of corruption and beheaded. Berthelot fled to Italy and was found guilty of fiddling the nation's accounts. The king grabbed his new château as he had done Chenonceaux. It contains fine Renaissance tapestries and furniture within. A *son-et-lumière* performance is given on most nights during summer.

To the 16C **Château de Saché** (6.5km SE) Balzac fled from creditors in the 1850s to write some of his novels, including *Le Père Goriot*. It contains a Balzac museum. Later the American sculptor Alexander Calder lived in the village. He originated mobiles and stabiles. You can see his outdoor works at **La Carroi**, to the N.

Azay-le-Rideau

BEAUGENCY
LOIRET Pop 7300

This lovely peaceful town with narrow medieval streets and a splendid 22-arch bridge over the Loire was a war target for centuries. The only Loire bridge crossing between Blois and Orléans, it was fought over by French and English, Protestants and Catholics, the Nazis and the Allies.

Beaugency

The English held it four times in the Hundred Years' War. The castle was built by Joan of Arc's companion Dunois. Now it has a museum of local clothes and furniture. Part of the 18C abbey became an hotel, but locals claim that the Devil still lives in the Tour du Diable next door.

There is a beach for river swimming and good fishing. There are music and drama festivals, also a summer *son-et-lumière*.

Meung-sur-Loire, 7km NE, is a pleasant little town on the river. The tower and transept of the Romanesque church are 11C, and the ruined 12C *donjon* it is where the 15C poet Villon was imprisoned. The town is named after the local 14C poet, Jean de Meung.

BLANC, LE
INDRE Pop 8100

Old town on the Creuse, built round a 12C castle which controlled the river crossing; now a centre for exploring La Brenne, a little-known area of pools, marshes, heathland and scattered sheep farms.

La Brenne is rich in fish and game. Its centre is the **Château de Bouchet**, a medieval fortress used by the English in the Hundred Years' War. The castle stands beside the Mer Rouge pool, named by an owner on his return from being held prisoner on the Red Sea during the Crusades. On an island in the pool is the rebuilt church of Notre-Dame de la Mer Rouge, to which there is still a pilgrimage each Aug.

The **abbey of Fontgombault**, 7km NW, was established by Benedictine hermits in the 11C, and contained some ninety monks in the 13–14C. Dismantled in the Revolution, it was restored in the 19C. The 15C abbey building and cloisters are still occupied by the order. The lofty choir is especially impressive.

BLOIS
LOIR-ET-CHER Pop 49,400

Prettily situated among rising hills, mostly on the N bank of the Loire, this old town is still a busy

Blois

agricultural market for wine, strawberries, wheat, vegetables and bulbs, and manufactures chocolate. The château, facing N, is a 13–17C jumble of styles.

Louis d'Orléans bought the château in 1391 after seducing the owner's wife and persuading her to hand over her husband's money. Charles, his eldest son, inherited it but was captured at Agincourt and spent 25 years as a prisoner in England, writing poetry. Returning to Blois, he demolished part of the old fortress, built a prettier mansion, surrounded himself with artists and writers, and married a girl of 14, thereby producing the future Louis XII.

In the 16C Louis XII and his wife Anne of Brittany made the château the centre of court life. He brought over the great Italian Mercogliano to design superb gardens – alas, later built over.

François I added some of the finest parts of the castle in Renaissance Italian style, including the magnificent external staircase.

In 1588 the duke of Guise, bloodthirsty head of the powerful Catholic League, called the States General (Parliament) to depose Henri III and make himself king. Henri exposed the plot and had Guise murdered in the château. He himself was murdered eight months later.

In 1632 Louis XIII banished his brother, Gaston d'Orléans, a perpetual conspirator, to Blois, and gave him money to rebuild the château to keep him quiet. He hired the great architect Mansart, but happily ran out of money before he could alter the whole François I wing. It is all superb and well worth exploring. A *son-et-lumière* performance is held on most summer nights.

BOURGES
CHER   Pop 79,400

An industrial city S of Orléans, it is a centre of chemical, aeronautical and metallurgic industries, a military town, and has a Michelin tyre factory. Its 12C cathedral of St-Étienne is remarkable and beautiful. Gothic, enormously wide, with five great portals on the W front, it has masterful uniformity, with repair work through the centuries beautifully matched except for some mistakes in the 19C. Inside it looks vast, 110m long with a nave 40m high, no transepts, and an unbroken line of columns to the far end. The glass windows are magnificent.

Bourges university was world famous when students from Heidelberg brought with them the teachings of Martin Luther and the Reformation. Calvin was there as a student, learned these new beliefs and began to preach them. Bourges, divided among itself in the Wars of Religion, did not recover until modern times.

A 15C Gothic secular building almost as great as the cathedral is Jacques Coeur's palace. The richness and variety of its decoration does not destroy its elegance and beauty. It was the house of a banker, treasurer to Charles VII, who was unjustly arrested by the king, escaped to the Vatican, and died leading a fleet against the Saracens to liberate the Greek isles.

Bourges has several beautiful public gardens, including one next to the cathedral.

CHAMBORD, CHÂTEAU DE
LOIR-ET-CHER

This vast fairy-tale palace on the Cosson river, W of La Ferté St-Aubin, stands in a park of 54 sq. km, surrounded by a wall almost 35km long. The lower part is squat and stolid. The top is a whirlwind of planned disarray in carved, decorated stone, a stone garden of turrets, dormers, bells, cupolas, gables and pinnacles, with 365 sculptured chimneys. Inside are 440 rooms, a double-spiralled staircase, so that two people going up and down never lose sight of each other but cannot meet except at the top and bottom, fourteen other great staircases and seventy smaller ones.

It was built in 1519 by the flamboyant François I, devotee of hunting stags and women, the theatrical king who put on the sumptuous show to outshine the English Henry VIII at the Field of the Cloth of Gold.

Chambord

He used it only forty days. But he probably needed all those bedrooms, for the whole court travelled with him; 12,000 horses carried them, their servants, crockery, baggage and furniture. It was very uncomfortable inside. Almost bare for years, it now has suitable and some historic furnishings, tapestries and paintings. It swarms with visitors in midsummer.

Henri III finished the building. Louis XIV stayed nine times. For him, Molière wrote *Monsieur de Pourceaugnac* to be performed here. The king did not like it until the ballet composer Lully fell off the stage into the orchestra. *Le Bourgeois Gentilhomme* had more success.

Louis XV gave it to the arrogant, luxury-loving Marshal Saxe, who had two regiments of cavalry, from Tartars to negroes from Martinique, running wild in the park.

The park now is a presidential game reserve for deer, roe and wild boar, part open to the public.

Son-et-lumière, with night visits of the château, are held from 1 May to 30 Sept., entitled "Conflict Between Night and Day". The castle is open most days.

CHAPELLE D'ANGILLON, LA
CHER   Pop 700

On the banks of the Petite Sauldre in Haut Berry, N of Bourges and on the edge of the wild Sologne (q.v.), it is notable for two earlier inhabitants. Maximilien de Béthune, later duke of Sully, great statesman and financier under Henri IV, lived in the **Château de Béthune**, a restored fortress covering the 11–17C. Alain-Fournier, whose literary repute rests on one great novel *Le Grand Meaulnes*, was born here in 1886. The book came out in 1913, and in 1914 he was killed as a French officer. His name is on the war memorial by the church. The novel's Domaine des Sablières, a mysterious castle which, when his hero tried to revisit it, had become a ruin, with a lake filled in, was probably a combination of the Béthune château and the nearby **abbey of Loroy**.

CHÂTEAUDUN
EURE-ET-LOIR   Pop 16,000

A market town for the rich agricultural regions of Beauce and La Perche, particularly for grain, it is perched on a spur above the Loir river. The château, built around the 12C, is a sombre fort from outside, attractive from the courtyard. Much of its more comfortable interior was the work of Dunois, companion-in-arms to Joan of Arc and half-brother of the poet Charles of Orléans, who gave him the castle. The castle and surrounding houses were burned in 1723, in 1870 by the Prussians, and in 1940 by the Nazis, but restoration has been excellent. **Brou** (22km NW) is another market town, grouped round its market (Pl. des Halles) and many half-timbered houses with carved woodwork. **Patay** (SW between Châteaudun and Orléans) is where Joan of Arc beat the English and captured John Talbot, Earl of Salisbury, victor of forty battles.

Châteaudun

CHÂTEAUNEUF-SUR-LOIRE
LOIRET   Pop 6000

Likeable market town with pleasant walks along the river rich in wildfowl. Little is left of the castle except the gorgeous park with red squirrels among rare trees and shrubs, including enormous magnolias and giant rhododendrons. The castle rotunda, now the town hall, has a Loire maritime museum in the basement, tracing the story of river traffic when it was more important than the roads. The mostly 11C church of **St-Benoît-sur-Loire** (9km SE) is one of the finest Romanesque buildings in Europe. Its W tower is famous for its carved capitals, and the apse and colonnaded sanctuary are artistic masterpieces.

CHÂTEAUROUX
INDRE   Pop 54,000

Capital of Bas-Berry (Indre), an industrial town making textiles, machinery, motor tyres (Dunlop) and cigarettes. Napoleon's loyal friend General Bertrand lived here and his house is a museum of Napoleonic interest. **Châteauroux forest**, 8km S, is a beautiful forest of oaks and other deciduous trees. At **Diors** (11km NE) in the ruined castle is the Museum of Three Wars – Franco-Prussian, World Wars I and II.

CHAUMONT-SUR-LOIRE
LOIR-ET-CHER   Pop 850

The little town S of Blois with fine views over the river valley has a fierce 15C fortress with great round towers staring down at it. Catherine de Médicis is said to have lived here when Henri II, her husband, was killed in a joust and she became regent, allotting one room to Ruggieri, her astrologer. More probably she bought it to exchange for Chenonceaux with her husband's mistress, Diane de Poitiers, who did not like Chaumont and soon left. Madame de Staël, the writer, lived here during her banishment from Paris by Napoleon – and also disliked it.

The cedars in the park are centuries old. The stables are elegant – lined in velvet.

CHENONCEAUX
INDRE-ET-LOIRE

Château de Chenonceaux, spanning the river Cher, is arguably the most beautiful house in the world. It was designed by a woman, Catherine Briçonnet, between 1513 and 1521, not to withstand attack or siege or for outward show, but to be lived in. Chenonceaux was said to be the first great château built to banish draughts, the curse of previous dwellings. Catherine died before she could occupy it and her son, Antoine Bohier, had to give it to François I in return for an alleged debt of his dead father. François spent money in millions and took it where he could find it.

His son, Henri II, installed his brilliant mistress Diane de Poitiers here. She made a superb garden and started the bridge over the Cher. Then Henri was killed in a joust and Diane, previously all powerful, was swept aside by the queen-regent, Catherine de Médicis, who took Chenonceaux from her. She made a vast park, filled the rooms with finest furniture, statues, ornaments and hangings from her native Italy and above all built the superb gallery on the bridge, 60m long.

It is impossible in this space to describe Chenonceaux, to tell all its history, its stories of intrigue, love affairs and politics, its fêtes and parties where nymphs, satyrs and cavaliers pranced, mermaids swam in the moat and duchesses with their hair down served them at table and in boudoirs. See it for yourself, read a long book about it, then see it again. It is magnificent and we owe a great debt to the Menier chocolate family who keep it up. There is a *son-et-lumière* in summer.

Chenonceaux

CHINON
INDRE-ET-LOIRE   Pop 8900

This delightful wine town of steep streets above the river Vienne has a near-surfeit of history. Richelieu owned it. The English Henry II died in 1189 in the castle, then named after St George. King Philippe Auguste of France did not dare attack it while Richard Lionheart lived, but took it from the weak King John after an eight-months siege. Charles VII moved his court here, listened to Joan of Arc's strange story, believed her and gave her an army. The château, partly ruined, is still magnificent.

The river bridge, partly 12C, spans an island where in 1321 all the Jews of Chinon were burned alive.

At La Devinière, a manor house nearby, the satirist, scholar, priest and physician François Rabelais was born and spent his childhood. It was here that he wrote his *Gargantua*, published in 1532. The house contains a Rabelais museum.

Chinon red wines, made from Cabernet Franc grapes, are mostly softer than the Bourgueil reds from across the Loire which are now fashionable.

Chinon

ÉPINEUIL-LE-FLEURIEL
CHER

Although the writer Alain-Fournier was born at La Chapelle d'Angillon (q.v.), he spent much of his early life in this village, 65km S of Bourges, where his parents were school teachers. The village (Ste-Agathe) where he set his great novel *Le Grand Meaulnes* is based on Épineuil, and the present village school contains a fascinating little museum devoted to him. The name used for the novel title comes from another nearby village, **Meaulne**.

FONTEVRAUD-L'ABBAYE
MAINE-ET-LOIRE   Pop 1900

The historic and magnificent abbey is slowly being restored. Napoleon, not noted for his cultural tastes, turned it into a prison. It remained so until 1963, and is now a government owned cultural centre. Set up in 1099 by Robert d'Abrissel, it had one building for nuns, another for monks and others for aged nuns, fallen women and lepers. An abbess was in charge, to the annoyance of some monks, and the list of thirty-seven residents included fourteen princesses. Queen Eleanor of

Fontevraud-l'Abbaye

Aquitaine spent some years here and it was a sort of Westminster Abbey of the Plantagenets; in the church are the tombs of Eleanor, Henry II, their son Richard Lionheart and John's wife Isabelle. The kitchens, in an octagonal tower with twenty chimneys, are ingeniously arranged to get rid of smoke and smells.

GIEN
LOIRET   Pop 16,400

On the Loire's N bank, it was rebuilt very well in original style, using stone and glazed pink brick, after terrible World War II damage. The 15C château of pink and black brick, in geometric style, was the home of Anne de Beaujeu, favourite child of Louis XI and later regent until Charles VIII reached maturity. It now has a hunting museum. The Joan of Arc church was rebuilt after war damage in a cunning blend of modern and Romanesque, using pink and black brick with the original 15C square tower. It has Max Ingrand glass. You can visit the ceramic works, founded 1820 and producing Nevers-style porcelain, bird and animal designs, and brown glaze earthenware.

ILLIERS-COMBRAY
EURE-ET-LOIR   Pop 3500

This rather gloomy little town, 29km N of Châteaudun, on the headstream of the Loir, is renowned as the 'Combray' of Marcel Proust's great autobiographical novel, *À la Recherche du Temps Perdu (Remembrance of Things Past)*. As a child he spent holidays in the house of his aunt, which has been reconstituted as a museum, with his own little room overlooking the garden, his aunt's room, the original kitchen and the old garden gate with its bell – all of which featured prominently in the first volume of the work. The surrounding countryside is also beautifully evoked in the book. The name 'Combray' was recently added to the town's name.

ISSOUDUN
INDRE   Pop 15,200

Important even before Caesar invaded Gaul because of its position where two rivers meet, it became a frontier town in the Hundred Years' War between French and English armies. The round keep was built by Richard Lionheart. It is nowadays industrial, yet quite attractive. A 16C hospital contains a 17C chemist's shop with a collection of Nevers ceramic medicine jars and two Trees of Jesse (genealogies of Christ).

LANGEAIS
INDRE-ET-LOIRE   Pop 4200

This little riverside town of narrow streets, a centre for Loire fishermen, is attractive off-season, but crowded and impossible for cars in high tourist season. Its 15C castle, little altered, was built for Louis XI by Jean Bourré, finance minister to three kings of France. With two great round towers, narrow entrance and drawbridge, it looks forbidding – a Gothic fortress. Inside is a house beautifully furnished with period pieces and Flemish tapestry. In the Grand Salon, in 1491, Charles VIII married Anne of Brittany, bringing that free province under French rule. Across the bridge are river beaches used for summer swimming or sunbathing. Langeais is known, too, for melons, and its suspension bridge.

Cinq-Mars-la-Pile (5km NE) has a mysterious "pile" – square tower 29m high, with four of its five pinnacles left. It may have been Gallo-Roman. The castle nearby was pulled down by order of Richelieu. The 18-year-old Marquis de Cinq-Mars was planted by Richelieu as a page to spy on Louis XIII but he became a king's favourite and four years later denounced Richelieu, who had him beheaded.

LOCHES
INDRE-ET-LOIRE   Pop 7000

A charming town on the banks of the Indre with a fine medieval city within; it refuses to be hurried even by masses of tourists. It is one of the most striking and interesting places in France, and you must walk round it, for its narrow lanes make driving almost impossible.

Richard Lionheart lived in the château of Loches. While he was a prisoner in Austria on his way back from a crusade, his brother John gave it to the king of France, Philippe Auguste. On his return Richard was so angry that he stormed it and took it in three hours. When he died, it took Philippe a year's siege to get the English out.

Later it became a sinister place. In the Tour Ronde and Martelet of the château, the kings of France kept political prisoners in appalling conditions. For betraying Louis XI, Cardinal La Balue spent eleven years in an iron cage, able neither to stand nor lie down, which ironically he had himself invented for others. Ludovico Sforza, duke of Milan, captured by Louis XII, spent eight years in an underground cell. The former patron of Leonardo da Vinci covered his walls with paintings; on release, he died, some say of sudden sunlight. And

Loches

two bishops in a dungeon lit by a solitary ray of sunlight hollowed an altar out of the wall.

See these sinister towers first, then the happier scene of the recumbent figure of the beautiful Agnès Sorel, mistress of Charles VII and model for Fouquet's *Madonna and Child*. In the great hall Joan of Arc persuaded Charles VII to go to Reims to be crowned, and in the anteroom is a copy of the manuscript record of Joan's trial.

You can walk round the ramparts (1km).

MEHUN-SUR-YÈVRE
CHER   Pop 7200

A little town on the Berry canal, making porcelain. Two towers remain of the "fairy castle" home of Duke Jean de Berry, 14C patron of artists, who included the Limbourg brothers, painters of illuminated manuscripts, and writers such as Froissart. A ceramic museum is in one tower. The 14C town gate, with a clock, is superb.

MEILLANT, CHÂTEAU DE
CHER

In a wooded park N of St-Amand, this château was built in the 12C but completely refurbished for Charles I of Amboise by Jocondo, who had worked with Michelangelo. So the exterior is ornately decorated with emblems, arms and cyphers while inside it is medieval, but again inhabited and beautifully furnished.

MENNETOU-SUR-CHER
LOIR-ET-CHER   Pop 950

On both the river Cher and the Berry canal, this dreamy old town, 16km from Vierzon, looks as if it is still living in past centuries. Encircled by 13C ramparts, with three town gates and three of the five original towers still standing, it has a delightful steep main road with 13C Gothic houses, half-timbered houses from the 15C, and 16C villas.

MONTARGIS
LOIRET   Pop 17,700

Attractive town with ramparts on several streams of the Loing river and its tributaries the Puisseaux and Vernisson, which run into a large lake. It is famous for *pralines* (almond sweets).

MONTBAZON
INDRE-ET-LOIRE   Pop 3000

A busy little town on the N10, notable for being on a pleasant riverside route from Loches and on to Azay-le-Rideau, and also because of two fin-de-siècle châteaux, hidden away from the crowds and cars, yet almost in town. The Domaine de la Tortinière and the Château d'Artigny are expensive, delightful hotels, situated in magnificent parks.

MONTOIRE-SUR-LE-LOIR
LOIR-ET-CHER   Pop 4300

A pleasant market town straddling the Loir river

W of Vendôme, Montoire has the ruins of a once-magnificent medieval castle and the Romanesque chapel of St-Gilles, part of an old priory with remarkable 12–13C murals and a lovely garden. There are fine Renaissance houses on either side of the river, and the Hôtel de Ville contains a model of the château in its original form. The surrounding countryside and villages have associations with the Renaissance poet Pierre de Ronsard.

The strange little fortified town of **Trôo** (6.5km NW), with some of its 11–13C defences intact, is situated on a slope and still retains old troglodyte houses, rising in tiers; the chalk cliffs are honeycombed with underground passages, known as *caforts (caves fortes)*, used as hiding places in times of war. The 11C collegiate church of St-Martin has an unusual tower with pierced openings. Nearby is the Grands Puits, a well with a splendid echo.

MONTRÉSOR
INDRE-ET-LOIRE   Pop 460

A gem of a village sloping up in an amphitheatre from the tiny Indrois river and surrounded by country sprinkled with woods. It has an ivy-covered castle, a Renaissance collegiate church, and a 12C covered market.

The peaceful early 16C château, with mullioned windows and great dormers, is set in a lovely garden walled by the inner girdle of medieval fortifications of a ruined castle which belonged to Henry I and Henry II of England. One wing has wonderful views over the countryside. The furnishings are original, from Renaissance to Second Empire, with French, Italian and Polish paintings. The 16C church is Gothic with Renaissance decoration, paintings and lovely windows.

Nouhans-les-Fontaines (8km E) is reached along the Indrois valley lined with alders, willows and poplars, with orchards on the slopes. Its 13C church contains the primitive 1C masterpiece by Jean Fouquet, the *Deposition*, a huge painting on wood, in subdued colours.

MONTREUIL-BELLAY
MAINE-ET-LOIRE   Pop 4300

On its way to skirting Saumur, 16km on, and flowing into the Loire, the river Thouet broadens below this little terraced town into a wooded basin in which the castle and church are reflected.

The original castle was built by Foulques Nerra, count of Anjou, around AD1000. It was dismantled, after a three-year siege, by Geoffrey Plantagenet, duke of Anjou, father of the English Henry II. The present castle is mainly 15C, a sturdy but elegant dwelling of towers and turrets, all enclosed by a turreted wall, and reached by a bridge over a moat. It has fine fireplaces and a grand staircase up which the duchess of Longueville rode on horseback. The other moat bridge leads to a 15C Flamboyant church with a single nave.

MONTRICHARD
LOIR-ET-CHER   Pop 3800

A pleasing town on the Cher, 8km E of Chenonceaux, its old houses and streets, especially Rue

Nationale, are more interesting than its ruined castle. In the tiny parish church of Ste-Croix the 12-year-old Jeanne de France, crippled daughter of Louis XI, married Louis d'Orléans, heir to the throne. As Louis XII, he, the church and the state pulled every legal trick to discard her so that he could marry Anne of Brittany to keep Brittany under French rule.

Le Gué-Péan (13km E, near Monthou-sur-Cher) is an attractive blue and white Renaissance château on the edge of Choussy forest, hidden in a wooded valley. Built round a courtyard, it is elegant, with arcades, fine windows and one pointed and one bell-shaped tower. Inside are interesting Louis XV and XVI furnishings, tapestries, paintings which include works of Dali, Fragonard, David and Gérard, and an enormous fireplace by Germain Pillon.

MONTSOREAU
MAINE-ET-LOIRE   Pop 450

The village, prettily mirrored in the Loire, surrounds a severe medieval castle with an undeserved notoriety. It was the property, in the 16C, of Jean de Chambes, whose wife Françoise was used by Alexandre Dumas as the model for the heroine of his novel, *La Dame de Montsoreau*. Dumas set the plot of the novel here, but in reality the events portrayed, including the killing of Françoise's lover, Bussy d'Ambois, governor of Anjou and persecutor of Huguenots, occurred across the river at La Coutancière, a château she preferred.

The Montsoreau château is now a museum of the fearsome Goums, the French cavalrymen recruited in Morocco.

NOHANT, CHÂTEAU DE
INDRE

Called the 'château' by local residents, this delightful 18C country house was where the novelist George Sand spent her childhood and teenage years. She returned to its peace and quiet to write, dying here in 1876.

As preserved, the house looks as if she has popped out for a few minutes. Dinner is laid for dinner, perhaps for a guest such as Balzac, Flaubert, Dumas the Younger or Liszt. Chopin's piano awaits the master's touch. Here he improvised and composed – the second Nocturne, three Mazurkas, the Sonata in B flat minor. In her bedroom is the 'desk' – a shelf in a doorless cupboard – where she wrote some of her masterpieces.

Drawings for the theatre and marionettes by her son Maurice Sand are there, and even the kitchen, with its old utensils, is interesting.

A George Sand museum is to be seen in the keep of the former castle of **La Châtre**, a town (pop. 5200) 36km S of Châteauroux, standing above the Indre valley in the wooded country which she called 'the dark valley'.

OLIVET
LOIRET   Pop 14,500

On the banks of the little Loiret river, 9km S of Orléans in a charming setting. Orléans people have always come here for fishing, boating, picnics, and walks along riverside paths past fine old houses and watermills. You can hire rowing boats or canoes. Cafés and restaurants give it the feeling of a modernized scene from a Renoir. Market gardens have fields of flowers and the floral clock by the bridge is composed of 5000 flowers.

Just past it is the new town of **La Source** and its new university campus, S of the superb floral park, full of old trees, fountains and modern sculptures, surrounded by massed blooms, including tulips, iris, dahlias and 200,000 rose bushes. The Loiret, which starts at St-Benoît, re-emerges here with water bubbling out at a temperature of 12-15°C. Flamingoes, ducks and numerous other web-footed birds winter here. A little train runs round the park in summer.

ORLÉANS
LOIRET   Pop 106,000

Terribly devastated in World War II, Orléans, the regional capital, has been well rebuilt but is essentially a commercial city, especially for food, wine and flowers from the surrounding country, and now an industrial centre, with new factories, including one making Michelin tyres. Banishment of the university to a new town has also taken away some of the original atmosphere. But because of the courage of Joan of Arc, it remains to the French the "heart of France". Paris is merely "the head".

When Joan arrived here with her troops in 1429 the English had been besieging it for six months and there was stalemate. The 10,000 French defenders were low in morale. The English had withdrawn all but 2000 tired and bored troops – not enough to encircle the city. Joan realized that if she could take the Bastille St-Loup the E side was wide open. She did this, crossed the river over a bridge of boats to take the Bastille St-Jean, and caught the enemy in crossfire. The English retreated and Joan entered Orléans.

Every year since 1430 Orléans has celebrated, on 7 and 8 May, Joan's victory with pageants, cavalcades, parades and flowers, and since 1921 these days have been a national holiday. She was not made a saint until 1920, thanks to Cardinal Touchet, whose statue is in the scarred cathedral, at the top of the splendid modern shopping street, Rue

Orléans

Jeanne d'Arc. The Maid's statue, by Foyatier (1855) stands in Pl. du Martroi.

The new Maison de Jeanne d'Arc, on Pl. Général de Gaulle, was built from ancient materials in 15C style and contains various documents and maquettes of the siege. The Musée de Beaux Arts in a 15C house includes fine paintings from that century, through David, Velazquez and Tintoretto to moderns such as Gauguin and Max Jacob, the Jewish poet-artist who lived at St-Benoît nearby, was converted to Catholicism and died in a Gestapo prison, despite Cocteau's efforts to get him released.

PONCÉ-SUR-LE-LOIR
SARTHE

A mystery château. Nobody seems to know who built it or when; and it was altered in the 18C. Although an Italian-French mixture, it has one of the finest staircases in the world, with delicate but ornately sculptured ceilings on the six flights, portraying reality, mythology and allegory. The château dovecote has 1800 holes with revolving ladders to gather the eggs. Imagine what local farmers felt when 1800 doves were released on their crops by *droit de seigneur*, so that killing them was a capital offence! Faded murals in the church are from the year 1180, one showing Christians fighting Moslems, which could relate to a crusade or to earlier battles when Charles Martel drove the Saracens from France.

RICHELIEU
INDRE-ET-LOIRE Pop 2500

La Fontaine, the chronicler of fables, commented on the scarcity of people in Cardinal Richelieu's 17C New Town, and it has remained quiet through the centuries except on cattle market days. Richelieu had it built in geometric precision around his château and magnificent gardens predating Versailles. He filled it with magnificent works by the greatest artists and sculptors and razed many châteaux in the vicinity to prevent them outstripping his own. His own was demolished in the 19C by an asset stripper.

Grande Rue remains, with twenty-eight identical houses, the town hall has a museum, and the Classical church has two towers topped by obelisks. There is also an immense park, with chestnut- and plane-lined avenues.

SANCERRE
CHER Pop 2300

A beautiful old hilltop wine town with gables and turreted houses lining narrow, steep streets, it has an enormous tower, last remains of its castle. From its lime-shaded terrace are unforgettable views of vineyard slopes, the Loire, and a curved viaduct taking a road to bypass the very old village of St-Satur. In 1534 Protestant Sancerre withstood a Catholic siege for seven months. The people ate powdered slate and leather.

The dry white wine from Sauvignon grapes, long recommended for drinking with fish, has become fashionable and inevitably pricier.

SAUMUR
MAINE-ET-LOIRE Pop 22,000

Between Angers and Tours, Saumur was a vital Loire crossing point from the Middle Ages, and

Saumur

the spectacular Louis X 14C château on a sheer cliff still overlooks the town. It looks best from across the river.

In the 17C it was a centre of Protestantism. The governor was Duplessis-Mornay, scholar, soldier and called by the Catholics "the Protestant Pope". Saumur declined after the revocation of the Edict of Nantes deprived French Protestants of their civil and religious liberties.

The castle houses the Musée des Arts Décoratifs, with excellent tapestries, porcelain and furniture, and a Musée du Cheval – a history of the horse. Saumur's cavalry school started in 1763 when the best horsemen in France were sent to form the Cadre Noir (Black Squadron). Now it is a tank school but the National Riding School still trains the Black Squadron and at the end of July they give a riding display with armoured colleagues who perform spectacular feats in tanks, armoured cars and on motor-cycles. The school houses a cavalry museum. A tank museum in another building shows World Wars I and II tanks from France, Britain, Germany, USA and USSR.

There are more tapestries in the Notre-Dame church and better ones (17C Aubusson) in the Hospice Jeanne Delanoue. The Jardin des Plantes is laid out in terraces down the castle slopes, garlanded with vines.

Saumur makes rosaries and wine. At St-Hilaire St-Florent, a suburb where rivers meet, you can taste the fruity white wine at the firm of Ackerman Laurance. Ackerman, an Alsatian, taught the locals to put in the sparkle by the Champagne method in 1811, the first time the process had been used outside that region. It is a pleasant wine, brut or demi-sec, but no substitute for champagne itself. Still white and red wines are also increasingly made.

At **Chênehutte-les-Tuffeaux**, a village between the river and steep cliffs, mushrooms are grown in former quarries dug out of tufa stone.

SOLOGNE

A huge flatland of pools, heaths and forests in the Orléans loop of the Loire, E to the Sancerre hills, S to the Loir river. It was once a wasteland of fever-ridden swamps, like Les Landes. When peaceful, it has a melancholy beauty. It is rich in wildlife – alas, too rich, for it has inevitably fired the French frenzy for La Chasse, hunting and shooting, so that gunfire breaks the tranquillity, private property and hunting reserves abound, and it has been described as a Parisian colony for smart-set sportsmen.

Napoleon III, when a prince, started the reclaiming of the desolate waste. In the grounds of his château at **Lamotte-Beuvron**, he set up a model farm, planted pines and birch, dug canals, cleared, dredged and drained pools, built roads and improved the soil.

Some 200,000ha are nowadays cultivated, producing cereals, fruit, vegetables and, increasingly, fodder for game. Pheasant rearing, too, is popular. For long the main industries were sawmills and packaging materials. Now there are factories producing plastic car bodies at Romorantin, armaments at La Ferté-St-Aubin and porcelain at Lamotte-Beuvron. Shooting, however, is the money-spinner. And the scenery is best in autumn when heather blooms.

From Orléans (18km) you enter the Sologne, which is well signposted throughout, at **La Ferté-St-Aubin** (pop. 5500), a pleasant place with old brick and timber houses on the river Cosson, which flows through the moats of the castle, rebuilt in the 17C to the plans of Mansart.

Avoiding the main N20, most sightseers cross the area by the tourist road D922.

Beyond the **Montevran zoo**, where animals roam in comparative freedom, is **Chaumont-sur-Tharonne** (pop. 900), a village perched on a mound around a 15–16C church. Among the many pools in the area is the hidden village of **St-Viatre**, once a place of pilgrimage to the relics of a 6C hermit. The 16C painted panels in the church recall his life and a wayside altar is dedicated to him.

Romorantin-Lanthenay is by far the biggest place (pop. 18,000). French humorists and newspapers have poked fun at it as the typical small provincial town but Romorantin has got its own back with its Michelin two-star *Hôtel Lion d'Or* and its Matra cars, which won the Formula One World Championship for France in 1968. To celebrate this victory, the town set up a motor-racing museum, heavily loaded towards Matra but showing how racing produced technical advances and having a splendid motor-sport library. Though new suburbs and industries (electronics, refrigeration and cine cameras) have been added, it is still a pleasant town, straddling the river Sauldre, where it divides into arms. François I spent his childhood here and later commissioned Leonardo da Vinci to design a palace, astride the river, for his mother; but she died. The Musée de la Sologne includes the story of the sabot makers who were still at work until very recently.

Villeherviers nearby has a population of only 360 but produces superb asparagus and cultivates dahlias.

To the S of Chambord (q.v.) across the forest of Boulogne is the charming Renaissance **Château de Villesavin** and below that the **Château de Cheverny**.

Still lived in and beautifully furnished with furniture of the period in which it was built, the 17C Cheverny gives a better picture of the life-style of old French aristocrats than do any of the "museum" châteaux.

The present owner, the Marquis de Vibraye, is a descendant of Hurault de Cheverny, who built it. Most of the original building remains, from sumptuous decorations by Jean Mosnier to Flemish tapestries, and the ornate King's Bedroom which, under *droit de gîte*, had to be held ready, though no king used it. White, "fat and friendly", it stands in a fine park near a forest.

Beauregard, nearby, is a pretty château, built in 1550 by François I. It has a gallery with 363 portraits of important people and a Delft tiled floor showing Louis XII's army.

E of N20 are the **Étang de Puits**, a huge reservoir lake among woods, used for rowing, sailing and regattas; **Argent sur Sauldre**, a small industrial town making machinery, furniture and lingerie and with a 15C château; **Aubigny-sur-Nère** (q.v.); **Nançay**, with an experimental station and a great radio telescope; and **La Chapelle d'Angillon** (q.v.).

In 1954 a brave attempt was made to turn the tide back to agriculture in the Sologne by the Grande Sologne Association. New types of hybrid corn have been tried, a few sheep have returned, and drainage has been improved; but the hunters and fishermen are there now, owning land and houses, and it is more profitable to sell or rent out infertile land than try to make a living farming it.

SULLY-SUR-LOIRE
LOIRET   Pop 5900

A charming town with a river beach on the edge of the Sologne, it faces, across the Loire, its medieval château, surrounded by water. Both have been restored after heavy damage in 1940–45. A long graceful suspension bridge spans the river. The fortress looks dark and sinister but inside its outer walls is a pretty Renaissance Petit Château, altered later by Henri IV's statesman, the duke of Sully,

Sully-sur-Loire

who built the tower. The château contains the finest medieval timber roof in France, erected in 1363.

Maurice de Sully, the Paris bishop who built Notre-Dame, was born here in 1120. Charles VII sheltered here with his mistress Georges de la Trémoille while Joan of Arc fought the English at Patay for him in 1429, and she hurried here to persuade him to go unwillingly to Reims to be crowned. A year later, having failed to take Paris, she returned and was kept a virtual prisoner for a month.

But Sully is remembered mostly for the man who took its name as duke, Maximilien de Béthune, who bought it in 1602. Successful commander of Henri of Navarre's Protestant forces at Coutras and Ivry, he became the first of the great statesmen who made France great and rich. When Henri took the crown as Henri IV, he became minister of state, attending to finance, industry, agriculture and public works. His greatest achievement was persuading the French actually to pay their taxes. In a dozen years he more than doubled the state's income.

One of his descendants, a liberal who loved new ideas, gave Voltaire refuge when he had to flee the court and built him a theatre. Voltaire chased the girls, wrote plays about them, and performed them, using the girls themselves as actresses.

TALCY

LOIR-ET-CHER   Pop 220

An isolated village on the Beauce plain, its severe-looking château is known for its 400-year-old wine press which is still working, a dovecote with 1500 pigeon holes, and its association with poets. In the 16C a Florentine banker, Bernardo Salviati, cousin to the Medicis, lived there. The poet Ronsard dedicated many sonnets to his daughter Cassandra – in vain. Along the road from Talcy to Mer are some 10,000 rose bushes.

TOURS

INDRE-ET-LOIRE   Pop 137,000

The inevitable march of industry, traffic jams, ugly concrete expressways to clear the traffic, and concrete suburbs to house industry and people, have all hit Tours to a degree which other towns of the Loire have managed to avoid – even Orléans. The new Tours covers 7km along the Loire and has spread S way past the river Cher. From silk, food and wine its industries have spread to metallurgy, plastics, electronics, chemicals, textiles, pharmaceuticals, motor tyres and printing. It is still growing. Yet the old part, which is being beautifully and expensively renovated after terrible damage in World War II, covers only about 300m W of Rue Nationale and the rest of the "tourist area" covers 300m E. The people of Tours still meet at the end of Rue Nationale in Pl. Jean Jaurès. Spring and autumn are the best times to see the city, not only because of summer crowds but in order to avoid the damp heat from its site in a bowl between two rivers.

It takes longer to explore the city than you would think because it has a lot of interesting smaller

St-Gatien, Tours

attractions rather than one big tourist trap. The city grew around the tomb of St Martin, the third bishop, who died in AD397 and seemingly set off a stream of miracles. As his body reached Tours, trees grew green, plants flowered, birds sang – in November. Hence a "St Martin's Summer". The basilica built above his tomb was destroyed in 1808. Two towers remain, Tour de l'Horloge and Tour Charlemagne, with 11C frescoes.

A monk from York, Alcuin, made Tours a centre of learning in the 8C. After 50 years in York, he was taken by Charlemagne to start a model education centre in Aachen, then sent to Tours as abbot. Tours had a medieval university and the modern university has 12,000 students, adding to the liveliness of the city.

The English and French fought over Tours through the Middle Ages, and Henry II of England built a château near the present Quai d'Orléans; but all that remains is the Tour de Guise, called after the duke of Guise ("Scarface") who escaped from prison here.

The cathedral, St-Gatien, was begun in the early 13C and not completed until the 16C, so it is a blend of styles from Romanesque to the beautiful soaring Flamboyant Gothic towers capped with Renaissance crowns. It is a truly pretty church, fairly simple inside, with warm and delightful medieval glass. There is a good view from the garden of the Musée des Beaux-Arts next door. The attractive cathedral close, with 15–16C canons' houses, was the setting of Balzac's novel *The Curé of Tours*.

The museum is in the 17–18C Archbishop's Palace. The rooms, decorated with Tours silks and Louis XVI panelling, contain fine furniture, sculptures, including Mantegna's *Christ in the Garden of Olives*, and paintings, with Rembrandt's *Flight into Egypt* and others by Rubens, Delacroix and Degas.

Many interesting sights of Tours include the

194

18C stone bridge over the Loire, the old timbered houses and medieval streets around Pl. Plumereau in the old city, the interesting museum of Touraine wines in a vaulted 12C cellar on Rue Nationale, and the fascinating Musée de Compagnonnage devoted to craftsmanship of all ages.

Vouvray (10km upstream on the N side of Loire) is the heart of steep vineyards. It still has a few troglodyte houses but most caves nowadays contain bottles, not people. The wine route (Vouvray route) is clearly signposted. Most caves welcome visitors and the vast cellars of **La Bonne Dame** hold two annual fairs – in mid Jan. for the trade, in Aug. for tourists. Wines from the Chenin grape (Pineau Blanc de Loire) are white, dry or demi-sec, still, pétillant (just sparkling on the tongue) or mousseux (sparkling). Mousseux wines are made by the Champagne method.

Montlouis, opposite Vouvray on the S bank, is on tufa slopes with caves and produces wine from similar grapes but usually lighter, not so fruity and more acidic.

Also near Tours is the priory of **Ste-Cosme**, where the poet Ronsard spent his later years and died.

USSÉ, CHÂTEAU D'
INDRE-ET-LOIRE

This fairy-tale château of the Loire is said to have inspired Charles Perrault as the setting for his *Sleeping Beauty*. It stands above the Indre, backing Chinon forest, near the village of Rigny-Ussé, and is perched on a terrace with gorgeous formal gardens which soften its grim look. So does the little forest of chimneys, pinnacles, pointed roof-tops and turrets. Ussé is another Loire castle turned from a Gothic fortress into a Renaissance home. The Renaissance chapel in the park is delightful.

VALENÇAY
INDRE   Pop 3200

Just S of the river Cher in Indre, the château was built in 1540 by Jacques d'Estampes, who knocked down the feudal castle he owned here after marrying a financier's daughter and her fortune.

In 1803, Napoleon told his minister Talleyrand to buy it to receive distinguished foreign visitors. Talleyrand had started in the church, under Louis XVI in 1775, and became a powerful minister in each political regime until the reign of Louis-Philippe in the 1830s, being made a duke by Louis XVIII and a prince by Napoleon. Today the château has a Talleyrand museum and magnificent furnishings, mostly of the two Napoleonic periods. In the fine park roam llamas and deer, with peacocks, cranes, flamingoes, black swans and parrots.

VENDÔME
LOIR-ET-CHER   Pop 18,200

A charming town for wandering, with little out-standing to see but a nice atmosphere. Below a steep hill, it is on the banks of the Loir river where it divides into many arms, spanned by several bridges. The ruined castle on top of the hill has a vast garden inside its walls. The old abbey church of the Trinity is a higgledy-piggledy mixture of architecture from the 11–16C but has a fine 12C separated tower, used, as was then customary, as a bell-tower and defensive keep; it is topped by a 4m-high iron cross. Inside, the 15C choir stalls with quaint carvings are interesting.

VIERZON
CHER   Pop 35,000

A communication centre on the edge of the Berry-Champagne region where the Yèvre and Cher meet and with a port on the Berry canal, it is inevitably industrialized but has many treasures. Industries include porcelain, glassware, knitwear, clothing, cement, fertilizers and agricultural machinery. On the hill above is an old town of winding streets and timbered houses, and a town hall in 17C buildings of the former abbey. The nearby river banks are lovely.

VILLANDRY, CHÂTEAU DE
INDRE-ET-LOIRE

Between Tours and Azay-le-Rideau, the castle is on the banks of the Cher near the point where it joins the Loire. Built in 1532 by François I's secretary of state, it was "improved" by various owners. It is known for its gardens – formal, French, mathematically precise, with boxwood hedges, pools with fountains, a water garden and canal flowing into the moat. The original French formal garden had been replaced by an English park, with clumps of trees, grassy slopes and calculated disorder. This century Dr Carvallo, founder of the Demeure Historique (Historic Houses Association) bought it and changed it all back to the way it was in the 16C, using the correct flowers, trees and varieties. It is said to be the only such garden in France.

Nearby **Savonnières** has a pretty little river beach and caves with small stalactites, draperies and an underground lake.

Villandry

BURGUNDY

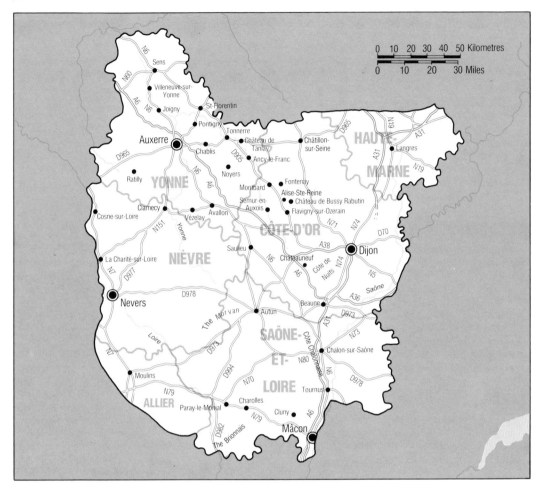

Extending south and east almost from Paris to Lyon, from the Loire to the Saône, and beyond to the Marne, Burgundy is a green and generous region, whose people work hard and live well. Although industries flourish in the main towns, agriculture remains the principal activity. Richly cultivated valleys, lush pastures with the heavy white-coated Charolais cattle, wilder areas of forests, rivers and hills – everywhere the countryside retains a rustic and unspoiled character.

Many of the quiet little provincial towns and villages are extremely picturesque with narrow cobbled streets, medieval houses, encircling ramparts – and very often a Romanesque church, some nearby Gallic or Roman ruins, and even some remnants of Neolithic settlement preserved in the local museum.

The Gauls had established towns and commerce in the Burgundy region by the time of the Roman invasion: it was partly because of this wealth that the Romans invaded. Under Vercingetorix, the Gauls put up a good fight against the occupation, but after the decisive battle at Alesia (52BC), the region was brought firmly under Roman rule. Autun became their provincial capital, a large, civilized and important town, as indicated by its

Roman ruins. In the 5C the warlike but cultured Burgundii ('barbarians' from the Baltic) moved in and made it their homeland. It remained for centuries a separate entity from the rest of France, and often a threat to it, even after it had become a duchy nominally subservient to the French crown (1016).

The many great Romanesque abbeys and churches which rise up majestically from tiny villages to dominate the surrounding landscape are the legacy of three centuries (11–14C) during which Burgundy acquired great religious influence and power. At Cluny are the remains of the largest and most influential abbey in the Christian world, founded in 910. At Cîteaux there are fragments of the abbey of the more austere Cistercian order which in 1098 broke away from the wealthy Benedictines at Cluny. The abbeys also had an enormous impact on the architecture of the region.

From 1364 to 1477 Burgundy was ruled in turn by four generations of the noble Valois family; the dukes were warriors and art patrons alike. By the end of their reign, during which for a time Burgundy had sided with the English against the French in the Hundred Years' War, the duchy controlled all of Franche-Comté, Alsace-Lorraine,

Belgium, Holland, Picardy, and Flanders. The cities of Burgundy, especially the capital Dijon, had become among Europe's foremost centres of learning and civilized life. Flemish artisans and craftsmen were particularly in demand, and thousands migrated to Burgundy, bringing with them, among other decorative techniques, the custom of glazed and patterned rooftiles.

When in 1477, Louis XI reasserted French control over the duchy, also gaining possession of its Flemish empire, Burgundy maintained its sense of separateness, and the arts and architecture continued to flourish. New restoration and building work was enthusiastically undertaken in the new Italianate Renaissance style, as can be seen in the lavish, elegant châteaux of Sully, Tanlay, Ancy-le-Franc, etc. And a traditional enjoyment of the good things in life became even more firmly established as the essential character of Burgundy, as it remains to this day.

For the very name of Burgundy brings to mind rich food and great wines. The distinctive feature of Burgundian cooking is meat cooked in wine sauces, and some traditional dishes have become classics of French cuisine – *boeuf bourgignonne*, and *coq au vin*, for example; fish from the many lakes and rivers also feature on restaurant menus, again in wine sauces, with abundant vegetables, intriguing varieties of mushrooms, and curiosities such as *escargots*, a Burgundian favourite, snails cooked after being fed on herbs for several days. Although cattle are raised almost exclusively for beef, an inevitable result is a wide selection of cheeses, many local to a single village. *Fromage blanc*, a tangy low-fat cheese, almost liquid, usually eaten with cream and sugar, is a popular family dessert.

Wines from the Côte d'Or vineyards south of Dijon have been acclaimed as among the best money can buy (and you need plenty of money to prove it!). While most are red, full-bodied, and the better for several years 'laying down', the whites too (Meursault, Montrachet, etc) are internationally famed. Even Burgundy's 'minor' vineyard districts – Chablis in the north and Mâconnais further south – are world renowned.

Though some of the wine-making villages have famous names, they are just small farming communities. Frequently wine is offered for tasting, *dégustation*; the cool vaulted cellars, often centuries old, in which the wine is matured, can usually be visited for a small fee. High point of the year for vine-growers is the *vendange*, the autumn grape harvest. After the new vintage has been made, on the third weekend in November, the Trois Glorieuses imparts a sense of occasion in the Côte d'Or. This is the three-day festival for merchants, growers and members of the Confrérie des Chevaliers du Tastevin: it begins with a huge feast at the Confrérie's headquarters at the Château of Clos de Vougeot on the Saturday; on Sunday, in Beaune, the new wines of the Hospices de Beaune are publicly auctioned amid much ceremony and excitement – this is an important indicator of prices for other growers and districts (followed by another big meal); finally, on the Monday, growers bring contributions of their own wine to yet another banquet, called the Paulée, held in the village of Meursault.

Other villages have wine festivals at about the same time, notably Chablis. There are Gastronomic Fairs too, of which the best known is at Dijon. An all-summer-long arts festival – L'Estivade – provides both visitors and residents with an abundance of entertainment in theatre, music, dance.

No part of Burgundy guards its festivals and village traditions better than the Morvan, a huge upland region in the very heart of the province, designated as a Regional Nature Park. The forests and lakes of these ancient granite hills have made Morvan an excellent area for outdoor recreation: walking, riding, sailing, camping. Yet in the main, tourism seems hardly to have touched the area. The park's small communities are determined to resist 'progress' and preserve their own identity.

The Paris-Lyon Autoroute du Soleil (A6) gives quick and convenient access to some of the most interesting towns in northern and central Burgundy, as well as to Dijon, and the towns of the Saône valley. For more leisurely travellers, the N7, the original old Lyon highway, takes an attractive route down Burgundy's western frontier on the bank of the broad river Loire. From Nevers it is an easy step into the peaceful countryside of the Nivernais and Morvan, and to pretty Brionnais with its dozen Cluniac churches. And for the even more adventurous, the canals of Burgundy are excellently maintained waterways passing through attractive scenery and beautiful old towns.

ALISE-STE-REINE
CÔTE D'OR   Pop 760

At Alésia, on Mont Auxois, now called Alise-Ste-Reine (2km from Les Laumes), Vercingetorix, chief of the Gauls, was finally beaten by Caesar in 52BC. Paying the price for earlier successes, he was captured, taken to Rome and died in prison soon afterwards. The site can be viewed, and there is a bronze statue of the warrior Gaul. Interesting items discovered here are displayed in the Musée Alésia in the modern village.

ANCY-LE-FRANC
YONNE   Pop 1100

The château at Ancy-le-Franc, in the Armançon valley, is one of the most superb achievements of the graceful art and decoration of the Renaissance.

This palatial house was designed by the Italian architect Serlio, employed by François I. It is entered by way of a square courtyard. On the first floor are apartments and galleries decorated in sumptuous style by Primaticcio; below are a dozen rooms splendidly adorned with frescoes and tapestries.

AUTUN
SAÔNE-ET-LOIRE   Pop 16,300

Autun, a lively town in the rural heart of Burgundy, was once an important Roman city (Augustodunum), the 'sister of Rome'. Even today it is only just large enough to extend beyond the ancient walls. Two city gates survive, Porte d'Arroux and Porte St-André, both remarkably ele-

Autun

gant, with arcaded galleries. Outside the town stands the so-called Temple of Janus, a curious isolated remnant of a powerful Roman tower (there is no evidence that it was a temple). Of Autun's Roman theatre, the largest in Gaul, only small fragments remain in an attractive park.

The centre of town is a magnificently spacious square, the Champs de Mars, with the florid Hôtel de Ville, a library with many ancient manuscripts, and the Collège where Napoleon was a student. On a slight elevation among the maze of narrow streets stands the cathedral of St-Lazare, outside which is an extraordinarily ornate fountain. The cathedral entrance is large and confident; an excellent tympanum above the door escaped the Revolution because it had long before been plastered-over and forgotten. Inside, the sturdy pillars have delicately carved capitals. Behind the altar a golden box holds what pilgrims believe to be the bones of Lazarus. Spiral steps ascend to the bell tower, giving a superb view of green rolling country all around. The adjacent Musée Rolin contains 16C sculptures and painting, and a large collection of important Gallo-Roman finds made here.

About 2km S, at **Couhard**, there is a strange Roman 'pyramid' of masonry, perhaps a tomb. The **Château de Sully**, 14km NE, can only be seen from outside, yet gives a remarkably complete picture of 16C Renaissance taste and design. With square towers at the corners, a beautiful courtyard, a wide moat, all in an extensive park setting, the whole impression is of elegance and harmony.

AUXERRE
YONNE Pop 40,700

Auxerre, on the steep left bank of the Yonne, looks its best from the other side of the river, Gothic spires rising high above the jumble of old rooftops. The St-Étienne cathedral, uninhibitedly Flamboyant, has a facade covered with exquisite tracery. Its doors and porches are superb, and inside there is more finely carved stone, and lovely rose windows. Faint traces of frescoes can be seen in side chapels. In the 11C Romanesque crypt, part of an older church, larger areas of frescoes have survived. A short walk away, the abbey church and cloisters of St-Germain, much damaged over the centuries, has a fine 14C belfry separated from the rest, and,

in the Carolingian and Romanesque crypt, still more intriguing frescoes, dating from AD850, and believed to be the oldest in France.

Many Renaissance houses, and some much older, line the picturesque streets and lanes and popular little squares. An 18C mansion, off Pl. Bart, houses the Musée Leblanc-Duvernoy, with Beauvais tapestries, chinaware and furnishings. Unusual modern painted statues by Auxerrois sculptor François Brochet decorate the town. One of them, in Pl. Hôtel de Ville, is of 'Marie-Noel', a poet much admired in France, who died here in 1967. Her statue is next to the 'Gaillarde', an archway and clock tower with black spires, originally a Gallo-Roman gateway. Tree-shaded boulevards have replaced the ramparts. The riverside quays make a lovely walk.

Auxerre

AVALLON
YONNE Pop 9200

Old Avallon is well placed within its magnificent fortifications above the deep valley of the little river Cousin. The Promenade de la Petite Porte, a terrace of lime trees just outside one of the town gates, gives a precipitous view of the surrounding country. A walkway starts here, encircling the ramparts with their towers and bastions. The quiet main street of the old town passes through an archway beneath the Tour de l'Horloge, 15C clock tower. The early 12C collegiate church of St-Lazare has a weatherworn facade. It is entered by going down stairs from the street, through a vast doorway, into a dark and sombre Romanesque edifice with interesting frescoes and capitals, and a 4C crypt. On a corner almost opposite the church is a particularly fine 15C half-timbered house (in which is the tourist office), one of many in the old town.

Even the 'new' part of Avallon, north of the walls, is mainly 17–18C with imposing mansions, boulevards, spacious promenades and squares.

BEAUNE
CÔTE-D'OR Pop 21,100

Beaune's ancient centre is a confusion of narrow cobbled lanes and attractive squares. There are fine old stone houses and mansions in almost every street. Medieval ramparts, still almost complete, enclose the town. Much of the central area has been turned into a pedestrian precinct.

The Hôtel-Dieu, most splendid of the historic buildings, was built in 1443, in Flemish Gothic style, as a charitable hospital. It was used as such until 1948, and now is one of three buildings of the Hospices de Beaune, which runs a free hospital and old peoples' home. The nursing nuns still wear the traditional medieval hooded costume. Though constructed mainly of wood, the Hôtel-Dieu is in excellent condition inside and out. It encloses a pretty courtyard, from which the coloured and glazed roof-tiles look astonishing and lovely. Inside, the barrel-vaulted wooden roof, long hospital ward and kitchen are impressive. In its 'museum' are the hospital's 15C tapestries and – masterpiece of Flemish art – Van der Weyden's *Polyptych of the Last Judgment* (1443).

The sombre collegiate church of Notre-Dame, originally in Cluny Romanesque style (early 12C), has been much altered and restored over the centuries, with 13C choir, graceful 14C flying buttresses, 15C frescoes in a side chapel, and a 16C dome. In the choir is a much revered 12C Madonna and five wool-and-silk tapestries made in 1474. Outside are peaceful cloisters.

The former Beaune residence of the dukes of Burgundy, the Hôtel des Ducs, has been turned into a museum of wine. Here the story of Burgundy wine is told, and tools of the trade exhibited, including huge wooden presses. Beaune is the principal commercial centre for the Côte de Beaune wine region. Many well-known merchants and growers have their cellars here, some being set into the ramparts. Most are open to the public, and offer tastings. On the third Sun. in Nov., which is the second day of Les Trois Glorieuses – the annual three-day ceremony to greet the new vintage – the auction takes place in the covered market of the prestigious new wines of the Hospices de Beaune. It is attended by buyers from all over France and from abroad.

Pl. Monge is the main square, with a 14C belfry and the 16C Gothic Hôtel de la Rochepot. The Hôtel de Ville, in a former 17C convent, contains museums of art and early cinematography. The popular Beaune Fair lasts from the first Sat. to the second Sun. in June.

Nearby **Aloxe-Corton**, **Pommard**, **Meursault**, **Puligny-Montrachet**, **Chassagne-Montrachet**, and other villages of the steep, terraced Côte de Beaune (southern part of the Côte d'Or), produce some of the world's greatest – and most expensive! – wines, especially whites. **Santenay**, on the S tip of the Côte, is an agreeable spa town. The **Hautes-Côtes de Beaune**, higher ground further W, produces less renowned wine in even prettier country.

On a hilltop beyond the vineyards, 18km SW, **Château de la Rochepot** is a fairy-tale castle of spires and turrets, built in the 12C and subsequently restored. The hill opposite has two dolmens; and the village below possesses an interesting 12C Romanesque church. 6km S of Beaune, the **Archéodrome** is an unusual archaeological museum with open-air reconstructions of Neolithic, Gallic and Roman buildings.

BRIONNAIS

South of Paray-le-Monial and Charollais, on the right bank of the Loire, the Brionnais is a rural region of gentle hills, leafy copses, streams, fields of pasture with white Charolais cattle, rustic farmyards and, most remarkably, more than a dozen magnificent Romanesque churches, one in almost every village. Most are based on the great abbey at nearby Cluny, and were built at about the same time, early 12C. A few are older, and from them it is possible to see how the Cluny style developed from earlier Romanesque ideas. A 100km marked route along the country lanes, 'Circuit des Églises Romanes', makes a pleasant day's drive, starting from Paray and calling at thirteen villages. There are other little towns not on the marked route but equally of interest for their unusual markets, fine restaurants, or attractive setting.

Anzy-le-Duc has one of the most beautiful churches, built early in the 11C, exquisitely simple and decorated with primitive frescoes; 11km away, the church at **Semur-en-Brionnais**, built after the Cluny abbey, has more elegance but less mystery. **Marcigny**, between the two, has old timbered houses, and a large, colourful open-air market. Tiny **St-Christophe-en-Brionnais**, near Semur, has an enormous livestock market each Thurs. morning, until recently the biggest in France, for the buying and selling of Charolais cattle. Southernmost town of the region, **Charlieu**, on the river Sornin, has ruins of a Benedictine abbey, several medieval houses, and impressive remnants of its 11C church. **La Clayette** is attractive with a 14C lakeside castle.

BUSSY-RABUTIN, CHÂTEAU DE
CÔTE-D'OR

Count Roger de Bussy-Rabutin, cousin of the influential woman of letters Marquise de Sévigné, was an art-lover, intellectual and libertarian. In 1649 he rebuilt his château with the finest, most elegant Renaissance taste, but keeping the impos-

Hôtel-Dieu, Beaune

ing older circular towers. His irreverent writings caused much annoyance to Louis XIV, and the *Histoires Amoureuses des Gaules* (1665), a satirical and risqué account of court life, was so scandalous that he was sentenced to a year in the Bastille, then ordered to remain in exile at his château.

Thus confined, he decorated the house with hundreds of paintings. The Salon des Hommes de Guerre has 65 portraits (mostly copies) of noted military men. The *Tour Dorée* is entirely filled with pictures by Mignard, Juste, Le Brun and others; and Bussy-Rabutin's Chambre, with the original furnishings, contains 25 portraits of celebrated women – including royal mistresses, his own former women companions, and a triptych of his second wife with Mme de Sévigné and her daughter. Beneath many of the pictures are lascivious and uncomplimentary verses by the count himself.

CHABLIS
YONNE   Pop 2400

The quiet little farming town of Chablis in N Burgundy gives its name to a world-famous crisp dry white wine, mostly still made by individual growers on family-run vineyards. The principal growing area extends about 8km from the town in each direction. Chablis is pretty and unspoiled, despite some wartime damage, and stands on the bank of the Serein. The Promenade de Patis is a shady riverside walk. In the village centre there is a 12–13C Romanesque church. On the fourth Sun. in Nov., Chablis celebrates the new vintage with its annual Wine Festival.

Chablis

CHALON-SUR-SAÔNE
SAÔNE-ET-LOIRE   Pop 58,000

Major industrial port on the Saône and Canal du Centre, and commercial centre of a rich agricultural region, Chalon is a busy modern town. Yet Vieux Chalon still exists, an attractive area of old buildings around Grande Rue, especially in the St-Vincent quarter, adjacent to the interesting former cathedral. Musée Denon, in an 18C convent in Pl. Hôtel de Ville, contains valuable collections of paintings, furnishings and local archaeological finds. On the waterfront, the Musée de Nicéphore Niepce (inventor of photography, born at Chalon) has exhibits of improbable early cameras and pictures. In mid-river is an island with port, 16C

hospital and 15C Tour du Doyenné, which can be climbed.

On 27 Feb. a very ancient commercial fair, the Foire aux Sauvagines, is held in the streets, shortly followed by a lively week-long carnival.

The Côte Chalonnaise, a ridge of hills W of the town, is a small but highly reputed vineyard region, its main wine villages being **Rully, Mercurey, Givry** and **Montagny**.

CHARITÉ-SUR-LOIRE, LA
NIÈVRE   Pop 6400

Once an important riverport, now a peaceful little town on the broad and stately Loire, La Charité has many vestiges of its former grandeur. It derives its name from the generosity it once showed to poor pilgrims. Of the huge 11–12C Romanesque church of Notre-Dame and its Benedictine abbey, known as 'the eldest daughter of Cluny', only a fraction remains. Yet even that is impressively large, and has a lovely spire on a domed crossing, and interesting pillars and capitals. In front of the church is a courtyard lined with cottages – all this was originally part of the nave. The curious isolated gateway and steps in Pl. des Pêcheurs was once the main entrance and facade.

Musée Adam, situated in a park, displays local prehistoric finds. A short length of ancient town fortifications remains, together with ruins of a castle, accessible from the park; a marvellous view can be enjoyed from the ramparts walkway of the church, the river and distant farmland. The oldest and most interesting cottages and streets are near the waterfront, and along Rue des Hôtelleries. A beautiful (but sturdy) stone bridge built in the 16C still carries the main road across the Loire. On the river bank S of the town a long grassy promenade, shaded by planes, is delightful.

CHAROLLES
SAÔNE-ET-LOIRE   Pop 3800

A rustic market town in S Burgundy, Charolles and its surrounding region known as the Charollais (spelt with two L's) gave their name to a peculiar breed of cattle raised for meat rather than milk – the massive and completely white Charolais (one L). Though now seen all over France, they are still particularly numerous in the pastures around Charolles, where they are the principal 'crop'.

Charolles nestles in green and rolling, partly wooded countryside. The Arconce and Semence rivers meet here, after much twisting and turning, and there are some thirty bridges in the little town. Ruins of the castle of the counts of Charollais are partly within a small park, from which there are good views.

CHÂTEAUNEUF
CÔTE D'OR

The 12–15C castle, W of Dijon, stands on a rock, encircled by vineyards, 11km SW of the village of Sombernon. You can still admire its massive walls, gateway towers and drawbridge, large guard room and chapel, and there are superb views of the surrounding countryside.

CHÂTILLON-SUR-SEINE
CÔTE D'OR   Pop 8000

Attractive despite war damage, Chatillon in N Burgundy stands on the divided stream of the young Seine and the rushing Douix, which emerges from rocks in a tree-shaded promenade above the rest of the town. Also on this ridge are a striking 11C Romanesque church, and ruins of a castle and a tower. The museum in a Renaissance house, Maison Philandrier, contains important local archaeological finds; the most dramatic, discovered Jan. 1953, is the Trésor de Vix, comprising 6BC grave-goods: jewellery, solid gold ornaments and a large decorated bronze vase.

CLAMECY
NIÈVRE   Pop 5800

At Clamecy on the Yonne, until this century, vast quantities of timber from the Morvan woodlands were floated N on the river. Now logs travel by road, but the days of *flottage* are recalled in the municipal museum. The old town has much character, with steep twisting lanes and timbered gabled houses. In the centre is the unusual 13–15C church of St-Martin, with Gothic Flamboyant facade, squared-off ambulatory and no transept.

The entrance to the town is by the Pont de Bethléem, named after the bishop of Bethlehem, expelled by Saladin in 1188, who established his see in Clamecy's Hôpital de Pantenor. The bishopric lasted for six centuries, until the Revolution.

Clamecy

CLUNY
SAÔNE-ET-LOIRE   Pop 4700

Today hardly more than a village, Cluny in rural S Burgundy once possessed the Benedictine abbey whose impact was felt throughout Christendom – in politics, religion, art and architecture. Founded in AD910 and reaching its zenith in the 11–13C, the abbey accumulated enormous wealth which

The abbey, Cluny

eventually weakened its moral authority and caused its downfall.

The abbey church, built (1088–1130) in a refined and distinctive Romanesque style, subsequently much copied, was the world's largest, 177m long, with 225 choir stalls and five naves, the highest of them 30m. After the Revolution it was demolished, leaving only the 62m-high octagonal Clocher de l'Eau-Bénite and other towers, and a part of the main abbey building. Even these fragments are tremendously impressive, and evocative of Cluny's magnificence. The Musée Ochier helps complete the picture.

Around the abbey, Cluny retains a number of remarkable domestic houses in Romanesque style, dating back to the 12–13C, and many other interesting buildings including stables of the National Stud.

The Renaissance **Château de Cormatin**, 12km E, has 17C apartments decorated in fantastically rich style.

COSNE-SUR-LOIRE
NIÈVRE   Pop 11,100

Beautifully located on the river Nohain and the Loire, Cosne is a pleasantly bustling small town with thriving light industry. It has an attractive centre, cropped plane trees lining the main street. The church of St-Agnan has good Romanesque features; St-Jacques has a curious square tower. There is an interesting museum of Loire river navigation.

CÔTE DE NUITS

The Côte d'Or, extending for 60km SE of Dijon, is a narrow ridge of hills with perfect conditions of sunlight, soil and drainage for growing the best varieties of grapes used in wine-making – Pinot Noir for red, Chardonnay for white. This 'golden slope' is divided into the Côte de Nuits, the northern part, and Côte de Beaune (see *Beaune*), the smaller southern part.

The villages or small individual vineyards (known as *clos* or *climats*) of the Côte de Nuits, their names world-famous, produce the greatest

Burgundy wines, acclaimed as the finest wines in the world.

The Route du Vin passes through almost all the picturesque wine villages, basking on the terraced hillsides; many have establishments offering *dégustation*, tasting. Along the route, **Chenove** has interesting wine-cellars of the dukes of Burgundy; **Fixin** has a pleasant lofty park (and a monument to Napoleon); **Gevrey-Chambertin** has a 13C church and 10C castle, and is a good starting point to ascend the steeply wooded valley known as the Combe de Lavaux.

The magnificent château of **Clos de Vougeot** stands in open country surrounded by its vineyards. Originally 12C, rebuilt in the 16C, the château belonged to the monks of nearby Cîteaux, who used it for their wine-making. The château is today the base of the Confrérie des Chevaliers du Tastevin, an exclusive gastronomic organization, founded to promote Burgundy wines. On the third Sat. of Nov., the first day of Les Trois Glorieuses, a lavish candlelight banquet for more than 500 guests is held in the vaults of the château. The Confrérie holds other banquets there throughout the year.

Nuits-St-Georges, commercial capital of the Côte de Nuits, is an unremarkable little town, though with an unusually late (13C) Romanesque church.

The **Hautes Côtes de Nuits**, plateau country on top of and behind the famous hillside, produces less renowned wines in a rural region excellent for touring.

Cîteaux, 12km E from Nuits, is the home of the ascetic Cistercian order of monks, founded in 1098. Their abbey was largely destroyed in the Revolution, and the order dispersed, but a century later it reassembled in what remained of the beautiful abbey. New buildings have been added and extensive grounds acquired.

DIJON
CÔTE D'OR   Pop 145,600

Dijon was from 1364 to 1477 the capital city of the mighty dukes of Burgundy, when it became a great centre of learning and art, with Flemish painters and craftsmen particularly to the fore. Later coming under the control of the French crown, Dijon entered an even more creative period. Today, as

Dijon

home of a super-prefecture controlling four *départements*, it is again capital of the Burgundy region. The city's extensive older quarters are among the most interesting in France, the ancient boundaries being marked today by a ring of main roads, following the course of earlier fortifications, from one square to another. Pl. Darcy, centre of modern Dijon (with tourist office), has pleasant gardens, and an elaborate 18C archway, Porte Guillaume, on the site of a city gate.

From Porte Guillaume, Dijon's chic main shopping street, Rue de la République, leads to the Ducal Palace. Completely rebuilt in 1682, the palace is partially used as the town hall. In front is the majestic Cour d'Honneur, with access to a 15C tower, Tour de Philippe Le Bon, which can be climbed for a view over the rooftops. The part of the building open to the public is mainly taken up by the Musée des Beaux Arts, a huge museum of French and Flemish art. The most impressive exhibits are a magnificently intricate gilded retable (1393), and the superbly carved ornate tombs of dukes Philippe Le Hardi and Jean Sans Peur with his wife. The palace kitchens have astonishing, massive chimneys.

Behind the palace is a network of narrow old streets and small squares, much of the area now a pedestrian precinct, extraordinarily rich in fine 15–16C mansions; particularly rewarding is a stroll in Rue des Forges and Pl. François Rude. In Rue de la Chouette, a street named for a small carved owl – which is supposed to bring luck if you touch it – set into the church wall, stands the 13C church of Notre-Dame, in Burgundian Gothic style. It has a curious facade with false gargoyles; above is a Jacquemart (clock with mechanical models) brought from Flanders. In a nearby square, the church of St-Michel, though mainly Gothic, has a Renaissance facade.

Around the 16C Palais de Justice are many more grand, well-preserved mansions, one of which is the Musée Magnin, complete with its original 17C furniture and decoration, and the walls hung with a private collection of 16–19C paintings. In Pl. St-Bénigne is Dijon's Gothic cathedral, with its coloured tile roof; it contains a remarkable 10C crypt. In the adjacent 12C abbey an archaeological museum displays important locally found treasures of every period from the Neolithic to the Middle Ages, including some excellent 15C sculpture from the former Chartreuse de Champnol monastery, a short distance from the city centre. Among the scant remains of the monastery is the Puits de Moïse, a hexagonal well surrounded by biblical statues. Just outside the ancient boundaries, the Jardin de l'Arquebuse is an agreeable botanic gardens with a flower-lined promenade.

Dijon's famous mustard is sold in all the *épiceries fines*. Cassis, the blackcurrant liqueur, is also supposed to originate here. All summer long Dijon enjoys a cultural feast, starting quietly with L'Été Musical (classical concerts throughout June), and exploding into life for L'Estivade (20 June–15 Aug.), a succession of artistic events, some formal, others in the street, some serious, others playful. In autumn, the first or second weekend in Sept. brings the Wine Fair, followed by the Foire Internationale Gastronomique, for the first two weeks of Nov.

There are pleasant walks and drives near Dijon along the Ouche and Suzon rivers and in the Côte d'Or wine country.

FLAVIGNY-SUR-OZERAIN
CÔTE D'OR   Pop 440

Tiny Flavigny, high on a rocky spur near Mont Auxois (see *Alésia*), 18km SE of Montbard, encloses within ancient ramparts narrow lanes lined with old turreted houses and mansions, and remains of an important 8C abbey, including the original Carolingian crypt. In a central square, the Gothic church of St-Genest has good choir-stalls and rood-loft. The town walls are entered through splendidly fortified gateways. Little aniseed sweets are traditionally a local speciality.

FONTENAY
CÔTE D'OR

In delightful wooded country, 4km NE of Montbard, the former great Cistercian abbey of Fontenay, built in 1118, was well restored in 1906. The cloisters are particularly beautiful, with double

Fontenay

pillars and Roman arches. The abbey church and other buildings, with bare simplicity and grace, give an insight into the disciplined asceticism of the Cistercians.

JOIGNY
YONNE   Pop 10,500

The narrow lanes of medieval Joigny climb steeply from the right bank of the Yonne, the newer part of town occupying the opposite bank. A tree-lined walkway runs along the riverside, and the 18C bridge gives a good view of the old town. Rue Gabriel Cortel, with many buildings dating back to the Middle Ages, reaches the 12C Porte du Bois, once the gateway of a castle; the churches of St-Jean and St-André have notable Renaissance additions; and St-Thibault, a church in Gothic/Renaissance style, curiously assymetrical inside, has a touching 14C statue, the 'Smiling Virgin'. Around St-Thibault some of the timbered cottages are over 700 years old; though many were damaged in the 1940 bombing, they have been carefully restored.

LANGRES
HAUTE-MARNE   Pop 11,200

Langres, in NE Burgundy, near the source of the river Marne, stands on a ridge in plateau country. Extensive ramparts, 4km around, give superb views from its walkway. Seven beautiful towers and six gateways punctuate the walls.

The 18C saw much building and restoration of grand houses in Renaissance and classical styles. A classical facade was added to the 12C cathedral of St-Mammès, which is dark inside but with some good features, including Roman arches, interesting capitals, and 16C tapestries. Opposite the cathedral, the Musée St-Didier exhibits local archaeology and more recent sculpture and painting. The Musée du Breuil de St-Germain has other fine art collections, and a section devoted to Diderot, philosopher and writer, born here in 1713.

MÂCON
SAÔNE-ET-LOIRE   Pop 38,700

A large thriving town on the river Saône, with much through traffic, Mâcon today retains few relics of its long history; but its many hotels make it useful for an overnight stop.

The church of St-Vincent was almost destroyed by Revolutionaries, leaving two octagonal towers and a Romanesque porch. A single remarkable Renaissance house, La Maison de Bois, survives in Pl. aux Herbes. The Musée Municipale des Ursulines, in a 17C convent, contains archaeological finds made at Mâcon and nearby Solutré. There is also a small museum devoted to Alphonse de Lamartine, the poet, born here in 1790.

Mâcon is the capital of a small wine area W of the town, the Mâconnais, which produces good basic reds and prestigious whites. At the N end of town, in a park by the river, Mâcon's Maison des Vins gives information on local wine, and tastings. The best known villages, all within 10km of the town, are **Pouilly**, **Fuissé**, **Loché** and **Vinzelles**.

The village of **Chasselas** gives its name to a grape used for cheaper wines.

In the same area, **Solutré** is the curious escarpment at the base of which an incredible number of animals bones – lying as much as 2m thick across an area of 4000 sq. metres – were discovered in 1866. Most are the skeletons of horses. It is presumed that the animals were deliberately massacred. Further excavations this century uncovered much earlier human settlements at the same spot. The Solutreans, dating back to more than 16,000 years ago, produced delicate stone flakes for spear points, decorated with laurel leaf patterns. President Mitterrand, with his family and friends, climbs the rock of Solutré every Easter.

MONTBARD
CÔTE D'OR   Pop 7900

Montbard is an important little steel-making town on the river Brenne and the Canal de Bourgogne. The scholar Comte de Buffon was born here in 1707, and later went to Paris as *intendant* of the royal gardens. He became a distinguished natural historian, and on his return to Montbard acquired the town's feudal château – which he almost completely knocked down in order to spend the rest of his life creating the lovely Parc de Buffon.

MORVAN

The unspoiled Regional Nature Park of the Morvan covers 175,000ha of extensive upland forests, lakes, rivers and remote pastures in the middle of Burgundy, reaching from Vézelay almost to Autun. The Cousin, the Cure, the Ternin, the Yonne, the Canche, and many other streams emerge from the thin layer of earth which conceals impermeable rock: not surprising, for on Morvan's higher ground there is precipitation on one day in two. The woodland is mainly handsome beech and oak, crisscrossed with marked foothpaths, and country lanes ideal for cycling or for drives.

Traditional customs and festivals (listed in the booklet *Morvan en Fête*, available from local tourist offices) have been preserved as much as possible by the region's villagers. At country fairs, locals quaintly dressed as Galvachers, formerly Morvan's travelling traders who had colourfully painted carts, make a reappearance.

At rustic little **Pierre-Perthuis**, in the northern part, the church overlooks the river Cure rushing

Morvan landscape

in its narrow gorge; the name comes from the Pierre Percée (pierced stone), a natural rock arch on the river's right bank. There are ruins of a 12C castle, and nearby is **Lac du Crescent**. **Lormes**, a hillside village on the eastern boundary, with excellent views, has some accommodation and is a good base for touring. **Lac des Settons**, in the tranquil centre of the park on the river Cure, is the most popular of the large reservoirs around which some provision has been made for holidaymakers in search of angling, watersports, walking, or just peace and quiet.

'Capital' of Morvan is **Château-Chinon** (pop. 2700), small town dominated by a hill, Le Calvaire, with panoramic views. A small folklore museum in the town has interesting exhibits of 18–19C local life. S of Château-Chinon the country becomes more mountainous. Among the higher peaks, **Mont Beuvray** (900m) is notable, for this was the site of Bibracte, the settlement and wartime retreat of the Eduens tribe of Gauls. Here Vercingetorix called a conference of the tribes and assumed overall leadership in their battle against Caesar. Much archaeological work has been done at the site. On the park's south-western boundary, **St-Honoré-les-Bains** is an attractive village spa, known to the Romans and still in use, which has become a good base for visiting Morvan.

The park's main information and exhibition centre is at **St-Brisson**, near Saulieu (q.v.), which is also just within the park boundary, and in some ways the best base for touring the region.

President Mitterrand was for many years mayor of Château-Chinon, only relinquishing the post when he assumed the presidency in 1981.

MOULINS
ALLIER   Pop 25,500

Capital of the duchy of Bourbon from 1368 to 1527, now prefecture of the Allier *département*, Moulins is a busy commercial town with an attractive old central area; 15C houses cluster around the cathedral of Notre-Dame, a curious squared-off Gothic building with exquisite artwork in the windows, and several good sculptures. Its 'treasure', a 15C triptych by Jean Hey ('the Master of Moulin'), can be viewed in the sacristy.

Tour Malcoiffée opposite the cathedral is a remnant of the 14C ducal castle; the adjacent *pavillon* of Anne de Beaujeu contains a museum of Art and Archaeology. A distinctive belfry with mechanical figures that strike the hours dominates Pl. de l'Hôtel de Ville, a small picturesque square. In a 15C house here is a folklore museum.

Crossing the Allier on the 18C Pont Régemortes (important checkpoint, in World War II, between occupied France and Vichy-ruled southern France), one passes through the **Forêt de Moladier** to **Souvigny**. This little town has an unusual priory church with tombs of Louis III and Charles I, as well as much excellent sculpture and woodcarving. The building dates mainly from the 11C, in Cluny Romanesque style, though with many 15C Gothic additions. In the interesting lapidary museum, note a fine 12C stonecarving depicting the months.

NEVERS
NIÈVRE Pop 44,800

Situated at the confluence of the Loire and the Nièvre (and close to that of the Allier), fortified Nevers had a long history of wealth and independence as the seat of a count and then a duke. A traditional reputation for ceramics is kept alive by a small number of craftsmen. Of the ramparts little remains, although a magnificent 14C gateway, the Porte du Croux, survives in excellent condition; it contains a small archaeological museum. (The less interesting Porte de Paris is an 18C triumphal arch, not a city gate). The municipal museum has a collection of Nevers faïence and ceramics, tracing its development across the centuries.

The large and unappealing cathedral in the heart of the old quarter consists of two dissimilar churches knocked into one; its main interest is that it contains an example of every architectural style from the 10C to the 16C! Much more attractive is the 15C ducal palace opposite, now the Palais de Justice, an early Renaissance château with large round towers. The convent of St-Gildard is where Bernadette Soubirous spent her life as a nun after her visions at Lourdes. Canonized in 1933, her body is preserved in a glass casket in the chapel.

The film *Hiroshima Mon Amour* was partly made in the narrow lanes and stepped alleys of Nevers. Many buildings date from the 15–16C and a 15C belfry overlooks the main shopping streets (pedestrianized). The 11C church of St-Étienne is plain and pleasingly simple, inside and out, combining the differing Romanesque styles of Burgundy and Auvergne. A big park adjoins the town centre.

Nevers is the capital of the Nivernais, a large rural upland area, mainly wooded, ideal for rambling or riding. It includes historic picturesque villages with Gothic churches, such as **Donzy**, **Varzy** and **St-Saulge**. **Pougues-les-Eaux** is a pretty little spa town.

Porte du Croux, Nevers

NOYERS
YONNE Pop 880

Situated 23km from Chablis along the Serein, Noyers is extraordinarily picturesque. The river winds almost completely around the small town. Part of the old ramparts remain, including sixteen distinctive circular towers. Along the streets and around the many little squares are numerous 14–15C houses in excellent condition, some timbered, others of stone. From outside the 15C Renaissance church of Notre-Dame there is a fine view of the river and fields beyond.

PARAY-LE-MONIAL
SAÔNE-ET-LOIRE Pop 11,300

Paray 'of the monks', rural market town in S Burgundy, is among the most popular places of pilgrimage in France. It was here that novice nun Marguerite Marie Alacoque, in 1673, claimed to have visions of Christ with his heart exposed, saying the words 'Here is the heart which so loved Man'. The cult of the Sacred Heart was adopted officially by the state in 1873, and in 1920 Sister Alacoque was made a saint. The room where she lived has been reconstructed and is preserved as a museum, the Chambre des Reliques. The Chapelle de la Visitation is supposedly where she had her visions.

The church of Notre-Dame, though now known as the Basilique du Sacré Coeur, built in 1109 from blocks of pale stone, is a scaled-down copy of the abbey church at Cluny, and is perhaps the best illustration of what Cluny actually looked like. Massive yet elegant, pure Romanesque, with two square towers and an octagonal central spire, the exterior is enchanting, and its location in a park on the bank of the pretty tree-lined Bourbince river enhances the impression. The interior is tall, graceful, austere, with slender columns reflecting a classical influence.

Paray's town hall, in the curious 16C Maison Jayet, has an extraordinarily ornate facade covered in amusing little sculptures. Facing it is a deconsecrated church with a distinctive tower, St-Nicholas, which has become a Fine Arts museum. In this quarter are several Renaissance houses.

Digoin, 12km W, is a small town with a long tradition of pottery and ceramics (interesting pottery museum), at an important intersection of three rivers and three canals, one of which crosses the Loire by way of a sixteen-arch aqueduct. S of Paray and Digoin lies the Brionnais (q.v.).

PONTIGNY
YONNE Pop 825

The Cistercians founded their second monastery in 1114 at Pontigny, 20km NE of Auxerre. Here Thomas à Becket fled after his disagreement with Henry II, with the result that two years later Henry threatened to expel all Cistercians from England, whereupon Becket moved to Sens. The Revolutionaries left the monastery in ruins, but remarkably the abbey church survived intact. It is an impressively large, terribly austere building in transitional Gothic style.

RATILLY, CHÂTEAU DE
NIÈVRE

Splendidly romantic, with massive round towers and encircling moat, and made of ochre stone, the 13C Château de Ratilly stands in beautiful wooded countryside, 28km NE of Cosne-sur-Loire. Once a hideout for Jansenists secretly printing their journals here, nowadays there are pottery and ceramics workshops in the château.

ST-FLORENTIN
YONNE   Pop 6800

A small cheesemaking town poised above the Armance and Armançon rivers, St-Florentin has some lovely streets, good views from the Promenade du Prieurie, and an interesting Renaissance church which, though much damaged, preserves many excellent features, especially the stained glass.

Stretching out to the N of the town is the extensive Othe region, mainly forested (apart from the apple orchards, used for cider). The Othe takes in a number of enticing little villages, rustic and pretty, with Gothic and Renaissance churches, such as **Berulle**, **Aix-en-Othe** and **Rigny-le-Ferron**. **Auxon** has a particularly fine 16C church.

SAULIEU
CÔTE D'OR   Pop 3200

Within the eastern boundary of the Morvan Regional Nature Park, Saulieu is an excellent base for touring in the park area. It is an old town with many picturesque corners. The ramparts have gone except for the Tour d'Auxois. The 11C abbey church of St-Andoche, despite unfortunate later alterations, retains some interesting original features including the detailed capitals and the saint's 5C sarcophagus.

Saulieu was long known as a *ville gastronomique*, a convenient halt on the ancient Paris-Lyon road; but this reputation has declined because of the autoroute. The museum beside the church has a room devoted to local gastronomy, as well as a section on the animal sculptures of the local 19C artist François Pompon.

SEMUR-EN-AUXOIS
CÔTE D'OR   Pop 5400

This peaceful little country town of cobbled streets keeps its character and charm intact despite easy access from the autoroute. The fortifications, and a defensive position on a high ridge above a bend in the Armançon, have made Semur not only virtually impregnable but also exceptionally attractive. From a walkway on the wooded ramparts there are good views; the town looks its best from Pont Joly, down below. Four mighty round towers mark the site of a 14C castle, dismantled in 1602; one of the towers contains a museum of local interest.

In the main square, the church of Notre-Dame, originally 11C, much damaged and restored in later centuries, has many interesting sculptures inside, and some good exterior stonecarving. In the streets around the church are several decorative wells and fountains. In Rue Buffon, two ancient gateways, the 15C Porte Sauvigny and the 13C Porte Guillier, combine to form a single archway.

Semur-en-Auxois

SENS
YONNE   Pop 27,000

Important settlement of the Senoni Gauls, a Roman provincial capital, Sens on the river Yonne later grew to become a great ecclesiastical town, seat of an archbishop whose diocese, until 1627, included Paris. Thomas à Becket spent some of his exile here, and the architect of its 12C cathedral, William of Sens, was commissioned to redesign Canterbury Cathedral after Becket's murder.

The cathedral of St-Étienne, early Gothic, has a squared-off castle-like exterior, with one tower conspicuously missing, and fine portals. The interior is tall and spacious, with excellent 16C stained glass by local master craftsman Jean Cousin. Its treasury includes some of Becket's liturgical vestments.

The town ramparts have been replaced by boulevards and promenades. Along Grande Rue (pedestrianized), main street of the old central quarter, and in the back streets, are dozens of fascinating timber or stone houses, including the remarkably ornate 16C Maison d'Abraham.

Sens

Château de Fleurigny, 15km NE, with moat and towers, despite alterations, remains in exquisite Renaissance taste. Jean Cousin made a window in its chapel, and designed the sculpted fireplace in the guard room.

TANLAY, CHÂTEAU DE
YONNE

Perhaps the most beautiful of Burgundy's Renaissance châteaux is Tanlay, in the Armançon valley 2km from Tonnerre. Built in the 1550s, in extensive cultivated grounds, it has exceptional elegance. It consists of a Petit Château, beyond which, within a moat, is the impressive Grand Château with sturdy corner towers and splendid courtyard. The interior decor is lavish. There are ruins of a 12–15C abbey in the grounds. Tanlay provided a refuge for leading Protestants during the 16C Wars of Religion.

TONNERRE
YONNE Pop 6200

Bustling Tonnerre rises up the steep banks of the Armançon and the Canal de Bourgogne. A Celtic, then a Roman settlement, today it retains a medieval character with narrow streets and an old quarter below the church of St-Pierre, from which there are extensive views. Near the church, the Fosse Diane is a curious spring of turquoise water, now a public laundry house. The 13C Ancien Hôpital, plain and functional from outside, contains a ward of impressive size with a remarkable oak roof.

Tournus

TOURNUS
SAÔNE-ET-LOIRE Pop 6700

Tournus, alongside the Saône, is an agreeable town, very ancient, now noted for the manufacture of kitchen equipment. Its remarkable abbey church, large and sturdy, with defensive towers, is within its own walled and magnificently fortified enclosure. In fact, it is three separate churches built on top of one another. The main section, the 10C St-Philibert, is entered through a low, dark narthex full of pillars. Inside, the nave is vast and bare, with wide side aisles, and the roof strangely barrel-vaulted crosswise. The windows are unexpectedly modern. Below is the crypt of a previous

church only a century older, while above the narthex, reached by outside steps, stands the 10C church of St-Michel.

Adjacent are other abbey buildings and a modest museum. The 18C pharmacy of Hôtel-Dieu hospital remains unaltered. In the town are some old streets with arcaded sidewalks. Ste-Madeleine, a tiny Romanesque church, has a wonderful unaffected simplicity.

In attractive country to the W are the picturesque villages of **Brancion**, with a 10C castle, medieval covered market and small 12C church, and **Chapaize**, with a tall 11C belltower.

VÉZELAY
YONNE Pop 600

On a hilltop at the northern edge of Morvan, visible from miles away, the 11–12C abbey church of La Madeleine in the fortified village of Vézelay was restored from its ruins by Viollet-le-Duc in the 19C. It has truly majestic dimensions, 120m long, with a tall wide nave entered from an immense narthex by gigantic wooden doors. The ceiling is beautiful, barrel-vaulted with voussoirs of alternate light and dark stone blocks. The large mutilated tympanum above the exterior doors is reproduced in undamaged form above the interior doors. There is little decoration, save for exquisite capitals. The choir, older than the nave, stands on an even older crypt.

Founded in 864, the abbey thrived for centuries as a halt for pilgrims on the Compostela route after relics believed to be those of Mary Magdalene, were brought here. In 1120 a catastrophic fire swept through the crowded church and killed about a thousand pilgrims. Vézelay's importance came to an abrupt end when, in 1280, it was discovered that the Magdalene relics were still at St-Maximin in Provence. Though much damaged by Protestants and local villagers, the abbey survived until the Revolution.

The village itself, climbing up the hill to the abbey church, has much else of interest: cobbled streets, 15–16C dwellings, a 17C clocktower, and impressive gateways in the fortifications.

Vézelay

JURA/FRANCHE-COMTÉ

The Jura is a beautiful place, an elongated wedge of France pressed hard against the Swiss frontier, a land of lakes and rivers and rolling forested hills.

Historically, this was a divided and much disputed land. During the Middle Ages it made up the Comté, that part of Burgundy which owed allegiance to the Holy Roman Emperor as opposed to the Duché, which was one of the great fiefs of the kingdom of France. The very name Franche-Comté did not come into being until the end of the 14C, and it was not until 1678 that Louis XIV finally wrested control of the Comté from the Hapsburgs, established the eastern frontier of France and Switzerland, and subsequently ratified his conquest by the Treaty of Nijmegen. As a result of all this strife, Franche-Comté remains a frontier country, one well supplied with castles and fortified towns, some – like mighty Besançon – embellished with fortifications by the Sun King's great engineer, Vauban, which still endure today, others little, half-forgotten places, basking quietly in the afterglow of peaceful days.

Those former jarring times now lie in the distant past. Today Franche-Comté is first and foremost a holiday region, a place to which thousands flock each year, to fish the rivers, swim or sail in the lakes, slide each winter over the long cross-country ski trails, or simply travel about to enjoy the quiet valleys and beautiful unspoilt villages, a notable local cuisine and some excellent little-known

wines, those tasty vintages from Arbois and the Bugey which go so well with the local trout, pork and cheese. The local people may be dour, but friendly enough to the passing stranger, especially one with a genuine interest in the beauties of the landscape and an eye for the more subtle charms of small, ancient villages, golden-stone Romanesque churches, grim castles, and everywhere the glint of lakes and the rushing ripple of mountain streams.

Those who like the excitement and bustle of the big cities might find Franche-Comté rather subdued, though Besançon is one of the great provincial cities of France, an important town since Roman times, and the other centres, Belfort of famous memory, Pontarlier, even little Ornans, are well worth a visit. That said, this is really a country region, rich and varied, enjoyable to visit and pleasant to remember.

ARBOIS
JURA   Pop 4200

Lying 50km S and W of Besançon, Arbois is a picturesque little town, the capital of the wine-producing heart of the Jura, and entirely encircled by vineyards. Much of the present town centre is medieval, and it still retains the relics of the old fortifications, the towers and ramparts of the outer wall, the Tour de la Gloriette, which date from the 13C, and the main church of St-Just, on the banks of the pretty river Cuisance, which winds through the town. Although he was actually born in Dole, Arbois also lays claim to Louis Pasteur, who went to school here from the age of five, and then worked in the town for much of his life, often helping the local *vignerons* combat the various diseases which attacked their vines. Today, Arbois is a tourist centre for the southern Jura, where wine remains the principal local industry. There are wine cellars offering tastings and bottles for sale, a museum of the Vine and Wine and an annual wine festival, the Fête du Biou, held during the first week in Sept. Sights to see in the town

Arbois

include the Pasteur family home in the Rue de Courcelles, the church of St-Just, and the old houses by the river which are best viewed from the 13C bridge, the Pont des Capucins. Good views of the surrounding countryside can be obtained from the high point of **Le Tourillon**, 3km E, and wine lovers should also venture 2km outside the town to see the mighty **Vigne de Pasteur**, Pasteur's vine, the grapes of which he used to carry out his experiments in fermentation, and which still produces excellent wine.

ARC-EN-SENANS
DOUBS Pop 1300

Arc-en-Senans, built to exploit the local salt mines S of Dole, is a most unusual place, an example of 18C town planning. No factory estate since created would look like this, alas. It was built in 1773 by Claude-Nicolas Ledoux, on classical lines, and designed as an example of French 18C architecture, although less than a tenth of the original plan was actually completed. The town is laid out on a circular plan with the house of the director of the royal salt works in the central position, and the other houses, warehouses and offices, the building of the carpenters, the salt warehouses, the directors' stables, set in the streets around the centre; an elegant composition. The buildings can still be visited and give a good idea of how elegant a commercial town this would have been had not the Revolution interrupted the building.

BAUME-LES-DAMES
DOUBS Pop 5700

This little town occupies an attractive position in the valley of the Doubs, NE of Besançon, and is a centre for the manufacture of pipes. That apart, it is a good place to stay in while touring the surrounding countryside and the green valley of the Doubs.

BAUME-LES-MESSIEURS
JURA Pop 200

Baume-les-Messieurs is barely a hamlet, just a scattering of houses at the point where three deep valleys interlink to form the great natural wonder of the **Cirque de Baume**. Apart from the outstanding scenery, the chief attraction here is the ancient abbey, founded in the 6C by St Columba. Twelve monks sent from Baume created the abbey of Cluny in the 11C, and the abbey church is a magnificent relic of Baume's former power and importance.

BELFORT
TERRITOIRE-DE-BELFORT Pop 57,700

Belfort, the 'strong castle', owes much of its fame to Louis XIV's great castle builder, Vauban, who was commanded by the king to make Belfort impregnable, a task he accomplished to perfection. Belfort, and the small *territoire* which still surrounds it, gained their place in French history during the Franco-Prussian War of 1870 when the garrison, under Colonel Denfert-Rochereau, was besieged

by the German army for three months, and only surrendered after the armistice was signed at Versailles. As a result, Belfort was not annexed by the Germans, and remained a French enclave when Alsace and Lorraine were handed over to Germany.

Thanks to its strategic position in the wide valley, or Trouée, which runs between the hills of the Jura and the Vosges, linking the valleys of the Rhine and the Rhône, Belfort has always been a fortified town, trampled by the passage of armies since Roman times. The town today lies in two parts, old and new, divided by the river Savoureuse. The old town is dominated by the vast fortifications erected by Vauban in the late 17C, as well as the mighty statue of a lion, 11m high and 2m long, which stands below the citadel and was erected to commemorate the heroic defence of the town in 1870–71. Even to the modern eye, Belfort is clearly a place of war, but one not unattractive and now much mellowed by time. The citadel is well worth visiting and contains an interesting museum of art and history, with works by Dürer and Courbet, while the old narrow streets of the town are full of attractive architecture. The cathedral of St-Christophe has an elegant 18C facade and there are pleasant walks along the banks of the Savoureuse. Belfort today is also an industrial centre, manufacturing textiles, typewriters and electrical goods. Of the hills which lie on either side of the city, the high peaks of Alsace, which lie to the N around the **Ballon d'Alsace** (1250m) are the most attractive and set in a good area for summer walking or winter cross-country skiing.

BESANÇON
DOUBS Pop 120,000

Besançon is the capital of Franche-Comté, the largest town in the region, and one of the finest provincial cities in France. It is an old town, dating back to Roman times, and it occupied a strategic site on an escarpment high above a tight loop in the river Doubs, which serves the city like a moat, with a wall and a Vauban citadel across the neck of land to complete the fortifications. Modern Besançon has spread out far beyond the old town up on the cliffs, and now occupies large areas of land on the far side of the Doubs.

During the Middle Ages, Besançon was a fortress city, and the seat of an archbishopric. The city was rebuilt in the 11C by archbishop Hugh de Salins; the present cathedral of St-Jean dates from the 12C and is a fine example of the early Gothic, with much subsequent rebuilding. Besançon was a free city of the Hapsburg Holy Roman Empire and ruled by the archbishop for much of the Middle Ages. It was annexed for the kingdom of France by Richelieu in 1635 and later fortified as an eastern bastion of the country by Vauban at the end of the 17C, after being ceded to France by the Peace of Nijmegen in 1678. The city enjoyed considerable prosperity as a trading centre and was noted for the manufacture of artificial silk. Today there is a good deal of light industry, notably in the manufacture of clocks and watches.

Most visitors will begin a visit to Besançon by walking up the Grand Rue through the Roman

209

arch of the Porte Noire to the cathedral and the citadel, standing high above the Doubs and completely dominating the town. The old moats and ditches now contain a small zoo while the citadel contains several museums, of Folklore, of Natural History, and most notably, of the Resistance. During World War II, Franche-Comté was a stronghold of the Resistance and many of those patriots captured in the fighting were imprisoned, tortured and shot within the citadel.

Less grim reminders of the past include the 11C church of Notre-Dame, the municipal library and the Hôpital St-Jacques, with its magnificent wrought-iron gate and railings. The Porte Noire, or Gate of Mars, is a Roman triumphal arch dating from the 2C and was probably built to honour Marcus Aurelius. Besançon is full of fine houses from all periods, and has many splendid public buildings, many in the French Renaissance style. Of the city museums, the Musée des Beaux Arts is one of the oldest and best endowed in France, famous for its large and excellent collection of works by Fragonard, Courbet and Boucher. The town's most famous son was Victor Hugo, born here in 1802, and his birthplace at 140 Grande Rue can still be visited.

Culture apart, Besançon today is a lively, bustling, provincial capital, with many excellent hotels, fine restaurants, bars, cinemas, parks and public gardens, even a casino, and well worth a couple of days for exploration and enjoyment. From Besançon there is good access to all parts of Franche-Comté, and into the high hills of the Jura which lie to the SE. The valley of the river Ognon, reached through **Voray**, is a beautiful, undiscovered place.

CHAMPAGNOLE
JURA Pop 10,100

Like all too many towns hereabouts, Champagnole, set below Mont Rivel in the valley of the river Ain, has suffered the experience of being completely destroyed by fire. The present red-roofed town dates only from the 19C and it has since developed into a centre for light industry, and as a starting point for summer tourists to the hills of the Jura Massif, which lie to the E. The town contains a fine medieval church, but is really best used as an excursion centre to the deep gorges of **Langouette**, which lie to the S, to the source of the river Ain a little to the NE, to the waterfall of **La Billaude**, and above all, to the spectacular waterfalls at **Hérisson** and the beautiful **Lac de Chalain**, situated to the S. The medieval town of **Nozeroy**, 19km E of Champagnole, is also well worth a visit.

CHAMPLITTE
HAUTE-SAÔNE Pop 1400

Those who love old buildings and graceful architecture will love Champlitte. Set on the slopes of a hill overlooking the green valley of the Salon, this is an old fortified town, which has now developed into a centre for the local wine trade. The village retains vestiges of the old walls, a Gothic church and convent dating from the 15C, and a fine 17C château which now contains the town hall and a folklore museum.

DOLE
JURA Pop 27,700

Before the coming of the French in the 16C, Dole was the capital of the Comté, and it still has the slightly regal air of a capital city, a pleasant place, of old, leaning houses topped with rust-red roofs. Louis XI of France burned much of the town in 1479, and it suffered still more during the 'Great Siege' of 1636 when Richelieu sent his great general Condé to reduce the city. The 'Great Siege' lasted three months before the French withdrew, but the town finally fell to the troops of Louis XIV in 1674, and Louis then transferred the seat of his governor to Besançon. Louis Pasteur, although claimed by Arbois, was born here in what is now the Rue Pasteur in 1822, and lived here until the age of five.

Dole occupies a pleasant location on the right bank of the Doubs, and much of the old, medieval town centre, which clusters closely around the church of Notre-Dame, is a maze of narrow, cobbled streets, and ancient leaning buildings. Dole is a place to explore on foot, starting at Notre-Dame, and visiting all the attractive places which lie just a short distance away. Among the most interesting are Pasteur's birthplace, the Pl. aux Fleurs, the convent of the Carmelites, and the Jesuit college.

The best excursions from the town lie in either direction along the picturesque valley of the Doubs.

LONS-LE-SAUNIER
JURA Pop 21,900

Lons-le-Saunier was the birthplace, in 1760, of Rouget de Lisle, composer of the *Chant de guerre de l'Armée du Rhin*, better known to history as the *Marseillaise*, that most stirring of anthems. Lons has yet another connection with the early days of the French republic, for it was at Lons that Marshal Ney, who had been sent to capture Napoleon as he marched on Paris after escaping from Elba, threw off his oath of loyalty to the Bourbons and declared again for the emperor. Ney commanded the Old Guard when Napoleon was defeated at Waterloo three months later, and was shot by the vengeful Bourbons in December 1815.

Today, Lons is a small, attractive town, and capital of the Jura *département*. The town has an excellent museum in the Hôtel de Ville with paintings by Breughel, Vouet and Courbet, and Rouget de Lisle's home still stands in the Rue du Commerce. The medieval **Château du Pin**, just to the N, and the beautiful landscapes of the **Cirque de Baume**, 19km E, are two worthwhile excursions.

MONTBÉLIARD
DOUBS Pop 33,400

Montbéliard is a pleasing mixture of ancient and modern. The town's origins date back even to the 8C, while the major local industry today is the manufacture of cars and bicycles by Peugeot, though the Peugeot family's associations with the town go back to 1810 when they ran a small steel mill here.

The first sight of the town is striking, for the red rooftops are dominated by the walls and turrets of a 15C *château-fort*, which is now the town museum with exhibits as diverse as relics of the Gallo-Roman era, and a room devoted to the work of Étienne Oehmichen, a pioneer of the helicopter.

MONTBENOÎT
DOUBS   Pop 180

Montbenoît, SE of Besançon, is a little place with a great heart, the capital of the Saugeais, a green valley set beneath the Jura hills. Montbenoît is famous for the abbey of St-Claude, which occupies much of the present village, and dates mainly from the end of the medieval period. The nave of the church is 12C but the choir, and most notably the exquisitely-carved choir stalls, date from the 16C, as does the cloister. Today, Montbenoît is a popular centre for walking and cross-country skiing.

ORNANS
DOUBS   Pop 4300

Ornans

Set in a delightful situation, along the banks of the river Loue, Ornans is one spot which every traveller to the Jura should certainly visit. Ornans is a very old town, with a charter dating from 1244, and many ancient houses, each with a wooden balcony overhanging the river which runs through the centre of the town. The town's most famous son is the painter Gustave Courbet, who was born here in 1819, and whose works can be found in art galleries and museums all over Franche-Comté. His birthplace, which is also a museum, can be visited. Other sights to see around the town include the Grand Pont over the river, and the 15C Hôtel de Grospain, now the town hall.

PONTARLIER
DOUBS   Pop 18,800

Pontarlier, 60km S of Besançon, is best regarded as a touring centre for the countryside round about. The town is pleasant enough, set on a bend in the Doubs, and much of the town centre dates back to the Middle Ages. Important sites include the Chapelle des Annonciades and a triumphal arch, erected in honour of Louis XIV. Pontarlier lies at the foot and centre of the Jura hills, offering easy access up into the massif, or S to the lake district around Champagnole. About 4km S is the 10C **Château de Joux**, which in the early 19C served as

a prison for the unfortunate Toussaint L'Ouverture, emancipator of St Dominique (Haiti), who was imprisoned here by Napoleon.

ST-CLAUDE
JURA   Pop 13,200

St-Claude has two claims to fame. Firstly, it occupies one of the most splendid natural sites in the southern Jura. Secondly, it is the capital for the ancient craft of pipe-making. St-Claude's pipes, often beautifully carved, are prized by pipe-smokers the world over, and the local industry, which dates back to 1560 when tobacco was first introduced into France, still flourishes today, owing this long tradition to the quality and abundance of the local briar.

St-Claude lies astride the river Bienne, 60km S of Lons-le-Saunier, at the junction with the river Tacon. Parts of the town date back to the early days of Christianity, at the end of the Roman Empire, when St Romain, an anchorite monk, built the first cathedral on this spot. St-Claude remained a religious and pilgrim centre until the Revolution. The St Claude who gave his name to the town was archbishop of Besançon in the 7C and built the local abbey which was destroyed by a Revolutionary mob in 1794. Only the cathedral of St-Pierre and some of the old houses remain from St-Claude's golden age of pilgrimage.

Apart from the cathedral, visitors can inspect the pipe museum, or obtain fine views over the town from the terrace in the Place Louis XI. Excursions and walks from St-Claude include trips to the waterfall of the **Queue de Cheval** (Horse's Tail), to the viewpoint at **Le Crêt Pourri**, and to the pilgrim chapel of **St-Romain** at **St-Lupicin**.

SALINS-LES-BAINS
JURA   Pop 4200

Salins is now a thermal spa and was once a centre for the medieval salt trade. The town straggles along the banks of the river Furieuse and still retains remnants of the medieval fortifications, including parts of the walls and several towers. In the first half of the 14C Salins was a thriving town, but the Black Death of 1349 devastated the population, which took generations to recover. The site is very attractive and places worth visiting in the town include the salt works, the Burgundian Gothic church of St-Anatoile, which dates from the 13C, the old hospital or Hôtel-Dieu, and the Promenade des Cordeliers.

VESOUL
HAUTE-SAÔNE   Pop 20,300

Vesoul lies in the very centre of the Haute-Saône, the most northern *département* of Franche-Comté, close to the frontier of Lorraine. The site has been occupied since pre-Roman times, and the legions of Caesar had a marching camp here. It remained a garrison town for the Hapsburgs until captured by the forces of Louis XIV in 1678. Today, the town is still a transport centre, straddling the road and rail routes to Switzerland, and a popular excursion centre for the northern Jura.

POITOU/CHARENTES

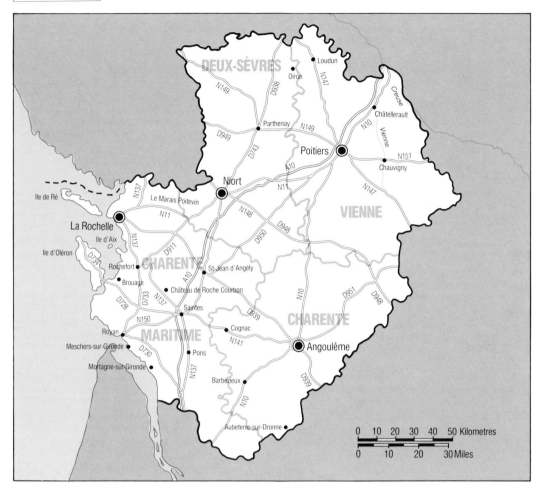

The flat plains and marshlands of Poitou, Charente and the Saintenage are lush and have huge horizons but are not beautiful.

Travellers through centuries have tended to hurry through to Bordeaux or to Spain, welcoming the flat lands to speed them on their way – medieval pilgrims making for Compostela, modern holiday-makers scurrying to the sun. Towns and villages look rather severe, as befits a land which listened to Calvin and was mostly ardently Protestant in the days of religious strife.

Protestant loyalties kept back industrialization. Thriving towns lost their artisans, who fled religious persecution, and many now have fewer inhabitants than centuries ago. Most became market towns for a people living off the land. But these troubles left this western area rich in three treasures – fascinating history, delightful Romanesque churches, and superb food. The Romanesque churches remained, partly because the Protestants did not believe in the frivolities of the Renaissance styles and partly because the communities were too poor for such restyling. So superb medieval churches abound. There are about a dozen around the Poitiers area alone.

The dramas of history continued into modern times, as Napoleon was persuaded to leave the isle of Aix to join the *Bellerophon* as a prisoner in 1815, and the Nazis made a last stand in 1945 against the Free French in Royan, so that the town was almost wiped out.

The cooking of this whole area is usually what the French call 'honest and direct'. Chefs simply do not need frills or much inventiveness. Some of France's richest land gives them superb butter and fine beef from Charente water-meadows, salt-grazed lamb from the marshes south of La Rochelle, and lovely vegetables and fruit, including Charentais melons. Fish is outstanding even for France – oysters from Marennes and the isles of Oléron and Aix, mussels from the farms of Boyardville Bay off Oléron, lampreys (eels) from the estuaries and *anguilles* (little eels) from the Marais Poitevin, sardines, tuna, masses of varied white fish from La Rochelle's fishing fleet, sturgeon, trout from many rivers, pork from around Angoulême. With these ingredients they cook simply in butter with cream and wine. And it is worth dallying in this tranquil part of France simply to recall what fine fresh food can taste like.

If the inland plains are quiet, the coast is interesting and in places lively. Two extremes in holiday resorts are there: La Rochelle, an old port, with lovely old and historic buildings, is a little paradise for gourmands and yachtsmen – one of the most pleasant coastal towns in Europe. Royan, completely rebuilt, offers modern accommodation, shops, churches, entertainments and a huge beach – ideal for the family holiday.

Then there are the three islands, Ré, Aix, Oléron – once for escapists, but so many people nowadays flock to them in summer that the true refuges are the agricultural villages of the mainland plains. Not even the new French drive for industrial technology has reached them.

AIX, ÎLE D'
CHARENTE MARITIME   Pop 170

A peaceful, car-free island holiday resort where the locals go shrimping, farm oysters, work in mother-of-pearl and tend vineyards producing white wine. For centuries it was a fortress, guarding approaches to the ports of La Rochelle and Rochefort. It was fortified by the greatest of military architects, Vauban, partly blown up by the British in the Seven Years' War, but repaired by engineers who included Laclos, later author of *Les Liaisons Dangereuses*.

In 1808 Napoleon ordered a house to be built for him (Maison de l'Empereur) when he visited the isle. It is now a Napoleonic museum. Two years later he ordered the building of a fort – La Rade, but it was not finished until 1837.

In July 1815, after defeat at Waterloo, he returned to Aix, hoping to escape to America, but a British naval force was in the vicinity. He spent four days on Aix saying goodbye to his brother Joseph, writing a letter to the Prince Regent (later George IV) claiming asylum, and arranging to give himself up to the captain of the *Bellerophon*.

The letter is in the museum on Aix. In a nearby African museum's garden is the white dromedary, stuffed after death, which Napoleon rode in Egypt.

ANGOULÊME
CHARENTE   Pop 50,000

An ancient town, already important under the Romans, has become the centre for a modern industrial experiment – Le Grand Angoulême. Heavy engineering factories are located in the country to give workers a healthier and happier life. Angoulême had 100 mills making watermarked paper until the Protestant workers fled after 1685, and still makes quality paper; also the famous *pantoufles charentaises* (felt slippers).

The old town stands behind high ramparts above the Charente river. You can drive or walk round them and get fine views across the Charente plain. At Promenade Beaulieu, overlooking Jardin Vert, is a plaque to France's first "para", General Resnier. In 1806, aged 73, he invented a wing-flapping machine and took off from this spot, hoping to find a way for Napoleon's troops to invade England. He ended in the river.

In the old town, among some fine old houses, is the 12C cathedral of St-Pierre, still magnificent despite some ruthless 19C restoration by Paul Abadie, architect of Sacré-Coeur and the "restorer" who added all the towers to St-Front in Périgueux. He also built Angoulême town hall on the site of an historic château, incorporating a 13C keep and a 15C round tower. Here was born, in 1492, Marguerite d'Angoulême, sister of François I, grandmother of Henri IV and a remarkable woman. Among other things, she wrote to Erasmus in Hebrew, Latin and Greek, was fluent in Italian and Spanish, and wrote stories imitating great writers.

Another Angoulême girl was Queen Isabella, wife of King John of England and mother of Henry III. In 1200 John virtually kidnapped her when she was 12. After his death she returned to marry a Frenchman, but is buried at Fontevraud with Henry II and Eleanor of Aquitaine.

St-Pierre, Angoulême

AUBETERRE-SUR-DRONNE
CHARENTE   Pop 420

About 10km E of Chalais, it is a peaceful village built into white chalk cliffs forming an amphitheatre above the Dronne river. It has fine views. The monolithic church was hollowed out of rock in the 12C to house relics brought back from a Crusade by the local lord, Pierre de Castillon. In the Revolution it became a saltpetre factory, then, until 1865, a cemetery.

BARBEZIEUX
CHARENTE   Pop 5100

This bright and cheerful town is the capital of Cognac brandy's Petite Champagne. Only this area and La Grande Champagne, a small area nearer to Cognac, may call their brandy Fine Champagne. Among old buildings, two attractive round towers remain of the 12C castle, restored by Marguerite Rochefoucauld in the 15C and now used as a theatre and museum. The town is known for marrons glacés and fruits confits (preserved chestnuts and fruits) and for chickens. At **Blanzac**, 15km E, in the Né valley, the 12C St-Arthémy church is surrounded by castle ruins.

BROUAGE
CHARENTE-MARITIME

Once the biggest salt port in Europe and rival to La Rochelle, this strange and melancholy place is sinking into the mud, the 17C fortifications built by Richelieu intact but overgrown. When the salt marshes which now surround it were sea, great merchantmen departed from the port. Samuel Champlain, born here in 1567 of a Protestant family, sailed to found Quebec. Silting commenced when the prince of Condé, Protestant leader, besieged it and blockaded its harbour, although it was still accessible when Richelieu used it as a base for his siege of La Rochelle. The death-knell came when Colbert chose Rochefort as his new port.

All that remains of the port are patches of quayside, mooring rings and a trickle of water which is just navigable at high tide to the sea 3km away. Silent watchtowers on the ramparts look

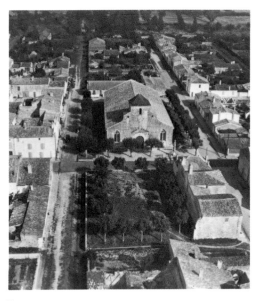

Brouage

down on wild flowers and grass between 17C houses. The salt pans are oyster farms with huts for workers built on stilts. **Marennes** is the green-oyster capital.

CHÂTELLERAULT
VIENNE   Pop 36,000

The beautiful Pont Henri IV, with twin towers, joins the two halves of the town across the river Vienne. Started in 1572, the bridge was not finished until 1609. Châtellerault, now important commercially, was a thriving port until better roads killed river traffic. Cutlery has been the main manufacture since the 11C. Shops still gleam with knives, scissors and table cutlery. Small arms, too, were made here until 1968, and metallurgy and electronics have recently been added.

Châtellerault

St-Jacques was a priory church, consecrated in 1066, but in the 19C two towers and a neo-Romanesque facade were added. It has 13C Angevin vaulting in the nave, a wooden effigy of St Jacques de Compostela, and a carillon of 52 bells.

René Descartes, the philosopher, whose logical method of thinking still influences French education, lived here as a youth. His family house is a museum. A very interesting motor and technical museum is in the former arms factory, with some particularly good examples of early steam and electric cars, bicycles, tricycles and motorbikes.

At **Vieux-Poitiers** nearby are small remains of a Roman wall and the place where in AD732 Charles Martel routed the Saracens and stopped the Moslem advance into Christian Europe.

CHAUVIGNY
VIENNE   Pop 6400

Beside the river Vienne is an industrial town making porcelain. Above, on a spur of rock fashioned for defence, stands the old town of Chauvigny, clustered round three ruined castles, Évêques, Harcourt and Gouzon, and the 12C church of St-Pierre, a lovely example of Poitevin-Romanesque in grey stone, but with bad 19C interior restoration.

Château de Touffou, 7km N, is of four different styles. It has two 12C keeps and four great 14C round towers; but the elegant Renaissance buildings linking the keeps give it an agreeable harmony. A 16C tower has beautiful frescoes showing farming scenes of the four seasons.

St-Savin, on the Gartempe river, 9km E, has a large, graceful Romanesque abbey church with what are said to be the richest and most complete medieval wall paintings in France. You can hire binoculars to see those in the high barrel vault. The crypt has superb frescoes at eye level. The Romanesque architecture, too, is excellent, with magnificent columns supporting upper galleries.

COGNAC
CHARENTE   Pop 21,000

The town which gave its name to the greatest brandy lies astride the Charente river, NW of Angoulême, and one of its biggest *chais* (cellars) producing Hennessy brandy lies astride it, too. You take a ferry from the main building to the maturing cellars. On visits to Hennessy you can see a film of brandy production, a museum of old instruments and barrels, and the world's largest reserves of old brandy still maturing in the *chais*. Microscopic fungi thriving on alcohol fumes have turned buildings in Cognac browny-black. Before modern ventilation, men working in the cellars used to get drunk breathing the fumes.

Cognac brandy is produced from white grape varieties, notably the St-Émilion, which has no connection with the Bordeaux wine of that name. The grapes of the Cognac region have a high acid content, and their juice ferments without addition of sugar or sulphur dioxide. The wine, hard and acidic, is distilled during the winter, over an open fire, very slowly; the liquid obtained is colourless, but after ageing in oak barrels it turns yellowish-brown. After three years in cask it may be blended, with the addition of sugar syrup, or decanted into old barrels for maturing. Most cognac brandies are from five to ten years old.

The best quality cognacs are from grapes in the Grande Champagne region, between Cognac, Jarnac and Segonzac, closely followed by those from Petite Champagne, a small area E of Cognac. Then come brandies from five other subregions, varying in quality.

Since 1795 there had been Otard brandy maturing in the cellars of what is left of the Château de Valois, birthplace and home when young of François I. Later it was a prison for Britons taken in Canada in the Seven Years' War; Their grafitti are still there. The town museum has two floors devoted to brandy. The old quarter of the town has some handsome 16–17C houses and a fine Romanesque fountain.

Boats run on the Charente from Whitsun to mid-Sept. to Saintes, passing the *prés* – lush water-meadows which nurture the cows that produce the renowned Charente butter, cream and cheese.

Jarnac, 15km E, is known for its brandy market, for Château Courvoisier, and for a notorious duel fought in 1547 between Gui Chabot, lord of Jarnac, and La Châtaigneraie, friend of Henri II. In front of the king, the queen (Catherine de

Cognac

Médicis) and the king's mistress (Diane de Poitiers), Chabot, who was losing, caddishly thrust his sword into his rival's hamstring. A stab in the back in France is still called "un coup de Jarnac".

Bassac abbey, 3km SE of Jarnac, was founded just after the year 1000, deconsecrated during the Revolution and only reconsecrated in 1947. The facade, Romanesque, was altered in the 15C for defensive reasons. Inside is a 13C statue of St Nicholas. Traditionally, girls kissed his feet to help them find a husband.

LOUDUN
VIENNE   Pop 8200

A strange little walled hilltop town with a Foulkes Nerra tower on top, 19km from Richelieu, Cardinal Richelieu's "new town". And there lies Loudun's interest. A local priest who made fun of Richelieu's project was found guilty of bewitching the nuns in a local convent and burned alive. Part of Loudun was pulled down. The all-powerful cardinal could hardly have guessed that just 300 years later English novelist Aldous Huxley would make the story of his ruthlessness the basis of a book called *The Devils of Loudun*, subsequently staged and filmed. This is another of the prosperous towns which never recovered from losing its Protestant artisans, as a result of the revocation of the Edict of Nantes. In the 17C Loudun had over 20,000 inhabitants.

MARAIS POITEVIN, LE

A strange, secretive marshland, drained by canals and dykes, stretching from just N of La Rochelle to S of Les Sables d'Olonne and inland to Niort. Monks started trying to drain the 'marsh of Poitou' back in the 13C but not until the 17C did Henri IV bring in a Dutch engineer to show how it could be done.

A hundred years ago a handful of people lived here. There are few roads, and flat-bottomed boats (*plattes*, propelled by poles) are still used for transporting people, cows and goats. Pastures beside dykes are lush and market gardens flourish, growing artichokes, courgettes, broad beans and haricots, but the people of the peaceful hamlets live as much by fishing for carp, perch, crayfish and tiny eels as dairy farming, though the cheese is well known. They will take you for peaceful *plattes* trips around the canals under willows and poplars.

Coulon is the best centre, with a charming square and a church dating back to Charlemagne. **Marans** is bigger but has factories, including one making cheese. A canal joins it to the sea.

Towards the coast, salt-meadow lamb is raised. At **L'Aiguillon-sur-Mer**, where there is a seabird sanctuary in the dunes, they grow flowers and raise mussels and oysters. The little resort of **La Tranche**, with a spacious beach, dunes and pines, has been noted for its garlic and onions. Recently they started to grow tulips and gladioli with great success. Les Floralies are held in the large park from Easter to June.

Le Marais Poitevin

MESCHERS-SUR-GIRONDE
CHARENTE-MARITIME Pop 1600

This pleasant seaside resort with a good beach, 11km from Royan, is sometimes crowded with excursionists who come to look at the Trous des Meschers – caves decorated with shells by prehistoric men, used later by pirates, refugees from religious persecution, and by fishermen. Most are nowadays summer residences, craft shops or restaurants.

MORTAGNE-SUR-GIRONDE
CHARENTE-MARITIME Pop 1100

The salmon arriving in the Gironde estuary to find spawning grounds are accompanied by big sturgeon, known here as *créa*. These are fished from this port for their flesh and their eggs for caviar, called *créat*. A Russian emigré taught the people of Mortagne and Talmont how to prepare caviar after World War I. Yachts use the port which has boat yards.

A mile inland is a hermitage of St-Martial, hewn out of rock by 4C monks. It has a chapel, other rooms and 75 stairs to a clifftop look-out. You can see the enormous Romanesque church at Talmont, on a cliff above the estuary.

NIORT
DEUX-SÈVRES Pop 60,000

The capital of Deux-Sèvres is a pleasant old provincial town, blazing with seasonal flowers. It was trading with England by AD900 and received its charter from Eleanor of Aquitaine in 1203. Two enormous towers and ramparts, left from a castle built by Henry II and Richard Lionheart, is now a museum of Poitou costumes. Mme de Maintenon was born here, probably in the Chaumont mansion.

Niort is the headquarters of one of France's biggest insurance companies. It grew rich, however, by tanning pelts imported from Canada. The breeches worn by the cavalry in the American Civil War were made in Niort. It is also an important agricultural centre with a big show in May.

OIRON
DEUX-SÈVRES Pop 800

The enormous Renaissance Château Le Gouffier in a simple village S of the Loudun-Thouars road should be better known if only because of its association with "Puss in Boots" (Le Chat Botté) by Charles Perrault. The castle's first owner, Claude Gouffier, Count Caravas, had such an extravagant life-style that he was the model for Perrault's Marquis de Carabas. He was also Royal Master of the Horse, and along the walls of the arcaded gallery in the left wing are inscribed the names of his finest horses. The château was later owned by Mme de Montespan, mistress of Louis XIV, after she was edged out of favour by her "friend" Mme Scarron. It has a fine gallery, with wall paintings of scenes from the *Iliad* and *Aeneid*, and a splendid Renaissance staircase.

OLÉRON, ÎLE D'
CHARENTE-MARITIME Pop 16,400

France's second largest isle after Corsica is reached by a 30km-long causeway with a toll, from the coast near Marennes. Not so attractive as Île de Ré (q.v.), it is popular with holidaymakers for its mild climate, huge beaches backed by pines, excellent fishing and oysters. Oyster-farming on the salt marshes is the main industry, and at **St-Pierre** they make the dry white wine to go with them. The chief port, **Le Château**, has 17C fortifications and a Vauban fort ruined by bombardment in 1945. An attractive little place, it is the biggest oyster port in France. St-Pierre has a 13C Lanterne des Morts and a house where Pierre Loti, author of *Pêcheur d'Islande (Icelandic Fishermen)*, spent his youth, being buried in its garden in 1923. **St-Trajan** is known for its three beaches, superb pine forest and mimosa in spring. **La Cotinière** is a charming little port. Inland are hamlets with green and white houses in the midst of vineyards, woods and marshes.

Île d'Oléron

PARTHENAY
DEUX-SÈVRES Pop 11,700

Parthenay, a medieval fortified town which was a halting place for pilgrims making for Compostela in Spain, is stacked up a hillside of pink granite above the river Thouet, and its old houses, churches and double ramparts look dramatic from the new bridge over the road which bypasses the old town. The pilgrims entered over the 13C arched bridge nearby. This leads straight to the old town, which has eight old churches. Today Parthenay is a market town, notably for cattle.

The citadel was one of those castles built in a night by the fairy Mélusine for her husband, whom she had met in the woods and married. Alas, she had not told him that as a punishment for killing her father she grew a dragon's tail every Saturday.

Parthenay

He was suspicious of her activities on that day and burst into her room, whereupon she flew out of the window and was never seen again. Of the castle, only three rampart towers remain.

POITIERS
VIENNE Pop 83,000

French history was changed around Poitiers. In AD507 Clovis, king of the Franks, supported by the church, defeated the Visigoths nearby. Then in 732 Charles Martel beat the invading Saracens.

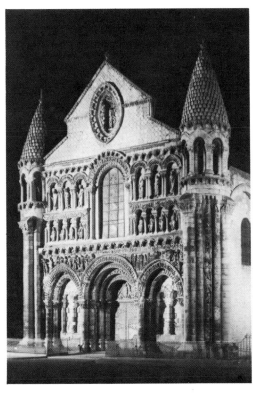

Notre-Dame-la-Grande, Poitiers

Poitiers became English when Eleanor of Aquitaine married Henry II in 1152. In 1356 the young Black Prince comprehensively defeated the French under King Jean le Bon in a bloody battle close by at Nouaillé-Maupertuis, taking twice as many prisoners as he had English troops, including the king himself; but du Guesclin took Poitiers back thirteen years later. Thereafter it remained French; and it was at the court of Jean de Berry, Count of Poitou, that Poitiers first became the city of art, frequented by sculptors, artists and painters. The university, founded in 1432, was surpassed in importance only by those of Paris and Lyon. Two great philosophers, Francis Bacon and René Descartes, were students here.

Poitiers suffered greatly in the Wars of Religion, being twice besieged, and did not really recover until after World War II, when new industries brought new life. Though situated between the beautiful valleys of the Clain and Boivre, it is not an attractive city but contains some gems of Romanesque architecture, with five major churches. Most famous is Notre-Dame-la-Grande on the market square, with a richly decorated facade, once brightly coloured, now damaged and blackened. The cathedral is largely Gothic, with 13C windows (one of the Crucifixion from 1170) and 13C stalls which are the oldest in France. Nearby is the oldest Christian building in France – the 4C baptistry of St-Jean, now a museum.

St-Hilaire-le-Grand, at the other end of the city, is an 11C building designed to take hundreds of pilgrims. The saint is buried in the crypt. Alas, a 19C facelift has done it no good.

The Palais de Justice contains part of the palace of the dukes of Aquitaine, including the magnificent 12C great hall and the 14C Maubergeon tower named after the mistress of one duke who imprisoned her there. Joan of Arc was cross-examined at the palace by learned doctors from Paris University after telling the Dauphin about her voices. They accepted her as genuine. It was in Poitiers that Calvin stayed and preached on his way to Geneva.

PONS
CHARENTE-MARITIME Pop 5400

This little hill-town was another pilgrims' halt on the way to Compostela, a seat of power until the Wars of Religion. The river Seugne, a tributary of the Charente, divides here into several branches. Across it is the beautiful Renaissance Château d'Ussons, dismantled in 1890 on its old site at Lonzac, near Cognac, moved here and rebuilt. Beyond it, the church at Avy has a 14C fresco of two pilgrims in traditional dress.

Southward is **Jonzac**, a trim little town astride the Seugne. Only a 15C postern and a tower are left of its castle. It is an important producer of the delicious Charente butter, and of Pineau de Charente, the pleasant aperitif made of young white or rosé wine mixed with brandy, said to have been invented by an innkeeper accidentally topping up a brandy cask with wine.

RÉ, ÎLE DE
CHARENTE-MARITIME Pop 10,300

Accessible by ferry and summer excursion boats from the old port of La Rochelle, this island, 28km by 5km, is noted for its market gardening, especially asparagus, fishing and oyster farming. It is a popular holiday resort, thanks to superb pine-shaded beaches and dunes, and families from La Rochelle take summer homes there.

Île de Ré

ROCHE COURBON, CHÂTEAU DE
CHARENTE-MARITIME

A fairy-story 15C château in woods near the Charente 16km NW of Saintes, it has a truly lovely setting, reflected in a long canal among French gardens with statues, carved yew trees, ponds and paths. Pierre Loti, who knew it as a ruin when he was a child, called it the 'Castle of the Sleeping Beauty' and appealed for it to be saved; in 1920 it was finally restored and its gardens reconstructed. There are remarkable, ornately painted ceilings and walls, especially in a bathroom at the base of a tower. An 18C clockwork spit still works.

ROCHEFORT
CHARENTE-MARITIME Pop 27,700

Colbert built Rochefort in 1666 as a naval base, arsenal and shipyard in defence against the English, and it is still a naval town, but also something of a spa. It stands on a great loop of the Charente by its estuary. Vauban's ramparts are mostly replaced by promenades. The naval museum in the 17C naval headquarters has models of ships built here. Most visitors come to see the museum devoted to Pierre Loti, the naval officer who wrote so superbly about sea life that he was elected to the Académie Française. He was born here, returned here later to live, the two houses being next door to each other. The Renaissance-style dining room has five Gobelin tapestries.

ROCHELLE, LA
CHARENTE-MARITIME Pop 78,000

La Rochelle is one of the most charming and picturesque cities in France, with a relaxed, cheerful and friendly atmosphere. A network of pedestrianized streets leads from the 14C walled Hôtel de Ville to the old fortified port, surrounded by lovely old buildings, cafés and fish restaurants. The port dates from the Middle Ages and is still protected by two towers, St-Nicholas and La Chaîne, from which a chain used to be lowered to prevent ships entering or leaving. La Lanterne, a 15C lighthouse, has views of town and port from a balcony half way up.

The old port, from which emigrants sailed for Montreal in the 18C, is used by small sardine boats and pleasure boats, a small newer harbour alongside by yachts, and a large newer basin by big fishing boats, and other merchant vessels. La Pallice, 5km W, created in 1900 in the lee of Île de Ré (q.v.), takes big merchant and naval ships. It has a long mole where the German battleship *Scharnhorst* was berthed in 1941 preparing for raids in the Atlantic. She was crippled by RAF bombers and limped back to Brest.

The town hall, grand and impressive, has 14C battlements and a Renaissance facade. The courtyard has a splendid staircase and statue of Henri IV. Leading to it is Grande Rue des Merciers, a street of fine old houses and arcaded pavements. The town possesses a multitude of small treasures, including a splendid Café de la Paix in Pl. Verdun, left over from the 19C, with ornate decor.

Melinda Messenger recalls pedalo escapes and honeymooning in the loo

I AM very restless and if I'm stuck in any one place for too long, I start to go stir crazy, so I really need a holiday for a change of scene. Wayne and I never plan a holiday in advance. It's always completely last minute and sometimes we've booked the flights only a couple of hours before check in. I'm always worried that if you arrange something months in advance, when the time actually comes you might not want to go any more. We went on this two-week trip to Grand Cayman, in the Caribbean, which we'd booked six months beforehand, but when we were due to leave, I didn't really feel like a holiday at all. It was a fantastically beautiful place, but our hearts weren't in it, so we came home early.

We were married a couple of years ago in Bali. We had two weddings: a Buddhist ceremony and then a civil wedding to make it all legal. The Buddhist one was in a temple and I didn't have a clue what was going on, because the whole thing was in Indonesian. I could have been saying anything for all I knew, but everything looked very nice. They wrapped us up in a gold cloth and tied ribbons on our fingers and it was all very relaxed.

We were married in the south,

in Sanur, and after the wedding we'd planned to go up into the mountains around Ubud. We'd found this beautiful villa, overlooking a ravine and a sacred mountain, and it was really romantic and perfect — but I got food poisoning and spent most of my honeymoon in the toilet.

After that, we made some trips up into the mountains — I remember it was quite strange, because people kept recognising me. We'd be in the middle of the Indonesian rainforest, and people would just stare. I kept thinking I must have something on my face. In America I get people coming up to me a lot, but it usually turns out they think I'm Pamela Anderson.

We had an awful trip to a Sandals resort in Jamaica once. There were lots of Americans there who just wanted to link up and do things together all the time — we spent most of the time trying to get away from them. We even went out to sea on a pedalo to get away from one couple and they followed us out there!

When I'm filming Fort Boyard, an adventure game show, we stay just outside La Rochelle. The area around there is beautiful and quite a well-kept secret. My favourite place is Châtelaillon-Plage, which has a lovely harbour and this amazing long sandy beach. Apparently, they made it longer and

sandier than it originally was
bringing in more sand fro
another beach down the coast.

My idea of heaven is walkin
— and fish and chips. We've ju
come back from Devon, where w
had a perfect holiday, going fo
long rambling walks across Dart
moor and finishing up in the pub.
We've got one of those baby back-
packs for Morgan, so we'd put
him in it, take the dogs and set off
for four or five hours a day.

I suppose I've got quite a spar-
tan streak when it comes to holidays — probably a legacy of family holidays I had as a child. We'd
always go camping on the Gower
peninsula or to a caravan site at
Harlin Bay in Cornwall. I still
think there's nothing to beat a
camping holiday. It feels like a
real adventure.

Before we had Morgan, we
would take off whenever we
wanted and go anywhere in the
world. We went to Jamaica, New
York, Sri Lanka, wherever we fan
cied, but now we can't really g
so far afield because flights wit
toddler are a bit of a nightm

La Rochelle

La Rochelle belonged twice to England. In the 17C it became rich and then, under Calvin's influence, became a Protestant stronghold. In 1573 the duke of Anjou (later Henri III) besieged it unsuccessfully for six months, losing 20,000 men, some to a machine which hurled boiling pitch and oil. Richelieu saw it as a threat to a united France and in 1627 persuaded Louis XIII to besiege the town. The Protestants were led by a fanatical and brave mayor, Jean Gulton. The architect Clément Métezeau had a huge dam built to cut off the town from supplies from the sea. The incompetent duke of Buckingham, who was supposed to bring an English relieving force, got no further than the Île de Ré.

When Richelieu finally entered the town after fifteen months, the houses were full of corpses. Only 5000 people out of 28,000 survived starvation, but La Rochelle remained Protestant. Today there is still a fairly large Protestant community which takes particular pride in the town's former tribulations and triumphs.

Apart from being the fifth biggest fishing port in France, La Rochelle builds ships, trains and cars. It is also increasingly popular for holidays. One of the attractions is the provision, free of charge both to residents and visitors, of the famous yellow bicycles, introduced by the mayor Michel Crépeau as part of a scheme to improve traffic conditions. The town beach is rather uninteresting but there are superb sands and dunes on the Île de Ré, accessible by car ferry from the old port, and a good beach at **Châtelaillon-Plage** 12km S.

A new marina is at **St-Minimes**, just S of the town. Every two years, over 1000 yachts from many nations take part in the Plymouth-La Rochelle race. There is a sailing week at Whitsun and a cavalcade and fête in May.

ROYAN
CHARENTE-MARITIME   Pop 18,100

Nothing can stop this modern beach resort spreading all along the 12km of fine clean sand of the Gironde estuary. It has everything going for it – south-facing, protected from Atlantic breakers by sandbanks, sheltered on the land side by a ring of pine forests, a splendid harbour luring yachts, two casinos, and curative thermal baths.

The fin-de-siècle resort was almost totally destroyed by air raids in 1944–5 when retreating German troops dug in here. Everything is new, including a spectacular and original church in concrete with a 65m belfry.

It has many hotels, holiday apartments, caravan and camp sites, and festivals and shows throughout the season. A Festival of Contemporary Art is held at Easter.

A road NW takes you through **Coubre forest** of pines along the coast beside Nazi blockhouses and wild Atlantic waves. By climbing 300 steps, you get a fine view from the top of Coubre lighthouse.

ST-JEAN-D'ANGÉLY
CHARENTE-MARITIME   Pop 9500

A Benedictine abbey was built in the 9C to accommodate the supposed head of John the Baptist (there is another at Amiens) and a town arose on the hillside above the river Boutonne to house and feed the pilgrims. It was a convenient day's walk from Saintes (27km). It received its charter under the English in 1199. Much was destroyed during the Wars of Religion, when it was a Protestant stronghold, but there are charming old houses in its narrow, winding streets. The Gothic church which was to have replaced the abbey was never finished. The beautiful Renaissance fountain came from a nearby château. St-Jean is a pleasant town, now producing biscuits and eau-de-vie, and a busy farming centre. The château of **Dampierre-sur-Boutonne** (17km) is on a river island; early 16C, it has two galleries, one above the other, the upper one being richly decorated.

SAINTES
CHARENTE-MARITIME   Pop 27,500

This ordinary-looking town across the river Charente is rewarding for anyone interested in history. Capital of a Gaulish tribe, it became an important Roman city. The 1C Roman arena is one of the oldest that remains, holding 20,000 spectators. The Arch of Germanicus, carrying dedications to Germanicus, the Emperor Tiberius and his son Drusus, was originally on a Roman bridge and was moved in 1842 when the bridge was demolished. Prosper Mérimée, inspector of Historic Monuments and author of *Carmen*, saved it. The archaeological museum nearby has some priceless Roman remains, well presented.

The old town, on the left bank behind broad quays lined with fine 17C houses, has a maze of little medieval streets. The Flamboyant Gothic 15C cathedral of St-Pierre has an unfinished 75m-high bell tower. The Dupuy-Mestreau museum shows local costumes and furniture and the Fine Arts museum has a painting on wood by Breughel and many Dutch, Flemish and French works. Over the river, the 12C church of the Abbaye aux Dames is beautiful, with a magnificent crypt. Its multi-storied bell tower is topped by a pinecone roof. The abbey, once a school for noble young ladies, among them Mme de Montespan, witty and outrageous mistress of Louis XIV, is still being restored.

Saintes has a good horse stud (Haras) with English thoroughbreds, Anglo-Arabs and Norman trotters (open mid-July–end Feb.).

MASSIF CENTRAL

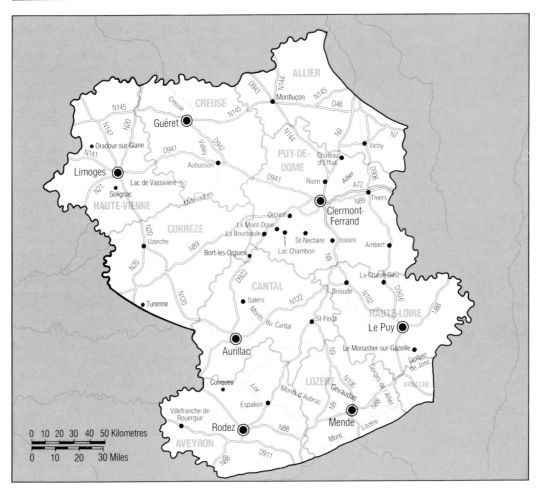

The great granite uplands of the Massif Central stand firmly between the north and the south of France. Difficult terrain for travellers in the past, these ancient hills – far older than the taller Alps or Pyrenees – have preserved an identity, and a rustic simple way of life which still endures. Throughout history, remoteness has protected the mountain rulers and given them a measure of independence. The Arvernes tribe of Gauls, under their chief Vercingetorix, whose capital was at Gergovia (very near the modern capital Clermont), proved troublesome to the Romans. During the feudal period, too, the local barons, many of them tyrannical, cruel and unrestrained, were beyond the control of the French crown. Not until the 17th century was the whole province joined to the kingdom, and even then, the subservience meant little. In 1665, Louis XIV attempted to 'try' the local *seigneurs* for their arrogance and excesses, in the 'Grand Jours d'Auvergne' at Clermont. However, proceedings were ridiculed by the accused, and the king's officers, unable to enforce sentences on those found guilty, ended up 'executing' pictures of the tyrants. Even this, though, proved a great delight for the populace.

Today the mountains are more easily accessible, and provide the visitor with endless opportunities for touring in green unspoiled country, for sampling the hearty cuisine of the region, and for walking, riding and sailing. In winter the hills are snow-covered and skiing is popular, while summer temperatures can be surprisingly hot. At all times of year, have a waterproof handy.

The most distinctive feature of this landscape is the *puy*, literally 'peak', a steep hill rising abruptly from the ground. Some are actually mountains, such as Puy Sancy, highest point in the Massif Central, but many others needles of rock, mounds or pyramids, jutting strangely out of the earth. All of them are remnants of volcanoes. For until as recently as 4000 years ago, the region was volcanically active – perhaps it still is.

There are three main *puy* areas. The Monts Dômes, in the north of the region, more than a hundred hills, domed and most with cratered summits, still resemble exactly what they are: small volcanoes which were erupting at the time, say, that animals were being sketched inside the Dordogne caves. The Monts Dore, south of them, are higher, weirder vestiges of older volcanoes which have been worn away by millennia of wind and weather. The Monts de Cantal, in the south, are even older, and the high peaks and pasture-covered rolling hills give little hint they are all fragments of a single unimaginably gigantic volcano which stood here. In Aurillac, capital of the Cantal, the Maison des Volcans, a permanent exhibition on volcanic activity, makes a fascinating visit. The Regional Nature Park of the Volcanoes of the Auvergne, largest of the French 'natural parks' (325,000 hectares), encompasses all three areas. The park is crisscrossed with footpaths, bridle tracks, and rivers.

Auvergne is the heart of the Massif Central. The least accessible part until recently, it remains a refuge of tradition and tranquillity. Nowadays it is allowed to take in the old Bourbon country, flatter country to its north, for administrative purposes, but the true Auvergne is an upland territory, hardly cultivated, and populated with a tough, self-reliant peasantry. One of the peculiar features of Auvergne (because it is volcanic) is the number of spas, thought to have been a major incentive for the Romans in their efforts to conquer the province. Most of the spa resorts, which flourished in the last century, preserve a sedate, fin-de-siècle atmosphere. Many still have thousands of visitors each year – tens of thousands in the case of Vichy – and the French Department of Health evidently accepts the value of the mineral waters, since many *curistes*, as they are called, are being reimbursed 70 per cent of the cost of their treatment by the Sécurité Sociale.

But above all, this is a village region. Apart from the spa resorts, and the ever-expanding city of Clermont-Ferrand, home of Michelin and much other industry, most communities are essentially small farmers occupied with rearing livestock and making cheese. Long-established traditions are kept very much alive: each village has its festival, usually religious in inspiration, but often with colourful processions, like the one at Estaing, where everyone puts on fancy dress. Sometimes couples, wearing clogs, can be seen doing the *bourrée* folk dance, accompanied by musicians on the *cabrette* (a sort of bagpipe), *vielle* (a decorated hand-held hurdy-gurdy), and fiddle. Livestock fairs, often held in quite out-of-the-way places, attract crowds of country people and have an exciting atmosphere. Laguiole and Nesbinals in the Monts d'Aubrac have especially big markets, and animals being driven to them often clog the hill roads.

The lack of remunerative employment, together with higher expectations in the modern world, has encouraged many youngsters to set off to France's big cities in search of work. It is said that there are more Auvergnats in Paris than in Auvergne – but that even there, they stick together and try to preserve their old customs. Most Auvergnats are conservative and, by tradition at least, deeply religious. Even today, villagers are proud if their parish church contains the relics of a saint (there seem to be a great many saints in this part of the world), and one of the most intriguing objects of veneration in these hills is the Black Virgin. Many miracles (indeed any fortunate events) are attributed to these ancient statues, entirely black, often of unknown age and origin, representing a grim Madonna seated rigidly upright, with a Child,

sitting equally stiffly on her knee and looking more like a small adult than an infant.

The Romanesque church architecture of the Auvergne developed a very rounded style, with domes, circular arches, and round chapels off the apse. An even more remarkable characteristic of many of them is the patterned decoration of the facade, achieved by using stones of different colours. The designs have a Byzantine look about them, which comes as a surprise in such an isolated region so far from the influences of the Eastern Church or of Islam. Le Puy, in its cathedral of Notre-Dame and church of St-Michel d'Aiguilhe, has two excellent examples.

A heavy and substantial type of cuisine has developed in the Massif Central, using local produce. Some of the village cheeses are seen at every market in France – St-Nectaire, Bleu d'Auvergne, and above all Cantal. Ham is worked into most dishes . . . mixed with cabbage to make a traditional soup, or with lentils and raw vegetables to make a *salade Auvergnat* . . . and also goes into a dozen kinds of sausage. Cantal, in particular, is noted for farmhouse-style dishes, such as *tripoux*, stuffed sheep's feet wrapped in pieces of sheep's stomach. Easier perhaps to stick to the trout and salmon from the region's many rivers.

The gentle hills of Limousin, in the west of the Massif Central, beyond the Dordogne river, have a slightly different character. For one thing, the people of this region are considered in France to be the very epitome of warm and generous, down-to-earth peasant stock. Their cookery follows suit, just as filling but more refined than that of Auvergne, and served in good measure. Liver pâtés (made rather cruelly by force-feeding) are the speciality of Limousin farmers. Often pâtés are mixed with chestnuts, or with truffles, those dense black underground mushrooms which are found in this area. The prestigious (because terribly expensive) truffle, and the unassuming chestnut are both very versatile, and make regular appearances in poultry dishes, sauces, omelettes, and even in pastry.

Aperitifs and liqueurs made from bilberries, gentian or *verveine* are a mountain speciality (especially around Le Puy), but not much wine can be produced (at least, not from grapes, though occasionally dessert wines made from other fruits are seen). Indeed the traditional drink in some parts used to be cider. But fortunately the Massif benefits from being surrounded by good vineyard regions – Beaujolais, Bergerac, Rhône valley – and likes to adopt all these as its own local wine. Fruits grow in plenty, and cherry or bilberry flans make a tasty dessert. The most delicious of them is *cla-fouti*, a sort of extra-light cherry cake, invented in Limousin and eaten everywhere in the Massif Central.

Writers and artists who loved solitude and quiet unspoiled country have found their way here. George Sand, especially, wrote much about the Massif Central landscapes, the Creuse valley which she loved, and the uplands of the Haute-Loire, '. . . a soil cut up with deep ravines, crossed in every way by lofty walls of lava, and furrowed by numerous torrents'. And it was from the airy hills of the Haute-Loire that Robert Louis Stevenson, who longed 'to get down off the feather bed of civilization', set out, accompanied by his donkey Modestine, to travel these hills on foot.

ALLIER, GORGES DE L'
HAUTE-LOIRE

The Allier winds through the Auvergne from the uplands of Lozère in the S to join the Loire on the borders of Burgundy. Though sometimes in rocky gorges, sometimes in broad watermeadows or fertile plains (Limagne), its character changes little: clean, fast-flowing and shallow, on a stony bed. The Clermont-Nîmes railway line runs beside the Allier for much of the distance, giving superb views; it can be explored in closer detail by following the minor roads which go from one riverside village to another. The most spectacular stretch is the gorge between **Chapeauroux** and **Brioude**, taking in several attractive towns and villages: **Monistrol d'Allier** (good views), **Prades** (remarkable location), **Langeac** (bustling country town with interesting church) and **Lavoûte-Chilhac** (riverside village with 11C bridge).

AMBERT
PUY-DE-DÔME   Pop 8000

Busy Ambert in the Dore valley has an interesting town centre with some unusual features. The 15C church of St-Jean is all in Gothic style except for one Renaissance tower. Another oddity is the circular town hall. Composer Emmanuel Chabrier was born here in 1841. In the 15–17C Ambert was devoted to paper-making, with over 300 mills in the area. Hand-made paper is still produced here, and 4km away at **Moulin Richard-le-Bas**, traditional paper-making methods can be watched by visitors.

AUBRAC, MONTS DE
AVEYRON

Vast numbers of cattle are raised in the pasture-covered Aubrac hills, together with the herds of sheep brought up for the summer along ancient drove roads. Impressive livestock markets are held in the main villages of **Nasbinals** and smaller **Laguiole** (pronounced Layole). Laguiole is also noted for cheese and for distinctive ivory-handled cutlery made by craftsmen. Other interesting villages are **St-Urcize**, **Prades d'Aubrac**, **Aubrac** and – just across the river Lot – **Espalion** (q.v.).

AUBUSSON
CREUSE   Pop 6200

Famous since the 15C for its carpet and tapestry-making, brought here by Flemish weavers, Aubusson, in the steep valley of the river Creuse, still prides itself on this craft. Large exhibitions of ancient and modern tapestries are given every summer. At its height, the industry was dealt an irreparable blow by the revocation of the Edict of Nantes, 1685, since most weavers were Protestants and had to emigrate immediately. However, it did not die completely, had a moment of prosperity in the 18C, and has experienced another revival in the 20C. The Maison du Vieux Tapissier is an old workshop preserved in a 15C house (off Grande Rue), but newer workshops actually in production can also be visited and purchases made directly from the craftsmen. Not quite all the present-day hangings consist of brightly coloured cheap and cheerful designs – a few stand out for their traditional skill and complex themes. Aubusson retains a small attractive old quarter around Pl. de la Libération, a 16C bridge, and ruins of its hilltop castle.

Little **Felletin**, 10km S, started tapestry-weaving before Aubusson, and this is still, together with diamond-cutting, the town's main industry. Felletin has the greater reputation for modern tapestry (summer exhibition in the 15C church), and the largest ever made – designed by Sutherland for Coventry Cathedral – was made here.

Aubusson

AURILLAC
CANTAL   Pop 33,200

Capital of the mountainous Cantal *département*, Aurillac is a modern town thriving on its big cattle and cheese markets, and has an important umbrella industry. Leading off the large main square are the few remaining streets of the old quarter, much damaged in the Wars of Religion. The abbey church of St-Géraud has been restored, and several Renaissance mansions have survived in good condition. The 16C Maison Consulaire contains the Musée du Vieil Aurillac. The town and river Jordanne look picturesque from the Pont Rouge, near which a statue by d'Angers commemorates the local shepherd Gerbert – who became Sylvester II, the first French pope (AD999), and introduced Arabic numerals to western Europe.

Musée Rames, S of the square, displays local archaeology and traditional Cantal country life. Above the town, the reconstructed Château St-Étienne has a fascinating museum on volcanic activity, the Maison des Volcans, inside the original 11C keep, and affords panoramic views.

BORT-LES-ORGUES
CORRÈZE   Pop 5000

Bort 'the organ pipes', on the main D922, takes its name from the spectacular cylindrical formations in the 3km-long, 100m-high escarpment on the other side of the river Dordogne, best seen from the S side of town. Though plain and industrial, Bort is a useful halt with several inexpensive hotels and restaurants. To the N is the immense, 120m-high Bort barrage and hydroelectric power station, largest of the dams constructed to tame the Dordogne.

BOURBOULE, LA
PUY-DE-DÔME   Pop 2400

A 19C spa on the rushing young river Dordogne, high in the *puy* country, La Bourboule is a cheerful town. Its speciality is allergies, and the treatment of children; its waters are exceptionally rich in . . . arsenic. Many buildings have magnificently gaudy early-20C exteriors, especially the casino and the silver-domed Grands Thermes. Numerous pink and blue bridges cross the river. The church of St-Joseph was built in 1888, but in pure Auvergnat Romanesque style, using ancient building techniques. La Bourboule has many sports facilities and is an excellent base for walks and drives in the Monts Dore (q.v.).

From the beautiful town park a cable car goes in just four minutes to the wooded **Plateau de Charlannes** (1250 m; good views and walks). In winter, La Bourboule is a cross-country ski resort.

BRIOUDE
HAUTE-LOIRE   Pop 7900

Brioude, a bustling old market town overlooking the broad fertile valley of the Allier, has attractive old houses and is noted for its salmon – trapped by a dam 2km upriver. The basilica of St-Julien in the town centre is the largest of Auvergne's Romanesque churches. The W front and towers are 19C reconstructions, but the rest dates from the 12–13C. It has fine side porches and doors, and superb interior chapels, walls patterned with the natural colours of the stone, and a lovely cobbled floor. There are 13C frescoes and a strange 14C statue of Christ as a leper.

Rustic little **Lavaudieu**, 9.5km SE, has beautiful remains of a Benedictine abbey with 14C frescoes.

CANTAL, MONTS DU
CANTAL

The *puys* of the Cantal, even the peaks of **Puy Mary** (1787m) and **Plomb de Cantal** (1855m) are mere fragments of a single gigantic volcano which, geologists believe, once existed here. Some of the hills are jagged and stark, others rounded. The climb to the summit of Puy Mary is not very difficult (from the hamlet of Vaisses it takes about 20 minutes). From the top is a fine panorama.

A 'buron', Puy Mary

Cantal is important cattle and cheese country. (Cantal is one of the cheapest and most popular cheeses in France, resembling cheddar.) 'Burons', simple stone huts in which the cheese is made when the cows are being left out on their summer pasture, can be seen on the hills.

Many of the area's old towns are interesting. **Mauriac**, on the fringes of Cantal, is small and pretty, with black lava houses and a Romanesque basilica, Notre-Dame des Miracles. **Salers** (q.v.) is an unusual village at the start of remarkable mountain drives to Puy Mary or Aurillac. The **Routes des Crêtes** follows the Jordanne valley through a striking landscape. The N122, following the Cère valley, passes through several small mountain towns (with cheap accommodation and restaurants): **Vic-sur-Cère**, **Thiézac**, skiers' and walkers' resort **Lioran**, from which there is a footpath to **Puy Griou** (1694m), and attractive **Murat** above the river Alagnon.

CHAISE-DIEU, LA
HAUTE-LOIRE   Pop 950

Situated 1000m up, above the forested hills of the Haute-Loire, the village of La Chaise-Dieu had an important Benedictine abbey which Protestants almost completely destroyed. Lovely cloisters survive, as does much of the large and sturdy 14C abbey church of St-Robert, in an unadorned Gothic style. Musical evenings are held here during the summer.

The choir, curiously, is larger than the nave, and contains the church's best features: fine 15C stalls, 16C tapestries and the marble tomb of Pope Clement VI, one of the abbey's monks. Drawn on the wall, an exceptional, 26m-long *Danse Macabre* depicts chillingly the ghostly, grinning Dead plucking the arms of the self-satisfied Living.

CLERMONT-FERRAND
PUY-DE-DÔME   Pop 151,100

Miles of bleak industrial and residential suburbs surround Clermont-Ferrand, major city of the Auvergne and headquarters of the multinational Michelin tyre company. The main N9 does not penetrate this outer layer and Clermont has acquired an unflattering reputation among through-travellers. Yet at the centre of the city, on a slight hill, is a fascinating jumble of old streets and squares with fountains, buildings of dark volcanic lava, and many superb houses of the 15–18C. Several of these grand mansions have courtyards open to the public: note particularly those in Rue des Gras, Rue du Port, Rue Pascal and Rue des Chaussetiers. Inside the Renaissance Hôtel Fontfreyde, the Musée du Ranquet contains an impressive collection of Renaissance and medieval art, as well as a display of items of everyday use from the 19C.

On the edge of Jardin Lecoq, the city centre's delightful park, are the Musée Lecoq (natural history) and the Musée Bargoin (archaeology, with good Gallo-Roman exhibits). Busy tree-lined boulevards encircle the central area, Blvd Gergovia (tourist office) being named for the nearby battle site where Caesar's troops were trounced by the proudly remembered Vercingetorix. A rousing statue of the warrior Gaul stands in Pl. de Jaude, the large main square.

At the heart of old Clermont rises the 13C Gothic cathedral of Notre-Dame-de-l'Assomption, a vast, sombre edifice of dark grey volcanic stone from nearby Volvic. Of exceptional technical finesse, very tall inside, with slender columns and lovely stained glass, the building was left incomplete until Viollet-le-Duc added the W front in 1855. A Romanesque crypt belongs to an earlier church on the site. Near the cathedral, in Pl. de la Poterne (excellent view of modern Clermont), the 16C Fontaine d'Amboise is laden with Gothic and Renaissance decoration.

Notre-Dame-du-Port, a century older than the cathedral, makes a striking contrast. Pure Auvergnat Romanesque, of warm ochre blocks and round stones from the Allier, with fine capitals, excellent sculpture and stained glass, it is an exceptionally beautiful church. Its Black Virgin heads a procession through the streets in May.

Outside this church, in 1095, in what is now Pl. Delille, Pope Urban II preached the First Crusade.

Montferrand was Clermont's rival and neighbour until 1731, when the two were amalgamated to form Clermont-Ferrand. Though now swept up in the modern suburbs, the small area of old Montferrand preserves numerous majestic 15–16C dwellings. Royat, on the city's W edge, higher and cooler than Clermont, is a pleasant spa, with

attractive gardens, Roman baths, and an 11C fortified church.

Plateau de Gergovie (7km S) has been considerably excavated to reveal details of Vercingetorix's battle in 52BC.

Immediately W of Clermont-Ferrand are the **Monts Dômes**, an assembly of *puys*, remnants of volcanoes, only 4000 years old. The highest, and oldest of these 112 separate peaks is the **Puy de Dôme** (1465m) with a magnificent ruined Roman temple to Mercury on top. It can be ascended by a hair-raising toll road or by an old Roman footpath. There are phenomenal views from the summit – said to take in eleven *départements*. The scientific philosopher Blaise Pascal, born at Clermont in 1623, proved his theories about air pressure by conducting barometric experiments at the top and bottom of the mountain. The Monts Dômes form part of the Regional Nature Park of the Volcanoes of the Auvergne, extending over a considerable proportion of western Auvergne. Taking in almost all the country from Clermont-Ferrand to Aurillac, it is the largest of the French natural parks.

Within the lunar setting of the Monts Dômes, there are rustic villages and tiny roads skirting the hills, with extraordinary views. **Pontgibaud** is a quiet village on the Siourle; it has a restored 12–15C château. **Lac d'Aydat**, in the southern part of the region, is a shallow lake naturally formed by lava blocking a river – it has become a popular spot for anglers. The village of **Volvic**, at the bottom of Puy de la Nugère in the N of the area, has interesting underground quarries, from which was mined the strong dark stone used to build many houses and churches in the region, including Clermont's cathedral. Volvic is also noted for its bottled spring water, sold all over France.

CONQUES
AVEYRON   Pop 400

Remarkably situated on a steep hillside above the river Dourdou in the glorious green countryside of northern Aveyron, the small village of Conques zealously preserves the picturesque cobbled streets, restored 14C houses and 12C town gates, which help to charm the coachloads of tourists. The village encircles the beautiful 11C Romanesque church of Ste-Foy, part of a former 8C abbey. In 1837, when Prosper Mérimée passed this way, the church was in ruins, with no roof, and collapsing walls. Thanks to his orders, it has been entirely rebuilt, and is now an exceptional building, with a high nave, a lofty choir, a triforium of twin arches, fine capitals and, on the superb W door, an impressively detailed 12C tympanum of The Last Judgment, with faint hints of its original painted colouring. (By contrast, the modern stained glass is uninteresting.) The treasury, one of the richest in France, contains quantities of jewels, gold and fine tapestries. Its centrepiece is a small statue of Ste Foy, seated in a chair, and with a curiously unprepossessing appearance, the entire object encrusted with gold and jewels. The head of the statue, dating from about the 5C, is said to contain the skull of the child saint herself. Amazingly, the statue was *stolen* from the church at Agen in the 9C by a monk who brought it to Conques –

Notre-Dame-du-Port, Clermont-Ferrand

Ste-Foy, Conques

and the theft then apparently justified by a succession of miracles attributed to Ste Foy!

The shell motif in the church stonework signifies that this was a halt for pilgrims on their way to St-James of Compostela, although it was also a pilgrims' destination in its own right.

CREUSE VALLEY
CREUSE

'Rien n'est plus beau que la Creuse', said George Sand of this river, which features in many of her novels. Claude Monet perhaps agreed, for he frequently painted here. Running in a winding ravine, the Creuse passes through a succession of tiny villages with spectacular views. Narrow roads make superb drives from one to another. The most rewarding section (about 46km) is from pretty **Argenton** to **Crozant**, a town long popular with artists. Along the way are ruined hilltop fortifications, especially impressive at **Châteaubrun** and at Crozant, where the huge castle was known as The Key to Limousin.

EFFIAT, CHÂTEAU D'
PUY-DE-DÔME

On the road from Aigueperse to Vichy, near the village of Effiat, this 17C château was built by one of Richelieu's ministers, the ambassador who arranged the marriage of Charles I of England to Henrietta Maria. He died before occupying it, his son was beheaded for treason, and his grandson was accused of poisoning the sister-in-law of Louis XIV. The château, handsomely furnished and with formal gardens, stands in a large park.

ESPALION
AVEYRON   Pop 4900

Espalion is built on both sides of the river Lot, the older part being on the S bank. A 13C bridge of attractive pink sandstone, now reserved for pedestrians, crosses the river. Hilltop ruins of a feudal castle, the Calmont d'Olt, dominate the town. The balconies of old riverside houses picturesquely overhang the water, and many of the town's cottages and houses have much character with their steep stone roofs and outside staircases. On the river bank a small Renaissance château, Le Vieux Palais, built 1572, contains a museum of local art and archaeology.

Perse, 1km S, has an attractive 11C church

made of pink sandstone, with a roughly carved tympanum of the Last Judgment, and an arcaded belfry. Nearby **Bouzols** is a village situated precariously on both sides of the canyon of the river Dourdou; it has an interesting church. **St-Come-d'Olt** is a fascinating fortified village, on the river Lot.

At tranquil riverside **Estaing**, 10km W, old village houses cluster around the rock on which stands the impressive 15–16C château, with its tall keep. Once home of the noble Estaing family (former president Giscard d'Estaing is a part-descendant), it is now occupied by a religious community. A Gothic bridge of five arches, with lovely simplicity, crosses the Lot. The first Sun. in July sees the lively Fête de St-Fleuret, when local people parade through the streets in fancy dress as saints, pilgrims and biblical characters.

Further W, **Entraygues**, in a richly cultivated setting at the confluence of the Truyère and the Lot, has a 13C bridge and a pleasant old quarter.

Espalion

GERBIER DE JONC
LOZÈRE

Gerbier de Jonc (1551m), a conical mountain rising above the hills of the Ardèche, gives a striking view across the surrounding wild and rocky country. The Alps can be seen if conditions are clear. A rough path leads to the top from the D122 (about 25 mins. each way). This is quite a popular excursion, perhaps partly also because of the mountain's odd and appealing name, of uncertain origin.

GÉVAUDAN
LOZÈRE

Much of the Lozère *département* was formerly known as Gévaudan, with Mende as its capital. The area acquired tremendous notoriety in 1764 as a result of several strange killings in open country attributed to a mysterious animal called the Bête du Gévaudan. The victims were horribly mutilated and partly eaten. Perhaps it was a wolf – several were shot in the effort to halt the Bête's activities – or perhaps it was a rogue bear (there were a few left in the Massif Central at that time), yet the suspicion remains that it might even have been a human 'beast', because all the victims were women, or in a few cases, children. In 1767, by which time over fifty people had fallen prey to the Bête, the deaths came to an abrupt end shortly after yet another wolf had been killed.

At **Marvejols**, a handsome old Protestant town with three fine city gates, there is a fanciful statue of the Bête du Gévaudan in Pl. des Cordeliers by the sculptor Auriscate. N of the town, the Parc du Gévaudan (open summer only) is an extraordinary wildlife park in rough mountain country, where animals now rare in Europe live and breed in near-complete liberty. They include buffalo, bear, wolves . . . and others.

GUÉRET
CREUSE Pop 16,600

Guéret (prefecture of the Creuse *département*) is a modern town near the beautiful Creuse valley. Its municipal museum, in lovely gardens, has exceptional displays of gold and silver ware, fine enamel and chinaware, a curious collection of 500 dolls in national costumes, and other rooms devoted to sculpture, painting and local archaeology. 17C Aubusson tapestries hang on the staircase walls. The 15–16C Gothic Hôtel des Moneyroux, one of the few relics of the town's past, is used for an annual exhibition of modern Aubusson tapestries.

Just 5km S is the beginning of the **Forest of Chabrières**, a rocky area covered with beech, birch and pine trees. **Moutier d'Ahun**, 16km SE, is a really remarkable 12C abbey church with much exquisite 17C woodcarving. Visit also the 12C village church of neighbouring **Ahun**.

ISSOIRE
PUY-DE-DÔME Pop 15,400

Issoire, a Protestant town virtually destroyed in the Wars of Religion ('Ici fut Issoire' – 'here was Issoire' – said a sign erected in 1577), thrives today by producing small aircraft and aluminium goods. An old quarter survives. In the Maison des Échevins, an exhibition traces Issoire's violent history. The 12C Romanesque church of St-Austremoine has an unusual square E end decorated with zodiac signs. The interior, though rather spoiled by some mid-19C paintwork, has excellent capitals, a 15C fresco and simple crypt.

Interesting villages nearby, to N and E, in the **Monts de Livradois** include **Vic-le-Comte**, **Usson** and **Nonette**, each with its château and handsome Gothic church. **Billom**, 20km N, once noted for its ancient university, now produces materials for the construction industry, and also specializes in growing and processing garlic. The church of St-Cerneuf, a Gothic edifice with fascinating 13–14C murals, dominates the central quarter. Surrounding streets and houses date from the Middle Ages – note especially Rue des Boucheries. The 15C Maison de Chapitre was a building of the historic university.

LIMOGES
HAUTE-VIENNE Pop 144,000

A large modern manufacturing town on the river Vienne, prefecture of the Haute-Vienne *département*, Limoges dates back to Gallo-Roman times. A large Roman arena has been uncovered in the public gardens, Jardin d'Orsay. The town suffered enormous destruction through the Hundred Years'

War, the Wars of Religion, the Revolution and World War II. A tradition of fine porcelain and enamelling has become a major industry, along with shoemaking, and there are support-industries for uranium mining. Porcelain remains its outstanding feature, with many shops selling excellent examples. Factories can be visited, and in the Musée Adrien Dubouche (by Jardin d'Orsay) an exceptional collection traces the worldwide history of chinaware. Enamelling is still done by craftsmen in their own small workshops (several around Rue des Tanneries and Rue Raspail).

In the Middle Ages, two rival districts developed – the *cité*, centred on the cathedral of St-Étienne, and the *ville*, around the church of St-Martial. The 13C cathedral, combining Romanesque and Gothic, is impressively spacious, with much good sculpture and stained glass, and a wonderfully carved rood screen. Around the chancel are three interesting tombs. The neighbouring 18C Archbishop's Palace, in splendid formal gardens, contains the municipal museum in which Limousin enamels from the 12C to the present-day are exhibited, together with local archaeology, and two pictures by Renoir, who was born here in 1841. Another local artist was Étienne de Silhouette, born 1709, who developed the style of drawing which has taken his name.

The *ville* district has kept more of its old character, with steep narrow streets, open vegetable market, and interesting churches. St Martial, who introduced Christianity to Limoges in AD250, is buried in a partly-4C crypt in Pl. de la République, centre of the *ville*. The oldest parts are Quartier Abbessaille, near the 13C Pont St-Étienne, and Rue de la Boucherie, in which there are still many butchers' shops, and the amazingly richly decorated chapel of St-Aurélien, dedicated to the powerful medieval Butchers' Fraternity.

The church of St-Pierre-de-Queyroix has a 13C belfry and 16C facade. The interior is curiously wide and short, with a low-vaulted roof; the 16C stained glass and 17C gilded retable are remarkable. The church of St-Michel-des-Lions takes its name from granite lions at the S door. A copper ball balances on top of the unusual belfry. Inside are three naves of equal size, with good 15C stained glass, and rather unnerving leaning pillars.

An international show of the Limousin breed of cattle is held in the town each Sept.

Solignac, 13km S, has a beautiful Romanesque abbey church. A little further is the **Château de Chalusset**, a ruined hilltop fortress, occupied by the English in the Hundred Years' War.

Limoges porcelain

MENDE
LOZÈRE   Pop 12,100

Prefecture of the Lozère, former capital of Gévau-dan (q.v.), Mende stands on the edge of the Cévennes, poised on a ridge above the river Lot and below the Causse Mejean. Boulevards have replaced the ramparts, of which the only relic is the Tour des Pénitents. Now overgrown and busy, Mende was originally built around the tomb of St Privatus, whose hermitage lies a short distance S of the town. His tomb is in the crypt of the cathedral (built 1365, much repaired 17C and 19C), a large structure with two towers, one adorned by a spire 84m tall. The interior, remarkably plain and simple, has twenty side chapels, a good rose window, 17C choirstalls and Aubusson tapestries of 1706. A pleasant old quarter surrounds the cathedral. The small Musée Ignon Fabre illustrates local archae-ology and country life. A very attractive narrow 14C bridge crosses the river Lot.

MILLEVACHES
CORRÈZE

The plateau of Millevaches, consisting of conifer plantations and broad open heath, has a bleak distinctive character. Sparsely populated, extend-ing from **Felletin** to **Ussel**, it has occasional hamlets, like Millevaches itself, with its simple church and thatched cottages. The name means not 1000 cows – cattle are few – but 1000 springs, a more accurate description, from a local Celtic word.

Below Millevaches lies the **Monedières Massif**, a range of low heather-covered hills. Caesar's troops burnt down the forest which originally grew here. Replanted, it was burnt down again in the Wars of Religion. Once more, trees are being planted, but the main cash 'crop' is wild blueberries.

MONASTIER-SUR-GAZEILLE, LE
LOZÈRE   Pop 620

From this little town, in the lace-making province of Velay, R.L. Stevenson and his donkey Modes-tine set off in Sept. 1878 for their *Travels* in the Cévennes. The town derives its name from the oldest monastery in Velay (7C, rebuilt 11C), much of which survives, including the abbey church (restored 15C). The exterior is a superb example of the Auvergnat Romanesque technique of decor-ation, using stones of different shades. By contrast, much of the interior is Gothic and Renaissance. The town hall, in part of the old abbey, keeps a very small 'Stevenson Museum'.

On his first day's walk, Stevenson went through **St-Martin-de-Fugères**, **Goudet**, **Ussel** and **Costa-ros**, to **Bouchet-St-Nicholas**.

MONT-DORE, LE
PUY-DE-DÔME   Pop 2400

The river Dordogne, still a rushing stream, flows between public gardens along one side of long, narrow Le Mont-Dore (alt. 1050m). Wooded mountains rise up all around the town. In summer this is a popular base for motorists and walkers

Le Mont-Dore

visiting the unspoiled Monts Dore region; in win-ter the town transforms itself into a ski resort, mainly for cross-country enthusiasts, though there is plenty of downhill skiing available too on nearby **Puy de Sancy** (1886m – highest point in the Massif Central). Le Mont-Dore has been a thriving spa, specializing in the treatment of asthma, for at least 2000 years. The thermal baths in the centre of town still attract many *curistes*.

Puy de Sancy, 4km S, easily reached by road or footpath, then cable car to the summit, makes a dramatic excursion with views across the volcanic mountain range. **Promenade Melchi-Roze** is a pleasant walk on the hillside above the town. The Monts Dore are high jagged peaks, all that remains of three huge volcanoes, now weathered away, once active in this section of the Park of the Volcanoes of the Auvergne. Wild, heavily wooded, with a multitude of lakes, rivers and streams, the area is much loved by walkers, and in winter, cross-country skiers.

There is much to see, either on foot or by car. **Besse-en-Chandesse**, a very attractively situated little mountain town, preserves ancient streets and houses of volcanic rock (especially Rue de la Boucherie). An impressive town gate and its sub-stantial barbican are among the remnants of former ramparts. The dark 12C Romanesque church, with 15C choir and 16C stalls, houses a Black Virgin . . . most of the year. On 2 July she is taken in solemn procession by sixty men up to a moun-tain retreat, **Chapelle de Vassivières**, 7km W, and brought back on 21 Sept.

At the W end of popular **Lac Chambon**, the village of **Chambon-sur-Lac** also has its 12C church. 3km away, a ruined, but still imposing 13C castle (open to the public) dominates the pretty, old-fashioned village of **Murol. St-Nec-taire** (q.v.) is a tiny hillside spa, noted for its church and its cheese. In the northern part of the Monts Dore, green hills seem to descend into the very centre of **Orcival**, a perfectly restored village much visited by tourists – and pilgrims.

MONTLUÇON
ALLIER   Pop 51,800

Montluçon, on the river Cher in the flat Bourbon country, is a large modern town with chemical, rubber and foundry works. A small old quarter on the right bank is not without charm. There is a museum of local history, with a fascinating collec-tion of beautiful old hurdy-gurdies, housed in a 15C Bourbon castle.

Tronçais Forest, 35km NE, is an area of over 10,000 hectares of handsome woodlands, mainly oak, interspersed with lakes. Numerous deer and some wild boar live in the forest. There are footpaths, campsites and picnic spots.

ORADOUR-SUR-GLANE
HAUTE-VIENNE Pop 1940

One of the most shocking places to visit, the village of Oradour, 22km NE of Limoges, survives as a monument to the German occupation in World War II. On 10 June 1944, 200 men of the SS 'das Reich' division entered the village, closed all its exits, and ordered the whole population, numbering some 650 people, to assemble in the village square. The men were then machine-gunned, or burnt alive in barns. The women and children were bolted into the church, which was burnt down together with its occupants. One woman, a boy, and about half a dozen men managed to escape alive.

A new Oradour has been built, and the old village left exactly as it was on that day. The cemetery where the victims are buried, and the small museum of a few of their personal effects, are disturbing. 'Do not forget', says a sign in German.

ORCIVAL
PUY-DE-DÔME Pop 380

This small village at the foot of the Monts Dore is chiefly notable for the huge, dark 12C basilica of Notre-Dame, made of volcanic rock, and a superb example of the Auvergnat Romanesque style, with rounded chapels and a central octagonal tower. Indeed, it can claim to be the loveliest church in the Massif Central. The interior – rather preciously equipped for visitors, even with piped Gregorian chants – contains exquisitely carved capitals. In the choir is a revered Madonna, seated in the rigid Auvergnat pose, but not coloured black. Instead, this Virgin is covered with silver and enamel. Known as Our Lady of Iron and Chains, she is sacred to prisoners who have finished their sentence. On Ascension Day she is the object of a huge pilgrimage: in the evening there is a torchlight procession, and a midnight Mass in the basilica. Near Orcival, at **Cordès**, there is a 15C Renaissance 'manoir', a wonderfully romantic building with conical towers and glorious gardens.

PUY, LE
HAUTE-LOIRE Pop 26,000

Le Puy, prefecture of the Haute-Loire and capital of old Velay, is one of France's more extraordinary-looking towns. The *puy* (called Rocher Corneille) from which it earns its name looms above the streets. On the summit stands an enormous, unappealing red cast iron statue, Notre-Dame-de-France, 16m high and weighing 110 tons.

Beside this peak rises another, finer point of rock topped with a 10C church, St-Michel d'Aiguilhe (literally, 'of the needle'), approached by 267 steps. This fascinating building is almost Byzantine in inspiration and decoration. It is an odd shape, the floor merely following the flat ground

available. Interesting arches give the structure support.

High on the slope of the Rocher Corneille stands the cathedral of Notre-Dame. The exterior is one of the best examples of the Auvergnat Romanesque custom of decoration by using stone blocks with different shades of colour. The effect is magnificent. A curiosity of the cathedral is that the nave is *above* the main entrance: access is up another flight of stairs, which pass the supposedly miraculous Fever Stone. The cathedral, an important halt for Compostela pilgrims, has an unusual squared-off shape, but oriental looking domes, and contains a Black Virgin (19C replacement for older statue), remarkable frescoes and much good sculpture. Alongside the cathedral are other abbey buildings, and beautiful Romanesque cloisters with older Carolingian capitals. The Maison du Prieuré has a permanent exhibition of 'Old Velay'. From here a steep path and steps ascend to the statue of Notre-Dame-de-France (which can be climbed inside). The view is spectacular.

The cathedral stands in the old part of town, surrounded by dark buildings, narrow streets and stairways, quiet squares and fountains. Little remains of the ramparts except the dark and squat Tour Pannessac: originally there were eighteen city gates and towers. Boulevards now encircle the old town, and separate it from the newer area, focus of which is the big Pl. de Breuil, with pretty public gardens, the Jardin Vinay.

Fine silk and cotton lace-making, a great tradition of Velay, survives in Le Puy, where dozens of women keep boutiques to sell their handiwork. The Musée Crozatier, in the Jardin Vinay, includes a large collection of lacework dating back to 16C. Another local product is strong sweet liqueurs made from local wild plants, especially *verveine* (verbena). Each Sat. a big open-air market fills Pl. de Breuil and many streets in the old town.

On a commanding rocky platform, the **Château de Polignac**, 6km NW, is an impressive sight. A large square keep, built 14–15C, dominates the fortress. On the site is a Roman temple to Apollo.

St-Michel d'Aiguilhe, Le Puy

RIOM
PUY-DE-DÔME   Pop 18,900

Riom has a grand history dating back beyond Roman times, and was capital of the Auvergne from the 14C until ousted by Clermont-Ferrand (15km S) in the 17C. It remains the region's judicial capital. The circular central area, its ramparts now replaced by tree-lined boulevards, has fascinating old streets, fountains, and opulent Renaissance mansions of black volcanic stone. Many of the courtyards of these great houses, erected by Riom's wealthy lawyers and judges, are open to the public.

Musée Mandet, an art museum, is housed in a 17C mansion. Opposite, the Musée Régional d'Auvergne contains an extensive museum of local country life. The Palais de Justice stands on the site of the Duc de Berry's 14C château and incorporates the chapel of the original building, with excellent stained glass and Beauvais tapestries.

The 15C Gothic church of Notre-Dame-du-Marthuret has a lovely 14C statu called the Vierge à l'Oiseau (Bird Virgin): a tender madonna holding a smiling child with fluttering bird. She is in marked contrast to the church's more revered and formal 12C Black Virgin. In the basilica of St-Amable are kept the relics of this obscure saint. On the Sun. following 11 June these are carried through the streets by 'Brayauds', local men in old-fashioned peasant costumes, at the head of a lively parade.

Mozac, a suburb of Riom, retains the 12C church of a Benedictine abbey; it has excellent capitals and, in the treasury, a 12C enamelled reliquary casket. **Marsat**, 3km SW, has another interesting 12C Benedictine abbey church, Notre-Dame-de-Marsat, with a very devoutly worshipped Black Virgin, in whose honour a popular festival is held on the Sun. after Ascension. **Châtelguyon**, 6km NW, is a 2000-year-old spa, still thriving, with thirty springs, and specializing in treatment of digestive ailments.

RODEZ
AVEYRON   Pop 26,300

Prefecture of the Aveyron *département*, Rodez is a big modern town. In the Middle Ages it was divided between the episcopal *cité*, and the *bourg* of the counts. So intense did the rivalry become that walls were erected to separate the two. Though eventually united, the two districts are still remembered in the names of the two main squares of the old central area.

A large cathedral in grey-red sandstone dominates the town centre from a hilltop. The lower level is a fortress-like Gothic, and the upper level decorative Renaissance. An impressive 16C belfry soars to 87m. The 14C Tour des Anglais is a relic of the English occupation of the town (1360–68). The dark interior has some interesting features: an unusual gallery, ornate organ loft, a brightly painted 16C stone Entombment, a good rood-screen (moved out of the nave), and 15C choir-stalls. Two tombs behind the altar date from the 5–6C.

In the bustling old lanes behind the cathedral, several Renaissance houses have survived. One of them, the Musée Fenaille, has collections of archaeology and Renaissance furnishings. The Musée Beaux-Arts has a modest selection of painting and sculpture. There is a popular Sat. market in Pl. de la Cité.

ST-FLOUR
CANTAL   Pop 9100

The extensive older part of St-Flour, poised on a high ridge, looks across the new areas of town, the confluence of two small rivers and the surrounding country. Numerous 16–17C houses line the streets of the Vieille Ville. Its centre is Pl. des Armes, in which stands a gloomy black fortress of a cathedral (built 1400 – at 881m, the highest in France). The facade consists only of two mighty towers. The interior is a massive hall with no transept. However, it contains some beautiful wood-carving; especially notable is the black Christ, of uncertain date (13C), called Le Beau Dieu Noir.

Also in Pl. des Armes are the Renaissance Maison Consulaire, containing a museum of furnishings and decoration and the Musée de la Haute-Auvergne, with excellent collections of art, archaeology, and traditional local life. The Terrasse des Roches, immediately behind the cathedral, has a stunning view.

S of St-Flour, the Truyère river runs through impressive wooded gorges with lovely reservoir-lakes. The valley is crossed 12km S by Boyer and Eiffel's amazing railway bridge, the 564m-long **Viaduc de Garabit** (completed 1884), spanning the gorge in a single arch. The small, prettily situated spa **Chaudes-Aigues** ('hot waters'), 32km S, has the hottest natural spring water in Europe – up to 82°C – emerging from 32 springs. There is not only a bath house (speciality, rheumatism), but free hot water supplied to every home.

St-Flour

ST-NECTAIRE
PUY-DE-DÔME   Pop 650

St-Nectaire, well known for the cheese of that name, is really two villages, in the steep wooded valley of the Courançon in the Monts Dore. Downstream, **St-Nectaire-le-Bas** is a tiny spa with over 40 springs (speciality, kidney complaints). Along the single street are the thermal baths, casino, hotels and shops. 1·5km higher up, in the older community of **St-Nectaire-le-Haut**, is the village church. This 12C building, one of the finest examples of Auvergnat Romanesque and in a beautiful setting, has exceptionally pleasing proportions, remarkable and harmonious exterior decoration, as well as a lovely interior with entertaining capitals and a valuable collection of 12C statues, reliquaries, enamels and other works in the treasury.

SALERS
CANTAL   Pop 470

Salers, at the NW corner of the Cantal mountains, is an unusual village of extraordinary grandeur. Fortified, with two 15C gateways, and situated in a commanding position, it was from 15C the judicial seat for the surrounding mountain areas. Judges and other dignitaries in residence here erected superb Renaissance houses of grey volcanic stone, many with turrets and towers. Grande Place, the small central square with an attractive fountain, is completely surrounded by these remarkable mansions.

The 15C Gothic church has a 12C Romanesque doorway, left from the previous building on this site. Inside are interesting tapestries and sculptures, including a 15C painted stone Entombment. The streets of the village are beautifully cobbled. Esplanade de Barrouze on the S side of town has superb views.

SOLIGNAC
HAUTE-VIENNE   Pop 4000

The little town of Solignac, 13km S of Limoges, has an interesting and beautiful abbey church of 1143, a remnant of the much-besieged monastery founded by St-Éloi in the 7C. This is a good example of the Périgord Romanesque style, with domes over the nave, and there are exceptionally fine 15C choir-stalls. The other monastery buildings were reconstructed in the 18C.

THIERS
PUY-DE-DÔME   Pop 16,800

Thiers has an exceptional appearance, climbing on terraces up the precipitous slopes of the Durolle valley. The town has for centuries been almost

Thiers

synonymous with knife-making; this has grown from an ancient craft to a thriving modern industry. The modern workshops are still located on the bank of the river Durolle. There is also a fascinating knife museum in the Rue de Barante. Papermaking, for which Thiers also once had a reputation, has all but died out.

Remarkably well-preserved and highly decorated old timbered houses line its picturesque steep narrow lanes. Those around Pl. du Pirou, especially the 15C Maison du Pirou, are particularly notable. Interspersed with them are cutlery shops with the most varied displays. From the Terrasse du Rempart there is a panoramic view. The church of St-Genès and the abbey church du Moutier are both unusual examples of the Romanesque style.

Between Thiers, **Montbrison** and **Ambert** is the region of the **Monts de Forez**, richly farmed on the lower slopes and densely wooded above with pine and beech. Clean, fresh streams rush down from the heights. At the W edge of the hills, the villages are busy with small-scale light industry. Higher up, the communities are more rustic and attractive. All this is good country for walkers and, in winter, for skiers.

TURENNE
CORRÈZE   Pop 500

The village of Turenne (16km S of Brive) was in feudal times the seat of a *seigneur* with absolute power over more than 1000 communities. Totally independent of the crown until as recently as 1738, the lords of Turenne even printed their own money. The village consists today of a picturesque cluster of 15–16C houses, some with turrets and towers, around the grim ruined castle on its lofty site. The castle's vaulted guardroom, and its mint, are especially interesting. One of the two imposing 14–15C keeps, the Tour de César, can be climbed to give a splendid view.

UZERCHE
CORRÈZE   Pop 3200

Uzerche is an ancient town encircled by a bend in the Vézère river. This position, together with the mighty ramparts and 18 towers which used to protect it, rendered the town unassailable. For this reason Charles V dubbed it 'Uzerche the Maid', and the town's motto, reflecting the same sentiment, is 'Non Polluta' ('never sullied'). Another saying is 'He who owns a house in Uzerche has a castle in Limousin'; apt comment not only because of the secure location but also because many of the town's dwellings do resemble little castles, with turrets and towers.

Only one of the fortified city gates survives, Porte Bécharie. Just inside it, Pl. des Vignerons (vinegrowers) is very picturesque. A Romanesque 12–13C church, standing on an 11C crypt and surmounted by a fine Limousin-style belfry, square at the bottom, octagonal at the top, dominates the centre of town; the interior has good capitals, and a barrel-vaulted roof. From a terrace in front of the church, Esplanade de la Lunade, impressive views extend across the river and surrounding hills.

VASSIVIÈRE, LAC DE
HAUTE-VIENNE

The beautiful 1000-hectare artificial lake of Vassi-vière, in the gentle wooded hills of Limousin, has a beach, campsites and some low-key tourist development, including facilities for watersports. A national regatta is held at Whitsun. Minor roads encircle the lake, making a pleasant drive of some 16km.

VICHY
ALLIER Pop 30,600

Best known of all French spas, Vichy in northern Auvergne has a lingering fin-de-siècle style and elegance which is unique. The beneficial effect of its waters on the digestive system have long been known – the Romans praised them – but only from the 17–19C did it become *the* fashionable place for a restful cure. *Curistes* still come in their tens of thousands annually. In the past they included some distinguished names: Madame de Sévigné, whose letters from Vichy give a valuable insight into 17C life; many members of the French royal families; and Napoleon III, who during his visits had the banks of the river Allier drained and turned into the pleasant parks and gardens which are one of the town's most appealing features.

Vichy

The centre of the town, too, is taken up by a public 'park' (entirely paved), the shady Parc des Sources. At the end of it is the magnificent greenhouse-like Hall des Sources in which *curistes* queue for their doses of water from the various springs, which emerge here from permanently running taps. The only palatable waters are from the Celestin spring, which is bottled and exported all over the world.

Dominating the Parc, at the N end, is the wonderfully gaudy Grand Établissement Thermal. At the S end is the once-opulent Second Empire casino, behind which is the pump room of the particularly vile Hospital spring.

Vichy acquired great notoriety as the seat of the pro-Hitler puppet government led by Maréchal Pétain. Few souvenirs of that era have been preserved. Cabinet meetings were held in the Hôtel du Parc, now residential (with the municipal tourist office on the ground floor).

Offering a surprising variety of hotels, chic shops, excellent restaurants and sophisticated entertainment, as well as extensive modern sports facilities on the other side of the Allier, Vichy has much to recommend it other than for a cure. There is much excellent early-20C architecture of considerable interest. One of the most unconventional and pleasing examples is the church of St-Blaise, a bright hall of blue mosaic, which is strangely amalgamated, inside, to a dark Romanesque chapel. In the older part, a 12C Black Virgin sits among her votive offerings. A small old quarter, Napoleon III's Vichy, with remains of a 15C castle, surrounds the church.

The town and its district have given the world a delicious vegetable soup – vichyssoise.

VILLEFRANCHE-DE-ROUERGUE
AVEYRON Pop 13,900

On the Aveyron river in an attractive area of gorges, Villefranche-de-Rouergue was rebuilt by Alphonse de Poitiers in the 13C as a walled *bastide* with a grid of straight lanes. It has since lost most of its walls and grown considerably, but preserves a great many fascinating old dwellings, especially around the cobbled market square – very lively on market days – Pl. Notre-Dame, with its arcaded houses and massive arcaded belfry of the church of Notre-Dame.

The church has a large nave, beautifully vaulted, with high narrow windows, and much remarkable stonework. The excellent, imaginative choirstalls (15C) are by André Sulpice. The 17C Chapelle des Pénitents Noir (in Blvd Haute-Guyenne), laid out on a Greek Cross plan, has a remarkably ornate interior with a painted ceiling and a gilded Baroque retable.

Best-known of the town's buildings is the 15C charterhouse, Chartreuse de St-Sauveur, now a hospital, out on the Albi road. Mercifully, it escaped the Revolution unscathed. In a pure but austere Gothic style, it has two chapels (with more Sulpice choirstalls), a vaulted refectory with curious stone pulpit, and two lovely cloisters.

Villefranche-de-Rouergue

LYON AREA

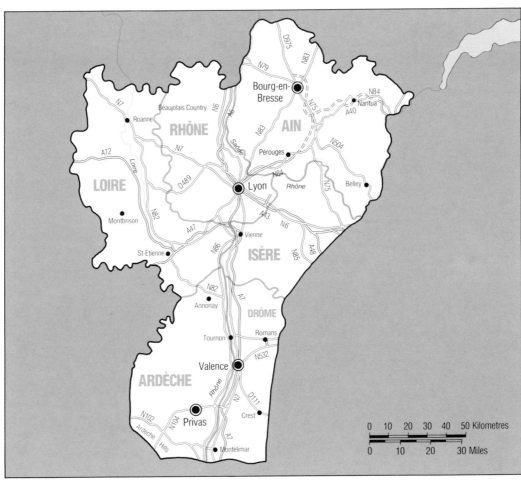

Travellers from the north catch the scent of something southern in the air as soon as Lyon is reached. From then on their journey along the Rhône, that mighty river highway, passes under an ever-bluer sky through a succession of vineyards, pretty orchards, and productive market gardens, interspersed with a considerable amount of industry, including oil refineries and nuclear power stations. Lyon itself, a great and civilized metropolis, has much to detain any traveller with an interest in art or architecture . . . or food. For this is a gastronomic city; within easy reach of it are the rolling vineyards and peaceful villages of Beaujolais, which supply one of the most vital ingredients of a good Lyonnais dinner.

Easy river access (from the north on the Saône as well as from the south) made the area important to the Romans, whose traces can be seen in several towns, especially Lyon and Vienne. Subsequently this became one of the smallest of French provinces, though one of the most industrious. From 1400, Lyon prospered with its silk weaving, and a frontier position on the old borders of France, Provence and Italy further contributed to the city's growth as a centre of trade, industry and finance. Despite considerable destruction inflicted in the

Revolutionary period, and in this century by retreating Germans, Lyon continued to thrive.

On the right (west) bank of the Rhône rise the steep hills of Ardèche (formerly part of the southern domaine of Languedoc). This rugged, largely unspoiled region of wooded mountains makes a striking contrast to the highly developed Rhône corridor. For the view alone, it is worth travelling on the west side of the river rather than on the teeming autoroute and route nationale of the eastern bank. Along the way are detours into the hills: particularly beautiful are the minor roads between

Tournon and Valence ('Corniche du Rhône'), with magnificent views, and again for some miles south of Valence ('Corniche de l'Eyrieux').

Further inland, on the edges of the Massif Central, are lakes, rivers and forests, criss-crossed with minor roads and footpaths. The flatter country to the east also has its charm: the farms of Bresse, remarkably unspoiled villages like Pérouges, and quiet rural routes meandering within sight of the snow-covered Alps.

ANNONAY
ARDÈCHE Pop 20,000

Capital of the Haute-Vivarais, Annonay lies in hills W of the Rhône, below the ruins of a castle. It is a busy town, principally occupied, as for centuries, with paper-making, tanneries, and textiles. The old quarter has cobbled lanes, arcades, and a 14C bridge crossing the rocky channel of the Deume. From Pl. des Cordeliers in 1783, the first ascent in a hot-air balloon was made by the brothers Joseph and Étienne Montgolfier, sons of a local paper merchant.

A superb 19km drive on a minor road follows the river Cance to join the Rhône.

BEAUJOLAIS COUNTRY

'Three great rivers,' goes the saying, 'flow into Lyon – Saône, Rhône and Beaujolais Wine.' This highly productive vineyard region, delightful rolling hill country NW of Lyon, has long supplied the gastronomic city with most of its vin de table.

Made with the Gamay grape, with few exceptions Beaujolais is a wine to be drunk young and fresh. Cheap-and-cheerful Beaujolais Nouveau, the area's latest marketing success, is for drinking between 15 Nov. and Christmas immediately after the autumn harvest. Finest of Beaujolais' three *appellations*, N of Villefranche-sur-Saône, is Beaujolais Villages, with its nine distinguished '*crûs*' – St-Amour, Juliénas, Chénas, Moulin-à-Vent, Fleurie, Chiroubles, Morgon, Côte de Brouilly and Brouilly. *Appellations* Beaujolais and Beaujolais Supérieur cover the area W and S of Villefranche.

The signposted **Route du Beaujolais**, running from **Crêches** (8km S of Mâcon) to Villefranche along rural lanes parallel to the N6, goes through many of the most noted villages. There are ample opportunities along the way for tasting at the *caves coopératives*, as well as excellent restaurants and good straightforward lodgings. S of Villefranche, the **Pays de Pierres Dorées** is so called because its fortified villages and feudal castles are built of honey-coloured stone. **Oingt** and **Ternand** are especially picturesque.

Belleville, once a walled *bastide* and preserving a beautiful 12C church, is the commercial centre of the wine country; industrial Villefranche was built in 1140 by the lords of Beaujeu, who made it their capital. Little **Beaujeu** itself, from which the region takes its name, was the earlier seat of the powerful local lords. Surprisingly, it is not a vine-growing village, though most of its neighbours are. It has an interesting church of 1134, and ruins of a castle dismantled by Richelieu. There is a small museum with an unusual collection of 19C dolls,

Moulin-à-Vent

and on a similar note, a statue has been erected of Gnafron, one of the two disreputable Beaujolais-swigging heroes of the popular Lyonnais puppet show.

BELLEY
AIN Pop 8400

A quiet town on the southern edge of the Jura plateau, among mountains, forests and lakes, Belley is remembered by the French as the home of Brillat-Savarin. This local judge (house preserved, 62 Grande Rue) achieved great eminence when aged 70, writing a major work on gastronomy, *La Physiologie du Goût*, published 1825. The poet Lamartine studied here. The cathedral, rebuilt 1864, has kept its 15C choir.

BOURG-EN-BRESSE
AIN Pop 43,700

Bresse, a flat area of farmlands NE of Lyon, is known abroad for its Bleu de Bresse cheese and much better known in France for its high-quality free-range chickens and eggs, supplied in great quantity to nearby Burgundy and Lyon. There are many dairy farms, too, and Bresse has developed its own creamy style of cuisine reflecting the local abundance.

Its capital Bourg, a large commercial town noted for animated cattle fairs and poultry markets, retains a small old quarter in the centre. The 16C church, with good choir-stalls and windows, has a remarkable pastel-coloured Renaissance exterior and a carillon which rings ten minutes before striking the hours of 8am, noon and 7pm.

Brou monastery church lies 1km SE. The exterior is fairly plain except for the Gothic/Renaissance portals and tympanum. The interior has beautiful vaults and is marvellously pale and light. Hidden behind a superb rood-screen is the extraordinary Gothic choir. Within are 74 oak stalls (1530–32), a masterpiece of wood carving, and three gorgeously ornate, Flamboyant tombs in white marble, carved in the most delicate, exquisite tracery. Centrepiece is that of Philibert-le-Beau – the choir, with its lovely stained glass, seems to have been built around him – with his wife Marguerite of Austria in an even more lavish tomb to one side, and his mother Marguerite of Bourbon on the other. Philibert and his wife are each represented twice on their tombs: once in worldly glory, and again, below, as dead bodies stripped of finery. Besides

Detail of Marguerite of Austria's tomb

the magnificence of the stonework, it is a very moving ensemble, commissioned in 1506 by Marguerite of Austria, who founded the monastery here after Philibert was killed in a hunting accident. The monastery building beside the church, after a spell as a prison, now contains a museum of local country life.

CREST
DRÔME Pop 7900

A little mountain town on the N bank of the Drôme, Crest has several stepped alleys and paths, one of which (off Rue de l'Hôtel de Ville) leads to an impressive hillside keep, ruin of the 12C fortress which guarded this valley. It retains vaulted chambers and grim dungeons. From the top is a fantastic mountain panorama.

Crest

LYON
RHÔNE Pop city – 418,500; conurbation – 1½ million

Lyon, France's second largest conurbation, capital of the Rhône-Alpes region, is a thriving and busy modern city, its sprawling industrial periphery devoted to synthetics, metals and chemical works; miles of oil refineries extend southwards and through-traffic still has to endure crowded, exhaust-filled tunnels beneath the central area. Yet

Lyon is also a magnificent, handsome town, sophisticated and civilized, with an enormous amount to see and do.

Two broad rivers, the Saône and the Rhône, skirting the two hills, Fourvière and Croix-Rousse, run majestically between busy tree-lined quays through the heart of the city, south of which they unite. The long narrow strip between the rivers (La Presqu'île) is the 'centre' of Lyon (though far from the middle of the urban area). Here life revolves around three large squares. Pl. Carnot has lawns, fountains, lively cafés, inexpensive snack bars and the Perrache main railway station. Pl. Bellecour is a huge area, with popular cafés, fast-food restaurants and shops along its sides, and a bronze equestrian statue of Louis XIV in the middle; NW of Bellecour is a 'red light' district. Pl. des Terreaux, with more cafés and shops, is smaller yet grander, surrounded by fine Renaissance buildings including the imposing Hôtel de Ville, and with a dramatic monumental fountain. The three squares are linked by chic shopping streets, including traffic-free Rue Victor Hugo and Rue de la République, but distances are quite long on foot, so take advantage of the excellent bus and métro systems.

In Pl. des Terreaux the extensive Musée des Beaux Arts, housed in the 17C former nunnery Palais St-Pierre, contains Greek and Roman sculpture, religious artefacts of the Middle Ages, Limoges enamels, and vast numbers of paintings from the 15C to the present-day, including El Greco, Rubens, Monet, Van Gogh, Renoir, Degas, Manet, Gauguin, Picasso, Matisse, and many others. S of Terreaux, in Rue de la Poulaillerie, is the interesting little Musée de l'Imprimerie et de la Banque (Printing and Banking), established by the Crédit Lyonnais, the bank founded here in the 19C. Between Bellecour and Carnot, in Rue de la Charité, the Musée des Arts Decoratifs has French and Flemish furnishings and ornaments. Two doors down, the Musée Historique des Tissus has one of the world's greatest collections of fabrics, with fascinating ancient Greek, Roman and Byzantine examples, 16C Persian carpets, oriental silkworks, and a vast range of Lyon silks from 1400 onwards.

Traditionally, the silkworkers – *canuts*, in local slang – lived (in wretched poverty) in tall houses on the hill of Croix-Rousse, still a densely populated, warren-like clothing district, N of Terreaux. Though slummy, the area has much character, and is laced with that curiosity of Lyon, the *traboules* – unnamed alleys and shortcuts that pass right through the courtyards and hallways of crumbling old apartment buildings.

Another area of *traboules* is across the Saône in Vieux Lyon. This picturesque district, well-restored, preserves numerous impressive Gothic and Renaissance buildings. Many of their courtyards, attractive with circular stairwells, are open to the public. Despite obvious charm, Vieux Lyon remains quiet and uncommercialized, though there are several nightclubs and good restaurants on this side of the river. The Musée du Vieux Lyon, in Hôtel Gadagne, tells the history of the city and also has an unusual display of puppets. Rue St-Jean, the main street of this quarter, is particularly attractive, and leads to the ornate cathedral of St-Jean, best of Lyon's churches. Initially 11C Romanesque, it was subsequently rebuilt in Gothic style, with a 15C facade, but has kept the original choir and possesses good 13C windows. Most intriguing is the wonderful 14C astronomical clock.

Close to the cathedral is Gare St-Jean, terminus of the funicular railway which travels inside the hill to the summit of Fourvière, the site of Roman Lyon, called Lugdunum. Ruins of an important theatre and odeon have been uncovered, and there is a good Gallo-Roman museum. A pompous 19C basilica, and a large unsightly statue of Notre-Dame stand on the peak of Fourvière, from which is a stirring view of the city, the two rivers with their embankments of fine mansions, and the modern business district of La Part-Dieu across the Rhône. In the distance the Alps are visible. The church tower can be ascended for an even more impressive panorama.

Formerly a run-down residential area and old barracks, Part-Dieu is now a model commercial centre. Also on this side of the river are outstanding sports facilities, the university and medical school, and the spacious Parc de la Tête d'Or, which has a huge rose garden. Beyond to the E lie many miles of residential districts.

Lyon's history has been long. There was a Greek settlement before the Romans arrived (43BC). Lugdunum grew to become a major strategic city. In the 5C, with the Roman withdrawal, it became part of Burgundy, and later, principal city of the Provençal kingdom. It has thrived ever since, thanks in part to its silk trade, despite efforts by Revolutionaries in 1793 to destroy the city. At the forefront of the Revolution in its early democratic stage, Lyon reacted against the authoritarian fanatics who subsequently rose to prominence. In consequence, Revolutionary Committees decreed that Lyon 'be no more'. The guillotine was set up in Pl. des Terreaux; thousands were executed and large areas of housing were destroyed. Fortunately, the downfall of Robespierre cut short the destruction.

Lyon has seen other rebellions bloodily put down: the 12C 'heresy' of Waldensianism began here and attracted many adherents; in 1843 an uprising by silk-workers against their working conditions resulted in hundreds shot dead in the streets when troops were called in; and in World War II Lyon was the HQ of the French Resistance. Left-winger Édouard Herriot remained mayor of the city from 1905–55. The libertarian spirit of the Lyonnais is shown perhaps by the popularity of the traditional local puppet show starring Guignol, his wife Madelon and their friend Gnafron, all three lovable rogues who hate work or authority but love a glass or two of Beaujolais.

In the 19C Lyon emerged as a major international banking centre, and its subsequent prosperity has been based on its financial role in the nation's economy and its diversified industrial development, with chemicals and metals having now surpassed textiles in importance.

Lyon is widely recognized as the gastronomic capital of France. An abundance of first-rate ingredients from the farms of neighbouring Burgundy, Bresse, Provence and the Rhône valley combines with a great tradition of cuisine to create a city with scores of excellent restaurants, the most renowned of which is the Michelin three-rosette establishment of Paul Bocuse, indisputably France's most distinguished restaurateur and leading exponent of the *nouvelle cuisine*. Local specialities include gratinée dishes, quenelles, chickens with truffles, many strange kinds of sausage, and braised trout from the alpine lakes. A unique Lyonnais phenomenon is the *bouchon*, a 'local' restaurant with a set menu of gourmet food, good table wines, a regular clientele and a discreet atmosphere.

Lyon has a very active cultural life, including a summer arts festival in which some events are held in the Roman theatre. The suburb of Villeurbanne is the birthplace and headquarters of Roger Planchon's world-renowned company, the Théâtre

Lyon

National Populaire (TNP), second only in prestige to the Comédie Française. And the city offers a wide range of popular entertainments at all levels.

A suburb N of Lyon, Rochetaillé-sur-Saône, has a château and park which house the Musée de l'Automobile Henri Malartre. This fascinating collection of some 200 vintage cars includes several unique models, many dating from before World War I. Most are actually inside the rooms of the handsome building, with racing vehicles in an adjoining hall. A number of extraordinary old bicycles and 'velocipedes' are on display on the second floor.

MONTBRISON
LOIRE   Pop 11,200

A pleasant manufacturing town E of the Monts de Forez, Montbrison is built around a once-fortified hill. The town was severely damaged in the Hundred Years' War and the Wars of Religion. The 13–15C church of Notre-Dame d'Espérance is imposing, with a good facade and large nave. Behind the church an unusual hall called La Diane has a vaulted wooden ceiling and painted heraldic panels, and contains a museum of local history and archaeology. In Blvd de la Préfecture, next to a small park, Musée d'Allard has a large collection of dolls.

Champdieu, 4km N, and **St-Romain-le-Puy**, 6km SE, have fortified churches. **La Bastie d'Urfé**, 13km N, is a château in elaborate Italian-Renaissance style, with magnificent stonecarving, Aubusson tapestries, superb gardens and a curious shell grotto.

MONTÉLIMAR
DRÔME   Pop 30,200

Montélimar promotes itself obsessively as the capital of nougat; but the town also has an attractive old centre, with narrow lanes and many 16–17C buildings. The ramparts have gone but a medieval gate remains. On a nearby hill are ruins of a 12–14C château.

Rochemaure (5km NW) is a ruined walled village with hilltop remnants of a feudal château.

NANTUA
AIN   Pop 3500

A small, bustling town on the edge of the Jura, Nantua stands at the end of the beautiful lake of the same name and is a popular tourist centre, with good food, delightful walks and water sports, and fine views of surrounding woods and mountains. The 12C church of St-Michel, formerly an 8C Benedictine abbey and mutilated during the Revolution, has an interesting porch, Renaissance chapel and unusual tower.

PÉROUGES
AIN   Pop 650

The fortified village of Pérouges (37km NE of Lyon), splendidly poised at the top of a hill, has survived with its medieval appearance amazingly unaltered. Its narrow, quiet cobbled lanes, flintstone cottages, a village square with an ancient tree and 15–16C houses, are staunchly defended by double ramparts. The walls are entered through the original two gateways, called Porte d'en Bas and Porte d'en Haut. Pérouges has provided the setting for a number of historical films, such as *The Three Musketeers*.

PRIVAS
ARDÈCHE   Pop 10,600

Almost completely destroyed by Richelieu in 1629 because of its incorrigible Protestantism, Privas was rebuilt and is today capital of the Ardèche *département*. It is a pleasant southern town in attractive country, between the banks of rivers Charalon and Ouvèze, 14km W of the Rhône. There are many 17C houses, and at the N edge of town are the few buildings which predate this time.

ROANNE
LOIRE   Pop 49,600

A large garrison and industrial river port on the Loire, Roanne is mainly notable for its great gourmet restaurant, the *Troisgros*, with the Miche-

lin three rosettes. In the city centre is a 14–16C castle keep and a good archaeological museum.

The Loire enters impressive gorges 5km S, flanked by minor roads. **St-Hâon-le-Châtel**, 12km W, is a hilltop 15C château and village, protected by remarkable fortifications with imposing towers and gates. N of Roanne lies attractive **Charlieu** and the **Brionnais** (see *Burgundy*).

ROMANS
DRÔME   Pop 33,900

An industrial town on the Isère, its principal manufactures being shoes and leather goods, Romans was made the subject of a fascinating historical study, *Carnival at Romans*, by Emmanuel Le Roy Ladurie, who used contemporary documents to examine life in the town in the year 1579–80; even at that time it was largely devoted to leather tanning.

In a vast former 17C convent, part of the town museum traces the development of footwear over the centuries; another section contains documents and maps recalling the wartime Resistance. The 12C abbey church of St-Barnard, by the river, has an interesting choir and some good Flemish tapestries. The town's attractive old quarter clusters around the church. On the opposite bank is Bourg-de-Péage, so named because there was once a toll to cross the river.

St-Donat, 14km NW, the scene of horrific German reprisals in 1944, lives on as a pleasant vineyard town, with ruins of a 12C castle. The 12–16C collegiate church has a particularly fine organ, on which concerts are given during the summer Bach Festival. The adjacent chapel of St-Michel has curious old geometric patterns on the interior walls.

ST-ÉTIENNE
LOIRE   Pop 206,100

Capital of the Loire *département*, and a major industrial city, St-Étienne stands in a flat colliery district within sight of green mountains on the borders of the Massif Central – and indeed calls itself the Ville Vert ('Green City'), which is, however, something of an exaggeration. It is best known to Frenchmen as the home of a successful top-class football team, nicknamed Les Verts. Once called 'the town which makes everything', its principal manufactures including fabrics, ribbons, elastic and steel goods, especially armaments, it has been badly hit by recession and many collieries have been shut down.

Vast and modern, St-Étienne is yet not without its appeal. Trams and trolley buses clatter along the surprisingly narrow main streets. There are relics of an old quarter, and in one of the central squares, Pl. du Peuple, interesting Renaissance buildings survive. Arts and theatre are active in a large Maison de la Culture set in a park. The Musée d'Art et d'Industrie is divided into sections dealing with a very wide range of subjects, from fabrics, coalmining, bicycles and armaments to modern sculpture and painting.

About 10km SW of St-Étienne, the main road enters a wooded mountain area, climbing to the very attractive forested pass called **Col de la République** or **Col du Grand Bois** (1161m), before descending again to the Rhône.

TOURNON
ARDÈCHE Pop 9700

The twin towns of Tournon and **Tain l'Hermitage** (pop 5600), the latter having better road and rail communications, face each other on steep rocky slopes across the Rhône; linked by a pedestrian bridge, they have virtually become one place.

Tournon is noted for its orchards and market gardens. It has an interesting old centre from which rises the square tower of the 14–17C Gothic church of St-Julien (good 16C triptych). The Lycée, in a Renaissance building, was originally founded in 1536 by Cardinal de Tournon. Mallarmé taught English at the school, 1863–66. Along the riverside is a pleasant esplanade shaded by plane trees. Tournon's castle, once a prison, now housing a local museum, has a superb view from its terraces of the old town, the broad curve of the river, and the Hermitage vineyards climbing the opposite bank.

Tain l'Hermitage takes its name from a 15C hermit's cell on the hillside. The vineyards produce a dry white and a famous robust red wine. The Côtes-du-Rhône *appellation* extends along the left bank roughly from the Côte Rotie, around **Ampuis** (near Vienne) to **St-Péray** (S of Tournon), and on the right bank around Tain l'Hermitage. Some distance S, the Côtes-du-Rhône district is resumed around Orange and Avignon (see *Provence*). Hermitage is generally acknowledged as the best that this (very variable) wine region has to offer.

On 14 July there is a jousting tournament afloat in the Rhône between contestants in rival boats.

A steam train runs the 33km from Tournon to **Lamastre** along the beautiful gorges of the river Doux.

VALENCE
DRÔME Pop 68,200

A large and busy town, capital of the Drôme *département*, Valence thrives on fruit and vegetable marketing and light industry. It has an agreeable southern atmosphere. Rabelais studied at the university here (closed 1793) and Napoleon went to the artillery school. Though once Roman (Valentia Julia), little is left to be seen of the town's past. Some interesting Renaissance buildings do remain in what is left of the old centre. The Maison des Têtes (1532), in Grande Rue, has an extraordinary facade of carved medallions. A large Romanesque cathedral, St-Apollinaire, not unattractive despite an incongruous tower (added 1862), stands next door to the bishop's palace, now a municipal museum with good Roman mosaics and some notable drawings by Hubert Robert. Unfortunately, the town is effectively cut off from the Rhône by the autoroute. Main roads run around the SE of the town centre, together with pleasant leafy promenades. Champs de Mars is a huge open space with a fine view across the adjacent Parc Jouvet, over the river, to Mont Crussol with 16C ruined

castle on its summit. In July each year the town has a festival of classical music.

VIENNE
ISÈRE Pop 29,100

Vienne, 27km S of Lyon, on the E bank of a bend in the Rhône, is a centre of light industry in a productive fruit-growing area. It is a modest town with a great past. Capital of the Allobrages tribe, it became an opulent and important Roman city, capital of provincial Gaul. Later it was capital of the Burgundiones (5–6C), and subsequently a powerful diocese. It has a formidable array of ancient buildings.

Vienne

At the centre of the town the Musée des Beaux Arts et d'Archéologie contains impressive Roman relics. Behind the museum, the Jardin Archéologique de Cybèle, with a decorated Roman double arch in pale stone, makes an agreeable park in which are remains of a forum and temple. From here Rue Victor Hugo ascends to the large Roman theatre, built into the hillside of Mont Pipet (good view from summit). In Pl. du Palais, the Temple d'Auguste et de Livie (AD41) is a curious rectangular hall still standing solidly with its Corinthian columns.

The town centre also has a number of good medieval and Renaissance buildings, and two remarkable early churches: St-Pierre (deconsecrated – now a museum with good local archaeological finds), 9C, built with Roman masonry; and St-André-le-Bas, also 9C and very weatherworn, with a handsome tower and beautiful cloisters, 12C Romanesque additions. The imposing 12–15C cathedral of St-Maurice, with no transept, is less appealing, though with much good stained glass and sculpture. From a square in front of the cathedral, a pedestrian bridge crosses the Rhône. On the other side, St-Romain-en-Gal has a remarkable archaeological site with Roman villas, market and baths. On the southern edge of Vienne is a curious Roman pyramid, once the centre of a chariot racetrack. Beside it now is the famous (and expensive) *Restaurant Pyramide*, annually awarded Michelin's highest accolade, three rosettes, founded by the late Fernand Point, true pioneer of the *nouvelle cuisine*.

During the summer Vienne has an excellent Festival of Music and Drama with plays in the Roman theatre and concerts in the cathedral and the St-André church.

ALPS/SAVOY

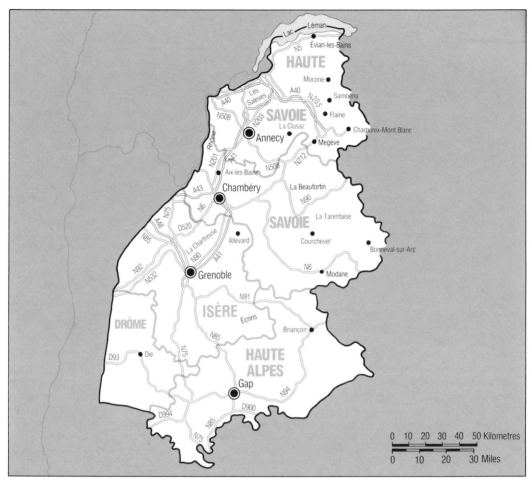

The Alps stretch for about 1200km from north of Nice in a great arc deep into Austria, nearly to Vienna. The French Alps reach from near the Mediterranean to Lac Léman, which we call Lake Geneva. But to most of us the French Alps are the old provinces of Savoie and Dauphiné, between the Rhône valley and the mountain frontiers of Switzerland and Italy.

The Dauphiné was sold to France back in 1349 on condition that the king's eldest son should rule it and become "Dauphin". But Savoie was a dukedom constantly fighting against France, several times occupied, but not for long, and stretching well into what is now Italy. It was united with Piedmont and in 1559 the dukes moved from Chambéry to Turin. Not until 1860 did the Savoyards vote to join France. You can see the Piedmont influence in town architecture.

Although many of the villages in Savoie are as picturesque as those of Switzerland, the Dauphiné villages are markedly more austere. Stone was used to build most of the old houses and balconies are for storing firewood for the winter. Until the arrival of tourism, the Savoie and Dauphiné were poor outside the big cities such as Grenoble, Chambéry and Annecy.

Communities were almost cut off from outside contact, so that as late as 1815 Napoleon, having escaped from Elba, was able to march northwards unhindered although nobody welcomed him until he got to Gap. The Route Napoléon still goes through wild country to Grenoble.

The climbers came in the 19th century. Some were scientists, like the Swiss Saussure, second man up Mont Blanc. He climbed it in a tailcoat! Some were rich young men looking for adventure, many of them British.

Then, after World War I, the fashionable sport of skiing spread in the French Alps so fast that Chamonix, not St Moritz, was chosen for the first Winter Olympics in 1924. The "worst" months of the year in the Alps began to be the best, the north-facing slopes most popular.

Hydroelectric schemes high in the mountains revolutionized alpine life after World War II. It changed wastelands into workplaces and playgrounds. Industry grew along alpine valleys. Grenoble's population multiplied five times. Electricity came to the higher mountain villages, supplying ski lifts so that the pistes could move up from under 1000m to over 2000m.

Subsequently entire resorts were built – little

concrete cities with hotels, big apartment blocks, shops, cinemas, bars, cafés, restaurants, with lifts sited entirely for the convenience and enjoyment of the skier. These new resorts are pleasant in summer; but they belong to the skiers.

The Savoyard cuisine makes much use of local beef, lamb, fish and mountain cheese, notably the Gruyères of Comté, the smooth Belfort and the small *tomme* cheeses. Vegetables and early summer fruits are plentiful, the latter much used in tarts and pâtisserie.

AIX-LES-BAINS
SAVOIE   Pop 22,500

In a charming situation beside the deep Lake Bourget below Mont Revard, Aix has not faded like so many 19C spas. Though not so fashionable as when rich Americans and British aristocrats filled it, it has remained lively as the weekend playground of the people of nearby Chambéry.

Aix-les-Bains

The modern thermal establishment here is renowned for treatment of rheumatism, sciatica and respiratory illnesses. The Romans had baths here and there are a few remains. The spa was revived in 1790, reaching its zenith around 1885. In Pl. de Revard is a bust of one distinguished visitor – Queen Victoria. The baths are open all year, but the season is April-Oct.

The lake has fine sailing, water skiing and fishing. Despite purification plant, the water can be polluted in summer, so swim in the pools.

Opposite the baths is a little town hall in a 16C medieval-style château of the former Marquis d'Aix. Built of stone from Roman ruins, it has a fine Renaissance staircase. The Musée Faure includes a magnificent collection of Impressionist paintings, with every painter of the school represented, plus some sculptures and watercolours by Rodin.

Boat tours of the lake visit the Benedictine abbey of Hautecombe, where the princes and princesses of Savoy were buried. On Suns. at 8.30am is a mass with Gregorian chant.

Opposite Aix, 9km round the bottom of the lake, is **Le Bourget-du-Lac**, a delightful hillside village with a little harbour and port from which steam boats used to go to Lyon by the Savière canal until 1859. It has an interesting 15C cloister next to the 13C church.

ALLEVARD
ISÈRE   Pop 2400

This little spa 475m up and 23km SE of Chambéry is a good centre for exploring alpine forest and mountains on foot or by car. Its waters are hard, cold, sparkling and sulphurous, used for treating all respiratory ailments. Founded in the 12C, Allevard used to produce iron for the French navy. On the border of Savoie and Dauphiné, it is at the opposite end of the Belledonne range from Uriage-les-Bains (near Grenoble).

ANNECY
HAUTE-SAVOIE   Pop 51,600

An alluring town at the top end of beautiful Lake Annecy and extremely popular as a holiday resort and place to live. It has grown fast, is very prosperous and makes costume-jewellery, ball bearings and razor blades. In the old town, bells are cast in the ancient Paccard foundry and exported round the world. Now a centre of nuclear energy research has been built almost alongside, with a 12C church between them.

The impressive château, much changed since the 11C, was the home of the counts of Geneva. On an island in the Thiou canal is a 12C castle, later used as law courts and now for exhibitions. There are several impressive old churches, including St-Maurice with 15C frescoes. Gardens give lovely lakeside walks. In Rue Jean-Jacques Rousseau is a bust of the philosopher in a cage of golden bars.

You can take a boat round the lake or drive round it – a superb tour, for the lake is almost surrounded by gorgeous mountain scenery.

Talloires is a beautifully sited, pretty and rather pricy resort at the narrowest part of the lake.

Lac d'Annecy

BEAUFORTIN, LA
SAVOIE

A secretive area NW from Bourg-St Maurice, surrounded by peaks. It has one main road from Albertville, through the capital Beaufort to Bourg-St Maurice, a lesser road from Beaufort climbing to the Saisies pass at 1633m, then down to Megève (q.v.) and occasional byroads to the few villages.

Beaufort (pop. 2000) clusters round its 17C church in typical Savoyard style with sculptured wood, including a fine pulpit. From here the Beaufort cheese, which the great gastronome Curnonsky called "the prince of Gruyères", has been exported to Geneva since the 18C. It is made in chalets in the alpine pastures of the Beaufortin and Tarentaise, not factory-made at Beaufort, and it is one of 21 French cheeses with an official *appellation d'origine*.

Two lakes for hydroelectric energy, created in the 1950s, have actually improved the scenery, especially the big wild **Roselend** lake alongside the road E of Beaufort – excellent for sailing.

BONNEVAL-SUR-ARC
SAVOIE   Pop 220

At 1835m, this is the highest village of La Maurienne mountain region and growing as a ski resort, partly because summer skiing is possible on the nearby glacier of Grand Pissaillas. It has ski lifts, a mountaineering and climbing school, two small hotels and furnished rooms.

BRIANÇON
HAUTES-ALPES   Pop 11,600

The citadel built at an altitude of 1326m for Louis XIV by Vauban must have been awe-inspiring in its day. Small wonder that, after Waterloo, it withstood an attack by an Austrian army 20,000 strong which had already taken Grenoble. It is the highest town in France, once guarding the frontier with Italy.

Briançon is at the meeting place of the Guisance and Durance rivers, and the gorge of the Durance is crossed by a spectacular bridge built in 1754. The newer town at 1200m leads up to the lovely old city with a double line of walls and steep, crowded streets.

Monetier-les-Bains (14km NW) is a mountain climbing centre. **Serre Chevalier** (6km) has 67 pistes for skiing at all levels and is suited to families; 61 lifts, three ice rinks and a covered swimming pool.

Montgenèvre (12km E) held the first international ski races in France in 1907.

CHAMBÉRY
SAVOIE   Pop 54,900

A delightful old town, 11km from Aix-les-Bains, so far avoiding much industrialization despite two motorways nearby connecting it to Lyon and Grenoble. It was capital of Savoy until the dukes moved to Turin. They kept their huge 14C château which still dominates Chambéry. Much of the imposing architecture is Piedmontese, with pebble-dash facades and turrets, courtyards and winding staircases.

Les Charmettes, 2km from Chambéry, is the house where Rousseau and Mme de Warens lived. He grew flowers, she kept bees.

Chambéry produces the pale, dry vermouth named after it and bottles wines from the surrounding vineyards of Apremont, Abymes and Chignin. Apremont white wines are highly rated but Chignin Bergeron from Roussane grapes is probably the best of Savoy.

CHAMONIX-MONT BLANC
HAUTE-SAVOIE   Pop 9300

In 1731 two young Englishmen, Windham and Pococke, discovered the tiny hamlet of Chamonix and its glaciers at a height of 1037m and informed fashionable society. A prize was offered for the first men to climb Mont Blanc, 4807m, Europe's highest peak. A local crystal cutter Balmat did it in 1786, followed next year by Saussure from Geneva. Climbing became the vogue.

The first winter Olympics were held at Chamonix in 1924. Today a network of lifts and rack railways serve 100 marked pistes (quite difficult) and give superb summer mountain rides. One cable car trip takes you to Plan d'Aiguille, an intermediate station, then to Aiguille du Midi, 1000m below the top of Mont Blanc, where the scenic views are breathtaking. There is summer skiing as well. From here you can take cable railways down to La Palud in Italy. This is at the Italian end of the Mont Blanc road tunnel, opened in 1965, 11.6km long and still the most popular route from France to Italy.

The Alpine museum is fascinating, but only opens 20 June–15 Sept. In the Anglican cemetery is the grave of the most famous Alpinist Edward Whymper (1840–1911).

Argentière, at the Swiss end of the valley, is an old village ski resort, pretty and less crowded.

Taconnaz glacier, Chamonix

CHARTREUSE, MASSIF DE LA
ISÈRE

A wild massif N of Grenoble and E of the little commercial town of Voiron, where skis are made. This mountain zone pioneered the generation of hydroelectricity – Savoy's "white coal" – which provided the stimulus for the early industrial development of Grenoble. The easy way to it is along N520 from Voiron to St-Laurent-du-Pont, then right along Gorge du Guiers Mort to **St-**

Pierre-de-Chartreuse, from where a road leads to the celebrated Chartreuse monastery, founded originally by St Bruno in 1101. You cannot visit it any more, but there is a museum nearby in the old guesthouse where Queen Victoria once stayed. The Musée de la Correrie shows a large-scale model of the present building dating from 1676. Avalanches drove the monks from the original site selected by Bruno. Chartreuse is Carthusian, a solitary order, and monks are allowed to talk only for two hours on Suns. In 1909 the state expelled them to the Spanish Pyrenees, but they came back in 1929.

They still make the very strong "elixir", used for centuries as a medicine for men and cattle, and once believed to bring long life, as well as the potent green and yellow Chartreuse liqueurs from mountain herbs. But these now age in caves in Voiron, where you can taste them.

A harder, shorter way to St-Pierre from Grenoble is by the tortuous N520 over the Col-de-Port (26km).

CLUSAZ, LA
HAUTE-SAVOIE   Pop 1700

For long a summer resort, this is now also an international ski resort at 1100-2600m in the Aravis range, surrounded by jagged crests. It is only 32km from Annecy, with a bus service. There are 38 ski-lifts to carry 25,000 skiers an hour, 45 pistes of all standards, nine cross-country tracks, a heated open-air pool (open in winter), 100 shops and five nightclubs – all built round a 17C church with an odd but attractive bell-tower.

St-Jean-de-Sixt (3km) is developing the old forgotten technique of walking on snowshoes.

A smaller, remoter resort is **Manigod**, 26km from Annecy through Thônes. A summer and winter resort, it has twelve ski-lifts, and is quiet and pleasant.

COURCHEVEL
SAVOIE

First of the serious purpose-built modern ski resorts, it was built in 1947 and has more of the alpine-village atmosphere than others built recently. It is a clutch of resorts at different levels in one of Les Trois Vallées. These valleys are connected with each other by a network of ski-lifts and pistes.

The main resort is Courchevel "1850". The complex has all the skiing, sports facilities, entertainment and nightlife of a fashionable and fairly luxurious winter and summer resort, including 61 hotels, 3000 self-catering apartments and seven nightclubs. Snow is consistently good. It is in the heart of La Tarentaise, which the French call the world's biggest skiing area, and is linked with Méribel, built in traditional style, with 55 pistes and a competition course. Courchevel has cableways to the top of La Saulire (2630m) with views to Mont Blanc 50km away.

DIE
DRÔME   Pop 4000

A pleasant old town in the lovely Drôme valley, at the S end of the Vercors range, once a Roman town, now known best for its sweet sparkling clairette wine, made from clairette and muscat grapes. A nice peaceful centre for discovering the wild rugged country of the Diois. Along the Drôme are orchards and vineyards. Die has Roman remains, including a triumphal arch.

ECRINS
ISÈRE

A wilderness of peaks, glaciers, valleys, SE from Grenoble and W from Briançon, it has been a national park since 1973. For long it was regarded as the poorest part of France, its peasants living on the starvation line. Geologists and mountaineers were the main visitors. The peaks were the last in Europe to be conquered – by Whymper in 1850, a remarkable American lady named Breevort in 1870 and the Grand Pic of Meije by a French team in 1877.

The park covers about 100,000ha with few roads – invaded by tourist cars in summer, impassable in winter. Ramblers' paths are marked. The little capital of the area is at the N tip – **Le Bourg d'Oisans**, a market town which holds a Mineralogy Fair on Easter weekend.

You can get a cable car to the **Meije glaciers** at 3200m from **La Grave**, a village at 1450m with magnificent views of this range. It has hotels, glacier skiing and a climbing school. The main ski resort is **Les Deux Alpes**, 30km W of La Grave, with a good snow and sun record, summer skiing on the glacier at 3568m, lifts to carry 40,000 skiers an hour, all grades of winter skiing, a slalom run, summer grass skiing, nightclubs, 40 hotels and 15,000 beds in apartments.

L'Alpes d'Huez, on a winding road N from Bourg d'Oisans, 63km from Grenoble, is another winter and summer ski resort, nearly as big as Les Deux Alpes and still developing.

ÉVIAN-LES-BAINS
HAUTE-SAVOIE   Pop 6200

One of the leading spas of Europe, in a fine position on the S shores of Lake Geneva, it was completely rebuilt as a spa resort by Baron de Blonay in 1865 when Baron Haussmann was modernizing Paris. It has everything to make it a fashionable resort – casino, golf course, sailing club, Palais de Congrès, swimming pool, nightclubs. Ornate old hotels remind Britons of their Victorian resorts. The treaty granting independence to Algeria was signed here in 1962. Waters are drunk to help the kidneys and alleviate arthritis. Évian water is non-sparkling, lightly mineralized, almost tasteless, and among the favourite French table waters.

There are boat trips round the lake and to many French and Swiss towns and villages around it. Just past **Thonon**, a smaller, quieter but very pleasant spa, is **Château de Ripaille**, where Amédée VIII, duke of Savoy, hid as a "hermit", then returned to die after being antipope. **Yvoire**, a hamlet rich in flowers and with some medieval houses, is one of the prettiest little places on the lake.

FLAINE
HAUTE-SAVOIE

A serious ski student's paradise, carefully designed in 1968, 1600m up in a white desert of the northern Alps. Already it has 31 lifts, 260km of pistes, and off-piste and ski touring with École du Ski Français. You can ski from your door.

GAP
HAUTES-ALPES   Pop 31,300

Important commercially and a busy route junction on the "Route Napoléon". You can see the house where he spent a night in March 1815 on his way to Paris after escaping from Elba.

GRENOBLE
ISÈRE   Pop with suburbs, 395,000

Anyone who last saw Grenoble in the 1950s would simply not recognize the city. Since 1960 it has been the boom city of France, its old city totally dwarfed by rows of skyscraping apartments and office blocks, concrete roads and fly-overs replacing cosy old streets, suburbs spreading year by year nearer to the surrounding mountains. Industry has moved into electronics, nuclear research and modern engineering. The population has multiplied five times in 35 years. The university (founded 1339) is now divided into three, with a total of 32,000 students, quite a number of them foreign. Grenoble is thus one of the largest French university towns.

The old city, between the Isère and Drac rivers, has not been obliterated. You can see that by taking a ride in one of the modernistic ball-shaped telecabins of the funicular to the old Bastille fort 475m up.

The hillside below the Bastille is a maze of *montées* (half alleys, half steps) which lead to student apartments, the Institutes of Geology and Alpine Geography, and the Dauphinois museum of daily mountain life through the centuries, housed in a convent founded in 1619 but, at the end of the 19C, a cabaret!

In the former Hôtel de Ville in the old town is a museum devoted to Stendhal, the writer born here in 1783. Nearby is the 13C church of St-André and the interesting Palace of Justice where the Dauphinois parliament used to sit. Another writer associated with Grenoble was de Laclos, who was garrisoned here and based his characters in *Les Liaisons Dangereuses* on the local aristocracy.

The modern Hôtel de Ville in Mistral Park has plate-glass walls, marble and mosaic patios, a fine fountain and sculptures. In this park are modern buildings and sports facilities made for the 1968 Olympics, including the superb skating rink. Much of Grenoble's modern building was prompted by the Games.

The city is blessedly rich in flowered parks. Art is not neglected. The Musée des Beaux Arts is one of the finest museums outside Paris. Its masterpieces include a superb Rubens, Sisley's *View of Montmartre*, Monet's magnificent *Garden at Giverny*, Picasso's *Femme Lisant*, great paintings of Utrillo, Modigliani, Renoir (*La Laitière*), Matisse's

controversial *Les Trois Aubergines*, and sculptures by Rodin and Cocteau.

A sadder little museum in Rue Jean-Jacques Rousseau, where Stendhal was born, is the Musée de la Résistance et de la Déportation. From 1940–45 Grenoble was a major centre of the French Resistance against the Nazis. Heroic deeds were performed in the Chartreuse (q.v.) and Vercors mountains, and many thousands were deported to suffer and die in Nazi concentration camps.

The Vercors was the centre of resistance, and by 1944 some 3000–4000 *maquisards* were conducting guerilla activities behind German lines. In June 1944 the Germans retaliated with a two-month campaign of considerable cruelty, in which many hundreds of French fighters and civilians were killed.

Grenoble's skiing area is in the Massif de Chamrousse. **Chamrousse** resort, 20km from Grenoble, was used for the 1968 Olympics. The 840m-long slope of Casserousse was the scene of Jean-Claude Killy's triple triumph. It stages, too, an international comic film festival, a dog-sled race in March and a snow-scooter race in Jan. **Uriage-les-Bains**, 10km from Grenoble, is a small spa in a pretty wooded valley beneath the forest of Prémol.

Take a trolley-bus from Grenoble to **Sassenage**, with its **Château Bérenger** (another allegedly built by the fairy Mélusine). This is the gateway to the magnificent **Vercors National Park**. Comprising alpine foothills, much of the park is green and gentle, but climbing with frightening steepness. From Sassenage you go through the **Gorges d'Engins** to **Lans** and **Villard-de-Lans**, a resort for walkers, climbers and fishermen, with cable cars to fine viewpoints over the Vercors range and the Dauphiné Alps.

Grenoble

MEGÈVE
HAUTE-SAVOIE   Pop 5300

Megève is the old-style ski resort which grew from a village after World War I. It was the most fashionable resort of the 1930s and despite the building of so many purpose-built resorts higher, with better snow and planned lifts and pistes, it remains popular and full. It has a superb range of hotels and restaurants, a casino, lively après-ski and livelier nightlife. There are gentle slopes for beginners and breakneck pistes. A cable-car takes you to Mount d'Arbois for magnificent views over les Aravis and to Mont Blanc. You can ski down.

Megève

Cableways and lifts connect with **St-Gervais-les-Bains**, a good centre for skiing, alpine excursions and taking sulphur baths for skin, nose, throat and ear problems. Le Tramway takes you up to 2386m at **Le Nid d'Aigle** (Eagle's Nest) where you can see the **Brionassay glacier** on Mont Blanc only 6km away.

MODANE
SAVOIE Pop 4900

Frontier town of customs officers, soldiers, tunnel engineers, and engineering works, it was for centuries a stopping place for travellers going by mule over the Mont Cenis pass to Italy. Then in 1871 a rail tunnel, the Fréjus, opened from here to Bardonecchia in Italy, later taking cars. It was the first tunnel through the Alps and the first for which compressed air was used in construction. Recently the new car tunnel to Italy was opened, 12.5km long, beating the record of the Mont Blanc tunnel (11.6km).

MORZINE
HAUTE-SAVOIE Pop 2900

In a lovely setting near the Swiss border, this ski and summer resort is at 960m and easily reached. Established since 1924, it has good snow for international competitions and is known for its restaurants offering Savoyard dishes. A road past the lake at Montriond or a cable-car lift take you to **Avoriaz**, a good resort built in 1966. It is designed in a modern version of traditional alpine style, its buildings covered in wood, and no cars are allowed, only horse-drawn sledges.

SALÈVES, LES
HAUTE-SAVOIE

Les Salèves is a French mountain area taken over by Swiss tourism. It runs along the Swiss border, but in France, S of Geneva, overlooking that city and the lake. A road runs along 34km of crests, but sometimes it seems that more people are climbing than motoring, though many climbs are not easy.

The road starts at **Annemasse**, an important French frontier commercial town (pop. 26,500), almost a suburb of Geneva. After it crosses the

Rhône, it climbs and zigzags to **Cruseilles**, 20km N of Annecy, a small town (pop. 2500) on the edge of mountain forests, through which flows the river Usses on its way to the Rhône. Nearer the Rhône on this road is a cable car to the *Restaurant des 13 Arbres* with superb views.

SAMOËNS
HAUTE-SAVOIE Pop 1950

Divided from the Swiss frontier by the Cirque du Fer à Cheval, this is a wild area of peaks and valleys where the conqueror of Mont Blanc, Jacques Balmat, disappeared mysteriously in 1834 when he was 72. He was looking for gold, rumoured to exist among these wild mountains, glaciers and waterfalls.

Samoëns is a lovely little place, winner of the "Most Beautiful Flowered Village" award. A real mountain market is held on Weds. in its medieval square. A superb alpine garden was given to the town in 1906 by a local girl goatherd who founded La Samaritaine departmental store in Paris with her pedlar husband and made a fortune. She had 250 gardeners to make it.

Above the town at **Folly Refuge** (2150m) is the entrance to a pothole where in 1981 the world record depth was broken – 1410m, finishing 70m under the streets of the town.

At **Sixt** (5km), named one of the "101 Most Beautiful Villages in France", the 12C abbey is now the hotel, with a vast refectory dining room.

TARENTAISE, LA
SAVOIE

This division of Savoie extends along the Isère river from Chambéry to the Little St-Bernard Pass. The main town is **Moûtiers** (pop. 4800), an ancient bishopric with a 15C cathedral containing a fine episcopal throne and rich treasury.

The little town of **Bourg-St-Maurice** (pop. 6700), 3km NE, dominates the upper Isère valley from 840m, but above it has been developed in recent years a place already better known – **Les Arcs**, a ski resort of three villages at 1600, 1800 and 2000m. Pistes are for all standards, but one run, Aiguille Rouge, has the world's largest vertical drop (2100m), and was one of the first resorts to use the *évolutif* method of teaching beginners. Pistes link with those of **La Plagne**, a resort started in 1960. This is a link-up of ten villages, from a concrete modern apartment village to old-style chalets. Its 86 lifts interconnect to avoid bottlenecks, and six serve a glacier for summer skiing. It is a skiers' world, with few cars, mostly N-facing with excellent snow conditions.

When they built the hydroelectric barrage at **Tignes** and created the huge Lake Chevril, they drowned the village of Tignes. The new village is beside the little natural lake of Tignes. It is a leading ski resort and, with glacier skiing on the Grande Motte, is one of the few in the world to be open twelve months of the year.

Val d'Isère (pop. 1700) to the S is a lively resort, with plenty of nightlife. It often has snow until the end of May and in summer is a base for drives or walks in La Vanoise national park.

DORDOGNE AND LOT

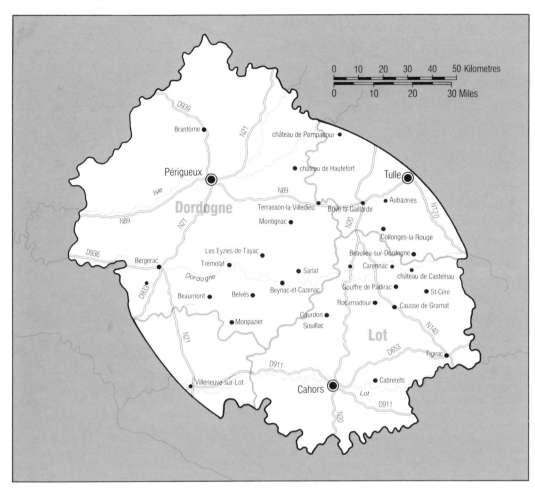

When, in the late 1930s, Henry Miller called the Dordogne "the nearest thing to paradise this side of Greece", it was truly connoisseur's France, known to a few Bordelais, fewer Parisians and a handful of Britons. It is now beloved by French and foreigners, but they use the word "Dordogne" so loosely that there can be real confusion.

The *département* of the Dordogne, created in 1790 and the third biggest in France, covers much the same area as the old province of Périgord, half-way between the plains of Guyenne and the Massif Central. But to local people the word "Dordogne" still means the river. They call themselves "Péri-gourdins" and the *département* "Périgord". Conversely, many visitors speak of the "Dordogne" to cover anywhere near the river and often way south to the river Lot and into Quercy, even as far as Cahors.

Rivers have made the history and the very landscape of this area. The Dronne, Isle, Auvézère and Vézère sweep from the hills into the beautiful Dordogne flowing west. Southward the Célé feeds the Lot flowing west to join the Garonne. Above ground, the rivers brought richer soil between the limestone and rocks of the plateaux and for centur-ies provided the main means of transport for goods

and livestock. Below ground, they cut the caves which were home to prehistoric man and which, through discoveries in the last century or so, have taught us more than any other area about our earliest ancestors. From their discoveries, archae-ologists have been able to follow the stages of development from our pre-hominid ancestors between ape and man, Neanderthal man living about 150,000 years ago and *Homo sapiens* from around 40,000 years ago.

Périgord was part of the Roman province of Aquitaine before Caesar invaded Gaul, and ruins at Périgueux show the prosperity of this Roman city of Vesuna. Charlemagne handed over Aquitaine, including Périgord, to a Count and, as a result, it came under the English crown. In 1152, Henry Plantagenet, Duke of Normandy, married the beautiful Eleanor of Aquitaine, former wife of Louis VII of France, and got Aquitaine as a dowry. A year later Henry was also king of England. His sons revolted against him, even Richard Lion-heart, and the family fights spread over the whole area. It is strange that some of the most interesting and handsome tourist attractions of the Dordogne, the castles, are there partly because of the English. Unlike the Loire, where châteaux were built for love these were built for war.

The Dordogne was a main battleground of the Hundred Years' War, started when Edward III of England claimed the French crown. Mostly the English held the south side of the river, the French the north side. Both armies pillaged the country, together with mercenary barons who fought for whichever would bring them the richest booty. Castles, towns and villages were built, taken, destroyed, rebuilt. At the end, Périgord especially was a country laid waste. Plague and disease had decimated its people.

The Wars of Religion following the Reformation were almost as destructive. Regarding the church as part of the Establishment of their lords, who charged them exorbitant rents for farms, many of the poor became Protestants. Bergerac was a Huguenot stronghold, changing hands constantly. Périgueux was Catholic, under Protestant rule. After the Edict of Nantes was revoked, taking away freedom of religion from Protestants, persecution and suffering were appalling, as was the destruction of churches.

The people of Périgord, Lot and Quercy were poor, proud but independent, as they showed in World War II. The Resistance was so effective that the St-Céré district was a major "depot" for dropping of arms by the RAF to distribute around France, and Colonel Buckmaster, head of the British organization, set up a French headquarters in St-Céré's *Hôtel de France* – now the *Coq Arlequin*.

This area has always been poor because of scarcity of mineral wealth and poverty of soil, despite its exceptional beauty and variety of scenery. Nowadays, modern farming methods and tourism have brought more prosperity.

By the late 1950s, farms had become uneconomically small because of French inheritance laws dividing land between children, and government agricultural policy, then loaded against small farms unsuitable for modern machines. The EEC brought fierce competition from small farmers of Italy and Germany. Sons could see little future in following their fathers into primitive cottages and working so hard for so little. More difficult fields were left fallow. In Quercy, whole hillsides of vineyards were abandoned. Cottages were empty and people from Bordeaux bought them very cheaply and modernized them for weekends and

holidays. Parisians and the British followed.

Dordogne and Quercy rely heavily on wild game, poultry and river fish for their cooking, with rich sauces.

Truffles have become too expensive for most cooks but other fungi, *cèpes, chanterelles* and *morilles*, make passable substitutes in many dishes. Traditionally, cooking was based on pork and goose, with duck tending to take over these days and turkey edging in. These are still used particularly in pâtés and in confit (potted meats), made by cooking them in their own fat and keeping them in earthenware pots. The method of making pâté de foie gras (goose liver) by force-feeding the geese has appalled foreigners, but many hide their consciences when faced with this delectable dish.

Beef comes into Périgord these days from Limousin and even steaks are served with the local Périgourdine sauce, magnificent when properly made. The real thing is of onions and shallots sautéed with goose fat, simmered with white wine and a little flour, with truffles added at the last moment. You can buy it in airtight containers from a village charcuterie. On meat or poultry, it goes well with the dark, strong, mature red wine of Cahors. So does Quercy goat's cheese, Chabichou.

AUBAZINES
CORRÈZE   Pop 670

Below Puy de Pauliac, on a promontory above the Corrèze valley, this tight little village grew around an abbey founded in 1152 by St Étienne (St Stephen); first Benedictine, then Cistercian. The abbey church, with superb carved tomb of the saint, remains, with some buildings occupied by Greek nuns.

BEAULIEU-SUR-DORDOGNE
CORRÈZE   Pop 1600

An archbishop of Bourges named this beautiful place on the Dordogne river bank around 850 and founded an abbey with monks from Cluny. They built the 12C church of St-Pierre in Limousin-Romanesque style with a magnificent sculptured doorway, showing Greek influence, by Toulouse craftsmen who carved others at Moissac and Souillac. The magnificent tympanum shows the Last Judgment, with prophets on supporting pillars and scenes from the Temptation and Daniel and the lion.

Queyssac, S of Beaulieu, a village among vineyards and woods, has vast views of the Dordogne valley to Castelnau, the Tours de St-Laurent and the Rocher des Pendus near Vic from the top of the castle tower.

BEAUMONT
DORDOGNE   Pop 1300

One of the first of Edward I's *bastides*, built S of the Dordogne river to defend Périgord (1272). Little remains except the church, originally fortified as a last line of defence, demilitarized last century but

for four corner towers and sentry walk. The attractive town market square has old arcades.

St-Avit-Sénieur (4km E) has a fortified church with rugged exterior, the remains of an abbey founded in 1214 in memory of a soldier-saint and destroyed four times in religious wars.

BELVÈS
DORDOGNE Pop 1700

On a hillside overlooking the Nauze valley, this quiet town, on the ancient road from Périgueux to Cahors, had a 9C Benedictine monastery; the present building is 14C. The main square has an old covered market. On one side is a 12C stone tower converted after the Hundred Years' War into a bell-tower and clock.

BERGERAC
DORDOGNE Pop 27,700

The biggest town on the Dordogne river was known for wine in the Middle Ages but has suffered in comparison with nearby Bordeaux. Despite damage in the Hundred Years' War when the Earl of Derby took it, much has survived around the market place in narrow streets, including the old port from which wines were taken by *gabarre* (flat bottomed barges) downriver to Libourne, and a restored monastery built between the 12–17C. This is now a Maison du Vin for tastings of Bergerac, Côtes de Bergerac, red Pécharmant and sweet white Monbazillac. A tobacco town, too, with a Musée du Tabac in the town hall, Bergerac now produces nitro-cellulose for paint, plastics and films.

Cyrano de Bergerac, a 17C writer and duellist, whose life was romanticized by Edmond Rostand (1868–1918) in his famous play of that name, has a statue in Pl. de la Myrpe.

Monbazillac (6km S) has a château (1550) housing exhibits of wine-making and local Protestant history, and vineyards where grapes are allowed to ripen to "noble rot", producing a sweet wine.

Bergerac

BEYNAC-ET-CAZENAC
DORDOGNE Pop 460

Beynac was one of the most powerful castles in France in the Middle Ages. Built on a rock commanding the Dordogne river, with superb views, it was taken in 1195 by Richard Lionheart. He gave it to the brutal Mercadier, who terrorized the countryside. Simon de Montfort, father of the English statesman, partly demolished it in 1214. Rebuilt, it was a French stronghold in the Hundred Years' War, skirmishing constantly with the English-held Castelnaud across the river. The interior is being restored. A superb wooden staircase has been reconstructed with slabs of 50-year-old oak. The impressive Salle d'État, where local barons met in council, and a curious naive 15C fresco of the Last Supper are being restored.

The château of Castelnaud towers over this magnificent stretch of the Dordogne, overlooking the village of that name, with picturesque old stone houses. Much ruined through neglect, it is being restored. Simon de Montfort took it during the Albigensian crusade. Catholic forces failed to capture it in the Wars of Religion.

La Roque-Gageac (5km E) is strung along the river and huddles against overhanging rocks. It is very pretty, but falling rocks destroyed some houses in 1956.

BRANTÔME
DORDOGNE Pop 2100

This beautiful little town is enfolded by two arms of the Dronne river. In summer, visitors far outnumber local people, so car parking is difficult. Red-roofed buildings, stone bridges, riverside gardens, tree-shaded walks make up its charm. Follow the dog-legged stone bridge to the monks' gardens and rose beds, loll outside the old monastery and watch the water tumbling over a narrow weir. Charlemagne may have founded the abbey in 780. It has been much changed and recently rather over-restored. The 11C bell-tower, square and gabled, is a delight. Caves under the belfry, used by the monks as a bakery and wine-cellar, have unusual religious bas-reliefs carved in the rock. Pierre de Bourdeilles, 16C adventurer, courtier, diplomat, was given the abbey for military services to the crown. He escorted Mary Queen of Scots back to Leith after her husband died. Then he retired to the abbey and, under the name of "Brantôme", wrote witty, cynical, often scandalous books about the court ladies and military leaders.

His family had built **Château de Bourdeilles** on a high rock 7km downstream from Brantôme, in the 14C. In the 16C they added within the fortifications a fine Renaissance house for a visit of Catherine de Médicis, who never arrived. Now it houses a collection of Renaissance furniture, travelling chests, armour and paintings. The Gilded Room has original rich decor by Ambroise Lenoble, painter of the Fontainebleau school.

At **Champagnac-de-Belair** (6km from Brantôme), a delightful 17C walnut oil mill, still with its machinery, is now a superb little hotel, Moulin du Roc, in a lovely waterside garden.

BRIVE-LA-GAILLARDE
CORRÈZE Pop 54,000

A lively commercial, railway and industrial town with traffic problems, it is particularly a market centre for fruit and market-gardening. But it hides old treasures, such as old turreted houses being restored near the tall 12C church of St-Martin and Hôtel de Labenche, a fine Renaissance house. It is an archaeological library, but you can see it from the courtyard – superb arcades with round arches.

CABRERETS
LOT Pop 220

A delightful hamlet 18km E of Cahors in an amphitheatre of rocks where the Célé and Sagne rivers meet. A pretty waterfall pours out of the rock by the road where an underground river surfaces. A ruined 8C medieval castle perched over the village, Château du Diable, is called Château des Anglais. The English used it in the Hundred Years' War to pillage the country. Château Gontaut-Biron, overlooking the valley, is not open to the public.

In 1922 two fourteen-year-old boys explored a rock cleft 3km W of Cabrerets used as a hideout in the Revolution and found caves used by prehistoric man. Walls of linked galleries have drawings of mammoths, bison, deer, horses, female bodies and human hands outlined in red and black. Further on are strangely shaped rock formations and bones of cave-bears. A mile of galleries are lit and open to the public.

Just S of the river Lot is **St-Cirq-Lapopie**, a dramatically lovely village perched high on a rock above the river. The castle, now ruined, defied even Richard Lionheart in 1199, but changed hands several times in the Hundred Years' War and was taken and destroyed in 1580 by the Protestant Henri of Navarre, future Henri IV of France. The hamlet has lovely old houses, and artisan shops in narrow streets.

CAHORS
LOT Pop 20,800

Cahors is in a magnificent position inside a great horseshoe bend of the Lot river, with hills above, some wooded, some with vineyards. Cahors red wine, which only received an *appellation* in 1971, was used once to fortify weaker Bordeaux. The weaker wines prevailed. Since a severe frost of 1956 enforced replanting, wines are now robust, smooth, full-flavoured and fashionable.

A commercial and university town in the Middle Ages, it was handed to the English in 1360 and became a near-deserted city. In the Wars of Religion in 1580 it was sacked by the Protestants. Until recent times, it was a sleepy old town, but industry has built up on the outer rim.

Much remains of interest, particularly the superbly beautiful Pont de Valentré, a medieval fortified bridge with three towers with battlements. Legend says that the Devil helped to finish it on time, and was tricked out of payment by the builder. Many fine old buildings include the cathedral of St-Étienne, also fortified, founded 1119,

Cahors

altered until 1500. It has medieval paintings, a supremely lovely medieval door, and carved ornamental cloisters, sadly damaged. Among famed sons of Cahors was Léon Gambetta, the statesman who defied the Prussians in 1870 and who has as many squares and streets named after him as Victor Hugo and de Gaulle.

CARENNAC
LOT Pop 400

Brown-tiled houses clustered around the remains of a priory on the banks of the Dordogne – a lovely hamlet. Fénelon, priest and writer, was prior from 1681, and wrote here his novel *Télémaque*, about the son of Ulysses. The prior's "château", a tower and a fortified gateway remain. The church of St-Pierre has a 12C doorway with a superbly beautiful carved tympanum of the Toulouse school. Peaceful cloisters beyond have Romanesque and Flamboyant galleries.

CASTELNAU, CHÂTEAU DE
LOT

It stands 11km from St-Céré on a spur above the river Dordogne where it meets the river Cère – a magnificent medieval pile with red stone ramparts, built in the 11C, extended in the Hundred Years' War until it was three miles around, had a garrison of 1500 men and 100 horses, and an annual rent of one egg, carried in pomp by four oxen to the Viscount of Turenne. Restored carefully between 1896–1932, it now has a lapidary museum, fine old Aubusson and Beauvais tapestries, and superb views from the ramparts (closed Tues.).

COLLONGES-LA-ROUGE
CORRÈZE Pop 380

A photogenic village built round a 12C Romanesque church, with cottages, inns, and turreted manor houses in red sandstone with red or blue schist roofs. About 2km N of Meyssac, off the Brive road, it was a retreat for the local lords of Turenne. Several restaurants packed in summer.

EYZIES-DE-TAYAC, LES
DORDOGNE   Pop 750

In a dramatic setting of steep hills and woods where two rivers meet, this market town slept until 1862 when Édouard Lartet and his English banker friend Henry Christy explored local caves. They not only contained human and animal skeletons, stone and bone tools and jewellery (now in local museums), but the walls were covered with incredible engravings and paintings. The town was dubbed the "capital of Prehistory". Prehistoric man, who came S to these caves for warmth in the second Ice Age, would get a shock if he saw the tens of thousands of travellers in cars and coaches who come annually to see his humble cave-homes. Font-de-Gaume cave has multicoloured paintings of animals from mammoths to reindeer; Grand Roc cave has remarkable stalactites and stalagmites; Les Combarelles has 300 animal drawings; Rouffignac has drawings and engravings of rhinos, mammoths, bison and deer; and Cro-Magnon is where skeletons of the Cro-Magnon race were found, establishing the characteristics of *Homo sapiens* around 40,000 years ago. These people, adaptable to many climates and environments, were hunters and food-gatherers, tall, long limbed and intelligent. There is a fascinating museum in a medieval castle of the Counts of Beynac.

FIGEAC
LOT   Pop 10,500

Busy, attractive town on banks of the Célé where Quercy and the Auvergne meet. The old part has half-timbered, balconied 14–15C houses, some with coats of arms, forged ironwork and mullion windows, two churches of mixed Gothic and Romanesque, and an interesting medieval mint. It was the birthplace of the Egyptologist Champollion who deciphered the Rosetta Stone, now in the British Museum. Figeac's museum has a moulding of the original.

GOURDON
LOT   Pop 5100

On the borders of Quercy and Périgord, and capital of the Bouriane, green, wooded land with deep *bocages*, the old town was built in terraces down from a castle razed in 1619. From the boulevards replacing the ramparts there are fine views all round. The most attractive square has a 17C town hall perched on a vaulted market and a fortified collegiate church of 1304 with a fine rose-window.

GRAMAT, CAUSSE DE
LOT

A wild, high limestone plateau between the Dordogne near Souillac and the Lot around Cahors, split open by two huge canyons. The beautiful Alzou canyon in the N has the remarkable medieval Rocamadour (q.v.), clinging to its face. The longer, almost fearsome Célé canyon lies to the S. The whole area is riddled with ravines, caves and underground streams. Truffles grow under stunted oaks. Grottes de Lacave, on the S bank of the Dordogne, are underground galleries with weird coloured stalagmites lit up and reflected in pools and waterfalls. You reach a 1.5km walk by lift and miniature railway.

Gramat (pop 3800), the capital, has the French police dog-training centre and holds a great sheep fair and markets for truffles and walnuts. S to the Célé is the wild Braunhie (pronounced "brogne"), almost a desert.

HAUTEFORT, CHÂTEAU DE
DORDOGNE

A 17C hilltop château above the Auvézère valley, in a magnificent park. Nearly restored after fire damage. More like a Loire château than a Perigordian castle. Superb old Flemish tapestries, restored. The 12C castle was destroyed in a feud between the owner Bertrand de Born, troubadour-warrior, and his brother, backed by rival Plantagenet brothers, Henry "Court Mantel" and Richard Lionheart.

MONPAZIER
DORDOGNE   Pop 560

Last of the *bastides* built by Edward I to defend Périgord (1284) and the best preserved. During the Hundred Years' War it often changed hands. After the Religious Wars, the peasants met at Monpazier to start a revolt, and 8000 teemed through the countryside, pillaging castles. The leader was caught by the duke of Épernon's troops and beheaded in Monpazier.

Now it is a charming, sleepy old town off tourist routes, except for those visiting **Château Biron** 4km S. The main market square, with lovely old arcades, is a delight. The Hôtel de France is in a fine old annexe of the castle. A fair is held on the third Thurs. each month. Biron, home of the Gontaut family who revolted against Henri IV, has a mixture of buildings ranging from the 12–17C. The massive stone-flagged kitchen is superb.

Monpazier

MONTIGNAC
DORDOGNE Pop 3200

The cave of Lascaux, near this town built on the Vézère, is one of the wonders of the world to those lucky enough to have seen it before it had to be closed. Discovered in 1940 by two boys exploring a hole under a tree, it has the finest collection of prehistoric art yet found. Animals are painted over one another, as if artists ran out of space. There are bulls of a species which died out 300 years ago, bison, stags, horses, including the tufted-mane horses of China, lions, ibex – all painted about 14,000 years ago. Until the cave was opened up, they were kept in perfect condition by constant temperatures and a chalky ceiling resisting water. Carbon-dioxide breathed out by tourists started to harm the paintings, so the cave has been shut since 1963. They have been reproduced in concrete with copies of the drawings in what experts believe are the same materials.

Montignac

PADIRAC, GOUFFRE DE
LOT Pop 150

Gouffre de Padirac is a chasm made by the heel of the Devil who challenged St Martin to jump the 100m gap on a mule. The mule made it; Martin was canonized. A refuge shelter in the Hundred Years' and Religious Wars, it was neglected until 1890. Today it is one of the most remarkable sights in the Dordogne. By lift and stairs, you descend over 100m to a chamber, walk to an underground river and take a boat over strangely translucent waters for half a mile to visit more chambers on foot. (Open spring holidays until end Oct.).

PÉRIGUEUX
DORDOGNE Pop 35,400

The white domes of the cathedral, as you enter the capital of Périgourdine food, of truffles and foie gras, also offer an architectural feast. Alas, too many buildings have been destroyed. The curious 12C cathedral, St-Front, looks slightly Byzantine, with five domes topped by cupolas, and more cupolas peering from between them; and the bare interior has Byzantine-style chandeliers. Sacré-Coeur de Montmartre is said to have been modelled on it. A Romanesque original, much

despoiled by wars, was "restored" by the 19C architect Abadie (called "The Wrecker"). He added seventeen towers. Medieval and Renaissance mansions survive around it.

The 12C church of St-Étienne-de-la-Cité was the cathedral until 1669. It had four domes, but two were removed by Protestants. Only two bays exist.

Périgueux

POMPADOUR
CORRÈZE Pop 1600

In 1745 Louis XV gave this 15C castle to his mistress Antoinette Poisson, Madame de Pompadour, with the title of marquise. She never came to see it. When she died in 1761, he established a stud alongside. Known as the "city of the horse", in the 19C it became the stud of Anglo-Arab horses introduced from Britain. Now the Puy-Marmont stallions of many breeds are stabled here for breeding. Race meetings and shows are held in summer. Only the terraces of the restored castle are open to view.

Ségur-le-Château (13km NW) – the ruins of the castle of the counts of Limoges, ancestors of Henri IV, is almost surrounded by the river Auvézère. Henri's great grandfather, Jean d'Albret, king of Navarre, was born here.

ROCAMADOUR
LOT Pop 800

This medieval city clamped on a 150m rock face is a tourist cliché but magnificent, despite too many visitors and souvenir shops. View it first from the road terrace at l'Hospitalet above, preferably at night when lit or in morning sun. You will never forget it.

From the castle at the top, the city descends through a maze of old houses, towers, rocks and oratories to a road still high above the river Alzou valley. Pilgrims have come since the Middle Ages to a little chapel dedicated to the Virgin. In 1166 the remains of a man were found under the chapel floor and entombed near the altar. Miracles started. The mystery hermit was called St Adour. Pilgrims came freely to seek purification or when ordered by an ecclesiastical court as a penance. In chains they climbed the 216 steps on their knees. It became one of the most important pilgrimages. The Plantagenet Henry III of England, many French kings, including Louis XIII and St Louis, and several other saints went there. Later, pilgrims kneeled at every step. A few zealots still do. It would be unwise even to walk up the steep steps after one of the meals offered in competing restaurants at the bottom.

Rocamadour's riches lured robbers. Henry, eldest son of Henry III, fighting his father, looted the shrine to pay his troops, then fled in remorse to Martel, where he died in agony on a bed of ashes.

Pilgrimages continued until the Wars of Religion when Protestants seized Rocamadour and destroyed the saint's body. But who was this mystery hermit? At first people believed that he was a hermit from Egypt, then St Sylvanus. In the 15C they decided that he was Zaccheus, the publican, husband of St Veronica who wiped blood and sweat from Jesus's face on the way to

Rocamadour

Calvary. They both fled to Limousin to avoid persecution.

Of the seven churches, the most important, Chapelle Miraculeuse, was rebuilt last century. The 15C town hall has a superb tapestry by Jean Lurçat (1892–1966).

ST-CÉRÉ
LOT Pop 4200

A happy little town with the Bavé river washing walls of flower-decked old houses. Built in the 9C at an important route junction, a trading centre in the 13C, it is still a market town for prosperous surrounding farms specializing in plums and strawberries; also a fine centre for touring and walking.

Defended by a series of castles, especially St-Laurent, whose two towers look down a steep hill to the old brown-tiled roofs of houses, it escaped remarkably from the ravages of wars.

St-Céré still has a medieval air, especially in the photogenic Pl. du Mercadiel and in Rue Paramelle, with wooden houses, 12C windows and 15–16C mansions.

St-Laurent towers (12C and 15C) were the home from 1945 until his death in 1966 of the artist Jean Lurçat, who revived and revolutionized the art of tapestry. Here he designed his richly coloured, firm-lined tapestries and his ceramics. You can see many of his works in the Casino bar in St-Céré. In

Hôtel Le Coq Arlequin is one of his greatest tapestries, of a puffed-up cock in a coat of many colours.

Places nearby include **Château de Montal** (3km), a 'phoenix' castle. In 1534 Jeanne de Balsac hired the greatest builders and artists to build it for a son away at the wars. Only his body returned. His grief-stricken mother had the windows blocked up. In 1879 an asset-stripper auctioned its treasures and some stonework. In 1908 a new owner repaired it and bought back treasures at ransom prices. A missing doorway was replaced with a new one by Rodin.

Autoire (8km) is a lovely hamlet in splendid surroundings – a waterfall, old houses, some half-timbered, villas, turreted mansions, clustered round a medieval church, with the Corrèze hills for backcloth.

Loubressac, an old fortified town (pop 400), is on a spur facing Castelnau castle and overlooking the river Bavé. It is an alluring place with narrow lanes between Haut-Quercy houses leading from a shady square to an old manor house on the tip of the spur.

Grotte de Presque (5km), a cave with several chambers, 350m long, is pillared with slim and thick stalagmites up to 10m high in strangely varying shapes.

SARLAT
DORDOGNE Pop 10,700

Still a fascinating town, Sarlat was sheer delight until increasing tourism from the 1970s onwards threatened to swamp it. Try to go off-season, when you can wander more easily along its narrow, steep alleys and streets flanked by medieval to Renaissance-style houses in honey-coloured stone. It is particularly fascinating to adventurous students of architecture, for it is not the well-preserved medieval town promised by the brochures but a charming mixture of styles spanning four centuries, all of which adds to its architectural and historical interest.

It was decaying sadly when in 1964 the French government decreed the whole town a monument, to be preserved and rehabilitated. In 1837 a road was built through the town, known as the Traverse, and you must turn off it on foot to find the best of the old buildings.

Sarlat grew around an abbey. In 1317 Pope John XXII, who came from Cahors, made it a bishopric and it stayed so until 1790. The Salignac-Fénelon family ruled it twice. François de Salignac asked his nephew, the writer-priest Fénelon, to commission a garden from Le Nôtre, Louis XIV's landscape gardener responsible for the gardens at Fontainebleau. Le Nôtre sent a pupil, Le Plantier; the public gardens are part of his work.

The old cathedral, a jumble of architectural styles, blessedly being renovated at last, was built mostly in the 16–17C, though its W belfry is Romanesque. But the little chapel on the S side, Chapel of the Blue Penitents, is 12C, part of the abbey. "Blue" penitents were monks from the upper classes. "White" penitents were lower-class monks whose 17C chapel is in Rue Jean-Jacques Rousseau, and has a museum of sacred art. Opposite is a lovely Renaissance house with spiralling tracery and delicate columns, called Maison de la Boëtie. Here the poet and lawyer Étienne de la Boëtie was born in 1530. He died at 33 and his friend the philosopher Montaigne wrote *On Friendship* in his memory. At 18, Étienne wrote *Contr'un*, an appeal for liberty which inspired Jean-Jacques Rousseau when he wrote *The Social Contract*.

The former bishop's palace on the S side of the cathedral, now a theatre, was the home of Cardinal Gaddi, who brought with him from the Medici court in Florence Italian artists and workmen who inspired many of Sarlat's Renaissance master-pieces. There are far too many beautiful and interesting buildings in Sarlat to see satisfactorily in a day, among them Hôtel de Maleville, made into a mansion from three houses in the 16C; Hôtel Plamon, a restored 14C Gothic mansion of a cloth merchant, with five arcades leading to a covered market; and the strange Lanterne des Morts, a 12C domed tower said to have commemorated a miracle performed here by St Bernard when trying unsuc-cessfully to convert heretical Albigensians.

For ten years in the Hundred Years' War Sarlat was an English garrison town and 300 coins were recently unearthed carrying the effigy of the Black Prince.

For centuries a goose market was held in Pl. des Oies (Goose Square) on Sats, but today confit, foie gras and terrine of goose and duck are more in evidence than the birds. But it is one of the biggest weekly markets in France, taking over most of the town. For the last week in July and first in Aug., the market square becomes an open-air theatre with performances of classics (Shakespeare, Molière, etc) by Parisian companies such as the Comédie Française.

Château de Montfort (6km S of Sarlat) – no longer open to the public – is in a spectacular position on a rock dropping sheer to the river Dordogne which also rings it. Destroyed by Simon de Montfort and by orders of Louis XI and Henri IV, it is a glorious muddle of 15C, 16C and 19C buildings and towers.

SOUILLAC
LOT Pop 4000

A busy little shopping and commercial centre beside the Dordogne river, serving hamlets and farmsteads hidden away on little roads around it, with tourists from *gîtes* and camp sites joining them in summer. It is traversed by the N20, too, so traffic can be horrific in summer, especially on Sats. But it is a jolly town with interesting little shops. It grew around the 13C abbey, destroyed in wars. The delightful abbey church has survived as the living parish church, though with a partial facade from the 17C. The uncluttered, harmonious single nave is light and spacious and contains an old doorway which is a masterpiece of Roman-esque sculpture, with men, saints and animals carved with intricate beauty.

For centuries the people of Souillac ran boats on the Dordogne, taking vine stakes, barrel staves, wine, corn and even cattle to Bordeaux. Laden with salt, they returned upstream pulled by oxen.

TERRASSON-LA-VILLEDIEU
CORRÈZE Pop 6200

This busy little town on slopes down to the river Vézère, 9km W of Brive, markets truffles and walnuts, especially at the important Thurs. mar-ket. Walnuts grow in plantations around it and, like poplars, sometimes line the river bank. There are two bridges, one modern, one 12C, and the old town is up the hill, dominated by a 15C church with splendid houses around it.

TRÉMOLAT
DORDOGNE Pop 540

In this charming village, so French that Claude Chabrol chose it as setting for his film *Le Boucher*, there is a bare-walled, stern 12C abbey church looking like a fort. A gloomy pile, damp and cold, contrasting with the lovely little Vieux Logis serv-ing delicious meals. Worshippers have fled to the restored little chapel of St-Hilaire, with bright modern windows by Paul Becker.

Nearby the Dordogne river loops through bare white cliffs – the **Cingle de Trémolat** – called by André Maurois "one of the wonders of the world". It is best seen from Rocamadour belvedere to the N. A bright marina from which regattas are held was once a haven for cargo barges making for Bordeaux.

TULLE
CORRÈZE Pop 20,600

A business and industrial town snaking in a narrow valley and for 3km along the river Corrèze. Its peaceful old hillside houses, medieval and Renais-sance, have seen a violent past. Involved in re-ligious squabbles for power when controlled by its abbey, it was later taken twice by the English, then sacked by Protestants in the Hundred Years' War and partly destroyed in the Revolution. Just after D-day in 1944 it was liberated by the pro-Commu-nist Maquis, but the Germans retook it, hanged 99 local people in the streets and deported hundreds, of whom 101 did not come back.

The elegant bell-tower, 73m high, survives from the abbey church. The medieval abbots made the abbey rich, but were constantly involved in law-suits. One replenished the coffers by borrowing from Jewish bankers in Brive, then, by controlling the court, had them arrested for usury, found them guilty and confiscated their property.

Gimel-les-Cascades (12km NE) enjoys a spec-tacular setting in a wild ravine; the river Montane tumbles over a series of waterfalls, dropping 130m.

AQUITAINE

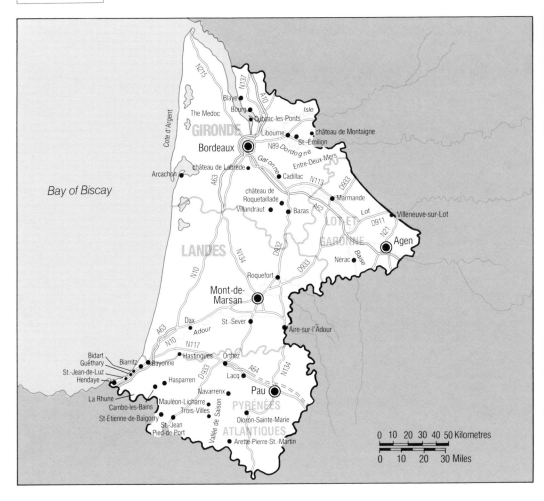

Roman Aquitania, 'land of waters', so called because of its rivers and Atlantic coastline, stretched from the river Gironde to the Pyrenees. During the next 2000 years, which included some 300 under English rule, it was to be extended, contracted and parcelled out in dukedoms. Not until 1964, when the name was revived for one of France's new economic regions, did this genial area of the south-west, where the climate is generally temperate and the tempo generally relaxed, where the fruits of sea and farm and vineyard contribute to the good life, regain its original identity. Today it extends roughly from Périgord to the Pyrenees, with its capital at Bordeaux.

Gaulish tribes were established here long before the Romans came. One of the main trade routes of Europe, linking Greece with the British Isles by way of southern France, ran through it. The Romans built cities and roads to link them, and established Bordeaux as a centre of the wine trade by laying out vineyards around the city, shipping wine from Médoc to the legions serving in Britain. The order and substance of that Gallo-Roman civilization crumbled before Visigoth, Saracen and Norse invasions which succeeded one another from the 5th century onwards.

English rule, which restored the prosperity of Roman days, began in 1152 with the marriage of Eleanor of Aquitaine, daughter of William, Count of Poitiers, to Henry of Anjou. Henry, the great-grandson of William the Conqueror, was heir to the throne of England. Within two years he became Henry II, and he and his queen reigned over a kingdom which stretched from the Tweed to the Pyrenees, including Normandy, Anjou and Touraine as well as Aquitaine. There were to be three centuries of claims and counter-claims between France and England, and spasmodic fighting along the Spanish frontier, but Aquitaine flourished. The wine trade prospered sensationally, its merchants enjoying exemption from customs duties, and there was constant commercial traffic between the two countries. But eventually the English were expelled at the end of the Hundred Years' War, in 1453. Yet the ancient tradition of tolerance persists, and there are few other parts of France where the English-speaking visitor is likely to feel so much at home or to be so sincerely welcomed as in Aquitaine.

Holiday-makers usually associate the province with the vineyards of the Médoc and the beaches that border the Atlantic coast. Less well-known are the great pine forests of the Landes where recreation, nature conservation and the commercial exploitation of the maritime pines have been happily reconciled.

There are small patches of cultivation in the clearings of the forest but the true agricultural area of Aquitaine is the rich land of the Lot-et-Garonne, to the east. This is a small paradise of orchards, vines and fields of corn, tobacco and tender early vegetables. Tiny towns and walled villages which recall the Middle Ages perch on the low hills through which the river winds.

In the extreme south-west, beyond the Adour, is the totally individual Pays Basque, where the visitor cannot fail to sense a new culture as well as enjoying a new landscape. The Basques are a race apart, and the French Basque country is only a small part of the much larger region that lies in Spain beyond the Pyrenees.

The whole of Aquitaine is an area of good eating. Locals will tell you that, given the excellence of the raw materials available to them, elaboration would be sacrilege. A famous exception is *sauce bordelaise*, the vital ingredients of which are red wine and shallots, which is the classic accompaniment to steak. The young lamb of the area and the free range chickens of the Landes need no adornment. Eastward, towards Gascony, is the area for *foie gras* (delicious eaten hot with tiny grapes), *confits* of duck or goose or pork, and terrines which may contain any or all of them. The cooking medium is more likely to be pork or goose fat than oil or butter. The edible mushrooms called *cèpes* grow plentifully round Bordeaux and this area has a speciality in its small, grey snails which are served in a thick sauce, the ingredients of which include white wine and concentrated tomato puree. Some of the more piquant dishes come from the far south-west, where the Basques, as they do in Spain, make lavish use of peppers and tomatoes. Some of the most memorable dishes are based on fish – trout and salmon from the streams of the Pyrenees, sole and turbot from the ocean. The oysters of Arcachon are justly renowned, as is *mouclade*, a delectable blend of mussels and cream. The local variety of fish soup is called *chaudrée*. In springtime lampreys are the great regional delicacy; a surfeit of them may be enjoyed along the Gironde or the Garonne.

AGEN
LOT-ET-GARONNE   Pop 32,900

This busy modern town on the Garonne, midway between Toulouse and Bordeaux, is the city of the prune, though this is a fruit very different from the wrinkled object with which most of us are only too familiar; more akin to the plum. The mild climate of the Agenais is ideally suited for fruit-growing and the prunes are produced from carefully selected fruit, gently dried.

Three Renaissance houses in the old quarter of Agen have been converted into a museum whose supreme treasure is a Greek marble statue of Venus discovered near Marmande in 1876. There is also a distinguished ceramic collection which includes, besides French and foreign porcelain and pottery, enamels by Bernard Palissy, the 16C potter, enameller, chemist and geologist, a native of Agen. Among the paintings are a group of canvases by Goya, including an outstanding self-portrait, and a number of Impressionist and Post-Impressionist pictures.

The cathedral church of St-Caprais has a striking 12C apse. Restoration in the 19C has given the interior a set of wall paintings that obscure the Romanesque sculpture. To the NW of the town a 500m viaduct of 23 arches carries the lateral canal of the Garonne over the river.

AIRE-SUR-L'ADOUR
LANDES   Pop 7200

This small town, at the junction of the N134 with the D935, has a foot in two worlds, being a market for ducks and geese, and the site of the Centre Nationale d'Études Spatiales. It was once the Roman settlement of Altuna and there are the remains of a Gallo-Roman pavement in the old bishop's palace, now the town hall. The former cathedral, of the 12C, was originally the church of a Benedictine monastery.

On the other side of the river, at Le Mas d'Aire, the church of Ste-Quitterie, a martyred princess of the Visigoths, has a rare example of early Christian art in the 5C sarcophagus where the saint's relics lie. Its carving, recognized as a masterpiece, shows, among other biblical scenes, the Creation of the World, with the Almighty wearing a Roman toga, as do other figures. The church itself, built in the 11C and restored in the late 19C, has an impressive Last Judgment in the tympanum of the W door and several Romanesque capitals in the interior.

ARCACHON
GIRONDE   Pop 13,700

Situated on a vast lagoon, this is really two towns, one the seaside playground of Bordeaux, 60km E, the other among the inland pine trees, a winter resort dating from the mid-19C, with a certain period charm and some delightfully dotty architecture. The summer town has a marina which can take 1800 yachts, greatly outnumbering the fishing craft. The aquarium contains a wide range of the marine life of the lagoon and the Atlantic, and the museum has departments of natural history and archaeology.

The oysters of the lagoon have been renowned since the 16C and the oyster beds are now among the largest in Europe, the stock having been renewed with "Portuguese" oysters from Canada and Japan after having been almost wiped out by disease during the 1970s. Mussels are also cultivated, clustering like grapes on stakes called *bouchots* which are planted in the mud-flats. The delta of the **Eyre**, on the S shore of the lagoon, about 10km E of Arcachon, is a nature reserve and bird sanctuary. To the SW of Arcachon, facing the lighthouse on Cap Ferret, the sandy shore has piled up into the 114m **Dune du Pilat**, Europe's highest, with a staircase to its summit.

Each year on the Feast of the Assumption (15 Aug.), Arcachon stages a Fête de la Mer.

ARETTE-PIERRE-ST-MARTIN
PYRÉNÉES-ATLANTIQUES

Arette is a popular winter sports station, 1640m up. Every year, on 13 July, a group of mayors from the Barétous in the Basse Soule meets with an equivalent group from Roncal on the Spanish side of the border at the Col de la Pierre St-Martin, 3km S of the village. They come to commemorate with a handclasp at a frontier post a treaty dating from 1375 which created what was virtually a free zone in which French and Spanish shepherds could graze their flocks, regardless of political frontiers. Originally the French representatives paid to the Spaniards the tribute of three heifers; today, less picturesquely, it has been commuted into cash.

BASQUES, PAYS

The Basques, though politically part of both Spain and France, are a separate and fiercely individualistic race, their origins shrouded in mystery. Their language, Euskara, is perhaps the oldest in Europe and quite unlike any other European tongue. It is still widely taught and spoken, reinforcing the sense of nationhood that links the populations on either side of the Pyrenees.

The French Basques are deeply attached to their language and culture. Tradition permeates every department of life, from local architecture to religion and recreation. The most typical of the villages are those of **Labourd**, in the western Pyrenees, where the sparkling white houses are timbered with reddish-brown beams and the red-tiled roofs have the wide eaves and gentle slope found in mountain country. They are always placed facing E, or SE, with their backs to the tearing W winds. Further E, in Basse-Navarre, stone is also used, and the house fronts are adorned with balconies; and beyond this, the tiled roofs give place to slate. The churches are remarkable. The common factor is the raised high altar, which, even in small village churches, is splendid with gold and ornament, and the single nave, with two or three rows of galleries round the walls. These are reserved for men; women and children are confined to the floor of the nave, though sometimes permitted to overflow into the gallery. Participation in services is enthusiastic, for the Basques delight in singing. To attend a mass being celebrated in Basque and hear the great surge of hymn singing from the galleries is to have the illusion of having strayed into a Welsh chapel. The most striking feature of the exterior is the type of three-pointed, trinitarian belfry found in the Soule. The churchyards are a reminder of the obscure roots of this people. Many of the older tombstones are discoidal, carved with patterns which often include the Basque cross, an adaptation of the swastika, itself of Eastern origin.

If the church is still the centre of village life, it is run close by the *fronton*, or pelota court, which is almost invariably near by – if, indeed, the church wall does not form part of it. The Basques, a tough and active people, are great games players, but pelota is more than a game, it is a part of life. Like squash and rackets, it is a variant of real tennis, played on an open-air court between two teams of three a side. The ball, slightly larger than a tennis ball, and made of rubber and wool covered with calf or kid skin, is struck with enormous force with a *chistera*, a narrow basket strapped to the player's wrist, sometimes with a gloved hand, occasionally with the bare palm. There are few more exciting spectator sports, none more deeply rooted in daily life. There is scarcely a daylight hour when the *fronton* is not occupied, whether by a couple of small boys just out of school or by the parish priest with his cassock hitched up.

Basque costume, nowadays, is worn only at fêtes – the beret and rope-soled shoes are so generally worn in France that they hardly qualify. Only rarely, in a country area, will a Basque be seen carrying the *makhila*, or swagger cane, which formerly served as cattle goad or swordstick, although one family still has the monopoly of their manufacture and the hereditary secret of tinting the medlar wood from which they are made. Folk music and dancing, by contrast, are very much alive, not preserved in the interests of tourism. Soule, the home of most traditions, is the area where one is most likely to see the *pastorales* and *mascarades*, a mixture of drama and dance, performed by an all-male cast, which last for hours. They originate in the mystery plays of the Middle Ages and their eternal subject is the conflict of good and evil, the protagonists ranging from the Devil to Napoleon. Contests in singing and musical improvisation are common, and may happen spontaneously at a feast. So too will dancing. Young Basques often let off steam in their marvellously athletic leaping dances, punctuated by piercing whoops. Or the dance may be elaborate and intricately beautiful, like the *danse du verre*, in which the participants, in brilliant costumes, circle about a full glass of wine, and, by turns, step on it for a fraction of a second without spilling a drop. The dances are the one cultural phenomenon in which there is a hint that the Basques may, after all, have their roots in Europe. The waving kerchiefs and jingling bells have their counterparts in English morris dancing. And the *zamalzain*, or horse man, is surely akin to the hobby horse, which comes from the common pool of European folk culture.

Basques

Most French Basques, apart from those engaged in the tourist industry, are farmers, growing corn and fruit, and raising sheep and dairy cattle, though some still fish for tunny. Smuggling, which used to be a profitable source of income, with livestock and liquor heading the list of contraband goods carried over the mountains and across the frontier into Spain, is now minimal.

BAYONNE
PYRÉNÉES-ATLANTIQUES   Pop 43,000

Bayonne, on the Adour, once a historic frontier fortress, is today an elegant, lively city with cool, arcaded streets, and also a thriving industrial port, dating from Roman times. It saw great prosperity in three centuries of English rule. Like Bordeaux, the city elected its own government after 1215 and did a substantial trade with Britain. Its return to French rule proved a doubtful blessing. The garrison surrendered to the French army seeing what they took to be a prophetic miracle – a white cross in the sky. The English market was lost, the citizens had to pay French taxes, and the laws were now written in French, not Gascon. It was to be nearly 200 years before the good times returned. Shipbuilding and arms manufacture flourished – at the beginning of the 18C Bayonne produced the bayonet which was adopted by the French army in 1707 – and local fishermen crossed the Atlantic to the Grand Banks of Newfoundland for cod. Privateers helped to swell the coffers of the local merchants which brimmed over after Bayonne was declared a free port in 1784. The city had to withstand fourteen sieges during the next three and a half centuries, and surrendered to Wellington in 1814, only after the fall of Paris. The modern port, greatly improved by dredging and the building of two deep-water breakwaters at the mouth of the Adour, is in full expansion, particularly as an outlet for the sulphur produced at Lacq.

Bayonne owes to Vauban its citadel and ramparts, now transformed into lawns and gardens. The Château Neuf dates from 1489, the more ancient Château Vieux, which was a Roman fort before it was a medieval donjon, has been transformed into a block of flats.

The Gothic cathedral of Ste-Marie, built from the 13–16C (the second of its twin towers added only in the 19C) has a splendid 13C apse with elegant flying buttresses and a double line of windows.

Some of the typical old houses of Bayonne, low and arcaded, are in the Rue du Pont Neuf. This is the place to sample the speciality of the city which is even better known than its hams, the fragrant drinking chocolate that was first imported from Spain in the 17C.

The Basque Museum, housed in a 15C building typical of the region, provides a comprehensive survey of Basque customs and culture – seafaring, costume, traditions, arts and crafts, and the great game of pelota. Bayonne's art gallery, the Musée Bonnat, is named after the portrait painter Léon Bonnat (1833–1922), who was a native of the city, and contains some of his work. It also includes 2000 drawings by European masters from the 15–19C and paintings or sketches by Leonardo, Rembrandt, Rubens, Goya, El Greco and Ingres, among others.

In the first week of Aug. Bayonne stages an annual Basque festival, with bullfights, pelota, singing and dancing.

Seven miles NW of the city, the Adour reaches the sea at **La Barre**, which can be spectacular in rough weather.

BAZAS
GIRONDE   Pop 5200

Bazas, above the valley of the Beuve, was a bishopric from the 5C until 1790, which accounts for its cathedral of St-Jean, built in the Northern Gothic style, during the 13–14C. It was rebuilt in the same fashion after being badly damaged during the Wars of Religion. On that occasion the citizens raised 10,000 crowns to buy off the Huguenot vandals who threatened to destroy the carving of the facade which is the best part of the building.

BIARRITZ
PYRÉNÉES-ATLANTIQUES   Pop 26,700

Halfway through the 19C Biarritz, within sight of the Spanish frontier, was a small fishing port, its empty beaches known only to local people who came out from Bayonne to bathe. Today the stretch of coast between the Rocher de la Vierge and the Plateau du Phare is one of Europe's more elegant and fashionable seaside resorts. The vogue began in 1854, when the Empress Eugénie brought Napoleon III there. He, too, was charmed; the Villa Eugénie, now the Hôtel du Palais, was built for his queen and her court, so writing the first page in a visitors' book which was to include many later crowned heads, including Victoria and Edward VII. Palatial hotels grew up, promenades

Biarritz

were laid out with hydrangeas and tamarisk, the golf courses proliferated. It all survives, its air of aristocratic yesterdays now invigorated by the surf-boarders who come to ride the Atlantic breakers. But although still frequented by the occasional aristocrats and film stars, it now attracts the package tourists as well, especially Spaniards, who come mainly for the gambling.

The Grande Plage remains the most fashionable of the three splendid beaches. The lighthouse on the Pointe St-Martin may be visited by day; the famous offshore Rocher de la Vierge (views N and S) is reached by a footbridge above the waves. The Plage des Basques is exposed to even heavier surf than the Grande Plage, whereas the small Plage du Port Vieux is in the shelter of the harbour. Above the Plage des Basques the promenade, La Perspective, has a remarkable view of the mountains to the S. There is a large collection of the species of the North Atlantic in the Musée de la Mer, situated on a promontory, and there are two casinos, as well as a number of heated indoor swimming pools as an alternative to the beaches.

Guéthary, on an inlet SW of Biarritz, was once a fishing port – the sailors' cross bears witness to that past. Now the elegant villas, most of them built in the Basque style, slope down to the sandy beach, with a terrace above it which gives wide views of the coast. The church, set in a commanding position on high ground, has unusually interesting furniture, including a 15C processional cross.

BIDART
PYRÉNÉES-ATLANTIQUES   Pop 3100

The clifftop village of Bidart, between Biarritz and St-Jean-de-Luz, is a tranquil haven from the relative sophistication of both resorts. White houses set in greenery look down on a stretch of shore that is blissfully undeveloped. The little square has the traditional Basque essentials of church and *fronton*, the pelota court which is a popular centre for competitions.

BLAYE
GIRONDE   Pop 4800

The Romans were the first to garrison Blaye which, from its height on the right bank of the Gironde, commands the point where the river broadens into the estuary. Two towers of the medieval castle of the Rudel family remain, as well as a legend. It concerns Jaufré Rudel, a 12C troubadour, who fell in love, sight unseen, with the Princess Melisande of Tripoli, and finally sailed to see her, only to die in her arms on landing. The enormous citadel is the work of Vauban: the medieval town was razed to accommo-

Blaye

date it. A house in its centre was the prison, from Nov. 1832 to May 1833, of the widowed Marie-Caroline, duchess of Berry, whose husband was a younger brother of the guillotined Louis XVI. In an attempt to dethrone King Louis-Philippe in favour of her posthumous son, the Comte de Chambord, last of the Bourbon line, she engineered an uprising in the Vendée. It was quelled and the duchess's credit was destroyed when she gave birth to a daughter whom only the excessively charitable assumed to be the issue of a secret marriage.

BORDEAUX
GIRONDE   Pop 211,200

Bordeaux, splendidly situated on the left bank of the Garonne, here 400m wide, is one of the great cities of France, its appearance and atmosphere elegant and gracious, rich in history yet proud of the post-war achievements that have revived its prosperity. Its estuary site, with access to a rich hinterland, predestined Bordeaux to be a major port from Roman times. It was a trading centre even before the Romans arrived, and they made it an imperial city, Burdigala, and the political capital of Aquitania: by the 4C it had a thriving university, and the poet Ausonius, who was born there, called it one of the great educational centres of Gaul.

Seven centuries of unrest followed the Romans, punctuated by invasions, culminating in that of the Norsemen in the 9C. Prosperity returned during the 300 years of English rule that began with the marriage of Eleanor of Aquitaine with Henry Plantagenet of Anjou, shortly to be Henry II of England. Bordeaux flourished under a system that gave its citizens virtual self-government – they elected their mayors from the early 13C – and exempted their wines from all customs duties. The Black Prince, son of Edward III, had his court at Bordeaux, during the Hundred Years' War, and his younger brother, Richard of Bordeaux, the future King Richard II, was born in the city. After the final defeat of the English at Castillon in 1453, the Bordelais rebelled against the limitation of their accustomed liberties, and the French kings found it politic to reduce the taxes which they had imposed on the wine trade and, a little later, to give Bordeaux its own *parlement*.

It is, nevertheless, to the central power that we owe the noble, stone-built city of today. The Intendants, or regional governors, instituted by Richelieu and Colbert, notably the Marquis de Tourny (1690–1760), decided in the 18C that the ancient city, crowded within its crumbling walls, must be rebuilt. They got little support from the rich but conservative merchants, whose wealth was now derived from the slave trade as well as from shipping wine, but, by the end of the 18C Bordeaux, besides masterpieces like the incomparable Grand Théâtre and the quayside square of the Quai de la Bourse, had acquired private houses worthy of the broad avenues and gardens laid out in the centre. The early 19C, after the setback of the Napoleonic Wars, which temporarily extinguished the port's trade, brought the building of the 17-arched Pont de Pierre across the Garonne and the

The Bourse, Bordeaux

laying out of the Esplanade des Quinconces, Europe's largest square, but this was an age of comfortable prosperity rather than enterprise.

Bordeaux's third golden age came after World War II, with the appointment of a dynamic young mayor, Jacques Chaban-Delmas, who had a distinguished record in the Resistance. Though opposed by conservative elements, including the local families owning the great vineyards, Chaban-Delmas, later to be prime minister, used his position in Paris to secure the necessary ministerial funds and decisions, introduced new industries, carried through the construction of a new deep-water port for tankers and containers, and led the revival of the city's commercial and cultural life. Modern Bordeaux is his justification. The city has gained two new bridges over the Garonne, with an accompanying spur to its industrial development, new motorways, a modern exhibition centre, a new university campus, some audacious housing development and, with it, an ambitious programme of conservation of the old town.

The Palais Gallieni, in the Rue Dr Albert Barraud, is the only relic of Bordeaux's Roman past. It is not, in fact, a palace, but the few surviving arches of a Roman amphitheatre, the rest being destroyed by the Revolution.

The Grand Théâtre, built between 1773 and 1780 on the site of a Gallo-Roman temple, is the most successful achievement of the "Bordeaux of the Intendants". It was designed by Victor Louis, and was to be the inspiration later for the Paris Opera House. The colonnaded facade, topped by statues of the Nine Muses and the Three Graces, has gaiety as well as dignity, the roof of the peristyle is coffered, and the double staircase leading up from the colonnaded foyer is lit by a glass dome. Around the theatre the plan of 18C Bordeaux opens out, the Pl. de la Comédie, built on the site of the Roman forum, the Allées de Tourny, a flowered promenade culminating in the Pl. de Tourny (unfortunately its 18C buildings have not escaped modern alteration), the Cours de l'Intendance and the Cours de Clemenceau. Hap-

pily, the Pl. des Grands Hommes, now housing the produce market, and the Pl. Gambetta (where the guillotine was set up during the Revolution) have fared better.

On the tree-lined Esplanade des Quinconces, opening on to the estuary, there is a monument to the Girondins, the moderate party in the National Assembly during the Revolution, which originated among the Bordeaux deputies. Twenty-two of them were executed on a trumped-up charge of being traitors to the Republic. There are statues of Montaigne and Montesquieu, the former of whom was mayor of Bordeaux from 1581 to 1585 and the latter a member of the *parlement* in the mid-18C.

The Pl. de la Bourse, on the waterfront, its 18C facades curving round the square with its fountain of the Three Graces, is a witness to the port's prosperity during that period. On either side, the tall houses of the wine merchants line the quays. The Hôtel de Tourny, set back a little from it, now houses the Musée de la Marine. The late 20C is represented by the huge Mériadeck ensemble, a resolutely contemporary complex of public buildings, shops, offices and flats, set around a paved area, relieved by trees, lawns, flower beds and fountains.

The Grosse Cloche, built in the 15C on the site of the Porte St-Éloi, which was part of the old town wall, is one of the few survivals of medieval Bordeaux. This was the town bell, sounded on all public occasions of sorrow or rejoicing, and to signal the opening of the vintage.

The cathedral of St-André, whose two slim spires are a landmark, is an 11C foundation but underwent so much building and rebuilding over the next 400 years that it is now a mixture of Gothic and Romanesque. There are 13C carvings on the S door, including a Last Judgment in the tympanum and statues of ten apostles in the embrasures. This was the Porte Royale through which François I and his bride passed after their wedding. The interior

St-André, Bordeaux

has a Romanesque nave and a soaring Flamboyant Gothic choir. The free-standing belfry, the Tour Pey-Berland, was added in the 15C.

The neighbouring Hôtel de Ville was originally the magnificent 18C palace of the archbishop Ferdinand de Rohan. Within a few years, it was to be confiscated and the Republic was proclaimed from its steps.

The bell tower of the basilica of St-Michel, built between 1472–92, is, with the spire which was added in 1862, the highest in the southwest, at 114m. The basilica itself, more than a century older, has an impressive W doorway below a great rose window, and glass by Max Ingrand to replace that destroyed during the bombing of 1940. St-Seurin has Gallo-Roman pillars and capitals, and 6C sarcophagi in its 9C crypt. The church itself, which is 11C, has retained some striking capitals. Ste-Croix, once the church of a monastery dating from the 7C, was itself built during the 12C, but restoration during the 19C has left only the S tower and the central doorway in their original state. Notre-Dame, a late 17C Jesuit church, which is a replica of the Gesù in Rome, has a particularly attractive facade.

The Musée des Beaux Arts, housed in the N gallery of the gardens of the Hôtel de Ville, is a considerable collection whose most important items include paintings by Perugino, Veronese, Rubens, Van Dyck, Delacroix, Nattier and Corot. The Musée d'Aquitaine, in the opposite wing, but shortly to be transferred to new premises, illustrates the life and culture of the region, from prehistory onwards. The scope of the Musée des Arts Décoratifs covers enamels from Limoges, ceramics from many parts of the world, metalwork, silver, glass and furniture.

For fifteen days in May each year Bordeaux stages a music and dance festival of international standard, and in May and Sept. exhibitions are arranged at the Galérie des Beaux Arts.

Musée des Beaux Arts, Bordeaux

BOURG
GIRONDE

Bourg was once an important port at the junction of the Dordogne and the Garonne which was engaged chiefly in the wine trade with England. The district still produces a more than respectable

table wine. Parts of the 13C fortifications remain in the upper town, where the terrace of the Château de la Citadelle, the old summer palace of the archbishop of Bordeaux, commands a superb view over the town and estuary. Rebuilt during the 18C and burned by the German forces in 1944, the palace has now been partly reconstructed and the surrounding ground is laid out as a park.

Half-a-dozen kilometres E are the prehistoric caves of **Pair-non-Pair**, which, excavations have suggested, are 5000 years older than those of Lascaux in Périgord. There are line drawings of horses, bison, mammoths and ibexes, also evidence of habitation by Aurignac man.

CADILLAC
GIRONDE   Pop 5000

Cadillac, on the right bank of the Garonne, a *bastide* town founded in 1280, still has part of its 14C ramparts. It is dominated by the enormous château of the dukes of Épernon, built between 1598 and 1620. Sacked during the Revolution, it later served as a state prison. It has been restored and is open to visitors, who can admire the eight monumental carved fireplaces. It is now the HQ of the Connétablie de Guyenne and the local white wines, Premier Côtes de Bordeaux et Cadillac, may be tasted in the W wing. The town's name is, of course, better known in the US as that of an automobile.

CAMBO-LES-BAINS
PYRÉNÉES-ATLANTIQUES   Pop 5000

Cambo-les-Bains, set in the hills 20km SE of Bayonne, and so an excellent centre for excursions in the Basque country, has a mild climate which ensured its development as a spa and health resort. This part of the town, Haut Cambo, is set on high ground above the Nive; le Bas Cambo, on its banks, is an old Basque village of great charm. The poet and dramatist, Edmond de Rostand (1868–1918), author of *Cyrano de Bergerac* and *L'Aiglon*, among other plays, settled at Cambo for the last eighteen years of his life. The Villa Anaga, which he built in the local Basque style, is now a Rostand Museum.

CÔTE D'ARGENT

The so-called Silver Coast of Aquitaine is the Atlantic shore that stretches from the Gironde to the Adour in 250km of unbroken sandy beaches. Its most attractive quality is its seemingly limitless space, for tourist development has thus far involved setting up a series of small centres rather than building a girdle of concrete to match the remaining fragments of the Atlantic Wall. West winds and the Atlantic rollers can make the swimming robust, but, immediately inland, there is a string of natural lakes which are equipped for water sports of every kind.

With the exception of Arcachon (q.v.) there are no large resorts. **Soulac-sur-Mer**, just S of the Pointe de Grave, was once a landing place for Compostela pilgrims, which accounts for the size of the 11C church of Notre-Dame-de-la-Fin-des-Terres, which was once that of a Benedictine abbey. The 12C choir has four capitals depicting Daniel in the lions' den. For decades it was buried in the shifting dunes, to be dug out and restored during the 19C. **Hourtin** and **Bombanne**, on the **Lac d'Houdin Carcans**, have, respectively, a station for pleasure boats and a comprehensively equipped leisure centre. **Lacanau-Océan**, as its name implies, is itself a beach resort, but no more than 5km from the **Étang de Lacanau**, which offers fishing as well as water sports. S of Arcachon, **Mimizan**, on the little **Étang de Biscarosse et de Parentis**, a harbour of some importance during the Middle Ages, has the ruins of a Benedictine abbey. During the 18C the sand overwhelmed the town: the 13C tower of the abbey rises from the dunes. **Lévignac** has a 14C church with a tower, which is effectively a donjon, and has retained the typical houses of the region, timbered and tiled. From the **Étang de Léon** it is possible to make a boat trip to the coast along the **Courant d'Huchet**, a river which passes through semi-tropical vegetation. **Hossegor**, close to the once considerable harbour of **Capbreton**, is the most fashionable of these lakeside resorts. Its name is a corruption of 'horse guards', recalling that some of Wellington's troops once stayed in the town. François Mitterand, president of the Republic after 1981, has a private house here, at Latche.

CUBZAC-LES-PONTS
GIRONDE Pop 4000

The huge **Château du Bouilh**, 5km N of Cubzac-les-Ponts, on the right bank of the Dordogne, was the first project to be taken on by the architect Victor Louis after his masterpiece, the Grand Théâtre at Bordeaux. It was never to be completed: the Marquis de la Tour du Pin, who had commissioned the building in 1789, was guillotined in 1794. Yet it remains impressive, particularly the pillared front above an arcade. The cellars are cut into the limestone and open to daylight. Downstream from the town, three bridges span the river. The oldest, a viaduct, 1046m long, was the work of the engineer Gustave Eiffel (1832–1923). The railway bridge, curving 40m above the river, came in 1889. Finally, in 1974, another road bridge was built as Eiffel's was too narrow for modern traffic.

DAX
LANDES Pop 19,700

The Emperor Augustus brought his rheumatic daughter to be treated at Dax, a much frequented spa on the Adour, on the S border of the Landes, where the Fontaine Chaude is still gushing out its mineral water at 64°C into an arcaded pool. A section of the Roman wall can be seen in the neighbouring park. The classical cathedral was built in the 17C to replace the Gothic one built by the English during their 300 years' occupation of the town: the richly carved N doorway of the old cathedral has been built into the N transept of the new. 9km NE, in the hamlet of **Buglose**, is the birthplace (largely reconstructed) of St-Vincent-de-Paul (1581–1660), the saint who might be claimed as the founder of modern social work.

Notre-Dame, Dax

ENTRE-DEUX-MERS
GIRONDE

The "seas" of Entre-deux-Mers are in fact rivers, the Garonne and the Dordogne, enclosing the area S of Bordeaux which produces mainly white wine. The attractively varied countryside is far different from the unrelieved vineyards of the Médoc. It is a region of *bastide* towns, among them **Créon**, which still has arcades on three sides of its market place. A little further SE are the ruins of the 11C abbey of Notre-Dame-de-la-Grande-Sauve, founded by St-Gérard. Part late Romanesque, part Gothic, it has interesting capitals in the choir. The late 12C parish church of St-Pierre has four splendid 13C statues in the niches of the apse. At **Rauzan**, the ruins of the Château de Duras, built early in the 14C by one of Edward I's captains, are being restored. The 12–13C abbey church of **St-Blasimon**, a few km SE, also ruined, has kept some remarkable carvings, including hunting scenes and the battle of the virtues and vices. Further S, the church of **Castelvieil** has a superb Romanesque doorway with carvings which include, among much else, the "labours of the month", ranging from pruning the vines to pig-killing. **St-Macaire** is a *bastide* which has kept to a marked degree the atmosphere of the Middle Ages along with its 13C walls, with three gate towers, and 15–16C houses. The church of St-Sauveur, late 12C, has an unusual "clover-leaf" E end. Further W is the 17C **Château de Malle**, with terraced gardens laid out at the same period and splendid wrought iron gates. The Commandérie du Bontemps de Sauternes et Barsac, whose function is to make known the wines of the region, has its HQ at the château.

HASPARREN
PYRÉNÉES-ATLANTIQUES   Pop 5600

Francis Jammes (1868–1938), the poet and prose writer, spent the last seventeen years of his life at Hasparren, some 20km SE of Bayonne; the garden of his house, Eyhartzia, is now a public park. The town itself is a copy-book illustration of how progress and tradition coexist in the Basque country. Once it lived chiefly on the tanneries which used bark from the neighbouring oak forests. Now oak forests and tanneries have vanished, but there are still boot and shoe factories. Since 1977, central heating appliances have also been manufactured. Amid the industrial development, the pelota matches continue and the cows are released to run through the streets during the *course landaise*.

HASTINGUES
LANDES   Pop 300

The fortified village set on its rock near the confluence of the Gave de Pau and the Gave d'Oleron was named after John Hastings, who built it as a *bastide* in 1289 at the command of Edward I. One of the fortified town gates survives. Near Bidache, a little further S, are the ruins of the Château de Gramont, which was occupied by the family of the same name from the 14C to the Revolution, by which time they were not simply lords of the manor but sovereign princes.

HENDAYE
PYRÉNÉES-ATLANTIQUES   Pop 11,100

Hendaye, on the bank of the Bidassoa, is a frontier post: across the river is the Spanish fortified town of Fontarabie. The wide sands and the bay of Chingoudy, the sheet of water into which the Bidassoa widens at high tide, make it an excellent holiday resort whose mild climate has produced a luxuriance of semi-tropical trees and flowers, palms, mimosa, eucalyptus, magnolia. Hendaye has associations with the novelist, Pierre Loti (1850–1923), who settled in the town after his retirement.

The **Île de Faisans**, in midstream, is owned jointly by Spain and France, the two countries exercising police duties and enjoying fishing rights in the river for alternating half-year periods. It was on the Île that the marriage contract between Louis XIV and the Infante Marie-Thérèse (see *St-Jean-de-Luz*) was signed.

LABRÈDE, CHÂTEAU DE
GIRONDE

The descendants of the writer and political philosopher, Charles de Segondat, Baron de Montesquieu (1689–1755), still live in this 12–15C château about 15km S of Bordeaux. Its Gothic severity is separated by a broad moat from the surrounding grassy meadows. Both the château and the park, which Montesquieu had laid out in the English style, remain substantially as they were during his lifetime, even to the setting out of his travelling trunks in the entrance hall, where twisted oak columns support a decorated ceiling. Montesquieu's library remains intact, its 7000 volumes in grille-fronted bookcases lining the walls of the enormous vaulted library which was originally the council chamber

LACQ
PYRÉNÉES-ATLANTIQUES   Pop 570

Flames from tall chimneys signal the industrial zone which has grown up in the valley of the Gave de Pau after the discovery at the end of 1951 of what was then one of the world's largest known deposits of natural gas. The field, which produces more than 5000 million cubic metres of gas a year, has transformed the economy of this area of the south-west, and brought about an influx of new populations. It has also created the new town of **Mourenx**, on the other side of the Gave de Pau, where some 10,000 technicians employed in the industrial zone have apartments in high-rise blocks. The Elf Aquitaine petrol company has set up a permanent exhibition illustrating the different uses of the gas and its products. Yet the Lacq reserves are already beginning to be exhausted, and with no major new finds expected, prospects for natural gas as a source of energy are dim.

LANDES, LES

This 14,000 sq km of pine forests enclosed roughly by the Garonne and the Adour, which some find depressing, others fascinating, is a man-made landscape. It was formerly a zone of scrub and marsh, inhabited chiefly by shepherds, who were said to maintain their pitiful flocks less for their wool or mutton than for the manure with which they fertilized the equally miserable plots around their huts. The Atlantic winds blew the sands of the coast inland, further impoverishing the coast and blocking the flow of the rivers, so that in winter the area became a bog whose inhabitants got about on the stilts now seen only at folk festivals. Change came towards the end of the 18C, when an engineer of genius, Nicolas-Thomas Brémontier, stabilized the coastal dunes by planting them with marram grass and marine pines and did the same for the sandy waste inland by planting reeds, broom and pines, with a screen of brushwood. When, from the mid–19C, the marshes were drained, the way was clear for large-scale afforestation.

Today this vast area, one of the most sparsely populated of France, is also one of the richest, the trees providing not only timber but also paper, resin and turpentine. The earthenware pots fastened to the trunks here and there mark the first stage in the process of collecting resin. Sheep are still pastured in the clearings, and there are cornfields as well as vegetable plots near the houses; but essentially the secondary industry of the Landes is tourism. Marked footpaths and bridleways have been laid out among the trees and there is fishing and canoeing in the lakes and rivers.

At **Marquèze**, in the S of the region, there is an open-air museum of Ecology where, on an 18-hectare site, scenes of daily life in the Landes during the 19C have been recreated. Small mixed farms have been laid out around typical houses of the region, some of which have been moved bodily from their original sites, and crafts like charcoal-burning are demonstrated. Part of the Landes has been designated as a regional park.

LIBOURNE
GIRONDE   Pop 23,300

Libourne, at the tidal limit of the Gironde, and once a busy wine-shipping port, is as English a town as any in Aquitaine. It was founded as a

Libourne

bastide in 1265 by the English seneschal, Roger de Leyburn, and named Libournia after him. The Tour du Grand-Port, on the Quai de l'Isle, was part of the 13C ramparts. The town hall is 15C and there are 16C houses in the Grand-Place.

About 9km W is the Renaissance castle of **Vayres**, which stands on a site first fortified by the Romans. It replaced a medieval castle, of which parts survive. Louis de Foix, who was responsible for the rebuilding, also designed the Phare de Cordouan, having previously established a permanent channel in the mouth of the Adour.

MARMANDE
LOT-ET-GARONNE   Pop 17,400

Marmande, on the right bank of the Garonne, is a busy market town in a fruit-growing area, known for the cultivation of the superbly flavoured tomatoes to which it has given its name. The church of Notre-Dame, whose earliest part is 13C, has a Renaissance cloister with a fine view of the river below.

At **Le Mas d'Agenais**, 15km S, once a Roman town, the 12C church of St-Vincent possesses a Rembrandt Crucifixion which may be seen on application to the *curé*.

MAULÉON-LICHARRE
PYRÉNÉES-ATLANTIQUES   Pop 3150

This old fortified town is famous for its sandals, boots, sabots and espadrilles, and nowadays makes rubber footwear as well as the famous rope-soles.

Gotein, about 5km S, has an example of the three-pointed bell-towers which were designed to explain the mystery of the Trinity to the Basques.

MÉDOC, LE
GIRONDE

N of Bordeaux, on the left bank of the Gironde, is a narrow strip of ungrateful soil, about 70km long, which produces some of the world's greatest wines. The vines of the Médoc thrive "with a sea view and their feet in the gravel", as the local saying has it; they are additionally sheltered by the pine forests from the force of the W winds. The term 'château', as applied to the homes of the great vintages, has not the usual architectural connotation here: often the buildings isolated among the stretches of low-growing vines are no more than large farmhouses or manors. An impressive exception is the **Château de Beychevelle**, rebuilt in the mid–18C on a site which had been fortified since the 14C. During the 17C it belonged to the dukes of Épernon, one of whom was High Admiral of France. The custom of passing ships dipping their sails in respect to him gave the château its name, a corruption of *baisse-voile*. **Fort Médoc**, just S of Beychevelle, is a massive, star-shaped strongpoint built by Vauban in 1689 to defend the approaches to Bordeaux. **Château Mouton-Rothschild**, near **Pauillac**, has a museum devoted to works of art in any medium which are related to wine. The items range from Roman glass to 15C tapestries from Strasbourg and jewelled miniatures which belonged to Catherine the Great. They include the château's own labels, designed by artists like Cocteau, Braque, Dali, Chagall and Henry Moore. They were paid, most suitably, in bottles of the vintage they embellished.

Vineyards of Château Lafite-Rothschild

MONTAIGNE, CHÂTEAU DE
DORDOGNE

Here, in his property E of St-Émilion, which was

more manor house than castle, Michel de Montaigne (1533–92) was born and died. During the last twenty years of his life he wrote the *Essays* which give us perhaps the best portrait we possess of Renaissance man at his most rational and civilized. Son of a prosperous merchant of Bordeaux, who, like his father, became its mayor, he was a lawyer and as member of the city's *parlement* was sent to the court of Henri III for a couple of years. At the age of 38 he retired to his country house to devote the rest of his life to peaceful study.

Most of the house is a 19C reconstruction of the original, which was destroyed by fire in 1885. Fortunately, the round tower which was Montaigne's retreat survives, though the library of 1000 books was scattered at his death. There remain about 50 Latin and Greek quotations, some now barely legible, which he wrote on the beams.

MONT-DE-MARSAN
LANDES   Pop 30,900

Mont-de-Marsan, at the confluence of the rivers Midon and Douze, S of the Landes, is famous as a centre both of the *course landaise*, a form of bullfighting in which the beast is played without being killed, and, during the second half of July, of the true Spanish corrida. The large racecourse stages a dozen meetings a year, among them the Grand Prix International on the last Sun. in Sept.

NAVARRENX
PYRÉNÉES-ATLANTIQUES   Pop 1200

This *bastide* town, on the Gave d'Oloron, is a centre for trout and salmon fishing and the scene every year of championships. Navarrenx did not get its walls until two centuries after its founding in 1540; they were built by the king of Navarre, Henri d'Albret. No town in the region was better prepared for war when the troops of Charles IX made war against the Protestants of Navarre.

NÉRAC
LOT-ET-GARONNE   Pop 7300

Only one wing now remains of the château of Nérac, about 30km W of Agen, where the legendary queen of Navarre, Marguerite d'Angoulême (1492–1549) reigned over a court which was at once entertaining and scholarly. The Renaissance front, with arcading and twisted pillars, and the vaulted ceilings of the ground floor rooms are enough to suggest the splendour of the whole, most of which was destroyed during the Revolution. The Promenade de la Garonne, the long walk beside the river, is said to have been the setting: "Navarre: a park with a palace in it" which Shakespeare chose for his *Love's Labour's Lost*. The promenade is now a public park, in which Marguerite is commemorated by a fountain. Her grandson, Henri of Navarre, who became Henri IV, has two monuments, an equestrian statue and, more obliquely, the Fontaine de Flourette, a memorial to a girl, daughter of a gardener, who drowned herself after, it is said, she had been seduced and deserted by the young prince.

Nérac

OLORON-STE-MARIE
PYRÉNÉES-ATLANTIQUES   Pop 12,200

Oloron, at the junction of the Gave d'Aspe and the Gave d'Ossau, SW of Pau, is on the road to the pass of Somport, an exhilarating route over the Pyrenees where today's travellers are following in the footsteps of the Compostela pilgrims and the Roman legions before them. Of Oloron's two churches, the 11C Ste-Croix and the 12C Ste-Marie, the latter is the more interesting. Its doorway, carved in Pyrenean marble to which time has done no more than add a sheen, is both a monument and a chronicle. It was raised by Gaston IV (1090–1131), viscount of Béarn, on his return from the First Crusade, to celebrate the taking of Jerusalem, in which he had played an important part. The carvings include a Vision of the Apocalypse, with 24 elders playing the viol and rebec, instruments used by the troubadours, and fascinating scenes from the daily life of the period, from smoking salmon to making cheese. Two Saracens in chains represent the invaders whom Gaston found in the Béarn when he returned from the Crusade and two Roman sentries the guards whom the Emperor Constantine posted for protection at the doors of Christian churches. Finally, there is an equestrian statue of Gaston himself.

ORTHEZ
PYRÉNÉES-ATLANTIQUES   Pop 10,500

One of the original pair of 13C towers still defends the bridge here over the Gave de Pau. Between 1194 and 1464 this quiet small town, 40km NW of Pau, was the capital of the Béarn and the seat of the counts of Foix. It even had a university. The 14C chronicler Froissart has left us an account of the court of Gaston Phoebus, most remarkable of the counts, which he visited in 1388. Never, he tells us, was he at one which pleased him more, nor was he ever more delighted by feats of arms. The town declined after the counts removed their court to Pau, and the Wars of Religion, followed by an epidemic of plague, saw the end of its splendours, including the closure of the university. Of the great fortress which Count Gaston VII built in the 13–

14C, only the Tour Moncade, on the N side of the town, remains. Just N of Orthez, Wellington, after his Peninsular campaign, defeated Marshal Soult's army. It was the last occasion on which the bridge tower served as a defensive point.

PAU
PYRÉNÉES-ATLANTIQUES Pop 85800

With its sensational southward view over the Pyrenees, this elegant town was the birthplace, in 1553, of Henri of Navarre, later to become Henri IV of France. He became one of the most effective and popular of French monarchs, ready to abjure the Protestant religion as a condition of succeeding to the throne ("Paris is worth a Mass") but wishing for his people the simple pleasure of "a chicken in every pot".

During the 19C Pau acquired a large British colony whose early nucleus was made up of retired officers of Wellington's army who had come to love the region during the Peninsular campaign. The mild climate soon attracted others, so that at one time the British made up 15 per cent of the population. They introduced foxhunting and steeplechasing, also the Continent's first golf course, laid out in 1866.

The castle built on a hill above the Gave de Pau, originally a hunting lodge of the counts of Foix, was enlarged by one of the most remarkable of them, Gaston Phoebus (1331–91), who built the brick keep on the left of the entrance. In the 16C Marguerite of Angoulême, Henri of Navarre's grandmother, turned it into a Renaissance mansion and laid out the gardens W of the castle. The royal souvenirs include the great tortoiseshell cradle in the room where, reputedly, Henri was born. There is a remarkable series of tapestries, Brussels, Gobelins and Flemish, from periods ranging from the early 16C to the 17C.

The Boulevard des Pyrénées, built on the initiative of Napoleon on a terrace above the Gave de Pau, is a 2km promenade running from the château to the Parc Beaumont, with its casino, and commanding a view of the range of the Pyrenees from the Pic d'Anie to the Pic du Midi du Bigorre.

The Musée des Beaux Arts has a varied collection, including pictures by Rubens, El Greco, Corot and Degas. The Musée Bernadotte is housed in the birthplace of Napoleon's marshal who, in 1818, accepted the invitation of Sweden to accede to its throne and, as Charles XIV, became founder of that country's royal house.

The Grand Prix de Pau, run over a 3km course laid out in the streets of the town, takes place during the three weeks of the Whitsun weekend every year.

Lescar is now virtually a residential suburb of Pau. The cathedral of Notre-Dame, where the kings of Navarre were buried, dates from the first half of the 12C. It has some fine Romanesque capitals and a 12C mosaic of hunting scenes in the choir.

The **Grottes de Bétharram**, 12km W of Pau, consist of descending galleries carved by an underground river. The guided tour, which includes a brief boat trip, highlights the remarkable limestone formations.

Château de Pau

ROQUEFORT
LANDES Pop 1800

This small town, 12km NE of Mont-de-Marsan, not to be confused with its better-known namesake in the Aveyron, has an 11C church which was a strongpoint as much as a place of worship. Its slit windows and defensive tower were a complement to the old ramparts with their two towers, one from the 12C, one from the 14C. Later the church was a centre for the Antoninians, a religious order whose members cared for the victims of the *mal des ardents*, a disease akin to ergotism, which was known also as St-Anthony's fire. The symbols of the order may be seen among the carvings of the Flamboyant S porch.

ROQUETAILLADE, CHÂTEAU DE
GIRONDE

Cardinal Gaillard de la Mothe, nephew of Pope Clement V, who raised this castle in 1306, gave it six towers like that of Villandraut (q.v.), 11km SW, which was built by his uncle. It is a near-perfect example of the work of the 19C architect Viollet-le-Duc, whose restorations ranged from the cathedral of Notre-Dame in Paris to the city of Carcassonne. Besides rebuilding Roquetaillade, he redecorated it with wall and ceiling paintings and supplied it with supposedly Gothic furniture. The castle is still inhabited.

ST-ÉMILION
GIRONDE Pop 3000

St-Émilion is a town as well as a vintage. The centre of the most celebrated of the wine districts around Bordeaux is a walled city on a hilltop whose faded russet roof tiles and houses of grey or gold stone retain their medieval air. Originally an 8C monastery, its prosperity began in 1199, when King John granted it a charter of privileges, which it lost when the English were driven out of Aquitaine. Its most remarkable monument is the underground church whose bell-tower rises above the town square. Benedictine monks created it between the 9C and 12C by enlarging existing caverns in the limestone. The brilliant frescoes which once decorated the interior were destroyed during the Revolution, when the church was used as a military saltpetre store. It was reconsecrated in 1837 but only a few bas-reliefs now relieve the ranks of rectangular pillars. The reputed hermitage of St-Émilion is nearby. The collegiate church has a 12C nave; the rest is Gothic, with a particularly good choir and transept, and a 14C cloister.

Every year the opening of the vintage is proclaimed from the tower of the 13C Château de Roy by the Jurade de St-Émilion, 24 officials dressed in their red medieval robes and flat caps. The Jurade was founded by King John and at one time administered the town. It is still responsible for controlling the quality of the wine, with the ultimate sanction of declaring a "non-vintage", which means that the wine must go for sale as unclassified vin rouge.

St-Émilion

ST-ÉTIENNE-DE-BAÏGORRY
PYRÉNÉES-ATLANTIQUES Pop 1700

This is a Basque picture village in the Vallée des Aldudes, with a Roman bridge over the river that divides it into two districts whose residents were once scarcely on speaking terms. The church of St-Étienne, originally Romanesque but rebuilt in the 18C, has an interior of surprisingly elaborate richness. Besides the three stages of galleries usual in Basque churches, it has three altars with richly gilded reredoses and a painted triumphal arch. Several centuries ago the village got a good deal of its wealth by manufacturing arms for the Basque

privateers – possibly they paid for the embellishment of the church.

ST-JEAN-DE-LUZ
PYRÉNÉES-ATLANTIQUES Pop 12,900

Relatively new as a holiday resort, with a splendid sandy beach curving round a deep-water bay, St-Jean-de-Luz, some 20km SW of Biarritz, has an ancient history as a fishing port. As early as the 13C – some say the 11C – its ships were whaling in the Antarctic and reached America long before Columbus. By the end of the 16C some 100 ships and 3000 sailors (out of a population of 14,000) sailed from this, the world's biggest whaling port. The fishing trade dwindled after 1713, when, under the Peace of Utrecht, France lost to England her fishing rights in Newfoundland, but the sailors and shipbuilders soon found alternative occupation in piracy. Today the small fishing boats which share the port with pleasure craft catch tunny, sardines and vast quantities of anchovies.

St-Jean was the scene of the marriage, on 9 June 1660, of Louis XIV and the Infanta Marie-Thérèse of Spain. The king and his court installed themselves at St-Jean a month before the event, the bride wore a gown of cloth of silver under a purple velvet cloak, and among her presents were, from the king, six sets of diamonds and precious stones, and, from Cardinal Mazarin, a solid gold dinner service and two state carriages, one drawn by six Russian, the other by six Indian horses.

The church of St-Jean-Baptiste, where the three-hour ceremony took place, is the biggest and finest of the Basque churches. It was built in the 15C and enlarged later. The rather restrained exterior belies the richness of the interior, which has the typical barrel roof and three tiers of galleries round the nave, in the centre of which hangs a votive ship. The raised altar has a magnificent reredos, a theatrical blaze of gold peopled with statues of saints and angels. The door by which the royal couple left the church after the ceremony was bricked up so that it should never be used by lesser mortals.

Among the fine houses which survive in the old town are the turreted Maison Louis XIV, built by the shipbuilder Lohobiague in 1643, and the brick and stone Maison de l'Infante, a Louis XIII house built by the Haraneder family, where the king and his bride respectively stayed before the marriage.

Ciboure, on the opposite side of the river Nivelle, was the birthplace of the composer Maurice Ravel (1875–1937).

The view SW from St-Jean is dominated by the 900m mountain of La Rhune, on the Spanish border, notable for its tendency to attract storms and to be almost always cloud-covered. Nevertheless it commands magnificent panoramas of the Pyrenees, the Atlantic and the Basque coast. In its neighbourhood are some delightful Basque villages. **Ascain**, with its monumental church tower, possesses one of the rather rare examples of a *trinquet*, or indoor real tennis court. **Sare**, with another splendid church, is a centre for the seasonal netting of migratory wood pigeons, the *palombes*, whose mass slaughter the law has recently been questioning. **Espelette**, a spreading

St-Jean-de-Luz

village with twisting, flowery streets, has a market for the sale of *pottoks*, the native ponies of the Pyrenees, and has won the title of prettiest village in France. In this it might well be rivalled by **Ainhoa**, to the S, its main street lined with red-tiled, white-walled houses.

ST-JEAN PIED-DE-PORT
PYRÉNÉES-ATLANTIQUES   Pop 1800

"Port" in this context means mountain pass, not harbour, for St-Jean is at the foot of the pass of Roncesvalles, where Roland and the rearguard of Charlemagne's army were slaughtered by the Basques as they returned from an expedition in Spain. It was also one of the pilgrim routes to Compostela, St-Jean being the last stopping place on French soil. The old town, clustered round the great citadel planned by Vauban, is enclosed by 15C ramparts. The New Town on the far bank of the Nive is defended by 17C fortifications, also by Vauban. There are 16–17C houses in the Rue de la Citadelle, and, beside the river, spanned by an ancient single-arch bridge, there is a memorable prospect of white houses, with the typical broad eaves and verandas, apparently growing out of the water.

ST-SEVER
LANDES   Pop 4800

St-Sever, looking out over the Adour from the edge of the plateau of Chalosse, is famous for its medieval abbey church which, unusually, has three apsidal chapels, increasing in scale towards the centre, at the E of each transept. The early 12C capitals are outstanding. They include a carving of Salome receiving the head of St John the Baptist, a prefiguration of the fate of St Sever, who is said to have been beheaded. In the choir and transept are marble pillars which come from the palace of the Roman governors of Morlanne.

SAISON, VALLÉE DE
PYRÉNÉES-ATLANTIQUES

This valley of the Haute Soule, leading S from Mauléon-Lichaure to the Spanish frontier, is the gateway to some of the wildest and loneliest areas of the Pyrenees, where flocks are brought to summer pasture and the wild ponies wander free. There are stunning views on both sides of the frontier and great beech forests like that of **Arbailles** and the 2300ha **Irat**, which, in the 18C, furnished the men-o'-war of both France and Germany with masts. The rare villages include the shepherd's hamlet of **Ste-Engrace**, surrounded by mountains. It was once a station on the road to Compostela, which explains the importance of its 11C church, once that of an abbey. The carvings on the capitals of the choir include hunting scenes and the visit of the Queen of Sheba, mounted on an elephant, to Solomon.

TROIS-VILLES
PYRÉNÉES-ATLANTIQUES

Mansard gave Trois-Villes, in the Basse Soule, its château, but Alexandre Dumas (1802–70) gave it its fame, for this was the home of the original Monsieur de Tréville, Captain of the King's Musketeers. About 12km E is **Lanne**, in whose château lived Isaac de Porthau, the novel's Porthos, and 5km beyond this, **Aramits**, of whose former abbey the fictional Aramis was a lay beneficiary.

VILLANDRAUT
GIRONDE   Pop 900

Clément V (1305–14), the Avignon pope, who was born in this small town on the SE edge of the Landes, built the six-towered castle whose magnificent ruin today dominates Villandraut. Clément is buried in the church of **Uzeste**, 5km S of Villandraut: he endowed it, which accounts for its cathedral-like proportions. There is a good Coronation of the Virgin over the S porch and, in the apse, a 13C Virgin said to have been venerated by the future pope. His white marble effigy, badly mutilated by the Huguenots, is behind the altar.

VILLENEUVE-SUR-LOT
LOT-ET-GARONNE   Pop 23,700

Its name, New Town, and its rectangular street pattern proclaim that this market town in a fruit-growing area was originally a *bastide*. It was built by the French in 1253 but quickly passed into the hands of the English, who built the bridge which can still be seen, though there is now a modern one upstream. Two of the town gates, both built of brick and stone, and crenellated and machicolated, remain from the old fortifications. The modern church of Ste-Catherine, also of brick, has 14–15C windows, salvaged from the former church, which are believed to be of the school of Arnaut de Moles, who made the famous windows of Auch cathedral.

Pujol, on a hilltop 3km SW of Villeneuve, is an ancient village which preserves within its walls timbered houses and two churches.

PYRENEES

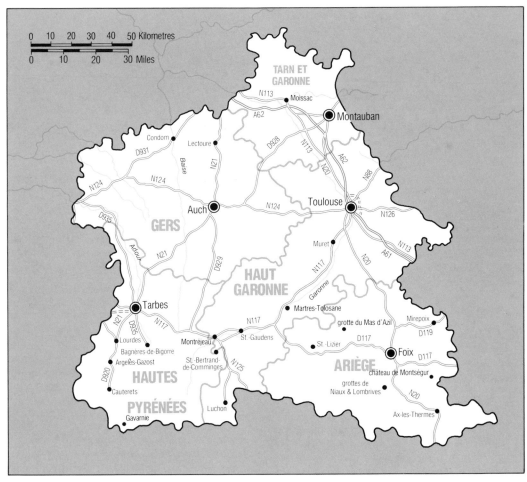

Mass tourism has not reached the Pyrenees and the many who love this, one of the more picturesque and varied areas of France, pray that it may never do so. It is essentially a land of contrasts. Against the line of glittering peaks that has been called the only view in Europe to rival that of Naples from the sea can be set the vineyards and orchards, the melons and strawberries of the northern plains and valleys. A few thousand feet above the stylish little spas there are flowery alpine meadows chiming with cowbells, and cols where French and Spanish shepherds clasp hands over the border to confirm common grazing rights dating from the 14th century.

In height, even the central section of the range, between the Ariège valley and the Vallée d'Ossau, does not rival the Alps: in majesty, however, it yields nothing to them. The tormented folding of the earth's surface in this region and the action of the glaciers which have scoured and scooped it have produced wild and magnificent landscapes like that of the head of the Vallée de Gavarnie (q.v.). Yet much of this high country is gentle and peaceful. Spring comes three or four weeks earlier than it does to the more northerly Alps and the narrow valleys that fan out to the north are sunny

and sheltered. The torrents – *gave* is the local word – that rush through them broaden into rivers like the Adour and the Garonne that flow through good agricultural land.

In the isolated mountain valleys there was traditionally a self-sufficient, intensely independent community life that led their people to treat their own counts and Colbert's tax collectors with equal firmness. Poor roads and distance from Paris meant that the industrial revolution scarcely touched the region: virtually it has passed in a step, industrially, from the past to the future.

The remote past has left evidence in cave dwellings which make the Pyrenees one of the most rewarding regions of France for the palaeontologist. History began with an invasion of Iberian and Ligurian tribes. There was an existing Gaulish civilization when the Romans came in the first century BC to impose their own, to build cities and to establish many spas. Christianity arrived after them: it was introduced in the third century AD and survived, however precariously, during the invasions, Barbarian, Saracen, Norse, that came after the collapse of Roman rule.

The civilization whose mark is still clear on the region, architecturally in churches, donjons and bastides, the "new towns" of the period, culturally in language and literature, is that of the 10th to the 13th centuries. Peace saw trade re-established; the resultant prosperity helped to give the counts of Toulouse a political power that made their court a nursery of troubadour art. It was the first Romantic era, but it was also an age of faith which found its expression in pilgrimages, the most famous of which was that to the tomb of the apostle St James at Santiago de Compostela in Galicia. The route passed through the Pyrenees and one of its legacies is the splendid basilica of St-Sernin at Toulouse; but the movement and the general climate of the period inspired much other church building, whether Romanesque or the red brick Gothic which is the most distinctive style of the region.

The bastides, in which Gascony is particularly rich, were towns built with a purpose, whether, like those established by or for Edward I, king of England and duke of Aquitaine, to mark the frontier between his territory and that of the French monarch, to settle an area or simply to provide necessary housing. Their methodical layout, recognizable today in small towns like Mirande, contrasts with the organic growth of most old towns.

The brutal 13th century crusade against the Cathar or Albigensian heretics (so called because the Albi region was one of their strongholds) ended that civilization and with it the power of the counts of Toulouse. The Cathars preached a dualist creed in which Jehovah and Lucifer were equal powers. They lived a life of extreme austerity, which was a reaction against the wealth and corruption of the church. After the murder of a papal legate near Nimes, in which Count Raymond VI of Toulouse, though nominally a Catholic, was suspected of being implicated, Pope Innocent III launched a crusade against the Cathars. The northern knights, who gathered under the banner of Simon de Montfort, seeing a prospect of gaining lands expropriated from heretics, waged a brutal campaign from 1209–18. The outcome, in 1271, was the union of the Languedoc and the French crown. With the treaty of the Pyrenees of 1659, the counts of areas such as Bigorre and Foix lost their authority and the whole region was united with it. Local life continued much as before, enduring the ravages of the Wars of Religion during the 16th century as it had endured the earlier savagery of Cathar repression.

The 19th century was a period of decline for the Pyrenees. A dwindling population, a lack of important industries, and remoteness from the main trade routes of Europe all contributed to the image of a backward area. The turning point came with the realization that the region had an inexhaustible source of hydraulic power in its mountain torrents. The way was open for the expansion of the present century, which took another bound forward with the discovery at Lacq, in 1951, of one of Europe's greatest deposits of natural gas.

Side by side with it has gone an intelligent exploitation of the other natural assets which fit the region so remarkably for the leisure industries which are the growth point of our own day. Mountaineering, which began as an elitist sport, today attracts more diverse enthusiasts. Parties of

St-Lizier

schoolchildren now join their elders in the Pyrenean resorts where the runs are excellent and where, traditionally, the atmosphere is one more of fun and friendship than of high fashion. In summer many of them are superb centres for mountain walking.

Less strenuous entertainment varies from casinos to music festivals, including a number of unusually interesting museums of local history and prehistory; and there are memorable spectacles in the limestone caves festooned with stalactites and stalagmites which underlie the area, several of which have been made accessible to tourists, as distinct from speleologists. Gastronomy, which, in France, ranks high among entertainments, is centred in the rich lowlands around Auch, the home of *foie gras* and other delectable products of goose, duck or pork. All three have a place in the *garbure*, the traditional peasant soup of Gascony, in which not only will the spoon stand up but some consumers find a fork necessary also.

The major achievement has been the creation, in 1967, of the National Park of the Pyrenees. Here, in a narrow strip running along 100 kilometres of mountain country on the Spanish frontier, is the essence of the region, the stunning landscapes, the fishing in rivers and lakes, the possibilities for long-distance walking and a range of animal and bird life that includes chamois, bearded vultures and golden eagles. There is even – they say – the last handful of brown bears in Europe.

AUCH
GERS   Pop 25,500

The capital of Gascony, an important city since Roman times, looks down on the valley of the Gers from a height on the W bank of the river. The Gothic cathedral of Ste-Marie dominates it, whether one looks up from the lower town at the pale gold building with its twin bell towers or across from the Pl. de la Libération at the imposing if slightly ponderous facade, but the interior

Auch

eclipses both. It glows with eighteen stained glass windows by Arnaut de Moles, a Gascon artist of the second half of the 15C. The richness and intensity of the colour is matched by the extraordinary naturalism of the figures which illustrate, above, the relation between the pagan world and the Old and New Testaments, below, scenes from the daily life of the period. The choir contains the masterpiece of the woodcarvers of the area, 113 oak stalls, carved with more than 1500 figures drawn impartially from the scriptures and from mythology. It was the work of fifty years, covering roughly the first half of the 16th century, and the craftsmen remain unknown. There are some splendid old houses in the narrow streets around the cathedral; from the terrace on its S side a monumental staircase of 232 steps leads to the river and the lower town. At its head the 14C Tour d'Armagnac, now used as a prison, rises to 40m; half-way down is a statue of d'Artagnan. Dumas based the character of his musketeer on Charles de Baez, who was born early in the 16C at the château of Castelmore, in Gascony.

Every year in June, Auch stages a music festival, including recitals on the celebrated cathedral organ, built in 1694 by Jean de Joyeuse.

Three interesting small towns lie within 20km of Auch. **Mirande** is a good example of the *bastides* established in the region during the 12–13C. It keeps the original rectangular plan and has an early 15C church whose tower could have served as a defensive point.

Simorre, to the SE, has 14–15C stained glass in its fortified brick church. The building itself, standing at the roadside like a veritable fortress, was energetically restored by Viollet-le-Duc during the 19C.

Gimont, almost due E, a little walled town on a hill, has the ruins of a Cistercian abbey and a 14C church with a brick tower. Our own century has added a large factory for canning the *foie gras* which is one of the specialities of Gascony.

AX-LES-THERMES
ARIÈGE   Pop 1500

Situated 15km from the frontier on the road from Toulouse to Andorra, this is a spa with 2000 years of history. The Romans used its hot springs and the steaming "bassin des Ladres", in front of the hospital, was constructed by St Louis for the use of his soldiers who returned from the Crusades afflicted with leprosy. Today the sulphurous waters are used for the treatment of rheumatism, respiratory ailments and certain skin diseases. Ax offers skiing in winter and mountain walking in summer.

The village of **Montaillou**, SE of Ax, with a ruined castle, was a site of a purge of the Cathars by a local bishop, and the subject matter for a famous account of medieval life by the historian Le Roy Ladurie.

BAGNÈRES-DE-BIGORRE
HAUTES-PYRÉNÉES   Pop 9900

This fashionable spa on the Adour, 22km SE of Lourdes, has a museum and art gallery, the former devoted largely to regional culture and folklore, as well as a casino. Since it is within easy reach of the majestic 2865m Pic du Midi, with a celebrated observatory on its summit, it is a fitting centre for the oldest of the Pyrenean mountaineering clubs, the Société Raymond, founded in 1865, a number of whose members were writers who have chronicled the early ascents. The church of St-Vincent is 15–16C, and there are remains of an earlier church. Near the town is the Grotte de Médous where the Adour flows through a cavern festooned with stalactites and stalagmites.

CAUTERETS
HAUTES-PYRÉNÉES   Pop 1100

This spa, some 25km SW of Lourdes, has ten warm sulphur springs and is a famous centre for climbers, mountain walkers and winter sports enthusiasts. It is a gateway to the central section of the National Park of the Pyrenees, and the converging point for five valleys which provide opportunities for delightful expeditions. The little town has a number of literary associations, providing romantic experiences for Victor Hugo, George Sand and Chateaubriand.

CONDOM
GERS   Pop 7800

This market town on the river Baise, a tributary of the Garonne, has a number of fine 18C houses, and thrives on Armagnac, the brandy of the Gers, subtly different in flavour from the better known Cognac. The town's Musée de l'Armagnac has documents which prove that the region was producing *eau-de-vie* as early as the first half of the 15C to justify its claim that Armagnac is the oldest French spirit, slightly predating Cognac.

The cathedral of St-Pierre, built, or rather rebuilt in the early 16C as one of the last late Gothic buildings in the Gers, narrowly escaped destruction by the Huguenots in 1569. The citizens raised

30,000 francs to ransom it. The great neo-Gothic cloister, with terracotta statues of saints and angels, was restored in the 19C after being badly damaged during the Revolution. Like the cathedral, it has pleasing painted roof bosses.

FOIX
ARIÈGE   Pop 10,100

The swift Ariège tears through Foix, the capital of its *département*, set among rock and wood and water at the junction of the D1 and N2. High above the town rises the trinity of towers, two square, one round, of the château built at the beginning of the 11C for the first Comte de Foix. It survived the Albigensian Crusade undamaged, but in 1272 it was taken by the king of France, Philippe le Hardi, whose sovereignty the count had refused to acknowledge. The château now houses a departmental museum and its terrace commands a sweeping panorama of the Pyrenees. The old town has some attractive narrow streets and a 14–17C church built on the site of a former abbey which marked the grave of its patron, St Volusien, an archbishop of Toulouse who was martyred at the end of the 5C.

About 6km NW is the entrance to the subterranean **river of Labouiche**, where you can make a 2–3km boat trip through galleries, illuminated to enhance the effect of the limestone formations.

Foix

GAVARNIE
HAUTES-PYRÉNÉES   Pop 170

This village 50km S of Lourdes is beautifully situated as a walking, climbing and skiing centre. From the village, but even more spectacularly from high viewpoints such as the Pic de Mourgat to the W, there is a panorama of the famous Cirque de Gavarnie, described by George Sand as 'primitive chaos'. This is an immense amphitheatre of glacial mountains rising several thousands of metres above the valley, a breathtaking landscape of ice, snow, rock and waterfalls. Among these is the Grande Cascade, Europe's highest, dropping a sheer 400m.

LECTOURE
GERS   Pop 4400

High above the valley of the Gers, some 30km N of Auch, this is one of the richest archaeological sites in the region. As late as the 6C it was a celebrated centre of pagan worship and the items in the town hall museum include twenty altars used for the cult of Cybele, the Great Mother, which was found beneath the cathedral when the late 14C Gothic choir was rebuilt in 1540. The cathedral lost its 90m spire in 1792, apparently less from Revolutionary fury than because the bishop of the period was bored with the responsibility of maintaining it.

LOURDES
HAUTES-PYRÉNÉES   Pop 17,700

Here, in the foothills of the Central Pyrenees, is the world's greatest pilgrimage centre, Rome included, which annually attracts some three million Catholics who come to worship or to pray for miraculous cures at the shrine where, in 1858, a 14-year-old peasant girl, Bernadette Soubirous, claimed that Our Lady had appeared to her on a number of occasions. The early pilgrimages to the grotto of Massabielle, where the visions occurred, seem to have been a spontaneous growth: they were formalized and blessed by the church in 1864. Today, although the town has been appallingly commercialized, the Religious City, in a park laid out within a loop of the Gave de Pau river, has a far different atmosphere. It owes more to the natural surroundings and to the devotion of the myriads of believers than to its architecture: the neo-Gothic basilica of the Immaculate Conception and the neo-Romanesque basilica of the Rosary, both late 19C, are seemly rather than distinguished. In 1958 the centenary of Bernadette's visions was celebrated by the building of the underground basilica of Pope Pius X, a feat of architectural engineering which can accommodate 20,000 people under a single span of concrete.

The most important of the six annual pilgrimages is on 15 Aug., with immense crowds, including hordes of cripples, participating in the processions, both by day and, with lighted torches, by night.

The medieval *château fort* on its rock on the opposite bank of the river now houses an admirable museum of the Pyrenees whose contents range from natural history and reconstructions of typical mountain villages to records of the early climbers, a number of them English, who first explored the range. The house where Bernadette was born can be visited and also a museum that shows a film of her life. There are funicular or cable railways to the two summits which give Lourdes so dramatic a setting, the Pic du Jer (948m) and Le Béout, both with magnificent views of the further ranges of the Pyrenees.

S of Lourdes there is spectacular mountain country where the valleys of the Gavarnie (q.v.) and the only slightly less impressive valley of the Héas penetrate deep among the highest mountains of the Pyrenees.

St-Pé-de-Bigorre, some 10km W of Lourdes, now a pleasant mountain resort, was once a stop on

Lourdes

the pilgrim road to Compostela, where the Cluniacs raised an abbey which was the most splendid building of the Pyrenees. The Romanesque church suffered so badly during the 16C Wars of Religion and a 17C earthquake that little remains except a tower and a transept.

The **Grottes de Bétharram**, about 15km SW of Lourdes, provide one of the most famous spectacles of the Pyrenees; an underground river which ultimately flows into the Gave de Pau has carved out of the rock a series of galleries with fantastic limestone formations. A visit includes trips by boat and by cable car.

Barèges, 1220m up, is the highest of the spas in the Lavedan, the area S of Lourdes. Its fortune was made in the 17C, when Mme de Maintenon, not yet the wife of Louis XIV, brought his son, the ailing young duke of Maine, there.

Argelès-Gazost, a popular spa between Lourdes and Cauterets, is surrounded by sensational mountain scenery. The 12C abbey church of St-Savin has a fine Romanesque doorway.

Luz-St-Sauveur, a small but lively spa in a sheltered situation on the Gave de Pau, owes its prosperity to the visits of Napoleon III and his court in the mid-19C. The striking fortified church, often called a Templar's church, was in fact the work of the Knights Hospitallers who made a fortress of the 12C building.

LUCHON
HAUTE-GARONNE   Pop 3600

Situated midway along the Route des Pyrénées, this is perhaps the most elegant and sophisticated of the region's spas, with a reputation for the treatment of respiratory ailments and of vocal cords, which makes it popular with singers and public speakers. It has been established as a spa since the 1C but gained much of its present charm in the 18C when gardens and avenues of limes were laid out. For those other than *curistes*, the town is an excellent centre both for walking and for motoring, with the Vallée de la Pique, the Vallée du Lys and the Vallée d'Oueil all at hand. **Superbagnères**, about 6km SW, at an altitude of 1800m, is a renowned winter sports station which, more recently, has become popular with hang-gliders. The views from here extend to the Maladetta massif over the Spanish border.

MARTRES-TOLOSANE
HAUTE-GARONNE   Pop 1900

Every year on Trinity Sun. this small town on the N117 W of the Garonne stages a battle between Christians and Saracens in memory of its martyred patron, St Vidian. His relics are preserved in the 14C church built on the site of the palaeo-Christian necropolis. Here, in the Gallo-Roman period, was the town of Chiragon, where a villa excavated during the 19C yielded a large quantity of busts and statues which are now in the museum of St-Raymond at Toulouse.

MAS D'AZIL, GROTTE DU
ARIÈGE

This immense cave, 15km NE of St-Girons, is one of the most significant prehistoric sites in the Pyrenees. The entrance to the cave was bored by the river Arize millions of years ago, and the road follows the course of the subterranean river for 400m through the cavern. Palaeolithic people lived here, as shown by the art objects and artefacts excavated and now displayed in the museum which is built into the limestone rock. The huge cave also provided later refuge for early Christians, Albigensian heretics and Huguenot refugees.

MIREPOIX
ARIÈGE   Pop 3600

Mirepoix, some 40km NE of Foix, is in Cathar country. As a centre of the Albigensian heresy, it was held for the count of Toulouse and destroyed in Simon de Montfort's crusade. The rebuilding of the town as a *bastide* at the end of the 13C was the work of Guy I de Lévis, whom Montfort appointed marshal of Foix. There is a charming central square surrounded by 13–15C houses with overhanging first storeys. The building of the cathedral extended over four centuries, from 1343 to 1865, but both the immense nave and the graceful Gothic spire date from the beginning of the 16C.

MOISSAC
TARN-ET-GARONNE   Pop 11,400

The abbey church of St-Pierre, Moissac, is a masterpiece of medieval architecture, lying among vineyards on the right bank of the Tarn, 15km N of Castelsarrasin. The abbey was founded early in the 7C as a filial of St Wandrille, in Normandy, but its splendour dates from the 11C, when it was united to the great abbey of Cluny and blessed with a succession of distinguished abbots under whom it became one of the greatest religious houses of SW France. Later it was to be occupied by the English during the Hundred Years' War, damaged by the Protestants during the Wars of Religion, pillaged under the Terror and, during the supposedly civilized mid-19C, threatened with the total destruction of its cloister to make way for the railway line to Bordeaux.

Just in time, the Beaux Arts intervened to preserve the calm enclosure where the capitals of the elegant pillars are a veritable gallery of 11C sculpture in their luxuriance and variety. Even

Moissac

they are surpassed by the carvings of the S door, built during the first half of the 12C, where the great Christ in Majesty on the tympanum is surrounded by the personages of the Vision of the Apocalypse. All that remains of the 11C abbey church is the lower part of the tower, built, like so many in this region, as a strongpoint. The upper part, like most of the church, is 15C Gothic.

MONTAUBAN
TARN-ET-GARONNE   Pop 53,200

This rosy brick town on the right bank of the Tarn was founded as a new settlement by the count of Toulouse in 1144. Strongly fortified and given a charter which conferred many advantages, it flourished to become, in the 16C, a high place of Protestantism. It was a brief triumph. After the fall of La Rochelle, in 1621, Montauban surrendered to the army of Louis XIII without giving battle.

The heart of the town is the Pl. Nationale, an arcaded oval built in the 17C to replace an earlier, half-timbered market which was destroyed by fire. There are attractive 17C houses and a seven-arched bridge which dates from the early 14C. The openings between the arches were planned to deal with flood water. After the Catholic reconquest of the town, the fortified church of St-Jacques-de-Compostelle became a cathedral and it remains more interesting than the present cathedral of Notre-Dame, a large, rather dull classical building.

Ingres (1780–1867) was born here. The Ingres Museum, housed in the former bishop's palace, which incorporates part of the original early 14C building, has a group of paintings, 4000 of the artist's drawings (shown in rotation) and sculptures by another native of Montauban, Antoine Bourdelle (1861–1929), a pupil of Rodin.

MONTRÉJEAU
HAUTE-GARONNE   Pop 3200

Built as a *bastide* at the end of the 13C, this attractive small town, which commands the junction of the Garonne and the Neste, is an observation point that looks over a sweep of meadow and wooded hills to the mountains massed behind Luchon. The gardens and the esplanade constructed as a corniche to take full advantage of the panorama would not shame a larger resort.

MONTSÉGUR, CHÂTEAU DE
ARIÈGE

The ruins of the castle of Montségur, 30km SE of Foix, perch on a high rock. This was the scene of the final, hideous defeat of the Cathars, a stronghold which sheltered the last adherents of the sect after de Montfort's crusade had effectively ended. In 1244 it fell, after a nine months' siege by the garrison of Carcassonne. More than 200 knights and their families, who refused to abjure their faith, were burned alive.

MURET
HAUTE-GARONNE   Pop 16,200

This town, on the Garonne, some 15km SW of Toulouse, was the scene, in Sept. 1213, of the battle in which Simon de Montfort and his Catholic crusaders crushed the Albigensians led by Count Raymond of Toulouse and King Pedro II of Aragon. Meanwhile, in the church of St-Jacques, St Dominic prayed. A commemorative tablet set up about 1km along the road to Seysses describes the battle not as a conflict between Catholics and heretics but as the defence of the liberties of the Languedoc. Muret was the birthplace of Clément Ader (1841–1925), the engineer who constructed France's first flying machine: a statue of Icarus, by Paul Landowski, commemorates its first flight in 1890.

NIAUX, GROTTE DE
ARIÈGE

Some 6km S of Tarascon-sur-Ariège is the cavern of Niaux, which contains the most important examples of prehistoric painting open to the public in France since the caves of Lascaux were closed in 1963. The paintings, of bison, horses and deer, date from the Magdalenian period, 12,000 to 16,000 years ago, and are astonishingly well preserved.

The huge **Grotte de Lombrive**, 3.5km further S, has a dreadful history. Here, eighty or so years after the fall of Montségur (q.v.) in 1244, the last of the Cathars were buried alive. The symbols which they carved on the rock are believed to be clues to the hiding place of the treasure which belonged to the community. According to one version it consisted of "gold, silver and a great quantity of money"; according to another it was spiritual and thought to have been the Grail.

ST-BERTRAND-DE-COMMINGES
HAUTE-GARONNE   Pop 230

This fortified village on its rocky height in the upper valley of the Garonne was once an important Roman provincial capital. Recent excavations have uncovered the remains of the forum, a temple, a theatre and thermal baths. Here, shortly after the crucifixion, Herod the Tetrarch, with his wife Herodias, was exiled by the Emperor Caligula, a punishment that can hardly have been insupportable in such idyllic surroundings. The Roman city was ravaged by the barbarians in the 4C and by the plague in the 6C; the cathedral of Ste-Marie was not built until the 12C, to be enlarged in the 14C. The peerless Romanesque cloister, its S side open to the mountains, whose columns include one of the four Evangelists standing back to back, and the 16C woodcarvings of the choir, are only two of the attractions of a remarkable building. There are 15–16C buildings in the steep streets of the village.

Some 2km NE of the cathedral is the Romanesque **basilica of St-Just**, flanked with cypresses that set off its remarkable apse and the red-tiled roof that contrasts with the slate of Ste-Marie.

About 8km from St-Bertrand is the **grotto of Gargas**, the 'cave of cut hands', so named because there are marks of mutilated hands all over the vault, evidently dating back to Palaeolithic times.

ST-GAUDENS
HAUTE-GARONNE Pop 12,100

Set on the N117, half-way between the Atlantic and the Mediterranean, this busy town has benefited materially, if not aesthetically, from the discovery of natural gas at St-Marcel 12km N. The 12C church, though much restored after the ravages of the Wars of Religion, retains some interesting sculptures on the N side of the exterior. There is a good museum, partly archaeological, partly devoted to local history and culture. At **Valentine**, 2km SW of the town, excavations have revealed a 4C Gallo-Roman villa.

Midway through the 19C, caves near the small town of **Aurignac**, 22km NE of St-Gaudens, yielded discoveries of paramount importance to our knowledge of prehistory in the form of Palaeolithic tools and weapons dating back 20,000 to 30,000 years. This flint culture was subsequently named Aurignacian. The town museum contains, besides the discoveries made locally by Édouard Lartet, Aurignacian material found elsewhere in SW France and in North Africa.

ST-LIZIER
ARIÈGE Pop 250

This picturesque village, looking down on the Salat, an excellent trout stream, once possessed two cathedrals, though the 17C Notre-Dame-de-la-Siège, on higher ground, was the bishops' private chapel. The late 11C St-Lizier, with its red brick tower, has Romanesque frescoes in the choir. In the 12C cloister, which has attractive carved capitals, Simon de Montfort, leader of the crusade against the Albigensians, signed the pact which led ultimately to the ruin of the house of Toulouse and, indirectly, to his own death during the siege of that city.

TARBES
HAUTES-PYRÉNÉES Pop 54,000

Tarbes, in the centre of a rich agricultural area on the Adour, some 20km NE of Lourdes, was a Roman settlement, but its growth into a considerable industrial and commercial town dates only from the 19C and the later development of tourism. Its turbulent history in the years between has left it with few old buildings and a church so much rebuilt that little remains of its 12C origins. Marshal Foch (1851–1929), the Allied commander-in-chief in 1918, was a native of Tarbes: his birthplace in the Rue de la Victoire may be visited. A more spectacular military display is that of the International Museum of the Hussars, which traces their history over 500 years and through most of the countries of Europe, with the aid of more than 100 models, meticulously uniformed and equipped. The national stud which was founded by Napoleon in 1806 to provide remounts for his army is in the town. Part of the 15C cloister of the Benedictine abbey of St-Sever-St-Rustan, NE of Tarbes, has been set up in the attractive Jardin Massey, with its wide views of valley and mountain, which was laid out for his own pleasure by Placide Massey (1777–1853), a one-time director of the orangery at Versailles.

TOULOUSE
HAUTE-GARONNE Pop 355,000

Midway between the Atlantic and the Mediterranean, with the Pyrenees as a distant backdrop, Toulouse, half treasure house of art and architecture, half industrial centre geared to aircraft, electronics and aerospace, with an expanding and cosmopolitan population, is the very type of regional capital of modern France.

There was a prehistoric settlement beside this curve of the Garonne. The Romans found an existing town which, under their rule and under the name of Tolosa, became the third largest of Gaul. St Saturnin, or Sernin, brought Christianity here in the 3C and in so doing found martyrdom; in the 5C Tolosa became the capital of the Visigoths, and later, after being captured by Clovis in 508, part of the Merovingian kingdom.

Its first great age began in the 9C, when it became the seat of the feudal counts of Toulouse, who enjoyed virtual autonomy in their province of Languedoc, which extended from the borders of Aquitaine to those of Provence. Their court was the centre of the most brilliant civilization of W Europe and the birthplace of the troubadour lyrics which brought literature out of the church and the schools and into the world. That civilization was destroyed in the 13C by the papal crusade against the Cathars (see *Introduction*). Toulouse was occupied by the army of Simon de Montfort and endured a period of terror. Count Raymond VI then reoccupied the city and in 1218 de Montfort was killed in an unsuccessful attack on the town. Count Raymond VI of Toulouse, as part of his penance, was ordered to maintain for ten years "four masters in theology, two in canon law, six masters of arts and two directors of grammar". So, in 1229, was born the university of Toulouse.

The fine *hôtels particuliers* which give the town so much of its character are for the most part a legacy from Toulouse's second age of gold. This came with the discovery, early in the 16C, of the possibilities of obtaining dye from the woad plant. The local merchants prospered and built themselves splendid houses. The period of prosperity did not last out the century, but buildings like the magnificent brick and stone Hôtel d'Assezat, the Hôtel du Bernuy, with its octagonal stair tower, the Hôtel de Clary, and the early Renaissance Hôtel Béringuer-Maynier, have proved longer-lived.

The rapid expansion of Toulouse during the past thirty years has produced some lamentable suburbs, high-rise concrete in a country of ruddy brick, but the old city on the right bank of the Garonne is virtually unmarred, with handsome old houses, courtyards and fountains, open squares and traffic-free streets, churches and museums. Its heart is the broad Pl. du Capitole, three of its sides lined with outdoor cafés, the fourth closed by the pillared facade of the mid-18C Capitole, or city hall, built of brick and stone. The right wing of its 128m length now accommodates the municipal theatre. The inner courtyard was the scene of the execution in 1632 of Henri de Montmorency, governor of the Languedoc, and one of the first noblemen of France, who had challenged the power of Louis XIII.

St-Sernin, Toulouse

The city has a remarkable number of churches, of which the masterpieces are the basilica of St-Sernin and the church of the Jacobins. The former, started at the end of the 11C and completed during the 14C, when the spire was added, is the greatest and most perfect Romanesque church of S France, a brick and stone building with a five-storey octagonal tower. The other example which inspired a school of Romanesque sculptors is the exquisitely carved Porte Miégeville on the S side. The interior, with its vast nave, wide transept and double aisles, shows clearly St-Sernin's origins as a pilgrimage church, planned to accommodate the crowds on their way to the tomb of St James at Compostela. Some early Romanesque paintings have recently been uncovered in the N transept and the wall of the crypt has seven marble bas-reliefs of the late 11C. There is a striking 12C gold Christ in the S chapel of the apse and 13C frescoes in the Lady Chapel. The marble altar table under the crossing is 11C.

The majestic Gothic brick church of the Jacobins was the mother church of the Dominican order, founded by St Dominic in 1215 in an effort to expunge the Cathar heresy by peaceful means. The order's first religious house was set up at Toulouse in 1216 and its church was started in 1230, to be completed by the end of the 14C. The 19C all but saw its destruction: after being taken over by the state during the Revolution, it became an artillery stable under the Empire. Restoration of church, cloister and conventual buildings has extended over the better part of a century, but the result is breathtaking. The exterior is as stern as a fortress. From the NE corner rises the great octagonal tower in which the bell of the Dominican University was placed in 1299. The interior is triumphant in its simplicity. It is divided into a double nave by a line of seven marble pillars sweeping up to the vault, where each forms the base of a complex of arches. There is 14C glass in the two small rose windows of the W end; the nave windows are by the contemporary master, Max Ingrand. Beneath the central altar of grey marble is the gold casket containing the relics of the most famous of all Dominicans, St Thomas Aquinas, brought here in 1974, the seventh centenary of his death. The cloister has also been restored.

The cathedral of St-Étienne, though it was the earliest Gothic church in S France, hardly compares with these two. A certain lack of unity is understandable considering that its building lasted over six centuries, and that it was never completed.

The church of Notre-Dame-du-Taur stands on the spot where St Sernin was martyred by being tied to the tail of a bull. Its curious gabled facade is a fascinating example of the ornamental effects that can be achieved in brick.

Toulouse is as rich in museums as it is in churches, with that of the Augustins installed in the former convent of the order in 14–15C buildings, with a 19C addition by Viollet-le-Duc. It has some remarkable Romanesque sculptures as well as religious paintings by Rubens, Perugino, Murillo and Delacroix among others. The Musée St-Raymond has pottery, sculpture and Roman mosaics, also an important series of portrait heads. The Musée Paul-Dupuy is devoted to the work of artist-craftsmen from the medieval period to our own, with a variety of objects ranging from coins and clocks to the early 17C pharmacy of the Jesuit College. The Musée Georges-Labit has collections of Far Eastern sculpture, ceramics and paintings; the Musée du Vieux Toulouse has local folk art and pottery; and the Musée d'Histoire Naturelle includes a department of prehistory.

Modern Toulouse has grown up with the aircraft industry. The city which has recently pioneered the Caravelle, the Concorde and the Airbus, had, fifty years earlier, seen the inauguration of the first regular mail flight between France and Morocco and, in 1930, the first commercial flight to South America.

LANGUEDOC-ROUSSILLON

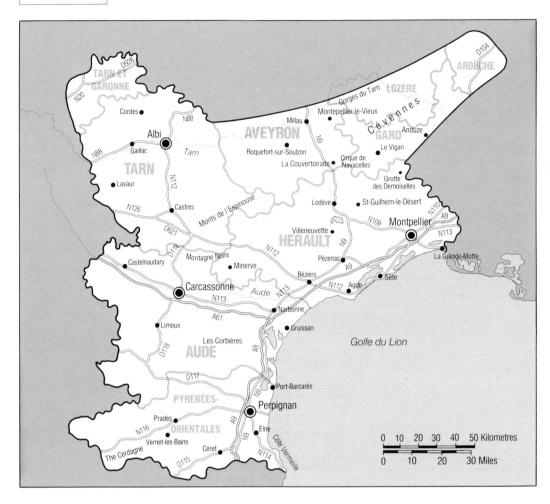

Historic Languedoc was a large and illustrious province stretching west as far as Toulouse, then its capital. But the modern 'region' of Languedoc-Roussillon includes only eastern or 'lower' Languedoc along the coast around Montpellier, now its capital, plus southerly parts of the Massif Central and, to the south, Roussillon (French Catalonia).

Languedoc's sun-parched coastal plain is the very epitome of southern France – an easy-going land of thyme and cicada, where cypresses stand beside red-roofed stone-walled farmsteads, and old men play *boules* in the shady squares of ancient sleepy villages. The coast itself is flat and dull, but has wide sandy beaches and big modern resorts. The plain and slopes behind are carpeted with mile upon mile of vineyard: the area produces 40 per cent of all French wine. Behind lies the country of the *garrigues*, dry stony hills covered with scrub. And farther north again rise the southern uplands of the Massif Central, crowned by Mont Aigoual. Here is the country of the *causses*, vast semi-arid limestone plateaux where sheep graze, providing milk for Roquefort cheeses and leather for Millau's glove industry. In places the *causses* are transected by deep winding gorges, those of the Tarn being the most spectacular. Just to the east are the

Cévennes, beautiful but lonely mountains where the local Protestants, still numerous, have not forgotten their ancestors' struggles against Catholic persecution in the 18th century.

Languedoc has long been a land of conflict – witness the mighty fortress of Carcassonne. Its plain lies astride one of Europe's oldest through-routes, for invasion, trade and, today, tourism. It was settled in c.600BC by Phocaeans from Greece who brought the culture of olive and vine. Then came the Romans who called the area Gallia Narbonnensis, with Narbonne as its capital, and made it a key province of their Empire. In the Dark Ages the Saracens arrived, a warlike people who were also highly cultured, lovers of learning and the arts, and thus were to be a major formative influence on the brilliant troubadour civilization that flourished in Languedoc in the 11th and 12th centuries. This was a golden era for Languedoc, then a powerful independent principality. But it was cut short in the early 13th century when the Cathar or Albigensian heresy aroused the wrath of the pope and the French king, and on their orders was brutally suppressed by Simon de Montfort. Languedoc was forcibly annexed to France. Its semi-autonomy as a province survived till the

Revolution, but its heyday was over. Yet the people here have strangely long memories: to this day they have not forgiven the Cathar massacres, and this remains the most anti-Paris of any French mainland region. People still feel 'colonized'.

The name Languedoc means 'langue d'oc', for its ancient tongue, Occitan, used 'oc' for 'yes' as opposed to 'oui' in the north. It was the heartland of the vast and vague region of 'Occitania' – and recent decades have seen quite an Occitan revival, both cultural and political. You can see 'OC' slogans daubed on walls by dotty extremists who want to create an Occitan nation. Most people are more realistic than this, yet many take pride in the local cultural revival which has produced Occitan writers, pop singers, folklore and theatre groups. Attempts, however, to revive the Occitan language may not get far. True, it has become an option in the *bac* and more young people are now studying it: but it is fast dying out in rural areas as a daily vehicle.

A few local traditions survive – some of them quite odd. You can find harvest festivals where people are pelted with flour and eggs or rolled in a pool of wine lees. The graceful old costumed folk-dances of Languedoc are still performed at some local festivals – but usually by students from the cities. However, the gastronomic tradition remains more authentically alive. Lavish with garlic and olive oil, it includes unusual country soups, spicy sausages, and above all, towards Toulouse, *cassoulet*, that marvellous stew of white beans with preserved goose and much else. The coast, especially the port of Sète, has a range of spicy fish and shellfish dishes.

All this good food is washed down by the region's wines, most of them quite cheap and many very pleasant (e.g. Corbières and Minervois), whatever their generally poor reputation in France. Yet the vine, Languedoc's major traditional source of wealth, is also its constant headache. The grape here grows so prolifically, needing so little care, that the many thousands of small farmers are used to an easy leisurely life and too often produce unsaleable surpluses. Since the coming of the EEC they have rioted repeatedly against the cheaper and stronger Italian wines flooding into France, and now they are equally alarmed at the threat of Spanish competition. The government has been trying, with some success, to get them to replace their poorer vines with 'nobler' ones producing better and more saleable wine: but the absurdities of wine economics are such that they still have a strong incentive to go on producing poor plonk, which adds to the EEC's wine lake and hence to the tax-payer's burden. Clearly, much of the region should no longer be under vine at all. The government in the 1950s created an ambitious irrigation network and persuaded some farmers to use this for moving over from wine to fruit growing: but this in turn has simply added to the EEC's peach and apple surpluses.

The government has been making other efforts, too, to diversify the economy of this rather sluggish area, so as to make it less dependent on the vine. Since the 1960s it has masterminded the building of a chain of eight mammoth new sea-resorts in modernistic style, with room for 280,000 tourist beds: the largest are at La Grande Motte and Cap d'Agde. The architecture may not suit all tastes – but at least the tourists have responded, and the region has grown richer. New industry, too, has settled, notably around Montpellier, which has grown from dozy provincial town into busy metropolis. The locals, conservative and suspicious, tend to look warily on this imposed 'progress' as Parisian 'neo-colonialism'.

You find few such complexes down in Roussillon, the French part of Catalonia, where the people tend to be more hard-working, serious, even dour – like their close cousins across the border, the Spanish Catalans. For many years Roussillon belonged to the kings of Aragon, before being united to France in 1659. It remains very Catalan: the arcaded squares, the dialect, the folk culture, will all be familiar to anyone who knows the Barcelona area. Country people still spontaneously dance the *sardana*, Catalonia's national dance, which alternates between joyous jig and stately ritual. The scenery is majestic and varied. Around Perpignan, the capital, is a fertile plain, a leading French market garden for early fruit and vegetables. To the south, the rugged Côte Vermeille has strange russet rocks. Here the Pyrenees tumble into the sea, and westwards they rise up to snowy peaks, where the remote and lovely abbey of St-Martin-de-Canigou nestles in the foothills of Mont Canigou.

Corbières vineyards

AGDE
HÉRAULT   Pop 13,000

An old fishing-port, 22km E of Béziers and 4km inland from the mouth of the Hérault. The former cathedral of St-Étienne, fortified, with battlements, was made with tufa-ash from Mont St-Loup at Cap d'Agde, an extinct volcano. On the coast at **Cap d'Agde**, 9km SE, is one of the largest – and pleasantest – of the big new Languedoc resorts. It is like an operetta stage-set of an old Provençal fishing-village, with pretty buildings in pastel shades; phoney, but agreeable. Next to it is the showpiece of modern tourism's fastest growth-sector: nudism. The nudist holiday-town here, Europe's largest, has casinos, nightclubs, supermarkets, the lot – and accommodation for 20,000 visitors.

ALBI
TARN   Pop 48,000

The mellow old city of Albi is world-famous for its Toulouse-Lautrec collection and, above all, for its huge and wonderful cathedral, built of pink-red brick like the *vieille ville* over which it towers. Albi in the 12–13C was a leading centre of the Cathar heretical movement which thus also took the name of 'Albigensian'. After the Cathars had been suppressed, the cruel Bernard de Castanet was in 1276 named bishop of Albi: he continued the Inquisition against them, and to reassert the power of the church built the great Romanesque cathedral, deliberately giving it stern fortress-like outer walls. This is still its aspect today, though the tall tower and the white Flamboyant porch were 15–16C additions.

The vast interior, by contrast, is a profusion of Renaissance gaiety, the work of artists from Bologna who covered walls, roof and pillars with multi-coloured designs. In the middle of the nave is a splendid rood-screen, intricately carved, and

Albi

behind it stands the huge choir, enclosed by walls decorated with delicate and sumptuous sculptures of biblical figures – as fine an example of Gothic art as exists anywhere. At the W end of the building, the gigantic fresco of the *Last Judgment*, by an unknown artist, said to be the largest painting in France, has sadly been blemished by the later imposition of the organ which obscures the central figure of Christ.

Next to the cathedral is the great episcopal palace, Palais de la Berbie, 13C and originally fortified. Today it houses the world's major collection of the works of Albi's celebrated son, Henri de Toulouse-Lautrec; after his death, the paintings were donated to the town by his mother and by a close friend, Maurice Joyant. Several rooms are filled with some of the finest creations of his Montmartre period. Nearby, also open to visits, is the house where he was born in 1864, son of Count Alphonse de Toulouse-Lautrec. It still belongs to the family. You can see photographs and other souvenirs, as well as the room where in 1878 he had the first fall that led to his deformity.

Albi today is an industrial town, with steel and glass works. In summer there is an excellent *son-et-lumière*, evoking the Albigensian crusades.

ANDUZE
GARD   Pop 2700

This little town on the S side of the Cévennes, near a gap in the mountains known as the 'Cévennes Gateway', was an important Protestant centre in the 16–18C. Nearby are two parks with exotic plants and tropical trees, notably huge bamboos: the former park of the Convent of the Cordeliers, and the park of Prafrance. The latter has 30 kinds of bamboo as well as trees from Asia and America: this unusual decor has been used in the shooting of many French films, including Clouzot's *The Wages of Fear*.

BÉZIERS
HÉRAULT   Pop 78,000

This big town, built on a low hill above the river Orb, existed even before the Romans came. They then built a forum and temples, probably on the site of the present *mairie*. Its great moment in history, a tragic one, was in 1209 when de Montfort's crusaders massacred 30,000 of the inhabitants. Today Béziers is the chief trading centre of the huge Languedoc wine industry; it also has one of the finest rugby teams in France.

The former cathedral of St-Nazaire, rebuilt in Gothic style after being sacked and pillaged in 1209, has two fortified towers and a lovely rose-window in the W façade; its terrace offers a good view of the river. The main promenade is the Allées Paul-Riquet, named after Béziers's most famous son (1604–80) who built the Canal du Midi. At the S end is the Plateau des Poètes, a park adorned with busts of poets. There are two good museums: the Musée du Vieux Biterrois et du Vin, with Greek, Roman and Etruscan amphorae found off the coast, and historical details of wine-making; and the Musée des Beaux-Arts, which has 140 Greek vases from Delos and paintings by Holbein,

Delacroix, Corot, etc. Spanish-style bullfights, where the bull is killed, are held from March to Sept. in the former Roman arena.

The **Oppidum of Ensérune**, on a hilltop 6km SW of Béziers, off the road to Narbonne, is one of the most important known pre-Roman settlements in France and was discovered in 1915. Excavations have revealed a Celtic (Gaulish) town dating back to at least 600BC, with a population of some 8000 in 300BC. The fascinating museum on the spot includes such finds as silos from the 6C BC, funeral urns from slightly later, and Greek pottery from the Aegean, proving that the Greeks traded here long before Roman times.

Carcassonne

Béziers

CARCASSONNE
AUDE   Pop 42,500

This is Europe's largest medieval fortress, and one of the best preserved. It is best seen at night, from a distance, when the great circle of towers and battlements, high on their hilltop, are floodlit. The newer town on the plain, the Ville Basse, is unexciting: but across the river Aude is the old walled city, La Cité. Part of its walls were first built by the Romans, then in the 5C the Visigoths enlarged it into a fortress (the present line of the towers is theirs). In the 9C Charlemagne laid siege to the town for five years.

The fortress fell to the anti-Cathar crusaders in the 13C, when Simon de Montfort used it as a command post for his massacres. St-Louis besieged and took the Cité, driving out its inhabitants, for whom he built the lower town. His son Philip the Bold then strengthened the fortifications, giving the place its present appearance. It was now self-sufficient and able to withstand any siege: a wheat-grinding mill was built, a mint coined money, smiths forged armour, while the Narbonne Tower held a cistern capable of holding six months' supply of fresh water. The cathedral of St-Nazaire was built, as was an open-air theatre, still used today.

After Roussillon was annexed by France in 1659, the fortress lost much of its military value

and fell slowly into ruin. Finally in 1844 the state commissioned Viollet-le-Duc to rebuild the battlements and cathedral – the world's first restoration on such a scale. Although this architect has been much criticized for being over-thorough, much of his detail appearing artificial, time has tended to mellow his work, which now blends less awkwardly with the original parts. At least he restored the original skyline of towers and turrets, to provide full romantic impact from a distance.

You can take a guided tour or wander free, admiring the elaborate fortifications of the two castellated walls, one inside the other, c.1.5km in circumference. There are 54 towers and two gates; the views towards the Pyrenees are splendid. The cathedral, over-restored in places, is remarkable for its stained-glass rose windows, fine statues, Romanesque nave and Gothic transepts. La Cité still has 500 inhabitants, mostly poorer people; its medieval streets are lined, inevitably, with brash souvenir shops, plus a few more tasteful craft boutiques.

CASTELNAUDARY
AUDE   Pop 11,000

A town on the Canal du Midi, famed as the heartland of the most succulent of all the many variations of *cassoulet* stew. It was burned by England's Black Prince in 1355 and was the site of a famous battle in 1632 when Richelieu defeated and captured the duke of Montmorency. St-Papoul, a village to the E, has an 11C Romanesque abbey with fine cloisters.

CASTRES
TARN   Pop 47,000

Since the 14C cloth-weaving has been the main activity of this lively industrial town on the river Agout; overhanging the river, and reflected in it, are picturesque old balconied houses. In the heart of the old town is the large baroque 17C cathedral of St-Benoit. The town hall next door, formerly the bishop's palace, contains, surprisingly, a museum with a fine collection of Spanish art, mainly Goya, bequeathed by a local artist. Close by are formal gardens designed by Le Nôtre, with elaborate topiary work.

Jean Jaurès (1859–1914), father of French Socialism, was born and educated in Castres, and in 1885 became its local MP.

Some 15km NE is the bizarre region of the **Sidobre**, where thousands of massive granite rocks

Castres

lie chaotically strewn over hillsides or in river-beds at the foot of wild ravines. Some stand delicately balanced; some, in odd shapes, have been given names like 'the three cheeses' or 'the curate's hat'. There are many quarries here, providing granite for the local stone-carving workshops (tombstones are a speciality).

CERDAGNE, THE
PYRÉNÉES-ORIENTALES

It is a strange and happy surprise to come upon this verdant upland plain, richly cultivated, in a region of austere mountains. The Cerdagne forms the bed of a prehistoric glacier lake, and this explains its contrast with the surrounding region. Its altitude is 1200–1800m: yet with its meadows, dairy herds and cornfields, backed by pine forests and snowy peaks, it seems more like a pastoral valley, and is the sunniest place in France. There is also much varied interest to tempt the visitor.

The plateau extends 25km from the Spanish frontier at Puigcerda to Mont-Louis. Starting at the western end, we come first to **Bourg-Madame**; nearby, the Spanish townlet of **Llivia** most curiously forms an enclave inside France, the result of a concession won by Spain when she ceded Roussillon in 1659. The area just to the E has been chosen, because of its high sunshine level, as the main site of French experiments with solar energy. France's largest solar furnace is being completed at **Saillagousse**. At **Odeillo**, near Font-Romeu, another big furnace dates from the mid-1970s and for some years was Europe's leading pioneer project in this crucial energy sector: it is a huge square building where 62 swivelling mirrors reflect the sun onto one giant concave mirror. Some of the scientists live in strange houses with ugly glass facades, heated by solar energy.

This sunlight also brings skiers to the Cerdagne – **Font-Romeu** is a well equipped resort where

Olympic champions train. It has a casino, and *sardaña* festivals in July and Sept. From here it is a 1.5km walk through the woods to **L'Ermitage**, shrine of the extraordinary Vierge de l'Invention. This austere Romanesque madonna is black with age, and from burial during the Arab invasions. The name 'Invention' (discovery) comes from the local legend whereby this virgin was accidentally unearthed, centuries later, by a bull scratching at the ground. Behind the altar of the chapel is the *camaril*, an 18C chamber decorated with a rare grace. A major pilgrimage procession takes place at the shrine on 8 Sept.; others are on 15 Aug. and the third Sun. after Whitsun.

The road from the Cerdagne to Perpignan skirts the big fortress of **Mont-Louis**, built by Vauban as a defence against the Spaniards. From here it is a short excursion to the hamlet of **Planès** where the little church is built curiously in the shape of a clover-leaf.

CÉRET
PYRÉNÉES-ORIENTALES   Pop 5000

This small town lies in a fruit-growing area near the Spanish border; with its *sardanas* and *corridas*, it is a lively centre of Catalan tradition. Around 1910 it was also an important centre of Fauvist and Cubist avant-garde painting: Picasso worked here for some years, and today several canvases by him are housed in the town's Musée d'Art Moderne, as well as others by Matisse, Chagall, Dufy, etc. There is a 14C bridge across the river Tech and a 12C church.

The little spa town of **Amélie-les-Bains**, 8km SW in the lovely Tech valley, has sulphur springs used medically since Roman times. One 19C *curiste* was Queen Amélie, wife of Louis-Philippe, and the town is now named after her. There are Roman thermal remains. A Mardi Gras carnival with masquerade, and a folk-dancing festival in Aug., are among other attractions. To the S are the **Gorges du Mondony**, while the winding mountain road NW to **Montbolo** offers spectacular views of the Pyrenees.

SW from Amélie stretches the remote and beautiful valley of the **Haut Vallespir**, a hilly region of meadows and of forests of beech and chestnut, whre Catalan folklore and handicraft traditions survive unspoilt. Among the special sights are the **Gorges de la Fou** and the quaint old village of **Prats-de-Mollo** (Romanesque church).

CÉVENNES
LOZÈRE, GARD

This celebrated mountain range of schist and granite stretches some 60km from NE to SW, and forms the SE flank of the Massif Central. The scenery -- bare plateaux cut by deep wooded valleys – is wild and beautiful, excellent country for hiking or camping: the local tourist authorities organize many cross-country hikes, where you can spend the night in upland hostels. The whole area is a conservation zone, the Parc National des Cévennes.

The main scenic route over the mountains, the high **Corniche des Cévennes**, runs from Florac to St-Jean-de-Gard and offers fine views most of the way, notably at the Col des Fausses and the Col de l'Exil: the road is narrow, with many hairpin bends, but quite passable. Westward lies the massif of **Mont Aigoual** (1567m), second highest peak of the Cévennes: a good road (open except in snowy weather) leads to the very summit, from where on a clear day the views are outstanding – as far as the coast, and sometimes even to the Alps and Pyrenees. In summer there is often mist or haze: best time to go is early in the morning. NE of Florac is the massif of **Mont Lozère** (1699m),

highest point of the Cévennes: here the summit, known as Finiels, is accessible only to mountain climbers, but a good scenic road leads up to the **Col de Finiels** (1348m) either from Le Pont-de-Montvert or Le Bleymard. **Villefort**, to the E, is an attractive holiday resort with a lake backed by heather-covered hills.

The Cévenols are tough, hard-working folk with a strong Protestant tradition. Since the 16C the Cévennes have been a centre of Calvinism, and after the revocation of the Edict of Nantes in 1685 many thousands emigrated to avoid persecution. Then in 1702 some 6000 Cévenol peasants (known as '*camisards*', meaning 'shirt-wearers') staged an armed revolt against their Catholic oppressors. This was put down, bloodily, in 1704. These events are today commemorated at the **Mas Soubeyran**, 6km N of Anduze on the S edge of the Cévennes, a farmhouse that once belonged to Roland, a leader of the Camisards. The Mas is now the Musée du Desert, dedicated to the memory of Protestant sufferings in the area: you can see Roland's room and his bible, and read about the 2500 local Protestants condemned for life to the galleys. Today, Protestants and Catholics cohabit easily, and the past is forgiven if not forgotten. Since 1968 the area has been settled by some 3000 middle-class 'drop-outs' from Paris and other cities, who have turned their hands to subsistence hill-farming and handicrafts, and are always ready to sell tourists their pottery, wood-carvings or honey and goats'-cheese.

Robert Louis Stevenson's journey through the Cévennes in 1878 took him from **Le Monastier** in the N, via **La Bastide-Purlaurens**, **Le Pont-de-Montvert** (where the Camisard revolt began) and **Florac**, to **St-Jean-du-Gard**. Organized tours today follow the same route – either with a donkey, or without.

Corniche des Cévennes

CORBIÈRES, LES
AUDE

These strange wild limestone hills form a NE spur of the Pyrenees, sprawling over a wide area between Perpignan and Carcassonne; forests of pine and cedar sweep down to lonely river valleys, and ruined castles stand gauntly on hilltops. The massif has given its name to the best wine of Languedoc: Corbières, red, fruity, and rich in alcohol. The finest vineyards are to the E, around Tuchan and Fitou.

In the N, the Benedictine abbey of **Lagrasse**, dating from the 10C, is now an old people's home; you can inspect the church, the fine central stairway, and the cloister with a huge pine tree in its middle. Much further S, just N of the Perpignan-Quillan road, are the wild **Gorges du Galamus**, and the **Grau de Maury**, a hill-pass with spectacular views. On the hills nearby are two ruined Cathar castles, both open to visits: **Peyrepertus**, and **Queribus**, where the Cathars made their last doomed stand in 1255.

CORDES
TARN   Pop 1000

'Cordes-in-the-Sky', as it is called, one of the major tourist sights of southern France, is an old fortified village perched high on a hill above the Cérou valley, 25km NW of Albi. It was built by a count of Toulouse in the early 13C as a defence outpost against Simon de Montfort's crusades, and later became a prosperous trading centre for leather, fabrics and dyeing. In the 15C, plagues and religious wars put an end to this golden age, and by the 20C Cordes was dying. It was saved in 1941 by an artist, Yves Brayer, who founded a colony of craftsmen and painters. The old houses were gradually refurbished. Today, some artisans and artists are still at work.

Cordes is now crammed with tourists and boutiques, but has not lost its charm. Along the Rue Voltaire and the Grand' Rue, climbing steeply through the village, are several fine old Gothic houses of the 13–14C – notably the Maison du Grand Veneur with its facade of sculpted hunting

scenes, and the Maison du Grand Fauconnier, now the *mairie*. The two little museums, Yves Brayer and Charles Portal, are worth a visit. For a splendid view, you should also climb to the top of the tower of the church of St-Michel, formerly the look-out post. From here you can see how, for greater security, the village was built with two rings of ramparts, outer and inner, each with a fortified gateway at either end.

CÔTE VERMEILLE
PYRÉNÉES-ORIENTALES

From Argelès northwards, the Roussillon coast is flat and dull, with big modern resorts. But further south, where the Pyrenees tumble into the sea, the 30km of coast from Argelès to the frontier are rocky, indented and rather beautiful: the rocks and hills are reddish, hence the name Côte Vermeille (Vermilion Coast). The four resorts, from N to S, are:

Collioure (pop. 2700): this picture-postcard fishing-village and bathing resort is much the prettiest place on the whole Languedoc-Roussillon

Collioure

coast. Despite its tourist hordes, it retains much of the old charm that once drew Matisse, Dufy, Picasso and others to work here and to paint the town so often (the Fauvist movement in painting was born here in 1905). The Hostellerie des Templiers, an inn with a lively ambience, has a collection of local paintings. The village with its cobbled alleyways lies below a big 12C castle that belonged to the Knights Templar; the church has nine richly gilded altarpieces; and in the bows of the fishing-boats drawn up on the pebbly beach are the great globes of the lamps used by the fishermen to lure their fish at night. Good sweetish local wine. Theatre festival in Aug.

Port-Vendres (pop. 5000): a commercial port (some trade with North Africa) and yachting centre, and good bathing.

Banyuls (pop. 4000): a congested but pleasant resort, famous for its sweetish wine, grown on the steep slopes above the town (the old wine cellars can be visited, and offer free tastings; wine festival in Aug.). There is an aquarium, and an important

Cordes

laboratory devoted to marine biology. The famous and prolific sculptor Aristide Maillol (1861–1944) lived at Banyuls. Yachting and bathing are good. There are fine views of sea and mountains from Cap l'Abeille, on the coast road 2km to SE; or, for a really stupendous view, take the narrow winding hill-road inland to the 14C Madeloc tower, and then drive back to the coast at Collioure.

Cerbère (pop. 1700): small fishing-port, on the frontier.

COUVERTOIRADE, LA
HÉRAULT

This medieval fortified village, today half ruined, makes a surprising sight in the middle of the vast flat plateau of Larzac. It belonged in the 12C to the Knights Templar, then to the Knights of St-John of Jerusalem. The ramparts, dating from the 14C, are still partially intact, but the Templars' castle and Romanesque church are largely destroyed and many of the ancient houses within the walls are empty. There is a small museum of local history.

On the main Millau-Montpellier road, 6km S, the village of **Le Caylar** lies at the foot of high smooth rocks that from a distance look like ramparts. The main road here has been dynamited through the rock face.

DEMOISELLES, Grotte des
HÉRAULT

This large and very lovely grotto, just off the Ganges-Montpellier road, was discovered in 1770; local peasants thought it to be the home of fairies or *demoiselles*, hence its name. Several caverns contain a profusion of huge stalactites and stalagmites of white calcite, in bizarre shapes, beautifully illuminated. One of them is known as the 'Virgin and Child' because of its shape. One vast cavern, 100m by 80m and 50m high, has been compared to a great cathedral. Visits all year.

The little industrial town of **Ganges** (pop. 3500), 7km to the NW in the upper Hérault valley, has been making silk stockings since the days of Louis XIV. Ten factories are at work today, though most stockings are now of nylon and rayon, not silk.

ELNE
PYRÉNÉES-ORIENTALES Pop 6000

This charming and ancient little town built on a hill, 12km SE of Perpignan, was formerly on the sea which has since receded 5km to the E. Named by Constantine after his mother Helena, Elne has had more than its share of history: Hannibal camped here in 218BC, the emperor Constantius was murdered here in AD350, and Elne was later sacked by the Saracens in the 8C and by the Normans in the 11C. The 11C cathedral of Ste-Eulalie has a fortified façade with battlements and offers a good view from its terrace. The adjacent cloister, 12–14C, is Elne's chief glory, notably its white marble columns adorned with carvings of bizarre animals.

St-Cyprien, 7km E, is the most southerly of the chain of modernistic resorts on this coast and has two golf courses and a country club.

Elne

ESPINOUSE, MONTS DE L'
HÉRAULT

This south-westerly spur of the Massif Central, rising to over 1000m, provides a mountainous backdrop to the Languedoc plain around Béziers. It is a wild, sprawling area, partly forested, and forms part of the Parc Natural Régional du Haut Languedoc, a conservation zone. Picturesque villages include **Olargues**, and **Fraisse-sur-Agout** which still has a few traditional low peasant cottages thatched with gorse and broom. To the E, it is worth visiting the **Gorges d'Héric**, or making the one-hour climb by footpath to the summit of **Mont Caroux** (panoramic views as far as the coast). NW of **Lamalou-les-Bains** is a forest planted in 1930 in memory of 560 writers, including Charles Péguy, who died fighting for France.

NW of the Espinouse are the two big artificial lakes and hydroelectric dams of **Raviège** and **Laouzas** (both suitable for bathing and sailing), and beyond them lie the Lacaune mountains. To the S of the Espinouse, the little town of **St-Pons** on the main Béziers-Toulouse road has an interesting cathedral, partly fortified, dating from the 12C and rebuilt in the 18C. Near **Corniou**, 5km to the W on the main road, the Grotte de la Devèze has delicate filigree-like stalactites and stalagmites, ochre-coloured from the iron oxide (open daily in summer; Sun. only in winter).

GAILLAC
TARN Pop 10,000

A pretty town on the river Tarn, with fountains in the squares, and houses of wood and brick along its narrow streets, Gaillac is reputed mainly for its fruity white and red wines, the best in the area (the cellars of the St-Michel abbey are open to visits). The imposing terraced Parc de Foucaud, by the river, was designed by Le Nôtre in the 17C.

La Grande Motte

GRANDE-MOTTE, LA
HÉRAULT   Pop winter, 4000; summer, 40,000

La Grande-Motte, 20km SE of Montpellier, is the largest, most sophisticated and highly publicized of the new Languedoc resorts: a space-age vision with motor-yachts and beach-parasols added. Coloured sun-blinds cover the honeycomb facades of its famous 10-storey ziggurat pyramids of holiday flats. Some of the newer ones are in weird shapes and colours: one resembles a giant fairground wheel, painted purple. Not everyone might choose to spend a holiday in these surreal pop-art surroundings, however bright the colours and lavish the amenities (boutiques, good restaurants, casino, watersports, etc). Yet the place is always full in high summer; it has camping sites for 15,000 people and a marina for 1800 yachts. It signals unmistakably the face of the New France.

To the W are the older traditional bathing-resorts of **Carnon-Plage** and **Palavas-les-Flots**, rather tatty and down-at-heel, with much sporadic modern building as well. **Maguelone**, 4km W of Palavas, is a curious ancient site on a narrow strip of land between sea and lagoon. It possibly began life as a Phocaean settlement in the 6C BC, became a flourishing town in the Middle Ages, but was destroyed in 1622 when its Protestant population was expelled. Nothing remains but the former cathedral, part Romanesque, part Gothic, restored in the 19C.

GRUISSAN
AUDE   Pop 1600

Built in an unusual circular shape on a peninsula and dominated by a ruined tower, this old fishing village, 10km SE of Narbonne, provides a quaint contrast to the ultra-modern resorts along this coast. Gruissan has its own new resort close by, built in a discreet style that harmonizes with the old village. To the S are salt-pans; to the N, the hills of La Clape with good views.

LAVAUR
TARN   Pop 8000

Memories of the Cathar massacres haunt this attractive town above the Agout river, 37km E of Toulouse. An Albigensian stronghold, it was besieged for two months in 1211 by Simon de Montfort; on its surrender, the defenders were burned or hanged and their leader, Lady Guirade of the Château Plo, was hurled into a well. The garden of Plo in the NE outskirts holds some remains of the château. The former cathedral of St-Alain, rebuilt in brick in 1254 after its destruction by de Montfort, contains a fine 15C altarpiece with scenes of the Passion. In a Romanesque tower on the S facade, a painted wooden figure, the Jacquemart, dating from 1523, strikes the hours and half-hours. The former bishop's palace is now a pleasant garden with old cedar trees and a terrace above the river.

LIMOUX
AUDE   Pop 11,000

A town on the river Aude, set amid vineyards, 24km S of Carcassonne; it is best known for its white sparkling wine, 'Blanquette de Limoux' (the local *caves* can be visited). Near the Romanesque church of St-Martin are narrow streets with carved wooden facades. On the Carcassonne road to the N is the church of Notre-Dame-de-Marceille, with a black marble Virgin (pilgrimage in Sept.).

Near **Couiza**, 18km S, is the hilltop hamlet of **Rennes-le-Château** where the local priest in the late 19C claimed to have found the key to a hidden treasure in his church; this has been linked to the mysteries of the Holy Grail, the Knights Templar and the Cathars. Further S, beyond **Quillan** (a good starting-point for excursions into the upper Aude valley), a highly scenic route leads through the wild Aude gorges to the Cerdagne.

LODÈVE
HÉRAULT   Pop 8000

Lodève dates from Roman times, when Nero had coins minted here to pay for his Roman legions. Since the 13C it has made textiles; today it is still a manufacturing town, and also a lively market centre. The huge cathedral of St-Fulcran, partly fortified, dates from the 10C; the Musée Jacques Audibert is devoted to geology and archaeology.

At **La Bourie-Noble**, 20km NW, in the wild and lonely hills of the *causses*, is the famous religious community of L'Arche, founded by the late Lanzo del Vasco, a leading disciple of Mahatma Gandhi. Here, in an isolated red-and-ochre converted farmhouse, a multi-national group of about 150 practise the shared, simple life in an atmosphere of patent joy and serenity. All money is pooled; the community weaves its own clothes and has no electricity, only candles. L'Arche is open to visitors. Further W, in the lovely valley of the Rob, is the artificial lake and hydroelectric dam of **Avène**, a good spot for picnics.

MILLAU
AVEYRON   Pop 22,000

On the river Tarn, roughly where the austere Massif Central meets the sunny Midi, Millau is a busy industrial and touristic centre, chief starting-point for excursions to the Gorges du Tarn. Since the 12C it has been a leading glove-making centre, using leather from the sheep reared on the nearby *causses*; today it still produces nearly half of France's annual production of some 350,000 pairs of gloves, much of it for export. The local museum gives details of this industry, also of the pottery made here in Gallo-Roman days. The Pl. du Maréchal-Foch has attractive medieval arcades; other interesting buildings are the Gothic belfry, once used as a prison, and the church of Notre-Dame with its modern frescoes.

The vast, barren **Causse du Larzac** stretches SW from Millau for 50km. Here, between La Cavalerie and Nant, is the famous Camp Larzac, a leading tank firing range of the French army, scene in the 1970s of a notorious ten-year tussle between military and ecologists. When the army announced its plan to extend the range by 35,000 acres, the 103 sheep-farmers involved were promised compensation but refused to leave. Their cause was eagerly taken up by scores of ecology and anti-militarist groups all over France who waged a national crusade. Thousands came each year to protest. Finally, when President Mitterrand came to power in 1981, one of his first acts was to cancel the army's scheme.

MINERVE
HÉRAULT   Pop 112

NW of Narbonne, a fascinating old hamlet on sa limestone cliff, dominating the vineyards of the Minervois that stretch for miles below and pro-dude some of the best Languedoc wine. There are ramparts, an 11C church, and a small museum of prehistory. But above all Minerve breathes sad Cathar memories: its ruined castle was a Cathar stronghold, besieged and captured by Simon de Montfort in 1210. He and his crusaders then burned alive 140 Cathars, watching the fires 'with great joy' (according to an eyewitness). Today the villagers still relate this story with bitter anger. At Minerve, as at Montségur, after 750 years, the martyrs' blood is not yet dry.

MONTAGNE NOIRE
TARN

This long range of high hills forms the extreme SW spur of the Massif Central and separates the plain of Carcassonne, to the south, from the rolling pastures of the Tarn, to the north. It is a wild region of forests, lakes and ravines; from the highest point, the **Pic de Nore** (1210m), SE of Mazamet, there are splendid views as far as the Pyrenees.

Mazamet (pop. 13,000) is the principal sheep-shearing and leather-dressing town of France. It uses local animals, as well as importing sheepskins from Australia and South America; the finished products are then widely exported.

MONTPELLIER
HÉRAULT   Pop 201,000

Capital of the Languedoc-Roussillon region and its largest city, Montpellier has grown since the last war from lazy provincial town to a commercial metropolis, with a major wine trade as well as ultra-modern industries (IBM is here, amongst others). The university is one of France's largest and oldest, founded in 1289 (Rabelais was a student), and is noted for medicine and chemistry.

The wide central square, the Pl. de la Comédie, with its paved piazza, is a smart meeting place for the local *jeunesse dorée*. Close by is a snazzy new commercial and shopping centre, the Polygone. Yet modern Montpellier has not lost its old seig-neurial charm: on a hill within the inner ring boulevard, the delightful narrow streets of the *vieille ville* are lined with elegant 17C and 18C residences. Here the chic Rue Foch leads to the Arc de Triomphe, built in 1691 in honour of Louis XIV. Just beyond is a formal garden, the Prom-enade du Peyrou, with good views over mountains and coast: there is an equestrian statue of Louis XIV, and an 18C aqueduct with a handsome

Promenade du Peyrou

Château d'Eau, adorned with Corinthian pillars and sculptures.

Just to the N is the Jardin des Plantes, the oldest such botanical garden in France (founded 1593), with a wide range of Mediterranean plants and flowers. Nearby are some of the older university buildings (the main campuses are now in the suburbs). Also in the old town are the Gothic cathedral of St-Pierre, dating from 1364, and two good museums: the Atger (drawings by Fragonard and other artists of the Midi) and the Fabre (collection of works by David, Ingres, Delacroix, étc).

The village of **Castries**, 12km NE, has an imposing 16C château with a garden designed by Le Nôtre. To the NW of Montpellier, the Cévennes foothills rise up from the plain – *garrigue* country of stony hills covered with scrub and brush. Here, a landmark from far away, is the **Pic St-Loup**, a conical limestone peak with a ruined white castle on its ridge.

MONTPELLIER-LE-VIEUX
AVEYRON

This amazing 'chaos' of huge rocks, strewn over the landscape 18km NE of Millau, looks so much like an old ruined city that it has been given the name of 'Montpellier-le-Vieux'. It was formerly the haunt of wolves, and peasants believed it to be a *'cité maudite'* haunted by the devil. Today it is haunted by tourists, and you pay to enter. The rocks have been given fancy names, like the 'Rabbit', the 'Sphinx', and – most celebrated – the 'Mycenae Gate', a high natural gateway of rock. The best view of the chaos is from the top of the 'Rampart' rock.

NARBONNE
AUDE   Pop 42,000

Narbonne, nowadays a quietish town devoted to the wine trade, was in Roman times a major city, one of the first to be colonized outside Italy and capital of the province of Gallia Narbonensis (roughly, today's southern Languedoc). Its port, now silted up, was then the busiest in the western Mediterranean.

There are several remarkable buildings. The town's glory, in some ways an oddity, is the cathedral of St-Just, begun in 1272 but never finished: when the choir had been built, the local consuls refused to let the nave be added – and so it remains today. It is one of the tallest Gothic cathedrals in France. The treasury contains fine 15–17C tapestries, including a Flemish one depicting the Creation. The 15C cloister leads to the massive fortified Palace of the Archbishops with its three square towers, 13–14C. In the palace are museums of art and ancient history, with Limoges porcelain and local prehistoric and Roman finds. The Musée Lapidaire, housed in a deconsecrated church, also sheds fascinating light on the Roman period. A handsome 16C building, the Maison des Trois-Nourrices (Three Wet-Nurses) is so named because the cornice of its fine Renaissance window is supported by very pneumatic caryatids.

About 15km SW, in a gentle valley of the Corbières, is the lovely 11C Cistercian abbey of

Fontfroide, with an elegant cloister and a quiet garden lined with cypresses. Today private property, but open to vistors, the abbey has been tastefully restored, with modern stained glass.

NAVACELLES, CIRQUE DE
GARD, HÉRAULT

This vast natural crater, some 350m deep, is one of the major scenic wonders of southern France. It has been formed by the winding river Vis, which enters and leaves the Cirque by narrow gorges on either side; all round are towering chalk cliffs, and at the bottom is a small village. Hairpin roads with steep gradients wind down into the crater, from **Blandas** to the N or **St-Maurice** to the S: if this drive is too giddy-making for you, just admire the view from the top.

PERPIGNAN
PYRÉNÉES-ORIENTALES   Pop 113,000

Capital of Roussillon and the largest Catalan town after Barcelona, Perpignan is a pleasant southerly city with palms and plane-trees lining its promenades. Not unsurprisingly, it much resembles Spain's Catalan cities. Legend claims that it takes its name from a cowherd, Père Pinya, who was magically led to found a town on this fertile spot.

St-Jean, Perpignan

In the 13C it was the seat of the so-called 'kingdom of Majorca': in the inner city, the vast royal palace, Gothic in style, with a square courtyard, can be visited. Other interesting buildings are: Le Castillet (citadel), a red-brick 14C fortress now housing a museum of local arts and traditions; the elegant 14C Loge de Mer, partly Moorish in style, long used as a trade centre where maritime disputes were handled; the 14C cathedral of St-Jean (fine wood and marble carvings); and the Hôtel de Ville, with a superb bronze nude by

Maillol in its patio. Worth a visit, too, are the Natural History and Rigaud museums, the latter devoted to the works of Hyacinthe Rigaud, Perpignan-born, who became court portrait painter to Louis XIV and Louis XV.

On summer evenings, the locals dance the *sardaña* in the little square beside the Loge. In June there is a lively Midsummer Festival. At **Thuir**, 12km SW, you can visit the huge cellars of Byrrh, makers of the well-known sweet apéritif.

PÉZENAS
HÉRAULT   Pop 8000

Today a major centre of the local wine and fruit-growing trades, Pézenas was formerly one of the leading towns of Languedoc: its fine ensemble of 15–17C houses, still largely intact, bears witness to its proud past. The États-Généraux du Languedoc held their first meeting here, in 1456. The town was later the residence of the governors of Languedoc, the Montmorency and Contis: Armand de Bourbon, Prince of Conti, held court in such style in the château of Grange-des-Prés (now ruined) that with its gardens and fountains it became known as 'the Versailles of Languedoc'. Molière, with his theatre company, came to play here several times in 1650-57, and was helped and sponsored by the prince. On the latter's death, the golden age of Pézenas ended.

After parking in the Pl. du 14-Juillet, the visitor can explore the old town on foot, to admire the stylish gateways and fine balconies of the mansions. Most notable buildings: Hôtel Lacoste, 15C (Gothic arches, imposing stairway, beamed first-floor ceiling); Tribunal de Commerce (wrought ironwork on the facade); Hôtel de Wicque (Renaissance façade); former Commanderie of St-John of Jerusalem (graceful corner tower); Sacristie des Pénitents Blancs (elegant 15C courtyard). Note also the Vulliod St-Germain museum of archaeology, furniture and popular arts, with some fine Aubusson tapestries; and the former Jewish ghetto around the Rue de la Juiverie.

There is a Molière drama festival in July, and various traditional events in Feb., June and Aug.

PORT-BARCARÈS
PYRÉNÉES-ORIENTALES   Pop 1618

Set on a narrow strip of land between the sea and the big Étang (lagoon) de Leucate, and 22km NE of Perpignan, Port-Barcarès is one of the largest of the modernistic new resorts on the Languedoc-Roussillon coast. It has a sailing and skin-diving school in the Centre du Nautisme, and also offers water-skiing and a yacht harbour with 200 berths. Chief curiosity is the *Lydia*, a Japanese owned former Greek passenger boat, now towed onto the beach to serve as casino, night-club and restaurant.

Port-Leucate, 3km to the N, another of the big new resorts, also has a water-sports school, sailing club and yacht harbour (500 berths). The nudist village of **Aphrodite** was created by the British, of all people! On the W side of the Étang de Leucate, and just off the Perpignan-Narbonne main road, the imposing fortress of **Salses** stands as a fine example of late-15C Spanish military architecture: at a time when Roussillon belonged to Spain, it was built by Don Sanche of Castille to protect his frontier against the French. Current work on a local quarry may close the fortress to the public.

PRADES
PYRÉNÉES-ORIENTALES   Pop 6000

Prades lies in an upland valley 43km W of Perpignan, in a fertile region of cherry, peach and apricot orchards. The great Spanish cellist Pablo Casals lived here for many years until he died, and today there is an annual music festival in his honour. Many of its concerts are held in the beautiful abbey of St-Michel-de-Cuxha, just S of Prades, which was the leading church of Roussillon in the 11C. It was abandoned during the Revolution and later pillaged, but in 1913 an American sculptor collected many missing pieces of the cloister which have been reassembled at Fort Tryon Park, Manhattan. The abbey is now restored and is occupied by Catalan Benedictines, who use it as a Catalan cultural centre. The cloister, though incomplete, is very elegant; the bell-tower is in Lombard style.

ROQUEFORT-SUR-SOULZON
AVEYRON   Pop 900

This village famous for its cheeses straggles along the foot of a high limestone cliff in the *causses* region. All genuine Roquefort cheeses are made locally and then matured in caves deep in this cliff: the caves of the leading firm, Société, can be visited.

Roquefort, blue-veined, with a rare heady, tangy taste, is to other cheeses what champagne is to other wines – expensive, too. Its special quality

Roquefort cheeses

derives from a unique combination of factors found only in these caves: the ancient fissures in the rock, which permit humidity and a cool, even temperature all the year; and a mysterious penicillin fungus which grows there naturally and is added to the young cheese to produce its special aroma.

Roquefort is made only from the pungent milk of ewes, some 800,000 of them belonging to 8000 private farmers, roaming the chalky uplands of the *causses*. The milking season is Dec. to July. The fresh milk is taken each morning to dairies near the farms where morsels of the penicillin are added to it, then it is churned. The young cheeses are later moved to the Roquefort caves and left to mature for three months; during this time the fungus grows, creating the veins and fermentation. Each of these great round cheeses, 8cm high by 25cm across, weighs some 3kg, and some 6 million are made every year.

ST-GUILHEM-LE-DÉSERT
HÉRAULT   Pop 200

This fascinating old village, historic, remote and very picturesque, is curiously situated in a ravine of the Hérault gorge, 42km NW of Montpellier. It was Guilhem, a trusty lieutenant of Charlemagne, who discovered the site after fighting victorious battles against the Saracens in the Midi. He founded an abbey here, which survives today, and gave it a piece of the True Cross which Charlemagne had received from the pope in Rome. The surrounding area is quite fertile: 'Désert' refers to the *garrigue* beyond.

On one side of the tiny village square, shaded by a large plane tree, stands the 10C Romanesque abbey, austerely beautiful inside. Only part of its cloister still stands: the rest was bought in 1906 by an American and moved to New York, where it is now in the Metropolitan Museum. Outside the village are the ruins of a château once owned by Don Juan, a Saracen who ravaged the area until killed by Guilhem: in the fight, the latter had the tip of his nose cut off and was thus known as 'Court-nez'.

Near the **Pont du Diable**, 2km S, is the celebrated **Grotte de la Clamouse**, discovered only in 1945. Part of the caves form the bed of the river. Erosion has left a profusion of stalactites and stalagmites in weird shapes, some of them looking like flowering bushes, today cleverly illuminated for visitors.

St-Guilhem-le-Désert

SÈTE
HÉRAULT   Pop 40,000

Sète, a lively town criss-crossed by canals, is France's largest Mediterranean port after Marseille, and Languedoc's leading fishing-port, mainly for sardines and tunny. The port was first built under Louis XIV, then enlarged in the 19C, and is linked to the Rhône by a major canal. This helps to explain the many industries in the area, such as oil refineries and chemical works. The port handles the bulk import of Italian wines, to the fury of local winegrowers who have sometimes blockaded it.

The old part of the town is almost Venetian, with graceful houses bordering canals. At the sea end of the Canal de Sète, the Rampe Paul-Valéry is lined with good outdoor fish restaurants. Here in the Vieux Port famous nautical jousts are held several times each summer, a tradition dating from 1666: young men dressed in white stand on high platforms fixed to big rowing boats, and each team tries to knock the other into the water, amid mirth and song.

Sète's many famous sons include Georges Brassens, the singer and, notably, the poet Paul Valéry. He adored Sète and is buried in the beautiful quiet cemetery high above the sea in the western outskirts: this was also the setting of one of his finest poems, *Le cimetière marin*. Beside it is the Musée Paul Valéry, which has souvenirs of the poet as well as some works by Renoir, Matisse, Dufy and others. The town's aquarium is also worth a visit.

Mont St-Clair (175m), one of the few high hills on the Languedoc plain, rises up in the western suburbs and affords fine views from its summit. To the west you see the huge lagoon of Thau, where oysters and mussels are bred. To the east is **Frontignan**, which earns its living mainly from two diverse liquids: oil refining, and a sweetish muscat wine.

TARN, GORGES DU
LOZÈRE

The most famous and spectacular gorges in France wind for some 45km from **Ispagnac**, near Florac, to **Le Rozier**. They are formed by a geological fault that separates the *causses* of Sauveterre and Méjean, and through it the river Tarn, rising in Mont Lozère, has thrust its way. A good tourist road today follows the entire length of the gorges, close to the river bed, offering dramatic and constantly changing views of the towering red and yellow cliffs, over 400m high at some points, and of the chaos of rocks that have slid into the river. Old romantic castles and pretty villages dot the route.

The excursion can be made in either direction, but perhaps it is best to go downstream, starting at **Florac**, a charming little Cévenol town in a fruit and vegetable-growing valley. The gorges proper start 9km below, at Ispagnac. Next we come to **Quézac**, with a handsome Gothic bridge across the Tarn. At **Castelbou** are the clifftop ruins of a château whose strange history is the subject of a *son-et-lumière* in summer.

The pretty village of **Ste-Énimie** lies in a fertile stretch of the gorge, with terraced orchards of peach and almond. There is an old monastery, now a school, and a small folklore museum. Just downstream on the other bank is another attractive village, **St-Chély**, close to two *cirques* with high cliffs and huge red rocks, and various caves. The 15C Château de la Caze, now a hotel, stands in a romantic setting above the river, with a leafy garden: it was built by Soubeyrane Alamand whose eight beautiful daughters were known as 'the nymphs of the Tarn'.

Ste-Énimie

From the village of **La Malène** a narrow, steep and giddily looping side-road leads up onto the Causse Méjean, where you can turn right and drive to the **Roc des Hourrous**, perched above the gorge, with marvellous views. From La Malène the main road continues downstream to **Les Détroits**, a defile of high, vertical, multi-coloured cliffs, probably the most dramatic and lovely section of the Gorges. The view is best from the river itself, and boats with boatmen can be hired at La Malène.

The gorge now widens into the **Cirque de Baumes**, a curving panorama of red, yellow, blue, grey and black tints. Here, at the **Pas de Souci**, the river almost disappears beneath a great chaos of rocks, the result of an earthquake in AD580. (According to legend, Ste-Énimie here chased Satan along the clifftop and called on the rocks to prevent his escape. They responded with a landslide, and one big rock, the Sourde, fell on him: but he managed to slip out from beneath and made his way back to Hell).

Beyond the *cirque*, **Les Vignes** is a village at a crossroads in a broad stretch of the gorge, with vineyards all around. One road winds up the cliffside to the W and leads to the **Point Sublime**, aptly named for its majestic view over the curving canyon. From Les Vignes the main road down the gorge passes below the ruined château of Blanquefort and the vast rock of Cinglegros, finally to reach **Le Rozier**, an ancient village at the confluence of the Tarn and the Jonte, where the Romans had a pottery. The road from here goes on to Millau. Across the Jonte is the quaint old village of **Peyreleau** where a square crenellated tower is all that remains of a former fortress.

From Le Rozier there are splendid hiking excursions to be made through the wild cliff country (*corniches*) of the Causse Méjean. You climb up

first to the abandoned hamlet of **Capluc** with its towering rock, then either hike N along the clifftop to the rock of **Cinglegros** or E to the great rocks of the **Vase de Chine** and the **Vase de Sèvres**. The paths are well signposted, but the trek needs several hours and is not for the inexperienced walker nor anyone afraid of heights.

The **Gorges de la Jonte**, though less spectacular than those of the Tarn, are worth a visit: a good road leads along them from Meyrueis to Le Rozier. It passes grottoes in the cliff-face; at **Les Douzes**, a high rock with a Romanesque chapel on the summit; and a fine viewpoint 1.5km W of Le Truel.

The huge underground cavern of **Aven Armand**, 11km NW of Meyrueis, on the *causse*, is at present closed to the public.

VERNET-LES-BAINS
PYRÉNÉES-ORIENTALES Pop 1400

In a beautiful setting of mountains and orchards, Vernet is a neatly laid-out but somewhat fading little spa, used for treating rheumatism and laryngitis. It was once much frequented by the British, including Trollope and Kipling. The old village, on a hill, has a castle and 12C church.

From Vernet it is well worth making the short excursion to the mountain abbey of **St-Martin-de-Canigou**, remote and austerely beautiful. It lies lost to view in the folds of Mont Canigou, Roussillon's highest Pyrenean peak (2784m), and from the hamlet of Casteil is accessible only by jeep or a 30-minute walk up a steep path. Built in the early 11C, it fell into ruins after the Revolution but has in this century been carefully restored and is now used for retreats by priests and laity (apply in writing).

The ascent of **Mont Canigou** itself is worth making, but you need to be a tough mountain hiker. From Vernet or Prades a very narrow, difficult road, open only July to Oct., winds up to the chalet-hotel of Les Cortalets (best go by jeep: these can be hired in the towns). From here it is a 90-minute climb by footpath to the summit, from where, on a clear day, the view is unbeatable.

VIGAN, LE
GARD Pop 4500

This small town in the SW foothills of the Cévennes makes a useful excursion base for the area. Like many of the surrounding towns, it is a traditional silk-making centre; some factories can ube visited (inquire at Syndicat d'Initiative). There is a small museum of Cévenol life and folklore; a fine promenade of big chestnut-trees; and a picturesque 12C bridge.

VILLENEUVETTE
HÉRAULT

This tiny 17C walled village, 3km SW of Clermont-l'Hérault, has an unusual history, for it was founded by Colbert as a cloth-weaving centre for the army. You enter through an arch bearing the words 'Honneur au Travail'. On the little square are workmen's cottages, with factory buildings in a nearby street. A path leads to a reservoir, formerly used to wash the new cloth.

PROVENCE

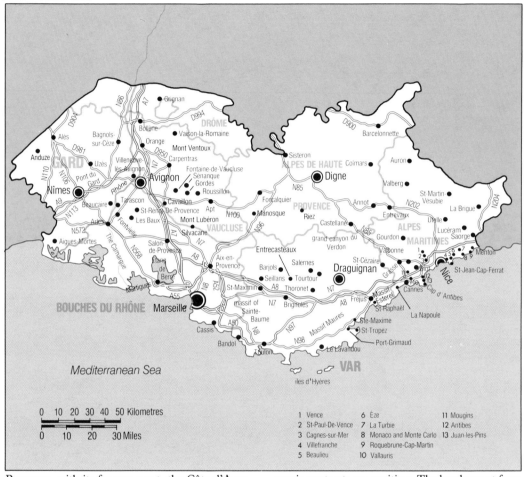

Mediterranean Sea

BOUCHES DU RHÔNE

GARD   DRÔME   ALPES DE HAUTE PROVENCE   ALPES MARITIMES   VAUCLUSE   VAR

0 10 20 30 40 50 Kilometres
0   10   20   30 Miles

1 Vence	6 Èze	11 Mougins
2 St-Paul-De-Vence	7 La Turbie	12 Antibes
3 Cagnes-sur-Mer	8 Monaco and Monte Carlo	13 Juan-les-Pins
4 Villefranche	9 Roquebrune-Cap-Martin	
5 Beaulieu	10 Vallauris	

Provence, with its famous coast, the Côte d'Azur, is many people's favourite part of France – and with reason. It is a sensuous land of dazzling white light, bright colours, strong tastes and immense diversity, where modern sophistication goes hand-in-hand with ancient peasant simplicity. And it is still remarkably unspoilt. Yes, much of it today *is* overbuilt and overcrowded, especially the coast in summer: but go just a few miles inland, and you find serene and empty landscapes where old hill-villages perch above gorges and the limestone plateaux roll to far horizons. For over two millennia Provence has been a focus of civilizations and each has left its strong mark, so that today no other corner of Europe provides so rich and intense a variety of interest and culture. Here are relics of Roman glories, of the troubadours' golden age, of the papal rule at Avignon, along with more recent wonders such as Monte Carlo's casino, the studios where Renoir and Picasso worked, modern nuclear stations, and the nudist beaches of St-Tropez.

Drive down from the north, and suddenly you enter that hypnotic, so different world of the Mediterranean. The air is drier, the light clearer, the sun beats stronger. The rolling hills are terraced with vine and olive and dotted with cypress; a scent of pine or lavender hangs in the air; old men in village squares drink *pastis* with black olives or play *boules* under the plane-trees. And the

scenic contrasts are exciting. The lovely coast from Menton to Marseille is all rocky coves and headlands where umbrella pines wave in the breeze and the wooded hills soar behind. Just inland are pastoral valleys bright with flowers in spring, and in winter with yellow mimosa. Much of the wide hinterland, further north, is mountainous – from the sub-alpine slopes behind Nice to the rocky plateau of Vaucluse, in the west, where a fertile plain full of orchards and vineyards lies alongside the wide Rhône and its delta.

The Greeks first settled this coast, at Marseille in c.600BC. They have left their traces, as have the Ligurian tribes who built towns in Provence long before the Romans arrived in the 2nd century BC. Julius Caesar founded a major port at Fréjus, and soon the Romans were colonizing their 'Provincia' (hence its modern name) in force, building the bulky monuments that still wholly or partly survive, at Nîmes, Arles, the Pont-du-Gard, Orange, Vaison, St-Rémy. Christianity first arrived in the 4th century, when Constantine the Great built a palace at Arles. Then in the 7th century the Saracens came, laying waste coastal towns yet bringing civilizing influences as well. Through the Middle Ages and Renaissance, Provence was ruled by its Counts as a semi-independent state quite separate from France, though it owed allegiance to the Holy Roman Empire, the Counts of Toulouse and others. Its golden age of prosperity was under 'Good King René' who in 1434–80 ruled as Count of Provence in Aix, his capital. In 1486 Provence was united to the kingdom of France, but until the Revolution kept some autonomy, with its own parliament in Aix. Today, it has again been finding some political identity, under the leadership of Gaston Defferre, since 1953 Socialist mayor of Marseille, the modern regional capital.

For centuries Provence has had a few local industries – for example, salt-works at Hyères, cork-making in the Maures, ochre quarrying near Apt. In the 19th century, heavy industry arrived: shipbuilding and engineering in the Marseille area. And since the war big modern firms have come in force: to the west, around Fos and the lake of Berre, oil refineries, steel and chemical works, and Europe's largest helicopter factory; also nuclear plant and hydroelectric dams in the Rhône valley, and high-technology research centres in the touristic setting of the Côte d'Azur. Drawn by the sun and scenery, many Parisians and other northerners have come to work here. Yet the overall tone is still set by the Provençaux themselves. Like other meridionals, they tend to be volatile and passionate; quick to pick a quarrel but just as ready to patch it up over a friendly *verre*; hard-working but none too punctual, and adept at twisting the rules. They talk French with the twangy accent of the Midi – *bong-jourr!* Just a few – older country people, or regionalist-minded city intellectuals – still speak the lovely old Provençal language, a form of Occitan, that until the mid-19th century was in common daily use. Alas, it has now largely died out.

Tourism is still the region's main industry. Cultural sightseers are drawn above all to the wonderful art-historical cities of the west, notably Arles, Aix, Avignon; also the lovely Cistercian abbeys of the hinterland and the modern art museums of the Côte. They may combine this with a villa or camping holiday in some quiet inland spot. In winter they go skiing in the Alps behind Nice, or make for the casinos and marinas of the madding coast.

The five major resorts on the coast, each with its own persona, are amusingly different: flowery Menton with its snug prettiness, rather genteel and old-fashioned; Monte-Carlo, all brash up-to-date Americanized glamour, high buildings and even higher society; Nice, the big commercial city, bustling and human; Cannes, smaller and smarter, a gleaming dynamo of up-market tourism; St-Tropez, the newcomer as resort, a disconcerting pot-pourri of mass vulgarity, genuine chic, out-to-shock trendiness and old-fishing-port charm. The beaches on the Côte vary too: sandy all the way west from Antibes, but shingle to its east, apart from pockets of not-very-fine imported sand. Thanks to the success of recent anti-pollution drives, nearly all beaches are now clean; but only from May to September is the sea warm enough for bathing. For touring and culture, spring and early autumn are the best times to visit Provence; in winter the mistral blows icily from the north, especially in the Rhône valley area.

In the hinterland, fortified hill-villages are a striking feature. Built in the Dark and Middle Ages for protection against marauders, they stand perched on crests or terraced along mountain sides. In safer times, the peasants began to leave them to live in the valleys, so that today many villages are partly ruined or abandoned. Recent trends, however, have been bringing a lot of them back to life. A few spectacular ones, such as Les Baux and Èze, have been engulfed by the tourist trade. Many others, now elegantly restored, their old alleys neatly paved and hung with flower-pots, have been absorbed by the post-war vogue for buying up rural cottages for conversion as summer or weekend homes.

In today's ecological age, the accent is on trying to preserve and restore the traditional rural architecture of Provence. Everywhere you see the old farmhouses, known as *mas*, and country houses, *bastides*: mostly they have stone walls, roofs of red terra-cotta tiles and, inside, red-tiled floors, beamed ceilings, solid wooden furniture, walls hung with copper pots – rather attractive. Many modern hotels and villas seek to imitate this effect, and in many rural areas you are not allowed to build a new house except in the traditional style.

This is one aspect of the bid to keep alive the old folk traditions which have been suffering from the impact of modern life: even in Arles, the lovely old costumes are today worn only for special fêtes. Every village still has its annual fête, and at some they still dance the *farandole*, with Provence's traditional musical instruments. Some fêtes include elaborate pageantry dating back centuries and lovingly perpetuated: e.g. the *bravades* at St-Tropez; the Passion scenes in the alleys of Roquebrune; the parade of the bizarre Tarasque monster at Tarascon; and the great gipsy festival at Les-Saintes-Maries in the Camargue. Western Provence also still has real fight-to-the-death bullfights, as well as the more harmless sport of *courses à la cocarde*, where agile young men compete to snatch a rosette off the bull's horns. *Boules*, a version of bowls, remains *the* popular sport in villages.

One special surviving Provençal tradition is the making of *santons* ('little saints'), costumed clay figurines: they represent figures of the Nativity story, or stock Provençal characters. Nowadays they are still made locally by craftsmen, and are used as ornaments or cribs in private homes, or as Christmas cribs in churches. Some villages, such as Les Baux, keep the tradition of a 'live crib' – a Nativity pageant on Christmas Eve, with villagers as the actors. *Santons* are among several old handicrafts that are today being revived in Provence – weaving, olive-wood sculpture, stained glass, silk-painting, ceramics, and others. Many craftsmen and artists have set up studios in the hill-villages.

Indeed, several great artists have found inspiration in the local crafts of Provence – Picasso, for example, in the ceramics of Vallauris. For other reasons, too, especially for its light and vivid colours, Provence has long been a magnet for artists. It has also produced several great names of its own, since early days – the Bréa family, 'primitive' painters at Nice in the 15th century; Charenton at Avignon; Froment at Aix; Pierre Puget, the sculptor, at Marseille; and others more recent, not forgetting Cézanne who was born at Aix and lived there many years. Other artists have come from outside to live and work, either in the Rhône area, like Van Gogh, or more often on the Riviera, like Picasso, Renoir, Chagall, Matisse, Dufy . . . the list is endless. Writers have come too, many of them foreign – from Petrarch at Avignon in the 14th century to Grahame Greene at Antibes today.

Last but far from least, Provence also attracts visitors with its *cuisine*, based on an agriculture of great diversity. Thanks to its sunshine and fertile soil, the lower Rhône valley is France's leading market garden – asparagus and tomatoes, peaches and strawberries, and the delicious sweet pink melons of Cavaillon. Plenty of wine is produced too: the Côtes-de-Provence are nothing special, but the area east of Marseille has some good wines (Bandol, Château Simone, white Cassis) and so does the Rhône valley (Gigondas, Châteauneuf-du-Pape, Tavel rosé). In the hinterland, sheep-grazing is prosperous: here in summer on the upland pastures the lambs graze on a diet of wild herbs, and these give the special aromatic flavour to the *agneau de Sisteron* that you find on many menus, often wood-fire grilled.

Varied and spicy, the Provençal *cuisine* relies heavily on garlic, on local herbs, and on olive oil which generally replaces butter in cooking. In rural areas, stews are common, such as *boeuf en daube*; rabbit may be cooked in a mustard sauce; chicken, some fish, even frogs' legs, are frequently prepared *à la provençale*, i.e. in a tomato and garlic sauce. A meal may well begin with a hearty soup such as *soupe au pistou* (with basil and garlic) or with the common *salade niçoise* (green peppers, eggs, black olives, tomatoes, tunny, anchovies, etc) or maybe with *crudités* (a basket of raw vegetables, with dressing). Fish of course holds pride of place. The complicated and expensive fish stews, *bouillabaisse* and *bourride*, are found mainly on the coast; but everywhere you will come across *soupe de poissons*, served with a strong garlic sauce. One very special Provençal dish is *aioli*, a garlic mayonnaise served usually with boiled cod and vegetables. Its very name sends Provençaux into fits of lyricism; the poet Mistral even founded a paper called *L'Aioli*, and wrote: "It concentrates all the warmth, strength and fun-loving gaiety of our people." Now who, after that, will dare admit to disliking garlic?

AIGUES-MORTES
GARD Pop 4000

A perfect example of a medieval town with ramparts, all intact. But whereas most such towns are on hills (e.g. Carcassonne), Aigues-Mortes stands amid salty marshes and lagoons – the name means 'dead water', from *Aquae Mortae*. It is a beautiful, haunting, somewhat sad town, which once lay on the sea and contained 15,000 inhabitants, but as a result of silting is now situated 8km inland. Louis IX, St-Louis, embarked from this spot for the Seventh Crusade in 1248. He built the city keep, the Tour de Constance; the ramparts were completed by his son, Philip the Bold. The old streets inside the walls still retain their original grid form.

The impressive round Tour de Constance is made up of two vaulted rooms. The lower one contains the Oratory of St-Louis, built into the walls, and documents of the saint at Aigues-Mortes. The upper room has souvenirs of the 14–18C period when the tower was a political prison, first for Templars, then for Huguenots and other 'heretics'. The Huguenots have left brave, pathetic inscriptions on the walls (*'au ciel, résistez'*). You can walk round the ramparts.

Le Grau-du-Roi, 6km S, is a picturesque fishing-village. Just to its S, Port Camargue is one of the big new Languedoc resorts; every villa has its own mooring in this elegant and spacious residential marina for 3000 boats.

AIX-EN-PROVENCE
BOUCHES-DU-RHÔNE Pop 114,000

Aix is a noble and lovely city of aristocratic grace: some call it 'the Oxford of France', others compare it to Florence. For 600 years it was Provence's dazzling capital: today, though no more than a sub-prefecture, it is still a major university town and centre of the arts. The many handsome classic buildings are somehow in harmony with the modern student atmosphere; and so intense is the ambience of the narrow streets of the Vieille Ville that one is largely unaware of the city's wider setting, where the plain of the Rhône delta meets the hills.

As with other towns called Aix, the name (pronounced 'aches') comes from the Latin *aquae*, for in 123BC the Roman consul Sextius founded a spa at the springs here and called it *Aquae Sextiae*. For a while Aix was capital of this part of Roman Gaul. In the 12C the Counts of Provence made it their capital. Then it knew its greatest glory under 'Good King René' in 1442–80. Though really a count, as exiled King of Naples he kept the royal title. A true Renaissance man – linguist, mathematician, patron of music and the arts – he developed Provence's economy, introducing the muscat grape and the silkworm.

Aix was the seat of the parliament and lawcourts of Provence for some 300 years, and thus acquired its graceful 17–18C mansions, built by moneyed prelates, nobles and magistrates. With the rise of Marseille in the 19C, Aix went into relative decline. But since 1945 it has grown hugely, as new suburbs and industries, and new campuses of the old 15C university, have spread across the plain.

The old part of town, compact and best visited on foot, contains most of the main sites. Here is the central avenue and focus of local life, the famous 17C Cours Mirabeau, one of France's noblest streets, though only 450m long. Built on the site of the old ramparts, it was later named after the Marquis de Mirabeau (1749–91), popular orator of the Revolution and once deputy for Aix. The street is shaded by four rows of plane-trees, meeting above to form an arbour, and along it are four fountains (at the E end, that of King René has a statue of him holding grapes).

SE of the Cours is the once aristocratic Mazarin Quarter, with its 17C Fontaine des Quatre Dauphins and lovely buildings such as the 13C church of St-Jean-de-Malte. Next to it, in the former Priory of the Knights of Malta, is the Musée Granet (named after a 19C Aixois artist) with many excellent French, Dutch and Flemish paintings. The big archaeology room holds Greek and Roman sculptures and a unique array of Celto-Ligurian sculptures from Entremont.

NE of the Cours, the large 17C church of Ste-Marie-Madeleine has an ornate interior: paintings by Rubens and Van Loo, and the wonderful 15C *Annunciation*, thought to be by Jean Chapus of Avignon (it is the centre of a triptych, the side-panels of which are abroad, but copies are in the sacristy). NW from here, the wonderful Gothic cathedral of St-Sauveur, rich in works of art, is in a curious jumble of styles, from 5C to 16C. All but one of the statues on the facade are 19C: the originals were destroyed in the Revolution, save for the central Virgin, spared because a cap of Liberty was stuck on her head. The cathedral's main treasures are kept locked, but the sacristan will show them: notably the rich 16C wood-carvings on the W doors, and Froment's celebrated triptych, *The Burning Bush* (1475). The 15 famous Brussels tapestries, woven for Canterbury Cathedral in 1511, then bought by Aix, are, alas, not on view. The delightful cloister leads to the former archbishop's palace, now a museum housing a famous collection of 18 Beauvais tapestries (17–18C): nine are vivid scenes from the life of Don Quixote, from designs by Natoire.

Vieil Aix, the lively old quarter between the Cours and the cathedral, is ideal for a stroll as many of its narrow streets are closed to traffic. Here the tiny cobbled Pl. d'Albertus is especially lovely. In the Pl. de l'Hôtel de Ville, with its flower-market, the former corn-market building has fine 18C carvings, while the 17C Hôtel de Ville itself holds the celebrated Méjanes Library of 300,000 books, including rare 15–16C volumes. At the top of the adjacent belfry are four rotating statues depicting the seasons: each in turn shows its face for three months. Nearby, in a 17C mansion, the Musée du Vieil Aix has one of the best folklore collections in Provence.

Outside the Old Town: the graceful Pavillon Vendôme, with its formal garden and atlantes on its facade, was built in 1667 as summer villa of Provence's governor, the Cardinal of Vendôme. The **Atelier Paul Cézanne**, 1km N, on a hill, is the studio where the painter came to work each day, from his home downtown. It has been refashioned just as it was when he died in 1906: you can see his easel and palette, hat and cloak and other effects, and some of the actual objects he painted (bottles, skulls, etc), but only three of his own works. Meanwhile, a modern artist of a totally different stamp is venerated – or, you could say, self-venerated – at the astonishing **Vasarély Foundation**, in the W suburbs. The self-aggrandizing Hungarian-born artist created this modern museum in 1975 to house and to explain his own works and theories, his experiments with the illusions of light and movement. Seven hexagonal cells display his geometric murals, rotating glass sculptures, polychromatic tiled mosaics, etc.

Aix-en-Provence

Aix is host to a major music festival, mid-July to mid-Aug. **Mont Ste-Victoire**, 8km E, is the lofty limestone ridge that Cézanne adored and so often painted, in such varied hues. Seen head-on from Aix, as he viewed it, it seems a white pyramid: it is really a long 16km wall of rock (over 1000m), as you can see from the autoroute to the S. To visit it, drive to **Les Cabassols**, then do a tough 2-hour hike up a mule-track to the monument on the summit (splendid views). At **Vauvenargues** is the 17C château briefly owned by Picasso (he is buried in its park). Near **Pourrières**, to the E, is the spot where the Roman general Marius defeated the Teuton hordes in 102BC, slaying 100,000, it is said (hence the mountain's name).

Entremont, 3km N of Aix, is the site of a major Celto-Ligurian oppidum, sacked in 123BC by Consul Sextius. Recent excavations have laid bare a gateway and bits of rampart. The aqueduct of **Roquefavour**, 11km W, a three-tier wonder 90m longer than the Pont du Gard and nearly twice as high, was built in 1842–47 to carry water from the Durance to Marseille.

ALÈS
GARD   Pop 44,000

Alès, on the SE edge of the Cévennes, was once a major coal-mining centre, but the mines are now mostly closed, and Alès has moved over to other industries, such as chemicals and lavatory-basins. The local silk industry too is now largely defunct. Louis Pasteur spent four crucial years here, 1865–69, evolving a remedy for diseases of the silkworm.

ANNOT
ALPES-DE-HAUT PROVENCE   Pop 900

Little streams burble down the paved alleyways of this exceptionally charming little town, a summer resort in a valley full of lilac and lavender, lime and chestnut, 32km NE of Castellane. The hills close by have bizarrely-shaped sandstone rocks. **Méailles**, 8km NW, is a pleasing hill-village.

ANTIBES
ALPES-MARITIMES   Pop 63,000

The ancient Greek trading-post of Antipolis faces Nice across the Baie des Anges and is still a busy commercial town and full of cultural interest. From the 14C it was a fortress town of the French kings when their foes, the Dukes of Savoy, held Nice: witness the seafront ramparts (you can walk along them) and the huge Fort Carré N of the harbour. The Vieille Ville with its narrow streets is full of character.

By the ramparts, the 13–16C castle of the Grimaldis, former lords of Antibes, is today a municipal Picasso Museum with a very fine collection. After spending the war in Paris, Picasso returned to his adored Mediterranean in 1945, but lacked a proper studio: so the curator lent him a room in the museum. Here for several months he worked joyously, then in gratitude left his output of that period on loan to the museum, together with some 200 of the ceramics he created at Vallauris. The museum contains some of Picasso's best larger canvases *(La Joie de Vivre, Ulysse et les Sirènes)*, as well as works inspired by the sea and Greek mythology, and a portrait of his daughter Paloma.

The museum of Archaeology, by the château, displays 4000 years of the town's history. The former cathedral, by the sea wall, mainly 17C, has an elaborate altarpiece by Louis Bréa.

Some 4km N of Antibes, on the coast at **La Brague**, are three noted pleasure-haunts: *La Bonne Auberge*, one of Provence's best restaurants; Marineland, a nautical zoo with aquarium, penguins, and performing dolphins; and *La Siesta*, a vast and stylish beach-club cum nightclub, open to the public and not too expensive, with imported sand, wave-shaped casino, and even a restaurant for dogs.

ANTIBES, CAP D'
ALPES-MARITIMES

Like the other lovely pine-wooded peninsulas on this coast, Cap-Martin and St-Jean-Cap-Ferrat, this one too is a preserve of the rich, mostly private estates with stately villas and subtropical gardens. But the ordinary visitor, too, can enjoy its sandy beaches, fine views and other delights.

At the S tip of the cape stands the most famous and glamorous of all the Riviera's luxury haunts of high society: the Hôtel du Cap d'Antibes, with its restaurant *Eden Roc*. It was the original for Scott Fitzgerald's 'Hôtel des Étrangers' in *Tender is the Night*. Today it is worth going for a drink, or a swim in the fabled pool, just to enjoy the diamond-studded nostalgia and the idyllic setting. Close by is a naval and Napoleonic museum; 2km N, the **Thuret** tropical garden.

Beside the lighthouse on the hilltop (fine views from here) is the extraordinary sailors' chapel of La Garoupe, full of ex-voto paintings by amateurs, made in thanksgiving or in fulfilment of a vow (e.g. pictures of miraculous escapes – a man falling from a tree, another saved from an angry dog, and a comic scene of a road accident). Well worth a visit.

APT
VAUCLUSE   Pop 11,000

In a wide valley 52km E of Avignon, this active town makes crystallized fruits and lavender essence and is a centre of ochre quarrying. It was a busy place in Roman days, too, as you can see in the museum of Archaeology; Roman baths lie beneath the sub-prefecture, and from the museum you can visit part of the Arena underground.

Apt was the site of the first shrine in France dedicated to Ste-Anne, mother of the Virgin, whose body was brought here, according to legend. There is still a pilgrimage, last Sun. in July. In the 11C ex-cathedral of Ste-Anne is a stained-glass window representing the saint, as well as a reliquary bust. The sacristy contains numerous treasures, notably an 11C Arab standard captured in the First Crusade.

The **Colorado de Rustrel**, 11km NE, is a succession of huge ochre quarries. A path off the D22 road leads to a good viewpoint.

ARLES
BOUCHES-DU-RHÔNE   Pop 50,000

Arles is essentially a museum town. Apart from its tourist trade, it seems a quiet, unsophisticated place: but its range of Roman and early Christian glories, and of Provençal folk traditions, is wonderfully varied and rich. Its old streets breathe the

Antibes

The Roman Arena, Arles

serenity of civilizations long past.

Arles became a key Roman centre thanks to its location. It stands astride an arm of the lower Rhône, on the N edge of the Camargue. It grew into a major port after the consul Marius dug a canal to the sea in 100BC; it also carried much of the land traffic between Spain, Italy and N France, being at the lowest point where the Rhône was bridgeable. For a while, under Julius Caesar, it was capital of Roman Provence, and under the later Empire it became a key trade centre: Constantine built a palace here, and Honorius in AD400 made it the capital of the 'three Gauls'. Later, early Christianity made Arles one of its crucial capitals: St Augustine was consecrated first Archbishop of Canterbury here in 597. But after the barbarian ravages of the Dark Ages it went into decline, and never recovered its status.

Almost all the main sights lie close together in the town centre. The Arena is one of the earliest (46BC) and largest (25,000 spectators) of the Roman world. Gladiatorial combats were held here, and fights with wild beasts (you can see the tunnels leading to their cages). In the Middle Ages the arena was fortified, with three towers added for defence, and a church and 200 houses built inside: its own stones were used for all this, and only in the 19C was it restored. The Roman Theatre is much more of a ruin, for in the Dark Ages it was pillaged and used as a quarry for other buildings. Just two tall columns survive from the original elaborate stage wall, and 20 rows of seats from an auditorium once holding 7000 people. Of the 4C Palace of Constantine, only the vast baths visibly remain, partly ruined but impressive in their grandeur, made of narrow layers of brick and stone. In the SE corner of the Pl. du Forum, two Corinthian columns are the relics of a Roman temple.

The former cathedral of St-Trophime dates back to Charlemagne's day, as can be seen from the lower part of the W facade. But it was rebuilt in the 11–15C and has a splendid Provençal Romanesque portal, with elaborate stone carvings. Inside, the Gothic flamboyance of the choir contrasts with the sober Romanesque nave; one chapel holds a 4C sarcophagus now used as a font. The church's graceful cloister is the most beautiful and famous in Provence: the capitals of the slender marble pillars are adorned with scenes from the Bible and Provençal legends. A chapel off the N side has superb Aubusson and Flemish tapestries. In the SE suburbs, the Alyscamps, a wide and peaceful path lined with sarcophagi, was originally a Roman necropolis (the name comes from 'Elysian fields'), then one of the great prestige burial-grounds of early Christendom.

Arles has four outstanding museums. That of Pagan Art, in a former church, has Greek and Roman tombs, mosaics and statues, found locally: notably, a Greek sarcophagus of Hippolytus and Phaedra; a statue of Augustus; and two casts of the famous Venus of Arles (the original is in the Louvre). The museum of Christian Art, in a former Jesuit chapel, contains richly carved sarcophagi, many from the Alyscamps: note the Tomb of the Trinity (a married couple). From the museum steps descend into the astonishing Cryptoporticus, a huge basement used by the Romans for storing grain milled nearby, some of which was sent to feed Rome's population.

The Musée Réattu, former 15C priory of the Knights of Malta, has a large and varied art collection, erratic in quality. By far the best exhibits are the set of satirical cartoon-like coloured sketches by Picasso, and five 17C Brussels tapestries eccentrically portraying the Wonders of the World. Good works too by Lurçat, Léger, Gauguin, etc. Last, but far from least, the Museon Arlaten gives a vivid and moving insight into the culture and traditions of Provence. This intensely personal folk museum was founded in 1896 by the poet Mistral, who labelled and explained many exhibits in his own hand: 30 rooms, deserving hours of study, include local costumes and lace bonnets, *santons*, legendary monsters, life-size tableaux of Provençal life – and, amazingly, golden tresses of a girl found in a tomb at Les Baux and dated to 1478.

Alas, the dark-eyed Arlésiennes rarely wear their famous lace bonnets and costumes in public now, except for festivals. The town still attracts some artists and musicians, though fewer than in the days when Bizet composed *l'Arlésienne* here, and when Van Gogh lived here (1888–90), painting frenetically and sinking into madness (in Arles he cut off his ear). The Arles that he painted, in *Café du Soir*, etc, has sadly been rebuilt; his bridge, S of Arles, was pulled down in 1926, though a copy has since been put up at Port-de-Bouc, close to Martigues.

Local festivals include the Camargue fête, last Sun. in Apr.; music and drama festival in the Roman Theatre, July; bullfight festival in the Arena, Easter; and bullfights roughly every other Sun., Apr. to Nov.

St-Gilles, 15km W, was in the Middle Ages a major centre for pilgrims to the tomb of St-Gilles the Hermit, who founded an abbey here in the 7C. The present church, 12C, has marvellous sculptures of the life of Christ on its broad W front. The spacious crypt, 11C Romanesque, holds what is believed to be the authentic tomb of St-Gilles. Of the E part of the abbey, little remains save the bell-tower: in it is a famous and unusual spiral staircase, Le Vis, the steps of which are roofed over, giving the effect of a curving funnel.

The former Benedictine abbey of **Montmajour**, 5km NE of Arles, built in the 10C on a low hill then an island by the Rhône, was powerful and wealthy in the Middle Ages, owning priories all over Provence. Later its glory waned and it was partially pulled down, but has since been partly restored. Note the high crenellated *donjon*, 14C; the 12C Romanesque church; the crypt built partly out of the rock; and the charming cloister with carvings of animals on the capitals. Just along the Fontvieille road, the appealing chapel of Ste-Croix is in the form of a Greek cross.

AURON
ALPES-MARITIMES

A sophisticated modern ski-resort, 98km NW of Nice, on a lonely plateau with high peaks all round. The lovely Romanesque chapel of St-Érige, dating from the 12C, has marvellously vivid 15C frescoes depicting Mary Magdalene, St-Denis (martyred in Paris in AD250) and St-Érige, archbishop of Gap. Best is the fresco of Christ in a robe decorated with lions, eagles and griffins.

Isola 2000, 38km SE, is a big new ski-resort built in modernistic style, with slopes suitable for beginners. The townlet of **St-Étienne-de-Tinée**, 7km N of Auron in a lovely mountain valley, was once a major religious centre – witness the three local chapels with good frescoes. Further N is the **Cime de la Bonnette** (2802m), one of the highest of all Alpine passes; here the oratory of Notre-Dame-du-Très-Haut has a popular pilgrimage in Aug.

AVIGNON
VAUCLUSE Pop 91,000

Avignon, heavy with history, is today also a lively and sophisticated modern city. It stands on a plain beside the confluence of the Rhône and Durance. Its great circle of ramparts, built in the 1350s, restored in the 19C, is less spectacular than Carcassonne's, but remains intact; and the main life of the city still takes place within these walls, even if four-fifths of the population now live outside them. Crowning all, in the heart of the city, is the gigantic palace that the popes built here, arguably Europe's most impressive medieval building.

Avignon was a trading centre even before Roman days. Later, pure accident made it into a major city, for it was chance that induced the papacy to move here in 1307, when it found life in Rome being made unbearable by the feuding between noble families. And it was the French king, Philippe-le-Bel, who induced the newly-elected Clément V, a French pope, to move here (hoping thus to increase French influence over the papacy).

Clément ruled from the episcopal palace. Benedict XII, elected in 1334, then set about making the move from Rome more permanent by constructing the Palais des Papes, which was finished in 1352 by his successor, Clément VI. This initiated Avignon's golden era as Christendom's capital, at a time when the papacy was given over to luxury and good living, flaunting its riches and tolerating carnal weaknesses. Avignon became a city of jollity and ostentation, even of crime – to the dismay of some of the more serious members of the papal court, such as Petrarch, the Italian poet: '. . . an abode of sorrows, the shame of mankind, a sink of vice. There God is held in contempt,

Pont d'Avignon

money is worshipped . . . Everything breathes a lie: the air, the earth, the houses, and above all the bedrooms.'

By 1377, when seven popes, all French, had ruled in Avignon, Gregory XI was persuaded to go back to Rome. Some dissident cardinals, however, preferred to stay in Avignon where they elected their own pope (i.e. antipope). Thus began the Great Schism of the West, as popes and antipopes bickered over papal lands and revenues and flung excommunications at each other. The last antipope was expelled by force in 1403, but carried on the fight in his native Spain, and the schism ended only in 1449. Avignon was ruled by a papal legate till the Revolution, when it was united to France.

With its high turreted towers and massive walls, the Palace of the Popes at first seems more military than religious. Inside, it is a honeycomb of chapels, halls, corridors. It is, in fact, two palaces, built within 20 years by two contrasting popes: the Old Palace, to the N, plain and sober, reflects the ascetic spirit of Benedict XII, a former Cistercian monk; the New Palace, to the S, far more ornate, was built by Clément VI, a lover of pomp and the arts. The building, damaged at the Revolution, and many of its frescoes vandalized, is now restored, though still bereft of much of its original sumptuous furnishing and decor.

Conducted tours begin in the Grand Courtyard, then go to the Consistory, where the pope held audience; off it, the chapel of St-Jean is partly covered with bright frescoes. Upstairs is the long Banqueting Hall where 150 people would enjoy a meal lasting up to eight hours, with minstrels and jugglers; six Gobelins tapestries now hang there. The tiny chapel of St-Martial, off the hall, has lovely dark blue frescoes by Giovanetti.

The papal Antechamber contains traces of its original vaulted roofing. The pope's little bedroom has gold and blue frescoes of squirrels, birds and foliage (all secular); its vivid mosaic floor is a copy of the original now in the palace museum. In the Room of the Deer (Pope Clément's study) are remarkable frescoes of bathing and games, fishing and hunting scenes – further proof of this pope's worldly tastes. Finally, the Grand Chapel has paintings by Mignard and Parrocel. Here the tour ends, and visitors can explore other sights on their own: the Indulgence window, where the pope would bless pilgrims below; the majestic Grand Audience Hall; and the beautiful vaulted Gallery of the Conclave, leading to the Conclave itself where the cardinals were locked up to elect a new pope –

as in the Vatican today.

Just N of the Palace, the 12C cathedral of Notre-Dame-des-Doms has an archbishop's throne in white marble and the Flamboyant Gothic tomb of Pope John XXII. N again, overlooking the Rhône, with fine views, is the rocky plateau of the Rocher des Doms, now a pleasant rose-garden. Below, jutting into the river, are the four remaining arches of the 12C Pont St-Bénézet (the rest of this famous bridge was borne away by floods in the 17C). This is the 'Pont d'Avignon' of the old song. Made for horses and pedestrians, it was far too narrow for people to 'dance in a circle' on it: probably the dancing was *'sous le pont'*, on the Île de la Barthelasse, a traditional recreation spot.

Close by, the former palace of the Archbishops of Avignon is now the Musée du Petit Palais, whose 20 rooms contain a superb collection of 13–16C works of the Avignon and North Italian schools (fine Italian primitives). Of Avignon's two other main museums, the Calvet is oddly eclectic: one room with hundreds of pieces of wrought-iron; another with Greek steles, vases and sculptures; and several rooms of 16–20C French painting. The Musée Lapidaire holds local Roman and pre-Roman finds: notably, the *Venus of Pourrières*, found near Aix, and the *Tarasque of Noves*, an Iron Age statuette of a man-eating lion.

Avignon's Vieille Ville, S and E of the papal palace, is an absorbing labyrinth of narrow streets, some now traffic-free, some full of smart shops, others lined with fine old mansions. Most interesting churches here are the Chapelle des Pénitents (rich carvings), St-Pierre (ditto), St-Symphorien (ditto), and St-Didier, with superb 14C frescoes and the celebrated 15th-century retable of the *Bearing of the Cross*, by Francesco Laurana. The charming cobbled Rue des Teinturiers runs by the river Sorgue whose old paddlewheels were in use until the late 19C to power local textile factories. The Rue des Marchands is an elegant pedestrian zone; the Pl. de l'Horloge and the broad Rue de la République are the centres of social life in this fashionable city which stays up late and retains its reputation for exuberance and gaiety.

Just S of the papal palace, the Fondation Jean Vilar is a fascinating little museum of post-war theatre, founded in 1981 in honour of the great director who led the French drama revival of the 1950s and founded the Avignon Festival. This, Europe's leading drama festival, spans the last three weeks of July; many plays are staged in the palace's Great Courtyard.

The old fortified village of **Barbentane**, 10km SW, has an elegant 17C château, less Provençal than Île-de-France in style.

BAGNOLS-SUR-CÈZE
GARD Pop 18,000

Bagnols, 33km NW of Avignon, is a sleepy old town onto which has been grafted – with an unexpected degree of harmony – a pleasantly built new dormitory suburb for the big nuclear centre of Marcoule, on the Rhône. Just N of Marcoule is a belvedere with superb views of the region. Bagnols's museum in the *mairie* has some good paintings by Bonnard, Matisse, etc.

BANDOL
VAR Pop 6000

An attractive, lively and sophisticated resort, with an animated fishing and yacht port, elegant promenade, sandy coves – and many amusing places to visit in the area. The rocky isle of **Bendor**, 2km offshore, was bought in 1955 by Paul Ricard, the flamboyant *pastis* tycoon, who transformed it into an unusual cultural-cum-tourist centre: it has a pastiche Provençal fishing-port, nautical club, good modern art gallery, 'artisans' village', and an interesting museum of wines, with items from 50 countries (including Norfolk *blanc*).

The isle of **Embiez**, 10km SE, off Le Brusc, also part of the Paul Ricard empire, is now a big modern sea-sports complex, with repair shipyard and research centre directed by Alain Bombard, the marine biologist. Nearby, **Sanary** is a pleasant family resort: Aldous Huxley used to live there. Beside the B52 autoroute, 3km NE of Bandol, is an exceptionally attractive little zoo, set in an 'exotic garden' of rare plants and trees.

La Cadière d'Azur and **Le Castellet**, 10km N of Bandol, are two charming hill-villages. Further N, just off the N8 highway, lies the **Circuit Paul Ricard**, Provence's best motor-racing track: events most weekends, several major races each year; museum of vintage racing cars; karting centre. The Dutch-owned *OK Corral* amusement park, c.9km further W, off N8, has ghost train, big wheel, 'Wild West' dramatic shows by actors – fun for kids from 4 to 84.

BARCELONNETTE
ALPES-DE-HAUTE PROVENCE Pop 3000

A small town in a majestic mountain valley, near the high ski-resorts of **Pra-Loup**, **Le Sauze** and **Super-Sauze**. In the War of the Spanish Succession, in 1713, the town was recaptured for France from Savoy through the skill of the Duke of Berwick, bastard son of James II.

BARJOLS
VAR Pop 2100

A market town 22km NW of Brignoles, known for its 33 fountains and shady trees: the plane tree by the *mairie*, 12m in circumference, is said to be France's largest. The Gothic facade of the 11C church has a 12C tympanum: at the Fête of St-Marcel, 16 Jan., there is dancing inside the church. Alone of all French towns, Barjols still makes the traditional *galoubets* (flutes) and *tambourins* (narrow drums) used in Provençal folk-dancing.

BAUX, LES
BOUCHES-DU-RHÔNE Pop 400

Half-ruined and half-deserted, unforgettable, mysterious, this most famous of Provençal hill-villages stands on a rocky spur of the Alpilles range. Its name comes from the Provençal *baou* ('rock'); hence the word 'bauxite', first discovered here in 1822. Best views are from the hill road to the NW or the valley road to the E. Over a million tourists a year visit this haunting domain, crowding its souvenir stalls, cramming its alleyways. It is best to visit very early, or out of season – or explore the ghost kingdom by moonlight.

From the 11C the lords of Les Baux, an arrogant and powerful feudal family, ruled over some 80 townships of Provence and as far as Sicily and Albania. In the 13C Les Baux was a leading 'court of love', with troubadours. In 1372 it came under the rule of the cruel Viscount Raymond de Turenne, a brigand who enjoyed kidnapping people and then making them jump to their deaths from his castle. Finally the French king led an army against him, and he was drowned trying to cross the Rhône. Later Les Baux became a Protestant stronghold, but this angered Richelieu, who in 1632 pulled down the castle and ramparts. Thus ended the greatness of Les Baux, which in its heyday had 6000 inhabitants.

Park below the village and enter on foot by the Porte Mage. All around are half-ruined Renaissance houses, such as the Hôtel des Porcelets, now a museum of Archaeology, and the Hôtel de Manville, now a museum of Modern Art. Note, too, the former Protestant chapel, and the lovely 12C church of St-Vincent, with a fine view of the valley from its terrace. Hewn out of the rock, the narrow Rue Turcat goes up to the 14C Tour de Brau, now a small museum of local finds. Here you enter the gaunt castle ruins, crowned by the 13C keep where de Turenne watched his victims leap down. In the valley on the W side are several luxury hotel/restaurants, notably the famous *Oustau de Baumanière* where the Queen and Prince Philip dined on their state visit to France in 1972. Here also is the little Pavillon de la Reine Jeanne, built in 1581 in memory of the second wife of King René, who for a while owned Les Baux.

On Christmas Eve, ever since the 16C, a Midnight Mass in the form of a Provençal Nativity pageant has been held in the church of St-Vincent.

Les Alpilles are a bizarre-looking range of arid hills with jagged chalky peaks, rising only to 450m but looking higher; the top point, with fine views, is **La Caume**, SE of St-Rémy. Wild scenery in the **Val d'Enfer** gorge, 2km NW of Les Baux.

Les Baux

BEAUCAIRE
GARD   Pop 13,000

Beaucaire's mighty 13C castle faces that of Tarascon across the Rhône. The towns were rivals for centuries, for Beaucaire was in Languedoc, and

Beaucaire

Tarascon in Provence. Built by Count Raymond VI of Toulouse, and partly pulled down by Richelieu in 1632, the hilltop castle is today half-ruined and unrestored; but the high *donjon* (keep) survives, and you can climb to the top of its curious triangular tower for fine views.

The annual Trade Fair, also created by Count Raymond, was for centuries the greatest in Europe, drawing 800 boats and up to 300,000 people from many nations, every July. It lasted till the mid-19C, when it fell victim to the railway age. It was held in the big meadow between castle and river, where it is today commemorated by a more modest annual fête, late July.

BEAULIEU
ALPES-MARITIMES   Pop 4300

No longer so glamorously fashionable as in pre-war days, Beaulieu still retains a certain sedate chic, with its floodlit palms and two famous luxury hotels, La Réserve and the Métropole. Lively casino, but stony beach. Many elegant villas: Villa Kérylos (open to the public), built in 1900 on a headland, is a copy of an ancient Greek villa; Villa Namouna was the home of Gordon Bennett, owner of the *New York Herald*, who commissioned Stanley to look for Livingstone; Villa Léonine was designed and built by the Marquess of Salisbury, British prime minister.

BERRE, ÉTANG DE
BOUCHES-DU-RHÔNE

Separated from the sea by the Estaque range, this huge salt-water lake covers 155sq. km yet is only 10m deep. Its shores have been colonized since Greek and Roman times and today are intensively industrialized: petro-chemical and other factories, four big oil refineries, and the terminal of the pipeline carrying crude oil to E France and SW Germany. Clockwise around the lake, the main points of interest are, apart from Martigues (q.v.):

Marignane: next to Marseille's international airport is Europe's largest helicopter factory, state-owned, famous for having developed a new system of labour relations, based on small separate work groups, somewhat like Fiat and Volvo. **St-Blaise:** excavations here have unearthed a Greek fortress of the 7C BC, possibly the oldest Greek settlement in France. **Miramas-le-Vieux:** at the N tip of the lake, a village on a rocky spur: good views, 13C castle.

The huge modern port and industrial estate of

Fos, 10km W of the lake, has been developed since 1965 by the Port of Marseille Authority as an extension of the city's own port.

BIOT
ALPES-MARITIMES   Pop 3000

A charming old walled town with an arcaded main square, set above a flowery valley; the church has two 15C retables of the Nice school, one by Bréa. Biot has for centuries been a centre of pottery and glass-making, still thriving today.

The Musée Fernand Léger, an imposing modern building in a hillside park, was built by the artist's widow soon after his death in 1955. The facade carries an arresting mosaic of sport, designed by Léger for a stadium in Hanover. Inside are 300 of his works, showing his evolution via Impressionism and Cubism to an obsession with machinery and robot-like figures. The mosaics and sculptures in the garden were made by Léger's followers, to his designs.

BOLLÈNE
VAUCLUSE   Pop 11,000

Tourists entering the province by the Rhône valley route can get their first true taste of Provence at this old town, set on a hillside above the river and the motorway. Its museum has drawings by Chagall and Picasso, while along the river to the N lies a different kind of modernism: huge hydroelectric works and a nuclear centre. Superb panorama from the hilltop château of **Barry** 6km N.

BRIGNOLES
VAR   Pop 10,500

Brignoles, 57km E of Aix, is a lively industrial and wine-marketing town, with vineyards all around. The museum in the ruins of the 11C château has a 3C sarcophagus. Nearby, white marble has been quarried since Roman days; this is also France's main centre for bauxite extraction.

Good views nearby from the summit of the **Loube** mountain, 8km SE.

BRIGUE, LA
ALPES-MARITIMES   Pop 500

Ceded to France only in 1947, the area round La Brigue and Tende was previously the private hunting ground (wild boar and chamois) of the Italian kings. La Brigue is an unrestored medieval village with vaulted streets, a Romanesque church with Lombard belfry and good primitive paintings, and a ruined castle above. The tiny chapel of **Notre-Dame-des-Fontaines** lies 4km E, alone in a lush valley full of orchards, streams and grazing sheep. The plain exterior belies the wonderfully rich interior, full of 15C frescoes by a Piedmontese priest, portraying the life of Christ with pathos and naturalism.

The well-named **Vallée des Merveilles**, in a remote setting 15km W of La Brigue, is one of the strangest places in Provence. This austere rock-strewn valley lies below the haunting **Mont Bégo** with lordly Alps all round three deep lakes. Most

mysterious of all, cut all over the rocks are some 30,000 engravings of totems, daggers and bulls, thought to be the work of Iron or Bronze Age tribesmen who came here on pilgrimage. Owing to snow, the valley can be visited only June to Oct. A full visit needs at least 8 hours: part of the journey must be made on foot (via well-marked paths), or you can hire a jeep. At the S end of the valley is a hostel with beds and simple food.

CAGNES-SUR-MER
ALPES-MARITIMES   Pop 35,000

A sprawling conurbation, in three sharply contrasting parts. On the coast, Cros-de-Cagnes, a fishing-village now swollen into a brash modern resort clogged with highways, high-rise flats and hypermarkets. Just inland is Cagnes-Ville, the main town. Behind is the little ramparted hilltop village of Haut-de-Cagnes, with a maze of alleys winding up to its medieval castle.

The castle, built as a fortress in the 14C by the Grimaldi family (see *Monaco*), who ruled here till 1789, was converted into a graceful château in 1620 and is now a remarkable and varied civic museum. You enter via a charming triangular courtyard, with a 200-year-old pepper-tree on one side. On the ground floor is a museum of olive oil and the olive-tree; on the first floor, the high ceiling of the Salle des Fêtes has an unusual *trompe l'oeil* fresco of the *Fall of Phaeton* by Carlone of Genoa. On the next floor, the museum of Modern Mediterranean Art has works by Chagall, Dufy, Vasarély, etc. In the Marquise de Grimaldi's former boudoir is a striking curiosity: 40 portraits of local cabaret singer Suzy Solidor by 40 different artists, among them Dufy, Cocteau and Foujita. The chapel of Notre-Dame-de-Protection has 16C frescoes.

In Cagnes-Ville, the nostalgic and poignant Musée Renoir is housed in Les Collettes, where the great artist spent his last years, 1907–19. The museum contains only one of his canvases, but several drawings and sculptures.

Cagnes-sur-Mer

CAMARGUE, THE
BOUCHES-DU-RHÔNE, GARD

This wide expanse of lagoons and marshy plains, in the Rhône delta, is a strange region, like none other in France. Birds and animals in great variety here lead their special life; sunsets linger on the far flat horizons; herds of black bulls and half-wild white horses roam the salty marshes, where few buildings are visible save the lonely whitewashed, thatched cottages of the herdsmen; and at dusk a flock of pink flamingoes may fly up from the reeds of a lagoon.

The Camargue comprises some 770 sq. km between the Grand Rhône to the E and Aigues-Mortes (q.v.) to the W. The N part towards Arles was desalinated after the war and is now France's main rice-growing area. To the S is the big lake of **Vaccarès**, screened from the sea by a maze of islands: the area is now a nature reserve, open to visits only by naturalists or students who must seek permission in advance. It contains many rare wild plants and flowers, and a variety of birds living freely in the open – among them, storks and cormorants, purple herons, and the Camargue's famous flamingoes. Outside the reserve it is possible to see some of its birds (best time early morning or late afternoon) and flowers by driving along the E side of the lake to the Gacholle lighthouse, from where in dry weather you can walk along the dunes to Les Saintes-Maries.

Most of the Camargue is split up into some 30 private ranches, each with its own *manade* (herd) of black bulls and white horses. Though fighting animals, the bulls are not bred to be killed in local *corridas*, but are used for the more harmless sport of *courses à la cocarde*, or sold for beef. Everywhere

The Camargue

you see the famous white horses – hardy, stocky, with broad flanks and short legs, yet nimble and manageable. Some are still wild; all are left free to roam in the open at night. They are hired out to tourists (at a price): N of Les Saintes-Maries are several good ranch-hotels where you can enjoy an equestrian holiday, going in groups for long rides across the marshes, led by a *gardian*.

The *manades* are run by these *gardians*, 'the aristocrats of the Camargue' – tough men and women with weather-beaten faces and a rather gipsy appearance. One duty of the *gardian* is the annual *ferrade* (branding) when the yearlings are brought to an enclosure to be branded with their owner's mark. **Méjanes**, on the NW shore of lake

Vaccarès, is a ranch owned and run as a holiday centre by Paul Ricard (see *Bandol*): besides *ferrades*, it offers mock bullfights, horse-riding, scenic railway, etc.

At **Pont de Rousty**, on N570 SW of Arles, is a good museum of Camargue life, installed in a graceful farm building. The Information Centre at Gînes, 5km N of Saintes-Maries, has a slide-show, etc, and a small aviary. Boat-trips can be taken up the Petit Rhône from a point 3km W of Saintes-Maries. The best time for a visit to the Camargue is spring or early summer: it is best to avoid the winter mistral and autumn mosquitoes.

The Camargue's 'capital', **Les Saintes-Maries-de-la-Mer** (pop. 2000), lying between the lagoons and the sand-dunes with their beaches, is a mixture of bathing-resort, pilgrimage centre and focal point of Provençal tradition. The customs and wildlife of the Camargue can be studied at the Musée Baroncelli, in the quaint old part of town at the foot of the towering church.

According to a 9C legend about how Christianity arrived in Provence, a boat with no sails or oars left Palestine and came ashore here, bearing Mary Magdalene, Mary Jacobé, Mary Salome, Martha and other saints, with their African servant, Sara. Most of them went off to evangelize Provence; but two Marys and Sara stayed on (hence the town's name) and were buried in the spot where the church now stands. The odd-looking fortified, crenellated church was built in the 11C as a defence against the Saracens; its high five-arch belfry is visible from far across the plain. Inside are the reliquary and the boat of the two Marys, and, in the crypt, a reliquary and strange costumed statue of Sara.

The town is Europe's gipsy capital, and Sara is their patroness. Each 23–27 May they hold their famous festival, coming here in thousands, still exotically clothed even though their caravans are now motorized. They hold a night vigil in the crypt, then carry the blue and pink statues of the saints, in their little boat, to the sea. Lesser pilgrimages are held on the weekend nearest 22 Oct. and first Sun. in Dec.

CANNES
ALPES-MARITIMES   Pop 72,000

Although its year-round population is only one-fifth of that of its rival Nice, Cannes too has the air of a metropolis, so grandiose and sparkling is its tourist industry. Much of the year it is as smart and sophisticated a resort as any in Europe: but when the mobs arrive, in high summer or at film festival time, then the golden image becomes more tawdry and the traffic unbearable – especially along La Croisette, the famous promenade where the palm-trees wave in the sea breeze. Westward lies the port and the old quarter, and behind are the sheltering wooded hills, now horridly overbuilt with high-rise flats, but still ensuring mild winters.

Cannes was only a fishing village on that fateful day in 1834 when Lord Brougham was obliged to stop there on his way to Italy, since the frontier W of Nice was closed due to cholera. So delighted was he with the warm climate and pretty coast that he built a villa and spent the next 34 winters there –

and soon scores of other lords and kings followed in his tracks, including the Prince of Wales and the Tsars. Great hotels were built, Cannes outshone all its Riviera rivals, and by the 1920s had coined the haughty ditty: 'Menton's dowdy, Monte's brass, Nice is rowdy – Cannes is class!'

Cannes

La Croisette, still Europe's smartest sea-promenade, is very much more the focus of elegant social life in Cannes than is the Promenade des Anglais in Nice. Rows of palms and pines stand between silver beaches on one side, luxury shops, cafés and hotels on the other. Here the *beau monde* takes its evening stroll, and here, too, are the great palace-hotels – notably the Majestic, with its marble bathrooms, and the wedding-cake Carlton, whose trendily informal bar is a great social centre.

At the W end of La Croisette, a huge new Convention Centre, opened in 1983, is the hub of the city's busy and lucrative conference trade, also the home of the winter casino and of the notorious annual Film Festival (once a glamorous event, now for the most part drably commercial). At the E end, on a headland, stands the Palm Beach summer casino, a big white oddity, looking, as the writer Archibald Lyall put it, 'as though a Foreign Legion fort had had a flirtation with the Doge's palace'. Under one roof it houses casino, disco, and cabaret, plus fashionable swimming-pool. Cannes also has two marinas full of wealthy yachts, miles of sandy beaches, and scope for every kind of sport. Main shopping street is the Rue d'Antibes.

To the W of the port is the hill of Le Suquet, its 11C tower floodlit at night. Here the Musée de la Castre houses an eclectic collection of antiquities, including Egyptian, Chinese, Polynesian and pre-Colombian. In the NE suburbs, the Observatoire de Super-Cannes (accessible by lift or by road) offers one of the finest views in Provence – as far as Corsica, on a clear day.

Main events: Jan., MIDEM fair (records and music); May, Film Festival; June, Café-Théâtre Festival; Sept., Yachting Festival; Oct./Nov., Golf Championship.

The two Lérins islands (**Ste-Marguerite** and **St-Honorat**), just offshore, reached by frequent boat services, are well worth a visit. St-Honorat, a 4C monk, founded one of France's first monasteries on the smaller, more distant island, which bears his name. By the 7C, with 4000 monks and a great library, it was one of the most powerful centres in Christendom. Subsequently it produced 600 bishops and 20 saints, including St Patrick of

Ireland. It closed after the Revolution, but in 1869 was bought by the Cistercians who still run it today. You can visit the museum in their big 19C monastery, also explore the 11C keep of the old fortified monastery, set romantically alone by the sea: it has a Roman marble cistern and arcaded cloisters. The island, peaceful and lush with flowers and trees, is ideal for a lazy picnic.

The Île Ste-Marguerite is named after St-Honorat's sister who headed a nunnery there. The 17C fort, built by Richelieu, was for centuries a state prison. Its best-known inmate was the mysterious 'Man in the Iron Mask', shut up there 1687–98, his identity unknown (was he indeed the bastard brother of Louis XIV?). You can see his cell, also that of the cowardly Marshal Bazaine who surrendered Metz to the Prussians in 1870; and the statue of six Huguenot pastors, all but one of whom went mad in solitary confinement. Today, the fort in summer is used as a youth, sport and cultural centre; it holds *son-et-lumière* shows, also concerts and opera performances.

CARPENTRAS
VAUCLUSE   Pop 25,000

This historic town, 24km NE of Avignon, was from 1320 to 1791 capital of the Comtat Venaissin, a territory then owned by the papacy, corresponding roughly to the modern Vaucluse. Of its old ramparts, only the Porte d'Orange now remains. Chief sight is the former cathedral of St-Siffrein, richly decorated inside with paintings by Mignard and Parrocel, gilded sculptures by Bernus, etc; the Flamboyant Gothic S door is known as the Porte Juive, since Jewish converts entered by it to be baptized. The nearby synagogue, the oldest in France (1367), was the centre of a big Jewish colony, powerful when the Jews managed the finances of the Avignon popes. The small Roman triumphal arch has unusual bas-reliefs of two captives, one wearing an animal skin, the other a tunic. More interesting than the town's two museums are the huge Inguimbertine Library (200,000 books and MSS) and the 18C Hôtel Dieu, its pharmacy adorned with comic paintings of monkeys.

The old village of **Venasque**, 11km SE, is notable for the 7C Merovingian baptistry next to its 13C church. Picturesque **Pernes-les-Fontaines**, 6km S, capital of the Comtat before Carpentras, has graceful fountains (as its name suggests) and a 16C bridge with a tiny chapel on it. The Tour Ferrande contains notable 13C frescoes.

CASSIS
BOUCHES-DU-RHÔNE   Pop 6000

An enchanting old fishing-port that has long been a favourite with artists: Dufy and Matisse painted it. It lies in a deep bay, sheltered by limestone cliffs, and has kept much of its old charm, despite the ugly holiday flats on the hillside and the hordes of tourists – including trippers from nearby Marseille who come mainly to gamble in the stylish new casino. The local white wine, greenish in hue, goes well with the local fish.

Just to the W lie the famous and beautiful

Calanques – deep fjord-like creeks, bordered by limestone cliffs. You can visit them by boat from Cassis; or drive to **Port-Miou** creek, (whose white rock was used in building the Suez Canal), then go on by foot to **Port-Pin** and **En-Vau**.

W of Cassis, the craggy cliff of Cap Canaille (360m) rises sheer above the sea. You can drive to the top, then along a *corniche* to the Grande Tête (396m) and down to **La Ciotat**, a sizeable ship-building town that has seen better days. These cliffs are the highest in France.

CASTELLANE
ALPES-DE-HAUTE PROVENCE   Pop 1300

A lively little market town in the Verdon valley, 63km NW of Grasse, with bare highlands all round. It is overlooked by a sheer 180m rock; the pilgrim chapel on top can be reached by a 30-minute footpath climb. Note the 12C church of St-Victor, and the high pentagonal tower, a relic of the old ramparts.

About 5km to the N, the Verdon has been widened to form the artificial lake of **Castillon**, suitable for bathing, with a hydroelectric dam. **St-André-les-Alpes**, further N, is a pleasant summer resort in a mountain valley, with plenty of sports. **Senez**, a tiny village 20km NW of Castellane, just off the N85, was – amazingly – the seat of a bishopric till 1790. The little Romanesque ex-cathedral has Flanders and Aubusson tapestries.

CAVAILLON
VAUCLUSE   Pop 21,000

Cavaillon, in a fertile sector of the Durance valley, is France's main market for fruit and vegetables, especially succulent pink melons. The Romans, too, traded here, as can be seen from the local finds (coins, pottery, etc) in the museum of Archaeology. The town has a small Roman arch, a synagogue with a Jewish museum, and interesting art in the part-Romanesque former cathedral.

COLMARS
ALPES-DE-HAUTE-PROVENCE   Pop. 300

17C ramparts enclose this charming townlet, in the high alpine valley of the upper Verdon, 71km NE of Digne. On either side are the medieval forts of Savoie and France, which guarded it in the 14C when it was on the French frontier. To the N, the road climbs up to the ugly ski-resort of Allos, then on to the Col d'Allos (splendid views).

DIGNE
ALPES-DE-HAUTE PROVENCE   Pop 16,000

Victor Hugo set the first part of *Les Misérables* in this 'dignified' little spa town that today treats rheumatism. The municipal museum is good on local history and archaeology; the 13C ex-cathedral of Notre-Dame-de-Bourg, in the outskirts, has a pretty rose window.

To the N, two roads (D900 and D900A) wind through the barren wild Pré-Alpes de Digne to the Col de Maure and on to Barcelonnette. The D900A is the more spectacular, but very narrow.

DRAGUIGNAN
VAR   Pop 25,000

A graceful old market town, 65km W of Cannes. It has a museum with Gallo-Roman remains, a 17C clocktower with wrought-iron campanile, and narrow streets, now traffic-free. 2km E is a major war cemetery for the Allied dead of the 1944 battles near here.

The church at **Les Arcs**, 10km S, has a fine 16C retable by Bréa. The restored Ste-Rosaline chapel has 16C choir-stalls and a modern bronze bas-relief by Giacometti.

ENTRECASTEAUX
VAR

As bizarre and beguiling a set-up as any in Provence is to be found in the château of this tiny medieval village in a valley 26km W of Draguignan. Note the 13C humpback bridge and the formal garden by Le Nôtre, then visit the austere prison-like castle, once strongly fortified. One of its local *seigneurs*, in the 18C, killed his young bride, then vanished into a Portuguese jail. After this the château fell into ruin, but in 1974 was bought by Ian McGarvie-Munn, Scottish nationalist, avant-garde painter, ex-commander-in-chief of the Guatemalan Navy (sic). He restored the place, which since his death in 1981 is run by his son as a museum of his oddly eclectic collections: Scottish bagpipes, Murano goblets, pre-Columbian ceramics, McGarvie-Munn's own Daliesque paintings (some pornographic) – and much else. Classical concerts are held in summer on the lovely terrace.

ENTREVAUX
ALPES-MARITIMES   Pop 700

A fascinating fortified village, built not on a hill, like most in Provence, but by the river Var on the main road, 72km NW of Nice. It has moats and three gates: you pass through one to enter the old village. The ramparts are by Vauban, built in 1695 when the Var was France's frontier with Savoy. There is a Vauban fort on the hill behind. The 17C cathedral, part of the ramparts, is plain outside but contains notable paintings, retable and choir-stalls; the 11C bell-tower was built by the Knights Templar. International festival of 16–17C music in Aug.; costumed procession at the Fête of John the Baptist, weekend nearest to 24 June.

The road along the Gorges de Daluis, to the N, offers superb views of towering red rocks. The medieval town of **Puget-Théniers**, 7km E, has a church with unusual 15C walnut woodcarvings.

ESTEREL, COAST AND MASSIF
ALPES-MARITIMES, VAR

The wild Esterel range with its toothy red-brown rocks, lying beside the coast between St-Raphael and La Napoule, is one of Provence's most distinctive sights. Believed to be a single chunk of volcanic porphyry, one of Europe's oldest land masses, eroded into jagged shapes, it is thick with wild plants and with forests of oak and pine which in recent years have suffered heavily from fires. Until the early 20C the only through-road was the Romans' old Aurelian Way – for centuries a hazardous route, since highwaymen and escaped convicts lurked in the wild ravines. Only in 1903 was a coast road built. If you don't mind rough roads you can drive into the heart of the lonely massif – to the weird rocky gorge of the Mal Infernet, N of Agay, or to points from where you can climb the main peaks, the Pic de l'Ours, Pic du Cap Roux and, further inland, Mont Vinaigre, all with spectacular views.

Main resorts on Esterel coast, E to W: **Théoule** is a lively place, with reddish sandy beaches. From here via **Miramar** to **Le Trayas** the coast is rather built up, but further on there are no beaches and the coast is empty and wild, as the waves dash against bright red rocks and russet crags soar behind. **Port-Galère**, 2.5km S of Théoule, is an extraordinary new holiday 'village' of flats and villas, grafted onto a hillside, designed by the architect Jacques Couelle. It is a honeycomb of uneven facades, yellow, white and pink, some looking like plasticine models or cave-dwellings, in juxtaposed local Mediterranean styles – Greek, Provençal, Moroccan, etc – to create a colourful, hypnotic fantasy that some may think ghastly but others will feel merges harmoniously with the scenery.

To the W, towards St-Raphael, the lively resort of **Agay** lies in a deep bay below the red rocks of the Rastel d'Agay. This has been a natural anchorage since Roman days, and the whole coast here is lined with sandy coves. By the main road at **Le Dramont**, 1km SW, a tablet marks the landing of the 36th US Infantry Division on 15 Aug., 1944. There are fine views from the nearby headland with its semaphore.

The large recently-created artificial lake of **St-Cassien**, between the massif and the Grasse-Draguignan road, is a popular bathing, sailing and windsurfing area.

ÈZE
ALPES-MARITIMES   Pop 2000

Èze, on the coast by the Middle Corniche, is the best-known and most heavily tourist-besieged of all Côte d'Azur hill-villages, largely because of its spectacular location, on a rock 400m sheer above the sea. It has been well restored, and its many tourist boutiques are not too vulgar. Narrow alleys lead up to the Jardin Exotique, with stunning views of the coast.

View from Èze

FONTAINE-DE-VAUCLUSE
VAUCLUSE

This famous fountain springs from a cavern where the river Sorgue emerges from the mountain at the foot of a limestone cliff. In a cascade of spray the waters surge up over a rocky barrier. In winter or spring it is a splendid sight, especially when the snows are melting or after heavy rain; but in the dry season there is little to see. Even so, the fountain attracts over a million visitors annually. The village of the same name, a short walk away, is submerged by tourists: little remains of the serenity that drew the Italian poet Petrarch to live here. A small Petrarch museum stands on the site of the house he lived in, 1337–53. There is also a speleological museum, and *son-et-lumière* mid-June–Sept.

L'Isle-sur-la-Sorgue, 7km W, is a town with running streams and grassy banks. The baroque church is worth a visit, also the 18C woodcarvings in the chapel of the old hospital.

FONTVIEILLE
BOUCHES-DU-RHÔNE   Pop 3000

Alone on a rocky hill above this little town, with views of the Alpilles hills and the plain of Arles, stands the old windmill that inspired Alphonse Daudet (1840–97) to write his famous *Letters*. He actually wrote them in Paris, but often visited the mill when staying in the village. The mill is still in good order; in its beams is Daudet's owl, now stuffed. The basement is a small Daudet museum.

FORCALQUIER
ALPES-DE-HAUTE PROVENCE   Pop 3500

Superbly sited on the slopes of a steep hill, Forcalquier was a powerful feudal capital in the 12C; its Couvent des Cordeliers was one of France's earliest Franciscan monasteries. The cemetery, 1km up the hill, is unusual for its tall box-hedges of neatly clipped yew.

The Observatory of Haute Provence, 13km SW, is a leading state astronomical research centre. The lofty ridge of the **Lure** mountain, 32km to the N, can be reached by car through dense woods: the **Signal de Lure** (1826m) offers spectacular views.

FRÉJUS
VAR   Pop 32,000

On a plain just inland, a dull modern town with, however, some of the most intriguing Roman remains in France – and medieval glories too. Founded in 49BC by Julius Caesar, *Forum Julii* became a major naval base under Augustus who moored here the warships captured from Antony and Cleopatra at Actium in 31BC. The sea has since receded: his port was near the modern town centre, and probably had quays 2km long, with a lighthouse and shipyards. You can still see one tower of the Porte des Gaules; the Porte d'Orée, to the SE, was probably part of the baths. The Lanterne d'Auguste, E of the town, is a medieval tower on a Roman base that probably stood by the harbour. The arena, the oldest in Gaul, has been renovated and is used today for bullfights.

Fréjus

Destroyed by the Saracens in the 10C, Fréjus was rebuilt by Bishop Riculphe who made it an important bishopric. Hence the splendour of the Episcopal City, an ensemble still in good condition. You must take a guided tour. First the guide opens the shutters of the Renaissance doors, to show the carved walnut panels with scenes of Saracen massacres and the life of the Virgin. The octagonal 5C baptistry has a sunken font and two doors: catechumens would enter by one, have their feet anointed by the bishop, then would pass out through the other door, white-robed, for their first communion. The enchanting 12C cloister has a garden with a well, a graceful bell-tower, and a beamed ceiling with tiny painted panels of animals, most of them destroyed in the Revolution. The cathedral, 10–13C, is rather austere. In the Archaeological Museum, the local Roman finds are less attractive than the exquisite Greek vases, brought to Fréjus by the Romans.

Festival: *bravade* costumed procession, third Sun. after Easter.

About 4km N, off the road to Bagnols, is a red-painted mosque, built in 1914–18 by soldiers from the former French Sudan, a replica of the famous Missiri mosque at Djenne. It is now empty and unkempt. Better cared-for is the Buddhist pagoda, 3km NE, by the N7, built as a shrine in the cemetery of 5000 Annamite troops killed in 1914–18; it has a large reclining Buddha and a garden full of cheerful stucco animals. Also off N7, 2km N, is a modern chapel decorated by Cocteau.

The ruined **Malpasset** dam, 11km N, off N7, was the scene of a tragedy in Dec. 1959 when the dam burst after heavy rain, causing floods to sweep through Fréjus, killing 400 people. You can still see the ruins, and the huge pieces of concrete strewn below it by the flood – a haunting sight. **Roquebrune-sur-Argens**, a picturesque hill-village 11km W of Fréjus, lies below the rocky Roquebrune mountain.

GORDES
VAUCLUSE Pop 1550

Many artists and intellectuals, from Paris and elsewhere, spend the summer at Gordes, a large and well-known hill-village on a rocky promontory above the Coulon valley, 38km E of Avignon. Terraces of old houses rise up to the fortified Renaissance château with its two round towers –

Gordes

austere-looking from the outside, but inside full of elegant detail. Victor Vasarély, the artist, who has a summer villa here, has installed in the château his Musée Didactique – more didactic even than his Fondation at Aix (q.v.). His theories on art and geometry are explained in sliding panels, and come alive in tapestries, mosaics and sculptures.

The **Village des Bories**, 3km SW, down a bumpy track off the D2, is an unusual and fascinating museum. A *borie* is a beehive-shaped primitive hut of rough stones, found in France only on the S slopes of the Vaucluse plateau and the N slopes of the Lubéron where they stand singly or in clusters. Some probably date from Ligurian days, but some were lived in till the 18C, possibly occupied at times by town-dwellers fleeing plagues. This 'village' is a group of 12 *bories*, whose last inhabitants left c.1820. It is now a well-designed and informative museum of traditional rural life. Beside the 16C **Bouillons** olive oil mill, 5km S of Gordes, is a museum of the history of stained glass, and a gallery selling stained glass by local artists.

GOURDON
ALPES-MARITIMES Pop 250

High on a rock above the Loup gorge, Gourdon is one of the most dramatically-sited of Provençal hill-villages. Seen from below, its old grey houses appear to be part of the rock. The place is very touristy, but worth visiting for the grandiose views from its terrace and for its 13C castle (good collections of armour and of naive paintings). A road winds down into the gorge, and another follows its bed, past high waterfalls.

The village of **Le Bar-sur-Loup**, just S of Pont du Loup, has a 15C Gothic church with an extraordinary diabolical 15C painting, the *Danse Macabre*, thought to have been done in a time of plague.

GRASSE
ALPES-MARITIMES   Pop 38,000

The world capital of the perfume industry calls itself 'the balcony of the Côte d'Azur': with its long looping boulevards, it is built in terraces along the S slopes of a limestone plateau, facing seaward across a wide vale of flowers, with fine views everywhere. Its sheltered position made it a fashionable winter resort in the 19C: Queen Victoria wintered here often, in the Rothschild villa or the now defunct Grand Hotel. Today, although full of trippers in daytime, Grasse is subdued at night.

In the Middle Ages the main industry was tanning. The perfume industry was then introduced on the initiative of Catherine de Medici (at first related to the tanning because of the 16C vogue for scented gloves). The cultivation of flowers was later introduced to provide the factories with raw materials. Today 30 local factories treat almost 90 per cent of the world's flower essences for perfumes, using mostly local flowers and importing others from 20 countries, such as patchouli from Java. They use annually some 500 tons of roses, 250 of violet, 200 each of mimosa and orange, 130 of local lavender. There are 120,000 rosebuds to a ton, yet this makes just one kilo of scent essence – no wonder good perfumes are expensive.

The Grasse factories are wholesalers, selling their essences in bulk to Dior and the other fashion houses in Paris, New York, etc, who then blend them into their own fancily-named varieties. But much research is done in Grasse, where the laboratory of one big firm, Fragonard, has experts who can distinguish 1500 different scents. The Fragonard factory provides free conducted tours daily, showing the main scent-making processes – distillation, *enfleurage*, extraction – and has its own perfume museum, with old scent bottles, etc, some dating back to classical Greece. The Molinard factory is also open to visits.

The Fragonard firm is named after the painter Jean-Honoré Fragonard (1732–1806) who was born in Grasse, lived and worked mainly in Paris, then returned to live in the villa that is now a small museum dedicated to him: this contains very little of his better work, but there are copies of the panels he painted for Mme du Barry.

The Vieille Ville is attractive, with narrow alleys, steep steps, and fine arcades in the Pl. des Aires. The quarter today is inhabited mainly by

Fragonard statue, Grasse

North African immigrants. On its S side, the former cathedral of Notre-Dame stands impressively on a hilltop. Mostly 12C, restored in the 17C, it has a handsome curving double stairway in front, three paintings by Rubens and, above the sacristy door, a *Washing of the Feet* by Fragonard, one of his rare religious works.

There are many attractive old villages in the lush and lovely countryside around Grasse. **Cabris**, 5km W, a beautiful village on a spur above the Siagne valley, has superb views, notably from the terrace of its ruined castle. It is a sophisticated place, its old houses neatly restored, and has long been a haunt of writers and artists. **St-Vallier-de-Thiey**, 12km NW, is a summer holiday resort on a pastoral plateau where the air is sharp and clear; good hiking centre. Just outside the hill-village of **Opio**, 6km E, is the Roger Michel olive oil mill. Down an ill-marked turning 2km to the S, off the D3, you come to the semi-ruined 11C chapel of Notre-Dame-de-Brusc, alone amid farmland and all boarded-up: beside it are the remains of a 6C baptistry. **Auribeau**, 9km S of Grasse, is a delightful hill-village above the river Siagne: from the terrace of its hilltop church you can admire the Tuscany-like landscape of little hills, with many-coloured flower nurseries and green vineyards. All round here is mimosa country: in Jan. and Feb. the hillsides are a blaze of golden blossom, both wild and cultivated.

GRIGNAN
DRÔME   Pop 1100

In the NW corner of Provence, 28km SE of Montélimar, this old village on a rocky hill is crowned by its impressive Renaissance château. This was once the home of Madame de Grignan, daughter of Madame de Sévigné the writer, who loved the place and often stayed here. She died here in 1696 and is buried in the castle's church (splendid view from its terrace).

HYÈRES
VAR   Pop 41,000

The name makes a good pun, for Hyères is indeed of yesterday. It is the oldest resort on the Côte (Napoleon, Queen Victoria, Tolstoy and R.L. Stevenson were among its fans) but today has gone out of fashion. Its avenues shaded with date-palms wear a faded air. Both Greeks and Romans colonized the place (see their remains in the municipal museum); later it was a port for the Crusades. The sea in those days came much closer to the present town, which is now some 4km inland. In the Vieille Ville, on a slope, you get some idea of the town's importance in the Middle Ages – notably around the handsome 12C Tour St-Blaise, part of a former fortified church, and the 12C church of St-Paul on a hilltop behind.

The ugly modern resort of Hyères-Plage is by the sea to the SE, next to large saltpans. Here an isthmus leads past the lively bathing-station of **La Capte**, where in summer orange and yellow tents fill the pine-woods, to the hilly Giens peninsula. It has a village crowned by a ruined castle. The poet St-John Perse used to live here. At **La Tour Fondue** is a fortress built by Richelieu.

HYÈRES, ÎLES D'
VAR

Three exotic and beautiful islands, where lush subtropical vegetation grows on rugged clifftops; they are known also as the Îles d'Or, because the cliffs glow yellow in the sun. Until the late 17C they were the haunt of pirates.

Porquerolles, the largest, covered with heather, myrtle and pine, is good for picnics and walks (or bicycles can be hired). The S coast is steep and rugged; the N has sandy coves. The one village, built as an army garrison in the 19C, has a big main square with the air of a colonial military post: in its little church is a sequence of Stations of the Cross, carved in wood by a soldier with a penknife, yet remarkably sophisticated. At the *Arche de Noé*, a famous old inn, now rather run-down, you can gawp at the star names in its visitors' book: Chaplin, Mountbatten, King Baudouin, etc.

Port-Cros, the central island, is the most beautiful and strange. Owing to springs, it is lushly vegetated: from the tiny port you can walk through bright green groves to the cove of Port-Man or the Vallon de la Solitude. Port-Cros is owned by the state as a nature preserve: staff run enterprising guided tours in summer, such as underwater scuba-mask explorations of fish and marine flora.

Île du Levant, to the E, has high cliffs and thick foliage. Most of it, closed to visitors, belongs to the French Navy. On the W side is Héliopolis, an early pioneering nudist colony.

JUAN-LES-PINS
ALPES-MARITIMES   Pop 63,000, with Antibes

This suburb of Antibes was made into a fashionable resort by rich Americans in the 1920s: this was the 'bright tan prayer rug of a beach' where Scott Fitzgerald set *Tender is the Night*. Today, few traces of that fabled epoch survive (save perhaps in the two luxury hotels, Juana and Belles-Rives), in what has now become a garish, noisy and rather down-market resort, a haunt of the young. Near the casino, two big open-air cafés with deafening Brazilian orchestras vie with each other in ear-splitting frenzy till 3am. By day, you can still enjoy Juan's fine sandy beach and sheltered position.

Golfe-Juan, 3km W, is another popular bathing-resort. Here on 1 March, 1815, Napoleon landed with 800 men on his return from Elba, and started off along the Route Napoléon to Paris: a memorial to him is by the harbour.

LAVANDOU, LE
VAR   Pop 4000

This old fishing-port has mushroomed into a sizeable bathing resort, with many high-rise flats, and has lost much of its charm. But there are miles of good sandy beaches.

Bormes-les-Mimosa, 5km NW, is a most elegant hill-village, its old houses all pastel shades of pink, blue and yellow – a change from the usual Provençal grey. Mimosa and eucalyptus groves are all around. Beyond the rocky headland of Cap Bénat (most of it military and closed to the public) is the solitary sea-girt fortress of Bregançon, now a

summer residence of the President.

LUBÉRON, MONTAGNE DU
VAUCLUSE

These beautiful hills, between Apt and the Durance valley, run for 56km from W to E. In the 13–16C they were the stronghold of a Protestant sect, the Vaudois: often violent, they destroyed churches in the area, till finally in 1545 François I sent a crusade against them and captured or killed some 2000.

The wilder and higher stretch is to the E, the Grand Lubéron, now a national park: here the peak of Mourre Nègre (1100m), accessible by car, offers stunning views. W of the Lourmarin-Apt road is the Petit Lubéron, a lush plateau with vineyards, beehives and lavender; a scenic road runs along the crest from Bonnieux to Cavaillon, past a forest of tall cedars.

There are many places of interest in the Lubéron. From E to W:

Fort de Buoux is a ruined fortress on a rock above the rugged Buoux gorge, S of Apt; this natural defence point was used by Ligurians, Romans, then Protestants. At **Lourmarin**, a village on the S slopes, the imposing château has fine chimneys and main stairway; concerts are held here in summer; Albert Camus, the writer, is buried in the village cemetery.

At **Bonnieux**, a village facing N, the otherwise uninteresting 19C church contains four magnificent 15C German paintings behind the altar, depicting the martyrdom of Christ. **Ménerbes**, further W, perched above the valley, today has an active colony of artists and intellectuals. Finally, the astonishing **Oppède-le-Vieux** is an ancient village clinging to the side of a rocky cliff. By the 1940s it was almost deserted, but then a few artists and architects took over some of the semi-ruined houses, restored them, and now live in them. Other houses remain in ruins: the contrast is eery.

LUCÉRAM
ALPES-MARITIMES   Pop 700

Though only 24km NE of Nice, this fortified village is still fairly unspoilt, and very picturesque; steep stepped alleys and old houses one above another are built into the mountainside. On the hilltop is the 15C church with rococo decor and six retables by the Bréa family. The splendid treasure includes an unusual 15C silver statuette of Ste Marguerite standing on a dragon.

Amid rock-strewn pine forests, the D21 winds up N into wild sub-alpine scenery, with splendid views. Here **Col de Turini** is a stylish little skiing and summer resort, **Peïra-Cava** a duller one. From the col there are fine mountain drives, to the **Pointe-des-3-Communes** (superb alpine views), and guided rambles in summer to the Vallée des Merveilles.

Coaraze, 19km SW of Lucéram, is another delightful hill-village, with narrow alleys, vaults and arches. Many artists work here: enamelled tiles are a speciality. The village square has enamelled sun dials: Cocteau designed the one by the *mairie*.

MANOSQUE
ALPES-DE-HAUTE PROVENCE Pop 19,000

A medieval town of narrow streets, on a slope above the Durance valley. A circular boulevard marks the site of the former ramparts, from which two fortified 14C gateways survive, notably the high Porte de la Saunerie. Manosque is today a busy agricultural town. The novelist Jean Giono (1895-1970) lived here for many years.

Caradarche, 16km SW, on the wide Durance river, is the site of a leading hydroelectric dam and nuclear research centre. **Gréoux-les-Bains**, 14km SE, a spa town on the Verdon, treats rheumatism, arthritis and chest troubles. The modern baths contain a Roman votive inscription.

MARSEILLE
BOUCHES-DU-RHÔNE Pop 878,000

Capital of the Provence-Côte-d'Azur 'region' and France's leading port, this mighty city is impressively sited around a wide bay, backed by limestone hills. In population it is France's second *commune* but third conurbation (Lyon is larger). It is busy and cosmopolitan, full of interest but noisy and congested, and much of it frankly ugly; the traffic-jams in its criss-cross of drab streets are among Europe's worst. Many Marseillais have mixed French and Levantine blood, for since Roman days the city has been a racial melting-pot. Today it has many thousands of Arab immigrant workers and French *pieds-noirs* repatriates from Algeria, two groups often on bad terms – the recent rise of racial tension in France has been sharpest here. The city also lives up to its reputation for gangsterism and violence. Yet the Marseillais are also industrious, volatile, earthy and humorous – as the film director Marcel Pagnol described them.

A proud people, too – proud of the history of France's oldest town, founded by Greeks from Asia Minor in 600BC. Massilia (as it was called) became the main Greek colony in the west, then played a key role in Roman history, siding with the hapless Pompey against Caesar. Marseille has always lived by trade: the Crusades brought it great affluence, and it came to vie with Genoa and Venice, but in 1721 it suffered heavily from a plague that killed 50,000 people. After 1789 the town backed the Revolution and sent soldiers to Paris where they sang Rouget de l'Isle's new battle hymn so fervently that it was dubbed *La Marseillaise* – and the name has stuck.

The city's greatest era of commercial success came in the mid-19C with the French conquest of North Africa and the opening of the Suez Canal: most of its grand buildings date from then. In the present century, the loss of empire and latterly the world shipping slump have brought a certain decline: some docks lie idle, many workers are jobless. Yet the city has developed and modernized hugely since the war, under its famous and powerful Socialist mayor, Gaston Defferre. Witness the new Métro and new university campuses. Industries include chemicals, engineering, and of course *pastis*. The main focus of life is La Canebière boulevard, sloping down to the Vieux Port, with the modern port to the N.

La Canebière, in the days of sea travel, was one of the world's great streets, when maharajahs, princes and sultans would use its big terrace-cafés as smart meeting-places. In today's jet age, the rich and mighty bypass the city, and the boulevard is a tawdry place lined with cheap stores and cafeterias. The Vieux Port, today used mainly by small fishing and pleasure boats, was the main port till the 19C and is still the city's heart. Two old forts stand at its mouth: St-Jean to the N, St-Nicolas to the S, the latter built by Louis XIV to help control the turbulent Marseillais.

The Old Port, Marseille

Nearby, the basilica of St-Victor provides vivid insights into early Christendom. It is a fortified 11C Gothic church, built above a 5C one, wrecked by the Saracens. This early church now forms the crypt, well restored and much in use. Here are catacombs with sarcophagi, also the tomb of two 3C martyrs, thought to be Volusianus and Fortunatus: only in 1965 were their skeletons discovered, and dated by experts to AD250! From here, the Corniche Président-Kennedy winds along Marseille's splendid southern sea coast, past rocks, sandy coves and smart villas. On the hill above is the city's major landmark, the 19C neo-Byzantine basilica of Notre-Dame-de-la-Garde, topped by a big statue of the Virgin, floodlit at night. This ugly church (Marseille's counterpart of Paris's Sacré-Coeur) is worth a visit (by bus or car) if only for the splendid view from its terrace, and for its absorbing array of sailors' ex-votos.

On the N side of the Vieux Port, the sector as far as the Rue de la Caisserie was blown up by the Germans in 1943, then rebuilt in ugly style: but some fine buildings have survived, notably the *mairie* with its 17C facade. N is an area of picturesque slums, and N again the twin cathedrals of La Major, forming a startling contrast: the delightful little Ancienne Major, pure 12C Romanesque, nestles in the shadow of the huge newer church, a late-19C neo-Byzantine wedding-cake with cupolas and pink-and-white striped stone. N again lies the modern port with its 19km of quays, handling 20 million tons of goods a year.

Marseille has many fascinating museums:
Built in the 1860s, the typically grandiose Palais Longchamp, with its big mossy fountain, houses a museum in each of its wings. The Musée des Beaux-Arts has one of the best collections in the French provinces. Note especially: Michel Serre's two graphic canvases of Marseille in the 1721

plague; good works by Rubens, Jan Brueghel, Corot, etc; savage political cartoons by Daumier (who was born in Marseille); vivid cartoon-like murals by Puvis de Chavannes; and two rooms devoted to Pierre Puget, the great Marseillais sculptor. The adjacent Musée d'Histoire Naturelle has stuffed animals, skeletons of whales, etc, and an aquarium of gaudy fish. Those who prefer live animals will find a large but unkempt zoo in the park behind the palace.

The Musée Grobet-Labadié, close by, houses a former local musician's eclectic but harmonious collection, which he bequeathed to the city: porcelain, tapestries, paintings, old instruments, etc, all rather beautiful.

Down by the old port, the extraordinary Roman Docks Museum is a real Roman remain, for it comprises the original docks in their actual setting, unearthed when this area was destroyed in the war. The quay and the *dolia* (grain storage jars) are just as they were; Roman amphorae and anchors from local wrecks have been added. To the E, the remains of the Greek town and port of the 3-2C BC have recently been cleverly transformed into a small public garden: you can walk on lawns amid the ruins of quays, ramparts, etc. The Musée du Vieux Marseille, in the 16C Maison Diamante (with faceted facade) has a rich and varied folk-art collection of Camoin playing-cards, 18C furniture, maps and models of old Marseille and, notably, a wonderful array of *santons*, Nativity cribs and tableaux. The Marine Museum has models of sailing and steamships; the Musée Cantini contains Provençal faience and modern sculptures.

Lastly, by the sea in the S suburbs, the Borély park contains a botanical garden and also the 18C Château Borély, with three interesting museums. That of Archaeology houses one of Europe's finest collections of Egyptiana, including mummies, as well as Roman and Greek ceramics, and a Minoan wine-pitcher of c.1400BC. On the floor above is the Feuillet de Borsat collection of 18C French drawings (Greuze, etc). In an outhouse, the Lapidary Museum has varied exhibits: its star item is a 3C BC sanctuary reconstructed from recent finds at Roquepertuse, near Aix (note the portico decorated with skulls). On the Blvd Michelet, 2km inland, is Le Corbusier's famous 17-storey 'dwelling unit' (1952), a pioneering work and one of the few that the great Swiss architect ever created in his adoptive land.

Festivals include the *santons* fair, last two weeks Dec.; and the international trade fair, early Apr. and last two weeks Sept.

Boats ply regularly to the **Château d'If**, the famous fortress on an islet 3km offshore, built in 1524. It was long used as a state prison, for such inmates as 'the Man in the Iron Mask': you are shown the carvings left by Huguenot prisoners, and a terrible windowless cell where those with life sentences were left to perish. NW of Marseille, the **Chaîne de l'Estaque**, one of the three barren limestone ranges that surround Marseille, has wild scenery that Cézanne often painted; the 6km **Canal de Rove**, tunnelled under the hill in 1920, has been out of use since 1963 because of a landslip. The limestone Étoile range, NE of the city, offers many fine views; also old windmills at Allauch,

and a Provençal folk museum at Château-Guibert. Just W of the industrial town of **Aubagne**, the French Foreign Legion today has its HQ: you can visit its museum. Finally, the bare and craggy Marseilleveyre massif encloses the bay on its S side: take the corniche road S to Callelongue, then – if you like tough treks – climb up to the massif's peak (430m) for a dazzling view of city and coast.

MARTIGUES
BOUCHES-DU-RHÔNE   Pop 38,000

This old fishing village has now swelled into a dormitory town for the new industries of Fos and the Étang de Berre; but the pretty canals of the old quarter have not lost the appeal that drew Corot and Ziem to paint them. On the central **Île de Brescon**, take a look at the Pont St-Sebastien and the Baroque church of Ste-Madeleine. Two small museums, Vieux-Martigue and Beaux-Arts, have folklore exhibits and canvases by Ziem. In the W suburbs is an imposing new suspension bridge. To the N, the chapel of Notre-Dame-des-Marins stands solitary on a hilltop where there are good views of the Berre/Fos industries.

MAURES, MASSIF AND COAST
VAR

This huge wooded massif of schistous rock lies along the coast for 56km from Fréjus to Hyères. Its name comes from the Provençal *maouro*, 'dark' (because of its glowering forests) and not from *Maures*, i.e. the Moors (Saracens) who held and pillaged the area in the 9–10C. The wild interior, still quite unspoilt, is covered with rare plants and flowers, also with forests of cork oak and chestnut that are the basis of two local industries: the making of corks for bottles and of *marrons glacés*. Winding through the heart of the massif, several scenic roads provide sweeping views of coast and hills: from Le Lavandou and Bormes, for example, go to the rocky peak of **Pierre d'Avenon**, or on via the **Col de Babaou** to the ruined monastery of the **Chartreuse de la Verne**; then go close to **La Sauvette**, the highest peak (780m), and on to **La Garde Freinet** and **Plan-de-la-Tour** (where the Club Méditerranée has one of its very few summer 'villages' in France). **La Garde Freinet**, an attractive village with a ruined Saracen castle, is frequented by actors, writers, etc: Jeanne Moreau has a villa here.

Save for the old port of St-Tropez (q.v.), the Maures coast was unpopulated till the modern tourist boom. Now it is one string of bathing-resorts whose high-rise blocks have only partly spoilt the gorgeous scenery. This is at its best on the Corniche des Maures, where **Cavalière**, **Rayol** and **Cavalaire** are lively resorts.

MENTON
ALPES-MARITIMES   Pop 25,000

Menton, set along a wide bay, is the warmest of Côte d'Azur resorts, thanks to the sheltering mountains behind which give mild and balmy winters. Hence the profusion of semi-tropical plants and fruit, including the famous acres of lemon groves. Gently nostalgic, Menton is also the prettiest and least brash of big resorts on this coast. An obscure fishing-village till the 1850s, it was then 'discovered' by the English gentry, followed by other aristocrats, and became a chic resort. Today the British resident population, once 5000, is down to 120; and the palace hotels along the front, the Balmoral, Bristol, etc, have been pulled down or turned into holiday flats. Yet echoes of the old days linger – for example, the Anglican church with its tea-parties, and Katherine Mansfield's villa near the Jardin Botanique Exotique.

To the W of the port is the graceful palm-lined Promenade du Soleil; to the E are new marinas and beaches. Behind rise the steep alleys of the Vieille Ville, where steps lead up to the 17C church of St-Michel and the chapel of the Pénitents Blancs, both imposingly Baroque. Menton is Jean Cocteau's town: by the harbour, the little Musée Cocteau has stage sets, tapestries and vivid harlequin paintings by this versatile artist; in the town hall, the Salle des Mariages was decorated by Cocteau in 1957 with appealingly joyous scenes of love and marriage.

The Musée Municipal has varied arrays of painting (moderate) and folk art, but is strongest on prehistory and archaeology: note the famous 'Grimaldi Man' skull (c.30,000BC), found in a cave on the shore. The big ornamental garden of Les Colombières, on a hillside, was laid out by Ferdinand Bac, humorist writer and alleged bastard son of Napoleon III: once no doubt lovely, it is now sadly run-down. The strange villa in its grounds, designed by Bac in Hellenic-cum-Roman style, has arches, statues and frescoes: it also has bedrooms to let with Roman-style sunken baths. Or you can take lemon tea and admire the view.

The lemon festival is held in Feb. and a chamber music festival in first half Aug.

On a hill top above the town, good view from the terrace of the Annonciade monastery (closed). To the NW, **Ste-Agnès** and **Gorbio** are strikingly situated hill-villages.

MONACO (AND MONTE-CARLO)

INDEPENDENT PRINCIPALITY   Pop 24,600

With the exception of the Vatican, no other sovereign state so tiny exerts such dynamism, or holds such wealth, as this 468-acre strip of land between mountains and sea, much of it now full of skyscrapers. Here Prince Rainier III still rules like a Medici from his palace on the headland of the Old Town which, like his principality, is called Monaco; across the harbour stands the newer district, Monte-Carlo. Monaco has its own stamps and diplomatic service; but it uses French coinage and relies on France for defence and most utilities. Only 4500 of its inhabitants are Monegasque citizens (most are French or Italian) and they pay no income tax.

Rainier is a scion of the Grimaldi family, once mighty, that won Monaco from the Genoese in 1308. It managed to remain independent when the

Monte Carlo

rest of the Nice area was ceded to France in 1860, but it lost prosperous Menton and this soon spelt bankruptcy. So Prince Charles III decided to build a casino (these were still banned in France). It was opened in 1865, on a bare rock named Monte-Carlo in his honour – and soon aristocrats were crowding here to enjoy the new sport of gambling. Monaco became rich, and famous, overnight.

It has stayed rich, but only by again adapting. In 1949, when Rainier, aged 25, came to the throne, Monaco was in decline. Since then he and his associates have astutely modernized the place. A giant new convention complex, built out over the sea, symbolizes the prince's policy of 'business tourism'; big banks have been enticed by the low taxes; new casinos, nightclubs, beaches and ports have been built on land reclaimed from the sea. In short, just as Victorian Monte-Carlo had an English flavour, so it is now Americanized — 'Las-Vegas-plage' is one sneer. Yet this town of many faces, though in some ways vulgar, also retains a true glamour, a hypnotic appeal for bejewelled high society. Ex-Hollywood star Princess Grace was its very symbol. Her death in 1982, in a car accident in the hills behind, slowed its pulse for a while. But today it throbs as fast as ever.

On the headland, the Royal Palace dates in part from the 13C but was rebuilt in the 19C – hence its mock-Moorish crenellated towers. Any day you can watch the changing of the guard, but the interior is open to visitors only when the prince is away: then you can see the arcaded courtyard, throne room, and the Brueghels, Holbeins, etc. The museum in one wing has souvenirs of Napoleon and of Monaco's history. The nearby Cathedral (1875–1903) is in showy Neo-Romanesque style but does hold two retables, c.1500, by Bréa. Close by is the huge and celebrated Oceanographic Museum, the world's finest: it was created in 1910 by Prince Albert I, a passionate oceanographer, who made 24 voyages in his big yachts and brought back many rare seabed species. Exhibits include skeletons of whales, elaborate displays of marine technology, and Europe's best aquarium with its 60 tanks of every kind of fish. The museum's director is Commander Jacques Cousteau, the explorer. Just W of the headland is a rather cramped little zoo, and, on the hillside, a fine Exotic Garden, with over 1000 kinds of cacti. Nearby are some stalactite-filled caves, once the homes of Neolithic people, and a small museum with relics found in the caves and elsewhere.

Beyond the harbour is Monte Carlo, where a smart formal garden with tropical trees slopes down to the famous Casino, its four towers rising high above a terrace by the sea. It was designed in neo-baroque style by Charles Garnier, architect also of the Paris Opera. Here in 1887 a Briton, Charles Wells, was 'The Man who Broke the Bank. . .' The *salles privées*, formerly reserved for special players and high stakes, are now no more private then the *salles publiques* and have the same entrance fee (but you must wear a tie). Although in some rooms slot-machines flash and click, and most of the gamblers are dressed any-old-how – yet the majestic decor, recently restored, recalls the age of white-tie-and-tails – an incongruous scene. The Casino building also contains an ornate Opera House by Garnier, once one of Europe's greatest: Diaghilev here created his Ballets Russes. Today there is still an opera company here, though no more ballet. Facing the Casino is the vast and opulent Hôtel de Paris, built in 1864 for the kings, queens and other grandees then flooding in. Although the sight of flowery Bermuda shorts amid the neo-baroque decor of the cathedral-like foyer is somewhat bizarre, it is worth going in for a drink or just for a peek – also to the Hôtel Hermitage, a Belle Époque wonder with its lovely winter garden foyer. For a total contrast, take a look too at the massive new 622-bedroom Loews Hotel, American-owned, American-geared, brash and amusing. Such is modern Monte.

The sea-promenade N leads past another contrast: the National Museum, in an elegant villa, with one of the world's best collections of dolls and mechanical toys, notably a big 18C Neapolitan crib with 300 figures. Further on is the gigantic new Sporting Club, oddly-named for, in fact, it is a series of night-clubs, summer capital of Monte-by-night where *le très beau monde* dances amid romantic settings of floodlit lake and trees at *Jimmy's* or *Chez Régine*.

Monaco has many other night-clubs, and every kind of sport despite its tight urban setting: beaches of imported sand, health centres, yachting, tennis, golf (on the plateau behind), etc. Festivals and other events go on all year round: notably: Jan., Monte-Carlo car rally; Feb., TV festival; Apr., Tennis championships; May, Monaco Grand Prix; Nov., Monaco national fête.

MONT VENTOUX
VAUCLUSE

Highest W spur of the alpine massif, the lonely pyramid of Mont Ventoux (1900m) dominates the E side of the Rhône valley, visible from far away. It is Provence's highest peak, apart from the Alps. Both from W and E good roads lead up to the summit, where there are radar and TV posts, etc. The views are unbeatable – from the Alps to the Pyrenees on a clear day. At night, lighthouses flash along the coast. To avoid the noonday haze, the best time to ascend in summer is early morning or late afternoon. In winter, skies are often clearer but the mistral howls. Near the summit are alpine flowers – even polar ones such as the hairy poppy of Greenland. Skiing at Mont-Serein and Château-Reynard.

Mont Ventoux

To the SE is **Sault**, a village on a rocky spur; SW from here are the wild and impressive **Nesque** gorges (good road along N cliff). S stretches the limestone plateau of Vaucluse, holed with some 200 caves.

N and NE of Mt Ventoux lies the lovely scenic region of the **Baronnies**: here limestone crags stand above fertile valleys where vine and olive, cherry, almond and lavender are cultivated. Good views from the Col d'Ey, N of Buis, and farther E from the Col de Perty and the Col St-Jean.

MOUGINS
ALPES-MARITIMES   Pop 10,000

This hill-village, 7km N of Cannes, is today the kernel of a wealthy and sophisticated suburban area where rather grand people have villas. Though much tarted-up, the village has not lost its character: it has a 15th-century fortified gate, and a Romanesque church with a fine view from its tower. The lovely chapel of Notre-Dame-de-Vie, alone on a hill to the E, has a 15C stone cross and Roman inscriptions. Picasso lived his final years, and died, at the *mas* of Notre-Dame-de-Vie.

Smart people come to play golf at the fashionable Cannes Country Club, nearby, or to eat – and be seen – at Mougins's many excellent restaurants. Best known of these is *Le Moulin*, a 16C olive-mill run with panache by its lordly patron-chef Roger Vergé, one of the pioneers of *nouvelle cuisine*.

NAPOULE, LA
ALPES-MARITIMES   Pop 10,000

A busy seaside resort between Cannes and the Esterel, with good sandy beaches and yachting marina, and one of Provence's best restaurants, *L'Oasis*. The big pinkish medieval castle by the harbour, floodlit orange at night, belonged to the bizarre American sculptor Henry Clews, who restored it, lived and worked there, and on his death in 1937 was buried there. Today it contains a museum of his work, notably his peculiar sculptured grotesques of birds, animals and gnarled naked humans – inspired, it is said, by Negro and pre-Columbian carvings. If you find them distasteful, you can at least enjoy the gardens. The château also houses a Franco-American cultural centre.

NICE

ALPES-MARITIMES   Pop 338,000

Protected by steep hills behind, the Côte d'Azur's capital curves round the gleaming shore of the Baie des Anges. It is not just the doyen of European coastal resorts but also a true metropolis, at once commercial, chic and down-to-earth, with a bustling all-year life of its own – thus in many ways more appealing then smaller resorts such as Cannes that are mainly for tourists.

Greeks in the 4C BC founded Nice, and to mark a defeat of local Gauls they called it Nikêa (from Niké, goddess of victory). Then the Romans built a sizeable town at Cimiez, on the hills behind, which the Saracens later wrecked. Nice began to prosper after c.1100, first under the counts of Provence, then under the Italian house of Savoy, and in c.1450–1550 was the focus of a major school of religious painting, led by the Bréa family. Nice suffered a terrible plague in 1631. It stayed under Savoy till 1860 and was then annexed to France by treaty and local plebiscite. By then Nice was a busy seaside resort, due mainly to the English, who had started to winter here in the late 18th century, led in 1763 by the novelist Tobias Smollett. In 1822 the large English colony built a coastal path which later became the famous Promenade des Anglais. The tourist boom grew faster after the railway came in 1864: led by Queen Victoria and the Tsars, aristocrats poured in, the Russians built their cathedral, and chic hotels with names like Westminster appeared along the front. A few traces of that splendour survive; but since the Belle Époque, Nice has had to widen its appeal and today caters less for princes and film stars than for the package tour and congress trade.

The town is in two very different parts. To the E of the dry Pailion riverbed, and below the rocky hill where the castle once stood, is the Vieille Ville with its curving alleys; W of the Paillon stretches the newer town and the mighty promenade with its palms and palace-hotels. It is no place for sea-bathing (the beach is shingle) but offers all the fun and culture of a big town, not least the celebrated Battle of Flowers and Lenten Carnival. There are many light industries and a new university.

The Vieille Ville, its narrow alleys full of little shops and bistros, is noisy, plebeian and rather Italian – you could be in Genoa. Here are some fine Italian baroque churches; the Opera House; and the Palais Lascaris, a handsome 17C mansion, sumptuously furnished. Here too, in the Cours Saleya, are Nice's lavish and colourful flower, fruit and vegetable markets; and, in the nearby Rue St-François, the even more exotic fish market. On the hill above, the Greeks put their acropolis and the dukes of Savoy then set their castle, which was destroyed in 1706 by Marshal de Berwick, bastard son of James II of England. Today the spot is a public garden. The naval museum, on the SW side, has paintings of 19C Nice. To the E is Nice's lively harbour, where ferries leave for Corsica.

The Pl. Masséna, heart of modern Nice, has arcaded Genoese-style houses dating from 1830. To the W is the graceful Jardin Albert 1er, and the animated Rue Masséna, now an attractive pedestrian zone and smart social centre. Take a peep inside the wedding-cake Hôtel Negresco, carefully restored to its original 1912 style (the bell-boys still wear white gloves and red breeches): its flamboyant ground-floor lavatories are worth a visit, and its restaurant, the *Chantecler*, is one of France's best for *nouvelle cuisine*.

About 1km inland, the sumptuous Russian Orthodox cathedral (1903) has five green-gold onion-shaped cupolas, and rich ikons around the altar. You can still hear old folks talking Russian here, even though Nice's once huge Russian colony is fading away. At Cimiez, on a hill in the N suburbs, is the old Roman settlement, now excavated: you can see the amphitheatre, and the remains of baths and of a temple of Apollo. The former monastic church holds three fine Bréa retables. Cimiez with its big villas used to be Nice's smartest quarter: the gigantic rococo hideosity just W of the Arena is the former Hotel Excelsior where Queen Victoria used to winter. Today it is a block of flats: *sic transit . . .*

Main museums in Nice:

The Masséna, housed in an Empire-style 1890s palace, contains Bréa primitives; also fascinating souvenirs of Nice's history, of the Carnival, etc, and of the city's two most famous sons, Garibaldi (1807–82) and Masséna, one of Napoleon's greatest marshals. The Chéret, Nice's leading museum of painting, has Italian and Flemish primitives, a wide range of Impressionists (notably Renoir), a number of works by the Van Loo family (who worked locally), and a splendid array of Dufys. Up at Cimiez is the celebrated Musée Matisse: he lived and worked for many years in Nice and Cimiez, died there in 1954, and lies buried in Cimiez cemetery. There are sketches, models, sculptures, and 30 paintings that span his career, leading up to the vivid colours of his later years. In the same building is an archaeological museum of local Roman finds.

Nice

Above all, Nice's cultural glory is the Musée Marc Chagall – the world's finest collection of the works of this sublime artist who was born in Russia in 1887. Opened in 1973, the museum was created specially for his 'Biblical Message', a suite of 17 big canvases painted in 1954–67. Twelve of them, in one room, evoke the *Creation* and other biblical themes; five others are inspired by the *Song of Songs*. His naive and lyrical sense of fantasy, his vivid sensuous colours, and the power of his humanistic and spiritual beliefs, based on his Jewish faith, combine to create a shattering effect.

Nice's main festival is the Carnival, dating back to the 13C: a mind-blowing spectacle of fantasy floats and grotesques, costumed ladies on white horses, noisy brass bands, coloured rockets, confetti, and much else – all, today, more professional than spontaneous. It fills the two weeks preceding Lent, culminating in fireworks on Shrove Tuesday and a flower battle on the day after Ash Wednesday (there are other flower battles in summer). Among other events are a major jazz festival in July and a wine festival in Aug., both at Cimiez.

There are good views of the coast and city from Mont Alban, Mont Boron and other hilltops behind Nice. The Corniches of the Riviera are three famous roads, one above the other, along the side of the steep coast between Nice, Monaco and Menton. The Basse Corniche follows the coast; above it, the Moyenne Corniche, N7, was built in 1910–14; the Grande (upper) Corniche, was first built by Napoleon on Roman tracks. A fourth and even higher road, the A8 autoroute to Italy, was added in the 1970s.

NÎMES
GARD   Pop 134,000

Nîmes's claim for itself, 'the Rome of France', may be excessive: but it does contain two of the world's best-preserved Roman buildings, the Arena and the Maison Carrée. Augustus, after his Egyptian campaign, settled thousands of veterans here: hence the crocodile chained to a palm-tree, on the city's crest today. This is now a large, dusty, not very elegant commercial city, its main industries being shoe-making, fruit-canning and textiles. A rough cloth for overalls was first made here in the 19C and sold abroad as 'de Nîmes' (the name was soon contracted to 'denim'). Nimes, at the border of Languedoc and Provence, belongs really to both. Like all Languedoc, it has always been fiercely hostile to the central power in Paris. In the 16C it was a main base of the Huguenot 'heretics' and then played a big role in the revolt of the Protestant *camisards*.

The Arena (21,000 spectators) is one of the best preserved of the 70 extant from Roman times. In the 5C if became a fortress; from the 13C, a tenement inhabited by 2000 poor people who built 150 houses. The Romans used it for chariot races, also for fights between gladiators and wild beasts – a tradition now resumed, with many bullfights in summer.

The Maison Carrée ('square house' – but in fact rectangular), built in Hellenic style by Agrippa in 20BC, is one of the loveliest and best preserved of surviving Roman temples. Since the Middle Ages

Maison Carrée, Nîmes

it has been used as the town hall, a private house, a stable, a church and now a museum (the walled *cella* contains local Roman finds, notably a statue and a bronze head of Apollo, and the 'Venus of Nîmes', found in pieces and reassembled). The temple stands on a raised platform: its peristyle of fluted Ionic columns has delicate carvings.

Just to the NW, the ornamental 18C Jardin de la Fontaine lies on the site where the Romans, finding a spring here, built baths, a theatre and temple. Of all this, only the vast ruin of the Temple of Diana survives. High on the wooded hill behind stands the curious Tour Magne, built by the Romans probably as a watchtower. From its top (today shorn of its original 10m section) there are breathtaking views of the city and mountains.

The gracious and picturesque old quarter of Nîmes, N of the Arena, contrasts sharply with the rest of humdrum modern Nîmes. There are lovely Renaissance houses in the Rues de Bernis, des Marchands and de l'Aspic, a pedestrian zone. The 11C cathedral of St-Castor has been largely rebuilt: but the friezes of scenes from Genesis, on its facade, are originals. Of the town's three main museums, that of Vieux Nîmes is devoted to costumes, pottery and bullfighting; that of Archaeology has objects depicting Gallo-Roman daily life; that of Beaux-Arts contains, beside some second-rate works by Rubens, etc, a big Roman mosaic found at Nîmes, believed to depict the marriage of Admetus.

The Feria de Pentecôte, held for five days over Whitsun (Thurs.–Mon.), with bullfights, folklore, concerts, dancing in streets, etc, is one of the great French festivals. There are jazz and folklore festivals, July–Aug., and bullfights to-the-death on most Sun. afternoons from May–Oct., in the Arena.

Source Perrier, 14km SW, is an underground spring, sole source of the famous sparkling mineral water. Today French-owned and selling some 650 million bottles a year, half for export, the spring was first commercialized by an Englishman, St-John Harmsworth of the newspaper dynasty, who bought it in 1903. The guided tour starts with a film showing production methods, including the quarrying of sand from Mont Ventoux to make the tapering green bottles.

ORANGE
VAUCLUSE Pop 26,000

The theatre and arch, two of the noblest of Roman monuments, dominate this pleasant old town which lies amid vineyards in the Rhône valley. The Romans called it *Arausio*, hence the name 'Orange' which has nothing to do with the fruit. By Augustus's time it was a prosperous city, with massive baths, temples, stadium and arena. In the 13C it became a small principality, and in the 16C was inherited by William, Prince of Nassau, ancestor of today's Dutch royalty. He liked the town so much that he called his dynasty the House of Orange – and so today, through former Dutch overseas connections, the name 'Orange' is still borne by a river and state in South Africa and by the Protestants of Ulster. The town was annexed to France in 1713.

When Prince Maurice of Nassau fortified his city in 1622, he used stones from the temples, baths, etc: hence little of these survive. Being part of the defence system, the arch and theatre were spared. The big triumphal arch was built to mark Julius Caesar's victories over the Greek fleet of Massilia which had backed Pompey, and over local Gauls; a high central frieze and nautical emblems depict these victories. The theatre, which held 7000 people, is the finest of any surviving from the Roman era. Its facade, an imposing wall of reddish sandstone, 35m high, has lost its three tiers of columns and statues: but the 3m statue of Augustus was replaced in 1935. The stone blocks above supported poles carrying awnings to protect against the sun. The best view of the theatre and

town is from the hill of St-Eutrope, to the S. The town museum has marble pieces of a Roman cadastral survey, the only one of its kind extant.

In July a music and opera festival is held in the Roman theatre (superb acoustics).

The vineyards around **Châteauneuf-du-Pape**, 13km S, once belonged to the Avignon popes, hence the name. Today they produce one of the best Côtes du Rhône wines. Only one tower survives of the summer villas built here by the popes. At **Sérignan**, 8km NE of Orange, is the former home of the entomologist J.-H. Fabre (1823–1915), now a museum.

PONT DU GARD
GARD

This noble Roman monument was built across the Gard in 19BC, by Agrippa, as part of the 48km aqueduct supplying Nîmes. Its building still amazes engineers, for its blocks of stone weigh up to 6 tons each. After some 19C restoration it is today in near-perfect condition, its arches of golden stone harmonizing with the landscape. The best view is from 90m upstream on the right bank; near here, a path leads to the upper tier of arches (the one that carried the water) which can easily be walked across.

Pont du Gard

PORT-GRIMAUD
VAR

This modern luxury holiday village, built since the 1960s on the shore of the bay of St-Tropez, is generally regarded as a major architectural triumph, a showpiece of the current return to the vernacular. The Alsatian architect François Spoerry has conceived a clever pastiche that is part Provençal fishing-port, part small-scale Venice. There are no roads, only canals and alleys, linked by graceful arched bridges; the houses are in a variety of gay colours, and the overall effect is one of great harmony. The place is built for yachtsmen: each house has its own mooring by its front door. Tourists can tour the canals in a hired boat.

About 5km W, the old hill-village of **Grimaud**, tastefully restored, is overlooked by the craggy half-ruined towers of an old Grimaldi castle. **Cogolin**, 3km S of Grimaud, is an active centre of cottage industries: corks, briar pipes, clarinet pipes, carpets, etc. Some workshops can be visited.

Orange

RIEZ
VAUCLUSE Pop 1600

This tiny town between the Durance and Verdon valleys was a major religious centre both in Roman and early Christian times. Some relics survive from those days. In a meadow on the W side of the town are the remains of a 1C Roman temple: four granite columns with white marble Corinthian capitals. Nearby, across the river, is a 5C Merovingian baptistry, similar to those at Aix and Fréjus (see entries). Westward lies the high Valensole plateau, main lavender-producing region of France – best visited in July, when hills and fields are purple with fragrant lavender.

ROQUEBRUNE-CAP-MARTIN
ALPES-MARITIMES Pop 12,000

This straggling commune consists of (a) Cap-Martin on the coast SW of Menton; (b) the modern resort; (c) the old hill-village of Roquebrune, high above the Upper Corniche. Cap-Martin with its pine and olive woods has long been a haunt of the rich and famous: the Empresses Sissi of Austria and Eugénie of France first made it fashionable; later residents or regular visitors have included Churchill, Yeats (he died here in 1939) and Le Corbusier (he was drowned off the cape in 1965).

In medieval Roquebrune, elegantly restored, steep stairways and alleys curve up under Romanesque arches to the feudal hilltop castle. Here two colourful costumed processions have taken place each year since 1467, in fulfilment of a vow made then by the villagers which is said to have saved them from the plague. The dates are Good Friday and 5 Aug.

ROUSSILLON
VAUCLUSE Pop 1000

Capital of the ochre country, where the earth and rocks are bright red for miles around; quarrying has slashed the cliffs into bizarre shapes, some now bearing fancy names such as 'Needles of the Fairy Vale'. Roussillon, a very pretty old hilltop village, has houses in every shade of red, pink and orange and has long attracted artists; today it is a fashionable centre of painters, writers, etc. Laurence Wylie, the American sociologist, lived here and wrote a famous book about Roussillon, *Village in the Vaucluse* (1961), describing the impact of modernism on an archaic peasant community.

ST-CÉZAIRE
ALPES-MARITIMES Pop 1500

A village on a cliff above the deep Siagne gorge; in its outskirts is a Romanesque 12C chapel with a Roman sarcophagus. The remarkable grottoes, 3km NE, formed by a glacier 4 million years ago, were discovered by chance in 1890. The many stalagmites and stalactites, cleverly lit, are in bizarre shapes ('the fairy's bed', 'the gulf of hell', etc) and also musical.

St-Jean-Cap-Ferrat

ST-JEAN-CAP-FERRAT
ALPES-MARITIMES

An entrancingly beautiful peninsula, with many rocky coves, and full of flowers, pines and palms. Nearly all of it has been acquired by the rich and famous for their opulent villas and exotic gardens, so it is unsuitable terrain for scenic walks: but you can walk round the Pointe St-Hospice, or climb up to the lighthouse for a splendid view. St-Jean itself is a lively fishing-village.

The Villa Mauresque, near the S cape, is where Somerset Maugham spent his last years, much provoked by inquisitive tourist intruders. The Villa les Cèdres, W of St-Jean, once owned by King Leopold II of Belgium, has a fine garden. Part of it is now a large and well-kept private zoo, with a wide range of animals in outdoor cages.

Star feature of this all-but-isle is the Ephrussi de Rothschild museum, in an Italianate villa designed by the Baroness de Rothschild to house her treasures, then bequeathed by her to the Académie des Beaux Arts. This rich collection, typifying the Rothschilds' eclectic tastes, ranges from the 14C to 19C: Aubusson tapestries, Sèvres and Dresden china, Renaissance and Victorian furniture, paintings by Fragonard, Renoir. The ornamental garden has lily ponds and exotic flowers. Concerts and plays are held in the villa in summer.

ST-MARTIN-VÉSUBIE
ALPES-MARITIMES Pop 1200

This alpine summer resort, 65km N of Nice, is quite smart yet preserves an old-world charm, notably in the Rue du Dr-Cagnoli. The finely decorated 17C church has a sumptuously dressed 13C wooden statue of the Virgin which every 2 July is taken in procession to the high and isolated 14C sanctuary of the Madone de Fenestre.

At the entrance to the charming hill-village of **Venanson**, 5km S, is the tiny chapel of Ste-Claire, its inside walls and ceilings covered with vivid 15C frescoes of the life of St Sebastian.

Le Boréon is the point of access for the Mercantour national park (no cars, dogs or guns allowed), a wildlife reserve where you can hike or, in summer, learn mountain-climbing. **Valdeblore**, 10km W of St-Martin, is a scattered modern ski-resort amid fine scenery, where you can learn to ski in winter and take rock-climbing or hang-gliding courses in summer. Alternatively, take the funicular to the Pic de Colmiane. Valdeblore's tragic name (*val des pleurs* – vale of tears) derives from the true tale of a local lord who locked up his wives and starved them to death, ignoring their tears.

ST-MAXIMIN-LA-STE-BAUME
VAR   Pop 4000

The great basilica of Ste-Marie-Madeleine, Provence's finest Gothic building, stands in the middle of this busy market town, named after the saint who, so the legend goes, accompanied the three Marys to Provence (see *Camargue*) and was then martyred in Aix. The tombs in its crypt have been worshipped as his and Mary Magdalene's: even if there is little real evidence for this, its four sarcophagi are certainly among the oldest Christian relics in France. The building of the abbey began in 1295 and took over 200 years. In the Revolution it was saved from destruction because Bonaparte's young brother Lucien was stationed in the town and used it as a military warehouse.

With its lovely high vaulted nave and polygonal apse, the church has a feeling of space and light. Note the 17C choir-screen, fine 18C organ, the big pulpit carved from one piece of wood, and the unusual 16C retable by Antonio Ronzen of Venice, its 16 panels depicting the life and passion of Christ against European backgrounds.

ST-PAUL-DE-VENCE
ALPES-MARITIMES   Pop 2500

A beautiful and famous hill-village that has kept intact its 16C ramparts: you can walk round them, above a landscape still rather gorgeous despite the rash of modern building. St-Paul has long been a magnet for artists. Today it is a highly sophisticated and cultured place, elegantly restored: mosaic-paved alleys, piazzas with fountains, and on the hilltop a 12C church rich in art: e.g. a *Ste-Catherine* attributed to Tintoretto.

St-Paul-de-Vence

Above all, St-Paul is a marvellous place for modern art. At the entrance to the village, La Colombe d'Or is a famous little luxury hotel, full of old-world character, whose owners, the Roux family, have been art collectors and friends of artists: hence the Braque by the swimming-pool, Léger in the patio, Picasso and Matisse in the dining-room, and many other such works that would be the envy of any museum. More important still is the Fondation Maeght, just NW of St-Paul, a superb and unusual modern art museum created in 1964 by the Paris art dealer Aimé Maeght and designed by the Spanish architect J.L. Sert. The very striking pink-and-white building with its curious inverted domes is set amid pine-trees in a beautifully landscaped hilly garden. Inside are fine works by Bonnard, Braque, Chagall and many others; outside, remarkable sculptures by Giacometti, Arp, Hepworth, mobiles by Calder, fanciful mosaics and fountains by Miro. The Fondation also has a library and a cinema for art films, and holds special exhibitions.

ST-RAPHAËL
VAR   Pop 24,000

Known as 'the Bournemouth of France', this biggish, sedate, rather unfashionable resort is popular with families because of its good sandy beaches and marina, and is sheltered by the Esterel massif. It was settled by the Romans (note the many amphorae in the museum of Underwater Archaeology) and has an elegant 12C church of the Templiers. Bonaparte sailed from here for his Elba exile in 1814; Gounod composed *Roméo et Juliette* here in 1866. Valescure, on the high slopes behind, was once popular with the English as a smart winter health resort, but its grandiose Edwardian hotels are now empty or used as flats. Its famous golf course, founded 1891, is still active.

ST-RÉMY-DE-PROVENCE
BOUCHES-DU-RHÔNE   Pop 8000

Birthplace of the astrologer Nostradamus, St-Rémy is an agreeable market town in a rich plain. It has two modest museums: Alpilles Pierre de Brun (folk art); and the Lapidaire (finds from Glanum, see below), in the former home of relatives of the Marquis de Sade.

St-Rémy is best known for the remarkable Roman remains, 2km S, at the foot of the Alpilles. **Glanum** is a Gallo-Roman settlement that shows clearly the diverse influence of Greeks and then Romans in Provence. It was wrecked by barbarians in the 3C AD, who left no high buildings standing, but the ground plan is easy to see. First the Gauls built Greek-style houses here in the 2C BC: their columns, peristyle and mosaics can be seen to the W of a Roman street. To its E are the Romans' buildings: baths, forum, altars, temples. They probably used Glanum as a spa.

Across the road are Les Antiques, two fascinating Roman monuments that somehow were spared the barbarians' holocaust. The arch, its top part missing, is decorated with sculptures of captives. The cenotaph, wonderfully preserved, has bas-reliefs of battles, a boar hunt and naval emblems: it was probably built as a memorial to Augustus's grandsons Caius and Lucius, who died young (note the togaed statues of two youths).

The former monastery of St-Paul-de-Mausole, just N of Glanum, has been a mental home since 1605. Here Van Gogh spent a year as a patient after cutting off his ear. You cannot visit his cell, but can admire the flowery garden where he painted, and the lovely 12C cloister and chapel. Albert Schweitzer, an Alsatian and thus then a German citizen, was interned here in World War I.

The pretty village of **Maillane**, 6km NW, evokes another great man of those days: here the poet Mistral was born, lived for many years, died and now lies buried. His house is now a museum.

ST-TROPEZ
VAR   Pop 6000

That modern myth, multi-faceted St-Tropez, means many things – a playground of the rich, a haunt of show-off eccentrics, a tawdry trippery funfair, or a picturesque old fishing-port in a lovely setting, beloved of artists. It is all this, and more; and it has had a long and strange history. Its name comes from Torpes, a Roman officer martyred by Nero; his headless corpse is said to have come to land here, and he is still honoured by an annual *bravade* festival when his body is taken from the church and carried in procession, amid much music and mirth.

Rebuilt by the Genoese in the 15C, St-Tropez was then for two centuries a semi-autonomous republic and even routed a Spanish fleet in 1637. France's greatest admiral, the Bailli de Suffren (1726-88), came from St-Tropez and is remembered by a statue on the Quai de Suffren. The town's cultural career began only in the 1880s when Guy de Maupassant discovered it; then painter Paul Signac settled here, followed in summer by Matisse and others, and by the 1920s the place was a regular summer haunt of artists and writers from Paris, such as Colette. In 1957 its exposure to the media limelight truly began when the young director Roger Vadim brought his little-known starlet wife Brigitte Bardot to shoot *And God Created Woman* on location. The film started a cult both for St-Tropez and Bardot (who still has a villa on the coast here).

The charming yellow, pink and white houses that line the quay are clever copies of the original ones, destroyed when the retreating Germans blew up the port in 1944. Today the Germans are back *en masse* as tourists, part of the mob that on a summer's day can reach 50,000, cramming the little port to goggle at the celebrities imperviously sipping champagne on their fancy yachts. Glamorous models and film-stars still flock in, with the fashion media in pursuit. The modern Hôtel Byblos, an opulent and exotic fantasy where mock-

Provençal hill-village merges with ancient Hellas and the Orient, is still the Côte d'Azur's most fashionable and glamorous hotel; its disco, *Les Caves du Roy*, is the smartest venue outside Monaco.

A moving reminder of the town's more decorous pre-Bardot days can be found in the excellent Musée de l'Annonciade, full of paintings by artists who lived and worked here – Signac, Bonnard, Matisse, Dufy, Van Dongen and others. St-Tropez, in many charming guises, features repeatedly in the canvases. The Citadelle, a 17C fortress, has an interesting maritime museum.

The main *bravade* is on 16–18 May, a lesser one on 15 June.

Gassin and **Ramatuelle** are two attractive hill-villages, albeit too often over-crowded, in the beautiful wooded peninsula S of St-Tropez: the elm in Ramatuelle's main square dates from 1598. Close by are the three ruined windmills of Paillas, on a hilltop where the view is sublime.

STE-BAUME, MASSIF DE LA
VAR

This, the most spectacular and mysterious of the craggy limestone massifs of southern Provence, runs for 16km from Aubagne to St-Maximin – bare and arid on its S slopes, thickly forested to the N. The word *baume* comes from the Provençal *baoumo* (cave), for ancient legend has it that Mary Magdalene, after landing in Provence (see *Camargue*), took refuge in a lonely cave near the summit and here spent her final years alone.

The best route through the massif's wild centre is the D2 from Gemenos, first passing the Parc de St-Pons (remains of a 13C Cistercian abbey), then looping up into a desolate zone of toothy white crags – the gaunt Fourcade rock and the sugar-loaf Pic de Bertagne with its domed white observatory. At the Plan d'Aups the landscape suddenly changes into a mild plateau with tilled fields and neat farmhouses. Further on is an old hostelry with Renaissance chimney-piece, now run as a Dominican centre. Here the lovely forest of Ste-Baume has giant beeches, a species very rare in southern France. Above soars the crest of the massif, with a stone monument on its peak, St-Pilon (1150m). This is sacred ground, for Mary's supposed cave is just W of St-Pilon. On 22 July midnight mass is still celebrated in a chapel in the cave. From the hostelry, you can walk along clearly marked paths, through the forest and up to the cave and St-Pilon (sweeping views).

STE-MAXIME
VAR   Pop 7000

Less exotic than St-Tropez to the S, but much more amusing and sophisticated than St-Raphaël to the N, this is a sizeable modern resort with a youthful clientèle, elegant tree-lined promenade, sheltered climate, and lots to do – water-skiing, yachting, sandy beaches, golf, casino, festivals, etc. To the N, round Les Issambres, the coast is lovely, with sandy coves and umbrella pines.

St-Tropez

SALERNES
VAR   Pop 3000

A little town, 23km W of Draguignan, which
thanks to local clay deposits has an active traditional industry of coloured enamel tiles for bathrooms
and other such uses. You can visit some workshops
and see the tiles being made. **Cotignac**, 13km SW,
lies below a reddish cliff pock-marked with strange
caves, some once inhabited.

SALON-DE-PROVENCE
BOUCHES-DU-RHÔNE   Pop 35,000

A lively old market town, 33km NW of Aix, noted
for its olive oil since the 15C. The astrologer
Nostradamus (1503-66) lived and is buried here
(church of St-Laurent): his home is now a
museum. Apart from this, Salon has mainly military connections: it has an air force training school,
while the museum in the 10C Château de l'Empéri
is devoted to French army history.

The medieval **Château de Barben**, 8km E, has
paintings by Van Loo and an Empire-style boudoir
used by Pauline Borghese, Napoleon's sister, who
lived here. Beyond **Lambesc**, a charming old
town, a road climbs to the **Chaine des Côtes**, a
former Resistance stronghold (monument).

SAORGE
ALPES-MARITIMES   Pop 300

Saorge, 52km N of Menton, is one of the most
startlingly situated of all Provençal hill-villages. Its
old houses, pink, yellow and grey, seem to be
clinging precariously to the mountainside, soaring
high above the main road. You approach it down a
side-road from Fontan, to the N. Worth a visit are
the baroque parish church and the Franciscan
convent.

To the S, the imposing **Gorges de Saorge**; to
the N, the even more striking **Gorges de Bergue**,
their red rocks eroded into bizarre shapes. Here
the Nice-Turin railway is a masterpiece of mountain engineering: some tunnels make loops inside
the cliff. **Sospel**, 30km SE, is a charming summer
resort in a green valley, with an arcaded square and
houses with balconies.

SEILLANS
VAR   Pop 1200

The ramparts of Seillans's ruined 12C château
were used for defence against the Saracens (the
town's name comes from the Provençal word for a
pot of boiling oil, which the inhabitants poured on
attackers). Today with its fountains and paved
alleyways Seillans is a gentle and charming place,
facing across a lush valley to the Esterel hills.
Many well-to-do people choose to live in the town.
Max Ernst lived and painted here.

Bargemon, 13km SW, also in lovely woodland
scenery, has 12C fortified gateways and is equally
sought-out by summer residents (notably British).
Built into the ramparts, the 14C church of St-
Étienne has three fine retables. **Mons**, 20km NE,
is another enchanting hilltop village and has wonderful views.

SÉNANQUE, ABBAYE DE
VAUCLUSE

Standing majestically alone in a narrow valley,
reachable only by minor roads over rocky hills
from Gordes or Venasque, this beautiful 12C
Cistercian abbey demonstrates better than its two
peers, Silvacane and Thoronet (q.v.), that austere
order's love of secluded locations. It is also the best
preserved of the three, partly because its history
has been less stormy: the only serious trouble was
in 1544 when Protestants from the Lubéron
attacked and damaged it, hanging some monks. It
was later repaired, then sold at the Revolution: but
the Cistercians bought it back in 1854 and today
still own and run it. The large and graceful church,
though bare of ornaments (in the Cistercian manner), is in use for services and concerts. The
arcaded cloister, monks' dormitory and chapterhouse with their Romanesque vaulted ceilings are
all delightful.

Despite its lonely setting, Sénanque today is full
of activity, for it houses a busy cultural centre,
lay and religious. There are concerts, mostly of
Gregorian music; contemporary art exhibitions;
lectures and seminars on religious and historical
subjects. The former refectory has a presentation
of Cistercian history; and, strangely enough, there
is a remarkable museum belonging to the Collections Sahariennes (centre for Saharan studies),
with details of Touareg life and culture, and of the
Tassili N'Ajjer cave paintings.

Abbaye de Sénanque

SILVACANE, ABBAYE DE
VAR

Along with Sénanque and Thoronet (q.v.), this is
one of Provence's famous trio of 12C Cistercian
abbeys. Its name comes from *silva* (wood) and *cane*
(reed) for it was built beside reedy marshes in the
Durance valley N of Aix. In the 12C it had 110
monks and was the most influential of the 'three
sisters', but later it ran into trouble: pillaged by
nomads in 1357, seized by bandits in 1590, it was
for long no more than a village church. Its setting
is less attractive than that of its sister abbeys, but
its Romanesque architecture is as pure and harmonious as theirs.

SISTERON
ALPES-DE-HAUTE PROVENCE   Pop 7000

Natural gateway to Provence from the N, ancient
Sisteron is dramatically sited at a point where the
Durance river thrusts its way through a defile
between the craggy Rocher de la Baume and the
hill to the W crowned by the famous citadel. Badly
bombed by the allies in 1944, much of Sisteron is
modern, but some old streets survive: at 20 Rue
Saunerie is the *hôtel* where Napoleon breakfasted
on his way north from Elba to Waterloo. Beside
the 12C church of Notre-Dame are three towers,
part of the former ramparts.

The massive 13–16C citadel, restored after the
1944 bombing, was called 'the most powerful
fortress in my kingdom' by Henri IV. Worth
seeing are its 15C Gothic chapel (with modern
stained-glass), the *tour d'horloge* (once a prison) and
the startling Devil's Watchtower, above the river.
The guardroom where the Gestapo shut up French
maquisards is now a small museum of the Resistance. Beautifully floodlit at night in summer, the
citadel is the site of an arts festival, mid-July to
mid-Aug.

To the E, the narrow road leading up the
Vançon valley to **Authon** offers spectacular mountain scenery. At **Château-Arnoux**, 14km S of
Sisteron on N85, is one of Provence's best restaurants, *La Bonne Étape*.

Sisteron

TARASCON
BOUCHES-DU-RHÔNE   Pop 11,000

On the edge of this otherwise dull town, the
turreted towers and sturdy walls of a great fortified
château stand above the Rhône – a truly romantic
medieval castle. The foundations are 12C but the
main part is 15C, built by King René when
Tarascon was on Provence's frontier with France.
He spent some years here. The castle was later
used as a prison – till as late as 1926 – yet has
survived nearly intact, and still has its moat.

The king lived in the lofty *logis seigneurial* with
its two round and two square towers. The inner
courtyard, intimate and graceful, has a loggia
(restored) where the king and queen would watch
troubadours and jugglers. The minstrel's gallery,
giving onto both court and chapel, was used for
both religious and secular singing. A spiral stairway leads to the beautiful upper-floor rooms: e.g.

the banqueting hall, with its painted wood ceiling
and fireplace for roasting; the priest's bedroom,
with a hole in the wall for baking bread; the chapel
with its oratories. The graffiti on the walls, in
several rooms, were made by prisoners, some of
them English seamen, in the 18C. From the roof,
supporters of Robespierre were hurled into the
river after his fall from power in 1794.

Opposite the castle, the lovely 12C church of
Ste-Marthe has in its crypt a 5C sarcophagus
revered (probably wrongly) as being the tomb of
Ste-Marthe. According to a 9C legend (see *Camargue*), after landing in Provence the saint went to
Tarascon and found it traumatized by an amphi-
bious dragon, the 'Tarasque', which was abducting
women and devouring their children. The knights
had failed to conquer it, but the saint did so: with
the sign of the Cross she sent it back to its lair in
the river, and it never appeared again. King René
later created the annual Fête of the Tarasque,
which still takes place every year, on the last Sun.
in June: amid much celebration, a green papier-
mâché monster is paraded round the town, its head
and tail waved by men inside it.

Tarascon is also famous in literature, as the
home-town of Daudet's (see *Fontvieille*) comic anti-
hero, Tartarin.

THORONET, ABBAYE DE
VAR

In a secluded woodland setting 17km NE of
Brignoles, this 12C Cistercian abbey, sublimely
beautiful, reflects to perfection that order's humble
and austere spirit. It is a Romanesque ensemble of
great harmony, simplicity and purity – even love-
lier than the two other great Cistercian abbeys of
Provence, Sénanque and Silvacane (q.v.). Visitors
can attend vespers in a plain but graceful little
chapel.

Save for some faded 17C frescoes, the church
itself (with its high vaulted ceiling) is devoid of
decoration or furnishing – in the Cistercian manner. On the S wall, outside, is a niche where local
inhabitants placed their dead. The enchanting
cloister, with cypresses and a hexagonal washing-
machine, leads to the early Gothic chapterhouse,
and beyond are library, refectory and dormitories.
The abbey had fallen into disrepair after the monks
were expelled at the Revolution, but in 1854 was
bought by the state and has since been carefully
restored.

TOULON
VAR   Pop 181,000

France's principal naval base lies in a dramatic
setting – around a deep natural harbour, ringed by
high hills with Vauban-style forts on top. The
French Mediterranean Fleet has its HQ here.
Though bustling and commercial, Toulon is a
fascinating town.

The *vieille darse*, oldest part of the port, is 16C.
Louis XIV then made Toulon a great naval base by
building the *darse neuve* or arsenal. Here, in the
17–18C, negroes, convicts, and political prisoners
such as Huguenots were forced to row the royal
galley as slaves.

Toulon

The harbour-front Quai Stalingrad was rebuilt after the war in hideous style, but is an amusing and lively area, full of little bars and bistros. From the Quai there are three-hour guided boat tours around the harbour, explaining the dry-docks, arsenal, etc. The Musée Naval, on the Quai, has naval mementoes. A better museum is in the 16C Tour Royale, 2km SE at the E entrance to the harbour and formerly part of its defences (note the black atlantes taken from men o' war, and the cannon used by Lafayette against the British at Rhode Island).

The Vieille Ville, N of the harbour, remains a mass of old alleyways, some of them now an elegant pedestrian zone, around the Pl. Puget, while others to the E, beyond the sombre cathedral, are more squalid. The leafy Cours Lafayette has a busy morning market. Here the Historical Museum of Vieux Toulon is worth a visit, while the Museum of Art and Archaeology (up near the station) contains oriental art, some local Gallo-Roman finds, and a range of 13–20C paintings.

Festivals, flower parade, Apr.; circus performers in Vieille Ville, July–Aug.; *santons* fair, Nov.

The limestone **Mont Faron** (550m) rises just behind Toulon: you can go to the top by funicular (from beside the Hôtel Frantel) or drive up steeply amid pines and rocks. Near the summit, in an old fort, is the Mémorial National du Débarquement, Provence's answer to the D-Day Museum at Arromanches in Normandy (q.v.). It offers many details and souvenirs of the Allied invasion of Aug. 1944. A small zoo is nearby.

The hinterland N of Toulon is wild and mountainous, ideal for excursions. Beyond **Ollioules**, off the N8, a narrow road winds up along the huge ridge of **Le Gros Cerveau** (marvellous views). The N8 goes through the arid, rocky Ollioules gorges, then a turning E leads up to the ruined and deserted ghost-village of **Évenos**, on a crag below a ruined castle. The D62 winds on E to the top of **Mont Baume** (800m), another splendid viewpoint.

The capes and peninsulas SW of Toulon are also beautiful. **Les Sablettes** and **Tamaris** are two little resorts in the SW suburbs, with good sandy beaches: George Sand wrote some of her novels at Tamaris. To the SW, alone above the rocky coast at **Cap Sicié**, stands the chapel of Notre-Dame-du-Mai (pilgrimages in May). The fortress of **Six-Fours**, on a hill to the N, is one of the many round Toulon built by Vauban. The old village of **Sol-liès-Ville**, 13km NE of Toulon, has a remarkable Romanesque church: its sculpted walnut organ is one of the oldest in France (1499).

TOURTOUR
VAR Pop 300

A medieval village 20km W of Draguignan, now a chic residential centre and something of a show-piece, its houses of local golden stone all scraped clean (like a Cotswolds show-village!). The two big elms in the main square were planted in 1638 to mark Louis XIV's birth. Tourtour has several smart hotels, notably in the elegant new holiday estate of St-Pierre-de-Tourtour.

TURBIE, LA
ALPES-MARITIMES Pop 2000

An old town high on the Upper Corniche, behind Monaco. The Romans' Trophée des Alpes, a mighty landmark on this coast, was built c.6BC to mark Caesar Augustus's victories over turbulent local hill tribes. Originally it stood 50m high, with a statue of Augustus on top. Later it was partly dismantled, then blown up by the French in 1705. More recently it has been partly restored, thanks to the generosity of an American, Edward Tuck. Its museum has details of Roman Provence and a model of the trophy in its prime.

At **Laghet**, 3km NW, the 17C sanctuary of Notre-Dame has interesting ex-votos. Near the summit of **Mont Agel**, 8km NE, is one of the best – and most fashionable – golf-courses on the Côte. Further N are the attractive old hill-villages of **Peillon** and **Peille**.

UTELLE
ALPES-MARITIMES Pop 700

From St-Jean-la-Rivière in the Vésubie valley, a road winds up steeply to this unspoiled old village on a hill, with fine views. Its large and handsome church has a vaulted Gothic roof and a beautiful 16C retable of the Annunciation above the N aisle altar. About 6km W is the lonely sanctuary of Madone d'Utelle, founded in 850, rebuilt 1806 (pilgrimages Whit Mon. and 16 Oct.).

The deep **Gorges de la Vésubie** wind for 10km from St-Jean to Plan-du-Var. One road follows the river, but the best views are from the upper road (D19) to Levens. Here the '**Saut des Français**' is a panorama point at the spot where, in 1793, rebels from Nice hurled Republican soldiers into the canyon.

UZÈS
GARD Pop 7000

With its numerous high towers and narrow streets, Uzès is one of the most delightful and historic towns in Provence. Its history is closely linked with that of its great ducal family, the House of Uzès, who date back to Charlemagne and today still live in their vast romantic turreted castle in the town centre, where the duke's red-and-gold flag proudly flies. With its 11C *donjon*, 14C Tour de la Vicomté, Renaissance facade, and Gothic chapel, the castle is an odd mix of styles and epochs.

All around are arcaded streets and noblemen's handsome houses, such as the Hôtel Dampmartin.

The Place aux Herbes is a charming square with plane trees, arcades and a fountain. Most curious is the 12C Tour Fenestrelle, a round six-storey campanile of a kind common in N Italy but not seen elsewhere in France: it is the one relic of the Romanesque cathedral destroyed by the Huguenots (Uzès was a Huguenot hotbed, and in revenge Richelieu pulled down its ramparts). If you prefer the modern, then visit the Rodo museum (vintage cars and model railway).

There is a music festival in July, and lively country fairs in alternate months, Feb. to Nov.

VAISON-LA-ROMAINE
VAUCLUSE Pop 5000

The Roman remains at Vaison are in many ways the most interesting in France, for they afford a vivid picture of Roman daily life. Back in Gaulish days this was already a busy town: then the Romans came and built it up as a residential centre with wealthy patrician villas, rather than a city of big public buildings like Arles or Orange. Later Vaison became an important Christian centre. Then the Counts of Toulouse built a castle on the hill across the river, and a medieval town grew up below it. The modern town lies between the castle and the Roman quarter.

Excavations have revealed two areas of the Roman town: the Puyman and Villasse quarters. In the former you can visit: the Maison des Messii, home of a rich family, with mosaic floors, baths, latrines, kitchen, etc; the Portique de Pompée, an elegant colonnade; the Nymphée, a basin above a spring. In the Villasse quarter is an elegant villa with paved hall, baths, and vestiges of hanging gardens; and a street with pavements, parallel to a colonnaded way once lined with shops. A Roman tunnel leads to the theatre whose stage was cut out of the rock. The excellent modern museum contains fascinating local finds: e.g. the marble statue of an armour-plated emperor; and a double-faced statuette, one side laughing satyr, the other bearded noble.

To the W stands the former cathedral, 12C Romanesque, austerely graceful, built on the visible foundations of a 6C church. The cloister holds a small museum of early Christian art. Across the river, the old castle is empty and closed: the narrow cobbled streets below it have recently been elegantly restored.

There is a folklore festival in July and a music and drama festival mid-July to mid-Aug.

Séguret, 10km SW, a small village of cobbled streets below a high rock, has a fine 15C fountain. The vineyards on the plain below produce some of the best Côtes du Rhône wine, notably Gigondas. SW of Séguret, the **Dentelles de Montmirail** are a curious range of jagged, toothy rocks.

VALBERG
ALPES-MARITIMES

This rather ugly summer and winter resort, 85km NW of Nice, is notable mainly for the modern murals in the little mountain church of Notre-Dame-des-Neiges. Nearby, **Beuil** has a richly decorated little church, while at Guillaumes are the

ruins of a 15C castle. Fine views all round. The deep and spectacular **Gorges du Cians** are lined with splendid jagged red rocks.

VALBONNE
ALPES-MARITIMES Pop 4000

A delightful old town with arcaded square, 13C church, and an unusual grid pattern of streets. It lies amid lush countryside, dotted with opulent villas; smart golf-course, too. The new 'scientific park' of **Sophia Antipolis**, 5km SE, marks an attempt by the government to promote the area as a focus of advanced technology: its modernistic research buildings, and its imaginative boarding-school and residential complexes, will interest lovers of modern architecture.

VALLAURIS
ALPES-MARITIMES Pop 21,000

Vallauris, 6km NE of Cannes, is almost synonymous with Picasso. Its age-old pottery industry was in decline when Picasso came here on a visit in 1947 and found one good local artist, Suzanne Ramié, running the Madoura pottery. His interest in her work led him to take up pottery himself, and he spent six years in Vallauris, decorating ceramics or twisting pots into inspired shapes (many examples are in the museum at Antibes, q.v.). This gave the local industry a new lease of life. Today the Madoura pottery, still owned and run by the Ramié family, sells copies of Picasso's ceramics and the produce of its own local artists.

The Musée Picasso is a small deconsecrated 12C chapel, its walls and ceiling covered by one of the artist's most inspired works, *War and Peace*, which he painted in his Vallauris studio in 1952. Rather like *Guernica*, it expresses his horror of war. Opposite, in a small square, is his strange bronze statue of a naked man holding a struggling sheep.

Musée Picasso

VENCE
ALPES-MARITIMES Pop 13,000

This ancient town lies in lovely hilly country, sadly now rather built up, NW of Nice. It has a mild climate and has long attracted artists and writers, especially foreign ones (D.H. Lawrence died here in 1930). It was a major Roman centre, and a bishopric as early as the 5C. The charm of the Vieille Ville, with its animated alleys, has not been killed by the tourist hordes: note the fountain in the Place du Peyra. The Romanesque cathedral has amusing satiric carvings on its 15C choir-stalls.

Not to be missed: in the N suburbs, the delightful little modern Chapelle du Rosaire, designed and decorated by Matisse, then aged 80, in 1950. Though himself agnostic, he did the work as a gift for the convent of Dominican nuns, next door, who had nursed him through an illness. As the light falls onto white ceramic walls, through stained-glass windows of patterned blue, green and yellow, the effect is magical. Visits Tues., Thurs.

The 'circuit of the *clues*' (a *clue* is a rocky cleft with cascading torrent) is a 160km round trip through wild, grandiose and varied mountain scenery – well worth making, if you have a car. Most of the way there is hardly a house in sight, save for the odd deserted hill-village.

Leaving busy Vence by the Coursegoules road, you climb onto an empty rock-strewn plateau, with stunning views. After the Col de Vence, the route leads through meadowlands, then loops down into the wooded Loup valley and up to **Gréolières** (the church has a 10C sculpted wood Virgin). The road zigzags up the side of a sheer gorge, onto a plateau with majestic subalpine scenery, where side-roads lead to the resorts of **Gréolières-les-Neiges** and **Thorenc**. After the **Col de Bleine**, with its views of lofty rock peaks, a turning leads to the deep **Clue de St-Auban**; the circuit continues above lush valley vegetation to the **Clue d'Aiglun** where there are clear pools for bathing, then passes the quaint village of **Roquesteron**. Finally, at **Le Broc**, you gaze down on the urban plain of the Var.

VERDON, GRAND CANYON DU
ALPES-DE-HAUT PROVENCE

Perhaps less beautiful and romantic than its rival, the Gorges du Tarn (q.v.) but deeper (700m) and more grandiose: here the river Verdon winds for 21km through an ancient crevice in the vast limestone plateau of upper Provence. The canyon's bed is impassable, but good tourist roads follow the clifftops on either side, and in many places you can park and then gaze at the green waters far below. Careful driving is vital: to avoid the exposed side, you should take the N road from E to W or the S road from W to E.

On the N side, coming from Castellane or Comps, the first good view is at the Point Sublime; beyond, a left fork follows the Route des Crêtes with 15 belvederes above the canyon. On the S side, the road from Aups or Moustiers winds up through Aiguines, with initial views of the canyon at the Col de l'Illoire. It then follows the Corniche Sublime, with more superb views: the best is at the Balcons de Mescla, vertically above the point where the Verdon and Artuby gorges meet.

A giddily exciting walk down the cliff and along a series of ledges above the river can be made along a footpath between the Point Sublime and the Châlet de la Malène, on the N side. This takes 8 hours, and is only for tough, experienced hikers unafraid of heights. The river bed itself is negotiable only by trained mountaineers with a guide.

The 15C village of **Moustiers-Ste-Marie**, 6km N of the W end of the canyon, is dramatically sited at the foot of a deep ravine, between whose cliffs

there hangs an iron chain with a gilded star in the middle: it is said to have been placed there by a local knight, to fulfil a vow on his return from the Crusades. A footpath inside the ravine leads up to the chapel of Notre-Dame, with a Renaissance door of sculptured wood. Since the 17C Moustiers has been famed for its faience, still made locally.

S of Moustiers, the Verdon widens into the big artificial lake of **Ste-Croix**, with its new hydroelectric dam. To the E of the canyon, **Trigance** and **Comps-sur-Artuby** are attractive old villages on the grandiose rocky plateau. S of Comps there stretches the big French army camp of Canjuers.

VILLEFRANCHE
ALPES-MARITIMES Pop 7000

This animated fishing-port, in a sheltered bay 6km E of Nice, was established in the 14C as a free port (hence the name). Tall Italianate houses line its charming harbour-front, below the Vieille Ville with its narrow stairways, some vaulted. The 14C chapel by the harbour, where fishermen used to keep their nets, was decorated by Cocteau in 1957 with remarkable pale frescoes.

VILLENEUVE-LÈS-AVIGNON
GARD Pop 900

A peaceful little town lying just across the Rhône from Avignon ('lès' means 'near'). In the 13–16C, when the river was the Franco-Provençal frontier, the French kings made it a fortress town. Hence its two great military posts, the 14C Fort-St-André, a fine specimen of medieval military architecture, and the tower of Philippe le Bel, on a rock above the river. The towers of both offer marvellous views of Avignon and its papal palace, best seen in the late afternoon sun.

Of the many 'sights', the most impressive is the vast Charterhouse, the largest in France, filling six acres. Founded in 1356, it once housed hundreds of Carthusian monks, but was then sold by lots at the Revolution. Today, largely restored, it has oddly varied uses. The SW part is a municipal housing complex of shops and flats. The N and E sector, with the main religious buildings, is run by the state as an historic monument cum cultural and scientific centre with modern seminars – it is a curious sight to find, say, biologists or economists sipping cocktails beside the pope's tomb. As well as this graceful tomb with its white marble effigy, do not miss the frescoes in the chapel of Innocent VI, and the monks' living quarters.

The Musée Municipale, in a 17C palace, has items from the Charterhouse, notably a 17C engraving of the intact Pont St-Bénézet at Avignon soon before its destruction. Best painting is Charonton's rich and elaborate *Coronation of the Virgin*, masterpiece of the Avignon school. Note also a ghoulish work by Mignard of monks being hanged. Nearby, in the sacristy of the 14C church of Notre-Dame, is a marvellous polychrome ivory statuette of the *Virgin and Child*, carved from an elephant's tusk and thus curved in shape.

In July there is a varied cultural festival in the Charterhouse – music, theatre, poetry, art, etc.

CORSICA

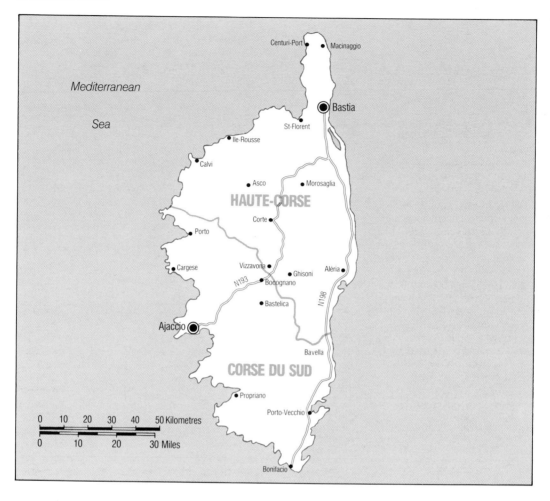

The island of Corsica is a mountain surrounded by sea. It is a region, comprising two *départements*, of metropolitan France, yet few of Corsica's 300,000 people think of themselves as typically French.

Corsicans have fought for their independence for centuries, against Pisans, Genoese, Turks, French, Mussolini's Italy and Hitler's Germany. It was ruled by the Genoese until 1768, when it became French. Napoleon, born in Ajaccio, is the hero of that city, but in fact he fought for France against Corsican independence, and did nothing for the isle when he was emperor. Outside Ajaccio, the hero is Pascal Paoli, whom Napoleon tried to defeat and who did set up an independent government for some years. Nowadays, despite occasional acts of violence, only about two per cent of the Corsican population seeks actual independence; the rest want more autonomy, and under a French socialist government a directly elected assembly has, during the past four years or so, been granted wider powers.

The term *vendetta* is a Corsican word, signifying the bitter and protracted individual and family feuds that have bedevilled Corsican society for centuries. Corsicans still have a deep and often hot-blooded sense of family and clan loyalties. In-

tensely religious, yet also superstitious, they take pride in their local festivals; they are passionately fond too of football and horse-racing. Towards foreigners they are proud but friendly.

As a tourist centre, Corsica could not fail once the money came for development, and within the limits of the money available tourism has grown fast in the last fifteen years. The island is not only extremely beautiful but also unusual. Its mountains look strange and disrupted. Many valleys are cul-de-sacs or even cut off except by old goat tracks. New roads have been built but most in the mountains are necessarily steep and zigzagging and some are still in bad condition. The scenery is best enjoyed by being driven around.

Its coastline of 1000km, a quarter the length of the French coastline, has some of the best sand beaches in Europe and cliffs rising 1000m sheer from the sea. Between are bays and coves giving shelter for boats. The clear seas are an invitation to underwater swimming. Few filing-cabinet concrete hotels have yet been built and in an underpopulated island there is no call for high-rise buildings, so tourism has not yet overwhelmed the towns and villages of old buildings, quiet squares and narrow streets. You can still walk in forests with carpets of wild flowers without meeting people, sit by pools among wild iris, and fish, undisturbed, in rushing mountain streams.

Corsica has three climates, according to how high up you go. Its "alpine" regions give superb mountain walks and mountaineering in summer. Skiing is just being introduced in a few small places in winter. Lower down, there is splendid walking and fishing in autumn and spring. The coasts are hot and dry in summer, with rain rare from June to October. Summer heat is not over-powering, and even in December most days are sunny. But May is the beautiful time, when snow is still on many peaks but the maquis is in full bloom.

In many places the maquis is true jungle where it would be very unwise to get lost: plants up to 3m high and trees entangled in an impenetrable barrier – cistus, heather, gorse, oleander, juniper, holly, thyme, mint, lavender, box and the beautifully flowered caper bush which can engulf and kill trees.

It was to the maquis that the independence fighters and the bandits fled to hide, but to Corsicans it is not a beautiful place to be admired. Their fathers fought a constant battle to prevent it overrunning their fields. It covers a quarter of the country and nearly half of all arable land, having taken over as poor farmers gave up after their sons had emigrated. Furthermore, many parts were malaria swamps. Not until the malaria mosquito was banished after World War II were some of the small holiday resorts even habitable. The population has still not reached the 1836 figure of 320,000, despite the settling of 15,000 people from Algeria when that country was lost to France.

Poverty meant that people could not afford to knock down old cottages and villages and rebuild. Nor did buildings fall into utter ruin, for people were living in them. That has helped tourism; and tourism has helped to reestablish agriculture. But Corsica's noticeable increase in prosperity has been due to the construction of dams for energy and soil irrigation. This, rather than tourism, provides optimism for the future.

AJACCIO
HAUTE CORSE   Pop 55,000

Although the capital of Corsica, and the most important commercial city, Ajaccio, founded by the Genoese in 1492, still has a small-town atmosphere, with unhurried people sitting in cafés just talking or drifting around squares watching the active play boules. The outdoor cafés under palms, the spacious squares and new hotels, the yachts in the harbour give it a permanent holiday look, all contrasting with the alleys of the old town near the fishing port. New buildings, especially hotels and apartments, have sprung up over the last fifteen years, a modern maritime station completed, and an attempt made to solve the parking problem, but one still gets the impression that business is not very important, especially during the early evening promenade in Cours Napoléon, for walking, watching, talking, exchanging glances and banter.

As you arrive by air or boat from Marseilles, Ajaccio looks like a huge amphitheatre, with the port as stage and the buildings as tiers of seats, with a backcloth of grandiose mountains, covered by forests with rock peaks. The big bay gives it a mild winter climate.

Napoleon Bonaparte was born here on 15 Aug. 1769, and the town is obsessed with him, especially when celebrating his birthday. Yet Ajaccio did not always think a lot of him when he was alive, especially when, as a young lieutenant of the National Guard, he deliberately provoked a shooting-affray near the cathedral to try to get himself made lieutenant-colonel. He also made an abortive attempt in 1793 to take Ajaccio from the Corsican independence fighters under Pascal Paoli.

Nowadays Napoleon is good for tourism. Many streets are named after him or his brothers. At his family home is the sofa on which he was born. Nearby in the Baroque cathedral is the font in which he was baptized, and a high altar given by his sister. In the Musée Napoléonien in the town hall is his baptismal certificate, a bronze death-mask made on St Helena, and busts and portraits of four generations of Bonapartes. In the Palais Fesch, named after Napoleon's maternal uncle Cardinal Fesch, the Chapelle Impériale, erected in 1855 by Napoleon III, is a mausoleum for the Bonaparte family, though Napoleon himelf is buried at Les Invalides in Paris. In another wing is a collection of 14–18C Italian paintings.

At the end of Cours Napoléon, Ajaccio's biggest square is now named after de Gaulle. In the centre is a statue of Napoleon as a Roman emperor, surrounded by his four brothers, known locally as "L'Encrier" – the ink-well. Other statues are in Pl. d'Austerlitz and Pl. Foch. On Casone hill, now a garden, a son-et-lumière about Napoleon is shown in the tourist season.

De Gaulle was here in 1943, following the freeing of Corsica by an all-French force from Algeria. The citadel, built under Henri II, is still used by the army.

Car ferries tie up beside Pl. du Marché where a market is held every morning. Ajaccio is a centre for sailing, scuba and boat trips. Boats take you round the island (3 hours), to the series of isles and reefs of **Îles Sanguinaires**, where the writer

Ajaccio

Alphonse Daudet lived in an old lighthouse in 1863, and the southern shore of the Gulf of Ajaccio, a beautiful coast with superb beaches and one small resort, **Porticcio**. This coast can also be reached by road and is accessible as far as **Portigliolo**.

ALÉRIA
HAUTE-CORSE   Pop 2400

An important Greek and Roman colony, now being excavated, its whole area of the Tavignano estuary on the E coast rotted away as a malaria-ridden swamp until mosquitoes were exterminated after World War II. Now it is a small resort area with long sandy beaches, large coastal lakes in which oysters and mussels are farmed, and vineyards and orchards. There are three "naturist" (nudist) holiday beaches. Jérome Carcopino museum, in a 1572 castle, has interesting finds cleverly displayed to trace early local history. At **Casabianda** is a reserve to protect endangered island flora and fauna.

ASCO
HAUTE-CORSE   Pop 120

An old bandit village 65km SW of Bastia, in a wild gorge, surrounded by wicked-looking rocky pinnacles and until recently cut off except by goat tracks, has miraculously become a small mountain resort with two hotels. Above it is **Haut-Asco** (1450m), a tiny summer and winter-sports resort with a ski lift and alpine-style self-catering chalets, a hotel and ski-renting shop. It is popular with climbers and mountain walkers. Some climbs are strictly for experts, especially up **Cinto**, highest point on Corsica (2707m), although there is a marked path for fit walkers. **Calacuccia** is a pleasant base for Monte Cinto. Fishing is excellent in the clear waters of the Stranciacone and mountain streams. Under an old Genoese bridge below Asco, the river forms a natural swimming pool. The scenery is ruggedly superb, with many waterfalls, wild flowers and trees of rare types, like *gymperus* juniper, responsible for the sweet, sticky white frost called manna of Asco. Excellent honey comes from valley hives. There is a reserve for mouflons (wild sheep); semi-nomadic shepherds graze flocks here in summer and drive them to the coast in winter.

BASTELICA
CORSE-DU-SUD   Pop 800

This old town at the end of the Prunelli valley, 40km from Ajaccio, is called "the true face of Corsica". It is surrounded by forest, upland pastures, beehives, cherry and apple orchards, and, of course, mountains. Its old red-roofed houses, school and domed church tower seem ageless. In front of the church is a bronze statue of the Corsican national hero, born here in 1498 – Sampiero Corso. A peasant's son, he became a mercenary for the French, successfully led Corsican volunteers for them in Italy, and saved the life of Henri II, who made him colonel-general of Corsican infantry. The French then betrayed him and handed over Corsica to the Genoese. With twenty-five Frenchmen he landed at Valinco and in three years almost freed the island. A typically Corsican family vendetta stopped him. As a young man he had strangled his wife for being unfaithful. Now her cousins murdered him on behalf of the Genoese. The inscription to him is by an Irish poet, William Wyse, nephew of Napoleon!

BASTIA
HAUTE-CORSE   Pop 45,000

Industrialized working town and port at the lower E side of Cap Corse, it suffers massive traffic jams and could do with a clean-up of many buildings. From its new port it exports citrus fruits, wine and tobacco and imports food from mainland France. Its industrial zone spreads 10km S, with engineering works and factories mainly making cars, cigarettes and processing foods. It trades extensively with Italy. It was the seat of the Genoese governor during the occupation, and the rest of Corsica has never forgiven it, even when Bastia won the French football cup a few years ago.

Bastia has the main airport in Corsica, so many tourists pass through. New hotels, holiday villages, restaurants, night spots and holiday apartments at **Biguglia** and **La Marana** beach have persuaded many to stay. This long Biguglia lagoon, with one small outlet to the sea, was malaria-ridden until twenty-five years ago. Now it is a blossoming resort with a wide beach of fine sand and shade of pine and eucalyptus on the tongue between sea and lake. The little town of Biguglia was the first Genoese capital. But the governor had to flee after a Corsican revolt, so he chose a rock to the N to build a citadel or *bastille* – hence Bastia.

The charm of Bastia lies in its old port and citadel. Around the port are high balconied houses in narrow crowded streets, often with washing strung across them. Cafés and restaurants line the quays, and fishing boats jostle yachts in the harbour. Under the high citadel ramparts are shady gardens with views over the harbour and town to the Cap Corse mountains. The former governor's palace is a museum of local history and geology.

Ores, marbles and granites include an orange ore from Matra called realgar. A German company mined it here before 1914 to make gas bombs used in World War I. Shown too is the flag of the independence fighter Pascal Paoli, carried at the final defeat of his Corsican Army by the French at Ponte Nuovo in 1769. The year before, he had had a remarkable victory over a superior French force at Borgo, on the heights above the Biguglia lagoon, where the French lost 600 dead, 1000 wounded, 600 prisoners and 700 guns. The Corsicans were incensed that Genoa had ceded Corsica to France without consulting the islanders.

BAVELLA
CORSE-DU-SUD

Truly breathtaking – a pass 1250m up, through a fierce wonderland of pointed jagged peaks, down to a pine forest. It is a nature reserve and part of a national park.

The nearest village is **Zonza**, with three hotels, 9km S, 100km from Ajaccio and 784m above sea level. Take RF4 from Zonza towards **Solenzara** on the E coast. After the **Bavella Pass**, the road plunges into a hollow to the old shepherd village of **Bavella**, then enters the forest. The pines are regrowing, the old trees having been decapitated by the wind. The road has hairpin bends and steep slopes but a good surface, and is spectacular right to the coast.

BOCOGNANO
CORSE-DU-SUD   Pop 320

A village among pines and chestnuts, streams and cascades 650m up, but only 40km from Ajaccio on a good road and served by rail. Napoleon was caught here by Paoli independence fighters when he was trying to destroy them, but a friend, the mayor, saved him.

It was home to the notorious Bellacoscias bandit family in the 19C. Last of them was Antoine, "king of the maquis", one of a family of eighteen children. He shot the mayor and took to the maquis, where he defied the authorities so successfully that famous people came to see him – Pierre Loti, Baron Haussmann and a princess among them. At 75 he gave himself up – and was found not guilty! He died in his bed in 1912 – aged 95.

BONIFACIO
CORSE-DU-SUD   Pop 2800

In a magnificent position, clinging to rocks at the far S of the isle, it has finally succumbed to tourism and its long jetty is lined with souvenir shops. But it has a magnificent harbour, protected by white chalk cliffs, with just a small opening to the sea; and the old town, a medieval fortress, is superb. It is like an island, enclosed in ramparts, almost surrounded by the sea, perched on a plateau 60m above the water and in places overhanging it, and it is reached through thick maquis. Count Bonifacio from Lucca in Tuscany, sent here by Charlemagne to fight the Moors, founded it in 828. Later the local people ruled themselves and lived by piracy. In 1187 Genoa took it by ruse and deported the

Bonifacio

local population. Now the people live by lobster fishing and taking tourists for boat trips to see impressive caves in the limestone cliffs, and the "stairway of the King of Aragon", said to have been cut in one night during a 15C invasion attempt. Car ferries run daily to **Santa Teresa** on the N tip of Sardinia (1 hour). You can see Sardinia and get fine views of Bonifacio from the lighthouse at **Pertusato**.

CALVI
HAUTE-CORSE   Pop 3700

Nelson lost his eye when bombarding this old fortified harbour in 1794, which could have been justice, for it is a beautiful little spot beside a bay which looks like a South Seas lagoon. An indigo sea is fringed by an arc of sand and pine trees, backed by mountains. The British, with Paoli's independence fighters, took it from the French after a seven-week bombardment.

The old 15C Genoese citadel, enclosed by impressive ramparts along which you can walk, is on a dramatic spur controlling the bay. It never

Calvi

recovered from the British bombardment and most of its old houses are deserted and falling apart. The former governor's palace is a Foreign Legion headquarters.

Calvi becomes very crowded with holiday-makers in midsummer. It is fashionable and pricy, with good watersports facilities and quite lively nightlife. Some of the holiday bungalows development in the pine forests behind has been haphazard and unworthy of this beautiful site.

During a night procession on Good Friday, people walk chanting, with hooded penitents carrying heavy wooden crosses. The procession is stopped three times for performance by the penitents of "La Granitola", a complicated movement in spirals (not quite a dance).

On 15 Aug. a religious ceremony sets off three days of secular festivities.

CARGÈSE
CORSE-DU-SUD   Pop 900

A fishing port 50km N of Ajaccio with several fine sand beaches within 1–7km, so a summer resort – hotels, a Club Méditerranée village and camping. Otherwise a sleepy little place with a tiny square completely shaded by a huge tree and two churches – one Catholic, one Greek Orthodox. The town was founded by Greeks who fled in 1676 from Turkish occupation of the Peloponnese.

CENTURI-PORT
HAUTE-CORSE   Pop 200

Sheer delight, this village of pink and silvery-grey houses round a tiny harbour of lobster boats. A new marina will make it gradually less of a hideaway, but it is remotely placed near the top of Cap Corse. You can taste the lobsters in local inns, but the rest go to the Côte d'Azur. A fake feudal château was built last century by a general, count Leonetto Cipriani, one of a flamboyant soldiering family. He fought for the duke of Tuscany. Another, fighting with Bolivar in South America,

Centuri-Port

ate a whole roast sheep as a bet.

CORTE
HAUTE-CORSE   Pop 5500

The very heart of old Corsica of the Corsicans, as opposed to the French. The buildings and statues of its old town are still pockmarked by cannon balls and bullets from the days of rebellion. Once the people came in from the maquis and held this town, the occupying authorities knew that they had trouble.

Built on a rocky spur above the meeting of two turbulent rivers, surrounded by granite mountains, with a citadel occupied today by the Foreign Legion, it still looks impregnable. But it is a place of peace now, with steep cobbled streets, steps, fountains, squares surrounded by old houses, and unhurried people. The more modern part below seems divorced from it.

The town centre is Pl. Paoli, with a statue of the freedom fighter who made this the capital of free Corsica from 1755 to 1769 and gave it a university. In Pl. Gaffori is a statue of Jean Pierre Gaffori, a local doctor who became a soldier fighting the Genoese and head of the first free government of Corsica but was murdered by assassins hired by the Genoese in 1752. His house is in the square. His wife and some Corsican fighters were besieged in it by the Genoese. The men were about to surrender, so she fused a barrel of gunpowder and threatened to light it. They were saved three days later by her husband. In the old governor's palace is a museum of Corsican history.

Corsica's second highest peak, **Monte Rotondo** (2625m) towers above Corte. A fair road goes to 1600m. A good walker can climb the rest in summer with proper equipment. The last 600m is rough (about 9 hours round trip). The N193 road from Bastia and Ajaccio to Corte is very winding but in good condition. There is also a railway.

The little mountain villages of **Castiglione** and **Popolasca** 20km N are old and picturesque. **Venaco**, 12km S, is a lovely area with superb fishing and tours on horseback, centred on the remarkable **Paesotel e Caselle** – shepherd's huts with full plumbing, restaurant and swimming pool.

GHISONI
HAUTE-CORSE   Pop 900

A mountain village in wild, remote country in central Corsica. Though 600m up, it is in a deep bowl below two frightening peaks, but in a lovely forest setting where two fierce-running rivers meet. Chestnuts give way to pines up the mountain slopes and the seeds are winnowed from the needles and exported. Trout fishing is excellent from June. There is a Logis de France. 12km E the Fium'Orbo river runs through the lovely **Strette** and **Inzecca gorges**. The **Sorba pass**, 10km N, offers superb forest views. **Monte Renoso** (35km) is for mountaineers. The walk to the summit and back takes 9–10 hours and it is advisable to stay overnight in shepherds' huts. Summit views can cover S Corsica and N Sardinia. Winter skiing at **Bergeries de Capanelle**, with ski lift.

The D69 road to Ghisoni from Corte is good but narrow and very winding.

ÎLE-ROUSSE
HAUTE-CORSE   Pop 2700

Pascal Paoli picked a winner when he built this town on the redrock of Pietra to annoy Calvi and Algajola, who were backing the Genoese. First it was a port for exporting olive oil, fruit, wine and cheese from the lush valleys to France. Now it is also a fashionable tourist resort, with white fine sand beaches, mild winters and not too much summer heat. Boats go to the Côte d'Azur, trains to Calvi past good beaches and camp sites. Calvi airport is only 20km. Île-Rousse is luring retired people from France, also the rich with two homes. A fair is held in Sept.

Algajola (9km towards Calvi) is a 15C fortified Genoese port with a tiny shaded square and a few little streets. But it has a vast sandy beach eastwards, and the big marina of **Sant'Ambrogio** with 700 villas attached, plenty of hotels and bungalow hotels, and a Club Méditerranée village, so it is lively in season.

Corniche Paoli, by D63, past the old hill villages of **Monticello** and **Santa Reparata-di-Balagna**, has excellent views.

MACINAGGIO
HAUTE-CORSE   Pop 500

Opposite Centuri on Cap Corse, this once important little harbour town is joined to it by a road which runs up the hillside and crosses the crest of Serra Passa (362m). When ships were smaller and made of wood, Macinaggio played a leading part in Corsican history and this top end of Cap Corse was one of the richest parts of the island. It decayed until recently when the port was renovated and turned into a yacht harbour. With the hamlet of **Rogliano**, it is becoming a holiday resort.

MOROSAGLIA
HAUTE-CORSE   Pop 1100

Pascal Paoli was born here in 1725, died in London in 1807 and was buried in Westminster Abbey – a British tribute to an ally who fought against Napoleon. In 1889 his remains were brought back to the house where he was born and laid under a stone. The room is now a chapel. Corsicans still go to pay their respects to their hero.

It is one of several attractive hamlets at around 700m, W of the **Castagniccia massif**, on the E coast below Bastia, an area where resistance fighters hid for centuries, against the Genoese, French, then Italians and Germans in World War II. The hamlets are surrounded by enormous chestnut trees. Just S beneath the highest peak, **San Petrone**, is the village of **Orezza**, which produces mineral water with iron content and delicious wild boar which feed on chestnuts from centuries-old trees. A monastery involved in the island history was deconsecrated in the Revolution, became a gendarmerie, then an Italian arms store in World War II. The Germans destroyed it when retreating, and it is now in ruins.

A hamlet in the Castagniccia massif

PORTO
CORSE-DU-SUD   Pop 300

The attractive little village of Porto, most photographed scene in Corsica, is at the centre of a wide gulf between Calvi and Ajaccio, flanked by cliffs of rose-red granite, strangely shaped, with peaks up to 1000m.

Porto is at the mouth of the Porto river, in a valley thick with eucalyptus trees growing to the edge of a small white-sand beach. A ruined Genoese tower stands on a rock jutting into the sea. Small hotels and houses are scattered in the woods. There are two camp sites and in season it is inevitably crowded, with the sound of more than a little night music. Boats take visitors round the bay and to **Girolata**, a simple langoustine-fishing village beside a Genoese fort.

There is a spectacular drive round the Corniche and another inland climbing to 1600m through the **Gorges de la Spelunca** to **Evisa**, a pleasant mountain-resort. The road S to **Piana** passes the strange calanques of huge crimson cliffs in twisted shapes.

Porto

PORTO-VECCHIO
CORSE-DU-SUD   Pop 8100

Beautifully situated in the subtropical SE at the head of a long fjord-like gulf, it has access to superb beaches, a good new marina, plenty of hotels and camp sites around the bay; and tourism is rivalling its traditional business of exporting cork from huge cork-oak plantations. Founded in 383BC by Greeks from Syracuse, it had a rough time, especially in the 16C when Algerian pirates used it as a base for their galleys. The Spaniards drove them out. Pirate raids, skirmishes between the Corsicans and Genoese and, above all, malaria made it a sorry place. It has thrived since the malaria mosquito was destroyed after 1945.

PROPRIANO
CORSE-DU-SUD   Pop 3100

The Phoenicians, Greeks and Etruscans used this natural haven in the Gulf of Valinco in the SW of

Propriano

Corsica, not to mention pirates and smugglers. It remained a small port until twenty years ago when its tourist potential was realized. It has a warm safe sea, tempting sand beaches, good fishing and watersports, pleasant hotels and lively little pavement cafés. Beside the old fishing boats, still landing languoustines, are pleasure boats and ocean-going yachts.

Filitosa, 20km NW, is a rarity – an important prehistoric site in a beautiful setting of the green Taravo valley, with olive groves and poplars, streams and pools with wild flowers on their banks. The megaliths were erected by people 8000 years ago, many with carvings and engravings, remarkable for representing three distinct periods of human prehistory on one site.

Sartène, 13km SE, keeps a medieval appearance with its tall fortress-like buildings. Hanging in the church are chains and a heavy cross. These are carried in the Holy Week processions by the chief penitent, who wears pink robes covering all but his eyes, which peer through slits.

Porto Pollo, round the bay from Propriano, is a small, pleasant holiday resort with a small beach, accessible sands, and several camp sites.

ST-FLORENT
HAUTE-CORSE   Pop 1200

"Give me the Gulf of St-Florent and two frigates and I will see that not a single vessel leaves Marseilles or Toulon," said Nelson. And the

Genoese had certainly built a formidable bastion on the neck of Cap Corse. It has been a Roman staging post, too. When steam replaced sail, it fell into a deep sleep. The harbour silted up. A few lobster fishermen lived in the centuries-old houses in narrow streets of the town. Within the last ten years, St-Florent has come to life, and the population has doubled. It is now a holiday resort – but a small, quiet, lazy one. The harbour area has been dredged, cafés and restaurants have opened round the quay, the beach has been cleaned and enlarged, and small hotels have been built just outside. There is water-skiing, scuba and very good sailing.

The port replaced the city of Nebbio, half a mile inland, a bishopric constantly attacked and destroyed finally in the 13C by the Saracens. All that remains is the 12C Romanesque church with a mummified body of St Flor in a glass case. Corsica's favourite wine comes from nearby Patrimonio.

VIZZAVONA
HAUTE-CORSE

A delicious area of forests, mountains and streams in the heart of Corsica, but only 45km from Ajaccio by a fairly fast road or a very fast train that tunnels under the mountain.

The village of Vizzavona has a few hotels, pensions and holiday houses owned by Ajaccio people, and a camping site. Skiing is becoming popular, though snow conditions vary. Climbing **Monte d'Oro** (2391m) takes a good 10 hours return and is for experienced, fit mountain walkers. There are many easier walks. Early May is a good time for walkers when wild flowers, especially violet cyclamen, bloom in the forest. **Vizzario**, 10km N, on steep slopes of a ravine, is another small resort. The railway, which continues through Venaco and Corte to Calvi, passes through magnificent scenery which cannot be seen from the road, especially on the way to Venaco.

Vizzavona

TOURIST INFORMATION

Walking and Rambling
There are some 20,000 kilometres of marked footpaths in France.
Detailed guide-books are available from:
– C.N.S.G.R., 92, rue de Clignancourt 7–5018 Paris
– I. G.N. (Institut National Géographique National) publishes
route maps:
107, rue de la Boétie–75008 Paris

1. Some of the routes suggested by the Comité National des
Sentiers de Grande Randonnée (C.N.S.G.R.)
Ile-de-France
– GR 1: Tour de l'Ile-de-France, 650 km around Paris
Normandy
– GR 2: Sentier de la Seine, Les Andelys to Le Havre
– GR 223: Tour du Cotentin
Centre
– GR 3: Sentier de la Loire
Auvergne
– GR 30: Tour des Lacs d'Auvergne
Brittany
– GR 34: Sentier du Tour de Bertagene 'Tro Breiz'
Poitou-Charentes
– GR 36: Sentier Manche-Pyrénées
– GR 360: Roman art in Saintonge
Auvergne, Languedoc-Roussillon
– GR 4: Sentier Méditerranée/Océan
– Grasse to Manosque via Gorges du Verdon
– Gard, Ardèche, Lozère, Cantal, from Pont Saint-Esprit to
Saint-Flour
– Avergne, Cantal, Puy-de-Dôme, Creuse, from Saint-Flour to
Aubusson
– GR 40: Tour de Velay
– GR 441: Tour de la Chaine des Puys, volcanoes of Auvergne
Rhône-Alpes
– GR 5: Sentier Hollande/Méditerranée
Haute-Savoie
Lac Léman–Col de la Croix du Bonhomme
Savoie
Parc National de la Vanoise
Hautes-Alps–Alpes de Haute-Provence
Modane–Larche
– GR 54: Parc National des Ecrins, Tour de l'Oisans
– GR 58: Tour du Queyras (Hautes-Alpes)
– GR 559: Lakes and Forests of the Jura
– GR 6: Sentier Alpes/Océan
Midi- Pyrénées, Aquitaine
6-60: Lozère, Aveyron, Lot: Meyrueis–Figeac
6-64: Lot, Dordogne, Quercy, Périgord
Noir: from Figeac to Les Eyzies
62-62 A: Sentier Causse Noir, Rouergue, from Conques to
Maubert
65: Chemin de Saint-Jacques de Compostella, Le Puy to Eauze
Auvergne – Languedoc-Roussillon
Midi-Pyrénées
– Haute-Loire, Lozère, Aveyron, Lot, Tarnet-Garonne, Gers
(Eauze)
66: Tour de l'Aigoual
67: Tour des Cévennes
68: Tour du Mont Lozère
Vosges
– GR 7: Sentier Vosges–Pyrénées
7: Vosges – Ballon d'Alsace
Burgundy
760: Tour du Beaujolais
– GR 9: Sentier Jura/Coté d'Azur
Corsica
– GR 20: Sentier de la Corse
Mont-Blanc
– T.M.B.: Tour du Mont-Blanc

2. The following organizations will give information on specific
routes and walks:
– Club Alpin Français (C.A.F.), rue de la Boétie – 75008 Paris
– Touring Club de France, 65, avenue de la Grande-Armée –
75016 Paris
– U.C.P.A. (Union des Centres de Plein-Air), 62, rue de la
Glacière–75013 Paris
– Chalets Internationaux de Haute-Montagne (C.I.H.M.), 15,
rue Gay-Lussac–75005 Paris

National and Regional Parks

1. National Parks
Languedoc-Roussillon
Parc National des Cévennes
Registered office: BP 4 – 48400 Florac

Midi-Pyrénées
Parc National des Pyrénées Occidentales
Registered office: BP 300 – 65013 Tarbes

Parc National de l'Ariege

Normandy
Parc National des Iles Chausey

Provence-Alpes-Côte-d'Azur
Parc National de Port-Cros
Registered office: 50, avenue Gambetta – 83400 Hyères

Parc National des Ecrins
Registered office: 7, rue du Colonel-Roux – 05000 Gap

Riviera-Côte-d'Azur
Parc National du Mercantour
Registered office: 17, rue Alexandre Mari – 06000 Nice

Alpes-du-Nord
Parc National de la Vanoise
Registered office: BP 105, 135, rue du Dr Julian – 73003
Chambéry

2. Natural Regional Parks
Alsace-Vosges-Lorraine
Parc de Lorraine
Registered office: Abbaye des Prémontrés, BP 35 – 54700 Pont-à-
Mousson

Parc des Vosges du Nord
Registered office: La Petite Pierre – 67290
Wingen-sur-Moder

Aquitaine
Parc des landes de Gascogne
Registered office: Préfecture des Landes – 40011 Mont-de-
Marsan

Auvergne
Parc des Volcans
Registered office: Château du Montlosier-Randanne – 63120
Rochefort-Montagne

Burgundy
Parc du Morvan
Registered office: Maison du Parc, Saint-Brisson – 58230
Montsauche

Brittany
Parc d'Armorique
Registered office: Menez-Meur-Hanvec – 29224 Daoulas

Champagne-Ardennes
Parc de la Forêt d'Orient
Registered office: Maison du Parc – 10220 Piney

Parc de la Montagne de Reims
Registered office: 86, rue Belin – 51000 Reims

Parc des Ardennes
Registered office: Chemin des granges moulues – 08011
Charleville-Mézières

Corsica
Parc de la Corse
Registered office: Préfecture de la Corse – 20188 Ajaccio

Languedoc-Roussillon
Parc du Haut-Languedoc
Registered office: 13, rue du Cloître, BP 9 – 34220 Saint-Pons

Nord-Pas-de-Calais
Parc du Saint-Amand-Raismes
Registered office: Préfecture du Nord-Pas-de-Calais, mission
régionale – 59039 Lille

Normandy
Parc de Brotonne
Registered office: 61320 Château de Carrouges

Pays-de-la-Loire
Parc de Brière
Registered office: 180, Ile de Fédrun – 44720 Saint-Joachim

Picardy
Parc de Picardie Maritime

Poitou-Charentes
parc du Marais Poitevin, Val de Sèvre et Vendée

Registered office: Syndicat Mixte, 4, rue Pasteur – 79000 Niort

Provence-Alpes-Côte-d'Azur
Parc de la Camargue
Registered office: Le Mas du Pont de Rousty – 132000 Arles

Parc du Lubéron
Registered office: avenue des Druides – 84400 Apt

Parc du Queyras
Registered office: avenue de la Gare, BP 3 – 05600 Guillestre et
Relais Inter, rue Carnot – 05008 Gap

Rhône-Loire
Parc du Pilat
Registered office: Moulin de Virieu, 2, rue Benay – 42410
Pelussin

parc du Vercors
Registered office: Maison du Parc, chemin des fusillés – 38250
Lans-en-Vercors

Alpes-du-Nord
parc du Vercors (see above)

Inland Waterways
Information:
– 'Tourisme Fluvial en France', brochure edited by the
Ministères des Transports, Sous-direction des voies navigables,
244, boulevard Saint-German – 75007 Paris
– Syndicat National des Loueurs de Bateaux de Plaisance, Yacht-
House de la F.I.N., Port de la Bourdonnais – 75007 Paris

Fishing
Information:
– Conseil Supérieur de la Pêche, 10, rue Péclet – 75015 Paris
– Union Nationale des Fédérations Départementales des
Associations Agréées de Pêche et de Pisciculture, 17, rue Bergère
– 75009 Paris

Horse-riding
Information:
– Association Nationale pour le Tourisme Equestre et
l'Equitation de Loisirs (A.N.T.E.), 12, rue du Parc Royal –
75003 Paris
1. Short riding holidays
– Touring Club de France, 65, avenue de la Grande-Armée–
75016 Paris
– U.C.P.A. (Union Nationale des Centres Sportifs de Plein-Air),
62, rue de la Glacière – 75013 Paris
– Cheval Voyage 8, rue de Milan – 75009 Paris

2. Horse-drawn carriage or caravan tours
Information:
– Cheval Voyage, 8, rue de Milan – 75009 Paris

Cycling
1. Hiring bicycles
– Information from local Syndicats d'Initiative and Offices de
Tourisme
– French railways (S.N.C.F.) hire bicycles at more than 112
stations

2. Organized cycle tours
Information:
– Fédération Française de Cyclotourisme, 8, rue Jean-Marie
Mégo – 75103 Paris

Clubs and associations:
– Bicyclub de France, 8, place de la Porte Champerret – 75017
Paris
– Le Touring Club de France, 65, avenue de la Grande-Armée –
75116 Paris
– Le C.I.H.M. (Chalets Internationaux de Haute-Montagne), 15,
rue Gay-Lussac – 75005 Paris

Railways of Tourist Interest
Information:
– A.F.A.C. (Association Française des Amis des Chemins de
Fer), Cour Souterraine Porte 9, Gare de Paris-Est – 75010 Paris
– A.J.E.C.T.A. (Association des Jeunes pour l'Entretien et la
Conservation des Trains d'Autrefois), BP 1 – 77650 Longueville
– A.F.T. (Association pour le Tourisme Ferroviaire), BP 1431 –
92154 Suresnes
– F.A.C.S. (Fédération des Amis des Chemins de Fer
Secondaires), 134, rue de Rennes – 75006 Paris

Grape-picking Festivals
These usually take place in September and October in most of the
areas near vineyards. Some festivals are held in spring and
summer, and on 22 January to celebrate Saint-Vincent, the

patron saint of vine-growers.

Alsace-Vosges-Lorraine
Grape-picking festivals:
Bas-Rhin
In October at Barr, Marlenheim, Obernai, Molsheim, Mutzig,
Scherwiller
Haut-Rhin
At Whir, Riquewihr, Ribeauvillé, in August: wine fair at Colmar,
in May: at Mulhouse, Guebwiller

Aquitaine
Dordogne
Wine festival at Sigoulès (summer)
Gironde
In June, wine festivals at Soulac, Montalivet, Carcans,
Maubuisson, Lacanau, Arcachon, Le Pyla
In June, gathering of the *confréries vineuses*: at Saint-Emilion, in
the Medoc and Graves, and end of July/beginning of August at
Sauveterre de Guyenne, Castillon, Lesparre, Saint-Croix-du-
Mont
In September, grape-picking festivals in Médoc, Saint-Emilion,
Sauterne, Fronsade, Blaye
Landes
Beginning of October, grape-picking festival at Pouillon

Auvergne
End of August, wine festival at Saint-Pourcain-sur-Sioule (Allier)

Burgundy
Côte d'Or
In September, vine festival at Dijon and festival of Sauvignon at
Saint-Bris-le-Vineaux
In November, 'Les Trois Glorieuses', wine festival at Clos-de-
Vougeot, wine sale of Hospices à Beaune, *fête de la Paulée* at
Meursault
Nièvre
In August, wine fair at Pouilly-sur-Loire
Saône-et-Loire
End of May, wine fair at Mâcon
Mid-September, wine festival at Saint-Jean-Devaux
End of October, Raclet festival at Romanèche-Thorins

Centre
Cher
In March, wine fair at Saint-Armand
Indre
In October, grape-picking festival at Pont-Chrétien-Chabenet
Indre-et-Loire
In March, wine fair at Chinon
15 August, wine festival at Amboise and Vouvray
Loiret
End of July, festival of Côteaux du Giennois

Champagne-Ardennes
Aube
22 January, festival of the Confrérie Saint-Paul, Saint-Vincent des
Vignerons du Barsuraubois
End of August, grape-picking festival at Bar-sur-Aube (every 4
years)
Mid-September, fair of the wines of Champagne at Bar-sur-Aube
End of September, days of sauerkraut and Champagne
Marne
21 January, festival of Saint-Vincent at Ambonnay
In May, Champagne fair at Rilly-la-Montagne

Franche-Comté
Haute-Saône
End of September, grape-picking festival at Champlitte
Jura
In July, grand wine festival at Arbois
Beginning of September, festival of new wines at Arbois

Languedoc-Roussillon
Aude
In August, wine festival at Largrasse and Narbonne
Gard
Mid-August, vine-growers' festival at Méjannes-le-Clap
End of September, grape-picking corrida at Nîmes
In April, wine fair of the Côtes du Rhône, fair of the wine of the
Gard at Villeneuve-les-Avignons
In May, wine festival at Roquemaure
Hérault
In August, Muscat festival at Frontignan
In October, festival of new wine at Béziers, internatinal wine fair
at Montpellier
Pyrénées-Orientales
In August, Muscat festival at Rivesaltes, wine festival at Estagel
and Baixas

Midi-Pyrénées
Gers
End of August, Armagnac fair
Tarn-et-Garonne
Beginning of September, wine festival at Fronton
End of September, chasselas festival at Moissac

Pays-de-la-Loire
Loire-Atlantique
Beginning of October, festival of grape-picking and new wine at
Le Loroux-Botteraux, Haute-Goulaine, Paulx, Saint-Etienne de
Montluc, Saint-Léger-les-Vignes, Ancenis, Chemere, Saint-
Philbert-de-Grandlieu
Mid-November, wine fair at Nantes
Maine-et-Loire
In February, wine festival of Anjou wines at Angers, Chalonnes-
sur-Loire, Saumer Mid-June, festival of vintage wines of Côteaux
de Layon at Saint-Aubin-de-Luigne

Poitou-Charentes
Deux-Sèvres
In March, wine fair at Thouars
End of November, grape-picking festival at Boullé-Loretz

Provence-Alpes-Côte-d'Azur
Bouches-du-Rhône
In September, grape-picking corrida at Arles
Var
In August, wine festivals at Cogolin, Sainte-Maxime
In September, grape-picking festival at Saint-Tropez
In October, grape-picking festival at La Motte
Vaucluse
In summer, festival of Côtes-du-Rhone
Villages at Vacqueyras
End of September, grape-picking festival at Chateauneuf-du-
Pape

Rhône-Loire
Ardèche
Beginning of September, wine festival at Saint-Peray
Loire
First weekend in November, wine fair at Saint-Haon-le-Vieux
Last weekend in November, wine fair at Chavannay

Where to Obtain Information
1. In France: from the various offices of France-Information-
Loisirs (F.I.L.)

Bordeaux
Office de Tourisme
12, Cours du 30 Juillet – 33000 Bordeaux
Calais Office de Tourisme
12, boulevard Clémenceau – 62100 Calais
Colmar Office de Tourisme
4, rue Unterlinden – 68000 Colmar
Evry Agora D'Evry
91000 Evry Ville Nouvelle
Grenoble Maison du Tourisme
Rue de la République – 38000 Grenoble
Lille Office de Tourisme
Place Rihour – 59800 Lille
Lyon Office de Tourisme
Place Bellecour – 69000 Lyon
Marseille Office de Tourisme
4, Canabière – 130001 Marseille
Metz Office de Tourisme
Porte Serpenoise – 57007 Metz Cedex
Nantes Office de Tourisme
Place du Change – 44000 Nantes
Paris Maison du Tourisme Vert
35, rue Godot-de-Mauroy – 75009 Paris
Paris Office de Tourisme
127, Champs-Elysées – 75008 Paris
Paris Centre National d'Art et de Culture
'Georges Pompidou' – 75191 Paris Cedex 04
Paris 8, avenue de l'Opera
75001 Paris
Pontoise Préfecture du Val d'Oise
95010 Cergy Pontoise
Reims Office de Tourisme
3, boulevard de la Paix – 51100 Reims
Rosny/s/Bois Centre Commercial Avenue du Général de Gaulle
– 93110 Rosny-sous-Bois
Rouen Office de Tourisme
25, place de la Cathédrale – 76100 Rouen
Strasbourg Office de Tourisme
Pont de l'Europe – 67000 Strasbourg

Toulouse Office de Tourisme
Donjon du Capitole – 31000 Toulouse

2. In France: regional tourist offices (Comités régionaux au
tourisme)

Ile-de-France
101, rue de Vaugirard – 75006 Paris
Alsace-Vosges-Lorraine
10, avenue de la Paix – 67000 Strasbourg
Aquitaine
24, allées de Tourny – 33000 Bordeaux
Auvergne
Maison de la Règion, 43, avenue Julien – 63000 Clermont-
Ferrand
Burgundy
Préfect – 21034 Dijon Cedex
Brittany
3, rue d'Espagne – 35100 Rennes
Centre
10, rue du Colombier, BP 2412 – 45032 Orléans Cedex
Champagne-Ardennes
2 bis, boulevard Vaubécourt – 51000 Châlons-sur-Marne
Corsica
38, cours Napoléon, BP 162 – 2000 Ajaccio
Franche-Comté
Place de la 1re Armée Française – 25041 Besançon
Languedoc-Roussillon
12, rue Foch – 34000 Montpellier
Limousin
41, boulevard Carnot – 87000 Limoges
Midi-Pyrénées
3, rue de l'Esquile – 31000 Toulouse
Nord-Pas-de-Calais
157, boulevard de la Liberté – 59800 Lille
Normandy
35, rue Joséphine – 27000 Evreux
Pays-de-la-Loire
3, place Saint-Pierre – 44000 Nantes
Picardy
9, rue Allard, BP 0342 – 80003 Amiens
Poitou-Charentes
3, place Aristide-Briand – 86000 Poitiers
Provence-alpes-Côte-d'Azur
372, rue du Paradis – 13008 Marseille
Riviera-Côte-d'Azur
55, Promenade des Anglais – 06000 Nice
Rhône-Loire
5, place de la Baleine – 69005 Lyon
Alpes-du-Nord
11 ter, avenue de Lyon – 73000 Chambéry
La Réunion
Prefecture de la Réunion – 97405 Saint-Denis

3. French Tourist Offices abroad

Belgium
Bruxelles (1060), 21, avenue de la Toison-d'Or
Brussels (1060), Guldenvlieslaan 21
Great Britain
London W1V 0AL, 178 Piccadilly
Netherlands
Amsterdam (1017 KX), Prinsengracht 670
United States of America
New York (N.Y. 10020), 610 Fifth Avenue
Chicago (Illinois 60611), 6645 North Michigan Avenue – Suite
430
Beverly Hills (California 90212), 9401 Wilshire Boulevard
Dallas (Texas 75258), World Trade Center, No 103, 2050
Stemmons Freeway – PO Box 58610
West Germany
D6 Frankfurt 1, Kaiserstrasse 12, Postfach 2927
D4 Düsseldorf, Berliner Allee 26

4. Offices in Paris
Office de Tourisme de Paris-Accueil de France, 127, avenue des
Champs-Elysées – 75008 Paris
Bureaux d'accueil et d'information, Gare du Nord; Gare de l'Est;
Gare de Lyon (S.N.C.F.), 127, avenue des Champs-Elysées –
75008 Paris
Automobile Club de France, 6, place de la Concorde – 75008
Paris
Touring Club de France, 65, avenue de la Grande-Armée – 75782
Paris Cedex 16

The information listed above was correct at the time of
publication. The French Tourist Offices will supply telephone
numbers and more detailed information.

INDEX TO GAZETTEER

PICTURE ACKNOWLEDGEMENTS

Anthony Blake: 60, 64, 75, 79 (below), 232
Bridgeman Art Gallery: 10, 19 (below), 20, 28 (above, Giraudon), 36 (Victoria & Albert Museum), 40, 43, 46, 48 (Giraudon)
Michael Busselle: title page, 73
J Allan Cash: 26, 31, 134, 138 (both), 147, 152, 249 (above), 292, 312, 323 (both), 324, 325 (below)
E.T. Archive: 16, 18, 21 (both)
Mary Evans Picture Library: 14, 15, 17, (both), 53, 54 (both), 55 (both), 56 (above), 57 (above, centre), 58, 59
John Foley: 110, 127, 129, 131, 135, 139 (above), 142, 144 (above), 145 (both), 150, 155 (below)
Food and Wine of France: 74, 76, 78 (above), 79 (above)
French Government Tourist Office: 87 (below), 88, 89, 92, 95, 97 (both), 98, 99, 104, 107, 109, 112, 113, 117, 118 (above left and right), 122 (below), 123, 124, (both), 130, 158 (both), 161, 164, 165 (all), 166, 167 (both), 169 (left), 170, 171, 172, 173, 175, 176 (below), 177, 178 (both), 179, 180, 182, 184 (both), 185 (above), 186 (above), 187, 188 (above), 189, 193, 194, 195, 198 (both), 201 (below), 202, 205, 206 (above), 208, 211, 213, 214 (below), 215, 216, 217 (all), 218, 219, 224, 225 (both), 227, 228, 229, 230, 234 (both), 237, 238, 239, 242, 243, 249 (below), 255, 257, (below), 261 (above), 262, 270, 281, 282, 286, 293, 294, 296, (both), 297, 299, 302, (left), 305, 311 (below), 314, 316, 317.

Sonia Halliday: 22, 29 (above left), 50
Robert Harding Associates; 19 (above) ,49
Michael Holford: 12, 24, 28, (below), 35, 45 (both), 70, 80, 86, 275
Angelo Hornak: 27 (below), 32, 34
Denis Hughes-Gilbey: 62, 63, 65, 68, 69 (both)
Lightbox Library: 6, 9 (right) 78 (below), 247, 248
The Mansell Collection: 56 (centre and both below), 57 (below)
Ronald Sheridan: 13, 25, 27 (above), 39, 42
Barrie Smith: 309
John Topham Library: 8, 29 (above right), 30 (above), 72, 77, 86, 87 (above), 90, 91, 93, 94, 96, 100, 101, 108, 111 (both), 114, 115 (both) 116, 118 (below), 122 (above), 125, 128, 132, 139, (below), 140, 142, 143, 144 (below), 146, 151, 153, 154, 155 (above), 159, 163, 165 (left), 168, 169, (right), 176 (above), 177, 181 (both), 183 (both), 185 (below), 186 (below), 188 (left, below), 191, 192, 199, 200, 201 (above), 202, 203, 204, 206 (below), 207 (both), 214 (above), 222, 223, 226, 231 (both), 235, 240, 246, 250, 254, 256, 257 (above) 258, 259, 261, 263, 264, 265, 267, 268, 269, 271, 273, 276, 277 (both), 278, 279, 280, 283, 284, 285, 287, 291, 298, 301, 302 (right), 303, 307, 308, 310, 311 (above), 313, 315, 318
Roger-Viollet: 33
Roy Williams: 9 (left), 137